GETTING PERSONAL — *selected writings*

PHILLIP LOPATE

Basic Books
A Member of the Perseus Books Group
New York

Books published by Basic Books are available at special discounts for bulk purchases in the United States by corporations, institutions, and other organizations. For more information, please contact the Special Markets Department at the Perseus Books Group, 11 Cambridge Center, Cambridge MA 02142, or call (617) 252-5298, (800) 255-1514 or e-mail j.mccrary@perseusbooks.com.

Designed by Jeff Williams
Set in 10.5-point Garamond MT by the Perseus Books Group

Library of Congress Cataloging-in-Publication Data
Lopate, Phillip, 1943-
  Getting personal : selected writings / by Phillip Lopate.
    p. cm.
Includes bibliographical references.
  ISBN 0-465-04173-6
  I. Title.

PS3562.O66A6 2003
818'.5409--dc21

2003013695

— To my wife Cheryl and my daughter Lily, always

CONTENTS

NOTES TOWARD AN INTRODUCTION

On the Confessional Mode

I HAVE ALWAYS BEEN ATTRACTED TO the confessional mode in literature and, with it, the whole dynamic of confidingness, rationalization, unreliable narration, and self-aggrandizement versus self-disgust. An irresistible title when I was an undergraduate (and a favorite novel of our set) was James Hogg's *The Private Memoirs and Confessions of a Justified Sinner*. I ate up Dostoevsky's *Notes From Underground*, Gide's *The Immoralist* and his autobiographical writings, *The Confessions of St. Augustine*, Rousseau's *Confessions*, Svevo's *Confessions of Zeno*, De Quincey's *Confessions of an English Opium-Eater*, Celine, Henry Miller, Kerouac. . . . I eagerly read the work of the so-called "confessional poets," such as Ann Sexton, John Berryman, Sylvia Plath and Robert Lowell, and disagreed with their detractors when they found something unclean about their self-revealing poems, just as, more recently, I could not agree with the backlash against the memoir by critics who felt it was too narcissistically self-indulgent. My own view is that, if anything, what is wrong with most memoirs and autobiographical poems is that they don't go far enough in their confessions; they myopically fudge the details, the close nitty-gritty of self-observation. I am endlessly interested in the wormy thoughts and regrets and excuses and explanations that people have for their behavior. "Confessional" is, to me, a descriptive term, not a derogatory one. (My first novel was called *Confessions of Summer*.) It was inevitable that I should be drawn to the personal essay, the form with which I am now most identified, because of its conversational and confessional attributes.

Honesty has been, for me, the one lodestar to which I never stop aspiring in print. I don't say I attain "honesty," but the very fact that I try to reach it gives my work, at least in my own eyes, a formal thrust, a dynamic, a topography. I want to get to the bottom of things. And as a reader, I have always loved that moment when the writer said something very daring, tore the cover off, told the *real* truth, and you had to gasp. Of course it is necessary to do more than merely confess and strive for honesty. (What, I wonder? Expanded argument tk.)

On the "I" Persona

I have sometimes been startled to hear a stranger, acquaintance, or even friend make some indulgent comment about me that seems drawn from assumptions about my character as it has appeared in print. For instance, they might say, "Oh, you wouldn't like to go on a nature hike," when in fact I am very susceptible to the charms of nature. I am not a committed curmudgeon, by any means. The contrarian role I have sometimes assumed in print, to throw my I-character into sharper relief or to distance myself from conventional thinking, has become a mental reflex, one part of my thinking pattern. But in daily circumstances, I am energetic and almost life-embracing; I regard myself as a blend of optimist and stoic. True, I like a little complexity and darkness with my optimism, though only in a Pollyannaish culture such as America's would such seasonings be regarded as "cynical." (This is beginning to sound smug.)

On Style

My prose style drifts in and out of beauty. I am not one of those to break himself on the wheel of the sentence. I do not try, as Isaac Babel did, to unleash a period with the force of a bullet; I simply end a sentence and start another. I sometimes listen in amazement to the advice other writing teachers give their students, such as: You should purge your work of passive verbs or adjectives. I would never think of doing such a thing to my own prose. Where my writing is lively (there's that "is" again—should I change it to something more active?), it's because what I have to say at that moment quickens into vigorous expression. A writer-friend told me she never begins a sentence with a gerund. Having started many such sentences this way myself, I paid her no heed; besides, archaic diction has always had a perverse appeal for me. I have never set out to exemplify the most up-to-date prose. I expect to be clear, and that's about it. It surprises and delights me when I come across a passage I wrote years ago that has a measure of elegance, concision, density of thought. "Knowing you can write well sometimes," the reader might ask, "why don't you make the effort to do it always?" I don't know. It goes against the grain to take myself or the art of prose so seriously; Flaubert's *le mot juste* makes me want to giggle. I believe in the aesthetically impure as an accurate reflection of reality, just as I believe in the acceptance of compromise as a political ideal. Perhaps it's not a question of intentions but my limitations as a writer. (This is beginning to sound defensive. You're going in circles, Bro.)

On the Difference Between Memoir and Personal Essay

Use that quote from Emily Fox Gordon's essay: "The memoir tempts the memoirist to grandiose self-representation. The essay, with its essential modesty, discourages the impulse. The memoir tends to deindividuate its protagonist, enlisting him to serve as a slightly larger-than-life representative of the sufferings of a group or community, while the essay calls attention to the quirks and fallibilities we take as marks of our essential separateness. The erratic zigzag of essayistic thinking—the process that Phillip Lopate calls 'thinking against oneself'—makes the essay proof against the triumphalism of memoir by slowing the gathering of narrative momentum. The essayist transects the past, slicing through it first from one angle, then from another, until—though it can never be captured—some fugitive truth has been definitively cornered." (Maybe I should take out the reference to me, especially since I stole the idea of "thinking against oneself" from Sartre or Cioran. I can no longer remember which. Just three-dot that part.)

On One's Proper Place in the Universe

Once, a woman who had started to go out with me decided to do some research. She was a feminist and she wanted to know where to place me on the scale of consciousness. She asked around town about me at bookstores, parties, asked her friends, and came back with a report that I had a clean bill of health; that is, I was not a male chauvinist. Somehow this miffed me a bit, because I know in my heart of hearts that I am a male chauvinist, and because there is something in this clean bill of health that suggested a eunuch. I must be giving off the wrong signal. Or maybe the women she had asked were not attractive to me; I had probably been understanding and polite with them while not making a pass—my sexual lack of interest had been misinterpreted as raised consciousness. On the other hand, I was pleased that they thought me all right.

Her report from the men she had asked was less flattering. Someone in a bookstore whom I hardly knew told her I was "arrogant." In fact, it turned out I had a general reputation for arrogance. It pleased me to hear this, too, since it meant I was throwing people off the scent; I know perfectly well how modest I am.

My modesty is something not to be questioned. It is not even modesty, but a correct evaluation of my talents. As a writer, for instance, I knew I would never be a Tolstoy, a Shakespeare, a Thomas Mann. Even Kafka I wouldn't come close to touching. If I worked like a dog all my life I would have written twenty books (so far, I'm up to fourteen) with some nice passages in them that will interest mainly graduate students of the future, the way that certain Creole dialect novelists of the nineteenth century are periodically rediscovered. Professors whose business it is to know everything about post-bankrupt New York will have to consult my texts. When I was younger it seemed to me that the luckiest stroke would be if, after I died, some discerning editor or critic were to put out an anthology, choosing the best of my essays, and pointing out that, while the books as a whole do not stand up, because "he never learned to shape his material into an overarching structure, or to cut," nevertheless a belletristic sensibility is at work here that is "interesting," or at least characteristic of its time.

Really, the goal of my whole life was one of those So-and-So Readers, which are eventually remaindered or sold at a steep discount in tony book catalogues. So how can you call a man like that arrogant? And now I actually have it: my own Reader! Yippee!

Afterword

By Dr. Horst Shovel

These scattered notes were found on the desk of my late friend, after his fatal aneurysm. They were meant to form the core of an introduction to his Selected Writings. On one of our last jogs around the Central Park reservoir, Phillip told me he was very excited about this project, which would at least compensate for the fact that some of his books had been allowed to go out of print. Too down-to-earth and sensible to let any bitterness regarding literary reputation or MacArthur fellowships affect him for long, he yet entertained hopes that he was poised to become much more famous than he had been.

My friend, whom I have known since our college days, was riddled with contradictions and inconsistencies: one moment generous, the next, guarded; alternately cocksure and uncertain; at times an egalitarian who could mix it up with janitors and bookies, at others an elitist snob who did not deign to disguise his boredom with the small talk of ordinary people. He once said to me, "Lev, you are the only man I know who is the same person in every circumstance." I took it as a compliment.

Of course, I am only a medical man, but I pride myself on being a good judge of literature. I can only second what Susan Sontag has said: "I am astonished that a writer of such greatness does not yet occupy the place he deserves." To be sure, she said it about another author, but that does not make it any less true in regard to my esteemed, under-valued friend. I hope that this posthumous collection will go some way toward rectifying that regrettable situation.

He often spoke of his desire to write an autobiography or formal memoir, when he retired from teaching, which would pull together the vagrant strands of his personal writing and raise them to a new, philosophical level: it was to be his crowning achievement. Now we have no choice but to cherish this smorgasbord of his best, or most characteristic, work as the informal version of the autobiography he never got around to writing.

― CHILDHOOD

My Early Years at School

IN THE FIRST GRADE I WAS IN A BIT OF A FOG. All I remember is running outside at three o'clock with the others to fill the safety zone in front of the school building, where we whirled around with our bookbags, hitting as many proximate bodies as possible. The whirling dervishes of Kabul could not have been more ecstatic than we with our thwacking book satchels.

But as for the rest of school, I was paying so little attention that, once, when I stayed home sick, and my mother had to write a letter of excuse to the teacher, she asked me what her name was and I said I did not know. "You must know what your teacher's name is." I took a stab at it. "Mrs. . . . . Latka?" I said, *latka* being the Jewish word for potato pancakes (this was around the time of Hanukkah celebrations). My mother laughed incredulously, and compromised with the salutation "Dear Teacher." As I learned soon after, my teacher's name was actually Mrs. Bobka, equally improbable. She wore her red hair rolled under a hairnet and had a glass eye, which I once saw her taking out in a luncheonette and showing to her neighbor, while I watched from a nearby table with my chocolate milk. Now, can it be possible that she really had a glass eye? Probably not; but why is it that every time I think of Mrs. Bobka my mind strays to that association? She had a hairnet and a very large nose, of that we can be sure, and seemed to have attained middle age. This teacher paid no attention to me whatsoever, which was the kindest thing she could have done to me. She had her favorite, Rookie, who collected papers and handed out pencils — Rookie, that little monster with the middy blouse and dangling curls, real name Rochelle. "Teacher's Pet!" we would yell at her.

Yet secretly I was attracted to Rookie, and admired the way she passed out supplies, as well as the attention she got.

Otherwise, I was so much in a daze, that once I got sent on an errand to a classroom on the third floor, and by the time I hit the stairwell I had already forgotten which room it was. Afterward, Mrs. Bobka never used me as her monitor.

The school itself was a wreck from Walt Whitman's day, with rotting floorboards, due to be condemned in a year or two; already the new annex that was to replace it was rising on the adjoining lot. But in a funny way, we loved the old school better. The boys' bathroom had zinc urinals with a common trough; the fixtures were green with rust, the toilet stalls doorless. In the Hadean basement where we went for our hot lunches, an overweight black woman would dish out tomato soup. Every day tomato soup, with a skim. Sometimes, when the basement flooded, we walked across a plank single file to get to the food counter. And that ends my memories from first grade.

In the second grade I had another teacher, Mrs. Seligman, whose only pleasure was to gossip with her teacher pals during lineups in the hall and fire drills (when *we* were supposed to be silent). Such joy came over her when another teacher entered our classroom — she was so bored with the exclusive company of children, poor woman, and lived for these visits.

By second grade, I had been anonymous long enough. One day we were doing show-and-tell, wherein each child bragged how he or she had been to the beach or had on a new pair of tap shoes. My parents had just taken me to see the movie *Les Misérables*, and Robert Newton as the tenacious gum-baring Inspector had made a great impression on me. Besides, I knew the story backwards and forwards, because I had also read the Classics Illustrated comic book version. As I stood up in front of the class, something possessed me to elaborate a little and bend the truth.

"Mrs. Seligman, I read a book called *Les Misérables* . . . "

She seemed ready to laugh in my face. "Oh? Who is it by?"

"Victor Hugo." I stood my ground. There must have been something in my plausible, shy, four-eyed manner that shook her. Her timing was momentarily upset; she asked me to sit down. Later, when there was a lull in the activity, she called me over to her desk.

"Now tell me, did you honestly read *Les Misérables*? Don't be afraid to tell the truth."

"Yes! it's about this man named Jean Valjean who . . ." and I proceeded to tell half the plot — no doubt getting the order confused, but still close enough to the original to give this old war-horse pause. She knew deep down in her professional soul that a child my age did not have the vocabulary or the comprehension to get through a book of that order of complexity. But she wanted to believe, I felt. If I stumbled she would dismiss me in a second, and I would probably burst into tears. Yet even then I knew (children know it better than adults) that in telling a lie, fidelity is everything. They can never be absolutely sure if you keep denying and insisting.

Just then one of her teacher pals came in, the awesome Mrs. McGonigle, who squeezed bad boys into wastebaskets.

"Do you know what? Phillip here says that he read Victor Hugo's *Les Misérables*."

"Really!" cried her friend archly. "And you believe him?"

"I don't know."

"What's it about? *I've* never read it. He must be very smart if he read it and I haven't."

"Tell Mrs. McGonigle the story."

"It's about this man named Jean Valjean who stole a loaf of bread," I began, my heart beating as I recounted his crime, aware that I myself was committing a parallel one. By this time I had gotten more than the attention I wanted and would have done anything to return to my seat. Mrs. McGonigle was scrutinizing me sarcastically with her bifocals, and I was much more afraid of her seeing through my deception than Mrs. Seligman. But it came to me in a dim haze of surprise that Mrs. Seligman seemed to be taking my side; she was nodding, and shushing the other woman's objections. Perhaps nothing so exciting had happened to her as a teacher for months, even years! Here was her chance to flaunt a child prodigy in her own classroom before the other teachers. I told the story as passionately as I could, seeing the movie unroll scene by scene in my mind's eye, a foot away from the desk.

"There's only one way to find out," interrupted Mrs. McGonigle. "We will take him down to the library and see if he can read the book."

My teacher could not wait to try this out. She rose and took my arm. "Now, class, I'm leaving you alone for a few minutes. You are to remain quiet and in your seats!" So they marched me over to the school library. I was praying that the school had no such volume on its shelves. But the librarian produced Victor Hugo's masterpiece with dispatch — as luck would have it, a sort of abridged version for young adults. I knew enough how to sound out words so that I was able to stumble through the first page; fortunately, Mrs. Seligman snatched the book away from me: "See? I told you he was telling the truth." Her mocker was silenced. And Seligman was so proud of me that she began petting my head — I, who had never received more than distracted frowns from her all year long.

But it wasn't enough; she wanted more. She and I would triumph together. I was to be testimony to her special reading program. Now she conceived a new plan: she would take me around from class to class, and tell everyone about my accomplishment, and have me read passages from the book.

I begged her not to do this. Not that I had any argument to offer against it, but I gave her to understand, by turning dangerously pale, that I had had enough excitement for the day. Everyone knows that those who are capable of great mental feats are also susceptible to faints and dizzy spells. Insensitive as she was, she got the point, and returned me regretfully to the classroom.

Every day afterward I lived in fear of being exhibited before each class and made to recount the deed that I had not done. I dreaded the truth coming out. Though my teacher did not ask me to "perform" *Les Misérables* anymore, nevertheless she pointed me out to any adult who visited the classroom, including the parents of other children. I heard them whispering about me. I bowed my head in shame, pretending that modesty or absorption in school-work made me turn red at the notoriety gathering around me.

So my career as genius and child prodigy began.

"Victor Hugo, *hélas!*" Gide said, when asked to name the greatest poet in the French language. I say "Victor Hugo, *hélas!*" for another reason. My guilt is such that every time I hear that worthy giant's name I cringe. Afterward, I was never able to read *Les Misérables*. In fact, irrationally or not, I have shunned his entire oeuvre.

_ 2

Willy

MY MOTHER WAS SEEING ANOTHER MAN. His name was Willy. It may have been childish confusion — I was eight years old at the time — or a trick memory plays on us, but I seem to remember the jeep he drove was also a Willys. This car has disappeared from modern life. I am unable even to picture it. But at the time it colored all my thinking about the affair. First, it was described to me as rugged, able to handle rough terrain, and so I came to picture the man himself. Second, the Willys had military associations, like my toy jeeps with green GI Joe soldiers jolted out of the wheel seat as the car went over the wooden runners separating one room from another.

My mother and Willy both worked in a war plant near the Brooklyn Navy Yard, manufacturing radio parts for the troops in Korea. My mother admired Willy for having been in the army, and even reenlisting for a second tour of duty. I come from a long line of draft dodgers. My paternal grandparents fled Russia around 1900 to escape military conscription. My father was excused from World War II because he had four small children. But Willy was not afraid of the service. Willy's only mistake, my mother said, was to marry a woman who was a complete bitch and only wanted his paycheck.

But now Willy was talking about leaving his wife and taking Mom and us kids to California, driving across the country in his jeep to the land of fruit trees and big defense factories.

And what about my father? Were we just supposed to leave him behind?

All that I understood about the Willy situation came to me from far away, and I kept forgetting what little I knew as quickly as possible, so that each time I heard about the affair, it seemed to be a novel, improbable rumor. I was still suffering from the childhood dreaminess that allowed me to ponder, for minutes on end, the order of dealing with socks and shoes, and even resulted once in my forgetting, when I had been sent out in a snow to bring back crumb buns and onion rolls, what I was supposed to buy, where the bakery was, and finally, as I looked about and saw everything covered with white, where my house had disappeared to! Not that I was stupid, but my attention was extremely selective. Car fins fascinated me. I was good out of vagueness rather than will. When it finally came to family matters, I relied on my older brother, Hal, to let me know if something important was starting to happen.

The girls had already met Willy and seen his jeep. One day after work, Mom had introduced them to her boyfriend and they went for a ride around Brooklyn, all the way to Coney Island. It seemed as though Mom was buying off the girls with this spin in a real automobile, saying: This is what our life could be like every day with your new "fun" father.

Somehow Hal and I had not been included in this pleasure jaunt. One more reason to detest our sisters when they came back with excited reports about Willy. What did girls know? Hal said. Their heads could be turned so easily by flashy things like cars. But in a way you couldn't blame them. Molly was just a kid—seven—hair still in ringlets, happy, goofy, a daredevil. And the baby, Leah, was three. She went where she was told, had no real mind of her own yet. A cute kid who liked to run around without panties and climb up the piano.

We lived on the top floor of a five-story tenement in Williamsburg, facing the BMT elevated train, or as everyone called it, the El. Our floors and windows would vibrate from the El, which shook the house like a giant, roaring as his eyes were being poked out. When we went down into the street we played on a checkerboard of sunspots and shadows, which rhymed the railroad ties above our heads. Even the brightest summer day could not lift the darkness and burnt-rubber smell of our street. I would hold my breath when I passed under the El's long shadow. It was the spinal column of my childhood, both oppressor and liberator, the monster who had taken away all our daylight, but on whose back alone one could ride out of the neighborhood into the big broad world.

My father usually took us somewhere on Saturdays—not because he especially wanted to, but because my mother hounded him to get us out of the house. She said she would go crazy if she didn't have a few hours of privacy. In the years when they were still getting along, Father and Mother used to send us to the movies on Saturday afternoons at the Commodore Theater when they wanted time alone together. But once the trouble started, my mother wanted my father out of the house as well. She nagged him and we ganged up too, like wild wolves smelling blood, until about noontime he would put down his book, and take us someplace on the train.

But first, however, he would show his resentment by an uncomfortable little ritual. When we reached the stairway to the elevated train, Father would line us up for inspection. He would find something dirty on our faces, and, wetting a finger, he would correct the offending smudge with his rough laborer's hands till our eyes watered from the pain. Or he would straighten our collar, grumbling aloud, "Your mother lets you go around like ragamuffins!" Never mind that his own fingernails were streaked by green ridges of dirt. His dissatisfaction with our appearance signaled to us that for the moment at least we were our mother's children, he wanted nothing to do with us, perhaps had never wanted us.

Strange, but I would feel a twinge of sympathy for him then. That he should be trapped into working like a dog to clothe and feed us useless kids.

Sometimes he would take us to his factory, which he referred to simply as "the Place." I have to go to the Place, he would announce, and everyone would know he meant his job. It was a ribbon-dyeing plant, with vats and troughs of ink — a business that trafficked only in color, scarlet and indigo. I thought of it also, because of the word *dyeing*, as a place connected to death, a dying factory, where my father gave up his life each day. But it was at work alone he seemed fully alive, lifting enormous spools of ribbons with his knotted arms onto a high shelf, moving through bins with purpose and direction, as he never seemed to move at home.

When he came home he wanted nothing except to eat, fall asleep, or read. Difficult, moody books — Faulkner, Schopenhauer, Dostoevski, James T. Farrell — were his favorites, and when he read it was the same as when he was sleeping. If you woke him accidentally from his nap, he would look at you with harsh nearsighted eyes, his glasses still on the sofa arm, like a boarder who didn't know where these children came from. Sometimes he made us laugh, tickling us with his long simian arms, or letting the girls comb his hair into bangs. Tall and gaunt, he reminded us of Abraham Lincoln. When he was in a joking mood, he would say strange things like "You are being inordinately obstreperous," using words we didn't understand for their humorous effect. It was our mother who would say the really important things, like "I want a quart of milk and some bread and bring back change" — statements to which you had to pay attention. My father drifted from ornamental language into silence. He would slip so far into himself that at the dinner table he would point, as if he had forgotten the words for sugar, knife, meat. "What's the matter?" my mother would say sarcastically. "You don't have a tongue?" We kids, hating her for humiliating our father in front of us, would nevertheless snicker at his strangeness; and he would frown at us with a ferocious look of being betrayed by the mob, that *Et tu Brute* stare.

My attempts to please him, and his to please me, always seemed to misfire. His tender moments had a self-defeating fragility, as though he expected to be rejected for having done something foolish. Since at home he was always under attack for his absentminded clumsiness, he developed an apologetic, apathetic manner, a humility that infuriated my mother even more. It was hard to reconcile in a single notion of "father" both the dread and the pathos he inspired — the first because he was still king of the household, meted out the disciplinary beatings and had a scary temper, the second because he seemed the butt of everyone's ridicule, almost an untouchable.

I remember, for instance, the incident of the marble cake.

We're sitting at the dinner table and eating marble cake. I love marble cake. My father is wearing glasses. He has a serious look, like a monkey concentrating on a metal puzzle. Suddenly he picks his nose, rubs the boogie into a green ball, and, in an absentminded manner, rolls it against his forehead.

"Stop that, you're such a slob!" my mother says.

At first he doesn't know what she's talking about. Then he realizes what he has been doing and his hand descends. We children look away.

"Is there any more marble cake?" I ask.

"No, that's all," says my mother.

My father pushes his portion toward me. "Here, you can take mine."

I stare at the plate, wishing I could eat it, but disgusted because he has already put part of it in his mouth. "No, thank you."

"Go ahead," he offers, "I'm not hungry anymore."

Still, I can't bring myself to eat it. I stare at the soggy end with regret; my father doesn't understand what's wrong. Finally a look of discouragement comes over his face and he leaves the table.

The particular Saturday morning I remember, we did not go to my father's factory. No, it was the Brooklyn Museum. As usual, my mother called to us out the window, remembering at the last moment some food to pick up on the way back. This time, though, at the El's entrance, there was no inspection. My father just took us by the hand, Hal on one side, me on the other, and swung our arms as though we were great friends. The girls ran ahead. Molly was the adventurous one in the family. She ducked under the turnstile with Leah in tow, pretending to be underage herself. On the platform, Molly started leaning over to watch the first sight of the train coming round the curve from Manhattan. Ordinarily, Father would have scolded her, but this time he gently took her hand, moving a safe step backward, and smiled at us boys. What in the heck was going on?

We got on the last car for Molly's sake. The girls raced over to the rear window to look out. Pop, Hal and I took two cane benches facing each other. I loved those old tan wicker seats, loved to run my hand in the weave and pick out the loose ends. I sat by the window, my legs rocking in excitement. To be inside the train while it was making one of those wide whooshing turns like a roller coaster that could easily jump the track and spill us down into the streets but never did, to look into *other people's* windows and fire escapes, to scrape past the moldy warehouses with their flaking olive walls, to stare down at the public square below every other El stop, with its pizza and delicatessen signs — all this was too marvelous to sit still for. Of course there were no elegant neighborhoods — wherever the El went it looked on or created blight, as who with money would want to live next door to it? — but poverty worse than ours was fun to watch from this height, and sometimes in the distance there would be blocks of trim private homes.

Father pulled out a pad of lined paper, and began writing. Usually he worked the crossword puzzle on the train, but today he was doing a poem. I remember having to memorize a poem for school: "In winter I get up at night / And dress by yellow candlelight." I asked Father what a poem really was. He said it was an expression of feeling, with certain rules that you had to follow. I sat quietly beside him and watched him composing. At one point, he took a pocket thesaurus from his coat and looked up a word.

"Who are you writing this for?" I asked timidly.

"It's for your mother."

"But it's not her birthday. Why are you writing a poem to Mom?"

"To get her love back. Shhh. . . ."

Hal gave me a brief nod, as if to say he understood everything and approved. Hal was like a wise old man sometimes; not a serene old man, but one who had seen too much pain and was afflicted with a permanent wince of understanding.

Looking over my father's shoulder, I read the first stanza:

Once in an antique time you seemed to love me,
Your quivering flesh I circled in my arms;
You panted out your gratitude — remember?
Such amorousness was but a false alarm.

I do not fear your look of proud contempt,
Albeit your motives seem so recondite;
I will not bore you with my sad laments
For disillusionment has banished spite.

"That's good, Pop," I said, not knowing what it meant. He accepted the compliment silently, continuing to work. I was fascinated by the way he kept crossing out words and moving lines around. Writing seemed suddenly sculptural, like modeling clay.

After a while I went to see what the girls were doing. Molly and I fought for the window; then we shared it. There was nothing I liked better than to stare out the back window of a train and watch the world be taken away. Later I turned around and saw Father and Hal in serious conversation, leaning toward one another.

Museums were something to be gotten through; room after room of early American portraits, men in blue uniforms with white socks and wigs, women in salmon-pink satin gowns, the George Washingtons and Mrs. Martin Van Burens. But we'd come here for Hal's sake. Hal was good at art in school. Though only eleven, he knew he wanted to be a painter. Hal would go right up to the canvas and study the brush strokes. And I would be proud of him studying the brush strokes, being influenced.

But after a while it was not so interesting, with the Egyptian jewelry and the Colonial bedrooms, and the corny French carpets on the wall; running after Molly, who was getting mischievous, and quieting Leah, whimpering with tiredness; and that burning sinus headache I always got behind the eyebrows in museums from the pearl-grey light diffused by the skylights on an overcast day.

Coming home on the train, Pop was still being so loving toward us boys that I decided to test him by curling up across him with my head on his lap. Who knows, maybe what I had wished for had finally arrived. Maybe a whole new feeling-life would spring up between us. I would no longer be afraid of him, and he would play ball with me in Prospect Park like the other boys' fathers, and he would be good to Hal from now on instead of yelling at him. He would be a whole new father. I cuddled against his arm, pretending to be asleep.

2.

A train had stopped outside our living room. It was level with our windows, so the passengers could look in on us, and we at them. Intensely real for a second, these strangers presented their solitude in the dim rushing light, leaving behind a single detail: the memory of crossed legs, a grey creased hat.

"Which is better, Hal, a Studebaker or a Hudson?" I asked.

"A Studebaker."

"Which is better, a Studebaker or a . . . Chrysler?"

"Chrysler," said Hal, unenthusiastically.

"Isn't it true, that a Russian MiG is better than a Sabrejet?"

"How should I know?"

He knew. He knew everything, my brother. "You do too know."

"I *don't* know. Why are you asking me all these stupid questions? And hold still."

"Am I allowed to look out the window?"

"No."

"Can I talk? I can talk at least."

"Only if I'm not working on your lips." My brother frowned and smudged the charcoal with his finger. He was trying to learn shading. Before, he had always done Battleships — dramatic murky black watercolors of storm clouds and aircraft carriers like those in the Brooklyn Navy Yard. But lately he had become interested in drawing people.

"Are you working on my lips now?"

"I'll tell you when I do."

"What did Daddy say to you? On the train yesterday?" I tried to sound casual, but I had been waiting for the moment to ask this question.

"I don't know if I should tell you."

"Why not?"

"Because. You might be too young."

"Oh, I'm not too young to model for you and I'm not too young when we go to the library. I'm not too young to play ball when you need someone to play with, but suddenly I'm too young. I hate that!"

My brother shrugged. "I tell you almost everything."

It was true. In spite of our three-year age difference, he treated me like an equal, his best friend — except when his friends were around. But those betrayals were rare. "Then why can't you tell me what Daddy said?" I persisted.

He looked up at me and looked down at the pad, without answering. Either he was turning it over in his mind, or he was too engrossed in drawing and forgot the question, or he was teasing me.

"I'm not going to stay still if you don't tell me what Daddy said."

"Okay, okay. You're the one who kept pestering me to draw you."

"You said you needed people to draw."

"Just let me finish this." He worked for a minute longer. When he looked up I sensed a change in him. "Daddy said Mommy wants to leave him because she loves somebody else. She wants to get a divorce." Hal's voice cracked, the way it did when he was close to tears.

"Why would she do that?"

He thought for a while, trying to gain control of himself, then answered with feigned calmness: "Because she's a bitch. I hate her. She wants to take us all to California with this stupid guy *Willy.*" He pronounced the name with disgust. "I don't want to go to California."

"*I* don't want to go to California."

"Sunshine — big deal! I'd rather stay behind in New York with the cold and snow. We can live here with Daddy."

"Yeah, we can live with Daddy," I said, not really sure what was going on.

"What Mom's doing isn't right."

"What else did Daddy say?"

"He said the men in the family should stick together. Like the Three Musketeers: all for one and one for all. Are you in on it?"

I nodded, but unsurely. I knew enough to stand in line with the men if we were dividing up that way. The only problem was, how could a little kid like me affect anything? "But did Daddy say what we should do?"

"No, not yet. But he said that if we men were *unified* — you know, that means if we stick together — that we could change Mommy's mind. She would never want to lose her children, because she loves us too much. So if we keep insisting and insisting that we won't go, she would have to give up all this stuff about Willy."

"I don't understand. Why couldn't she just take us, even if we didn't want to go?"

"Because, jerk, she doesn't want us to hate her! Anyway, I have a plan."

My neck was stiff; I got up and stretched. Then I wandered over for a peek at Hal's drawing. "It doesn't look like me but it's nice."

"I still have trouble with noses. So do you want to hear my plan?"

"Sure."

"We don't talk to Mommy. Just ignore her. Pretend she's dead."

"What if she yells at us?"

"So? Let her scream away."

"All right, but . . . what if she beats us with the ironing cord for not answering her?"

"Then she'll beat us," Hal said grimly. "Are you in on it?"

"I'm in. But, why don't we try to get the girls too?"

"Forget the girls. They're undependable."

"Yeah, I guess."

"Besides, we don't need everyone. All we need is to keep the plan and not give in. Come on, I need you in on it."

"I'm in on it. But the only thing is — won't it hurt Mommy's feelings?"

"So what if it hurts her feelings!" Hal said fiercely. "That's the whole idea, isn't it?"

Hal had everything figured out, but it still baffled me. For instance, I was puzzled about his taking Father's side, because Hal had never seemed to like our father very much. Hal was always arguing with him and trying to get in the last word, with Mom quieting them both. It had even come to blows between them recently. Hal brought home a report card with low marks in arithmetic, and Father punished him with a beating, and Hal actually had the nerve to punch him back! Mommy had had to tear Daddy off him. And now we were all allies against her, trying our hardest to hurt her feelings.

Well, it was time I stopped being such a baby. I was a soldier in Hal's regiment, and if the order came down to ignore her, then that was what I would do.

When Mom came home from work, around four as usual, she asked us what kind of day we had had at school. Hal caught my eye, shook his head no, and walked out of the kitchen. I followed him.

"I'm talking to you," said my mother. "Don't I deserve an answer?" We heard her rattling pots around. "What is this, a pigsty? Doesn't anybody wash a dish? I'm supposed to do everything around here? I'm speaking to you boys! Come in here."

I felt my body strain to obey but Hal signaled no.

"You hear me? If you don't get in here in five seconds I'm going to smack your bottoms with an ironing cord. And I mean it. You know I don't kid around. One . . . two . . . "

"We don't have to talk to her," I whispered.

"Three . . . Ah! so you decided to make an appearance. What do you call this? The table's a mess, the sink's full of dishes, the stove has — soup stains all over it. Whose idea was it to make tomato soup? Don't you know that when you make something you have to clean up after yourselves?"

I almost started to say, Hal was drawing me and we didn't get to it yet. Since Mom was partial to our artistic efforts, that would have been a good enough excuse. But Hal's bashful, demoniacal grin reminded me to keep silence.

"What's the matter, you two got lockjaw? You'll answer me good when I whack your fannies. You don't want to talk to me? So go take a flying leap. *Ich hub dir.* See if I care," she said, her eyes watering. "See if I answer when it's: Mommy, I need money for this, I love you, Mommy, I need a quarter —"

Hal squared his shoulders and walked out of the apartment. He had guts! Behind him I flew down the steps as fast as my feet would take me, and Mom stood at the top of the banister, yelling like the witch in *Hansel and Gretel*, "Boys, where are you going? Boys, come back here!" There was a new tone in her voice. For the first time it sounded as though she was begging us.

We ran past the Spanish family that lived underneath; the young mother who had long black braids and made strong Bustello coffee opened her door in her slip to see what was the matter. She looked up at my mother screaming to us. We raced down the third floor, and past the second-floor apartment of our landlady, mean old Mrs. Einstein. We were still running, out the front door, past old miser Einstein's sweatshop on the first floor where the elderly foreign women bent over their sewing machines, when we realized we had nowhere to go.

We hid in the cellar for an hour. Then we came up reluctantly for dinner. But Hal and I snubbed Mother all that night. During the next few days, though she pretended to be indifferent, we could tell the routine was getting to her. You could see her will crumbling.

By myself I would have given in long ago, but I stayed close to Hal, because Hal alone had the vision to defy this all-powerful Empress of our childhood. It was not so much that we were afraid of her. No, what took vision was to defy someone who had been so good to us. Mama had wrapped us in our snowsuits when we were small, and pulled us to market in a sled (lashed together so that we would not fall out). She had protected us the time an ugly grey rat got into my bunk bed, by chasing him with a broom; she had set the mousetraps and thrown out the poor filthy beasts with snapped necks when no one else would touch them, not even my father. It was she who got up on cold mornings without steam and lit the stove to warm the room for us, and made us hot cocoa before school; and when we came home and lay on the floor covering page after page with drawings, she was the one who applauded them all and kept us in crayons and pens.

When you depend upon someone for everything, it's not surprising if your helplessness collects hostility. But that resentment alone would not have taken us very far. We needed to fan our imagination, Hal and I, with propaganda about Mother as an evil woman, a Delilah. I had seen enough movies Saturday afternoons to know that there was a type of woman who was "bad." Oversexed. Went from man to man. It was necessary to keep this picture sharply in mind whenever my mother appealed to either of us with her hurt, "human" expression.

In the evenings, Hal would go to Father and they would have a private talk. I gathered that Father approved of what we were doing. Meanwhile, he was trying in the only way he knew how to win back Mother's love: there were more poems, one a day, begging, cajoling, accusing.

I would come across them unexpectedly all over the house, these onionskin sheets with blots of ball-point ink where my father's hand had rested. Mother would read the poems to herself with a half-sneering, half-pleased look.

3.

On the third afternoon of the pact against our mother, I came home from school to an empty house. Hal had stayed after school for Art Club, Leah was at nursery school, and Molly was running through the streets with her band of friends, boys who played hooky from school.

I took out my pack of warplane cards. I slipped the rubber band off and touched their frayed, greasy edges: the B–29, the Shooting Star, the Thunderjet, the Sabre. Olive and khaki, their very drabness signified awesome power. On the back of each bubble-gum card were statistics about speed and bombload, the name of the builder and a little history. I was particularly fascinated by Sikorsky, the renegade count and White Russian who had come over to our side. On the bottom of the pile was my favorite card, the Russian MiG, with its dread butcher's belly, like Stalin himself. I had a secret sympathy for the enemy — not because my parents were pro-Rosenberg and even knew some Communists, but because I believed what they taught me in school, that the Russians *were* treacherous, and I admired them for their villainy, just as I admired the Joker in Batman comics. Children are obsessed with fairness. I envied the Soviets their freedom to be mysteriously unfair, unfair without a qualm, which at the time I wished I could be.

Then, too, the war was like a baseball game, with its own bubble-gum cards: Americans were the Yankees, the "good guys," who always won. I, being a Brooklyn Dodger fan, hated the Yankees. The Russians were the underdogs. The Americans were bland and righteous and strong — they were like Willy, all wanting to drive to California and take my mother away from this dark Kremlin household under the El.

But the Russian MiG would shoot them down. Ha ha! I was just setting up my cards for a battle in the air when I heard Mom come in. I knew who it was by the sound of her high heels. "Anybody home?" she called. I heard her kick off her shoes and unzip her dress. That was the first thing she did when she came home, got out of her work clothes.

"Oh, it's you," she said as she opened my bedroom door. How I wished Hal was there to direct me! "Why don't you come in the kitchen, I'll make you some cocoa." I followed her into the kitchen.

"Did you have a nice day at school?"

I nodded. A nod didn't count.

"Where's your brother?"

I shrugged.

"I'm worried about him. Are you sure you don't know where he is? It's after four . . . if he doesn't come home soon I'm going to have to call the police."

I bit my lip; that would be awful, to have the police arrive. It would be my fault. Looking at the front door, I prayed that he would come in.

"I saw Molly downstairs playing hopscotch, and I told her she had to be up by five. But I'm worried about that brother of yours. Where could he be? I'm just going to have to call the police, that's all —"

"He had to stay after school!"

My mother smiled. She couldn't control her delight at having tricked me into speaking. Then she put her arms around me and kissed me. "I've missed you, honey. Let's make up."

"Okay."

She poured me the cocoa and watched me drink it. "This is good," I said, feeling weak-willed and embarrassed.

"Come inside my room," she said. "I want us to have a talk. And I have to change my clothes."

I followed her into her bedroom and sat on the mattress beside her. My mother was wearing her black nylon slip, out of which she seemed to burst. There was a large expanse of freckled cleavage, and her skin close up had soft pores and a smell of buttermilk. I did not like to look at her heavy thighs, the insides of which were riddled with purple varicose veins that made me think of blood poisoning — they came from standing on her feet too much at work, she said — but my eyes kept seeking them out nevertheless. Perhaps it was the desire to overcome my pity and repulsion that made me stare at them. I began to wish she would put on her clothes, as she said she was going to, but instead she kept sitting beside me half dressed, sighing and reaching for the right words.

"Tell me, why haven't you and Hal been talking to me? Am I such an ogre? Have I done anything to hurt you?"

"It's not that. We wanted to help Daddy."

"I figured your old man had been talking to you! What did he say?"

"I don't know, he talked mostly to Hal."

"Did he tell you I was going to leave him?"

"Yes," I said in a small voice.

"And that I was 'running around with another man'? . . . I could kill him! What right — what right does he have to use my children against me?"

"He didn't tell us not to talk to you. That was Hal's idea — and my idea," I added scrupulously.

"But you kids are being used."

"But we don't want you to leave Daddy."

"You don't know the whole story," she said, and let out a powerful sigh.

"Well, tell me."

My mother smiled. "I almost think I could explain it all to you, you seem so understanding sometimes. Naw, forget it."

"No, explain it," I said. I put on my most thoughtful "listener's" face, as I had watched adults do, scrunching up my brow — and waited.

"I'm unhappy, baby. You know the old expression, I feel like I'm being torn to pieces? That's me. A piece here, a piece there. I don't know what's right. I met a man. . . . And he makes me happy. I know you think of me as an old lady. But I'm only twenty-eight. I got married young, I was a — teenager, and I started having babies right away. I'm not saying I didn't want to have babies, of course I did. Your father was the one who. . . . But that's beside the point; what I'm trying to say is that I have years and years ahead of me. I don't want to be unhappy for the rest of my life."

"Why can't you be happy with Daddy?"

"Because I can't. He's miserable, and he's dragging me down. It's no use. You think I haven't tried. You know what living with your father is. He doesn't care about anything but the game on the radio and the book in front of his face. He married me because he needed a *mother*, someone to cook for him and wash his socks. He doesn't lift a finger to help me around the house. Oh, it's not all his fault, I know that. Your Pop had it rough when he was your age. His mother died young, and his stepmother made him wash floors. Like Cinderella. His father, Grandpa — well, you know, Grandpa's no bargain either. A real bastard, cold as they come. No one gave Bert much love, and as a result he — never learned how to show affection. But meanwhile, I'm the one who's paying for what his family did to him! It's like I've got five children to take care of instead of four, and your father's the most helpless of all."

"He sometimes helps you clean up."

"Oh, it's more than that," she said. "A woman needs — to be satisfied by a man — needs tenderness." Mom looked at me with hungry blue eyes. "He doesn't go out of his way to — do for me. A woman — likes to have a man who has manners. Who will open a door for her occasionally, make a nice compliment once in a while, be — considerate. That's all; just to show a little consideration. When you grow up, try to remember that."

"I will."

"I know you will, honey; you're already considerate."

I was flattered that Mom thought I would grow up to be the sort of man she admired. At the same time, I had the feeling that I was being sidetracked and was not advancing Dad's case enough. "But he writes poems to you, doesn't he?" I said.

"With sixty-four-dollar words that I don't understand? Where's the heart? Where's the *warmth*? I can't even read them without a dictionary. They make me feel stupid. . . . Who's he trying to impress, me? No, he's showing off his great brain.

Sure, he's smart. I married your father because he was the most intelligent man I knew. I wanted to have bright children. That part worked out fine. But did I know he would turn into a zombie? He used to be fun. We would go to nightclubs and he'd explain to me all about art and — and current events. . . . What did I know? I was a dumbbell working in a beauty parlor, I never even finished high school. And here was this guy Bert, who knew everything. I'm grateful to him for improving my mind. But now — he's given up. He's stuck in that lousy factory job and all he ever talks about is the Place. He gets up, goes to work, comes home, sleeps — like a robot! He's *got* a good brain, why can't he use it? I *tried* to get him to go back to college. It's hopeless. And I'm drowning. We're all drowning. You want me to drown? Look, try to see it from my side. I found someone who's crazy about me. So he's not as intelligent as your father. Maybe it's just as important to be kind and — and decent and . . . "

I said nothing, and my silence seemed to force her doubts to surface. Let's face it, in our family intelligence *was* what counted; we weren't about to trade it in for something as insipid as kindness.

"I don't know what your father has told you about Willy," she said. "You've never met him. You've never given him a chance. He's a very sweet man. He loves children. He's willing to take care of all of you, to break his back for us. Don't you want to go to California? It's warm all year round, it's not freezing like this — hellhole!"

"But I like the snow," I said. "And I don't want to leave Daddy."

"Try to understand. See it from my side! I'm not saying we're going to leave Bert. I haven't made up my mind about that. But if this is my only chance, I'd be a fool not to take it. Wouldn't I. . . . I don't *know* what I want to do, that's why I'm telling you this. Nothing is decided, honey. I'm all mixed up." She kept talking in circles and looking beseechingly into my eyes, as if I had the answers for her. It was then I think I learned that if you stay very quiet and listen to the confusion of others and nod from time to time, people will think you understand. They will go away feeling better.

Much of what she said sailed over my head, but I understood the main part: that she was unhappy. In years to come, whenever I've found myself reenacting this scene of listening to someone (usually a woman) in torment between two courses, my mind has gone back to Mother in her black slip. When I was in a mood to rebel against my personality, I would reproach my mother for taking away my childhood by placing me in the position of her judge and pardoner, and by telling me things that perhaps were not suited to my age. But what's the point of blaming, when it is questionable who seduced whom? She needed someone to talk to, and I would have sold out my "golden childhood" a dozen times over for a compliment like the one I received.

She said: "You know, I keep forgetting that I'm talking to an eight-year-old. It's as if I were speaking to someone older and wiser. You've made me feel a lot better."

I blushed. I had found a new way to make my mother love me.

"Baby, promise me you'll forgive me for making such a mess of things? That you won't hate me?"

"I love you," I said.

She squeezed me against her and kissed me, murmuring, "Precious, precious." I stood there accepting her warm, embarrassing kisses. Then she said with sudden impulsiveness: "Let's celebrate! I don't feel like cooking. Why don't we go across the street and buy some specials." (Specials were the fat kosher hot dogs we loved.) "And pastrami and salami and lots of pickles, sour ones, the kind you like."

"Do you have money?" I said. I hated to ask the bald delicatessen man across the street to "put it on my mother's bill."

"Of course we've got money. Here, take a ten-dollar bill, I'll write out a list for you. And if you see anything you like — just for yourself — like a piece of strudel or knish, throw that in, too."

I dreaded the moment when Hal would come home and see us talking; but he accepted the new situation without a word, and never demanded an explanation, even in private.

I felt optimistic that everything would work out now. Because we had had this heart-to-heart talk, and I had taken Father's side and she seemed chastened, I assumed that the trouble was settled. It was my first instance of placing excessive faith in the medium of confession. Mother continued seeing Willy, she still made herself look pretty when she was about to leave for work, she still hummed to herself.

My father, meanwhile, had become desperate. The poems had stopped; now he made threats, which my mother laughed at. She seemed to be daring him, like Carmen and Don José. One afternoon she kept needling him:

"Come on, Bertram, why don't you get off your bony ass and put down the goddamn book, *As I Lay Dying* or whatever it is, and help with the cleaning. Make like a human being! Who do you think you are — Sitting Bull?"

"All right!" Those were his only words, and they came out in a strangled, tortured voice garbled by phlegm. Then, strangely, he went back to reading.

"No, it's not all right. Why the hell should I slave on the weekends cleaning up when I work all week same as you. You know, if you were half a man, you would bring in enough money so that I could stay home and keep this place decent and look after the kids —"

"All right, all right!" he yelled. It was amazing how a man of his extensive vocabulary could exist inside those two words for days at a time.

"I'm sorry I brought it up, Your Highness. I didn't mean to disturb your train of thought. I don't know why I bother. It's like talking to a stone wall. I feel like putting on my hat and coat and saying goodbye and never coming back."

"Then go! Go to your lover-boy."

"What is that supposed to mean?" she said.

"You know what it means," he muttered.

"I'd rather not discuss it here like this, if you don't mind."

"Then I'll go. If you don't want me around so much, I'll leave you alone."

"Always making promises, never coming through," she said with a bitter laugh.

My father got up without a word and left the house.

4.

One thing we had never expected was for *Father* to run away. By dinner time he had still not returned, and we all felt guilty.

"Where did Daddy go?" Molly asked Mom for the third time.

"Who the hell knows?"

"What is Daddy doing now?"

"Maybe he's hanging himself, maybe he's run off with a blonde. How the hell should I know?" Whenever Mother felt worried, her language became coarser. "Maybe an A-bomb will drop on our heads and we'll all be dead. What am I, a fortune-teller? Come on, get into your pajamas. Hey, September Morn! Put some clothes on."

"I'm taking my bath," Leah said indignantly, with a lisp, stark naked as usual.

"All right, take your bath." Mom turned on the radio and we listened to "The Green Hornet." We were allowed to stay up later than usual because of the family catastrophe.

The next evening, my mother got a phone call; she made me run for a pencil to write down the number. He had moved into a YMCA room. "Oh, for crying out loud!" we heard her say into the receiver. "Why don't you come home? You know we can't afford two rents." It seemed he wanted her to agree to stop seeing Willy before he would promise to return. Mother resisted: "I can't make guarantees! What are you trying to do, force me by running away? That's so childish, Bert." They argued back and forth; but what struck me was that my mother kept saying "Please take care of yourself" and "Don't do anything foolish" and "We'll work it out."

She agreed to meet him alone for dinner, after work Tuesday night.

Five nights later, on Friday night, my father returned home. No one said, "How was the Y, Dad?" We allowed him to sink back into the family routine. He was sheepish and, for the most part, silent, and we had had too-recent evidence of his fragility to risk upsetting him.

As far as I was concerned — as far as I knew — the episode with Willy was closed. I assumed Father would not have returned unless some satisfactory agreement had been reached. But again I assumed wrong. He had merely given in, tired of his protest at the Y. We had underestimated Mother's stubbornness. She went on seeing her lover. That is, until one shocking night, which ended everything to do with Willy.

5.

My father was beating my mother. She had come home after midnight and he had lost no time smacking her; then he threw her into their bedroom. She screamed but did not run away. Strange to think of him shoving her around because she was the larger — we used to call them Fat and Skinny; but he was stronger, of course.

Through the locked door, and from the other end of the five-room apartment, in the girls' room where we all gathered, we could hear our father beating our mother with an open hand. His slaps came down on her plump body, the flat sound of his hand smacking her reverberating flesh. And Mother's cries: "Enough, enough!"

"I'll tell you when it's enough!" I could picture his spittle dripping at his mouth, the way it did when he lost control.

My brother and my sisters and I held hands. We could see nothing, we could only hear the sounds, which made it worse. It seemed like the end of the world. Little Leah began to wail. Molly and I held each other tighter, frightened but excited by the violence as by a fight in the school yard. Hal's fists kept clenching and unclenching. He looked demented. Suddenly his high-pitched voice startled us. "Leave her alone! *You stop hitting my mother!*"

"Don't, Hal, he'll hit you too," I whispered. "He'll murder us all!" I tried to hold Hal by the arm but he pulled away, screaming: "You leave my mother alone or I'll kill you!"

We heard our mother say: "Bert, the kids are listening. Don't shame me in front of them!"

"You should have thought of that sooner," Father said, growling. Remorselessly he continued his beating, like a man with a long day's work ahead of him. He had found a rhythm for the blows. When would it be enough? How would he know when the job was finished?

At the other end of the apartment we saw the crazy elevated train blazoning our ceiling with its orange headlights. Maybe passengers could look right in their bedroom and see the beating. Our whole living room was lit up with the train's lurid glow, like a bonfire. Crackling and flaming, the train pulled out, leaving us again in darkness.

Leah was crying hysterically. Molly and I tried to do something to comfort her. "It's all right," we took turns saying, "it will be over soon" — as much for our own benefit as for hers. Hal gazed fiercely in front of him. Rocking himself back and forth, he seemed to be measuring the strength in his small arms. But what could he do against Father? Besides, it seemed wrong to me that he should get in the middle of their fight. Mother had to take her beating like the rest of us. Something about the way she was moaning and weeping made me sense that they knew what they were doing, that this had to be done, and that they would respect the limits. They were both playing their roles in concert, with more cooperation than was usual between them. "I swear I'll never go back," she pleaded. "I just had to tell him it was over, Bert!" And he: "If you go back I'll kill you!"

He called her every name under the sun, and with each name his hand re-claimed its harsh beating rhythm. He had found the words at last.

Part of me identified absolutely with my mother; another part was experiencing a sort of sweet revenge. But the greatest part of which I now remain aware told me that this is how it is, this is the mystery you must understand.

How different my hypnotized response was from Hal's. The hero of my childhood, he thought he could act to rescue our mother. And in a way he did. He dashed to the other end of the house, through the frightening no-man's-land separating us from them, and pounded on their door. "Stop it! Stop hitting her! I'll call the police!"

In the end that voice must have gotten through to my father. He left off. But my mother continued sobbing for another hour. We heard her through the door, each sob feeding involuntarily on the last, winding down bitterly to a questioning whimper, like that of a crying doll pushed forward at the waist.

6.

And after that they remained together. Whether that was providential or a tragedy depends on whom you talk to; I for one was glad. It seemed to my childish mind that a beating had saved the family, though that was probably not the case. There were beatings all through my childhood, and disturbances between my mother and father were to occur again and again — but none came so close to splitting us up as the Willy episode, and none seemed to end quite so suddenly. I came away from that night with both a heightened respect for power and a nausea for violence. The peculiar part, though, was that it seemed to me my father's will had been broken, not my mother's, that night. Afterward he acted more defeated, as though the beating had smashed up something in him. And she seemed to pity him more.

Some say that life is a blessing; others, that the truth of life is cruelty. The strong have an air of believing both: they celebrate their ability to overcome experiences of a particularly coarse, violent nature with a heady realism; or else they compress their former exposure to horror into a steady stream of gentleness. Myself, I am made uncomfortable by the notion that mankind is, at bottom, brutal. I would prefer to honor the ironies, pleasures and civilities of life. Yet I cannot get beyond certain brutal memories from childhood whose rumble I still hear going on in my head like an inner trembling. And maybe I hold on to them too much, also, out of pride.

Often I have a dream where I have gotten off an elevated train at the end of the line; the tracks curve to a stop above my head like a hanging comma. Where am I? In the distance there seem to be nothing but empty lots, undeveloped property at the edge of the city line. I turn back in the other direction and examine the storefronts under the El, looking for the old corner delicatessen and the Marcy movie house with its familiar marquee. But in this dark crisscrossed world I recognize nothing. This is a part of Brooklyn I have never been to before. Should I walk back under the tracks until they get to Williamsburg? Should I move on into the rock-filled empty lots? Try something new? The dream always ends there, without my making up my mind.

― 3

Samson and Delilah and the Kids

I GREW UP IN THE ERA OF THE GREAT JEWISH LOVERS. *Samson and Delilah,* *David and Bathsheba, Solomon and Sheba* were burning up screens across the land. I never managed to see *David and Bathsheba* (though I knew the coming attractions by heart), because the movie industry in its wisdom decreed that I was too young for this adulterous tale. Inconsistently, they let me into *Samson and Delilah* when I was seven.

I still remember my excitement when I first saw the poster announcing its imminent arrival in our neighborhood. "See Samson battle a lion with his own hands! See Samson tear down the Temple of Dagon! See Delilah tame the strongman!" I was so crazy about movies that I saw everything connected to them as a *promesse de bonheur:* lobby stills, newspaper ads on the entertainment pages, and especially the ten-foot billboards displayed outside the Commodore, where giants held at bay an encircling, ungrounded chaos of tempting panoramas.

My tolerance for celluloid had been built up over the long Saturday matinees that my siblings and I attended regularly, and which included a double feature, seven cartoons, newsreels, coming attractions, and a Flash Gordon or Hopalong Cassidy serial. "O dark, dark, dark, amid the blaze of noon!" (*Samson Agonistes*) By the time we had stumbled onto the street, sated with the blood of scalped cavalrymen, the highballs served by Veronica Lake, the dynamite set off by a Bugs Bunny in drag, it was already dinner time. We would walk under the El past the discount stores serving our ghetto in Williamsburg, Brooklyn; past Stevens Bakery, which specialized in white icing; past the fish restaurant with its grotesque lobster tank in the window; past the tough shoeshine boys on the corner, past the synagogue, quickly and

---

This essay was written originally for an anthology of essays about the Old Testament, *Congregation,* in which each author was asked to establish personal ties with a biblical text. I chose to focus on the Samson story, both because it seems to me one of the key narratives in the Bible (its richness attested to by the many plays, operas, epic poems, films drawn from it), and because I suspected the Samson and Delilah dynamic had helped to shape me as a man, like it or not.

guiltily, because it was *Shabbes*, and make our way back to the tenement where we lived, debating our favorite scenes all the while.

If you ask me what the Bible meant to me as a child, I can tell you it signified two things: those awkwardly drawn comic strips the *Brooklyn Eagle* would run (next to "Dick Tracy" or "Mary Worth") each Sunday, "Tales from the Scriptures," featuring stern, bearded patriarchs and women with pitchers on their shoulders, and the biblical spectacles we were constantly told cost "millions" and had "casts of thousands." Whatever possessed Hollywood to turn out all those biblical/Roman clinkers throughout the fifties? The postwar audience's abandonment of a neo-realist aesthetic for the escapist anodynes of costumed bloodshed, the advent of widescreen technologies that cried out for spectacle, the more conservative political mood, the irresistible formula of having one's cake (sin) and eating it too (piety), the collapse of the studio system and its replacement by international package deals—all must have contributed to the zenith of this ill-fated genre.

Cecil B DeMille's *Samson and Delilah* (1949) was one of the first of the postwar biblical spectacles. Watching a VCR tape of it some thirty-five years later, I am struck by how dioramic and artificial (if entertaining in a kitschy way) it looks now, its drama as stylized as Kabuki, its sets like an old World's Fair made of endless lathe and temporary grandeur. The virtues of the biblical epic—which DeMille had a large hand in shaping—were mainly to be found in art direction, costumes, and special effects. DeMille began in the silent era, and there is an echo of Griffith's Babylonianism in the idol-gargoyled Temple of Dagon.

"Before the dawn of time . . ." intones the narrator in the opening shot; we see clouds, and marching feet, and are treated to a little lecture about the struggle between tyranny and freedom. Biblical epics tended to be made after both world wars, when America, as "leader of the free world," had a need to wrap itself in the sanctimonious mantle of previous Chosen Peoples. Curiously, the word "Jew" is never mentioned in the DeMille film, nor are the words "Hebrew" or "Israelite." Samson's people are referred to only as "Danites," in what may have been nervousness about anti-Semitism during the McCarthy era.

Samson and Delilah boasted one of those "international" casts: the star (Hedy Lamarr) spoke Viennese-scented English, her leading man (Victor Mature) hailed from Kentucky, and all the Philistine opponents of Judeo-Christianity had, in the curious convention of such films, British accents (George Sanders, Angela Lansbury, Henry Wilcoxin).

A DeMille scholar told me that the director had wanted to make *Samson and Delilah* ten years earlier but that he couldn't secure the financing. By the time the deal had come together with the actress he wanted, a certain freshness had gone out of Lamarr: she looked bruised by another decade's strain of holding together her glamour. But her worldly, mocking Viennese air had some of Dietrich's alluring melancholy, especially when it came up against the younger, oafish Mature: it was the Old World seducing the New World, yet again.

Hedy's basic Delilah costume consisted of a sleeveless halter that stopped just below her breasts, a long skirt, usually with a slit to show off her nice legs, and, anachronistically, a pair of pumps as well. After she becomes a Bad Woman she is never seen without a feather-duster plume, which she waves around to make her points, and which is color-coordinated to match her silver, turquoise, rose, and sapphire gowns. At times she seems to act mainly with her midriff (midriff eroticism being a staple of these epics, rendered more piquant by the code rule forbidding umbilici on-screen), or with her eloquent shoulder blades, as she leans against a wall, thrusting her breasts forward. Even though she seems rather diminutive next to Mature, she is altogether luscious with her upturned nose, saucy gazes, and spit curls.

Mature responds with a supercilious sneer like a country bumpkin who knows they are putting something over on him but isn't sure what, and hopes his cynicism will distract attention from his slowness. It was about this actor that David Thomson wrote, memorably if cruelly: "It is too easy to dismiss Mature, for he surpasses badness. He is a strong man in a land of nine-stone weaklings, an incredible concoction of corned beef, husky voice and brilliantine—a barely concealed sexual advertisement for soiled goods. Remarkably, he is as much himself in the cheerfully meretricious and the pretentiously serious. . . ." Here, however, he seems bewildered, his eyes look dead when he is called upon to say things like "You—daughter of hell!" He wears a green leather jerkin that leaves most of his chest uncovered, and his broad body, by our more stringent, Schwarzenegger standards of muscular definition, looks fat. (Incidentally, there is nothing in the Bible that says Samson was a brawny, muscular person. Since his strength came from God's spirit inhabiting him, the theological point might have been better made by casting Mickey Rooney or Arnold Stang.)

Yet, by that familiar phenomenon that makes it difficult to picture a story's characters afterward except in the physical shape of the actors who played them on-screen, however miscast they may have been, the past-her-prime Lamarr and the stalwart ham Mature will always remain in my imagination the quintessential, the *actual*, Samson and Delilah.

As a child I was a very forgiving moviegoer. If a picture had one or two scenes that excited my imagination, I would simply evacuate the duller parts from consciousness and concentrate on these privileged images, carrying them around like mental slides long afterward and consulting them solacingly in bad moments. Such a scene was the destruction of the Philistine hall in *Samson and Delilah*, where the pillars crumbled in sections like gigantic white Tootsie Rolls. For me, Samson was essentially a Superman figure. Just as I would jump off a chair and pretend to fly like the Man of Steel, so I used to play at tying my hands together and ripping the ropes off; eyes closed, I would grit my teeth and fantasize pulling a building down by straining with all my might. I had dreams of toppling P.S. 11, breaking everything I hated into rubble, like the newsreels of bombed Berlin. (As it happened, many blocks in Williamsburg already looked that way, torn down to make way for the future Brooklyn–Queens Expressway.)

I prayed to get back at everyone who had humiliated me in one blow, like poor Samson, the blind giant. Not that I had so many enemies, but every child suffers from powerlessness, bossed around by adults, older brothers, classroom bullies. There was one tormentor, Ronald, big for his age, who used to beat me up after school. I would imagine ways to torture him, a new one each night like Scheherazade. As I grew older I began to concoct more subtle revenge fantasies, sometimes even letting my prisoner go. Curiously, this reprieve gave me a greater *frisson*: I enjoyed the idea of playing cat and mouse with my victim, one day vicious, the next unexpectedly benevolent. Control, restraint, sadism, creativity. I was only a few years from eroticizing this fantasy with a chivalric twist.

In sixth grade I was attracted to a girl with a Roman nose named Felicia, as were all the boys, since she already had the curves of a woman. She was from a better family than ours, her father was a lawyer, and she carried herself rather haughtily. "She thinks she's Cleopatra—or Delilah!" we would say behind her back, because she knew all the boys fancied her. Secretly, I imagined myself drawing daily closer to the beautiful Felicia and impressing her with my intelligence. One afternoon when I tried to make friendly conversation she ridiculed me, saying that I wore the same clothes, the same ugly sweater, every day. It was true. I had taken no notice of what I had on, and neither, apparently, had my parents.

After she had humiliated me, I began to have dreams in which Felicia would knock on my door, completely naked and defenseless. Someone had stolen her clothing. Not only did I not take advantage of the situation, I would immediately throw a coat or blanket around her shoulders and escort her home. This chaperonage would sometimes take us down dank castle steps in which I would have to protect her honor by sword fight. Never did I ask her for so much as a kiss in payment—though sometimes she would reward me with a feast of kisses.

The closeness with which dreams of gallantry and revenge were tangled in my brain must be why, even today, when I remember to act in a polite manner (for instance, giving up my seat to a woman in the bus) and am thanked for being "chivalrous," I instantly feel a twinge of guilty conscience. But then, I am chronically guilt-ridden about my virtuous side, if you will. "You were always a good boy," my mother has told me so often. "You I never had to worry about." Even as a baby, before I had any choice in the matter, I was "good": when my mother was in the maternity ward, when all the other babies were wailing from the air-raid sirens, I quietly found her breast.

One of my earliest memories, from about the age of four, is of my older brother and younger sister experimenting with matches. "They shouldn't be doing that," I thought. Sure enough, the kitchen curtain caught fire. There was smoke, flames; my mother came home in the nick of time and doused the fire with pots of water. When it was over she demanded to know what had happened. My brother and sister pointed fingers at each other. "I didn't do anything," I kept telling her. Finally she said, "I know, cookie, I know you didn't." The question years later is, *Why* didn't I do anything? Why was I such a goody-goody? Was I good because I chose to be or because I was too timid, too programmed to do otherwise?

There were rewards for being the "good" boy, but sometimes it came as a mixed blessing; I was both my mother's favorite and the one to whom she paid the least attention, because I didn't cause her trouble. By nursery school, I had already developed a reputation for honesty. "Phillip never lies," my nursery teacher said. My mother, pleased to hear it, nevertheless insisted healthily, "Every child lies." "Not Phillip," said this woman, whom I had clearly managed to make fall in love with me.

One day, not long thereafter, I was jumping up and down on my parents' bed, using their mattress as a trampoline. I was no angel, I wanted to have a good time, to break the rules, to become an evildoer! (In Part 2 of *The Brothers Karamazov*, which Dostoevsky never got to write, the saintly Alyosha was supposed to turn into a great sinner.) In mid-jump I heard my mother coming. "What were you doing?" Were you jumping on my bed like I told you not to?" "No, uh-uh," I protested "I *saw* you do it!" she exclaimed. "Don't fib to me." Though I got a beating afterward we were both relieved: he lies!

In Judges, the story of Samson begins with his mother's barrenness. An angel appears to the wife of Manoah and tells her she is going to have a son, but she should drink no wine nor eat anything unclean, and "No razor shall come upon his head, for the boy shall be a Nazarite to God from birth; and he shall begin to deliver Israel from the hand of the Philistines." (Judges 13:5) She runs and tells her husband what the stranger has said, and Manoah gets the angel to repeat these instructions a third time. Then a puff of smoke, flames, and the couple realizes that the stranger is indeed an angel of the Lord; they fall on their faces to the ground. This angelic visitation to a barren woman is a recurrent biblical formula; only in the context of Judges, with its dense narrative style, does the incident's leisurely redundance surprise. Why is a whole chapter of twenty-five verses "wasted" on this business? Certainly no other judge is accorded such preliminary buildup; it is almost as though the whole Book of Judges were taking a breath before launching into the Samson story.

In a way, also, the chapter lets us know that before Samson is even born he is in God's debt. His body itself doesn't quite belong to him—it's a sacred weapon for God to inhabit with His spirit when He so desires. Moreover, without any choice in the matter, Samson is pledged to be a Nazarite: one who is consecrated, abstinent, separate from others, pure. No wonder Samson acts "bad": he is trying to make a space for his own life, inside the one already owed to his parents and God.

So he indulges in skirt-chasing. All his troubles—but also all his heroic deeds— stem from whoring and womanizing. He falls in love easily, and, it seems, purely on a physical basis. Like Portnoy, he is drawn to *shiksas*. In our very first encounter with the adult Samson, he has just seen a woman in Timnah, the daughter of Philistines, and wants her for a wife. His parents object: "Is there not a woman among the daughters of your kinsmen, or among all the people, that you must go to take a wife from the uncircumcised Philistines? But Samson said to his father, 'Get her for me, for she pleases me well.'" (Judges 14:3)

Now, this first time he is exonerated from blame, because the text immediately assures us that Samson's romantic entanglement was the doing of the Lord, who "was seeking an occasion against the Philistines." Later, in the Delilah episode, this cosmic alibi is withdrawn; Samson will be made to stand completely alone with his mistake. Everything in the Samson story happens twice, sometimes thrice; repetitions establish his character patterns. Thus, if he had let only Delilah wheedle a secret out of him, that would be one thing, but before he does so he gives the woman of Timnah the answer to his wedding riddle, "because she pressed him hard."

Samson is a man women nag. For all his strength, he seems not to engender their full respect, much less their obedience. They know how to play on his guilt with tears and reproaches ("You don't really love me or you'd tell me your secret"), to twist him around their fingers. And ultimately, they betray him. Not only does the woman of Timnah broadcast the riddle's answer, forcing Samson to pay everyone the betting price, but she cuckolds Samson by giving herself to "his companion, who had been his best man." (Judges 14:20) Delilah does even worse: she ruins him. Sandwiched between these two women is the harlot in Gaza, who also endangers Samson by keeping him occupied while his enemies surround his house. He escapes by lifting the city gates on his shoulders, but he is clearly tempting fate.

Samson also is a man who seems to enjoy being righteously angry. "If you had not ploughed with my heifer, you would not have found out my riddle," he tells the wedding guests, kills thirty men, and stomps off "in hot anger." Later, when he returns to Timnah and finds his wife has been given to another man, he rejects the offer of marrying her younger sister. "This time I shall be blameless in regard to the Philistines, when I do them mischief," he says, then ties three hundred foxes together, attaches lit torches between their tails, and lets them burn up all the Philistine orchards and grain. The Philistines retaliate by torching his wife (who had already abandoned him) and her father. Samson retorts: "'If this is what you do, I swear I will be avenged upon you, and after that I will quit.' And he smote them hip and thigh with great slaughter." The implication is that any destruction, however disproportionate, is "justifiable" if interpreted as retaliation. No wonder Samson allows himself so often to be betrayed: it frees him to do what he wants.

I grew up in a household where there was much arguing and yelling, even hitting. But it was necessary, as we learned from imitating my mother, always to lay a groundwork of self-righteousness before any explosion. "I am only doing this to you because you did X and Y to me first." Within the never-ending chain of injured feelings that is family history, it is not always easy to find the beginning of a causal series, which is why the person with the loudest voice or the longest memory is generally able to make the best tit for tat. My older brother, Hal, whose voice is very strong, was for a while the undisputed king of righteous explosions. Fortunately, Hal would fulminate so long on the heinousness of the wrong done him that it was possible to get out of the way of any serious physical harm before he swung into action. We were much more terrified of my father, who was phlegmatic, quiet, and withdrawn for the most part; but if he blew up you had less than a second's warning. When my father got physical the slaps and punches came hard and fast, as in a street fight. He had powerful, bony hands and sharp elbows, and in anger he seemed to lose control, with white spittle foaming at his mouth like a mad dog—or at least that was how it looked to a child. Curiously, he always tried to get out of spanking us; he had no heart for premeditated disciplining, leaving such beatings to my mother.

She would take out her ironing cord—a black-and-white fabric switch, which we thought of as a live creature. What was interesting about the way she beat us was that she would herself grunt and make awful faces each time she picked up her arm. "You had enough?" she would demand, after each blow. "Gonna try that again?"

It was a dialogue; we were supposed to respond correctly so that she would know when to quit. My brother would take his punishment like a man; howling only when he was in pain. I was more of a faker: very early I caught on that it was all symbolic, and I would scream and carry on from the first hand-raise so that she would let me go with next to nothing. My sister Molly, however, would laugh in my mother's face, would giggle or hum a tune to herself, refusing to concede even when I could see tears welling in her eyes, until finally my mother would stop, baffled, her arm exhausted.

I am struggling to find the pattern between all these pieces. I have the sense that the Samson story and my family story touch in odd ways; I try to put the stencil of one over the other, and, while they occasionally overlap, just as often the connection seems farfetched. Nonetheless, I am convinced that at the center of both is the mystery of power relations between men and women. I start to write "How did it come about that I started mistrusting women, or thought they would betray me?" But then I pause: Do I really? Aren't I often less guarded around women than I am with men? Let us say that a part of me still fears (hopes?) that women are treacherous creatures. I know that growing up, watching the unhappiness between my parents, watching my mother disparage my father every day and my father refuse to let her go, made me cautious toward the opposite sex. Then, too, my mother was very insecure as a young woman: we would climb into her lap and she would suddenly push us away, saying "Don't start that 'Mommy I love you' crap, you're only being lovey-dovey because you want something out of me. Okay, what is it this time? An ice cream? A quarter?" Naturally, I learned to be skeptical of affection, almost to *want* a barbed hurt to accompany love. As for my father, he had been treated wretchedly by his stepmother, who put him to work all the time, so he was both desperate for maternal warmth and suspicious of any feminine softness. When these two hurt, insecure people, the black sheep of both their middle-class families, came together to live in poverty and raise their own family, the results were not pretty.

My parents had a bookcase which held a few hardcovers and a library of Pocket Books, whose flimsy, browning pages would crack if you bent down the corners. I can still picture those cellophane-peeling covers with their kangaroo logo, their illustrations of busty, available-looking women or hard-bodied men or solemn, sensitive-looking Negroes; with titles like *Intruder in the Dust, Appointment in Samarra, Tobacco Road, Studs Lonigan, Strange Fruit, Good Night, Sweet Prince, The Great Gatsby, The Sound and the Fury.* . . .

Father brought home all the books, it was his responsibility; though Mother chafed at everything else in the marriage, she still permitted him at the time to be her intellectual mentor. I have often wondered on what basis he made his selections: he'd had only one term of night college (dropping out because he fell asleep in class after a full day in the factory), and I never saw him read book reviews. He seemed, all the same, to have a nose for decent literature. He was one of those autodidacts of the Depression generation, for whose guidance the inexpensive editions of Everyman, Modern Library, and Pocket Books seemed intentionally designed, out of some bygone assumption that the workingman should—must—be educated to the best in human thought.

My father had an awed respect for the power of good fiction, especially when it was able to mirror uncannily the conflicts in his own life. He would often marvel at Kafka's story "The Judgment," in which the patriarch tells his son to jump off a bridge—obviously because *his* father, my grandfather, had treated him like dirt. He never stopped praising *The Brothers Karamazov*, which had the status of the Bible in Brooklyn at the time. Again, I suspect its patricidal theme excited him more than Dostoevsky's philosophy. He did dip into one philosopher, Schopenhauer, and would occasionally read aloud one of the gloomy German's misogynistic aphorisms. These were usually to the effect that women had no capacity for ideas, that their only cleverness was in tricking men to perpetuate the species. (My mother gave an odd sort of credence to this theory by boasting that she had "seduced" my father into siring us—finagling away the contraception, I suppose—since he hadn't really wanted children. Four times she tricked him? Whether true or not, it was her way of making us feel indebted to her and opposed to him).

In any event, Schopenhauer's *bons mots* were his single means—a delayed one, at that—of answering Mother's nagging. My father was one of those dependable Jewish workingmen of his generation who regarded housework or any physical task around the house as anathema. (In his case, the phobia may have been increased because of his chore-filled childhood.) He would not "lift a finger around the house, if it killed him!" my mother would say. It was she who had to bang the nails, unstick the windows, lay the linoleum, complaining while my father sat, the soul of passivity, reading a book or napping. It enraged her partly because she had to go to work, too, and partly because my father was so able-bodied. As a young man he was tall, wiry, and very strong, like Samson. In his factory he could lift huge bales; at carnivals he would ring the bell, he triumphed at arm wrestling. Yet he became a weakling as soon as he arrived home; his kryptonite was family life. If my mother said something sarcastic to him, like "Why don't you get off your bony ass and do something?" or "What do I need you for? You're not married to me, you're married to your easy chair and the goddamn ball game!" he would merely sink deeper into a defeated shrug. But I believe that behind his stoical, resigned mask there raged a fierce misogyny.

What I would call the *Blue Angel/Of Human Bondage* plot—the educated or sensitive man who is dragged down by a coarse, sluttish vixen—had a particular vogue with my father's generation. One of the books he often touted to us was Ludwig Lewisohn's novel, *The Tyranny of Sex*. When I was sixteen and still a virgin I read it, naturally, to find out what was in store. Its lumpy, post-Dreiserian naturalist style disappointed, and I remember feeling the author was weighting the scales a bit too unfairly against the wife. Nevertheless, the luridly compelling story remained with me: a man becomes attracted to a woman, wants to sleep with her, and the next thing he knows he is married, cuckolded, in debt, his dreams for himself have flown out the window, his wife has become a slattern, no longer even attractive, a nagging shrew—in short, woman as swamp, quicksand.

Given the atmosphere in my home, I found the Samson and Delilah story the most natural in the world. Already I had imbibed from my father his sense of sexuality as a nightmarish tyranny, robbing a man of his strength, just as I had absorbed from my mother a rebellious, defiantly flirtatious, erotic appetite for life.

My mother had bought a piano, and she practiced her songs on it, preparing for the far-off day when she would become a professional entertainer. She sang mostly torch songs, the kind Helen Morgan made famous: "The Man I Love," "Just My Bill," "I Must Try to Make the Man Love Me," "Bewitched, Bothered, and Bewildered," "I Want a Sunday Kind of Love." With her pretty, tremulous voice, she would pour all her yearning and disappointment into these bittersweet verses. The message was unmistakable, even to a little kid: she was not happy with my father, she was still looking for something better, for "romance."

I loved to listen to her practice, glancing over her shoulder at the rising and falling syllables of the sheet music. All day in elementary school, her songs would go round in my head. At recess I would play tag or punchball to the rhythms of her longing.

One day, when it was too rainy to go outside, the teacher herded us into the auditorium and staged an impromptu talent show. Each child was urged to perform in front of the combined second and third grades. There were rampant cases of stage fright; some kids started to entertain, then giggled and hid their faces; others came on and rattled through a comic ditty or radio jingle so fast you couldn't make out the words. I wanted to sing. I faced the group and, hearing my mother's semitrained voice in my ears, I let her guide me through the melody.

Some day he'll come along, the man I love
And he'll be big and strong, the man I love

I could sense the teachers snickering, trading looks that said "We know how *this* one's going to turn out." My classmates started laughing. I realized too late that the song was for a girl, they would think me a sissy. I had no choice but to finish. At least I could try to sing on key and with feeling, as my mother did; maybe I would seduce them into liking it.

When the last contestant was finished, the teachers awarded me "first prize," a comic book. I, part Delilah, wondered if I would ever become a real man.

My mother was bawdy: she reveled in calling a spade a spade. She had a store of witticisms about excretory malfunctions, and she would tell smutty Hollywood stories—the scandals of her youth—about Fatty Arbuckle's Coke bottle and Mary Miles Minter, George S. Kaufman ("Oh, he must have been hot stuff!"), and Mary Astor's diary read aloud in divorce court. All this was a little hard for me to take. I particularly found it embarrassing when my mother let slip her physical appraisal of men. If we were watching a baseball game, say, on television, and Ted Kluszewski with his cutoff sleeves stepped up to bat, she would say, "Look at the shoulders on that guy! That's for me!" or "Boy, that Campy's built like a brick shithouse. He's gorgeous." The drama of the baseball diamond would be spoiled; I would suddenly be forced to see it from a sexual perspective, and imagine Mother having trysts with the local butcher, the baker, the ballplayer, whoever possessed a massive physique. (It didn't help that we all knew my mother was having extramarital affairs. Later on, I came to see that she had done the right thing for herself in scraping together a little happiness by going outside a marriage that was irredeemably bleak and frustrating, but when I was coming into puberty myself I sympathized with my father and thought her "cheap," a Bad Woman.) These comments about male physique made me feel especially inadequate, since I had narrow shoulders and a scholar's untoned body. If being a man meant having a body like Victor Mature or Roy Campanella, then forget it, I would never make it. Fortunately, my mother had another erotic ideal besides the powerful bruiser: the sensitive, poetic "gentleman" with manners and an English accent—Leslie Howard, her favorite, or James Mason. I at least had an outside chance at this ideal. If I speak gently today, to the point of habitually mumbling, it is probably because I am still trying to be Leslie Howard for my mother.

Samson "loved a woman in the valley of Sorek, named Delilah." But nowhere does the text say anything about Delilah loving Samson back. Indeed, immediately after this first sentence introducing Delilah, the Philistine lords approach and say: "Entice him, and see wherein his great strength lies, and by what means we may overpower him, that we may bind him to subdue him, and we shall each give you eleven hundred pieces of silver." In the Bible, Delilah is literally a *femme fatale*: she comes on, performs her treacherous function, and disappears from the narrative. We are left to guess whether she betrays Samson just for the money or because it is her nature. Virtually all later adaptations soften the harsh functionalism of the biblical Delilah, both by "humanizing" her with ambivalent motives of love, jealousy, revenge, and politics, and by having her visit Samson after he is in captivity. But the first Delilah is the pure Delilah, a dark female force who destroys men with her sex. Like a dominatrix, she is remarkably straightforward about her intentions: "Tell me, I pray thee, wherein thy great strength lieth, and wherewith thou mightest be bound to afflict thee." (Judges 16:6)

Fair warning. Samson receives even more evidence of her treacherous intent when, after fending her off with a false explanation of his strength, she calls in the soldiers, who had been hiding in her inner chamber, to seize him. Any man with half a brain would leave at this point. But no: three times Delilah entices Samson to give her his secret, three times he puts her off with fabrications, and three times she summons the Philistine troops to ensnare him. (The fourth time works the charm.)

The mystery is: What happens to Samson's famous self-righteous anger during this period of the three wrong explanations? Either Samson likes the danger, finds it spicy, or has come to expect nothing from women other than constant betrayal. Or does he simply overestimate his power to resist Delilah's coaxing (which would be foolish, given his past history)?

His hanging around her obviously booby-trapped tent has a comical side. Later dramatizations of the Samson story refrain from showing all four of Delilah's interrogations about his strength and his answers, partly because it would be dramatically redundant, but also because it would get farcical, and Samson would lose too much stature. Any man who puts up with that many consecutive betrayals is not a tragic hero but a *shlemiel*.

Although not necessarily. In fairy tales, it often happens that characters make the same mistake three times (for instance, misuse their wishes), and at the end of each mistake there is no accrual of wisdom. The point is made that human nature keeps screwing up the same way over and over. Seen from this perspective, Samson is Everyman: his continuing to stay with Delilah after he knows she will betray him is no more unusual than, say, a woman who remains with a husband who beats her, or a man who puts up with a wife who continually cheats on him.

Saint-Saëns's operatic Samson is so sexually fixated on Delilah, like Don José on Carmen, that he can't pull himself away, however much he realizes that she intends to ruin him. And she, for her part, betrays him because that seems the inevitable melodramatic outcome of all fatal passions. But this "fatal passion" explanation, so nineteenth century, seems incomplete. The biblical Samson takes too much active pleasure inventing the three lies about his strength for him to be seen as merely a passive moth drawn to the flame. Gradually, he himself allows Delilah to get a little "warmer," the third time actually referring to his hair, telling her that to tie up seven locks into a web would subdue his strength. In a way, the two are like children playing a game. Each time she notifies him "The Philistines be upon thee, Samson," she is in a sense calling out a ludic formula, such as "Tap, tap, Johnny, one two three!"

There is an undeniably playful element in this part of the Samson story. One could say that the strong man is experimenting with disarming himself and seeing how close he can come to being trapped, a Houdini who ties himself up in order to escape. After all, Samson delivers himself voluntarily into his captors' hands not once but twice: the first time was earlier in Judges, when his own people betrayed him to the Philistines and he ended up smiting a thousand with the jawbone of an ass.

The strong would seem to have a need to experiment with the limits of their strength—to experiment, indeed, with their weakness, as though it held a key to self-knowledge. Often in stories the great warrior "forgets" his duty to fight, detained in the arms of a beautiful woman: Samson and Delilah belong in the same company with Ulysses and Circe, Antony and Cleopatra, Lord Nelson and Lady Hamilton. Yet in these trysts, isn't the strong man measuring his fortitude against an opponent he recognizes as potentially more dangerous than an enemy general?

The strong man enters the erotic interior of the tent, the boudoir, with the understanding that other rules prevail than those on the battlefield. Here he hopes to be refreshed, but also tested in an intriguing manner. With a too-docile love slave, there would be no stimulating tension, no edge to the encounter. An experienced wanton like Delilah cannot offer the challenge of her virginity, so there must be another kind of advance-retreat. Like the geisha who are celebrated for their pert replies, wheedling, and jealous tantrums, the woman to whom the strong man surrenders must be in command of an entire repertoire of catlike capriciousness.

He enters the dark interior of her body to explore, to reconnoiter like a soldier moving laterally across a field; but by the end he has become soft and feminized, his ejaculated penis small. The strong man enters the tent, secretly, to become a woman. Lovemaking allows him to be tender, to loll about in bed, to be playful and "effeminate," to exchange sexual roles:

I yielded, and unlocked her all my heart,
Who with a grain of manhood well-resolved
Might easily have shook off all her snares.
But foul effeminacy held me yoked
To her bond-slave.

— Milton, *Samson Agonistes*

Afterward, the man resents the woman, wanton or not, for several reasons: because she has witnessed his "weakness"; because he needed her in the first place; and because she can go much longer than he can, sexually speaking—she has no sword to break. Men take revenge for their dependency by projecting their sexual needs onto women, reviving the figure of the insatiable temptress, the castrating Delilah.* Proverbs warns "Give not thy strength unto women" and "The horseleach hath two daughters, crying, Give, give. There are three things that are never satisfied, yea, four things say not, It is enough: The grave, and the barren womb, and the earth that is not filled with water, and the fire that saith not, It is enough." (Proverbs 30:15, 16) The Bible is filled with a sexual-economic fear of women, not unlike the general in *Dr. Strangelove* who practices celibacy so as to hold on to his "precious bodily fluids." The Samson story would seem to admonish us that sex with women depletes the hero of his strength—if not through one "castration" (the postcoital shrunken penis; the depleted fluids), then indirectly through another (the cut-off hair).

Yet while the message of Samson's fall, like Adam's, would seem to be cautionary and misogynistic, underneath we experience his time with Delilah as a liberating fantasy. That is why the story has such continuing claims on us. Don't we secretly rejoice at his having the good sense to follow the route of his desire, to free himself from the "good-boy" Nazarite onus by putting himself in temptation's way?

After all, Samson has always been a loner. "If a leader, he was one from a distance. Almost everything he did was as a private individual," writes the Israeli Talmudist Adin Steinsaltz. And Robert G. Boling, in his Anchor Bible commentary, notes: "The whole structure of the Samson segment is different from that of the other judges. There is no participation by Israelites in his elevation to judge and no mention of Israelites taking the field behind him." He is so alone, he might as well be an artist. The first time he comes to grips with another human being and doesn't run, doesn't go off angry or bloodthirsty, but stays, is with Delilah. It is progress of a sort.

The retreat of lovers from the world has always been perceived as both an alluring ideal and a dangerous threat to society, which must be punished—if not by the authorities, then by the dynamic of romantic love itself. In the Japanese film Oshima's *In the Realm of the Senses*, a geisha and a bouncer run off together. They become so immersed in making love that they rarely go out, they forget to eat, they become mystics in the pursuit of higher and higher pleasure. But the logic of ecstasy seems to dictate ascending risk; normal intercourse is no longer enough, they experiment with short strangulations to intensify the orgasmic rush. In the end, the

---

*Not that castration fear should be seen solely as a projection of male insecurity. There really are psychologically castrating women, analysts tell us. My mother belittled my father every day of their marriage. She was certainly provoked—he had a maddeningly taciturn, withdrawn, ungiving nature—but she took to provocation like a duck to water: "What are you good for? What do I need you for? You're like a mummy. Get lost, why don't you," she would say, "take a hike." One day he did, and jumped into the East River. Someone fished him out, fortunately, before he could drown. The police brought him home in his wet clothes.

woman strangles her lover fatally and, realizing he is dead, cuts off his penis and runs through the streets with it. It is unclear from the film whether the man has submitted to the woman's homicidal castrating tendencies or whether she has been the instrument of his suicidal desires. They have reached a point of such fusion, such boundarylessness—the desideratum of lovers, according to poetry—that it is pointless to speak of one "doing" anything "to" the other.

I would like to offer the possibility that a similar sort of collaboration or collusion existed between Samson and Delilah. Not that "she done him wrong," but that together the lovers were able to bring about the desired fatalistic result, which they had been working up to in practice three times. This interpretation is, I realize, perversely revisionist, it has little support in the text. What the good book does say is that Delilah pressed Samson until "his soul was vexed to death." Finally he opened his heart to her. "A razor has never come upon my head, for I have been a Nazarite to God from my mother's womb. If I be shaved, then my strength will leave me, and I shall become weak, and be like any other man." (Judges 16: 16) The irony is that Samson's great folly consists in nothing more than telling the truth—and telling it to one he loves.

"And she made him sleep upon her knees; and she called for a man, and she caused him to shave off the seven locks of his head; and she began to afflict him, and the strength went from him." (Judges 16: 19) She places his head in her lap, that maternal gesture. He is finally "unmanned" by surrendering to his need for mothering. This is at the heart of the male fear of Woman: that she will touch him in that sore place and open up his bottomless need for mother-love, which he had thought he had outgrown, and he will lose his ability to defend himself.*

I hated getting haircuts. When my mother took me, it seemed that the barber would pay more attention to her than to me. And when I was big enough to go alone, I still felt invisible in the large barber chair, always imagining that the barber must be bored cutting a little boy's head, or annoyed that he would not be getting the full fee, or inattentive because he'd been working all day and wanted to close up early.

One time, when I was around eleven, I went to get my hair cut at a barbershop near the Havemeyer Street markets. I had heard that this particular barber was twenty cents cheaper than most, and I hoped to use the money I saved for a treat. The barber turned out to be a tiny old man with a *yarmulkah* and a palsied shake to his hands—no wonder he was so cheap. His fingers had liver spots on them, like my grandfather's; I was tempted to get up and run, but the cover sheet was already around my shoulders. He brought the scissors close to my head, trembling, stopping

---

*Is it only my *mishegoss* that associates the Samson story with Oedipus? Both men dealt with riddles, both suffered ruin by sleeping with the wrong woman, both were blinded. Maybe the two legends came about in the same period or influenced each other.

at an arbitrary point where he jabbed them into my temple. As he clipped he would make a hundred tentative approximations in the air, like the outlines in a Giacometti drawing, before he landed. When he shaved the nape of my neck, he nicked me. "Oh, did I cut you?" he said "I'm sorry."

I couldn't wait to escape. The second after I paid him I darted out of the shop and ran several blocks. Finally I stopped in front of a luncheonette. I had twenty cents to spend: I read all the signs above the counter, grilled cheese sandwich, burger and fries, bacon lettuce and tomato . . . I had never tasted bacon. Though my parents did not keep a strict kosher household, we lived in an Orthodox Jewish neighborhood and eating pork was taboo, it just wasn't done. I ordered a BLT, feeling sinful but defiant, telling myself I deserved to break the rule because I had had to suffer that haircut, therefore my sin would be canceled out, I would be "blameless."

I wanted to say something earlier about tests of weakness. Even as a child, I had a strange experimental tendency to indulge a lassitude at the most inopportune moments. Once, when I was about nine, I let myself dangle upside down on a swing and refused, as it were, to exert the necessary muscle traction to grip my legs to the seat. I fell on my head and had to have several stitches taken. Superheroes fascinated me as much for their sudden enfeeblements as for their vast powers. I would picture being in the presence of kryptonite and the voluptuous surrender to weakness. All my childhood illnesses were rehearsals for this crumbling of the will, this letting go of the effort to be a little man.

As an adult, I still often experience the temptation to go weak as a babe, or to let my body get into incredibly clumsy positions, knowing full well that with a little extra effort I could manage the action better. I will forgo putting down one kitchen object before picking up another, and in my awkward maneuvering let food spill. Or I will go limp as a beanbag when having to extricate myself from the back seat of a car. Or sometimes, when I am helping several people lift a heavy piece up the stairs, I will suddenly become dreamy, forget to hold up my end. It isn't goldbricking exactly, because I'm not generally lazy about work. It's a way of resisting life on the physical plane.

A manly man will pick up a tool and perform a task with just the right amount of well-focused energy. I, on the other hand, view all implements as problematic, and all chores as a test of manhood that I am half-eager to fail. My mechanical ineptness is so fertile that it borders on creativity. I have no sooner to pick up the simplest can opener than I feel all vigor drain from my hands. I struggle to concentrate my sluggish fingers, to make a go of it; I tell myself "Even a child can do this." I force myself to grip the can opener and sink its sabertooth into the metal. Then, all too quickly, growing impatient, I bludgeon my way around the circle, starting half a dozen punctures. Soon the whole top is a twisted mess and I am tearing it off with my bare hands, cutting my flesh in the process. From lassitude to excessive force, with nothing in between. In all this feigned weakness and physical inattention, one sees a reluctance to leave the boy-man stage, as well as a perverse intellectual vanity, since what is not given to the body must be given to the mind.

Why does Delilah betray Samson? That is the problem all adaptations of the story have sought to solve.

The most complex answer, and the most noble Delilah, are found in Milton's *Samson Agonistes*. She is the secret hero of that great poem. First, the poet raises Delilah's status by making her Samson's wife. Though this allows Samson's father, Manoa, to quip, "I cannot praise thy marriage choices, son," and the blinded hero to roar when she visits him in prison, "My wife, my traitress, let her not come near me," she herself behaves with sympathy and dignity. She begs his forgiveness several times, offering a spectrum of explanations. The first is that, being a woman, she was subject to "common female faults . . . incident to all our sex, curiosity" and the urge "to publish" the secrets she learns. Then she says they were both weak, so they should both forgive each other. The strong man has very little sympathy for this excuse, retorting that "all wickedness is weakness." Then, more tenderly, she brings up the "jealousy of love"; she has seen his wandering fancies and wanted to hold him near her, to keep him from all his "perilous enterprises." She swears, too, that she was tricked by the Philistines, who assured her that no harm would come to her husband. He accuses her of betraying him for the gold. Dalila vigorously denies this, claiming that the magistrates had told her she had a "civic duty" to "entrap a common enemy," and the priest had appealed to her further on religious grounds, asserting that Samson was a "dishonorer of Dagon." He bats this argument away indignantly, saying that she had a primary duty to her husband, not her country. Dalila answers, abjectly, "I was a fool, too rash, and quite mistaken . . . Let me obtain forgiveness of thee, Samson." She paints a picture of the life they could lead from now on: she thinks she could secure his release; true, he is blind, but "Life yet hath many solaces, enjoyed/ Where other senses want not their delights/ At home in leisure and domestic ease. . . ." He refuses to be caught again, ensnared by "Thy fair enchanted cup." Dalila: "Let me approach, at least, and touch thy hand." Samson practically jumps out of his skin. The extremity of his reaction, threatening to "tear her joint by joint," betrays how much feeling he has for her still. Sorrowfully, she notes: "I see thou art implacable. . . . Thy anger, unappeasable, still rages." It is a beautiful matrimonial scene; she understands full well the function and operation of his rage. When he tells her that her name will be notorious forever, she allows herself a proud parting shot: if she is to be infamous among the Israelites, her own people will commemorate her as a heroine. And she compares herself to Jael, who in the same Book of Judges, "with inhospitable guile/ Smote Sisera sleeping through the temples nailed."

Indeed, any judgment of Delilah is complicated by the fact that her behavior seems structurally not so different from Jael's, or from Judith's decapitation of Holofernes. All three actions occur in a tent, with a guileful woman bringing a warrior down while he sleeps. Yet Delilah's "sisters," narratively speaking, are admired and celebrated, while she is reviled as the epitome of sluttish perfidy. History is written by the winners.

The Saint-Saëns opera also makes Delilah a Philistine patriot, but adds the dimension that she is the apostle of Love and is jealous of Samson's primary devotion to God. She carries on like a forlorn Dido about to be jilted by her Aeneas (*Mon coeur s'ouvre à ta voix* . . .), weeping and appealing to his pity.

In the movie, DeMille's scriptwriters introduce yet another motive by conveniently making Delilah the younger sister of the woman of Timnah (played by Angela Lansbury). The tomboyish Delilah develops a schoolgirl crush on her older sister's fiancé, Samson. When he rejects her as the replacement for the errant Lansbury, she is a woman scorned, and vows to get even by becoming a great courtesan. But her anger fades away during the idyllic period after she has seduced Samson; indeed, the scenes of the lovers dallying by the stream and inside Delilah's commodious tent are so charmingly playful that it becomes difficult to believe her subsequent betrayal, except as the reemergence of some innate "Delilah" nature. The Hollywood version has the lovers reunited, and it is a contrite Delilah who leads Samson to the pillars, gladly volunteering to die with him!

Why do men want Delilahs? If not in their homes, then in their fantasy lives? Why is the Bad Woman, the deceitful betrayer in all her *film noir* guises, always able to sell movie tickets? Because she is beautiful and sexy? So might be a virtuous woman. Because one yearns to be swept away by a passion stronger than one's reason, which can only be proven if it goes against one's own best interests; because by losing control one can turn around later and blame her, *she* tempted me, she snatched away my willpower; because one never takes her seriously as a partner for life, and so there is no threat of having to make a commitment; because, while she may destroy you, she will not smother you with admiration or doting affection, which makes you feel like a fraud; because her treacheries are exciting in an operatic (if ultimately tiresome) way, they keep you feeling alive and angry, and anger is an aphrodisiac; because she confirms your worst ideas about women; because you want to feel alone, to guard your solitude; because she is full of surprises and that keeps you off-balance; because you who have hurt women so often dream of being a victim, of being punished for your crimes; because, while Delilah may lack the domesticity and compassion of the woman in Proverbs whose "price is far above rubies," she possesses other arts: the ability to sustain an appearance of glamour (which is a function of the imagination as much as good looks); the control of scents; the manipulation of interior spaces; the ability to keep the humdrum everyday world at bay; sometimes the art of dance and playing an instrument; a refreshingly candid lack of decorum; the naughtiness of a young girl or a kitten or anything but a fully adult woman (who would remind you of your own death); a touch of androgyny when called for; a keen insight into men; and a thorough knowledge of sex.

All my life I have been searching for a woman who will live up to—or down to—this bad-girl archetype. Instead I have met, on the one hand, a succession of kind, sweet, devoted women (worse luck), or, on the other, hassled, self-absorbed, remote women (worse still). I am still waiting to encounter Hedy Lamarr's Delilah, with the headband around her forehead and her many teases.

Actually, I did come close to finding a Delilah type. She was capricious, sexy, smart, crazy, abusive, and pretty, and she tortured me for seven years. We started with a strong erotic spark, which later grew to be rooted in mutual anger—mine at her infidelities, hers at my refusing to take her "seriously." During all this time I was very productive, managing to put her provocations and scenes in the back of my mind and working out of that bottomless pit of creative energy, the feeling of being unloved, *le chant du mal-aimé*. As it happened, Kay was a writer, too, but her work did not get published very often. She would become furious and throw tantrums when she saw my poems in magazines unless I placated her for half an hour about how much better her poems were—which I rarely did. Once she asked me point-blank: "How are you able to wield so much power in the world? Teach me, how does one get literary success?" I shuddered. It was Delilah's question: Where does your strength come from? I was tempted to say my literary prominence was hardly so grand as to merit envy; but I had to admit that, compared to her, I was "successful." She felt that as a woman she had been kept in the dark about worldly power and now she wanted to become more like men, initially, perhaps, by sleeping with them. Myself, I was able to do very little for Kay as a poet—not that I tried very hard. She hated me at times with a palpable shocking openness that was, if nothing else, different: most people like me. My own feelings were a murk of pity, lust, and confusion, revulsion at her misconduct and disgust at myself for staying in the relationship. But I admit that, in a way, it kept me amused.

So Samson is captured and blinded, and made to grind wheat in the prison house, like a beast of burden. "Howbeit the hair of his head began to grow again after he was shaven." Odd that the Philistines, having paid so dearly to learn that the secret of Samson's strength resided in his hair, should let him grow it back again. In any event, the foreshadowing detail has been planted, and the stage is set for the final catastrophe. The rest we know well: the Philistines trot him out for sport on their feast day to Dagon, and Samson tells the lad who leads him: "Let me feel the pillars on which the house stands, that I may lean against them." It is a very satisfying narrative invention, this meeting of architectonics and apocalypse. Samson prays to the Lord for his strength to be returned, "only this once, that I may be avenged upon the Philistines for one of my two eyes." The Lord complies, and the house topples on everyone in it. "So the dead which he slew at his death were more than they which he slew in his life." (Judges 16: 30)

A good death. To redeem a whole misspent life by the manner of one's dying—to take this inevitable poll tax, mortality, and turn it into a *tour de force* of accomplishment—has been a dream of many suicides through the ages, from Samson to Sydney Carton to Mishima. However, Samson redeems himself not just by destroying slews of Israel's enemies, which is nothing new for him, but by his self-awareness, contained in his words: "Let me die with the Philistines." He does not pray to God, as he might have: "Let me destroy them in such a way that I can get off harmless." His conscience considers his sins, his follies, his own betrayal of his potential, and logically asks for the death penalty. We tend to forget that Samson was also—in whatever sense we care to take it—a judge ("And he judged Israel twenty years"): his last judicial act is to pronounce sentence on himself. When he says "Let me die with the Philistines," he also seems to be alluding to his taste for Philistine women: I have eaten *trayf*, it is only just that I go down with the *trayf*-eaters. With his last noble words, he exiles himself from his own people and joins the Diaspora of the dead. A bitter ending, but he has come a long way from the young, self-righteous man who petulantly exclaimed, before wreaking havoc, Now am I blameless for the harm I will do them. Like a hero in a Greek tragedy, he has finished his journey from warrior pride to humility by taking responsibility for violating the tribal laws.

I have said that my father was a physically strong man; this made his inability to deal with my mother or manifest any ambition all the more puzzling to me as a child. It often seemed to me that, in another situation in life, he would have realized a heroic potential. Though he never went into the army (excused from service because he had too many children), he would have made a good soldier. He was intelligent and stoic and did not shirk duty. I am not romanticizing, I hope, when I say that he would have run into a burning building to pull us out, without giving any thought to his safety. I still get shivers remembering one occasion when he risked his neck. We were locked out of our house—someone had lost the keys during a family outing—and my father went next door to see if he could leap from the neighbor's fire escape to ours. It was no small distance, if he slipped and fell he would hit solid cement. We couldn't see how he was doing because the fire escapes were all on the back side of the building and we waited in the front vestibule. My brother Hal started whistling the Funeral March. "Hope you like being a widow. Was that a splat?" he said, cocking his ear. Ordinarily, sarcasm and gallows humor were the preferred family style, but this time my mother chewed her lips and stared through the locked glass door, holding her mouton coat closed at the throat. She had tried to talk my father out of the attempt, insisting they could call the police to break down the door, but my father wouldn't hear of it. This was his job. I remember my mother's terrified, tear-streaked face while she waited in suspense. Molly said, "Ma, I don't think this is such a good idea," and my mother slapped her across her face for saying what all of us were thinking. Eventually we saw my father's trousers coming downstairs, the whole of him shortly after. When he let us in, we kids cheered: "Our hero!" "Don't give me that bullshit," said my father, modestly and gruffly. It did not take my mother long to recover her acid tongue: "Big show-off! You could have gotten killed, dummy!" But her agitated concern during those few minutes he'd been gone was a revelation to me. Maybe she cared about him more than she let on.

My father is now seventy-six, my mother sixty-eight. Two years ago she finally gave herself a present she had been wanting for over forty-five years: a divorce. Not that I blame her: she was, as she said, tired of being a full-time unpaid nursemaid to someone she didn't love. She kicked my father out of the house, and he went to live in a less-than-desirable nursing home in Far Rockaway. He has been depressed and emaciated, and he misses the city streets. Recently, we heard of the possibility of an opening in a much better old-age home near Columbus Avenue, in the middle of Manhattan. There is a long admissions procedure; it is as complicated as getting into an exclusive prep school. My mother took him to his interview herself, crowing afterward that the director mistook them for father and daughter. So far his chances look pretty good: my father is not very outgoing, but he is ambulatory and in his right mind. We all have our fingers crossed. So far the home has raised only one objection, my mother tells me: they would want him to shave his beard.

YOUTH

4

The Countess's Tutor

RECENTLY I BROUGHT A FRIEND TO SEE the old neighborhood in Fort
Greene, Brooklyn, where I lived from age eleven through high school, in the
mid–1950s. Fulton Street was just as funky a slum as I remembered: its bars and fortune tellers, processed-hair parlors, fried chicken joints, and street-corner winos
unchanged. Imagine my chagrin, however, when, prepared to show off the other
"mean streets" of my youth, I found the crummy six-story apartment building of
my early adolescence converted into condominiums, with a concierge, no less, at a
lobby desk. The last time I'd bothered to check, fifteen years before, that double-
winged apartment house on Washington Avenue had looked abandoned: windows
boarded up, yellow brick façades blackened like singed eyebrows by a suspicious fire.
I had half expected to see it torn down, but no, this time it was clean and gleaming,
its stone-carved gargoyles displayed to perfection. I asked the concierge for permission to take the elevator to the top floor, where my family, all six of us, had lived
miserably crammed together. He said yes, provided we didn't bother the present
occupants. I assured him I had absolutely no desire to peer inside: just the door
would suffice. We rode the elevator in silence, I noting with satisfaction its still-ugly
paint job. But I was in for a shock when I faced the old door: 6A had been changed
to the letters PH1. Had I known then that I was living in a future penthouse, how
different my sense of destiny and entitlement might have been.

Something is wrong with the world when the tenements of our youth have
become the prewar desiderata of the next generation. Then again, maybe the apartment building had been initially intended as discreet, middle-class luxe, and had only
gone into decline midcentury, the period during which my family inhabited it, and
was now restored to its original economic niche.

But that was not what I was thinking about. No, I was remembering the last time
we had been inside that door, when my mother sprayed the kitchen for cockroaches
in one final skirmish before moving out. We had fought the roaches so many years,
unavailingly, but at the penultimate moment we got hold of a powerful DDT spray
gun and cleared the food out of the kitchen. At first there were only a few. Then like

a locust storm the roaches began pouring out of the stove, from behind the refrigerator, across the ceiling. They were dropping at our feet, doped and spinning, and
we smashed them under our shoes like raisins, two at a time. It was a regular killing
field: wherever we stepped, we slaughtered. . . .

Then I gazed at the old staircase, and began remembering the time I descended
with heavy heart of brother-responsibility, to defend my younger sister Leah who
said she had been robbed by two black boys. I walked her around for blocks, asking
her every time we approached a knot of boys, "Are those the ones?"—as if I ever
could have wrested anything from them but a beating. (Years later, she confessed
that no one had robbed her; she had spent the money on ice cream.)

We had moved there ostensibly because our family of six needed more room.
But you don't move four growing white kids into a black slum just for the extra
space. The flight from our previous Jewish neighborhood in Williamsburg (itself a
patchy ghetto) had all the stigma of exile. My parents had gotten in trouble with the
last landlady and had been kicked out, simple as that. One afternoon, the landlady
(who lived beneath us: always a mistake) burst into our apartment while both our
parents were away at their jobs. She had two policemen with her. We kids had been
running around half-naked—playing strip poker, as my brother and I liked to do
with our younger sisters—but as soon as we saw her and the cops we hid under our
beds. "You see what I mean?" she kept saying, sweeping her arm in all directions.
"It's a madhouse, a pig sty, there's no supervision, the kids run wild, it looks like it
hasn't been cleaned in months. I just want you to be a witness." I poked my head out
but they ignored me, taking flash photographs at the disarray. I began to see the
excesses of my family from an outsider's perspective. Still, what had we done? We
had let the house get messy—by no means criminal neglect, or even destruction of
property. In a less house-proud setting, no one would have even thought to complain.

When the invaders left, we came out of our hiding places and roared with laughter. Obviously, some of this merriment was a defensive shock. But beyond that, we
were genuinely convulsed, mimicking the outrage on our landlady's face, the cops'
picture-taking gestures, like welfare blacks after a caseworker's home visit, who
simply cannot get over whitey's uptight silliness. My parents, though, did not find
the incident funny at all. They had to take a day off from work to answer Mrs.
Jacobson's charges in court. The upshot was that we were given three months to
move.

So I could never get out of my mind the notion that we were living in a black part
of Brooklyn as punishment—thrown out of the Eden of Williamsburg for being
slobs. My mother remained an indifferent housekeeper after coming home tired
from her clerical job, and we kids continued to run free and not be too fastidious,
either. But this time nobody seemed to care: we could mess up the place as much as
we wanted. The result was that the kitchen table especially acquired an intriguing
fecundity of detail.

The focus of our family life was the kitchen table. Hardly a surprising revelation: I have often read accounts of ghetto upbringings, Hispanic, African-American, Jewish or Italian, which boasted of the kitchen as the warm center, dispensing nourishment, conversation, and community. However, in our case the kitchen table had something sinister and pathological about it, due to the inconceivable density of objects on its top. Originally it had been used as a pantry annex, to catch the surplus from cupboards, but what had started in one corner of the table spread to another, so that pretty soon nothing was put away except strict perishables. Everything else was left on the table, where we "could get at it easily": jelly jars, Ritz crackers, dirty dishes, matzo boxes, playing cards, coffee pot, crayons, schoolbooks, radio, tax records and insurance papers (which always got spots of jam on them), mucilage, twine, sewing machine, vitamin bottles, seltzer canisters, U-Bet chocolate syrup, maple syrup, record albums from the Masterpiece of the Month Club, and whatever else had wandered into our life at the moment.

Whenever anything like a set of keys had been lost, we would first conduct a thorough search of the kitchen table, and they would usually turn up there. On the other hand, certain prized objects, such as bracelets or baseball cards, might slip out of sight for months, in the same way that Erik Satie's priceless compositions fell behind his piano and disappeared for years.

There is no question that the table's chaotic state "expressed" something about our family's character; but what, other than our being slobs? It was our Noah's ark, our survival raft, our environmental artwork; an overcompensation for our being poor, a visual refutation of material deprivation. The table also called attention to my mother's struggle against being overweight: because she was unhappy with her marriage and her job and herself, she went on eating binges, absentmindedly downing whatever was left around, a whole box of chocolate-covered marshmallows at a time. But it was not only my mother who "rounded" out a meal, or assuaged interprandial hungers, with edibles that took no preparation: the whole family had an addiction to noshing in a dreamy, unconscious way. My father would pop one Fig Newton after another in his mouth, staring off into space, while remaining thin as Kafka's hunger artist—a fact which naturally enraged his corpulent wife. Father's pensive passivity, his geological resistance to housework, played its part in this assemblage. But if you asked our parents how the table came to be so messy, they would have a simple answer: the children. It was the children who never cleaned up after themselves, who expected their mother to do everything like a slave, who brought whatever homework or game they were working on to the table for the sake of finding company there.

In truth, we did use the kitchen table as our school desk. And even I, who had the family reputation for being fussy, because I tried to keep a section of the bedroom I shared with Hal free from clutter, would no more have thought of cleaning off the kitchen table by myself than of pruning the trees in Brooklyn. Still, we were ashamed of the mess, and whenever anyone came over to our house, which was rare, we apologized about the table immediately. Less and less did we invite any of our classmates over, fearing they would not understand. My parents, for their part, seemed too fatigued by work to bother with friendships. They withdrew into themselves and gave free rein to their mania for disappointment.

"Well I know I got religion, certainly! I know I got religion, certainly Lord! well I know I got religion, certainly Lord, certainly, certainly, Looord." Sunday mornings we would wake up to the ebullient, hand-clapping sounds of gospel music from the clapboard tabernacle down the block. We'd open the window and hear a free concert of "Mary Don't You Weep," "Great Day in the Morning," or "I Got a Mother over Yonder" (which we would sing to our mother just to irritate her). That modest-looking church used to attract renowned groups on tour. My older brother Hal, who was already fast becoming a gospel and jazz aficionado, would say, "Omigod, they're going to have the Blind All Stars and Claude Jeter next month, and after that Sister Rosetta Tharpe!"

The other church, the Baptist one across the street, was more staidly established. From the window of the bedroom I shared with Hal, I would stare down every Sunday at the dignified black parishioners, the men in dark suits, the women in cheerful white dresses and splendiferous hats, lingering sociably on the iron balustrade steps, in a manner I would now characterize as "Southern." They represented normalcy to me (an attribute in short supply in our household). I see that the indispensable *AIA Guide to New York City* has deemed that church across the street architecturally noteworthy, even awarding it a star. "1860. Ebenezer L. Roberts. A pinch of Lombardian Romanesque decorates a highly articulated square-turreted English Gothic body. The brownstone water tables (white-painted) against red brick are perhaps too harsh." Picky, picky. I've since become interested in architecture, but as a child I never would have thought to notice. In fact, I never realized back then that the whole neighborhood of Clinton Hill (no one called it by that pretty name back then) which I took to be a dilapidated slum was, according to the knowledgeable *AIA Guide*, awash in "Romanesque Renaissance beauties." Perhaps all those fieldstone mansions and bay-windowed brownstones, all those granite pediments, cylindrical turrets and mansards several blocks away on Clinton Avenue, must have registered subconsciously, but my reality was more class-bound: we were barely scraping by, and we stuck out as downwardly mobile whites in an area 90 percent black and poor.

The neighborhood today remains a curious clash of chic townhouses and run-down shacks. The first wave of improvements occurred in the 1970s, after we'd left, when community-minded architecture students at Pratt Institute, the college in the heart of Clinton Hill, took to restoring the more usable handyman's specials. Since then, the area has drawn middle-class blacks and adventurous whites, who bask in the Brooklyn Academy of Music's proximity. Even the Mohawk Hotel, which I'd remembered as a seedy SRO, has been co-oped. None of this is to deny the edge of danger, the continuing reality of high crime, the off-balance sense you still get when you walk these streets.

Back then, we thought of ourselves as living on the border of Bedford-Stuyvesant, a notoriously tough, blighted turf over which two mighty youth gangs, the Bishops and the Chaplains, rumbled. I had to be careful where I walked because I would be shaken down by roving bands when I strayed beyond the streets where I was recognized. They would suddenly form a line in front of me. The curious thing was that sometimes they would let me pass, if I said the right thing, pressed the right button, sounded neither too fearful nor too flippant, but just respectful enough; they would laugh and say "We was just playing with you" and let me by. Other times they took every penny I had. It didn't have to be a violent encounter if you played it right: more like a loan to a neighbor you knew would never be paid back.

Actually, getting robbed was a straightforward transaction, almost preferable in a sense to the teasing, ominous game of "What you lookin' at?" You had to answer "Nothing" (or "You," if you were feeling cocky: I was never that cocky). But even "Nothing" would not necessarily let you off the hook. You might be told: "What you mean, nuthin'? I seen you lookin' at me. Don't you lie or I smash your face in." It was always on the tip of my tongue to ask, not out of provocation but curiosity, "What if I were looking at you, what would it mean?" It was somewhat of a mystery: How could I be harming anything by my gaze? Was it like the aborigine's suspicion of being photographed? Or a king whose subjects were forbidden to look upon his splendor? If you did not finesse the answer correctly, you might be drawn into a fistfight, which was the whole point of the exercise: the challenge to one's honor. Though I considered my honor not worth a thrashing, and regularly refused to take offense at the daylong slights to my mother's virtue, my situation was complicated by the fact that I loved to stare at people. So I always had a guilty conscience, because I *had* been looking at the one who called me out.

I learned the art of cowardice partly by watching my braver brother Hal, and deciding to do the opposite. One memory remains particularly vivid. Hal and I had entered the vestibule of our apartment building, where they buzz you in. Standing in front of the doorbells was Pete, the toughest kid on the block. Everyone, child and adult, was afraid of Pete. Even in idleness, his body conveyed a coiled power and swiftness, with the muscular shoulders of a professional prizefighter. His brown bullet-head was completely smooth: if he butted you with his skull alone, it might knock you out.

"What you lookin' at?" he said to my brother, baring his teeth in an almost friendly, almost ingratiating grin.

"Nothing. Okay?"

My brother tried to get past him and put the key in the lock. Pete blocked his way. "I saw you was staring at me. Why you looking at me? You some kind of fairy? Don't lie. Be a man. Admit you was looking at me."

I want to say, *Come on Hal, tell him you're a fairy, apologize, whatever he wants, just get to the other side of that door.*

Instead Hal answered, in a heated voice (I knew that temper of his well), "Okay, I was looking at you. What of it?"

"You want to fight?" Pete asks tantalizingly. It's an invitation: almost like, you want to dance? He thrusts his finger against my brother's chest. Hal raises his fists in the time-honored manner. *Meshugina.* "Hal, don't fight him! Come on—"

Neither pays attention to me. Pete grabs him fast as a cat, before Hal can change his mind, and they tangle. Hal's glasses fall to the tiled floor. I grab them and put them in my pocket. My brother is taller than Pete and tries to tie him up with his long arms, but the tussle lasts only a matter of seconds before Pete breaks away and throws several expert jabs at Hal's face. A combination. My brother goes down. Pete is on him instantly, straddling him, punching his face, moving straight down like a pile driver onto Hal's nose. I am thinking, *I must save my brother, I must save my brother, but how?* I start beating Pete on the back. My arms have an eerie lassitude, my punches lack force. Pete shoves me against the wall with one arm, while the other continues to pummel Hal. My brother's nose is gushing blood. I start to scream, "Help! Stop them!" Maybe someone bigger can break up the fight. Pete starts banging my brother's head against the hard tile floor. This is the worst part. I can only watch, with a sick feeling building inside. Hal's face is all pink, his eyes are weird and groggy. Each time his head hits the stone floor with a thud, I register the pain. We're close, Hal and I, like that story, "The Corsican Brothers": what happens to one, the other feels equally. Same time, some little part of me is glad to see my brother getting it. The tyrant of my youth. See, idiot, you shouldn't have taken up his challenge. I admire Pete's ability to fight, even as I am horrified by his lack of emotion. He has no malice toward my brother, doesn't even know him, this is just his way of enjoying himself—beating up a white boy. He might even get as much a kick out of bloodying a black boy, on a slow afternoon.

"You'll kill him! QUIT IT!" I'm yelling. An adult, Mack the super, runs in. Pete rises with a smile on his face and holds his hands out, as if to say, I'm clean. He darts out the door smooth as a leopard.

I help my brother up. "I'm sorry, Hal. I couldn't stop him! Are you all right?"

"I'm all right. Motherfucker sonofabitch."

"Here's your glasses."

"Next time I'll kill him," says Hal.

Of the three other white tenants, besides ourselves, in our apartment building, two were a very cultivated foreign couple (the man a professor of Spanish, I think), who spent part of each year in Peru and took an interest in Inca handicrafts. You would have thought that such a refined pair, who read books and appreciated classical music, would have been a godsend to my parents, who did the same. But not only did we never make friends with them, we ridiculed them endlessly behind their backs. The woman, Tiva, was said to have been caught "sun-worshipping" on the roof, naked to the waist and raising her arms to the sun. She was probably just practicing yoga. As often as I sneaked up to the tarred roof to catch her in this rite, I never saw her do anything but innocently drawing in her notebook, fully clothed. Since the Peruvian singer Yma Sumac had made a big splash with her exotic, scale-ascending records, my sister Molly, who was the official bestower of nicknames behind people's backs, dubbed her Yma.

I thought Yma harmless, but was terrified of the remaining white person in the building. She lived with our black superintendent, Mack, so we called her Mrs. Mack for starters, and later, thanks to Molly, The Dragon Lady, because she smoked constantly and curled the smoke back up her nose. Also because she had a surly, evil look, with tiny pink eyes embedded in a face rolling in fat, and huge dimpled arms that she used to lean on while looking out the window for Mack. She would chase us kids away when we tried to throw a spaldeen ball against the cornice beneath her window. She always wore the same faded housedress, and when you were foolish enough to get close to her, she gave off a strong body odor. Since Mack himself was a patient, squatly muscular man who tolerated children and in consequence was well liked by them, we wondered how he could have got stuck with such a repulsive sow. It was said that some black men had a "thing" about white women, but surely her complexion couldn't balance out her many other deficits. Yet there seemed an undeniable physical passion in that relationship, a powerful glue, you sensed it when you saw them together.

I could understand the attraction of white women to blacks. I looked up to blacks also, as a rule; it was the beginning of my "white Negro" period, and I had no difficulty romanticizing them as a superior race, stoically graceful and creative. The nearest exemplar of that Paul Robeson type was our neighbor across the foyer, a tall, noble, coal-black schoolboy athlete named Melville, who was the best track star at Boys High School, the best scholar, outrageously handsome, with that friendly, populist manner of the naturally aristocratic. My boyhood heroes were the Dodgers' Jackie Robinson and Don Newcombe. By the time I was twelve, my brother had introduced me to rhythm and blues, we would thrill on the radio to Mickey & Sylvia and Sam "The Man" Taylor, and from there it was but a short step to the worship of Bird, Coltrane, Bessie, and the blind gospel singers.

One day Hal came home all excited. He had just learned that the drunk we sometimes stepped over, near the corner of Fulton and Washington, the wino who slept in the alley beside the gospel church, was a former bop pianist who had once recorded with Bird! Admittedly, a minor bop pianist; but still . . . My brother, who usually responded with an ironic snort when misfortunes fell on our own family, was so touched and angered at the fate of this black musician, at the way society had undervalued its jazz artists and permitted them to end up in the gutter, that he vowed to do something about it. What? I was curious to know. At the very least, he would talk to the man, tell him how much his music had meant to him. And I, at the very least, never came upon the sleeping ex-sideman afterward without reverently tiptoeing around him.

There was a difference, of course, between these demigods and the everyday blacks you came across, who might stare you down with a scowl; but here too I made my adjustments. After living on the block awhile, it seemed to me my neighbors knew who I was, felt I belonged, and left me alone. The row of brownstones next to the Baptist Church served as a perfect backdrop for punchball games— there was just enough room from end to end to hit a decent-sized fly ball for a homer—and the black kids would let me into their games, if they were short of players. "Easy out," they would taunt me. "He ain't gonna hit it." I would bunch my fist together, pretending it had the hard bony strength of theirs. To hit a punchball far does not require massive biceps: there is a knack in the knuckles or the wrists which I never learned, though sometimes I would get lucky.

Each time I thought I was becoming comfortably invisible, or that race didn't matter, I would be brought up short. In Williamsburg I had joined a Hebrew choir; loving to sing, I continued to perform in it after my family moved to Fort Greene. One night, I was coming home from a gig at a Bronx synagogue; this was shortly before my bar mitzvah, my voice hadn't changed yet. Though it was late, I decided to walk the mile from Fulton Street and Franklin Avenue, rather than make the three train transfers which would put me a block away from home. Franklin Avenue happened to be an elevated train station: at the bottom of the steps awaited the one corner I was afraid of, a dark, rough crossroads that felt menacing even on ordinary nights.

This particular night, there was a crowd at the foot of the El steps, listening to an angry black orator. He stood on a makeshift raised platform decorated with signs for the U.S. Labor Party, a Communist front. Usually I liked crowds, I trusted them, I was curious about speechmakers. But this crowd had a nasty growl to it. The orator was whipping them up about Emmett Till, the Negro boy who had just been lynched down south. I knew about the case, my parents talked about it often, we were outraged at the bigots who had lynched Emmett Till. But suddenly that didn't matter: I had to traverse a semicircle about thirty yards around the crowd, inconspicuously.

"Now they took that twelve-year-old Negro boy and strung him up and choked the sweet life out of him, just because they *said* he looked at a white woman. Said he *looked* at a white woman. And our government sits by and don't do a thing. And so I ask you. What are *you* going to do about it? What are *you* going to *do* about it?"

Everyone was yelling for revenge against whites. I tried to make myself small, harmless, childlike. The thought struck me that I was the same age as Emmett Till. An eye for an eye. I began inching around the edge of the crowd, silently as I could, when some people started yelling: "Hey, here's one!" "Look at that white devil!" "He got some nerve coming round here." The crowd now turned away from the speaker to stare at me.

"Leave him alone," growled the speaker. "He's just a kid."

"Emmett Till just a kid!" yelled someone.

"Our business is with the ones in power. Let's not confuse the issue," the speaker said wearily. The crowd turned back to listen. I scurried across the street. He had saved me—whether out of compassion or ideological purity, I would never know.

I had lived on Washington Avenue for three years, and was approaching fourteen, when a new white family moved into the building. By that time we had made casual friendships with many neighbors, and almost resented the presence of this new white contingent, who, we felt obscurely, had no business living there. You would almost think we wanted to shut the door after us and keep the neighborhood from tipping. But it was rather that, like good American Jews, we had assimilated—albeit to a black ghetto—and the fact that these newcomers were Jews who spoke with a heavy Polish accent, looking fresh off the boat, made us uncomfortable. They would draw attention to our being Jewish, to the whole idea of Jewishness.

Sure enough, the Janusches were delighted when, after probing my mother in the hallway, they found out we were Jewish. Too delighted, for my taste. Confirming my worst fears, they made remarks about the "schwartzes" surrounding us, about their not knowing how to "keep clean." Occasionally I saw the newcomers in the darkened orange-walled lobby, entering while I was leaving: Mr. Janusch, a bone-slender man with a mustache, who wore suit and tie, fedora and topcoat, even in balmy weather; his stout wife, who seemed always loudly bossing him or Georgie, their pudgy ten-year-old son. The boy spoke reluctantly to his mother in Polish; but whenever he saw some other kid coming, he would break into a very American whine, "Oh, Ma!"

After a few months, I got the peculiar impression that Mrs. Janusch was watching me. Why, I had no idea; but whenever our paths crossed she would stare at me quickly and shrewdly. She had a penchant for black fur collars and feathery ruffs, which set off her chubby but almost pretty face in the theatrical manner of middle-period Elizabeth Taylor. Her jet-black eyes flashed imperiously, as though she were used to giving orders in the old country. My sister Molly had immediately dubbed her The Polish Countess.

One day, as I was getting the mail, Mrs. Janusch pounced on me from nowhere.

"Excuse me, you go to *chader?*" she asked, using the Yiddish word for Hebrew school.

"Not anymore, I had my bar mitzvah a year ago," I said, blushing. "I go once a week to a Bible discussion group for kids who have been bar mitzvahed."

"And do you lay tefillin?" she asked, referring to the morning devotional prayers with leather phylacteries which are the duty of young Jewish men.

"Only sometimes. Not so much lately."

"But you read Hebrew well. Your mother tells me you were in a Jewish choir?"

"Yes, until a little while ago," I said, flattered she should know that.

"What did you do in the choir?"

"I . . . sang in the high holidays, weddings, bar mitzvahs, concerts."

"And why did you quit?" she asked keenly.

"I got tired of it," I lied. The truth is, my pride had been hurt because they wouldn't give me more solos. My voice was too American, it didn't have that plaintive shtetl melisma.

"Everyone says around here that you're very smart."

"Around here—"

"Don't deny it. Do you know my son? Georgie? Do you think you could teach him to read Hebrew? He knows the letters already, but . . . either he is slow or he just doesn't bother. His father is ashamed that he can't take him to shul with him."

"I don't understand Hebrew either. Just a few dozen words."

"But you read it fast, yes? That's all his father wants. Besides, Georgie likes you."

"How can you tell? We've never even had a conversation."

"I can tell by the way he looks at you. Mothers know. How do you say in English? He *looks up to you*. If *you* teach him to read Hebrew, Georgie will be interested."

"I'm not sure I know how to. I've never taught before."

"Think about it. I will speak to your mother. I will pay, of course."

She worked out the deal with my mother. I would get $2.50 a week to tutor Georgie, and, since summer vacation was about to start, Molly would also be paid $2 to make his lunch. $2.50 was good money for me in those days—two-and-a-half times my weekly allowance. The choir had only paid me twenty-five dollars a *year;* I could make that now in ten weeks. Besides, the idea of teaching appealed to me. At school I loved to stand in front of the class and deliver a report or recite a poem. Mixed in with the tiresome need to show off was, I believe, a genuine pedagogic urge in nascent form. But I was still uncertain how to go about it. Should I prepare lessons in Hebrew, use learning games? I knew none. I would have to bluff—a thought that planted butterflies in my stomach.

My first lesson was scheduled for a Sunday afternoon. The Janusches had asked me to come at four, but they were still sitting down to their midday roast when I arrived, so I was told to wait in the boarder's room for ten minutes. This was a small room at the end of the hall, which they had rented out to an old tailor. Every Sunday he went to visit his sister in a nursing home in Queens. The room had an odor of stacked dust and incontinence. On the floor were dirty black socks rolled into balls, brown cardboard suitcases, prayer books, fabric remnants, used tea glasses, and old Yiddish newspapers. I occupied myself trying to puzzle out the captions on their front pages. There was a photograph of the Kremlin chiefs stiffly reviewing an army parade. "La-zar Ka-ga-no-vich," I translated the Yiddish letters into English. Whether the daily's slant was pro- or anti-Communist I had no idea: I could only tell that, though printed in New York, it was fascinated with all things Russian.

The room's dishevelment stood in contrast to the rest of the apartment, which was immaculate, with highly polished ebony furniture. Yet the Janusches had suggested that the first lesson take place in the boarder's room. Perhaps they wanted to spare Georgie the embarrassment of looking on. In any case, the room did have the appropriately musty air of a synagogue back room reserved for minyans, small prayer groups.

I was sitting in a deep velveteen armchair, uncomfortably scratchy, a faded rose color with duskier splotches where the fabric had been rubbed against the grain, when Georgie entered. I immediately stood up, closed the door behind him, and picked up a prayer book. "Read this." He looked at me with imploring eyes, as though I was about to drag him to the slaughterhouse. I was calm but stern: if anything, reassured by his fright, which quickened my sense of power and made me feel less of a fraud. He began stumbling through the syllables. Right then, I decided I would spend the first few sessions simply listening to him read and gauging his level—the old diagnostic "stall," which all teachers in the dark use, but which is nevertheless good practice. His forehead beaded over with sweat as he read. I put my hand on his shoulder: "Start again. This time just read the first paragraph. Slowly; don't rush it."

He began again, and I corrected each of his mistakes in a neutral voice, while looking over his shoulder. He would bite his lip when he stumbled, or punch his arm, muttering, "Dummy." He was making mistakes more from nerves than ignorance of the Hebrew alphabet. I knew I would have to reduce his level of fear somehow. My strategy was to get him to read one paragraph perfectly, build up his confidence this way, then move on to the next. The inspiration that struck me that first lesson was the simplest of thoughts: All he needs is practice!

By the end of the first hour, he could read the first three paragraphs of the daily prayer, the Shema. I returned him to his parents. I don't know whether they had been listening at the door, but they greeted us with pleased expressions. Georgie's piglet eyes looked shiny yet sleepy. "Now can I play outside?" Georgie's mother kissed him on his blond cropped head. Then she squeezed his cheeks together with one hand and yanked his head up to her lips with the other: a real mother-son smooch. The quiet Mr. Janusch smiled his gold-toothed grin at me and looked away apologetically.

The Janusches lived two flights below us, so that it was possible for Molly to stick her head out the window and call up the courtyard shaft: "Phee-leeps, Gee-org is ready for you!" She did this in a thick Polish accent, mimicking the Countess's mispronunciation of my name. I would put down my library book (that summer I was making my way through *100 American Plays*, one a day, encountering the brittle humor of George S. Kaufman and Philip Barry, planets remote from Fort Greene) and run downstairs, where Georgie would have just finished his lunch, usually tomato soup and a grilled cheese sandwich. Molly, being the good kid she was, sometimes left an extra lunch for me.

I was fired with ambition now to make Georgie a smooth, rapid reader of Hebrew. I had visions of his being called up to the Torah and impressing everyone:

"Who is that little kid? Where did he learn to read so well?" But his progress was less than astonishing. For one thing, without his parents in the next room, Georgie proved harder to control—I practically had to sit on him to keep him in one place. For another, the kid was sly and used every stall device he could.

We would begin by chatting for a few minutes. If I told myself this was to gain his friendship and cooperation, in truth I was in no hurry to start working either. But eventually the time came to get down to business. It was then that Georgie would do his damnedest to undercut the lesson, through a combination of coyness and mischief. "Oh, please?" he would beg, pressing his fingers together.

"That's the Christian sign of prayer—that won't do you any good. Come on, get in the other room," I'd say. Then he would try to make me chase him around: daring me, he would dart toward my reach and pedal back. Admittedly, Georgie was not very fast, but sometimes he could squirm out of my grasp like the greased little piglet he was. He seemed to crave rough-and-tumble physical contact with an older male, which perhaps he never got enough of from his father. There was a clownish side to him, too, that made me laugh against my will, and which he used to his best advantage (just as, I suppose, I used his liking for me to make him study). Other times, my amusement at him vanished without a trace—usually when he was being too coquettish or "cute." There are maneuvers that may charm an adult, which fall on deaf ears before another child.

Nevertheless, if Georgie sometimes miscalculated by forgetting I was still a child, he remembered it enough to exploit my weakness. He was in possession of a secret about me: that I also wanted to play. I had made the mistake one day of taking him outside to play punchball after he had done particularly well with his lessons. After that it was always: "Aw, why can't we just skip it this time and play punchball? I won't tell, I promise." Instantly, the nerves in my arm quivered, as I imagined belting a pink ball down the block and rounding the bases. "No; we have to study."

A deal was eventually worked out. I would use the punchball game after lessons as a carrot to keep him donkeyishly praying. If he read x number of pages without a mistake, we could cut ten minutes off the end of the lesson. Sometimes, however, I gave in to temptation and we went out before our goals had been met. Then we would try to scare up a game with whatever kids happened to be in the vicinity. If there weren't enough players for punchball squads, we would resort to three-box baseball or hit-the-dime, usually on the sidewalk outside Mack's window. The super would let us play, it was only Mrs. Mack who gave us a hard time.

One reason Georgie was so keen on our playing outside together was that I protected him. He had already acquired a reputation on the block for being both obnoxious and defenseless. A chunky kid who tried to whine his way into every game, he seemed a walking invitation for a stiff punch. Molly joked that we were really getting paid to see that the brat didn't get beaten up. There might have been some truth in that: since Georgie was friendless and lonely, his mother had hired him a few companions.

The synagogue for which I was preparing Georgie, the Fort Greene Jewish Center, was housed in a dignified, red-stoned Romanesque structure with a pointed roof and stained glass windows. The small, scattered congregation, a speck of Orthodoxy in an indifferent ocean, had been forced to buy an old church until such time as it could muster the resources to build a new edifice. (It seems that the old building has since returned to its former use, from the sign outside it that says ÉGLISE HAITIENNE.)

I usually entered the synagogue through the back door, which was a block closer to my house and opened onto a gymnasium, the unofficial domain of the teenagers. Here the Saturday night socials for young people were held: a phonograph with felt turntable would sit onstage, and I would station myself by it, pretending to be monitoring the choice of 45 rpm dance records, while the other boys tried to feel up the more precocious twelve-year-old girls. Here also the Boy Scout troop met. I had gone to only one meeting of the chapter and, turned off by the unsupervised aimless rowdiness of the Scouts, all these doltish Jewish boys wrestling each other on the floor and engaging in sadistic behavior, I sneaked out when no one was looking. The gym was also where the kiddush of wine and honey cake (and sometimes herring) was set out, on folded tables with white paper tablecloths, after bar mitzvahs.

You had to cross the lengthy gymnasium floor with its basketball hoops and folded bingo tables to enter the synagogue proper. But once there, you came upon the Old World. It was one of those happy accidents that the church interior had duplicated the classical architecture of Eastern European Orthodox synagogues: the carved wooden railings, the steps leading to the raised ark in the middle, the balconies reserved for women and children, all had a curiously nautical flavor, like the deck of a clipper ship. The old men in the front benches would chant in hoarse singsong the first words of a prayer, "*Ashro yishraw v'seycha*," then rock back and forth in their ancient bobbing motion, davening, mumbling the rest of the passage under their breath. It was these old men who were the spiritual (albeit not the socioeconomic) heart of the community. They kept an eye on tradition, and would grumble at the little mistakes the youthful Rabbi Dorfman made in the service, or criticize his patriotic, optimistic sermons. I shared their contempt for this nasal, smiling rabbi, with his seminary vocabulary: "Let us now partake of the repast." But the old men were no kinder to me. After my bar mitzvah, when I had not only read the traditional haftarah portion but led the whole morning service (having learned the sung texts in my Hebrew choir), and there was even some talk around the congregation of my becoming a boy cantor, and doing this every week, since they were too poor to employ a regular cantor year-round, I was accepting compliments when two of the elders crooked their fingers at me and said I should not have repeated a certain phrase more than twice, it was a sin! They knew.

These old men were small and wrinkled as dwarves, and they seemed to have nothing to do with this country. I liked them for that, and for the furious looks they darted at us boys who ran in breathlessly from the gym, causing the leather door to creak. (You were supposed to stand waiting at the diamond-shaped window cut into the door, and only enter during a break in the service.) Except for a few grandfathers who grinned toothlessly at anything young, most of the old worshippers showed no sentimentality toward children. Perhaps because they were equally small, they seemed to feel endangered by these wild beasts without reverence for the Law.

From my favorite pew, last row right, underneath the balcony's shadows, where I could watch everyone (including a girl I liked, Merrily Waxman) without being seen, I would look out at the old men, and wonder what beautiful thoughts were in their minds as they read the same prayers that left me cold. I wanted to believe, the way they did. But all that incomprehensible Hebrew did nothing for me, and the English translation opposite was no better: incessant praise for a God who needed to be flattered and told all the time how great He was. I knew this was not the only way to think about it, but it was too late, I was on the slippery slope of disbelief.

And yet I kept coming back to synagogue. No one forced me to—certainly not my parents, who told me, even on high holidays, "You go, it's not for us, honey." Or my older brother, who already called himself with pride an atheist. But the year after a young man goes through bar mitzvah is a crucial time, in which he is specifically instructed to strengthen his faith. Precisely because I was no longer strapped to the bar mitzvah conveyer belt, and my participation was voluntary, it seemed to me I was duty-bound to try. I even rose a few times at dawn and lashed the leather thongs of the phylacteries around my wrists and read the morning prayers. But I felt embarrassed, as though I were trying to behave like a nomadic shepherd in the modern world.

Only in the synagogue did I not feel embarrassed about practicing Judaism. There I felt bored, but that seemed appropriate. Everyone else was. And sometimes a mysterious shiver went through me when I put on the tallith, the ceremonial striped shawl, I felt a warmth which was more than the weight of the cloth. I instantly became more stoop-shouldered under that silken pressure, as though bypassing manhood and progressing straight to a pious, bent old age. When the Torah was paraded around the synagogue, I scrambled like everyone else to touch it, kissing the shawl's fringes to my lips and pressing them against the holy scroll as it marched past my aisle. I was kissing God.

At other times, all this Jewish ritual meant nothing to me. Why was I drilling Georgie in sight-reading Hebrew? What did he need it for? As far as I could tell, his parents were not particularly religious; they didn't even light Sabbath candles. It all seemed so mechanical, this skill of reading Hebrew rapidly without a mistake.

Receiving my wages one week, I noticed that Mrs. Janusch, in her black orchid summer dress, had numbers on her arm. Which did not seem unusual. Ever since I was small, Brooklyn had swarmed with concentration camp refugees. You'd go into a store and the man behind the counter would be gruff and ill-tempered, then you'd notice the numbers on his arm. The Polish Countess was not the sour type, but she was imperious: maybe she thought a lot was owed her for having been through the camps. In any case, it began to make sense to me that she would want her son to know how to carry himself as a Jew, having paid such a steep price for it herself.

Each time Mrs. Janusch counted out my wages, she tried to lure me into heart-to-heart talks about Georgie's progress in Hebrew:

"Do you think he's slow?" she'd ask.

"He's all right. He's getting it."

"But he's lazy. He doesn't practice enough when you're not here. I wonder if he has the brains to amount to anything. No, it isn't brains that is the problem—"

"Certainly, he's a smart kid."

"You mustn't think because intelligence comes easy to you, it is the same for everyone."

I blushed. Not that I was modest; I certainly thought I was smarter than her son. But she should not have been the one to tell me that. Why all these interrogations about Georgie? Leave the poor kid alone! What I didn't understand was that her constant parental concern masked her adoration of him. I misread it as something flirtatious passing between her and me. I resented her warm way of cornering me, especially as I found her, in spite of myself, attractive. My youthful tendency to caricature adults as grotesque told me she was a fat, silly foreigner; but my fourteen-year-old eyes kept being drawn to her bosom. She would give me those penetrating looks. Remembering, it all returns to me, the terror of that deep, probing look her woman's eyes imposed on me as a boy.

The one time Mrs. Janusch came too close was when she told me that I was my mother's favorite. It shamed me to hear this woman, an outsider, put into words what I had always suspected, even as I rejected her assessment with all my might. Far from feeling pleased at the honor of being thus singled out, I held it deeply against her.

One day, Georgie and I were taking a breather from reading Hebrew by going over some Bible stories. I had just read aloud the one about Joshua praying to have the sun stop in the sky, when he said: "That's impossible. That's a cock-and-bull story."

"Why do you say that?"

"Because, if the sun stopped, everything would fall off the earth and we'd all be dead. Joshua'd be dead too." My pupil seemed so proud of his cleverness, I had to smile.

"Maybe it is scientifically impossible. But don't you think that if God wanted to, He could do something which was scientifically impossible?"

"No, because that's what impossible means. It can't be done."

"Except in the case of miracles."

Georgie looked puzzled. "I don't get it. You gonna tell me—"

"Look, we read in the Bible that the earth was created in six days. Scientists like Darwin say that's impossible. So there are two explanations. One is that, if you believe God is all-powerful, He could do anything He wants. He *could* have made the earth in six days, and He could have even strewn fossils around it that looked like they came from millions of years apart. I'm not saying He did, but He could have. The other explanation is that each of those six days stood for so many thousands of years. So the Bible tells the truth, but in a roundabout way."

"I get a beating when I do that."

"It's not a fib. It's more like a code. The Bible substitutes one thing for another. Six days means six million years. Maybe making the sun stop is the code for an eclipse. Everyone got confused in the midst of battle, thinking Joshua had made the sun disappear."

"So which is right, the miracle or the eclipse?"

"That's for you to choose."

"You're the teacher, you're supposed to tell me. I'm just the smart-aleck kid."

"I don't know what the answer is, I wasn't around at the time."

"The way I see it, a code is just another way of saying it's a cock-and-bull story."

"You love that expression, don't you?"

Georgie's challenging of the Joshua story amused me. Essentially I agreed with him, though my own doubts about the Bible were caused less by scientific contradictions than moral concerns: the stories where God seemed to come off as a bully. For instance, the Sodom and Gomorrah story. Why wouldn't God go along with Abraham's plea for mercy? I had thrashed this out one week in the study group for post-bar mitzvah kids at the Fort Greene Jewish Center. These discussions were conducted by Max Drucker, a somber, intelligent man with silver hair and a pencil mustache, whose leg wound in World War II forced him to limp with pain. It was Drucker who had suggested to my parents that I become a cantor. First, because I had a good voice, and second, because cantors did not have to fight, but could serve on the side, like chaplains. This did not seem to me sufficient career motivation; but I was pleased that he thought enough of me to make the suggestion. Maybe because he did like me, and I respected him as a scholar, I found myself arguing with him at every session. Drucker listened patiently. He was the kind of intellectual opponent who conveys the impression, for all his seeming receptivity, that it is only a matter of time before the other person gives in to superior reason. He was stubborn; I was too. The difference was that, when it came to Judaism, he knew what he was talking about and I didn't.

"Mr. Drucker, maybe the grown-ups in Sodom and Gomorrah were bad. But I don't think God should have destroyed the babies or little children, when they were just copying their parents."

"You are saying our environment influences behavior," said Drucker. "But does that excuse it?"

"Well, if you come from a long line of family members who view evil as the norm, you probably act evil, just to fit in. Couldn't God understand that?"

"It is not a question of God's understanding. God understands all. But let us discuss *your* understanding for a moment. Yes, we are shaped by environment, but also we are responsible for our actions. Into each person God puts a *seed*, an awareness of good and evil. We are given free will, which differentiates us from machines, and it is up to each of us to follow the good."

"But doesn't it take a while for that awareness to develop? And in the case of babies or small children—why didn't God give them a decent chance?"

"It is not for us to sit in judgment of God's actions. If God destroyed Sodom and Gomorrah, He must have been convinced that the people in it were past redemption."

"But why does God see people in such black-and-white terms?" I whined. "Most people are a combination of good and bad."

"Some people are evil," said Drucker, sounding more experienced.

"But God made the world, so He made the evil in it, too. It was part of His plan for those Sodom and Gomorrahites to be bad in the first place."

"No. He gave them the choice, and they chose to ignore Him, to sin and blaspheme. You see the difference?"

"But if He left evil around in the world as a temptation, and then made man into a creature who was too weak to resist, then it was a foregone conclusion man would fall into the trap."

"You and I are talking about two different things here. I am not discussing how evil got to be in the world, which is an interesting theological problem for some other time, but specifically Sodom and Gomorrah, a place where men and women not only fell in the trap, but fell up to their ears. They were extraordinarily evil. And without exception. Let me give you an example, closer to home. Your argument reminded me of the Nuremburg trials. After World War II ended, the biggest Nazi criminals were rounded up and put on trial." He paused for effect. I nodded, tired of this analogy: in postwar Brooklyn, every minor infraction led straight to Buchenwald. "And after they got through pointing their fingers at each other, which was a nauseating spectacle in and of itself, they all came up with another excuse. They were just following orders. They were just conforming to the 'norm,' as you say, of behavior in Nazi Germany. I remember one of them even testified that if there had been protests from the ordinary German people, they might have thought twice; but nobody raised a word of protest. This Nazi officer was trying to say that in an environment where everyone is guilty, no one is guilty. That is a common but erroneous conclusion. In fact, the opposite is true. In an environment where everyone is guilty, everyone should be punished!" Here, Drucker turned red in the face. "Only in that way can we have justice. And that is the meaning of God's destruction of Sodom and Gomorrah."

Meanwhile, the other post-bar mitzvah boys, who came every week perhaps because their parents had badgered them, or because they liked to play basketball with each other afterward, looked resentfully on. They thought Drucker a gimpy wheeze-bag, and me a show-off, period. They would have been surprised to know how much it pained me to rip holes in my faith, how much I wished I could have been one of them.

By September, Georgie had become fluent enough at reading Hebrew for me to bring him to synagogue, where he was called to the Torah and read aloud for two minutes, during a special Young People's part of the service. His parents were so pleased that they urged me to continue "teaching him Hebrew" (a language I still insisted I did not know), and, additionally, to help him with spelling, a subject he was poor in. I was glad for the chance to diversify my pedagogic repertoire.

For an hour each afternoon, after the regular school day, I would enter the Janusches' clean, dust-free apartment. Sometimes Georgie would be hiding and would leap out at me. Georgie's success at the Torah had changed him, made him cockier. "It's a snap," he would say, when I reproached him for not trying enough, and I let him coast for awhile.

With the cold weather, too, a new craze began: marbles. It started on a rainy day. Punchball being out of the question, Georgie took out his set of marbles after the lesson, and I fell in with him. I had never gone in for marbles when I was his age, so their charm lay ready to hit me full-force. There were black agates, eerie and formal as obsidian, and gray-green combinations the color of cats' eyes, and smoky whites, clouded over like glaucoma, and one pure purple.

I loved getting down on my knees with Georgie and matching him shot for shot. The basic idea was to be the first to reach certain destination points—the table leg, the fourth parquet tile, the standing lamp—while knocking out, like croquet, one's opponent's marbles. But we kept making up more elaborate rules. The dining room floor was our playing field, and we spent much of the game under the oak dining table, with whose leaves and brackets I became well acquainted. The room looked different from this vantage point: we had turned its stuffy order into a shooting range. From sheer anarchy we would send marbles flying under the radiator or into the bedroom of Georgie's parents, which was a zone expressly forbidden to us. A sliding door separated the dining room from their bedroom; sometimes a marble would get stuck in the runner's grooves, or go bouncing merrily past and roll under the bed. Then one of us would crawl underneath and feel for the marble. Should we lose it and his parents happen to find it there, "we would be in bi-i-i-ig trouble," Georgie said.

I knew I was forfeiting much of my dignity and moral authority, scrambling around after my tutee on all fours. But perhaps this is why I liked the game: it equalized us. We had marble tournaments that went on for hours, and, once the sport had gotten into my blood, there were days when temptation led me to suspend lessons altogether. This was serious: I was giving Georgie ammunition for snitching. Nor did I like forgoing my duty and cheating my employers. But the game held such seductive power over me, Georgie knew he had only to propose marbles for my will to buckle. That fall, I lived for marbles, their neutral temperature and lightness in my hand, the skill involved in controlling the length and curve of flight with a finger-flick, their resemblance to jewels, the hilarious way they kept rolling and ending up in unforeseen places, their momentum, their comic resilience, like a cartoon character falling off a cliff and dusting himself off again, their self-contained indestructibility, all the more curious in that they were made of glass.

I sensed myself entering a morally confused place where the rules were becoming too flexible, and might ultimately undermine my ability to control him. What complicated the discipline issue was that Georgie seemed to be undergoing a change for the worse. Perhaps mimicking his public school classmates, he grew every day more vulgarly American in speech. He had the immigrant's quick ear for slang, and the child's need to adapt. He would imitate Porky Pig or Bugs Bunny by the hour, until I wanted to thrash him. If I told him to read a page in Hebrew, his response was "Thuffering thuccotash!"

"Come on. Be serious," I'd say.

"B-b-b-biya-bibiya-biya. That's all, folks!"

He would latch onto a phrase, like "Duck, you thucker!" and use it every minute, the way a small child repeats a naughty word on a car ride just to get on your nerves. He became devoted to pig Latin. Everything was *ouyay an'tcay*, and so on. "Shoot, Sarge!" was another of his pet sayings, used to decoy me out of demands. If I had a hard time locating the authentic Georgie underneath these robotic pop quotations, I could not help but appreciate it as a strategy. All this spewing of cartoon lines and radio jingles was a clever resistance to after-school tutoring, a payback for robbing him of his playtime.

I needed to find other incentives to keep him involved. But instead I began to lose patience with him. My hold on his respect was loosening, and the more saucy he acted, the more I wanted to slap him into line. The first time I hit him, he was quite surprised. So was I. "Well, I told you to pick up the book!" I said hotly, hoping my self-righteous tone would drown out what I had done. It seemed a momentary aberration, one which would never be repeated.

Yet there was something about his chunky body and squealing laugh that made me want to punch him a few days later, and a few days after that. It wasn't *only* that he was so provoking; in fact, I don't think I ever got angry enough at his behavior to really paste him. No, I *liked* Georgie; I just wanted to plant my fist somewhere in his flesh. I have mentioned already what I took to be Georgie's longing for physical contact with an older male, his propensity to come very close to me and then wheel away. Well, I discovered, much to my surprise, that I had a similar longing: to catch the kid and squeeze him in a tight hug, to graze his head with a noogie, a playful head-knuckle, and finally, quite simply, to hurt him. In retrospect, I wonder if this wasn't some sort of homoerotic play or sadomasochistic dance on both our parts: he would taunt, I would punch. It was a pattern I had mastered with my older brother, only this time I was the one dealing out the blows. I suppose I could say in my defense that my "environment," with its violent imprintings, had taught me to act this way; but what kind of bullshit excuse is that? I was supposed to be the good boy, the smart one. Was this the only way I could shrug off the burdens of responsibility, the premature maturity that had been placed on me, and prove to my elders I was not to be trusted? Another bullshit excuse. Was it my revenge against his mother for stigmatizing me as the favorite? Who knows? Each time I lost control and punched Georgie—usually with a single swift blow—I found myself a stranger. I was amazed at the brutality surfacing inside me.

"Don't tell your mother, okay?" I first threatened, then pleaded. He looked at me with a silent, wounded expression: the dark superior understanding that the abused has of the abuser.

My hunch was that he would not tell his mother. In the meantime, I made a vow never to hit him again. I became tolerance itself in our lessons. Georgie seemed placated; inwardly I rejoiced at my narrow escape. "Just let me get away with this one thing, Lord," I prayed to the God of Abraham and Isaac. At the end of the week, I went down to the Janusch apartment to pick up my wages. The Countess had taken off her work clothes and was sitting at the dining room table in a black slip. Her feet were soaking in a basin of water. She looked weary as she counted out the bills.

"Georgie tells me that you hit him."

"I . . . did lose my temper, yes—"

"Not once but several times," she cut me off. "I am very disappointed in you." She looked me hard in the face, to let me understand that, in addition to my sins against Georgie, I had personally violated *her* trust.

What could I say? I agreed completely. "I'm sorry."

She nodded. "You cannot work for us anymore."

I had prepared myself for her reproach, yet oddly enough, I had not expected such a total break. It was on the tip of my tongue to ask for another chance; but there was that in me that recognized the justice of her decision. It was over, this episode of our lives. I got up and left.

In the days that followed, I felt sick to my stomach. It was that squeamish sensation of guilt that comes from not only knowing you did wrong, but knowing your true nature was found out. I would encounter that same sensation other times in my adult life, when I had to ask myself: How could I have done or said such a cruel thing? I would cringe, I would laugh in disbelief, to cushion the feeling, perhaps, and I would never learn a thing from any of it, except that I should not be surprised when some foulness leapt out of me. Like the people of Sodom and Gomorrah, apparently, I was one of the evil ones.

Anticipation of La Notte: The "Heroic Age" of Moviegoing

ONE HAS TO GUARD AGAINST THE TENDENCY to think of one's youth as a time when the conversations were brighter, the friends truer, and the movies better. I am quite willing to let go of the first two, but it does seem to have been my luck to have come of age during a period of phenomenal cinematic creativity. I like to think of the early sixties as the "heroic" age of moviegoing, if one can call heroic an activity that consists of sitting on one's bum and letting one's thoughts be guided by a parade of cinematic sensations.

It was in 1959, while a junior in high school, that my craving for celluloid and my avocation as a film buff began. Certainly I had always liked going to movies; my parents had sent us off, when we were children, to the neighborhood double feature every Saturday morning. But the notion of motion pictures as an art form only struck me when I was about fifteen. I bought Arthur Knight's survey, *The Liveliest Art*, and went about in my thorough, solemn way trying to see every movie listed in the index. One thing that attracted me to film history was that it was relatively short, conquerable, compared to other artistic fields. The Thalia Theater's repertory schedule became my summer school catalogue that year, and I checked off nearly everything as a must-see, still happily unable to distinguish beforehand between the worth of an *M* and a *Captain from Koepenick*.

I went so far as to subscribe to a series of Russian silent films at the Kaufman–92nd Street Y, defiantly attending *Earth* the night before an important exam. But Dovshenko's poetic style put me to sleep; even now I have only to picture waving wheat and apple-cheeked, laughing peasants for my eyes to start to close.

In my last two years of high school I was restless and used film showings as a pretext to get out of Brooklyn, away from my family, and explore the city. The 92nd Street Y, the Sutton, and the Beekman introduced me to the posh East Side, the Art and the 8th Street Theater were my ports of entry to Greenwich Village, I learned the Upper West Side from the Thalia and the New Yorker. It was a Flaherty revival at Columbia University that first gave me the idea, walking through the campus afterward, to apply there for admission.

Sometimes a film club ad would lead me to some church basement in Chelsea, to watch an old Murnau or Preston Sturges, projected by a noisy Bell & Howell set up on a chair in the back of a rec room. Often I was the youngest member of that film addict crowd, whose collective appearance made me wonder what I was getting myself into. They were predominately male, lower middle class, with the burdened look of having come straight from work with their rolled-up *New York Posts* and ink-stained trousers; they had indoor faces with pendulous eye bags, sharp noses ready to sniff out the shoddy, and physiques that seemed at once undernourished in some parts and plump in others, the result of hasty delicatessen meals snatched before screenings. They looked like widowers or young men who had never known love—this was the fraternity I was about to join. Some seemed abnormally shy, they would arrive a few minutes early and sit as far away from everyone else as they could; at "The End" they would leave without a word. Occasionally, one of the old, bald-headed veterans would engage me gregariously in spasmodic conversation—an exchange of film titles, punctuated with superlatives, snorts, complaints about the projection or the sight lines—and I would come away touched by his kindness for having talked to an ignorant kid like me, and perhaps for this reason would feel sorry for him.

Whether the film had been glorious or dull barely mattered, so long as I could cross it off my list. The development of a taste of any sort requires plodding through the overrated as well as uncovering the sublime. If the movie had been genuinely great, I would leave the screening place inspired and pleasantly conscious of my isolation, and wander the streets for a while before taking the subway home. I came to love the way the gray city streets looked after a movie, the cinematic blush they seemed to wear. When the film had been a disappointment—well then, all the more was it a joy to get back to the true world, with its variety and uncanny compositions.

At Columbia, I discovered the general appetite for films was much higher than it had been at my high school; even the average student was willing to experiment with difficult fare. I remember going down to the Village one Friday night with a bunch of other dateless freshmen to see Kurosawa's *Ikiru*, part of a memorable season of Japanese premieres. Before the movie, just to get in the mood, we ate cross-legged on the floor at a Japanese restaurant. I adored *Ikiru*, with its perversely slow framing scene of the wake and its heart-wrenching flashbacks; but it also meant a lot to be sitting before it in a row of studious boys who I hoped would remain moviegoing friends. My own gang, as in *I Vitelloni*—except it didn't happen with this bunch. It took a while before I found my real film companions.

From time to time, film criticism would appear in the *Columbia Daily Spectator* by an upperclassman, James Stoller. His articles were so stylistically mature and so informed that they seemed to me to be written by a professional quarterly critic rather than a college student. I developed an intellectual crush on this Stoller: if his opinion differed from mine, I would secretly revise my own. I had been, for example, avoiding Satyajit Ray's films because their packaging suggested what Andrew Sarris called "dull UNESCO cinema." But Stoller wrote that the *Apu* trilogy was great, so I went, and he was right.

Finally I decided I had to meet James Stoller. Palms sweating, I summoned the courage to call his room from the phone downstairs in his dormitory. I explained that I was a fellow film lover. Could I stop by sometime and talk with him? Sure, come on up, he said.

It shocked me to see the great critic living in so tiny and shabby a room: a double-decker bed; a narrow desk, which he shared with his roommate; a single chair; and books. We had no place to sit but the lower bunk bed. It always surprised me—having come from a ghetto—that parts of Columbia should look so seedy and run-down. I suppose I was expecting the Ivy League to be a step upward.

Stoller himself gave an impression of fastidious hesitation and social awkwardness. I had come prepared to play the role of the freshman ignoramus and so was puzzled when he reacted incredulously to my praise of his articles, retreating into a modest shrug. When I asked if he had been yet to Michelangelo Antonioni's *L'Avventura*, the *cause célébre* that had just opened and which I was dying to see, he said he had, and fell silent. "Well, what did you think of it?" I prodded, expecting him to erupt with the equivalent of one of his articles. "It's—terrific, I guess, I'm not sure, I need to watch it a few more times. . . . Go see for yourself." He was uncomfortable being put on the spot.

I rushed to see *L'Avventura*. It was the movie I had been preparing for, and it came at the right time in my development. As a child, I had wanted only action movies. Dialogues and story setups bored me; I waited for that moment when the knife was hurled through the air. My awakening in adolescence to the art of film consisted precisely in overcoming this impatience. Over-compensating, perhaps, I now loved a cinema that dawdled, that lingered. Antonioni had a way of following characters with a pan shot, letting them exit and keeping the camera on the depopulated landscape. With his detachment from the human drama and his tactful spying on objects and backgrounds, he forced me to disengage as well, and to concentrate on the purity of his technique. Of course the story held me, too, with its bitter, world-weary, disillusioned tone. The adolescent wants to touch bottom, to know the worst. His soul craves sardonic disenchantment.

I rushed back to Stoller, now ready to discuss the film. He listened patiently and with quiet amusement to my enthusiasm. Indeed, this turned out to be our pattern: I, more ignorant but more voluble, would babble on, while he would offer an occasional objection or refinement. It was only by offering up chatter that I could get him to correct my misconceptions and to educate me cinematically.

This was not yet the era of film appreciation courses. Nor would we have dreamed of taking any offered; it was a point of pride to gather on our own the knowledge of our beloved, semi-underground subject, like the teenage garage-band aficionados of today.

Stoller introduced me to his friend Nicholas Zill, a film-obsessed sophomore, and we soon became a trio. Zill was a mischievous, intelligent boy of Russian Orthodox background who was given to sudden animated inspirations. The three of us took long walks together in the Columbia neighborhood, leap-frogging in our conversation from one film to another. Once, coming to a dead stop on the sidewalk, Zill asked me in horror, "You mean you haven't seen *Diary of a Country Priest?*" At such moments I felt like the baby of the group.

Zill and I both shared a zest for the grotesque, or what has been somewhat ponderously called "convulsive cinema," "the cinema of cruelty." I must say, these predilections were kept to the level of aesthetic appreciation; in our daily lives we were squeamishly decent, even if Zill, a psychology major, seemed to like cutting up rats. Nothing pleased us more than to talk about the beggars' orgy in *Viridiana*, or the maiming finale in *Freaks*, or choice bits in *Psycho*. We would go on in this perverse vein until Stoller was forced to remonstrate (which was probably why we did it). Stoller always championed the humane, the tender, the generous, and domestically observant moviemakers: Renoir, Ophuls, Truffaut, Satyajit Ray, Cukor, Borzage. It was typical for a powerless student like me to be drawn to Buñuelian fantasies of surrealist immorality and Raskolnikovian license. Much rarer was it to find balanced humanity in a nineteen-year-old, like Stoller. If I have come around over the years to his point of view, at the time I was looking for antisocial shivers, sliced eyeballs.

Nick Zill wanted to make movies—as I suppose we all did—but he went further in imagining bizarre film scenarios. He had already shot a film in high school; I remember it only as a disorganized romp of him chasing pretty girls, or was it pretty girls chasing him? In any case, he had registered an organization called Filmmakers of Columbia with the Campus Activities Office, so as to be able to borrow equipment and accept university funds should one of his projects ever get going. Filmmakers of Columbia existed only on paper; there were no meetings, even the title was pure wish fulfillment. As it happened, there *were* a number of "isolated" Columbia filmmakers (i.e., not in our circle) around, the most notable being young Brian DePalma. We did not know whether to consider DePalma's hammy experimental shorts like *Wotan's Wake* intentional or unintentional jokes, but we agreed that he had no future as a film director and that he was not a seriously knowledgeable, rigorous *cinéaste* like ourselves.

Sometimes I would go over to my friends' rooms and pass the time looking through their film magazine collections. Stills on glossy periodical stock particularly fascinated me. To stare at a shot from *Gilda*, say, with Rita Hayworth in her sheath dress before a palm-treed nightclub stand, was to enter a fantasy as satisfyingly complete, in its own way, as having seen the movie. A single frame, snatched from twenty-three others per second, is not intended to possess the self-complete wholeness of an art photograph, but for that very reason it evokes more the dream of continuing motion. Stills from the silent era, with their gestural intensity and powder-white ingenues' faces; soft-lit glamour shots from the thirties; the harsh key lighting and seamy locales of the forties—all were infinitely suggestive of the way the reigning fashions, film stock, decor, directorial style, and technology blended to produce a characteristic period image.

The desultory quality of these browsing sessions showed we were perhaps not so far removed from that age when we'd collected comic books and baseball cards. The point was not to read the articles straight through (one could always go back for that), but to be splashed by a sea of information: film festival roundups, news of film productions, historical rediscoveries. By leafing through these magazines together we shared a mood of sweet latency, imagining the films we had in store, like provincials dreaming of life in the capital. Cinema was a wave originating elsewhere, which we waited to break over us. This waiting had something to do with the nature of adolescence itself; it also reflected the resurgence of European films at the time.

To be young and in love with films in the early 1960s was to participate in what felt like an international youth movement. We in New York were following and, in a sense, mimicking the cafe arguments in Paris, London, and Rome, where the cinema had moved, for a brief historical moment, to the center of intellectual discourse, in the twilight of existentialism and before the onslaught of structuralism.

In retrospect, I may have undervalued the American studio films of the early sixties. At the time, having just lived through the Eisenhower fifties, I was impatient with what seemed to me the bland industrial style of most Hollywood movies (then symbolized by the much-maligned Doris Day); I could spot Art much more easily in foreign films, with their stylized codes of realism (sex, boredom, class conflict, unhappy endings) and their arty disjunctive texture. It took a certain sophistication, which I did not yet have, to appreciate the ironies behind the smooth-crafted surfaces of the best Hollywood genre movies. Our heroes in the French New Wave explicitly credited Hollywood films with the inspiration for their own personal styles, of course, but I accepted this taste partly as a whimsical paradox on their part without really sharing it, except in the case of rebels like Samuel Fuller or Frank Tashlin, whose shock tactics made them "almost" European.

Sometimes, instead of studying, I would end up in the film section of the college library poring over books on movies by writers like Béla Balasz, Raymond Spottiswoode, Siegfried Kracauer, Hortense Powdermaker—even their names were irresistible. Or I would struggle through the latest *Cahiers du Cinéma* in the periodicals section. As if my French were not imperfect enough, the *Cahiers* critics confounded me further with their profundity-mongering style, rarely passing a simple judgment without at the same time alluding to Hegel. I was never sure that I fully understood anything in *Cahiers*, except for the interviews with salty old Hollywood directors, and the rating system, with stars like a Michelin guide: ** *á voir,* *** *á voir absolument,* and a black dot • for *abominable.*

Sight and Sound was a breeze in comparison, although I was ashamed to admit to my friends how much I got from the English journal. It was considered stodgy and rearguard, perhaps because it was the official organ of the British Film Institute, but probably more because it took issue with *Cahiers du Cinéma's auteur* line—and we were deeply devoted auteurists. (I am using this term as shorthand for a critical approach recognizing the director as the main artist of a film, and looking at the body of a director's work for stylistic consistencies.)

I hesitate to raise a last-ditch defense of the auteur theory, so tattered has its flag become in recent years. Suffice to say that I remain loyal to the ideals of my youth. Say what you may against the auteur theory, it was good for adolescents: it gave us a system, and—more important—it gave us marching directions; it encouraged hero worship; it argued for the triumphant signature of selfhood in the face of conformist threats; it made clear distinctions between good and bad; and it blew the raspberry at pious sentiment.

Andrew Sarris's auteurist breakdown of American directors, which first appeared as a special issue of Film Culture, spring 1963, influenced us deeply partly because of its ruthlessly hierarchical ranking system: Pantheon Directors, Second Line, Likable But Elusive, Esoterica, Less Than Meets the Eye, and that most sinisterly fascinating of categories, Fallen Idols. It was here we learned to curl our lips at respected names like Fred Zinnemann, David Lean, and Stanley Kramer—liberal directors whose hearts and themes may have been in the right place but whose earnestly conventional handling of *mise-en-scéne* seemed unforgivable.

Ah, *mise-en-scène!* That camera style that favored flowing tracking shots and pans, wide angles and continuous takes; that followed characters up staircases and from room to room, capturing with rich detail their surroundings: the unfolding-scroll aesthetic of Mizoguchi, Ophuls, Murnau, Dreyer, Welles, Renoir, and Rossellini. Not only did this style seem deeper and more beautiful because it allowed more of a spiritual, contemplative feeling to accumulate than the rapid montage style, it was, if you bought all the arguments (and I did), more ethical. Why? Because it was less "manipulative." It offered the viewer the "freedom" to choose what to pay attention to in a long shot, like a theater spectator, rather than forcing the point with a close-up detail. The deep-focus style could also be seen as sympathetic to a progressive, left-wing political view, because it linked the characters inextricably to their social contexts. In retrospect, some of these claims seem contradictory, a result, perhaps, of the admirable critic André Bazin's need to reconcile his own Catholicism and Marxism and film tastes, however farfetched the synthesis. There also seems something curiously puritanical about the austere aesthetic of refraining from making cuts—something finally self-defeating, as well, since movies will always be assembled from pieces of spliced film.*

---

*This antagonism toward montage was carried to extremes by the *auteur*-ist *New York Film Bulletin*, which swore that it would trade all of Eisenstein for any one sequence in a Stanley Donen musical.

Nevertheless, I was so impressed by the style of slow cutting that each time a shot, having started to build up a pleasurable suspense in me, was broken by what seemed to me a "premature" cut to change the angle, I would wince, as if personally nicked. Watching television at home with my parents, during a filmed series like "Maverick," I would call out the cuts, just to prove my thesis that the editing followed a predictable metronomic pattern of one shot every four seconds or so. Threatened with bodily harm if I kept up this obnoxious routine, I maintained the practice silently in my head.

It would infuriate me when the *Times's* critic, Bosley Crowther (our favorite arch-Philistine), based his argument solely on content without saying a word about a film's visual style. How could he reject a film because he found the characters unsympathetic, or because of its "controversial" treatment of violence, organized religion, sexuality? Clearly, the real ethical questions were things like: Why did the director cheat with so many reaction shots? Why that gloopy slow-motion sequence?

For a certain kind of youth, the accumulation of taste becomes the crucible of self, the battleground on which character is formed. I must mention how much we hated Ingmar Bergman. Although his films had done more than anyone else's to build an audience for art films, his own popularity condemned him in our eyes: he was the darling of the suburbs and the solemn bourgeoisie who ate up the academic symbolism of *Wild Strawberries*. I once debated a fellow student for six hours because he called *The Seventh Seal* a great movie. Now I have come to love certain Bergman films (especially the early ones, like *Monika* and *Illicit Interlude*), but then, no, impossible. It was precisely because Bergman was so much an *auteur*, but not "our kind," that he posed such a threat. Like political radicals who reserve their greatest passion for denouncing liberals, we had to differentiate ourselves from the Bergmanites.

Our man was Godard. His disruptive jump cuts and anarcho-classical sensibility spoke directly to our impatient youth. Belmondo in *Breathless* was our heroic mouthpiece, whether talking to the camera or lying on the pavement: underneath that fierce hoodlum's exterior we recognized a precocious, wounded film addict. With their cinematic self-referentiality, Godard's films showed me my brothers, those equally unhappy captives of shadows. I confess I also found solace in Godard's portraits of women as either fickle betrayers or masochistic victims, which dovetailed nicely with my own adolescent fears of the opposite sex.

Even when Godard seemed momentarily to flirt with the Right, this didn't bother me. At the time I was fairly apolitical: one should not confuse the early sixties with the late. By 1968, the students at Columbia would have more important things to argue about than the merits of Gerd Oswald's *Screaming Mimi*. But in 1960–64, our politics *were* the *politiques des auteurs*. We looked for our morality in form: "The angles are the director's thoughts; the lighting is his philosophy" (Douglas Sirk).

It may seem arrogant to identify more with the directorial/camera viewpoint than with the protagonists', but that was precisely what the *auteur* theory encouraged us to do. Besides, if I could take the position of "I am a camera," this identification had less to do with superiority and more with fear and shyness, that shyness which in adolescence cooks up to pure alienation. If I went to a party, I would pretend to be filming it because I was too timid to approach the girls I liked. In classrooms where the professor droned on, I would escape by thinking, Where would I place the camera if I were making a documentary of this? Always my camera would start well back from the action, not only because of a preference for the long-shot aesthetic, but also because I felt so far apart from the vital center of life. Around this time I even had a dream in which I was directing a movie sequence inside a greenhouse: I was sitting behind the camera on a mechanical dolly, and I kept calling for the camera to be pulled farther and farther back, against the technicians' murmured warnings, until finally I crashed through the glass. Had I been perceptive, the dream might have warned me that I was on the edge of losing control; instead, I accepted it as a satisfying omen that I was going to become a film director.

It is a truism that moviegoing can become a substitute for living. Not that I regret one hour spent watching movies, then or now, since the habit persists to this day, but I would not argue either if someone wanted to maintain that chronic moviegoing often promotes a passivity before life, a detached tendency to aestheticize reality, and, I suppose, a narcissistic absorption that makes it harder to contact others. "Only connect," people were fond of quoting Forster at the time. For me, "connect" meant synchronizing my watch with the film schedules around town.

Often I would cut classes to catch an afternoon matinee at one of the little art houses in the Carnegie Hall area. Putting my feet up in the half-empty theater during intermission, I would listen in on the conversation of the blue-haired matinee dowagers: "I couldn't make head or tails of that movie the other day!" "I'm glad you said that. And they don't need to show such explicit stuff on-screen." Many an afternoon I shared with those old ladies, wondering what they were making of the capricious, Hitchcockian 360-degree tracking shots in, say, Chabrol's *Leda*. Or I would roam around Times Square, up and down 42nd Street (then a mecca of cinema gold, both foreign and domestic), enjoying the reverse chic of seeing a sacred Melville, Franju, Walsh, Losey, or Preminger film in such sordid surroundings.

In retrospect, the mystery to me is, how did I pay for all those movies? Even taking into consideration student discounts, early-bird specials, and the fact that movies were so much cheaper then, I must have spent a good part of my food money on tickets. But at least I could keep up with Stoller and Zill.

Nick Zill had been living in a railroad flat on West 106th Street, along with three other roommates. Since one of Nick's roommates worked in an art film distribution company, he was able to bring sixteen-millimeter prints home to screen.

The first time Nick invited me over for a screening in their living room, I stumbled over bodies and wine bottles to find a space on the floor. The idea of being part of a small, "invited" group watching a bona fide rare movie, Renoir's *La Marseillaise*, was heaven. I had been infected early on by the mystique of the lost, the rare, the archival film; one had only to advertise a movie as "forgotten" and I could barely stay away. Like an epicure dreaming of delicacies he has never tasted, I would fantasize being elected president just so I could order a screening in the White House den of Visconti's *Ossessione* (then tied up in litigation) or Eisenstein's *Bezhin Meadow*, or all of Louise Brooks's films, or that Holy Grail of *cinéastes*, the eight-hour *Greed*. And here I was, ensconced in a similar lucky place, the very hardness of Nick's wooden floor a mark of privilege. Most of the West 106th Street audience had a less reverential attitude, drawn simply by the lure of a free movie.

When Nick told me he was moving, and that I could take over his room if I wanted, I jumped at the chance to become a resident member of the West 106th Street film club. Perhaps I should have thought twice about it. In this dilapidated tenement building, which the city has since torn down, the rooms were so dark and closetlike that Zill once used one for a sensory deprivation experiment, locking his younger brother in and covering the windows. My own room looked out on a brick wall, and its only light source was a naked bulb that hung from the ceiling like a noose.

I mention the squalor of our living conditions because it seems somehow connected to the movie hunger. Not only did the silver screen offer a glamorous escape, it sometimes did just the opposite, held up a black-and-white mirror to our grainy, bleakly uncolorful lives. One found romantic confirmation in the impoverished locations of Italian neorealist and French New Wave pictures. If the hero in *Diary of a Country Priest* (which I had since seen) could die in a humble room like mine, the shadows forming a cross on the cracked walls above his pallet, then my own barren walls were somehow blessed, poeticized.

Do what I might, however, I was unable to find more than a few moments a week of daily life charged with that poetic transcendence I had come to expect from the movies. I wanted life to have the economy and double meaning of art. But more often I simply felt torn by a harsh, banal pain that had no cinematic equivalent. As the unhappiness increased, I began, almost in mechanical response, to think of killing myself.

If I reflect back to what brought on this crisis, I have to admit that it all feels very remote by now; I am no longer the teenager I once was; every cell in my body has since changed, biologically if not cognitively. Still, I can try to piece together the reasons. Some of my pain, I suspect, came from the fact that I had been a "star" in high school, while my first year at Columbia, surrounded by other high school stars, plunged me into such anonymity as to make me misplace all sense of self-worth. Too, I was living on my own for the first time. Though I had run away from home,

I think I felt "abandoned" by the ease with which my parents had let me go. They were too financially strapped to help me, and I was wearing myself out at odd jobs while studying full time. In the process I managed to lose forty pounds: a six-footer, I had gone from 165 pounds to a gaunt 125, as though trying to prove, against my own assertions of independence, that I was unable to take care of myself properly. Malnutrition may have affected my mental outlook more than I realized; in any event, I began to feel utterly hopeless and tired with life. I saw patterns of despair everywhere: in the street, in the sky. The arguing and drug taking of my roommates filled me with distress, contempt, and self-contempt for failing to forgive them. The urge to destroy myself took on an autonomous momentum and ironclad logic of its own. In retrospect, I was suffering from a kind of disease of logic, predicated on an overestimation of my reasoning powers; another way of putting it is that I was living entirely in my head.

Some of my unhappiness had to do with virginity. I was unable to break through to women—not only sexually but on all levels—to ask them for the least human companionship. Going to Columbia (an all-male school at the time), and immersed in this milieu of latent homosexuality, which was threatening my identity in its own way, I was frightened of women yet filled with yearning for them. It pained me even to see lovers taking liberties on the screen. Movies, saturated with the sensual, mocked me by their constant reminder that I was only a spectator.

At the same time, movies helped push me deeper into a monastic avoidance of the body. In the cinematic postulant, there is an ascetic element that exists, paradoxically, side by side with the worship of beauty: a tendency to equate the act of watching a film with praying.* One day I was at my job at the library, cataloguing book slips, when, light-headed with over-work and lack of sleep, I heard someone address me from behind. "Are you a Benedictine?" I turned around and no one was there. It seemed I had had an auditory hallucination, but even if I had merely overheard a scrap of conversation, I was spooked by the sense that someone was mocking me, unmasking my shameful monkish nature.

In Godard's *Masculin-Féminin* there is a scene with the hero, Paul (Jean-Pierre Léaud), sitting in a movie theater watching a Swedish film. On the sound track are his thoughts: "This wasn't the film we'd dreamed of. This wasn't the total film that each of us carried within himself . . . the film that we wanted to make or, more secretly, no doubt, that we wanted to live." Paul's confusion between movies and reality, his yearning for an alternate existence, his absorption of all the social distress and pain around him, and his inability to connect with women, driving his chic girlfriend away with his gloomy overseriousness, add up to the fate of many Godard

---

*Years ago, the Anthology Film Archives even constructed a Temple of Cinema in which each seat was separated from its neighbors by a black partition, not unlike a stiffened monk's cowl, which made contact with one's companion nigh impossible and forced the viewer into solitary contemplation of the mysteries.

heroes: suicide. Unless I am mistaken, suicide was in the air, in the cinematic culture of the early sixties; perhaps it was no more than a facile narrative solution for movies made by young men who were fond of indulging their existential self-pity. In any event, I fell right in with the mood.

Between screenings of Vigo's *L'Atalante* and *Zéro de Conduite* at West 106th Street, I told my older brother that I was thinking of killing myself. Distressed, he counseled patience, but it was too late to listen. Vigo's dream of a man and a woman drifting down the Seine in a houseboat, touching each other, seemed insultingly unreachable.

A few nights later I swallowed twenty sleeping pills with the aid of a quart of Tropicana orange juice. I had already written a suicide note with quotes from Paul Goodman and Freud—I can laugh at it now—and I lay down to die in my sleep. But stomach pains kept me awake: the beef stew I had eaten earlier at Columbia's dining hall (it is that wretched institutional food I have to thank for being alive today) and the acidic orange juice refused to digest. After an hour's uncomfortable attempt to ignore the stomach and think easeful, morbid thoughts, I leaned over the side of my bed and vomited—whole chunks of beef stew and carrots in a pool of orange juice. Then I called out to my roommates and told them what I had done. They rushed me to St. Luke's Hospital, where my stomach was pumped—so unpleasant but revivifying an experience that when the resident asked me in the middle of it why I had tried to do myself in, I was unable to think of a single reply. I stayed in the hospital's psychiatric ward for two weeks.

The afternoon I was released, my brother met me at the hospital and we went straight downtown to see a double bill at the Bleecker Street Cinema: *Grand Illusion* and *Paths of Glory*. Still movie-hungry after a two-week drought—or else piggishly over-indulgent, like a tonsillitis patient demanding all the ice cream he can eat—I insisted we race uptown to see *Zazie dans le Métro*, the Malle film that Stoller had praised in a recent review. What an orgy! I had gotten suicide out of my system, but not cinema.

I must backtrack a little. Before the suicide attempt, at the beginning of my sophomore year, Stoller, Zill, and I had agreed that Filmmakers of Columbia should run its own film series at the college, both to show movies we wanted to see and to raise money for future productions. Zill had surprised me by proposing that I be made president of the organization. Granted, his fear of being held fiscally responsible for our new venture may have had something to do with offering me this honor, but I accepted it with pride.

We began sending away for film rental catalogues and, when they arrived, poring over them like kids let loose in a candy store. We were free to order any movie we wanted to see, provided it was available in sixteen millimeter—and provided we occasionally considered commercial factors. It might be interesting, for instance, to rent all of the Brandon catalogue's Eastern European arcana, but if nobody came to *Ghetto Terezin* or *Border Street*, we would still have to shell out the seventy-five dollars' rental. The decision was made to balance our schedule with obscurities like Griffith's *Abraham Lincoln* and *Border Street* on the one hand, and moneymakers like Hitchcock's *Notorious* and *Rock Around the Clock* on the other. We booked the films, wrote the blurbs, ground out a flyer, and held our breaths.

Nick called me at the hospital, unable to believe, among other things, that I had attempted suicide two weeks before the opening of our Filmmakers of Columbia series. Shouldn't that have been enough to live for? No, I insisted stubbornly. Nevertheless, I got swept up immediately and fortunately into the venture, making business phone calls from the psychiatric ward while Zill and Stoller ran around town distributing flyers.

The first night of the film series drew a sellout crowd for Kurosawa's *Drunken Angel* and Kenneth Anger's *Fireworks* (a homoerotic short that had not been seen in New York for many years). I was so excited counting the money we made that I couldn't watch the movies. The next day, the dean called me into his office and told me he had heard about *Fireworks*, and to "keep it clean from now on."

A happier period began for me. Stoller introduced me to a woman named Abby, and we started going out together. Though the affair lasted only three months, it served its purpose. I also began writing film reviews for the *Columbia Daily Spectator* and stories for *Columbia Review*, the literary magazine, and no longer felt so neglected on campus. Moreover, the film series was a big hit, and was to continue successfully for years—helping to put me through college, in fact. Susan Sontag, who was then a religion professor at Columbia and already a force in the New York cultural life— especially to us *cinéastes*—gave her blessing to the series by periodically attending. Stoller and Zill gradually withdrew from the activity, although they continued to offer programming suggestions. And Jim Stoller provided one of our most memorable evenings by agreeing, after lengthy persuasion, to play piano behind Pabst's *The Love of Jeanne Ney*; it was a treat to see him overcome his compulsive modesty and perform in public.

We were all waiting impatiently for the sequel to *L'Avventura*. *La Notte* was said to feature a dream cast of Jeanne Moreau, Marcello Mastroianni, and Monica Vitti. Meanwhile, the art theaters kept our excitement at a boil by showing some of Antonioni's early films, like *Il Grido* and *Le Amiche*, which only deepened our admiration for our own "Michelangelo."

By the time the first ads appeared announcing the premiere of *La Notte*, I had worked myself into such a fit of anticipation that my unconscious mind jumped the gun: I began dreaming, for several nights in a row, preview versions of *La Notte*. When I finally saw it, the film became a normal extension of my dream life. Several of us went on opening night, waiting in line for an hour for tickets. I was with Carol Bergman, a Barnard girl whom I'd fallen in love with (and would marry a year later), and I held her throughout the film, perhaps undercutting the full impact of Antonioni's despondent message. It was great to see an Antonioni movie through the comfortable bifocals of being in love; when one is happy, one can look at both comedy and tragedy with equanimity.

Primed to adore *La Notte*, I did. Especially the ending, with the camera pulling away from Moreau and Mastroianni groping each other desperately in the lush grass at dawn. We left the theater quoting the Master's latest koan: "Sometimes beauty can lead to despair."

It was Jim Stoller, as usual, who saw problems with Antonioni's new direction before the rest of us did. After voicing objections, in his *La Notte* review, about the "sloppily paced" party sequence, the "leaden and insistent" symbolism, and the academic "discontinuous editing" in the walk sequence which was "used to develop a series of explicit, one-to-one meanings as in Eisenstein," Stoller went on to raise a more telling objection. Antonioni, he felt, had stacked the cards by denying any reference to a worthy model of behavior, any "point worth aspiring to," if only in the past, and any real engagement between the characters.

Of course I disagreed at the time, finding Stoller's demand sentimental. More to the point, this was disloyalty! I tried to argue him out of his position. But the words "card stacking" continued to roll uneasily around my brain.

My own disappointment with Antonioni came later with *Blow-Up*, though that derived partly from a misunderstanding, having wrongly elevated him to the level of philosopher in the first place. I had followed the lead of the press, which trumpeted his every quote as a weighty pronouncement: "Eroticism the Disease of the Age: Antonioni." Even his interview silences were reported as evidence of deep thought. It was partly the burden placed on Antonioni to be the oracle of modernity that forced him into ever more schematic conceptions. When his subsequent films exhibited signs of trendy jet-setting, hippie naïveté, and sheer woolly-headedness—even if the visuals remained stunning—I, like many of his fans, felt betrayed. It took me years to figure out that most film directors are not systematic thinkers but artistic opportunists. Maybe thanks to Coppola, Cimino & Company, we have reached a more realistic expectation of directors today; we are more used to the combination of great visual style with intellectual incoherence. But at the time we looked to filmmakers to be our novelists, our sages.

Film enjoyed as never before (or since) the prestige of high culture. English professors with whom I had difficulty making office appointments would stumble across my legs in Cinema 16 showings; they would interrupt themselves in class to gush about a movie; they would publish essays comparing Resnais's ordering of time to Proust's.

The euphoria and prestige that surrounded films in the early sixties seem, in retrospect, deserved. The French New Wave—Godard, Truffaut, Varda, Chabrol, Rivette, Resnais, Malle, Rohmer—had all burst on the American scene at once; Antonioni, Visconti, Rossellini, Fellini, Buñuel, Bergman, Welles, Minnelli, Satyajit Ray, Wajda, Losey, Torre Nilsson, and the Brazilian Cine Novo group were already operating in high gear, the New American Underground of Brakhage, Mekas, Warhol, Anger, etc., was in its heroic phase; and the lingering activity of such old masters as Renoir, Dreyer, Ford, Hawks, Lang, Hitchcock, and Ozu provided a sort of benign historical link to the golden age of silent cinema. A whole apparatus had sprung up to support this moviemaking renaissance; the art-house circuit, new movie journals, museum and university studies, and, like a final official seal of legitimacy, the establishment of the New York Film Festival.

I covered that first New York Film Festival in 1963 for the *Columbia Daily Spectator*. The air at Lincoln Center on opening night was alive with high hopes, with the conviction that we were entering a fat time for movies. Everyone, from dignitary to hungry film buff, seemed grateful to the ones who had given us a film festival; New York City was finally linked with Europe.

It was a banner year. The festival premieres included Buñuel's *Exterminating Angel*; Olmi's *The Fiancés*; Polanski's *Knife in the Water*; Ozu's *An Autumn Afternoon*; Bresson's *Trial of Joan of Arc*; Resnais's *Muriel*; Losey's *The Servant*; Rocha's *Barravento*; Mekas's *Hallelujah the Hills*; Marker's *Le Joli Mai*; Kobayashi's *Harakiri; ROGOPAG* by Rossellini, Godard, Pasolini, and Gregoretti; Blue's *The Olive Trees of Justice*; De Antonio's *Point of Order*, and Melville's *Magnet of Doom*. There were also first-shown retrospectives of the uncut Ophuls's *Lola Montez*, Mizoguchi's *Sansho the Bailiff*, Kurosawa's *I Live in Fear*. At the time, I did not appreciate what an unusually fortunate confluence of circumstances was reigning in the cinematic heavens; I thought it would go on forever with the same incandescence.

At college, I was still struggling with the question of whether to become a writer or a filmmaker. While writing came easily to me, I felt I had to try to make my own movie. I could not remain always a sponge for others' celluloid visions. So I adapted one of my short stories to a screenplay, took the profits from the film series, and gathered volunteer actors and technicians.

Orson Welles once said that *Citizen Kane* succeeded because he didn't know what could or couldn't be done in motion pictures. I wish to report that my movie didn't work for the same reason. I chose an impossibly complicated scheme: three unreliable narrators in the space of a twenty-minute film. Completed in my senior year, 1964, *Saint at the Crossroads* was "over two years in the making": in addition to the usual problems with a tiny budget and a volunteer crew—camera leaks, personality clashes, absenteeism, inappropriate weather—the fancy synch-sound equipment we had rented for the dialogue scenes failed to synchronize. Sound was our undoing; in the end we had to rent a dubbing studio. The visuals, however, were very pretty, largely due to my cameraman, Mark Weiss, who alone on the set knew what he was doing. There was an obligatory Antonioniesque sequence in Riverside Park where boy and girl, walking together, grow farther apart with each shot. They reach the pier where an elaborate tracking shot surrounds them as they kiss, then shows each looking away moodily at the water. . . .

I stayed up all night with the sound man to do a final mix, rushing to complete the film for its scheduled premiere. We finally got the mix done at eight o'clock Saturday morning—just in time for me to grab a taxi to my job as a weekend guard at the Metropolitan Museum. As the cab approached the museum, I looked out, blinking my eyes in the morning light, and saw Susan Sontag and three men in tuxedos, laughing with champagne glasses in their hands as they tripped around the fountain. Right out of *Last Year at Marienbad*.

Saint at the Crossroads premiered at Columbia, paired with Fellini's *Il Bidone*. Many of the exiting spectators were heard to remark "The sound was a problem," then lower their voices as they saw the filmmaker standing by. Once more Stoller came to the rescue, salving the pain with a positive review of *Saint at the Crossroads* in the *Spectator*. Admitting there were some "technical infelicities and rather disorienting violations of film grammar," he went on with a friend's partisan eye to discover "some very considerable achievements. If Lopate continues making films—as he should—he will soon, or next, give us something of surprising originality and power." No thanks: I had had my fun; I would become a writer. It was easier and cheaper to control pens and paper than actors. Besides, I could not stand the prospect of again disappointing so many volunteers because of my inexperience. Making that one twenty-minute film had taught me the enormous difference between having an aesthetic understanding of film and being confronted with the demands of transferring three dimensions into two on an actual set.

Gershom Scholem once characterized youth movements by their chatter, as distinguished from true language: "Youth has no language. That is the reason for its uncertainty and unhappiness. It has no language, which is to say its life is imaginary and its knowledge without substance. Its existence is dissolved past all recognition into a complex flatness." I am not sure I agree, even looking back with memory's foreshortened lens, that this period of my youth was complexly flat; it seems in some ways to have been unusually rich. But certainly we had no real perspective, which is why we called on movies to be our language and our knowledge, our hope, our romance, our cause, our imagination and our life.

EARLY MARRIAGE AND BACHELORHOOD

6

Washington Heights and Inwood

from *Waterfront*

WASHINGTON HEIGHTS IS one of the most dramatically hilly sections of Manhattan. Here, for once, the grid has been obliged to adjust to topography. There are steep stairs linking one street to another, as in European cities; and the catacomb-like subway stations with cavernous, arched ceilings and elaborate tile-work are built into the rock-face at such a depth as to require elevators. Certain east-west thoroughfares, such as West 181st Street, accommodate the land by gently curving to their termination at the peak of the cliffs. West 181st Street, once the heart of a Jewish neighborhood, retains a few kosher food stores and restaurants; and the street still acts as an unofficial barrier, dividing the southern end of Washington Heights, which is largely hospitals and Hispanic tenements, from the more Irish and Jewish northern end, with its middle-class cooperative enclaves and nursing homes.

If you walk downhill towards the river on West 181st Street, you come to Cabrini Boulevard (formerly Northern Avenue), one of New York's tucked-away treasures. Here are some remarkable apartment house enclaves, built during the 1920s and 30s, when city developers still thought it economically viable to erect castles for the middle class. On the eastern side of the street is the older Hudson View Gardens, a Tudor extravaganza in brown brick, with simulated half-timbering of dark brown wooden diagonals crisscrossing the façade. The apartment houses were built by George F. Pelham in 1924–25, and stand at attention along the street-wall, correctly if somewhat stodgily, like a regiment of Tudor cottages on growth hormones. Across the way from them, on the western side of Cabrini Boulevard, is Castle Village, built by Pelham's son, George F. Pelham II, in 1938–1939. This is a more frankly up-to-date and, to my mind, fascinating high-rise apartment complex, stretching all the way from West 181st to West 186th Street. It has been maintained in tiptop shape: the white window frames all look newly painted, the apple-red brick facades spanking clean. The "architecture" of Castle Village, if one should even call it that, attempts nothing ambitious; it is meant to convey cozy comfort, familiarity. The one original touch is that all five buildings are in the shape of a cross, which maximizes river views (eight out of nine apartments get them on each floor).

It was this X shape that caught the eye of Lewis Mumford, and prompted him to write a "Sky Line" column about Castle Village in *The New Yorker*. Unlike the architectural critics we have today, who focus obsessively on the plum commissions assigned or not assigned to two dozen international cutting-edge stars, Mumford was curious about the everyday built environment actually going up around him. After praising the enclave's attention to "Light, air, space, gardens—the substance and ornament of all good architecture," and the "simple vernacular of our period: wide, steel casement windows; a plain, unadorned façade," Mumford nit-picked the color of the brick, the "barricade"-like repetition of five identical, large buildings and the X plan's space-wastage compared to "a zigzag or sawtooth layout." He concluded even-handedly: "The builder of Castle Village is to be congratulated for going as far as he has gone, but he is to be reproached for not going further, since he had perhaps the finest site remaining in New York for residential purposes."

It remains a fine site, with the cruciform buildings set discreetly back from generous grounds. What captivates me most about Castle Village is the broad lawn sweeping down to the ledge that overlooks Fort Washington Park, the George Washington Bridge and the Hudson River. In the late afternoon, this secluded garden is a pleasance out of an Italian countryside, with quaint stone fence, benches, sitting nooks and magnificent trees, which give form and shade to the whole. Whether the public has or has not the right to enjoy this view—a sign on the lawn says "For Residents Only"—I always partake, and no one ever stops me. The former, Gothicized estate of Dr. Charles Paterno that once rested on the site may be gone, but you can still imagine, from the grounds' placement and from one remaining fragment, a pergola on the northern end of the garden, its picturesque configuration atop this hill overlooking New Jersey.

If you continue north along Cabrini Boulevard, past Mother Cabrini High School and Cabrini Chapel, the buildings suddenly cease along the western side of the street and give way to a mysterious wooden railing, which overlooks a steeply treacherous, pathless and largely impassable forest on the border between Fort Washington Park and Fort Tryon Park. When I lived in Inwood, in the mid–1960s, I used to be fascinated by this stretch of rural wildness. With no trouble at all, merely editing out distant traffic noise, I could imagine it the setting for some feral hermit's existence. At twenty, prematurely plunged into my first marriage, I was soothed by the wilderness glimpsed from Cabrini Terrace, so at odds did it seem with the surrounding *gemütlich* apartment buildings and bungalows of Washington Heights and Inwood, where elderly German Jews lived on reparation checks, and doctors' families occupied the spacious ground floor. These amiably middle-class homes soothed me as well, but in a different way: we were lucky to have found refuge amidst them. Upper Manhattan, though thoroughly respectable, wasn't fashionable enough to be pricey; and financially needy newlyweds such as ourselves could still find decent apartments at bargain rents. I remember living there with Carol during my last year at college, 1964, and several years after, and that feeling of still technically being on Manhattan Island, but far removed from the careerist energy and pulse and glamour, "the rat race," as we enviously called it; how poet-friends from the East Village had to be coaxed to visit us, and took several books with them on the subway uptown, as if for a three-days' journey; how I'd show them around, proud of the area's obscurity, its backwater charm: those private bungalows on Payson Avenue, with bricks the color of dried blood and casement windows with black hinges overlooking hilly Inwood Park, which Carol and I, mocking their pro-priety, would nonetheless fantasize retiring to in old age.

The dream of that first marriage was to bypass youth and ascend straight to a responsibly shared life in double work-harness. The goal seemed reasonable at the time, since we got along so companionably, but it proved impossible because we were way too young and exaggerated our maturity—a fact that only surfaced when life began to test us.

I was twenty-two when the screws tightened. I mention my age partly to exoner-ate myself in advance for bad behavior. It was not that I behaved so despicably, which could at least allow me the retrospective allure of villainy, as that I was so pas-sive and overwhelmed and inadequate to the challenge. My wife was also young at the time, but she behaved with far more womanly self-respect; age is not the whole story. Nevertheless, we were babies: two baby literati, presuming ourselves writers with no assurance from the world that we ought to have. For the moment, we sup-ported ourselves by free-lance editing, tape transcribing, ghostwriting—"taking in wash," we called it. We barely survived, using nearby Columbia-Presbyterian Hospi-tal's emergency room as our family physician; and when starvation threatened, Carol went out and got a full-time job. I'm especially embarrassed to recall that part: but there seemed to be an implicit understanding between us, typical of the period, that I was the literary genius of the house and needed to hone my writing, whereas she could develop hers any old time.

One day Carol came home and told me she was pregnant. We had been won-dering what had happened to her period, but I took the firm position that there was no point in worrying about what might not be the case. Now it was the case. What to do? We began by taking long walks, up and down the hills of Manhattan's northern tip, analyzing the pros and cons. I cannot think of those discussions without associating them with the terrain, the Cloisters and Fort Tryon Park where we picnicked if the weather was good, the frozen-in-time residential sec-tions of Inwood, and our feverish agonizing, dropping our voices in the presence of passersby when our vocabulary became too explicit ("curetage," "trimester"). One night on Broadway, near the Dyckman House, we were stopped in our tracks by a couple clouting each other outside an Irish saloon, and we were unsure how to take this: as a recommendation to start a family or not, since everything that crossed our path seemed an omen.

The most painful part of these increasingly nippy walks (it was autumn, edging over into winter) was that neither one of us seemed able to express a strong opinion about what he or she wanted. We had that young lovers' symbiotic habit of sympathizing with the other's viewpoint; and, like detectives hired to shadow one another, we watched carefully for signs of deep, unequivocal feeling, the better to support it. Not sure what my true feelings were, I told myself: If Carol really wants this baby, I will back her up, we'll somehow make ends meet. I had always imagined having children someday. The fact that the opportunity had come sooner rather than later—well, I could adjust to the challenge of fatherhood, I guessed. I had a great desire to be an adult. I also wanted to act nobly in a crisis, to shoulder my end of responsibility, or at least to appear in public to do so. Why should Carol have to make a sacrifice and give up a baby she wanted? If, however, she feels not yet emotionally ready for a baby, or thinks it would get in the way of her career, I'll support her decision to end the pregnancy. So far, she said she wasn't sure she *did* want it. But perhaps she was only saying that because she was uncertain whether she could depend on me, my being such an egotist. If I were to start saying I was *sure* I wanted this baby—which felt in any case like the mature, adult thing to say—she would undoubtedly—or most probably—come around to a certainty of wanting it. My pretend-decisiveness would conquer her hesitation, and, once the baby was born, she would, I felt confident, become a wonderfully devoted mother, and this devotion would in the end dissolve what remained of my own ambivalence. In fact, she might never even notice my ambivalence if I played the pro-baby role with enough conviction.

But of course, nothing goes unnoticed in marriage. And the fact that it was thought of as a role, not intrinsic to my character, meant that it could be superceded by another role ("If you really want this abortion I will support you all the way"), which is indeed what happened, until the two roles began alternating in such quick succession, as we went over and over the same ground, that in the end, understandably, she stopped listening to me. She turned inward. I began to sense a quiet will gathering inside her and hunkering down; we were no longer belaboring the topic as much. In truth, I began to miss that operatic agonizing; a part of me could have gone on and on with it. About that time, my wife began seeing a woman psychotherapist, and I suspected that they were working it out between themselves. Whether or not this suspicion was correct, the day came when Carol calmly informed me that she had made up her mind to have an abortion. It was fixed, final, no more discussion.

As abortions in 1966 were illegal, we would have to become outlaws. We asked around, and heard about a saintly woman physician named Dr. Elizabeth Something-or-other, in Philadelphia. Carol made an appointment to see her, and we took the train to Philadelphia. At first it seemed like a tourist adventure: we talked about seeing the Philadelphia Museum, and exploring a city neither of us knew. On the day in question we were too nervous to look at paintings, but we killed an hour or two walking around the historic district, admiring the old iron lampposts and cobblestone streets and Federal-style row-houses in which ordinary people still lived; and, with that hunger for normal life which must have sprung from the desperate little act we were contemplating, I predicted aloud that we would someday come to live here, in one of these same charming historic townhouses, as a reward for our current hardships.

The doctor's waiting room was crowded. We sat there patiently, and finally it was Carol's turn. I glimpsed Dr. Elizabeth for a few seconds, beckoning my wife inside: she was an elegantly poised brunette in a navy blue angora sweater, nicely put together (I placed her in my harem of erotic fantasies instantly, jerk that I am). Thirty minutes later Carol re-emerged, looking thoughtful and sad. For some reason I can no longer remember, Dr. Elizabeth had refused to perform the abortion. Perhaps she felt the police were watching her too closely, or she had decided to perform abortions only for in-state women, or else truly indigent cases. Whatever her reasons, they could not have been mercenary, because afterwards we did not think critically of her, only of ourselves: you would think we had failed a stiff entrance exam. We had a hollow feeling, as though our insides were already scraped out, while we waited at Union Station to catch the return train. Someone at the food counter had on a soul station, Diana Ross singing "My World Is Empty Without You, Babe," and this, too, seemed an omen.

Back in New York, Carol found another abortionist on the Lower East Side, and went alone to the appointment. The first curetage did not take; she was obliged to return to the same bungler (we could not afford two fees) and have it done all over again. I shudder to think how close we came to tragedy. No, I don't want to think about it. Half a lifetime later, she's alive, I'm alive. Both married to different people.

I cannot say that the abortion alone inflicted a mortal blow to our marriage (there would be others); but it did uncover veins of mutual mistrust we had not known existed. It left me feeling ashamed of myself, aware of my untrustworthiness and eager to cover it up better next time. And I think it left Carol not only wounded and weary, but resentful—either because I'd been unable to protect her from the sorrow she had gone through, more or less alone, or because my failure to lobby harder for baby and family had alerted her to a secret (even secret to myself at the time) inconstancy on my part toward the marriage, a footloose streak that would one day lead me to go off and fulfill some bachelor destiny.

"Destiny" is what you know about your life in hindsight. Or maybe it's the stubbornness that takes over once your character, colliding with the world's barriers, has coalesced into a set of rigidities. "There is a point beyond which there is no going back. That is the point that we must reach," said Kierkegaard. He was speaking of faith, but I would apply the same idea to love, monogamy, or the decision to have a child. Precisely what I was missing as a young man—now I have it almost too much— was a conviction of limits and the irrevocable: many paths seemed equally provisional, equally capricious (like the choice of trails from the Cloisters down to the street below), and so I felt a fraud asserting any one in particular.

_ 7

My Drawer

I AM LOOKING THROUGH THE TOP DRAWER of my bedroom dresser this morning — something I almost never do. I have a reticence about examining these articles, which I don't quite understand; it's as though the Puritan side of me said it was a waste of time, if not faintly indecent. Since I have moved my socks to another drawer there is even less reason to visit these redundant objects. Six months go by without my doing any more than feeling around blindly for a cuff link. My top drawer is a *way station* in which I keep the miscellanea that I cannot bear to throw away just yet, but that I fully intend to, the moment things get out of hand. So far the drawer can take it. It is too early for triage. But this morning I have an urge to make an inventory of the drawer, in a last attempt to understand the symbolic underpinnings of my character.

In it I find a pair of 3-D movie glasses. A silver whistle. A combination lock in good repair but whose combination has long been lost. A strip of extra cuff material for the legs of my white linen suit — should I ever grow an inch or two I can sew it on. One plastic and one aluminum shoehorn. A button that says BOYCOTT LETTUCE. Keys to old houses and offices. My last pair of glasses before the prescription changed — who can throw out a pair of eyeglasses? Two nail clippers. Cuff links. A pair of rusty unusable children's scissors. A windproof lighter I won at an amusement park; too bad I don't smoke. Oh, and lots more, much more. But before I go on, shouldn't I try to approach this mess more systematically — to categorize, to make generalizations?

One category that suggests itself is gifts I have no particular affection for, but am too superstitious to chuck out. (If you throw away a gift, something terrible will happen: the wastebasket will explode, or you'll never get another.) They include this pair of cloth finger puppets that I suppose were meant to give me endless hours of delight while sitting on my bed pretending to be Punch and Judy with myself. Because I work with children, people keep bringing me juvenile toys — magic sets, mazes with ball bearings, paddle-balls — confusing the profession with the profession's clients. Over the years I have been given a whole collection of oddities that do not really amuse me or match my sense of perversity. Nothing is trickier than bringing someone a novelty gift, since each person's definition of cute or campy is such a private affair.

Now we come to my "jewelry." Most of these items wandered into my possession toward the middle of the sixties, during those few seconds in American history when it was considered progressive for men to wear medallions and layers of necklaces. In my top drawer I find an imitation-elephant-tusk necklace, a multicolored string of Amerindian beads, and a hodgepodge of what I can only call spiritual amulets — tangled-up chains and rings that are supposed to contain special powers or that symbolize the third eye. Usually these ornaments were given to me with the explanation that most men the donor knew would be too uptight to wear jewelry like this in public, but that I was free enough to be at peace with my feminine side. Little did they know. Each and every one has landed in my top drawer, enough for me to open my own jewelry stall at a street fair.

Other mementos of hipper days include a large brown-velvet King's Road bow tie, a pack of moldering Bambu cigarette papers, and both DUMP LBJ and IMPEACH NIXON buttons. I find it hard to throw away political buttons — as hard as it was in those days actually to wear them. There is also a badge from a conference, with the words "Hi! I'm —" and my name on it. Toward the back of the drawer are my war medals: my high-school American history award, with its pea green / navy blue / red tricolor; my yellow-and-white-ribboned English award; the silver badge from the Fire Department for best fire-prevention essay. Glory days! They do cheer me up when I see them, though they are as useless now as the keys that no longer fit my door.

The keys belong to the category of things I kept to be *on the safe side*. For instance, an official bank card for cashing checks, no good to me now since I no longer go to that bank, but what if it were to fall into the wrong hands? I find also a wristwatch case with midnight-blue lining that seemed too pretty to part with, and that would make an excellent box for safety pins or — whatever. Oh, and a suede-looking drawstring purse that once held a bottle of over-priced shampoo (I seem particularly susceptible to these packages for luxury items). I realize I'm fooling myself when I say I will someday find a use for these containers. How can I when I ignore them for months at a time, and forget that they're there? They live a hidden life in the back street of my consciousness. Perhaps the drawer's purpose is to house objects that arouse only half-digested desires never fantasized all the way through. That is why I must not look into it too often. These are secret fantasies even I am not supposed to understand.

Even more than desire, these objects seem to have the power of arousing guilt; that is, they have fixed me with the hypnotizing promise not to throw them away. I find myself protecting them with an uneasy conscience, like someone whom I caused to be crippled and who now has the upper hand. I suppose if I were to examine the derivations of each of these keepsakes, many would call up some road not taken, some rejection of possibility. Or perhaps they are secretly connected to each other by surrealist logic, like the objects in a Joseph Cornell box, and if I were to lay them out on top of the dresser I could put together the story of my subconscious mind.

When I consider my peculiar, fitful relation to the drawer as a whole, I have to think back to the original top drawer: the one in my parents' house when I was seven and eight years old. There was nothing I liked better than to sneak into their bedroom when everyone else was out of the house, and to approach their large, dark mahogany dresser, with its altar top composed of the round reversible mirror, the wedding photograph, the stray hair-curlers, and the Chinese black-lacquered music box where my mother kept her Woolworth jewelry. Then, taking my time, I would pull open the three-sectioned top drawer by its brass handles. What was so fascinating about rifling through their drawer? I used to find nothing very unusual: some objects of obscure masculine power, like my father's leather traveling case, a shaving brush, a pair of suspenders, a wallet with photos of us, the children. Then I would go over to my mother's side of the drawer, and visit her bloomers and her gypsy scarves. I would pick up each item and smell the perfume: Arabia! Then back to my father's side, for some clues into his stolid, remote, Stakhanovite personality. In the middle section was no-man's-land, with elastic bands, garters, pipe cleaners. Once, it seems to me, I found a deck of pornographic playing cards. Am I imagining this? Isn't this rather what I kept looking for and *not* finding? I know I came across the rumored box of prophylactics, which my older brother had assured me would be there. Yet these balloons did not thrill me much, or as much as they might have if I had only been seeking "dirty things." I was searching for, not clarification, but a mystery, the mystery of masculine and feminine. Certainly I was looking for the tools of sexuality that held together the household, but this went further than mere rude instruments; it included everything that made my mother so different from my father, and that still enabled them to share the same life, as they shared this drawer. The drawer recorded without explanation the ordinariness of this miracle that had given birth to me.

And now I live alone — Oedipal child that I am. The contradictions of my top drawer stem from my own idiosyncrasies and not from any uneasy cohabitation of two creatures of the opposite sex. To pry through their things, I see now, was a kind of premasturbation. Where better to indulge than in the bedroom of one's parents? Even now I must be affected by that old taboo against self-abuse — in going through drawers, at least — which explains why I go through my own top drawer with embarrassed haste.

My drawer has its secrets as well. To honor the old prying and bring it down to earth, so to speak, I keep a box of prophylactics. Also, toward the back, I am ashamed to admit, are a few of those ads handed to me in the street for massage parlors: "Beautiful Girls — Complete Privacy — One Price. . . . Tahitia — Gives You Just What You Expect!" and an awful color photo of two women in a bubble bath with a grinning curly-headed man. These are also kept just in case, to be on the safe side. Here is a squashed-up tube of diaphragm cream, with just enough in it for one more go. Kay must have left it behind, as she did this frayed pair of panties. Do you know we almost moved in together, before we broke up for the very last time? And finally, the most forbidden object of all: the five-and-ten I.D. heart with Kay's name on it. Since I have forbidden myself to brood about her anymore, I must open and shut the drawer very quickly to skip seeing it, and inevitably I do catch sight of that heart-shaped button, the sort that high-school sweethearts wear. She gave it to me in our first year, and thinking I didn't love her enough, she accused me of being ashamed to wear it in front of my friends. She was right, of course — I have always been wary about advertising my heart on my sleeve, whether political or amorous. Kay was right, too, that in the beginning I did not love her enough. And now that I do, and she loves me not, I faithfully continue to wear her pin, in my top drawer. It has the place of honor in that reliquary, in my museum of useless and obsolete things that stand ready to testify at any moment to all that is never lost.

_ 8

Osao

SATURDAYS I TRY TO USE FOR WRITING. Sometimes the release from every-day work stirs up all I want to say; but sometimes just the opposite happens, and I cling to errands like doing the laundry. It was the second kind of Saturday, and I was looking for excuses so as not to confront my brain, as I walked to the Xerox shop. I know the man who owns the shop, Pak. He is a Korean who came to the United States as an exchange student, got his doctorate, and taught philosophy in midwestern universities for several years, before becoming a New York City shopkeeper.

His choice of the medium of xerography has always seemed to me to have a wry secret connection to his philosophical training. With his waxy skin indoor-pallid, his eyes baggy from serving these insatiable and unreliable machines, his short athletic body making half turns in the constricted space behind the counter, he seems to have become a kind of Xerox ascetic. Actually, I am making him sound more retiring than he really is: the shop does a brisk business. It is not as if he is "burying" himself, in fact he has quite a few entrepreneurial sidelines — used typewriters, off-set printing jobs, a half interest in the restaurant upstairs.

All the world seems to come to Pak's shop on Saturday. Most of the steady customers are self-employed, work at home, and hang around the Xerox place as a substitute office. The show people in the neighborhood, the dancers, the choir directors, want reviews and résumés multiplied; the music students have to have their scores duplicated on the folio machine; the nervous organizers of Balkan and Ukrainian support committees need hundreds of copies of their letters of appeal.

Though it purports to be cut-and-dried, a Xerox parlor arouses in some people a craving for special treatment, an undefinable "sweet tooth" to be indulged, like a bakery of the word. That particular Saturday, there was a small old lady with dark lipstick who had income-tax forms she wanted copied. From the excited way she talked, it might have been her first outing in years. When Pak yelled, "Anyone with offset jobs?" she asked in a panic, "What's that?" and a lady next to her said, "It's printing."

The old lady was none too pleased when she got her copies back. "It's so light I can barely read it!"

"That's because you use pencil," said Pak, making it sound "pen-soo" in his soft Korean accent.

"But it usually comes out darker than this!"

"No machine in the world do any better on pencil."

He turned to hand someone else his copies, but she stayed. "It's not in order! I don't see a third page. Couldn't you make this one darker?"

"I'll try, madam." He was remarkably patient (one might say, *philosophical*), even offering to charge her only for the dark sheets. But still she clogged up the counter, turning the pages this way and that, and pulling everyone else into her confusion.

In spite of the fact that I had nothing to do but waste time, I got carried along with the general impatience and kept staring at my watch, furious that it was taking so long.

Pak nodded at me when I handed him five poems. "How is Poet? You got any more big advances?"

"No, and I never had any in the first place."

"Don't tell me. You must be writing big money-maker."

All this was standard: I was getting rich, I was getting famous, and only my innate stinginess prevented me from buying all the used typewriters in his shop. But this time, as he handed my change back, Pak added something in an undertone, so that the other customers wouldn't hear it:

"I have a Korean friend who needs help translating poems into English. She's very nice. Just few poems."

"I don't know any Korean."

"No, no." He laughed. "She has already translated into English. This is just to give it — 'final poetic polish.'" Pak looked down at the floor, as though shy about asking a favor. "Can she call you? I told her you were 'sensitive young man,' fine 'poet,'" he said, giving the last word a faintly ridiculing, caricatured twist. "All right?"

"Sure, why not." I was hoping this woman would be beautiful and it would lead to an adventure. "Tell her to phone me in the next hour. I'm going straight home from here."

It was a time in my life when I had no love interests. I was between girlfriends and I had not slept with anyone for months. I had vowed to myself that the next passably attractive woman who crossed my path, I would chase.

By the time I got back to my apartment I was already picturing her as one of the Utamaro beauties hanging on my wall calendar, the voluptuous pearl divers, the decorous geishas. What is it about such out-of-the-blue assignations that raises all one's hopes of at last finding the woman of one's life? I prepared myself for disappointment: she was probably homely and wrinkled, or one of those cross matron-auntie types in Ozu movies. I equipped her with a hunchback, a patch over one eye, pock scars and sparse grey hair; I had so fertilely and successfully distorted her in every way that by the time the phone rang that afternoon I was surprised to hear a voice fresh, intelligent, and "pretty." Let me explain what I mean. Generally I can tell just by the phone voice whether someone I have never met is physically attractive. There seems to be a way that people who have received compliments all their lives put themselves forward, or rather, only part of themselves forward.

I began straightening up. She would be over any minute. I had to act professional. Pretend I was a private detective waiting for some client.

I went to answer the doorbell.

"I am Osao," she said with a trace of deprecation, as if apologizing for the fact that she was only this one person, as if she too were in on the joke of the multiple forms to which my imagination had subjected her.

There was about her the maturity of a woman in her mid-thirties, probably a few years older than I was, which was not necessarily a mark against her. From the way she stood at the front door, from her no-nonsense manner, I had a momentary image of her as a nurse, or someone used to making house calls, an impression that I later learned had no basis in fact. She had straight black hair, cropped short, a high-cheeked, pretty face and round black eyes that warned, "I am nobody's fool." I walked in front of her down the hall, and I noticed, turning for an instant, her full figure just at that shadow line between voluptuous and plump.

To be honest, I could not yet make up my mind whether I was or was not attracted to her.

She was not what I had expected, being neither as seductively Oriental as my most dreamy fantasies, nor as homely as my efforts to preempt and contain disappointment. I had to deal with a solid professional woman of the kind I met often in my teaching rounds: clearheaded, with no wish to appear glamorous (a wrap denim skirt seemed to signify preference for practical uniforms); yet there were faint touches of a will to beauty if one wanted to notice them.

She sat down on the couch, and I offered her tea, both of us smiling, perhaps at the comedy of my making this Asiatic gesture. From the stove, I noticed her looking around my apartment; perhaps she was doing her own kind of anthropology. What generalization and conclusion she was coming to I would have loved to know.

She got up to look at a poster of a celadon statuette from a museum exhibition. "Is that Korean?"

"Yes," I said.

She sat down, contented. I brought over the teacups.

"Did my friend explain to you what the job was?" she asked, getting down to business the moment I sat beside her, as though aware of the romantic interpretations to which her entering this strange man's house might be put, and wishing to steer far away from that level.

"You said something on the phone about your father and a calligraphy show."

"My father is having his first exhibition of calligraphy in America, at the Korea Society. You know the Korea Society?"

"Oh yes. I think I've been there once."

She looked at me doubtfully. "His show is in two weeks. Maybe you will be able to come?"

"I'd love to come. When is it?"

"Friday, July twenty-first, is the opening. Two weeks from yesterday," she said, and then added, "He is staying in my house in the meantime." From her tone I inferred that her father's visit was not an unmixed blessing.

"Do you not get along?" I asked.

"Oh, yes. This is the first time he is in New York so he is happy to see the sights. He walks around all day. But when I was younger we always used to fight."

"What about?"

She blushed. I wondered if I was going too quickly. But her explanation was ready: "My father is a difficult man. He is very — old-fashioned in his thinking. He is very proud to be old-fashioned. He has the typical Korean 'male chauvinist' attitude toward women."

"In what way?"

"Oh, you don't want to hear about that. I think I should discuss the price with you. How much do you usually get for work like this?"

"I don't know, I've never helped translate Korean poems before."

"These are Chinese. My father would never bother with Korean poems." She smiled. "He considers them not — *refined*, is that the right way to say it?"

"Unrefined, yes."

"You must forgive me, my English is very bad."

"It sounds perfectly fluent to me."

"Hardly fluent." Osao made a face. "Shall we discuss a fee?"

"Let me see what it is first, then I'll have a better idea."

She took out a sheaf of folded papers from her black plastic pocketbook. First, she had translated the original Chinese into Korean, then she had translated the Korean into English — but she would not let me see these until she had apologized for how awful they were. Each time I reached over to take the papers from her hand, she pulled them back, explaining that she had no instinct for poetry, she was completely "uncreative," her grasp of English was shameful, after living here fifteen years; I was not to worry about hurting her feelings, she knew she had done a terrible job, that was why she had sought professional help. At last she handed over the poems.

"But these are not bad," I said, reading the translations. "They're almost there." I saw that merely by quickening a phrase here and moving a line-break there, by finding a plainer diction, taking out the archaisms — by "de-poeticizing" them, in a word — they could be made into classical Chinese poetry to suit modern taste; that is, the kind that is currently being translated and imitated by American deep-image pastoral poets. The style was not my own, but it amused me to take up the challenge of mimicking that limpid, reverent surface.

We set to work. Going through the poems line by line, we tested, rewrote, crossed out. Again and again she asked me the reasons behind my suggestions, until I began giving them automatically. I much preferred this sitting alongside each other, addressing a common task, to the earlier clumsy probing — I always prefer getting to know someone by our working together. And we were making headway, through the waterfalls and winding streams that always seemed to separate friends, the mournful bird cries that reminded the poet of his native province to which he would never return, the flower that peeped up through the snow; we were zipping right through the Confucian sayings, the advice on how to live a well-ordered life, the nonresistance teachings of the Tao. Meanwhile, Osao made sardonic sideswipes at the ideas, which she thought outrageous (much more so than I did).

"What does 'I make my spirit supine' mean?" I asked.

"Oh, that is more of that same junk," she said bitterly. "The Chinese scholar gentleman is supposed to do nothing. He just 'contemplates nature.' And sends his wife and children out to work! It is so passive, it makes me crazy. That is their idea of the good life: 'Do nothing'!"

"Yes, but what is the exact literal meaning behind 'I make my spirit supine'? That doesn't sound right. . . . Can we go back and look at the original character?"

She frowned and turned over the pages. Several times I had made her put the strict literal translation of the Chinese character back into the text, and I saw now she thought there was something lazy or dishonest about this. "It says, 'stand-soul-against-wall.'"

That sounded good to me; but on the other hand, it had associations with a firing squad. "We need a more 'American' way of saying it. How about just 'I *loaf*...'" I suggested, thinking of Whitman's "I loaf and invite my soul."

"What does that mean?"

"It's sort of like wasting time, idling your life away. And 'loaf' can also be like a loaf of bread," I said enthusiastically, if irrelevantly. The more I thought of it, the more I loved sneaking in this tribute to Whitman that no one else would notice.

Osao agreed to the change. We had half-a-dozen more short poems to get through. Sitting next to her, I began to feel a dry warmth rise between us, as though we had been riding together on a dusty road inside a stagecoach. I had to stop myself from acting on the impulse to clutch her hand in her lap. There was that sexual current that exists between different races, and something else, the amorous gratitude I often feel toward a woman colleague working well with me. I wondered what she did for a living. When we were finally through, I asked her, and she said, "I teach high school," as though she were absolving me of any need to show further interest in her.

"What's wrong with teaching?" I said. "I work in public schools, and I find it very stimulating."

"You teach, too?"

"As a visiting poet. But there's something I like about the atmosphere of public schools."

"Oh, I love it!" She did a turnabout. "Especially I like my students. But . . . "

"What subject?" I asked, glossing over her *but*; anyone who worked in the schools did not have to have that *but* explained.

"Bookkeeping. Algebra. My father has all the creativity; I have a good mind for the practical. I told you I was not artistic!"

"But I can't believe you've never done anything artistic. Your translations are sensitive. You must have written at some time."

"When I was younger I wrote poetry," she confessed. "But not for many years. Oh, I wish I could. I have tried many times. I envy people who express themselves in writing. Like you." She blushed.

"I'll teach you how to write," I said.

Osao laughed. "You don't know how hard it would be, that's why you say that."

"No, I mean it."

"Come, let's talk about the fee."

"Nothing." I smiled.

"Please, you must let me pay you something," she said as though it were a cultural insult even to consider accepting my offer. She took out her checkbook.

"Why? It was fun for me. How can I take money for this? It was just an hour of work and I wanted to do it."

"But you should still be paid for your work, even if you enjoy doing it."

"That's true, but in this case, the fact is — I refuse. I can be very stubborn."

"Well, all right," she said, "then perhaps you will at least let me invite you to dinner?"

I could not have planned it to work out better if I had tried. "I would love that."

"Sometime soon? Next week maybe. While my father is still here. That way it will be more interesting for you."

I didn't know why she had to pretend that she needed an added attraction to engage my interest. And I was a little put out to hear that the father would be around; but the more I thought about it, the chaperon aspect seemed to add spice to the evening ahead. We agreed to make it next Friday, at Osao's.

I kept thinking of the way she moved down the hall after we said goodbye, her walk centered in the haunches, confidently sensual. Would I be able to win such a mature woman? What would our first dates be like? And afterward? Would she put up much resistance — or would her experience make everything fall into place? I imagined being sucked into one of those strange "realm of the senses" undertows of sexual obsession: the older woman and the younger man; the inescapableness of flesh. And, on the other hand, if it all worked out, I would propose marriage (I had always toyed with the dream of marrying an Oriental woman); we would go to Korea and live there for a while, then come back here. I could see us taking a summer house together on Martha's Vineyard; our children were all beautiful, our youngest daughter in her neat shirtwaist dress and hair ribbon was a famous child violinist. How she looked at me, my Eurasian daughter, with her wistful, slightly crossed almond eyes.

Osao lived on a down-at-the-heels-looking block between Broadway and Amsterdam Avenue, in the shadow of the Cathedral of St. John the Divine. Crumbling, pre-Depression apartment buildings muscled out the last moment of sun. A boy went by me on a skateboard, yelling a warning that hung suspended like a screech pasted on mid-air. It gave me a shudder to walk on this block, reminding me of my student days at Columbia, the grim, malnourished, overcast quality of life then. I fished out Osao's address. Hers would be that dejected grey stone structure with a courtyard, a dry fountain and a right and left entrance. Mothers talking in Spanish stood in front with baby carriages, and I passed by them in my white suit as quickly as possible. I was afraid they would know where I was going, could read on my face my seducer's intention, and would gossip about Osao behind her back.

The hall was so ill lit that I had to feel my way up the staircase. Why was she living in such a squalid place? Teachers made good enough salaries to afford better. Was she banking her money? Perhaps she was politically committed, a Maoist, wanted to "live with the people." I tried to see the lodgings through her eyes, as reassuring, the warm fried-onion smells of family life reminding her in her homesick moments of dense parts of Seoul. All this as I was searching the dark green doors for her number.

I knocked at the door, and Osao let me in. "You're early," she said. She had on a white blouse and brown skirt, and her eyes were shining.

"I hope not too early."

The small room was an obstacle course of papers and books, with a few throw pillows on the floor. "Excuse me, the couch didn't arrive from Macy's. It was supposed to come Wednesday and I stayed home to receive it but the delivery took it to the wrong place. I'm so embarrassed."

"That's all right; I'm used to sitting on floor pillows."

"Can you make it?" She offered me a hand. "I don't want you to get your beautiful white suit dirty. You look so elegant, I feel ashamed."

"Oh, but you look very nice," I said, annoyed at myself for not getting this in sooner. Because her compliment had come first, mine sounded forced.

"I don't. I look horrible." Which was not true at all. Either she was very modest, or very vain. "I had no time to get ready. You're early!" she said again, though in strict fact I wasn't. "Can I get you some Scotch, or a beer?"

I told her a beer would be fine. She disappeared into the kitchen.

The apartment was a chain of tiny doorless chambers: kitchen, living room, dining room, and bedroom. I looked around the living room. In addition to stacks of what appeared to be manuscripts (was she taking in typing on the side?), there was a small black upright piano, the kind my mother used to play, with sheet music composed by — if I squinted my eyes I could see — Bloch. Next to it stood an ebony-and-gold screen; on the wall was a framed calligraphy scroll, and above my head a mounted advertisement from the thirties of a couple silhouetted in violet before a round moon, and the slogan "Don't Get Caught Unprotected!," which I took to be evidence of Osao's sense of humor. There were signs in the decor of a certain level of cultivation, which reassured me; or, to put it more bluntly, there was nothing of such appalling vulgarity as would have made me pause before considering an involvement with this woman. Still, the surroundings gave little information about her personality — except, perhaps, that they reinforced an earlier impression of downward mobility. This seemed too cramped a cage for her.

I thought of all the times I had been to apartments like this, paying a first visit to a woman I was interested in — seen pinched rooms and cracked walls only partly disguised by visual reminders of a past family ease, or a largesse of soul uncontained by present hardships — and I tried to figure out to what degree it was proper to equate the person with the box drawn tightly around her. So connected seemed the fit of fate, personality and decor, however temporary or unfair the match may have been, that I wondered if it was even possible to see someone as distinct from his or her surroundings.

"Where is your father?" I called out.

"He is resting. He will get up for dinner. He is looking forward to meeting you!"

I started to pull myself up to join Osao, when she came in with a tray: "No, no, sit. Sit! I will bring you what you want." Apparently I was to be served like a sultan. Along with the beer, she brought a salad of shrimps and radishes, and there were unfamiliar stuffed delicacies handsomely arranged by color on the plate. "As you can see I am not used to this sort of thing," she said self-consciously, by which I took her to mean being a hostess, or waiting on men. But, all her nods toward Women's Lib to the contrary, the impression I received was that she had been perfectly well trained to serve the man, almost like a geisha. And I noticed for the first time, in the lamplight, as she bent down to replace a plate, that her cheeks had a thick layer of whitish-pink powder, and she had done something to her eyebrows, blacking them in sharply.

"Sit down, please, Osao," I bid her.

"I am not finished yet," she said, hesitating between staying and going.

"But you can talk for a minute?"

"Yes . . . I am afraid this will be a boring evening for you."

"I'm expecting just the opposite. What makes you think so?"

"I am not very talkative tonight. I am not good at making conversation. My language skills are so poor!"

"Why do you say that? You speak perfect English, from what I can gather."

"Don't you find me —" she paused, almost coquettishly searching for the right word — "don't you find me 'verbally underdeveloped,' to use the jargon of our trade?"

I laughed, first because the complexity of her diction so belied her assertion, and second because the word *underdeveloped* had made me think of her opulent figure. "Hardly. Your speech is not my idea of verbally underdeveloped," I said.

"You are just trying to be nice to me."

"No, I assure you." I was puzzled by this insistence on "deficits" that seemed to go beyond modesty. Or was her self-disparagement only a routine Korean expression of good manners? To change the subject I said, "You play the piano?"

"I — used to. I have given it up. I don't have the time. The school day takes everything out of me. Don't you find?"

"Sometimes. I don't teach every day, so it's not as wearing for me."

"You are lucky! You can keep your enthusiasm up. I need to find my enthusiasm again. . . . I used to love teaching. You must be a wonderful teacher."

"I have my good days, and my bad days. What are all these stacks of papers?"

"My thesis," she said perfunctorily.

"You're writing a doctoral thesis too?" I was surprised by this wider ambition, which made her even more desirable. "What field?"

"In sociology." She wrinkled up her nose.

"Why do you make a face when you say 'sociology'?" I asked.

"No, not sociology — it's the thesis. It is taking so long! I have no time to do it. I have finished all my research and statistics but I have such a hard time to write it up. That is why I envy writers!"

"I'm sure you'll find a way to write it when you give yourself some time."

"No — it is a real problem for me. I would ask you for some advice, but I know that must be horrible for you. Besides, I have to cook! I didn't know if you are vegetarian or meat eater, so I made both!" she laughed. I followed Osao into the kitchen so we could continue talking, though I sensed she was uncomfortable about my going in there.

Sweat blistered across her forehead, and she had fallen silent, turning all her attention to a head of lettuce in the sink. At first I thought that she was merely concentrating very hard on the cooking, but then I realized that she was averting her eyes, embarrassed for some reason. The customs here were strange, and I had better tread lightly. "Would you rather I went inside?" I asked finally.

"No, no," she protested.

"What's the matter?"

"I am ashamed to have people over here. Because of the *****!" Her nervous giggle drowned out the word.

"Because of *what?*"

"Because of the bugs, the roaches! *You* know. I'm so ashamed for people to see them. If I see one I start screaming! You must think I'm a crazy woman."

"But everyone has them in New York."

"I will never get used to them." She shuddered. "Please, promise me if you see one you will close your eyes!"

"I promise," I said, smiling.

Osao, relieved, went back to her cooking. Everywhere there seemed to be pots spitting froth from under their lids, vegetables waiting to be diced on the wooden cutting board, meat dumplings steaming, fish broiling, and Osao controlling it all, checking, chopping, spooning.

"Can't I help?"

"No, please. My father would be shocked if he even saw you in the kitchen! He is old-fashioned and thinks the woman should do everything. A typical Korean male, like your friend Pak."

"Pak thinks that way too?" This was a new insight into my Xerox man. "How long have you known Pak?"

"I know him well enough," Osao said, with an ironic smile. "He is a strange man."

"Yes, he is a strange man," I said eagerly. "But in what way do you find him strange?"

"It is really not fair to talk about him."

"Why not?"

"I went out with him once a long time ago."

"For how long?"

"It was nothing serious, believe me. But lately, every time I run into him I get the feeling he does not approve of me." She stopped short, regretful at having said even this much.

"Why wouldn't he approve of you? . . . Go on, you can tell me. Do you think I'll think badly of you? I assure you I won't."

"It's not that," she said meditatively. "It's just I don't like to talk about these gossip things, do you?"

"What things?"

"*You* know: 'affairs of the heart.'"

"What else is there of any interest to talk about?" I said.

"It's just that . . . Pak does not approve because he knows I have a friend. I live with a man friend." She turned away to wash the broccoli.

This was bad news. Still, there was the possibility that the man was nothing but a roommate, a foreign friend who had nowhere else to go, perhaps even gay.

"Why is it wrong to have a male roommate?" I asked disingenuously.

"I don't think it is wrong. But in our community everyone talks about everyone else, and it is considered not the proper thing for a single woman to live with her boyfriend." Again the stab. "Pak has a double standard, like most Korean men. He has affairs with American girls but he thinks Korean girls should be pure before their marriage. I mean, I am no girl anymore — look at me!"

"He's probably jealous. He's probably still in love with you." I was teasing her but really talking about my own disappointment.

"Oh, no, he was never in love with me," Osao said, quite firmly.

"And the man you're living with — is he American?"

"No, he's Korean."

"Oh." I watched her finish off the meal preparations. I felt I had nothing more to say; the major purpose of the evening was defeated. I had to find a way to get through the rest of the visit without too much bitterness. So there would be no love-making after all, no trip to Korea, no violinist daughter. It began to embarrass me that I should lose all interest in Osao just because I discovered she was "taken," when a half hour before I had been trying to decipher everything about her. Why couldn't I still figure out the mysteries of her personality by paying close attention? Her hands were squeezing the dumpling dough with strong shapely fingers, capable and quick and a little plump.

"You have very nice hands," I said, feeling good that I could pay her a compliment even after the chase was lost.

"Really? I think they're common. No, you are the one who has beautiful hands," said Osao, looking down at mine as if I had paid her a compliment only to have one returned. "See? You have long sensitive fingers. Mine are ugly." She held hers up to the light matter-of-factly.

"I can't agree," I said. She gave me a look that stated I didn't know what I was talking about; she had made a study of the subject. And now that she had raised the point, I did think my hands were nicer than hers.

Just then we heard some stirring from the inner rooms.

"That must be Father," she said.

She led me into the dining room to meet him. A thin elderly man stood at the end of the table waiting for us to come toward him. He was not very tall; he had thin lips and badly broken teeth and the fiercely staring eyes of someone who is fresh-wakened from sleep, and he was wearing a dark green drip-dry suit jacket over a white shirt with a thin olive tie. The dominant impression he gave was of severity, but there was a bit of the artist-dandy in him: one could see he thought highly of himself. Osao spoke to him in Korean, and his face immediately relaxed into a leathery smile and he shook my hand.

"I am Woo," he said.

"I am Lopate." I turned to Osao. "He speaks English?"

"He speaks a little English," she said. Her father said something to her in Korean, looking at me, and I asked her to translate. "He thanks you very much for the translations, and he would like to invite you to the opening."

He nodded at the end.

I tried to react with surprise and delight, though Osao had already invited me.

Her father began looking over the dinner table with a grumbling, severe expression.

"I think he wants his beer. My father always has one beer in the evening," she explained. She asked him in Korean, and he nodded concisely. "I will be back in a minute."

Now we were left alone. The old man regarded me with steady curiosity. Apparently it was not considered rude in his culture to stare at someone in this way, or else it was a prerogative earned by age. After a while his focus relaxed, and he lit a cigarette and looked away, as though I were not in the room. I thought this as good a way as any of handling the awkward situation.

Osao returned with two bottles of Kirin, then she left me alone with him again. The old man poured the beer into his glass, filling it only halfway with the liquid, drank precisely half of that, and set the glass down.

I thought I would try a conversation. "Is this the first time you have been to America?" I asked slowly.

His lips formed a tired smile, and he shrugged to indicate either that he hadn't understood — or if he had, what was the point of starting so exhausting an effort?

We stared past each other into the middle distance, like travelers on opposite sides of a train platform.

The dining table took up almost all of the room. There was a bookcase behind me filled with Osao's sociology classics, a typewriter table, a mirror, and a picture of the Mona Lisa. The incongruous cliché of that image in this household made me want to laugh, until I realized that it was the exact counterpart of my Utamaro calendar, a tribute to the opposite culture's icon.

The old man had taken his wire-rimmed spectacles out of his pocket and now he put them on; an act of sociability, I thought. Actually, he was not so old, only about seventy, and seemed to be in strong physical and mental condition. He must have known quite a bit about life, and about art. Too bad, I thought, that I understood so little about calligraphy, or I would be able to tell whether he was a skillful, cautious, middle-of-the-road practitioner, still worthy of respect, of course, or a giant in the field, a master. What did they call them in Japan? "A living national treasure."

I told myself I was sitting across the table from a living national treasure.

He began picking his teeth. A cockroach darted across the tablecloth. He looked at it, stern and a little sad. I remembered that I was supposed to close my eyes when I saw one. The calligrapher stared toward the kitchen with a reproachful, grizzled look. This was one of those relentless cockroaches that insist on exploring each check of the tablecloth. I banged my knee against the table leg to make him go away before Osao returned. Nothing happened. It was definitely bad manners to kill a cockroach in another person's home. At last he scurried off at a much bigger noise: the door had opened, and I turned and saw the man of the house.

The guilt I felt at that moment for having had designs on his woman made me want to stammer out an explanatory introduction that I was "only so-and-so," only this minor person not to be taken seriously. Osao came from the kitchen in her apron and put her arms around him, and I looked away.

She introduced me flatteringly. I rose to shake his hand.

"I am Jhun," he said, motioning me to sit. He joined us unceremoniously, taking a chair at the foot of the table. "Tired!" he exclaimed. He had a sympathetic, frank, workman's face, a face I trusted immediately, and he wore the standard white shirt with sleeves rolled up in a tight buckled square above the elbow. I was struck by his massive forearms.

Dishes began appearing on the table. There was clear noodle soup, shrimps, asparagus, beans, dumplings, broiled fish, rice, cabbage. Jhun ate with the rapid shoveling motions of exhausted laborers everywhere, lifting his face from time to time with a good-humored, inclusive grin of appetite. Now I noticed that Osao's father was refusing to look toward Jhun's side of the table, as though he did not approve of the man's eating habits or the man himself. Jhun winked at me. As formal as the old calligrapher was, Jhun seemed to be informal.

"Hot!" he warned, as I reached for the cabbage.

I took some in my mouth, and tried it gingerly, then reached for my glass of beer. Jhun laughed and clapped his hands. "Too hot! I told you." Then he shared the joke with his "father-in-law," who grinned reluctantly also; and I went along with it, fanning myself. I was providing the Occidental comic relief. Jhun laughed till there were tears in his eyes. "Hot! Be careful!" Osao, who had finally allowed herself to join us, laughed too, but in a smoothing-over way, as though to mute the barking edge of her lover's voice. I sensed that she was a little ashamed of him. Jhun spoke in an urgent guttural Korean, almost buffoonishly emphatic, and yet there was a shrewdness in his eyes. I liked him. I could not guess exactly how old he was; his face was boyish but his hair was grey.

"Tired?" I asked him.

"Tired! I thought I get away sooner. But — trouble in the store."

"Jhun runs a clothing store in Harlem," Osao explained.

"You know — cheap bargain, garments." The word *garments* sounded strange in Jhun's Korean accent, since I heard it all my life with a Yiddish inflection.

"How do you like working in Harlem?" I asked.

"Harlem very bad." He shook his head. "Every day getting worse. Air bad. People fighting, killing. Even stabbing! Bad people up there." He continued to describe the life with sad, earnest disgust. It was a primitive analysis, one that I imagined Osao with her graduate training in social sciences must feel disdainful of, or at least superior to. She said nothing during his discourse, but began to clear away some dishes. I noticed that the father, our distinguished national treasure, was frowning more deeply than ever. I caught his gaze resting on me from behind the glasses on his narrow, austere face.

He asked his daughter something in Korean, and Osao went red with discomfort, while Jhun guffawed.

"What did he say?" I asked.

The calligrapher continued to demand answers in his curt, worldly voice, and Osao continued to protest, with obvious displeasure, at his line of questioning. They were arguing back and forth. Meanwhile Jhun was enjoying himself immensely, even winking at me to show there was nothing to worry about. (Though whether it was a good-humored wink or a nervous twitch I was no longer sure.)

"What is he saying?" I asked again. It was obvious they were talking about me, and I had to pull Osao's sleeve to get her to answer.

"Stupid things. For instance, he wants to know if you live at home with your family."

I laughed easily. "Did you tell him I didn't?"

"Yes. He is very curious about you. He asks all sorts of questions about your personal life. He is really being impossible tonight."

"Like what? Tell him I'll answer anything he wants to know."

"You mustn't encourage him," said Osao.

"No, tell him. I don't mind."

She translated the information. Her father cleared his throat, and spoke, looking at me.

"He wants to know if you are married."

"No."

He looked at me with great interest. Then he spoke to Osao.

"He wants to know why you are not married."

"Tell him I once was but am now divorced."

She shook her head, almost refusing to convey this dangerous information, but in the end translated. His eyes grew no wider. He turned to his daughter and began to lecture her. Jhun could barely keep from rolling on the floor.

"What's he saying?" I demanded. "What's he saying?"

"He says he does not understand why you don't go back and live with your family now. Or else, why you don't marry again. He says he does not understand my life either. You must excuse my father," Osao said. "He thinks he is the greatest because he fathered eleven children. All of them happy except me."

The father nodded in my direction and asked if I had any children. Now *I* was beginning to feel uncomfortable; I cast about for some way to take the heat off.

"He thinks you should get married again to have someone take care of you," said Osao, mechanically. "He thinks you must be lonely living this way."

"Why don't *you* two get married?" I asked Osao, to turn the spotlight on her. It was also the kind of coward's question one asks of a woman one would like to sleep with, when one is afraid to speak directly.

"Because. Korean men expect the women to be good housewives, to be home all the time, to keep everything clean. As you can see, I am not good at that." She turned to face the kitchen, ready to bolt if necessary.

"But do you expect that?" I asked Jhun.

"Oh, he is different," she answered for him. "He is not like most Korean men."

"Then why don't you get married?"

"Because she don't trust men," Jhun said, smiling bitterly.

"I don't trust *you*," said Osao.

"Me? What you know about me? You think you know me but you don't. You don't know what is inside me." Jhun actually smote his chest, pleased to be declaring this to her in front of everyone. "What you know about trust? You don't know what I would do," he muttered.

She looked around the room for something to deliver her from this conversation that, if nothing else, seemed to go against her sense of appropriate table talk. But Jhun was not willing to let her off so easily. He turned to me for confirmation. "We think we know what is inside another person? What we see? Cheap. A mask. China doll mask!" He snorted. "You don't know what I would do," he repeated boldly.

"Oh? Maybe I am wrong," said Osao.

"Maybe I am wrong, maybe I am wrong!" he said, mimicking her. "You will never find out, because you don't trust men enough. *All* men."

I felt sorry for Osao, and partly responsible for getting her into this. "Why don't you trust us?" I asked glibly, trying to make light of the situation, to turn it into a kind of parlor game.

"I have had too much experience with men," Osao answered, taking my lead. She had found the proper, generalized tone to get her out of her personal discomfit. "I know what men are like. All too well. And you think this one is any better? You should see what he thinks about women."

"Oh, that." Jhun held his head like a coconut, shaking it from one side to the other. "She will start again. It's not true. I think women are pretty good."

"Yes, I know," said Osao, with a touch of jealousy. Then she left for the kitchen to replenish our beers.

"What you do?" Jhun asked me, point-blank but friendly.

"You mean for a living? I teach."

"I teach too. Martial Arts!" he proclaimed.

Looking at his brawny arms, I was not surprised. As he talked about giving lessons at a kung fu center, I began to see his relationship with Osao in a different light. I pictured them having a passionate and athletic, if combative, life in the bedroom. Perhaps only a muscleman like Jhun could satisfy her particular sensual needs — an idea that relieved me by offering an explanation for why I would never win Osao.

Jhun had many ancedotes about the funny Americans who wanted to learn kung fu, and who thought they could fly through the air because they had seen it in a Bruce Lee movie. Osao, who had returned from the kitchen, seemed entertained by these stories, chiming in from time to time, but her father was more bored than ever. He was obviously interested only in certain things close to him and, like a distinguished guest at a dinner party who is not allowed to show his stuff, became annoyed and hurt when the topic strayed too far from him. I thought it was time to draw the old man back into the conversation.

"Tell your father I greatly admire the art of calligraphy," I said.

When Osao translated my comment, Woo's face brightened.

"But I know so little of it," I hastened to add.

"That's not true. I was amazed how much he knew about Eastern culture," she told Jhun, "probably more than either of us."

"Not so," I said. "Please — ask your father if he would tell me something about calligraphy."

She conveyed the wish, and he sat even straighter than was his wont, and talked for a moment or two, then waited for the translation.

"He says that all Oriental philosophy comes down to two essential things: Yin and Yang."

The father nodded happily. I had been hoping for something more heady than this, but tried to look the proper acolyte. He called for paper to be brought to him, and took out his fountain pen.

"He is drawing the symbols for Yin and Yang," Osao noted.

The calligrapher spoke again with sober ease, as though this were the reason he had been called to the United States — to make this explanation — and he was finally getting a chance to relieve himself of his mission. Osao translated concurrently: "'All calligraphy must have a feeling of motion.'"

The old man began to draw. At first I could make little out of the characters, which seemed almost negligently sloppy notations filling the page. Then I began to see, not so much beauty, but motion. The old man stopped to grin at me. Then his hand began moving incredibly fast. Jhun was leaning forward, watching like a child at a fair. "He's fantastic, eh?" Jhun said proudly.

"What happens if you make a mistake?"

The old man did a gesture of crumpling up paper. With amusement he looked into my face for a reaction, waiting to see how I would take this iron law. Then he spoke again. Osao translated: "He says, 'Calligraphy is not just writing straight symbols like the alphabet, but is taking off from the original symbol by mental ideas — associations.'" When he gave a demonstration of how a commonplace character was transformed into something entirely different through a set of metaphorical associations, I saw that it was very close to the process of writing poetry.

"He says it is impossible to learn calligraphy unless you study with a master," Osao said. "You cannot learn it from a book. You must get it from a few people like him. . . . Now he is telling about his teacher, and his teacher's teacher. . . . The tradition he belongs to . . . goes back to the seventeen hundreds . . . the first great master of his school . . ." There followed a name I could not hope to remember. What a shame that I was the recipient of this teaching, since so much was lost on me, while another person, a student of calligraphy or one of those reverential American Buddhists, would have been in ecstasies every second. Nevertheless, what I got, I got.

"He says a master only takes a few pupils at a time. He is willing to take you as a student." The old man bowed formally. "My father is paying you a great compliment!" Osao explained. "He is not usually like this."

"I am very flattered. . . . Tell him that I would love to study with him, but I would have to move to Korea, and there isn't enough time for me to learn properly in the short time he's staying."

She translated this, and he nodded again. Then he made one more speech.

"What did he say?"

"He is inviting you to come to his show next week."

So the evening ended, with my third invitation to the exhibit.

The day of the opening came, and I was wavering back and forth about whether to attend. What business did I have dipping into their lives like a tourist? I would just feel out of place. In the end I went, perhaps to complete a loop in my own mind.

Not far from the door, past the table where one was supposed to hand in one's invitation card, Osao stood next to her father in a kind of receiving line, greeting guests. She looked stunning. Her beautiful gown of orange-and-black swirls, three-quarter length with black silk trousers underneath, suggested a traditional national costume at the same time that it seemed the height of Paris fashion. I was almost shy coming up to her, she looked so regal; her magnanimous black eyes glistened with quality. So she was a great beauty after all! The bracelets on her arms, the jewels in her ears, sent a secret pang to my heart. I waited for her to turn and notice me — she was talking to an otterish-looking young Korean whose television-blue shirt with white collar somehow rubbed me the wrong way — they were dallying like cousins. When she saw me she broke away, excusing herself to that pampered puppy, and received me with all graciousness. Her father, in a light blue seersucker suit, was standing so straight he appeared to be leaning backward. As I came up offering my hand he seemed happy and touched to see me, and opened his mouth wide in a great grin, his teeth just as broken as ever, the creases around his eyes lifted high in greeting. All the energy of his happiness at this encounter seemed to be ignited and spent in that wonderful smile, and I realized from the speed with which his eyes fixed on another guest that he had nothing to say to me. I had already performed my role simply by showing.

Osao, being the good hostess, quickly introduced me to an elderly Korean couple who happened to be standing next to me on the line, and made a few cementing remarks in an attempt to hitch us together — I was a writer who was interested in Oriental culture, this man was in the business of importing objects from Asia, we must have much to talk about. . . . The couple and I tried dutifully conversing, but I was conscious always of Osao, and eventually excused myself to visit the food tables, from where I could keep an eye on her and stuff myself. The affair had been admirably catered with hot stuffed dumplings, vegetable platters and light, dainty sweets; everything was delicious. No wonder that Korean who bribed American congressmen made such a splash with the parties he gave. This looked like the same crowd, well-off executives, diplomats, businessmen stationed comfortably in America with their begowned wives. I would have loved to eavesdrop, but no one was talking English. Nevertheless, one could imagine the talk from the stylized gaiety among the carefully coiffed women, pulling each other off to the side like brides-maids, and the bluff heartiness among the men (learned here, perhaps), their shoul-der-patting manner, fresh from the office, whiskey in hand. The language of prop-erty is everywhere the same. How did Osao fit in? If they were a cut or two above her in social standing, tonight she made her way through this crowd unapologeti-cally. The artist's daughter, checking with her quick black eyes to see who was enjoy-ing himself and who needed help, seemed everywhere at once, laughing, mixing. As the sole hostess of this sprawling, thickening reception, she was managing brilliantly — too brilliantly, in a way, for a high-school bookkeeping teacher.

Tired of spying on her, I began to apply myself to the art on the walls. It gave me a special pleasure to read underneath each scroll the neatly typed cards with our translations on them, and to remember some of the farfetched word choices. How unassailably orthodox they looked. Who would ever guess? As for Mr. Woo's callig-raphy, I was honestly unable to judge. As I went from piece to piece, trying to detect the principles of connoisseurship behind these disciplined executions, I met an exclusion so total that I began to feel dizzy, and to fight this I forced myself to be more engrossed than ever, by setting the problem for myself of which scroll I would buy, if the price were right.

Osao was suddenly at my side. "How are you enjoying it?"

"Oh, I love your father's work. I was just thinking of buying one."

"No, you don't mean that."

"Yes. What are the prices? Are they very expensive?"

"They are not so bad. . . . And since you helped us — but we talk about that later. First meet Stephen. I think you and he must like each other, you have so much in common." She pulled me over to a lank, fastidiously tailored American in a three-piece suit who worked for a private foundation. It bothered me that she had lumped us together in her mind. "Stephen, this is the man I told you about, the poet who helped me do the translations." He shook my hand limply with as little apparent lik-ing for me as I had for him. Osao left us alone together, and I asked him how he had come to know her. His responses were haughty and reluctant — and yet, didn't he see, we were the only two Americans, everyone else was jabbering in Korean. At last I steered him onto a subject that caught his enthusiasm, the ballet.

Just as he was about to loosen up, there was a request for silence. The ceremo-nial speechmaking began. Each of the dignitaries and honored guests was intro-duced, said a few words, received applause. Mr. Woo stood at attention throughout, severe, expressionless, as though at a military flag raising. I came alongside Osao and asked her, during a particularly long oration by a porcine man with a crew cut, what was being said.

"Oh — he is just telling the story of Father's life. That he studied with so-and-so who studied with such-and-such. . . . That he received all 'firsts' as a young man in school. . . . That he was in the navy. . . ." She whispered in my ear, discreetly, so as not to attract attention. The orator's voice droned on, Mr. Woo stood alone with his fingers locked behind his back, isolated as the this-is-your-life encomiums rained down on his pointy head.

Then the artist himself came forward to speak, and was roundly applauded.

"What's he saying?" I whispered.

"The same thing as before," she answered with a dimpled smile. "It is mostly a — *regurgitation*. Did I say it wrong?"

"No, you said it right."

After the speechmaking had ended, I asked, "Where is Jhun?"

"He had to work late. He will probably come later." She seemed unconcerned.

Some emergency pulled her away, and I was again at a loss. Art openings are among the most difficult social situations to pierce. There are of course the "regulars" who know everyone in the gallery and need not give more than a five-second glance at the art before settling into serious, loud partying; but if one is not lucky enough to be in that crowd, one may have to join the "strollers," who wander around the wall edges like moths, pretending deep hypnotic attachment to this pattern or that texture.

I had imagined that we would all go out afterward for dinner at a little piano bar known only to Koreans, just the artist's private party. But it did not seem to be working out that way; the reception was breaking up into groups, the room was clearing, and I left before I could learn whether I would have received one of those last-minute whispered invitations accorded to the inner few.

There followed all the next week a series of telephone conversations, back and forth, about the scroll I had chosen. Since I would not hear of taking it for free, it reverted to its original market price. Eventually, with Osao's coaxing, the artist knocked off a hundred and fifty dollars for me, so that I had the satisfaction of getting a bargain.

What was I doing buying this scroll in the first place? I did not collect art, nor was I in a financial position to start. The whole transaction was a mystery to me, one of those blind impulses I make myself follow in order to understand, in the end, what it was I was thinking about. Certainly I had in mind some way of prolonging a connection with Osao. Yet the scroll was more than a pretext to get to her: I wanted it. By owning some part of the old calligrapher, his daughter, and Jhun, perhaps I would find it easier to settle my accounts with them, and turn away.

On the phone Osao would become chatty, as if we were old friends. Just at the point when the business details had been completed, she would prolong the conversation, asking me about each of the different areas of my life. She seemed boundlessly curious about how I put the whole thing together, how I moved from part to part. I was not sure why she wanted this information, but I sensed her hunger to keep the conversation alive. "What have you been reading?" she would say, or "That sounds like you're having a good time!"

Jhun was a sincere, honest hunk, but she must have found him a limited conversationalist. How giddy she became on the phone! Sometimes she wanted so much to laugh that anything I said she interpreted as witty. Between us, through everything, I thought I saw the thin, hopeful strand of flirtation. No, I told myself, she just wanted more American friends, like that prune, Stephen. She was collecting American male aesthetes; or she was trying out her conversational skills with native speakers. Each time the phone rang and I heard Osao's voice, I asked myself, What is going on with her? Yet somewhere inside me I still hoped we would be thrown together as lovers — and I must have communicated that hope. Even when a woman has no intention of giving in to him, she may all the same want the one who has once desired her to remain under her gaze.

I had arranged with Osao to come by Saturday night and pick up my scroll, hand over the check, and have dinner. The old man had already flown back to Korea, Osao, that evening, seemed under a cloud. We had little opportunity to talk, because, as it turned out, several of Jhun's buddies joined us for dinner. They arrived in a noisy bunch, and began attacking the dishes Osao put in front of them with the same voracious hunger I had seen in Jhun. They were all Korean, and behaved toward each other with the joshing, boyish spirits of fraternity brothers. One lean-necked man was kidded incessantly, and he always laughed it off calmly. It turned out he had studied literature in his youth, a fact they thought immensely comical — they tried to get him to recite some poems. "He is also poet," Jhun said and nodded toward me. They offered me and the shy ex-literature student more and more liquor, to get us drunk enough to recite poems. They made many jokes about one another's capacities for drink and food.

Jhun was in his element, in the middle of all this noisy leg-pulling — a leader, in fact. But I no longer liked him as much as the first time we had met. Without the old man's disapproving formality to set him off, he seemed less striking.

I managed to learn that all except Jhun were employed in the garment district, mostly as crew managers. They made fun of the Puerto Ricans who worked under them. So this is how Koreans in the garment industry spend their Saturday nights, I mused. Watching them eat and laugh, trying to follow, however remotely, the line of discussion, I told myself it was an honor to be allowed to witness one of those hidden subcultures whose aggregate makes up New York City — so much of which will always be unknown, even to a native New Yorker like me.

At one point the discussion grew heated. I listened to the argument with the lost wonder of a man in a foreign port, at an outdoor café, surrounded by local bravos. But this was *my* city, damn it; I wasn't supposed to feel like a stranger. Jhun's voice became loud with skepticism and cynical experience. I wondered if they might be talking about Korean politics. Osao had left the room again — she had probably heard this a hundred times before. I turned to the man next to me, the tall bespectacled ex-poetry student, whose neck had been clipped so closely by the barber that its furrows appeared plucked clean.

"What are they saying?"

He answered that they were arguing about money. The fastest way to get it, the easiest way to lose it, the opportunities they had stupidly passed by, the ones they knew who pretended to be poorer than they were, but had actually socked away quite a pile . . .

For a while they would translate into English for me. But I got tired of asking them to translate; I didn't want to make a pest of myself. Now, there is some pleasure in watching people converse in a language unknown to you. The gestures, the tones of voice, become everything. And if the speakers are émigrés who are obliged to talk all week in a language not their own, it is wonderful to observe the sudden happy ease with which they explode into chatter. Yet, for this very reason, it is impossible ever to trust the sincerity of émigrés fully once you have seen them with their own kind. All that they can never share with you is suddenly quite exposed.

Osao returned with another six bottles of beer in her hands, as she had been doing all night, and they took them without a word of thanks. The last time I had seen her, at the reception, she had had the look of an empress; tonight she could have been the barmaid. Her remoteness did not seem to bother anyone. From time to time she gave me a look that showed she realized it was not working out for me. But she had no idea what to do to make things better.

Eventually I said I had to go, pushing back my chair, a little drunk, clutching my wrapped framed scroll.

Osao followed me out.

"I am afraid this has been a dull evening for you," she said at the door.

This time I did not contradict her, as I smiled and took her hand to squeeze it goodbye.

"Think good thoughts and pursue them earnestly." The Confucian message on the scroll now hangs above the portal to my bedroom.

One day months later I received in the mail a snapshot of the gallery reception, in which I appeared next to Osao and her father. With a note: "You were the best-looking in this picture, so I couldn't resist sending it to you."

I had a very busy winter, working to meet deadlines, taking on new projects at school; I went back to my old girlfriend, or rather, she agreed to take me back, one last time; there were feuds in my family, the city underwent a budget crisis; in short, I forgot about Osao.

Not true. I didn't forget about her, but I saw no way to go forward with her. We didn't have enough intellectual interests in common to make a friendship, and besides, I had enough platonic friends in my life as it was. What I had wanted from her was a love affair. Once the sexual route was blocked, I made her over into a static figure of pathos, forever serving beer to Jhun's friends, and I sealed her in a chamber of my mind with those other fondly regretted would-be romances that were destined never to attain carnal form. She had become, to be frank, an episode in my memory that had rounded to a satisfactory closure.

At the end of May my phone rang.

"This is*****," a strange voice said.

"How are you?" I stalled, hoping the caller would give me a better clue in what she said next, while I tried to process the sounds through my memory bank. This time the caller saw through my scheme.

"It's Osao! Osao Kim. Don't you remember me anymore?"

"Osao, of course I remember you!"

"No wonder you forget. You are so busy, you never call me!" she said. "I think you must be leading a very exciting life to have forgotten poor Osao" — this in a theatrical pouting voice that was, like a geisha's, too teasing to be taken seriously. Was I supposed to call? She made it sound as though we were actually close friends and I had neglected her.

"I'm sorry. I *have* been busy."

"Never mind; I called to tell you I have moved. I have a new number. Do you want it?" she said suspiciously.

"Yes, certainly," I said. She gave it to me, and added that she had a house now in Queens. A whole house to herself. It was much prettier than that last place — she should have moved years ago. So, I thought, she made the leap to suburbia. Good for her.

"What are you doing with your life these days? Did you see the new Woody Allen movie?" she asked.

"Yes —"

"I thought it was very funny. Did you like it?"

"Yes, it was very good." Though I had deep reservations about the film, there was something so vulnerable in her voice, asking to be accepted into the club of knowingly neurotic New Yorkers, that I decided to praise it warmly. "I thought there were some very clever things in it—"

"I saw it twice. It reminded me of you, even, a bit."

"Really?" I said, stung. Did she think all Jewish New Yorkers were alike? "Oh, I don't think I'm like Woody Allen."

"No, just the sense of humor, you know."

"Perhaps. Oh, I keep running into your friend Pak," I said, "at the Xerox shop."

"Who? Oh, I don't see him anymore, now that I am all the way out here in Queens." Obviously she was not too interested in Pak. "What else has been keeping you busy?"

"This time I'm going to get that question in first. What are *you* doing with yourself these days?"

"Nothing. I am getting awfully lazy. I go to work and come home and eat. I have gotten terribly fat. You would not recognize me."

"I'm sure you still look pretty," I said, my courtier wits working slowly.

"No, it's true, there is nothing to do around here so I eat. I've gained lots of weight. It is nice out here — but boring!" She laughed, and I started laughing with her. There is something so infectiously comic at times about negativity. Besides, it was good to hear her voice; I remembered my fondness for Osao.

"Why don't you try exercise?" I said.

"I know, I thought of jogging but they would think I was a crazy person if I ran around the block. This is not the Upper West Side, you know. People are so proper and conventional here. Besides, it does not look nice, a middle-aged woman with too much weight running around in shorts!"

I wondered why she was trying to make herself sound so unattractive to me. "But at least you got away from the cockroaches."

"There were a few, but I got rid of them. It's very clean here. You should come see it."

"It must be a big change for you."

"Yes, at first it was, but now I am getting used to it. I think it was time for me to move," she added in an official voice.

"How is Jhun fitting in?"

A silence. "We do not live together anymore. I thought you knew."

"No, I had no idea. . . . Then are you taking the house by yourself?"

"Yes, I prefer to live alone. I am through with men. No more men!" she declared.

"That's hard to believe," I said, trying to sound light-hearted, though my throat was swelling up as at the presence of danger. "You're too young to enter a nunnery."

"No, I mean it. No more the other way. The only men I want in my life now is if they would be friend to me."

It sounded like an offer — perhaps the simple offer of friendship she had been making all along. Or was it a disguised invitation for more, now that Jhun was gone? Either way, I found myself weighing every word. What could I say? Whatever was meant, I did not have the heart to take her up on it. How could I admit that my fantasies about us were already used up? We were too different somehow, talking to each other was too awkward. Or maybe there was some defect in my character, some cowardice when I was faced with the possible love of a mature woman. Whatever, no matter, I knew I would never come through for her.

"How is school?" I asked.

"School is school. They are making me the treasurer because I have good head for figures, so I won't have to teach as many classes. But you don't want to hear about that."

"No, I do, that's why I asked."

"You are just being polite. So, well, what have you been doing? You must have gone to lots of plays, movies —"

"I *have* gone to a lot of movies. But at the moment I can't remember any of them."

"There is nothing around here. But I go into town sometimes . . . "

Again it seemed she was hinting. "Why don't we go to a ballet sometime?" I asked. "You said you liked the New York City Ballet."

"But how will we get tickets? They say it's very crowded this year, all sold out."

"No, I can get tickets. I can try to get tickets," I amended. "It's in my neighborhood. I can walk over and ask."

"You're so lucky!"

"So, how shall we — you want to call me and tell me the next time you'll be in Manhattan?"

"I can come anytime. It's up to you. You're the one with the busy exciting life!"

"Very funny. Okay, I'll call you when I find out about the availability of tickets."

We hung up. I never called her back. I knew I wouldn't, even while I was making the offer, and I think Osao understood it too. But I felt like a heel. Obliging on the surface, I was underneath just like her artist father, disapproving and aloof. Maybe that was what she wanted from me; maybe I hadn't disappointed her after all.

You see how tempted I am to thrash around in my own guilt and promote some sense of shame in lieu of a larger meaning. The truth of the matter is, Osao and I could never have worked out. There are those newly struck acquaintances that, for all the goodwill of both parties, peter out after a month. And there are those "bonsai loves" that, like the bonsai tree, perfect in its own limited way, are doomed to grow no higher than one's knee.

— 9

Never Live Above Your Landlord

LAST WEEK, THE WRITING WORKSHOP I give for teachers at P.S. 90 met at my apartment. (We rotate houses, and my turn had finally come up.) Just after the class began—everyone seated in a semicircle, discussing one of their poems—there was a banging on the door, followed by the gruff voice of my landlady, Mrs. Rourke, who unfortunately lives right beneath me: "What's going on in there?"

I apologized to the group for the interruption and went to see what was on her mind. "Did you want to speak to me?" I asked, shutting the door behind me.

"What's going on? How many people you got visiting you?"

"Just about ten. They're quiet."

"Well, you can't have that many. This place isn't zoned for a school! It's against the law."

"There's no school, these people have never been here before."

"I don't care, you can't be going back and forth like this opening the door."

"No one else is coming. Don't worry."

"My husband wants to talk to you," she concluded, with the irritated snarl of W. C. Fields. They both talk that way, like Fields on a tear.

After the class I go downstairs and knock on their door. They're watching television; he's in his yellow terry-cloth robe and sandals. I make the mistake of thinking he will be more rational and calm than his wife. Addressing my comments mostly to him, I explain that I run a workshop of eleven people who meet in each other's homes, and that every three or four months it may fall on me to invite the group over. Is that all right? In fact, I know I have the legal right to visitors in my apartment, but I start by framing the request as a favor. She, suddenly well disposed, interrupts: "Jimmy, what do you think? He wants to know if it's okay."

Her husband moves his head stiffly like a G-man and looks at her intently, without answering.

"I'm bringing it up now," I explain, "so that the next time—"

"I understand, you don't want to be embarrassed," she sympathizes. If she understands this much, why did she run upstairs snapping at us like a cocker spaniel earlier?

"Right, I don't want to be embarrassed, or humiliated, in front of my guests."

"Well, it's nice of you to come and talk about it with us," she says. "What do you think, Jimmy?"

Mr. Rourke looks congenial, up to a point. Then, suddenly, his thick eyebrows knit, his voice fills with anger: "When we ask for a few extra dollars in rent you complain."

"The guy next door to you is paying fifty dollars more!" she jumps in excitedly. "And he doesn't get no separate bedroom like you. You got the Presidential Suite."

"We don't want them coming here. What we're afraid is, you got a school of some kind up there. You're running a professional office upstairs!" Rourke yells.

"The government doesn't think so. I can't even take it off my income tax."

"I don't care what the government thinks. I'm telling you, you are using it as an office. You're typing day and night. The ceiling's starting to come down. I may have to put in a whole new ceiling!" he says. (I smile at the idea that my pecking away can be causing such structural damage.) "You fill all our garbage cans with your papers—"

"Now wait a minute, that's an exaggeration."

"—And then you slam the door and the whole house shakes. I told you, mister, to fix that door, but nooooo, you don't want to. You don't want to do a lot of things!"

"Would you like to fix the door?" I ask. "It's your building."

"No, you fix it. You're a professional man."

"But let's return to the question I asked—"

"Jimmy, you're wasting his time. He wants to know about the visitors."

"We don't want 'em. They're strangers, they can't come in here."

"Mr. Rourke! I've been living here for four years, and I've had one party in all that time and a few small meetings. The group I had over tonight is very quiet. They just read and write."

"They're weird. They're bohemians, who knows? We don't want their crazy kind—"

"Have you seen them?"

"I've seen 'em all."

"You must have a periscope."

"I've seen them, and I don't want 'em around!"

"First of all, they're not bohemians. You know what they are?" I pause, and answer triumphantly: "They're *schoolteachers*."

"Schoolteachers!" Now he's really angry. "They're the stupidest of the lot. I only had two years of college myself, don't get me wrong, I'm no intellectual. But schoolteachers are the most ignorant goddamn bunch of all. They can't even speak the king's English! All a New York City schoolteacher can say is 'Be that as it may.'"

"Be that as it may! Be that as it may! That's all they know," she chimes in.

"Let me tell you something: I used to run an antique shop," he says. "And the worst people who ever came in were schoolteachers and doctors. They're the kinds that give us the most trouble. We used to sell fine art sometimes, if it was included in the estate. Watercolors by John Singer Sargent, and Bierstadt. You ever heard of Bierstadt?"

"Yes. Albert Bierstadt, nineteenth-century American landscape painter."

"Well, these—schoolteachers would ask to see everything in the store." His left eyelid with the mole started twitching just at the memory. "And then they wouldn't buy a thing. And they never even heard of John Singer Sargent!"

"But"—I almost said, *be that as it may*, and caught myself—"my understanding is that I have a legal right to invite people into my home any time I want, as long as they're not rowdy."

"I'm tellin' ya, we don't want 'em! You squawk about a few extra lousy dollars in rent. If you don't like it, why don't you move out? That's all. Buy your own building."

"I think you're overestimating my income—"

"You got plenty of money. You're a professional man. Buy your own building upstate somewhere, one of those old one-room schoolhouses. That'll solve your problem."

"All right, I won't have them over again."

He doesn't want to hear this now, he's too incensed. "Go buy your own building!" he repeats.

"I said I won't ask them over. I'm agreeing with you."

"When that door slams, the whole house shakes."

"And go easy on the toilet, Mr. Lopat," she inserts. I give her an odd look: Does she want me to flush less, or shit less? "Sometimes you let the seat drop and we can hear it down here. It makes an awful racket!"

Meanwhile, their dog, a poodle, has come up and begun licking my shoe. All I can do is watch him and smile, as Mr. Rourke continues to rant. "Aries, get away from there," Mrs. Rourke cries.

"You understand, I'm not trying to be unfriendly," concludes my landlord.

"I think you *are* trying to be unfriendly," I reply, as I start to leave.

"Well, get the hell out of here!" he yells. When I reach my landing, he is still yelling. He'll cool off by tomorrow.

Although I consider myself a good tenant, clean and quiet and unobtrusive, my landlord and landlady, because of our close proximity, hear every sound I make, and cannot bring themselves to stop resenting the fact that I come in the door, that I take off my shoes, that I open the refrigerator—in short, that I live and breathe. The ideal tenant is, to them, someone who sends in the monthly rent check punctually but does not occupy the premises. I discovered this when they began fondly reminiscing about the previous tenant, a Hungarian architect who spent half the year building prefab condos in Barbados. Certainly their property must take much less wear and tear when no one is in it; alas, I can never live up to the standard set by my "invisible" predecessor, my Rebecca, as it were. When I finally complained that the tiny kitchenette in the corner of my main room had no sink and that I had to go into the bathroom to wash the dishes, they were quick to inform me that the architect never used the cooking facilities, he took all his meals in restaurants.

On the one hand, although the Rourkes rent self-contained units to a fairly transient population in the middle of Manhattan, my landlords have the almost charmingly old-fashioned, busy-body mentality of the owners of a "respectable" boardinghouse, entitled to pry into the degree of wholesomeness of their tenants. On the other hand, they seem never to have quite accepted that the entire house is not their dwelling. A thin, four-story brownstone, its scale is such that it could be a one-family home—and indeed, it began that way. When my landlady mops the stairs (she's a tireless housekeeper, I'll give her that), I hear her muttering to herself about this tenant or that, as though they were her poor relations who had overstayed their welcome.

Sometimes I watch my landlord tending the garden outside their basement apartment. From my window, I have a good overview of him, padding around, usually in his yellow robe, squat and bowlegged as an old Japanese retiree, perfectly at peace with his roses or tomato plants. At such moments I find him admirable. When I want to get in his good graces, I ask him what he's planting this year. Rourke gives me a half-hour botanical lecture: he has shrewd eyes, and certainly realizes I don't understand or care about all this gardening lore. But such are the ways we find to get along, when we are getting along.

Once, during the winter, I came upon him in front of the house; he had just cleared a path in the snow and was admiring his shovel work. We stood around talking, and he told me he had been a semipro baseball player down in Florida before World War II. I assumed, since he is only a few inches taller than five feet, that he had played shortstop, but no, he was a first-baseman. I admired and liked him this time, too.

Sometimes I listen to his fights with his wife. (They must listen to mine as well.) Their fights are usually about money: one accuses the other of being too softhearted and letting an electrician or merchant gyp them. I've never heard them making love. Maybe they don't anymore, or maybe they do it very quietly.

The wife is both shriller and easier to get around. It's a tired literary device to characterize someone with an animal metaphor, but what can I do when I have such a mutt of a landlady? After scratching on my door, she bolts into the living room, her dirty-blond-gray hair plastered at odd angles from her head. "Mr. Lopat!" she barks. She has a harsh way of saying my name that stops me in my tracks, like a flashlight pointed at a burglar.

I am resigned to her letting herself in with her keys whenever she wants. One time, however, it made for some embarrassment; I was entertaining a pretty woman visitor, on my lap. Mrs. Rourke took her in immediately—sniffed her out, I should say—and proceeded to ignore her. "Mr. Lopat! Were you watering your plants too much?"

"No."

"'Cause it's leaking over our heads. Something's leaking. Did you just water your plants?"

"No!" I said, starting to get annoyed. "I wish I had; they needed it."

"Let me take a look." She bounded over to the window on her thick little ankle-socked legs and stuck her snout under the radiator. "The board's warped! It's leaking all over. I'll go get Jimmy."

Moments later, Mr. Rourke entered with his tools, grinning from ear to ear, enjoying, it would seem, the comedy of their interrupting a romantic scene. "Will you look at that?" he declared, kneeling by the radiator cap.

"Jimmy, it's leakin' all over! I thought it was the plants but he says he didn't water the plants."

"I know that! What are you telling me that for? Don't talk nonsense, Kate. . . . How do you like that! It's been turned a full turn since the last time. Maybe you got ghosts here. I hope you're not afraid of ghosts, mister."

"No."

"Nor am I. Well, but how do you explain who did it?" he asked roguishly, the implication being that I had monkeyed with the valve. He tinkered a minute more. "I'll have to come by tomorrow and look at it." They exited as suddenly as they had appeared, back to their kennel, I suppose.

Whenever anything goes wrong with the plumbing (the pipes in the brownstone are very old), the Rourkes always try to make me feel defensive, as if it were my fault. An anally shaming connotation is given to clogged drains. One day this note was slipped under my door:

> Please do not use the wash Basin to empty the dirt and cat litter in. Use a Pail and throw it *in your toilet*.
> This Past week the Basin was Packed full of junk. and we used *$9.95 worth* of Drain Power. Then I had to get my Plumber to dislodge the dirt. Let the water run to clear the drain in that sink. Please throw the stuff in the toilet and flush. Next thing the Pipes will get leaking.
>
> Mrs. Rourke

My answer:

> Dear Mrs Rourke:
> What makes you think I am emptying cat litter and dirt in the wash basin!! This is an absurd contention. Please make sure you know whereof you speak before you start making baseless and, frankly, fantastic accusations.
>
> Sincerely,
> Phillip Lopate

I held my breath for the next few days, thinking that perhaps I had gone too far this time. Yet when I ran into my landlady in the hallway, she was almost respectful. Not that our epistolary relationship ended there. I keep all the notes she slips under my door, among which is this quaintly worded favorite:

Please stop that
jungle drum music.

———

or whatever it is.

———

I'm going out of my mind.
Bang Bang Bang.
Mrs. Rourke

Since I don't often listen to music I was a bit insulted at the time, but I turned off the jazz station I had on.

All these skirmishes are part of the "class struggle" that we are obliged to wage as tenant and landlord. The trouble is, underneath everything, we like each other, which complicates the purity of the antagonism. That murkiness began the very first day, when I answered the Rourkes' ad. I had come dressed in suit and tie, to radiate respectability; I instantly fell in love with the apartment, with its high ceilings, garden window, floor-length mirror, and genteel-seedy Edwardian furnishings. I noted the ornate molding with rhythmical slits, which Rourke proudly told me was called "dentile" work. He seemed delighted to have impressed me, a seemingly educated person, with his knowledge. Perhaps it was nothing more than that which softened him. Or perhaps they saw me, for one split second, as a sort of son. Whatever the reason, when I told them it was twenty dollars a month more than I could afford, they let me have the apartment anyway, at the lower figure.

Since then they have been playing "catch-up," trying to undo that first mistake of generosity. They grumble as though I had swindled them, refusing to acknowledge that their real bafflement is at their own initial charity. My rent has been raised many times, but it is still a bargain compared to the other rents in the building, and in light of how expensive the neighborhood has gotten. Nevertheless, I bellow like a gored bull whenever they confront me with a new increase, because I believe that it is my role to make them feel guilty for bringing up such demands, just as it is theirs to make me feel reluctant about suggesting repairs.

Once, after giving me a song and dance about rising fuel oil costs, Mrs. Rourke admitted (or I got her to admit) that this was a good time for landlords. "But we got to take in all the money we can. Supposing they put another freeze on us. Like in forty-four. So you have to charge now whatever you can get away with, 'cause it could end any minute."

"It's going to last for the indefinite future, in Manhattan at least."

"Come on, forty dollars more ain't gonna hurt ya. It's a business—you understand. If you moved out I could raise it thirteen percent extra. Everyone wants to live on this block. I got these guys living upstairs in single rooms, they pay more than you. They work for the UN and they only make twenty-three thousand."

"But I don't even make *twenty* thousand."

"But you got the possibility to make a lot more, 'cause you're on your own. These guys that work for the government or a corporation, what do they have to look forward to? They get together and drink beer at—P. J. Clarke's or someplace, and they talk about who's gonna get a raise. But you're on your own, you got all kinds of ways to make money. You could make a million. All you got to do is write garbage, trash. That's what the public wants."

"Okay, I'll try."

"Try, Mr. Lopat. You can do it."

"You could, too, probably."

"What am I going to write about? My 'misspent youth'? All the things I didn't do and should've?" she said, laughing and, much to my surprise, giving me a wink.

She does have her kindly side. Sometimes I come home and find that the bathroom floor has been scrubbed, or the dishes washed. She also fed my cat one weekend when I went away; apparently Milena resisted the dry food I had left out and was yowling in a sulk. Mrs. Rourke went out and bought her some canned liver, in spite of the fact that she hates my having a pet in the apartment.

Yesterday, Mrs. Rourke came in to investigate something and stayed to chat for over an hour. I was feeling tired and relaxed, and I encouraged her to talk. She practically told me her life story. Afterward I wrote down everything I could remember, as close to verbatim as possible. Herein, then, is

The Landlady's Tale

I don't like to rent to women. Because they're always picky, picky, they start finding fault with this and that. They want tiles in the bathroom. Men are more easily satisfied. You can tell a man something and he'll agree or disagree, but that's that. He says to himself, she probably had a headache today. But a woman, she's vindictive, she remembers.

I had one woman in here, she was a nice-looking girl, blond and slim, she said to me, "If I get this place I'll never give you a moment's trouble." So, fine, she took the place and the next thing I know she's complaining, there's no heat. I says, Okay, I'll come up and fix it. "Oh," she says, "you can't just come into my house, you have to tell me first. You have to notify me. And you can't come today, you have to come Friday." So all right, I figured forget it. The next thing I know she's all upset. She's seen a cockroach. I said why don't you get an exterminator? She said, "I know my rights, you have to supply me with an exterminator." Oh, she was screaming like she'd never seen a cockroach before. I said, "What are you scared of a little cockroach for when you got that big gorilla sleeping in your bed?" Ha! She was so surprised when I said that. But I'd seen him coming in and out, a guy like a gorilla with a big beard. He belonged to that Puerto Rican Independence party. He had these tapes going on loud, Viva-this and Down with Anaconda-that. One day I knock on the door and I says to him, "Listen, I didn't rent my rooms for this. If you want to play your anti-American speeches why don't you put down a few bucks and hire a meeting hall?" He said to me, all red in the face, "Don't you bother me, get out of here!" I was a little scared. He could be a bomber! Could blow the whole building up! He had all these guys with Castro beards coming in and out, sitting on the stoop. Agitators. I says to him, "Listen, I'm not afraid of you. If you keep this up I'll call the FBI and have you investigated."

So the next thing I know the girl comes to me and says, "Mrs. Rourke, you got the wrong idea! He doesn't sleep with me." So I went in with my Instamatic when she wasn't there and I took pictures. He had his shoes lying on the floor and his pants and underpants! I wasn't planning to do anything with the pictures, but just if she started something. So she moves out real fast. Left me a nice note. She was a sweet-looking girl, you know. I went in there to clean up and it turned out she had shut the radiator off! That's why it was always so cold. But she wouldn't let me in to check. That's why I don't like women tenants. A friend of mine owns a building down the block, number forty-four. She rented it to a girl and the girl has her gurus coming up and down. Two o'clock in the morning they start meditatin'. Making noise, like O-maa-aa-wuuu. When everybody's sleeping. My friend says, "Oh, I want to kill that woman!" But what can she do? Nothing.

This friend of mine's daughter went to Vegas. To my way of thinking she was very plain-looking. No hips, no bust, no face, no legs, nothing. She met this insurance man who was a millionaire and she married him! I don't know what he saw in her, the daughter. Maybe it was one of those things—an attraction. Maybe he liked the way she threw the dice. He died. He had a heart attack, all of a sudden a sharp pain! The artery bursted. Now she's got a million. See, maybe if I went to Reno and been at the right spot I could've been rich by now. But instead I came to New York and I'm still struggling. I didn't plan to stay in New York. I just came here to make something of myself and get out. I came from Pennsylvania. I wanted to get into show business. But I was too short. Too short for a Roxyette. Nowadays they take 'em small. Then it was a certain look they wanted: tall, baby face, a little plump, you know. Now they like that starved look. I had a friend back then who was a big model, Babe Casey. She was a gorgeous girl. You must have seen that Unguentine ad, you know, with the girl bending over. That's her. Edna. They called her Babe though. She went into the Ziegfeld Follies. Then she married somebody rich from down South. She's probably passed on by now. Anyway, she got me a few jobs posing for ski ads. Twenty-five bucks an hour. Good money. In those days, though, you had to bring your own clothes on the job. If it was a ski shot you had to go out and buy a pair of skis.

Meanwhile I was working at the Downtown Athletic Club, waiting on tables for their luncheon meal. They only paid you a dollar an hour, but the tips were what made it. I could come home sometimes with thirty, forty dollars in change. They were always after me. One old guy says to me, "What kind of lipstick you like?" I says, "Any kind I can get!" He left me a five-dollar tip. Another guy had a big Packard, rode around with the hood down. He says to me, "How'd you like to be living in the Essex House?" "Fine," I says, "but what do I have to do for it?" Besides, I noticed that this guy had a different girl with him every time I saw him. So if you did what he said, you'd be living at the Essex House, and the next thing you knew he'd be sending up his friends to entertain. Sure! Before you knew it you'd be living the life of a real hustler. I wasn't interested in sleeping with men. Oh, I'd go on dates. When I was hungry! My girlfriend and I were living in the same residence hotel, and she was a beautiful thing, looked like Jean Harlow. The men would invite her out to dinner and she'd say, "But you have to take my girlfriend, too." We'd go to the Roxy together and then have a big meal on them and never see 'em again. Hello and good-bye, that sort of routine.

I had one fella who was after me, Ripley's secretary. You know Ripley's Believe It or Not? He was the guy who used to research it. A brilliant man, everybody said. He came to the Athletic Club, he would write me poems. All about my hair. A lovely guy. The other girls said, "Gee, you're lucky. That's the man for you, Kate, he'll make a great husband." But I didn't love him. He had gray hair. And I was eighteen.

I would always tell the men what they wanted to hear. To get a tip, you know? One customer would say, "What are you doing tomorrow?" I'd say, "Oh, it's my mother's birthday and I've got to take her out. If only I could take her somewhere special!" He'd leave me five dollars. You have to make up something interesting, that's what men like. They don't want to hear the same old story. One man says to me, "Will you be here next week?" I says, "Not only next week, I'll be here forever." That kind of thing.

Then I met my husband. I was living in this residence hotel on the same floor as my girlfriend, and there was a man in the middle between our two rooms. Rosenzweig. We used to share the wash basin. He'd say, "Girls, are you going to be in there for long?" And my girlfriend would say, "Yes we're going to be in there for very long. You don't like it?" He says, "I can't stand it anymore!" She was always trying to get a rise out of him. So one day he was trying to be friendly, and he invited both of us into his room. I saw he had a caricature on the wall of himself. This Mr. Rosenzweig had an unusually large—nose. And it was all there in the cartoon. I says, "That's very good, it's a good likeness." He says, "Oh, that's by my friend Jimmy Rourke, he's an artist. He's from Florida. He's coming into town next week, and if you girls are nice I'll introduce you to him." My girlfriend says, "Ah, we don't want to meet any friend of yours." She was always trying to get him riled up.

So the next weekend he left his door open next to the wash basin, a signal that he was inviting us to join them. They were going to a baseball game. So we all went to the game, and that's how I met Jimmy. I knew right away. I told my friend, "I found somebody I want to marry." We went together for a year. We were like two puppies. Oh, we had a lot of fun. What I liked about him was that he was so easy. If we were walking along and I saw a Max Factor makeup kit in the window that I liked, he went right inside and bought it for me. Never asked for a thing in return. Not even a kiss. Most men, they would say, "How about a kiss first?" I said to myself, Here's a man.

When we got married we both had jobs, so we took an eight-room apartment on West 105th Street. The rent was only fifty-four dollars a month then! I fixed up one part and rented it out to an Irish couple as a one-bedroom apartment. They were paying eleven dollars a week, which was a lot of money for the time. Then I heard about this building we're in now. A friend told me about it. It was owned by a Jewish woman with big legs. It was getting too much for her, she was getting too old to run the place. So we bought it. Then we went into antiques. We ran antique stores for thirty years. All the dealers knew me, they used to call me Kiss-Me-Kate.

I had a friend who was an interior decorator named Gladys, she used to bring her clients around. What she would charge 'em! She'd bring in this judge's wife, Mrs. Gold. And tell her: "You have to have this Biedermeier in your home." The woman would say: "Vat I gotta haf dat ugly ting in my house?" Gladys would tell her, "But it won't look like this when I get through with it. I have the finest Italian artist who's going to transform it into the most beautiful thing you ever saw. Just write out a check for six hundred dollars, that's what I paid Mrs. Rourke for it." She'd bought it from me for two hundred! I says to her when we're alone, "Gladys, don't you have no shame at all?" She laughs and says, "Why should I? I have to take that dumb woman to lunch and all around town in cabs and I keep picking up the bill. My husband and I play cards with the judge and her. And we lose. We lose all the time, on purpose. Nah, I got no time for pitying her." "Well, that's a different story," I says. So we both had a good laugh.

When Jimmy and I sold our business we had some money to invest. But we missed our opportunities. I could have had that office building on 72nd Street for ninety-eight thousand dollars. The one with the beautiful iron doors. But Jimmy said it was too expensive. To him everything was always too expensive. You know what it's worth now? A million! The point of it is: invest. And there's nothin' like real estate. Oh, what we could have picked up after the war. But you're young and you don't want responsibilities. Invest while you're young, that's the point I'm making. I used to have this friend, Mr. Hermann, he was a stockbroker. And a real gentleman. Oh, Jimmy didn't like him! Thought he was paying too much attention to me. One time we were at a dancing party and I asked Mr. Hermann if he had any good tips for investments. He took me into his arms and started whirling me around the room, and all the while he was whispering in my ear, "Gold! Gold! Gold!"

The next thing I know, gold is going up through the ceiling. I should've listened to him. He gave me another good tip: there was a place just across the street, a penthouse. It used to be where servants hung the wash. I could have picked it up for twenty-five thousand, put in another thirty-five thousand and we'd have had a beautiful roof apartment. The sun would be shining in on us every day. I told my husband, "Jimmy, I want to move there." He says, "Go ahead. I'll even sign the papers. But I'm staying here. I'm not going to move into no roof apartment. We'd get mugged." I says, "What do I want to go live there by myself for?" You know what I think? Jimmy was jealous! Anything to do with Mr. Hermann, he didn't trust.

Besides, he doesn't want to change. I heard about other places to fix up. Now I can't be bothered. I'm close to seventy, I don't want to start a whole new enterprise. We talk about who we're going to leave this house to. There's my niece, but she's still like a hippy. She's over thirty and she's taking art lessons! That's not so bad, but she's been married and divorced and got two kids and now she's getting the government to pay for her art lessons. I sort of feel she's missed the boat. Know what I mean? It's too late for that, you get past a certain point in life. . . .

I says, Jimmy, let's leave it to the dog!

There was an old guy who lived in the Dakota, left a fortune that way. The will saw that so much every month would be spent on feeding and care of the animal. So this fella who was taking care of it, he drew a good salary, he was living high, all he had to do was walk the dog and feed it. And the dog died. So the fella was devastated. He went to the lawyer and said, "What am I going to do?" The lawyer thought and thought, and finally he said, "I'll tell you what to do. Get another dog that's almost like the one who died and take care of him."

I'll stop here, because my hand is tired. In any case, you get the idea. Twenty-four hours later, her chatter still flows on and on in my head, she's so real, Mrs. Rourke, with her innocence and her Unguentine ads, her obsession with making money and her inability to go in for the kill. Why aren't I real the way she is? She's a character, all right, and she has certainty, however narrow its intellectual base. *Ils sont dans le vrai*, said Flaubert, the visionary artist envying the bourgeoisie out for a Sunday walk in the park. How tiresome. No, I don't envy the Rourkes exactly, but I'm fond of their postwar-America outlook. I envy their past; the very word "postwar" in fact gives me a jolt of warmth, with its promise of young married couples starting off on a new life. My parents were still hopeful in 1945; I was two years old, barely able to toddle, certainly unable to appreciate the tonal brilliance of forties *film noir* or bebop that mean so much to me now. I suppose we often have a nostalgic affinity for the cultural era when we were still in the womb or barely out. A Freudian would say it was the Oedipal desire to crawl in between one's parents' lovemaking, to be in on one's conception. But the Rourkes—to think of them as a young couple, a union of baseball and the Ziegfeld Follies, with all the world ahead of them, only to end up finally, by imperceptible declensions and fateful turns, that most morally suspect of creatures, New York landlords. Well, they're honest ones, at least. Still, what happened to Jimmy's artistic ambitions? Or the children—why are there no children? Don't leave it to the poodle, for God's sake! Think of your poor, put-upon tenant, your long-lost son!

_ 10

On Shaving a Beard

I HAVE JUST MADE A CHANGE THAT FEELS AS DRAMATIC, for the moment, as switching from Democrat to Republican. I have shaved off my beard. Actually I clipped it away with a scissors first, then I went in for the kill with a safety razor. The first snip is the most tentative: you can still allow yourself the fantasy that you are only shaping and trimming, perhaps a raffish Vandyke will emerge. Then comes the moment when you make a serious gash in the carpet. You rub the neighboring whiskers over the patch to see if it can still be covered, but the die is cast, and with a certain glee the energy turns demolitionary.

As I cut away the clumps of darkness, a moon rises out of my face. It lights up the old canyon line of the jawbone. I am getting my face back. I lather up again and again and shave away the bristles until the skin is smooth as a newborn's—the red irritation spots where the skin has reacted to the unaccustomed blade seem a sort of diaper rash. When I am done, I look in the glass and my face itself is like a mirror, so polished and empty are the checks I feel a little sorry for the tender boy-man reflected before me, his helpless features open to assault. The unguarded vacancy of that face! Now I will have to come to terms again with the weak chin, the domi-neering nose, the thin, sarcastic-pleading lips.

I look down at the reddish-gray curls in the sink. The men in my family have always been proud that our beards grew in red though the tops of our heads were black. It seems an absurd triviality for Nature to waste a gene on, but it is one of the most tangible ways that my father has felt united to his sons and we to him. A momentary regret passes through me.

Never mind: I have taken an action. I grew the beard originally because I had been restless and dissatisfied with myself; I shaved it for the same reason. How few cut-rate stratagems there are to better our mood: you can take a trip, go shopping, change your hair, see every movie in town—and the list is exhausted. Now I will have to be contented for a while. It is summer, the wrong time to start growing a beard again.

Because of the hot weather, I also have a ready-made excuse for anyone who might ask why I gave up my beard. I know the real reasons are more murky—they go to the heart of my insecurities as a man and my envy of others of my sex. When I meet a man I admire and he is wearing a beard, I immediately think about emulating him. The tribe of bearded men have a patriarchal firmness, a rabbinical kindly wisdom in their faces. They strike me as good providers. They resemble trees (their beards are nests) or tree cutters. In any case, mentally I place them in the forest, with flannel shirt and axe.

So I join this fraternity, and start to collect the equivalent of approving winks from other beardies, fellow conspirators in the League of Hirsutes. It feels good to be taken for an ancestor or pioneer. Then the novelty begins to wear off, the beard start to itch, and I realize that inside I am no more rooted or masculinely capable than before. I start to envy clean-shaven men—their frank, open, attractively "vulnerable" faces. Some women will trust you more if you are clean-shaven; they profess to see beards as mephistophelian masks, hiding the emotions. Early in the relationship, this may be a good reason to keep a beard. At a later point shaving it off becomes tantamount to a giddy declaration of love.

Other women, on the other hand, will tell you that a kiss without facial hair is like a roast beef sandwich without mustard. They consider beards a mark of virility, trustworthiness, and bohemian sensitivity. Obviously, the image systems break down in the face of individual tastes. Nevertheless, it is still possible to say that beards connote freedom, telling the boss off, an attitude of "gone fishing"; men often grow them on vacations, or after being booted from the White House staff, like Ehrlichman. (Even Admiral Poindexter grew a mustache.) Clean-shavenness, on the other hand, implies a subscription to the rules of society.

A major division in the bearded kingdom exists between those who revel in no longer having to bother with maintenance, letting Nature have its luxuriant bushy way, and those who continue to keep a razor nearby, prudently pruning or shaving the checks every few days. A well-clipped beard on a kindly man looks as proper as a well-kept lawn on Sunday. On the other hand, there are beards with a glint of cruelty—beards trimmed to Caligulaesque exactitude. I had thought to be one of the pruners, but went too far, lacking the razor-sharp finesse.

Having shaved the beard off, I take my first cautious steps into society. I am dreading those who will ask why I did it, then settle back for a long soul-bearing explanation. What will I reply to those who are quick to say, "I liked you better the other way"? My impulse is to step on their toes, but we must not punish honesty. Once, when I was teaching in P.S. 90, I shaved off my beard, and the children, who were familiar with me as a hairy man, were so outraged that all through the first day of the new regime they ran alongside and punched me. Children are good at expressing a sense of betrayal at change.

Those who are bearded for the long haul either tend to view the new me with something like a Mennonite's disapproval at backsliding, or are relieved that one who had appeared a member of the brotherhood was exposed in the nick of time as a turncoat. A few friends, who pride themselves on their observational powers, make helpful comments like: You look fatter. You look thinner. You look younger. You look older. The majority nothing. At first I think they are being polite, not meaning to broach a subject that might make me self-conscious. Then, of frustration at their not having noticed, I finally call my naked face to their attention. They say: "I *thought* there was something different about you but I couldn't put my finger on it. Besides, you keep going back and forth, Lopate, who can keep up?"

11

Getting a Cat

1.

AFTER SO MANY YEARS OF LIVING ALONE, I broke down and got a cat. I really didn't want a cat. Once I was in Jungian therapy and the therapist said to me, "You should get a cat." He was a very decent man, I gained a lot from him, I listened respectfully to everything he said, except when he gave me practical advice like this. "You should try it. You'll learn interesting things about yourself. . . ." And then he slid away into his mysterious smile. One might almost say, a Cheshire cat smile.

You can't imagine how many people have been offering me their superfluous kittens over the years. Why was everyone so eager to give me a cat? I saw them all smiling, rubbing their hands: "Ah, he'll get a cat, very good, it's a good sign, means he's settling down."

By what Darwinian logic was I supposed to graduate from one to the other? Maybe I was to start with a cat, then go to a sheep dog, next a pony, then a monkey, then an ape, then finally a Wife. It was far more likely that, if I got a cat, I would stop there. What annoyed me was this smug assumption that because I lived alone, I was barren; I needed to start making "commitments" to other living creatures, to open my heart to them and take on responsibility. As far as I can piece it together, the idea seems to be that we should commit ourselves to something in this black hole of a universe. We should make an effort to join the Association of fellow creatures. Now, "commitment" comes into popular discourse when belief in love starts to slide. They're not so sure anymore, the experts, the theologians, that there is such a thing as love. So they tell you you should build up to it — practice. Throw your arms around a tree. Myself, I still believe in love, what do I need commitment for? So this was one reason for my not getting a cat. Plus my apartment is too small — there are no doors between the rooms — and I sometimes have to travel on the spur of the moment. Most important, I didn't feel I needed a cat.

Very well, you might ask, how did it happen that I got a cat?

It was partly a misunderstanding. I was in the country one weekend, where one is always more prone to sentimental longings and feelings of incompleteness. That's why I stay out of the country as much as possible. But I was visiting a friend; and there was an old man also staying at the house, a respected old writer, a lovely man whom I'll call Claude. This old man has beautiful silky white hair. He moves with graceful modesty, slight of build and wearing threadbare sweaters with holes in them, not because he can't afford any better but because he has already stopped caring about making an impression. He lives alone and seems wonderfully self-sufficient, except for his cats. He and I were standing inside the threshold of his bare country room and bending over a box where the mother cat was sleeping with her four kittens. The children were all sleeping head to foot, with their tails in each other's mouths so that together they looked like one big cat.

They made, I had to admit, a cute effect. I was trying to get a suitably fond expression onto my face and he was explaining about their delivery.

"There was a lot of hard labor involved. Usually she likes me to be around — some cats don't. There has to be a box ready. She knew just what to do. She ate the umbilical cord, and the afterbirth, which is supposed to be good for them. Then she licked off the first kitten and was ready for the next. Each kitten comes in a different sack . . . they're not like humans that way."

"Hm," I said, impressed with his knowledge of nature. Each kitten had a different coloration: one grey, one black, one cinnamon orange, and one whitish. A Mendelian demonstration. I liked the grey cat, because he was so straightforward, your basic alley cat. I was also drawn to the milky-orange one but distrusted her because she was *too* pretty.

Claude's hand, which was large and sensitive, pale veined with brown spots — I shook it every chance I got — descended to stroke each of the cats along its furry back.

"What are you going to do with all the kittens?" I asked idly.

"I'll give away as many as people want, and let her keep one to raise; and the rest will have to be taken to the vet to be killed. That's the difficult part," he said. The fold above his eye twitched as he talked, and he turned his face for a moment deliberately toward me, with a politeness and candor that showed he was not afraid to look me in the eye. "But she isn't willing to do it," he said, "and so I have to. I don't need more than one cat, you see."

I was so taken with this, with his acceptance of the world as it was, that I wanted to have one of his cats. I spoke up like a fool who raises his hand at an auction just to participate, to release the tension, and offered to take a kitten. He looked at me with a kind, piercing gaze, and asked if I was positive I wanted one. I said I was absolutely sure, trembling at what his look of examination might have told him about me. For a while he pretended I hadn't made the offer at all, in order to let me gracefully off the hook. But I kept forcing myself toward a firm statement that I wanted one of his kittens — the grey one probably. Although the cinnamon-orange one was pretty too. And suddenly I became horribly torn between these two animals, as between two ideals.

If I took the grey alley cat, I would be opting for everything that was decent peasant stock, dependable, ordinary and hardworking in myself. The idea pleased me. But I would be turning my back on beauty. I stood over the box, wondering if I should be ruled by a flash of prettiness, mystery, the gamine, the treacherous, as I had been so often in my life, or if, by embarking on this new, "more mature" stage of commitment, I would do better to choose sturdier virtues for companionship. In the end I picked the grey, partly because I was feeling guilty for having wanted to go back on my promise to him, after noticing a new, more fetching piece of fur.

Two or three days later, back in the city, grimly contented, coolheaded, myself again, I realized I had made a terrible mistake. I didn't want a cat! I wanted to be this old man. I wanted to grow up more quickly and be done with my idiotic youth and literary ambitions and sexual drives that bossed me around, and — I wanted to be Claude, gentle, pure. I must have fallen in love with his white beard and his spotted hands; and under his spell, in their charmed propinquity, whatever he had warmed with his glance that moment I probably would have coveted. Fortunately it was only a cat; it might have been worse.

I had to find a way to tell him I was backing out of the deal. For a long while I did nothing. I sat on my hands. Finally I wrote a card to him saying that I hadn't forgotten, that I hoped he was keeping the grey kitty for me — but maybe it was the orange one I really wanted, I couldn't make up my mind. It was a scatterbrained, sloppy note, and I hoped it would convey the impression of an irresponsible young man who cannot be counted on for anything he says. You may be amazed at this subterfuge, but it was the closest I could get to telling the truth.

In any case he did not get the hint. Like Death coming to call, Claude telephoned me once he was back in New York, and said that it was time for me to stop by and collect my kitty.

With a heavy heart, I rode down in the taxi next to the black metal carrying box that friends had lent me, my Black Maria. I had already provisioned my apartment with the supplies that Claude, in a moment of doubting me, had called to remind me to have ready as soon as the cat should enter its new home. I climbed the stairs to Claude's loft, wondering how the old man managed them every day. He opened the door to me with a peculiarly impish smile.

I wanted to get this over with as quickly as possible. "Hello, kitty," I said, bending down to pet the grey kitten.

"No, that's not your cat. I gave that to someone else. Here's your cat," he said. "There she is — she was under the bed! She's a very timid creature. Not like her brother Waldo, the grey. *There* she is! *There* she is." He held her in his arms, and poignantly gave her over to me.

I need not say how grateful I was that it was the orange one. She was warm in my hands, and gorgeously, obscenely pretty. Old Claude must be some student of the human heart.

The rest was odds and ends, formalities of transfer. She had already had her first distemper shot but I was to take her again in four months. I would be better off not giving her too much milk at first. She liked Purina tuna most of all the brands he'd tried. She was a good jumper — a first-class jumper; but as she had been up to now in the shadow of her brother Waldo, she seemed retiring. That would probably change. He had noticed it sometimes happened with girls, when they had brothers, that the boy kittens would be very active and dominate them. A good thing was to get an empty crushed pack of Winstons, which she liked to play with. Did I smoke? he asked. No, I said. "Well, then get your smoking friends to save them for you. She also likes to play with a little toy ball, and I'll give that to you." He located the ball, and his last empty cigarette pack, and give me a box of dry cat food and would have piled on several cans of tuna if I had not stopped him and said I had plenty at home. "Very well," he said, simply and with loss. "I guess that's it."

We were caught in such an emotional moment that I wanted to throw myself into his arms and comfort him, or be comforted myself. Instead, I shook his hand, which was always a good idea.

"Goodbye, *****," he said, calling her something like Priscilla, or Betsy. I didn't want to hear; I wanted her named existence to begin with me. "You're going off to your new home," he said. "Have a good time."

"Won't she be lonely for her brother and her mother?" I asked.

"Yes . . . but that's life," he replied, smiling at both the threadbareness of the phrase and the truth of it.

He walked me to the door and stood at the top of the stairs with me. "If you have any questions, ask people who have cats for advice. They'll be more than happy to give it to you, and most of it will be wrong — but that's all right, they'll all have dozens of tips. And of course you can call me anytime you want if you're having problems with her. I know very little but I can hold your hand."

2.

And so I settled down to my comfortable married life. After she had overcome her first shyness, the girl began to demonstrate her affectionate nature. She would take my finger in her mouth and lick it, and move on to the next finger, and the next. Her little pink tongue, rough as a wash-cloth, would sand away at my skin until it became sore. Then I would push her away, and pick up my book.

But a little while later, I would try to entice her back. "Come here, Milena," I would say. She would look uncertainly, mistrustfully up at me. I would wave my hand in the air, a gesture that hypnotized her each time, and wiggle my fingers until she jumped at them. Then I'd *catch* her and clutch her to me and squeeze her. She didn't like to be squeezed, or at first even petted; she would immediately turn around and start licking the hand that tried to stroke her.

In the evening she would curl up on my lap and close her eyes and make that motor-running, steady-breathing sound. I didn't have the heart to move, with her on my lap, purring like that. Moreover, she held her paw on my wrist, as if to detain me. How could I reach for a pencil?

On first arriving, she had investigated every corner of my apartment, going around the perimeters of the living room into the bedroom, the kitchenette, and finally into the bathroom, where she took note of her cat box. I was wondering when she would begin to use the box. The first day passed, and the pebbles were unruffled. Then another day came and went, without commission, and I thought she might be so nervous from the move that she was constipated.

On the third day I sat down on the couch; something was wrong. My nostrils opened. Right next to me on the sofa was the most disgusting pile of shit. I nearly retched. I cleaned it off distastefully and dropped a piece of it in the cat box, so that she would know that was the proper place for it. Then I lowered her into this same cat box and she hopped out of it as quickly as from an electric shock. This was too much. Claude had assured me that she was toilet trained! I sprayed the sofa with Lysol disinfectant. She kept returning to the spot like the criminal she was, and sniffing the upholstery, trying to puzzle out the two different smells, and backing away, bewildered.

That afternoon I called Claude, to get the exact name of the cat litter he'd been using. I told him what she had done. He said, "Oh, dear, that must be disagreeable; I'm so sorry to hear it . . ." Never mind, I thought, just tell me the name of your cat litter. It turned out to be another brand; so, hoping this would make the difference, I went from supermarket to supermarket until I had found the preferred gravel. I lugged twenty pounds of it home with me and poured a deep, cloud-releasing stratum in her box.

That night I couldn't sleep. I was so revulsed by the image of finding that bundle on the couch, I felt as if my house, my sanctuary had been ruined. Why had I gotten a cat? That night my dreams were full of unpleasant surprises.

In the morning I awoke to the smell of a stack of her shit on the white brocade armchair. This could go on for weeks. My work was suffering, I couldn't concentrate, I couldn't do a thing until I had broken in that cat and shown her who was master. I bet she knows that's her box, I thought, but she just prefers taking a crap on a nice comfy armchair or a sofa surrounded by pillows. Wouldn't we all? She must think I'm a total sucker.

I sponged the chair, again sprayed with Lysol, deposited a piece of her droppings in the cat box. Then I grabbed her by the neck, not so gently, and dropped her into the gravel. She jumped out like a shot. I caught her and put her in again. She hopped out, whining. I threw her in again. Romance of education: she was the wild child, Helen Keller, I was the stubborn tutor. I was willing to treat it like a game: you jump out, I'll throw you back. She bounded, I caught her. My arm was stuck out like a fence to grab her as soon as she escaped. Each time she grew a little slower in leaving the box, a little more pensive and frustrated. Staring at me with her big, victimized pussycat eyes. "That look is wasted on me," I told her. She fell in the gravel, defeated. She seemed to chew over the situation for a half minute. Then she sat up in the posture of evacuating, and lowered her bottom ever so gradually. She got off (it was a little pee) and carefully kicked some pebbles over the spot. Hurray!

After that we had no more surprise "bundles." Life fell back to normal, or let us say, my new normal, which seemed to consist of my spending days running to the store for cat food and litter, and buying a vacuum cleaner to swoop up the cat's hairs so that my allergic friends could visit me, or locating the right scratching post before it was too late. Milena had found the underguts of a chair and was taking clumps of stuffing out of it for sport. In fact she was doing nightmarish things to all the furniture. Since I live in a furnished apartment, I was terrified of what would happen if my landlady came snooping around. My landlady is not fond of signs of life in any form. I had been afraid to ask her permission in the first place, and had sneaked in the cat on the *fait accompli* principle. If I had asked her, I knew, she would have said no; this way she would either have to accept it or start costly eviction proceedings.

One afternoon, as I was walking up the stoop of my house, where my landlady lives also, unfortunately, directly beneath me, she told me that "there was someone knocking" at my door. I thought this was odd; but then I noticed the scowling, misanthropic expression on her pudgy face and the two tufts of dirty-blondish hair sticking angrily out of her ears (God, she looked like a bulldog!), and via this animal association I realized that she was referring in her elliptical way to my cat. She followed this "knocking" statement with: "No cats, Mr. Lopate. We can't have cats here. They smell up the place and destroy the rugs and we can't have cats here, you understand?"

I said nothing, and proceeded past her into my apartment and closed the door, trembling with anger. I was ready to fight her to the bitter end. I turned to Milena, all innocent of the threat against her. "Don't worry," I said. "I won't let her throw you out. We'll move first." So our destinies were tied. "But you must," I said, "you must control your destructiveness. We live in this woman's house, don't you see; this is her furniture! If you go tearing large holes in everything it will cost me a fortune. Look, I bought you a scratching pad; can't you bring yourself to use it?"

In the meantime, something had to be done. I consulted friends. Some advocated declawing, others were aghast at the idea, with a foaming passion that made you suspect they were talking about something else. Anyhow, someone said, a kitten her age was too young for the operation. When I learned that it was indeed an "operation," that she would have to go to the hospital for it, I postponed the project indefinitely. Instead, I clipped her toenails and coaxed her to try the new scratching post (I had replaced the cardboard stand with a fabric one). The man in the pet shop said, "If you put some catnip around the base she'll be sure to like it." I bought a container of fresh catnip — anything for my baby girl. I spread the leaves up and down the scratching post. She did love the smell; she licked at the catnip and slept on the fabric base when she needed a rest from her more exhausting vandalisms.

3.

After that, a strange, sullen period began for us. At times I thought I loved her, at other times I would be completely indifferent to her. I would kick her off the bed when she tried to sleep with me, because I wanted to be alone and not worry about rolling onto her. But always when I had almost forgotten she was there, she would crouch into my vision.

She had the annoying habit of trying to stop me when I dialed the phone, as if jealous of my speaking to anyone else. She would smudge the dialing circle with her paw, forcing me to dial the same number several times. We often got in each other's way. She and I competed for the bright red armchair — the one I considered my "writing chair." Milena always seemed to be occupying it just as I was getting ready to lower myself. Sometimes I would come home after work and find her sleeping on that chair, a lazy housewife. She would blink her eyes as I turned on the light.

When I totally ignored her, she began knocking down my knickknacks. She would tear through the house. She seemed to be taking over the living space and squeezing me into a small, meaningless corner. I resented having to smell her all over my apartment. At my typing desk, in the kitchenette, there was that warm, cloying, offensively close odor from her shed hairs. And I got cross at her for not raking under her shits. Cats were supposed to be "fastidious creatures" and do that instinctively. It seemed a violation of the contract.

I was looking for violations, I suppose. In the back of my mind I kept thinking that I could send her away. It was hard for me to grasp the idea that I was going to have to care for her always. Until one of us died.

Claude called from time to time, "to hold my hand," as he put it. He was very sweet. I was delighted to have the chance to talk more often with him, even though our conversations were rather specialized. Once he suggested that I spread baking powder through the cat litter to cut the smell. Not a lot on the top surface — she wouldn't use it if you did — but a little throughout the mixture.

All this lore of cats! It was too much to take in; and it was only the beginning. As Claude had predicted, everyone had instructions for me.

Now, there were four things I could never stand to hear people going on about: one was their dreams, two was their coincidences, three was their favorite restaurants and meals, and four was their pets. And I never did like going over to a friend's house and in the middle of an intense conversation watching the friend's eyes turn senile with fondness as he interrupted to draw my attention to the cute position his cat had gotten herself into.

Now that I had this cat, every visitor started off with fifteen minutes of reaction to her. Women friends, particularly, made much of Milena. One commented that it was rare to find an orange female. Another said the cat was so elegant that she herself felt "underdressed" around her. Kay, my old flame, remarked: "Your cat is so gentle. I can't get over how delicate — how attuned she is! Oh, she's exquisite."

I felt abashed for not having perceived this special "attunedness" in Milena. From my point of view she was doing a kitten's job adequately, she was holding down the role, earning her can a day, but not setting any records. They all seemed to want to find something unique about Milena, whereas I, on the contrary, liked her precisely because she was just a cat. True, she had an appealingly pathetic stare: those black pupils with two concentric circles of olive around them. But I resisted the flattering appraisals, which seemed to me as farfetched as newborn-baby compliments. I had no idea how fond and proud I had grown of her until I came up against a nonbeliever.

My friend Emily remarked, without having seen her: "She's not as nice as my cat, is she?" and assured herself no, as if it were self-evident. I was furious. Not that my cat is so great, but why should hers be better? Emily was my model of the delusional cat owner. She had theories about how her cat knew her moods better than anyone, stayed away from her when that was the right thing to do, comforted her when she was down, intuitively kept her claws in — a miracle of a domestic cat that didn't need to be declawed, spayed or altered or anything else cats usually need to be, because it was so considerate and discreet. Her cat was a Colette novel. Often, people hurt Emily with their rudeness or selfish insensitivity, but her cat — never. Her cat sets the standard, I thought sardonically, that all of us, her friends, must chase after and miss. When Emily shuts the door on her last visitor of the night, she curls up with her kitty cat, the understanding one.

This would never happen to me, I vowed. First of all, I have no fantasies that Milena understands me. How could she, when our interests, our hobbies, our yearnings, are so different?

I don't pretend to guess her secrets. I watch her.

There she is, chasing a fly.

Now she knocks a spoon off the table, a Magic Marker from the desk, and starts kicking it about. Everything is a toy to her. She drags her booty through a square hole she has scratched in the white brocade armchair. I don't know how to stop her from gouging the seat covers. This one tear-hole particularly has a use in her play. What does it mean to her? Someone said to me, "Kittens have such imaginations. They think they're in the jungle!" Is that it? Are you thrashing through the Amazon brush chasing enemies? Milena, you have your toy, you have that rubber ball with chimes inside. But to you, all the world is your plaything.

Milena can do all kinds of tricks. She can tear a paper towel into shreds and strew it over the apartment. She can stand on her hind legs and turn on the lamp. It's the truth.

When I go into the bathroom she likes to come in with me. Even when I shut the door she manages to squeeze inside. She crawls into her cat box and inspects the gravel surface, then sifts through to see if the droppings are still there. They're her property, her valuables in the safe-deposit box. You're like a rich old dowager, Milena, with your orange-and-white mink coat and your jewels.

Then I come out of the bathroom with my robe on and she starts squeaking. She wants to eat! Take your time, you'll get it. She's so eager that she doesn't let me scoop out all her canned food. She gets in the way so that I can't even put the rest on her plate — a clump of it drops on her head. You see that? If you'd only let me . . .

Now the cat is quiet. She has gotten what she wants to eat, her tuna. She sits in a pool of sun. The days are getting shorter and shorter. Winter is coming, Milena, I explain to her.

12

Against Joie de Vivre

OVER THE YEARS I HAVE DEVELOPED A DISTASTE for the spectacle of *joie de vivre*, the knack of knowing how to live. Not that I disapprove of all hearty enjoyment of life. A flushed sense of happiness can overtake a person anywhere, and one is no more to blame for it than the Asiatic flu or a sudden benevolent change in the weather (which is often joy's immediate cause). No, what rankles me is the stylization of this private condition into a bullying social ritual.

The French, who have elevated the picnic to their highest rite, are probably most responsible for promoting this smugly upbeat, flaunting style. It took the French genius for formalizing the informal to bring sticky sacramental sanctity to the baguette, wine, and cheese. A pure image of sleeveless *joie de vivre* Sundays can also be found in Renoir's paintings. Weekend satyrs dance and wink; leisure takes on a bohemian stripe. A decent writer, Henry Miller, caught the French malady and ran back to tell us of *pissoirs* in the Paris streets (why this should have impressed him so, I've never figured out).

But if you want a double dose of *joie de vivre*, you need to consult a later, hence more stylized, version of the French myth of pagan happiness: those *Family of Man* photographs of endlessly kissing lovers, snapped by Doisneau and Boubat, or Cartier-Bresson's icon of the proud tyke carrying bottles of wine. If Cartier-Bresson and his disciples are excellent photographers for all that, it is in spite of their occasionally rubbing our noses in a tediously problematic "affirmation of life."

Though it is traditionally the province of the French, the whole Mediterranean is a hotbed of professional *joie de vivrism*, which they have gotten down to a routine like a crack *son et lumière* display. The Italians export *dolce far niente* as aggressively as tomato paste. For the Greeks, a Zorba dance to life has supplanted classical antiquities as their main touristic lure. Hard to imagine anything as stomach-turning as being forced to participate in such an oppressively robust, folknik effusion. Fortunately, the country has its share of thin, nervous, bitter types, but Greeks do exist who would clutch you to their joyfully stout bellies and crush you there. The *joie de vivrist* is an incorrigible missionary who presumes that everyone wants to express pro-life feelings in the same stereotyped manner.

A warning: since I myself have a large store of nervous discontent (some would say hostility), I am apt to be harsh in my secret judgments of others, seeing them as defective because they are not enough like me. From moment to moment, the person I am with often seems too shrill, too bland, too something-or-other to allow my own expansiveness to swing into stage center. "Feeling no need to drink, you will promptly despise a drunkard" (Kenneth Burke). So it goes with me, which is why I am not a literary critic. I have no faith that my discriminations in taste are anything but the picky awareness of what will keep me stimulated, based on the peculiar family and class circumstances that formed me. But the knowledge that my discriminations are skewed and not always universally desirable doesn't stop me in the least from making them, just as one never gives up a negative first impression, no matter how many times it is contradicted. A believer in astrology (to cite another false system), having guessed that someone is a Sagittarius, and then told he is a Scorpio, says "Scorpio—yes, of course!" without missing a beat, or relinquishing confidence in his ability to tell people's signs, or in his idea that the person is somehow secretly Sagittarian.

1. The Houseboat

I remember exactly when my dislike for *joie de vivre* began to crystallize. It was 1969. We had gone to visit an old Greek painter on his houseboat in Sausalito. Old Vartas's vitality was legendary, and it was considered a spiritual honor to meet him, like getting an audience with the pope. Each Sunday he had a sort of open house, or open boat.

My "sponsor," Frank, had been many times to the houseboat, furnishing Vartas with record albums, since the old painter had a passion for San Francisco rock bands. Frank told me that Vartas had been a pal of Henry Miller's, and I, being a writer of Russian descent, would love him. I failed to grasp the syllogism, but, putting aside my instinct to dislike anybody I have been assured I will adore, I prepared myself to give the man a chance.

Greeting us on the gangplank was an old man with thick, lush, white hair and snowy eyebrows, his face reddened from the sun. As he took us into the houseboat cabin he told me proudly that he was seventy-seven years old, and gestured toward the paintings that were spaced a few feet apart on the floor, leaning against the wall. They were celebrations of the blue Aegean, boats moored in ports, whitewashed houses on a hill, painted in primary colors and decorated with collaged materials: mirrors, burlap, Life Saver candies. These sunny little canvases with their talented innocence, third-generation spirit of Montmartre, bore testimony to a love of life so unbending as to leave an impression of rigid narrow-mindedness as extreme as any Savonarola's. Their rejection of sorrow was total. They were the sort of festive paintings that sell at high-rent Madison Avenue galleries specializing in European *schlock*.

Then I became aware of three young, beautiful women, bare-shouldered, wearing white pajama pants, each with long blond hair falling onto a sky-blue halter— unmistakably suggesting the Three Graces. They lived with him on the houseboat, I was told, giving no one knew what compensation for their lodgings. Perhaps their only payment was to feed his vanity in front of outsiders. The Greek painter smiled with the air of an old fox around the trio. For their part, the women obligingly contributed their praises of Vartas's youthful zip, which of course was taken by some guests as double entendre for undiminished sexual prowess. The Three Graces also gathered the food offerings of the visitors to make a midday meal.

Then the boat, equipped with a sail, was launched to sea. I must admit it gave me a spoilsport's pleasure when the winds turned becalmed. We could not move. Aboard were several members of the Bay Area's French colony, who dangled their feet over the sides, passed around bunches of grapes, and sang what I imagined were Gallic camping songs. The French know boredom, so they would understand how to behave in such a situation. It has been my observation that many French men and women stationed in America have the attitude of taking it easy, slumming at a health resort, and nowhere more so than in California. The *émigré* crew included a securities analyst, an academic sociologist, a museum administrator and his wife, a modiste: on Vartas's boat, they all got drunk and carried on like redskins, noble savages off Tahiti.

Joie de vivre requires a *soupçon* of the primitive. But since the illusion of the primitive soon palls and has nowhere to go, it becomes necessary to make new initiates. A good part of the day, in fact, was taken up with regulars interpreting to first-timers like myself certain mores pertaining to the houseboat, as well as offering tidbits about Vartas's Rabelaisian views of life. Here everyone was encouraged to do what he willed. (How much could you do on a becalmed boat surrounded by strangers?) No one had much solid information about their host's past, which only increased the privileged status of those who knew at least one fact. Useless to ask the object of this venerating speculation, since Vartas said next to nothing (adding to his impressiveness) when he was around, and disappeared below for long stretches of time.

In the evening, after a communal dinner, the new Grateful Dead record Frank had brought was put on the phonograph, and Vartas danced, first by himself, then with all three Graces, bending his arms in broad, hooking sweeps. He stomped his foot and looked around scampishly at the guests for appreciation, not unlike an organ-grinder and his monkey. Imagine, if you will, a being whose generous bestowal of self-satisfaction invites and is willing to receive nothing but flattery in return, a person who has managed to make others buy his somewhat senile projection of indestructibility as a Hymn to Life. In no sense could he be called a charlatan; he delivered what he promised, an incarnation of *joie de vivre*, and if it was shallow, it was also effective, managing even to attract an enviable "harem" (which was what really burned me).

A few years passed.

Some Dutch TV crew, ever on the lookout for exotic bits of Americana that would make good short subjects, planned to do a documentary about Vartas as a sort of paean to eternal youth. I later learned from Frank that Vartas died before the shooting could be completed. A pity, in a way. The home movie I've run off in my head of the old man is getting a little tattered, the colors splotchy, and the scenario goes nowhere, lacks point. All I have for sure is the title: *The Man Who Gave* Joie de Vivre *a Bad Name*.

"Ah, what a twinkle in the eye the old man has! He'll outlive us all." So we speak of old people who bore us, when we wish to honor them. We often see projected onto old people this worship of the life force. It is not the fault of the old if they then turn around and try to exploit our misguided amazement at their longevity as though it were a personal tour de force. The elderly, when they are honest with themselves, realize they have done nothing particularly to be proud of in lasting to a ripe old age, and then carrying themselves through a thousand more days. Yet you still hear an old woman or man telling a bus driver with a chuckle, "Would you believe that I am eighty-four years old!" As though they should be patted on the back for still knowing how to talk, or as though they had pulled a practical joke on the other riders by staying so spry and mobile. Such insecure, wheedling behavior always embarrasses me. I will look away rather than meet the speaker's eyes and be forced to lie with a smile, "Yes, you are remarkable," which seems condescending on my part and humiliating to us both.

Like children forced to play the cute part adults expect of them, some old people must get confused trying to adapt to a social role of indeterminate standards, which is why they seem to whine: "I'm doing all right, aren't I—for my age?" It is interesting that society's two most powerless groups, children and the elderly, have both been made into sentimental symbols. In the child's little hungry hands grasping for life, joined to the old person's frail slipping fingers hanging on to it, you have one of the commonest advertising metaphors for intense appreciation. It is enough to show a young child sleeping in his or her grandparent's lap to procure *joie de vivre* overload.

2. The Dinner Party

I am invited periodically to dinner parties and brunches—and I go, because I like to be with people and oblige them, even if I secretly cannot share their optimism about these events. I go, not believing that I will have fun, but with the intent of observing people who think a *dinner party* a good time. I eat their fancy food, drink the wine, make my share of entertaining conversation, and often leave having had a pleasant evening, which does not prevent me from anticipating the next invitation with the same bleak lack of hope. To put it in a nutshell, I am an ingrate.

Although I have traveled a long way from my proletarian origins and talk, dress, act, and spend money like a perfect little bourgeois, I hold on to my poor-boy's outrage at the "decadence" (meaning dull entertainment style) of the middle and upper-middle classes; or, like a model Soviet moviegoer watching scenes of prerevolutionary capitalists gorging themselves on caviar, I am appalled, but I dig in with the rest.

Perhaps my uneasiness with dinner parties comes from the simple fact that not a single dinner party was given by my solitudinous parents the whole time I was growing up, and I had to wait until my late twenties before learning the ritual. A spy in the enemy camp, I have made myself a patient observer of strange customs. For the benefit of other late-starting social climbers, this is what I have observed.

As everyone should know, the ritual of the dinner party begins away from the table. Usually in the living room, cheeses and walnuts are set out, to start the digestive juices flowing. Here introductions between strangers are also made. Most dinner parties contain at least a few guests who have been unknown to each other before that evening, but who the host and/or hostess envision would enjoy meeting. These novel pairings and their interactions add spice to the postmortem: Who got along with whom? The lack of prior acquaintanceship also ensures that the guests will have to rely on and go through the only people known to everyone, the host and hostess, whose absorption of this helplessly dependent attention is one of the main reasons for throwing dinner parties.

Although an after-work "leisure activity," the dinner party is in fact a celebration of professional identity. Each of the guests has been preselected as in a floral bouquet; and in certain developed forms of this ritual there is usually a cunning mix of professions. Yet the point is finally not so much diversity as commonality; what remarkably shared attitudes and interests these people from different vocations demonstrate by conversing intelligently, or at least glibly, on the topics that arise. Naturally, a person cannot discourse too technically about one's line of work, so he or she picks precisely those themes that invite overlap. The psychiatrist laments the new breed of egoless, narcissistic patient who keeps turning up in his office (a beach bum who lacks the work ethic); the college professor bemoans the shoddy intellectual backgrounds and self-centered ignorance of his students; and the bookseller parodies the customer who pronounced Sophocles to rhyme with "bifocals." The dinner party is thus an exercise in locating ignorance—elsewhere. Whoever is present is *ipso facto* part of that beleaguered remnant of civilized folk fast disappearing from earth.

Or think of a dinner party as a club of revolutionaries, a technocratic elite whose social interactions that night are a dry run for some future takeover of the state. These are the future cabinet members (now only a shadow cabinet, alas) meeting to practice for the first time. How well they get on! "The time will soon be ripe, my friends. . . ." If this is too fanciful for you, then compare the dinner party to a utopian community, a Brook Farm supper club, in which only the best and most useful community members are chosen to participate. The smugness begins as soon as one enters the door, since one is already part of the chosen few. And from then on, every mechanical step in dinner-party process is designed to augment the atmosphere of group *amour propre*. This is not to say that there won't be one or two people in an absolute torment of exclusion, too shy to speak up, or suspecting that when they do their contributions fail to carry the same weight as those of the others. The group's all-purpose drone of self-contentment ignores these drowning people—cruelly inattentive in one sense but benign in another: it invites them to join the shared ethos of success any time they are ready.

The group is asked to repair to the table. Once again they find themselves marveling at a shared perception of life. How delicious the fish soup! How cute the stuffed tomatoes! What did you use in this green sauce? Now comes much talk of ingredients, and credit is given where credit is due. It is Jacques who made the salad. It was Mamie who brought the homemade bread. Everyone pleads with the hostess to sit down, not to work so hard—an empty formula whose hypocrisy bothers no one. Who else is going to put the butter dish on the table? For a moment all become quiet, except for the sounds of eating. This corresponds to the part in a church service that calls for silent prayer.

I am saved from such culinary paganism by the fact that food is largely an indifferent matter to me. I rarely think much about what I am putting in my mouth. Though my savage, illiterate plate has inevitably been educated to some degree by the many meals I have shared with people who care enormously about such things, I resist going any further. I am superstitious that the day I send back a dish at a restaurant, or make a complicated journey somewhere just for a meal, that day I will have sacrificed my freedom and traded in my soul for a lesser god.

I don't expect the reader to agree with me. That's not the point. Unlike the behavior called for at a dinner party, I am not obliged, sitting at my typewriter, to help procure consensus every moment. So I am at liberty to declare, to the friend who once told me that dinner parties were one of the only opportunities for intelligently convivial conversations to take place in this cold, fragmented city, that she is crazy. The conversation at dinner parties is of a mind-numbing caliber. No discussion of any clarifying rigor—be it political, spiritual, artistic, or financial—can take place in a context where fervent conviction of any kind is frowned upon, and the desire to follow through a sequence of ideas must give way every time to the impressionistic, breezy flitting from topic to topic. Talk must be bubbly but not penetrating. Illumination would only slow the flow. Some hit-and-run remark may accidentally jog an idea loose, but in such cases it is better to scribble a few words down on the napkin for later than attempt to "think" at a dinner party.

What do people talk about at such gatherings? The latest movies, the priciness of things, word processors, restaurants, muggings and burglaries, private versus public schools, the fool in the White House (there have been so many fools in a row that this subject is getting tired), the undeserved reputations of certain better-known professionals in one's field, the fashions in investments, the investments in fashion. What is traded at the dinner-party table is, of course, class information. You will learn whether you are in the avant-garde or rear guard of your social class, or, preferably, right in step.

As for Serious Subjects, dinner-party guests have the latest *New Yorker* in-depth piece to bring up. People who ordinarily would not spare a moment worrying about the treatment of schizophrenics in mental hospitals, the fate of Great Britain in the Common Market, or the disposal of nuclear wastes suddenly find their consciences orchestrated in unison about these problems, thanks to their favorite periodical—though a month later they have forgotten all about it and are on to something new.

The dinner party is a suburban form of entertainment. Its spread in our big cities represents an insidious Fifth Column suburbanization of the metropolis. In the suburbs it becomes necessary to be able to discourse knowledgeably about the heart of the city, but from the viewpoint of a day-shopper. Dinner-party chatter is the communicative equivalent of roaming around shopping malls.

Much thought has gone into the ideal size for a dinner party—usually with the hostess arriving at the figure eight. Six would give each personality too much weight; ten would lead to splintering side discussions; eight is the largest number still able to force everyone into the same compulsively congenial conversation. My own strength as a conversationalist comes out less in groups of eight than one-to-one, which may explain my resistance to dinner parties. At the table, unfortunately, any engrossing *tête-à-tête* is frowned upon as antisocial. I often find myself in the frustrating situation of being drawn to several engaging people in among the bores, and wishing I could have a private conversation with each, without being able to do more than signal across the table a wry recognition of that fact. "Some other time, perhaps," we seem to be saying with our eyes, all evening long.

Later, however—to give the devil his due—when guests and hosts retire from the table back to the living room, the strict demands of group participation may be relaxed, and individuals allowed to pair off in some form of conversational intimacy. But one must be ever on the lookout for the group's need to swoop everybody together again for one last demonstration of collective fealty.

The first to leave breaks the communal spell. There is a sudden rush to the coat closet, the bathroom, the bedroom, as others, under the protection of the first defector's original sin, quit the Party apologetically. The utopian dream has collapsed: left behind are a few loyalists and insomniacs, swillers of a last cognac. "Don't leave yet," begs the host, knowing what a sense of letdown, pain, and self-recrimination awaits. Dirty dishes are, if anything, a comfort: the faucet's warm gush serves to stave off the moment of anesthetized stock-taking—Was that really necessary?—in the sobering silence that follows a dinner party.

3. Joie's Doppelgänger

I have no desire to rail against the Me Generation. We all know that the current epi-curean style of the Good Life, from light foods to running shoes, is a result of mar-ket research techniques developed to sell "spot" markets, and, as such, a natural out-growth of consumer capitalism. I may not like it, but I can't pretend that my objections are the result of a high-minded Laschian political analysis. Moreover, my own record of activism is not so noticeably impressive that I can lecture the Sunday brunchers to roll up their sleeves and start fighting social injustices instead of indulging themselves.

No, if I try to understand the reasons for my antihedonistic biases I must admit that they come from somewhere other than idealism. It's odd, because there seems to be a contradiction between the curmudgeonly feeling inside me and my periodi-cally strong appetite for life. I am reminded of my hero, William Hazlitt, with his sarcastic, grumpy disposition on the one hand, and his capacity for "gusto" (his word, not Schlitz's) on the other. With Hazlitt, one senses a fanatically tenacious defense of individuality and independence against some unnamed bully stalking him. He had trained himself to be a connoisseur of vitality, and got irritated when life was not filled to the brim. I am far less irritable—before others; I will laugh if there is the merest *anything* to laugh at. But it is a tense, pouncing pleasure, not one that will allow me to sink into undifferentiated relaxation. The prospect of a long day at the beach makes me panic. There is no harder work I can think of than tak-ing myself off to somewhere pleasant, where I am forced to stay for hours and "have fun." Taking it easy, watching my personality's borders loosen and dissolve, arouse an unpleasantly floating giddiness. I don't even like water beds. Fear of Freud's "oceanic feeling," I suppose—I distrust anything that will make me pause long enough to be put in touch with my helplessness.

The other repugnance I experience around *joie de vivrism* is that I associate its rit-uals with depression. All these people sitting around a pool, drinking margaritas—they're not really happy, they're depressed. Perhaps I am generalizing too much from my own despair in such situations. Drunk, sunbaked, stretched out in a beach chair, I am unable to ward off the sensation of being utterly alone, unconnected, cut off from the others.

An article in the Science section of the *Times* about depression (they seem to run one every few months) described the illness as a pattern of "learned helplessness." Dr. Martin Seligman of the University of Pennsylvania described his series of experiments: "At first mild electrical shocks were given to dogs, from which they were unable to escape. In a second set of experiments, dogs were given shocks from which they could escape—but they didn't try. They just lay there, passively accept-ing the pain. It seemed that the animals' inability to control their experiences had brought them to a state resembling clinical depression in humans."

Keep busy, I always say. At all costs avoid the trough of passivity, which leads to the Slough of Despond. Someone (a girlfriend, who else?) once accused me of being intolerant of the depressed way of looking at the world, which had its own intelligence and moral integrity, both obviously unavailable to me. It's true. I don't like the smell of depression (it has a smell, a very distinct one, something fetid like morning odors), and I stay away from depressed characters whenever possible. Except when they happen to be my closest friends or family members. It goes without saying that I am also, for all my squeamishness, attracted to depressed people, since they seem to know something I don't. I wouldn't rule out the possibility that the brown-gray logic of depression *is* the truth. In another experiment (also reported in the *Times's* Science section), pitting "optimists" against clinically diagnosed "depressives" on their self-perceived abilities to effect outcomes according to their wills, researchers tentatively concluded that depressed people may have a more realistic, clear-sighted view of the world.

Nevertheless, what I don't like about depressives sometimes is their chummy I-told-you-so smugness, like Woody Allen fans who treat anhedonia as a vanguard position.

And for all that, depressives make the most rabid converts to *joie de vivre*. The reason for this is that *joie de vivre* and depression are not opposites but relatives of the same family, practically twins. When I see *joie de vivre* rituals, I always notice, like a TV ghost, depression right alongside it. I knew a man, dominated by a powerful father, who thought he had come out of a long depression occasioned, in his mind, by his divorce. Whenever I met him he would say that his life was getting better and better. Now he could run long distances, he was putting healthy food into his system, he was more physically fit at forty than he had been at twenty-five; now he had dates, he was going out with three different women, he had a good therapist, he was looking forward to renting a bungalow in better woods than the previous summer. . . . I don't know whether it was his tone of voice when he said this, his sagging shoulders, or what, but I always had an urge to burst into tears. If only he had admitted he was miserable I could have consoled him outright instead of being embarrassed to notice the deep hurt in him, like a swallowed razor cutting him from inside. And his pain still stunk up the room like in the old days, that sour cabbage smell was in his running suit, yet he wouldn't let on, he thought the smell was gone. The therapist had told him to forgive himself, and he had gone ahead and done it, the poor *schnook*. But tell me: Why would anyone need such a stylized, disciplined regimen of enjoyment if he were not depressed?

4. In the Here and Now

The argument of both the hedonist and the guru is that if we were but to open ourselves to the richness of the moment, to concentrate on the feast before us, we would be filled with bliss. I have lived in the present from time to time, and I can tell you that it is much overrated. Occasionally, as a holiday from stroking one's memories or brooding about future worries, I grant you, it can be a nice change of pace. But to "be here now," hour after hour, would never work. I don't even approve of stories written in the present tense. As for poets who never use a past participle, they deserve the eternity they are striving for.

Besides, the present has a way of intruding whether you like it or not. Why should I go out of my way to meet it? Let it splash on me from time to time, like a car going through a puddle, and I, on the sidewalk of my solitude, will salute it grimly like any other modern inconvenience.

If I attend a concert, obviously not to listen to the music but to find a brief breathing space in which to meditate on the past and future, I realize that there may be moments when the music invades my ears and I am forced to pay attention to it, note after note. I believe I take such intrusions gracefully. The present is not always an unwelcome guest, so long as it doesn't stay too long and cut into my remembering or brooding time.

Even for survival, it's not necessary to focus one's full attention on the present. The instincts of a pedestrian crossing the street in a reverie will usually suffice. Alertness is all right as long as it is not treated as a promissory note on happiness. Anyone who recommends attention to the moment as a prescription for grateful wonder is telling only half the truth. To be happy one must pay attention, but to be unhappy one must also have paid attention.

Attention, at best, is a form of prayer. Conversely, as Simone Weil said, prayer is a way of focusing attention. All religions recognize this when they ask their worshipers to repeat the name of their God, a devotional practice that draws the practitioner into a trancelike awareness of the present, and the objects around oneself. With one part of the soul one praises God, and with the other part one expresses a hunger, a dissatisfaction, a desire for more spiritual contact. Praise must never stray too far from longing, that longing which takes us implicitly beyond the present.

I was about to say that the very act of attention implies longing, but this is not necessarily true. Attention is not always infused with desire; it can settle on us most placidly once desire has been momentarily satisfied, like after the sex act. There are also periods following overwork, when the exhausted slave-body is freed and the eyes dilate to register with awe the lights of the city; one is too tired to desire anything else.

Such moments are rare. They form the basis for a poetic appreciation of the beauty of the world. However, there seems no reliable way to invoke or prolong them. The rest of the time, when we are not being edgy or impatient, we are often simply *disappointed*, which amounts to a confession that the present is not good enough. People often try to hide their disappointment—just as Berryman's mother told him not to let people see that he was bored, because it suggested that he had no "inner resources." But there is something to be said for disappointment.

This least respected form of suffering, downgraded to a kind of petulance, at least accurately measures the distance between hope and reality. And it has its own peculiar satisfactions: Why else do we return years later to places where we had been happy, if not to savor the bittersweet pleasures of disappointment? "For as you well know: while a single disappointment may elicit tears, a repeated disappointment will evoke a smile" (Musil).

Moreover, disappointment is the flip side of a strong, predictive feeling for beauty or appropriate civility or decency: only those with a sense of order and harmony can be disappointed.

We are told that to be disappointed is immature, in that it presupposes unrealistic expectations, whereas the wise man meets each moment head-on without preconceptions, with freshness and detachment, grateful for anything it offers. However, this pernicious teaching ignores everything we know of the world. If we continue to expect what turns out to be not forthcoming, it is not because we are unworldly in our expectations, but because our very worldliness has taught us to demand of an unjust world that it behave a little more fairly. The least we can do, for instance, is to register the expectation that people in a stronger position be kind and not cruel to those in a weaker one, knowing all the while that we will probably be disappointed.

The truth is, most wisdom is embittering. The task of the wise person cannot be to pretend with false naïveté that every moment is new and unprecedented, but to bear the burden of bitterness that experience forces on us with as much uncomplaining dignity as strength will allow. Beyond that, all we can ask of ourselves is that bitterness not cancel out our capacity still to be surprised.

5. Making Love

If it is true that I have the tendency to withhold sympathy from those pleasures or experiences that fall outside my capabilities, the opposite is also true: I admire immoderately those things I cannot do. I've always gone out with women who swam better than I did. It's as if I were asking them to teach me how to make love. Though I know how to make love (more or less), I have never fully shaken that adolescent boy's insecurity that there was more to it than I could ever imagine, and that I needed a full-time instructress. For my first sexual experiences, in fact, I chose older women. Later, when I slept with women my own age and younger, I still tended to take the stylistic lead from them, adapting myself to each one's rhythm and ardor, not only because I wanted to be "responsive," but because I secretly thought that women—any woman—understood lovemaking in a way that I did not. In bed I came to them as a student, and I have made them pay later, in other ways, for letting them see me thus. Sex has always been so impromptu, so out of my control, so different each time, that even when I became the confident bull in bed I was dismayed by this sudden power, itself a form of powerlessness because so unpredictable.

Something Michel Leiris wrote in his book *Manhood* has always stuck with me: "It has been some time, in any case, since I have ceased to consider the sexual act as a simple matter, but rather as a relatively exceptional act, necessitating certain inner accommodations that are either particularly tragic or particularly exalted, but very different, in either case, from what I regard as my usual disposition."

The transformation from a preoccupied urban intellectual to a sexual animal involves, at times, an almost superhuman strain. To find in one's bed a living, undulating woman of God knows what capacities and secret desires may seem too high, too formal, too ridiculous or blissful an occasion—even without the shock to an undernourished heart like mine of an injection of undiluted affection, if the woman proves loving as well.

Most often, I simply do what the flood allows me to, improvising here or there like a man tying a white flag to a raft that is being swiftly swept along, a plea for love or forgiveness. But as for artistry, control, enslavement through my penis, that's someone else. Which is not to say that there weren't women who were perfectly happy with me as a lover. In those cases, there was some love between us outside of bed: the intimacy was much more intense because we had something big to say to each other before we ever took off our clothes, but which could now be said only with our bodies.

With other women, whom I cared less about, I was sometimes a dud. I am not one of those men who can force themselves to make love passionately or athletically when their affections are not engaged. From the perplexity of wide variations in my experiences I have been able to tell myself that I am neither a good nor a bad lover, but one who responds differently according to the emotions present. A banal conclusion; maybe a true one.

It does not do away, however, with some need to have my remaining insecurities about sexual ability laid to rest. I begin to suspect that all my fancy distrust of hedonism comes down to a fear of being judged in this one category: Do I make love well? Every brie and wine picnic, every tanned body relaxing on the beach, every celebration of *joie de vivre* carries a sly wink of some missed sexual enlightenment that may be too threatening to me. I am like the prudish old maid who blushes behind her packages when she sees sexy young people kissing.

When I was twenty I married. My wife was the second woman I had ever slept with. Our marriage was the recognition that we suited one another remarkably well as company—could walk and talk and share insights all day, work side by side like Chinese peasants, read silently together like graduate students, tease each other like brother and sister, and when at night we found our bodies tired, pull the covers over ourselves and become lovers. She was two years older than I, but I was good at faking maturity; and I found her so companionable and trustworthy and able to take care of me that I could not let such a gold mine go by.

Our love life was mild and regular. There was a sweetness to sex, as befitted domesticity. Out of the surplus energy of late afternoons I would find myself coming up behind her sometimes as she worked in the kitchen, taking her away from her involvements, leading her by the hand into the bedroom. I would unbutton her blouse. I would stroke her breasts, and she would get a look in her eyes of quiet intermittent hunger, like a German shepherd being petted; she would seem to listen far off; absent-mindedly daydreaming, she would return my petting, stroke my arm with distracted patience like a mother who has something on the stove, trying to calm her weeping child. I would listen, too, to guess what she might be hearing, bird calls or steam heat. The enlargement of her nipples under my fingers fascinated me. Goose bumps either rose on her skin where I touched or didn't, I noted with scientific interest, a moment before getting carried away by my own eagerness. Then we were undressing, she was doing something in the bathroom, and I was waiting on the bed, with all the consciousness of a sun-mote. I was large and ready, the proud husband, waiting to receive my treasure. . . .

I remember our favorite position was with her on top, me on the bottom, upthrusting and receiving. Distraction, absentmindedness, return, calm exploration marked our sensual life. To be forgetful seemed the highest grace. We often achieved perfection.

Then I became haunted with images of seductive, heartless cunts. It was the era of the miniskirt, girl-women, Rudi Gernreich bikinis and Tiger Morse underwear, see-through blouses, flashes of flesh that invited the hand to go creeping under and into costumes. I wanted my wife to be more glamorous. We would go shopping for dresses together, she would complain that her legs were wrong for the new fashions. Or she would come home proudly with a bargain pink and blue felt minidress, bought for three dollars at a discount store, which my aching heart would tell me missed the point completely.

She, too, became dissatisfied with the absence of furtive excitement in our marriage. She wanted to seduce me, like a stranger on a plane. But I was too easy, so we ended up seducing others. Then we turned back to each other and with one last desperate attempt, before the marriage fell to pieces, each sought in the other a plasticity of sensual forms, like the statuary in an Indian temple. In our lovemaking I tried to believe that the body of one woman was the body of all women; all I achieved was a groping to distance lovingly familiar forms into those of anonymous erotic succubi. The height of this insanity, I remember, was one evening in the park when I pounded my wife's lips with kisses in an effort to provoke something between us like "hot passion." My eyes closed, I practiced a repertoire of French tongue-kisses on her. I shall never forget her frightened silent appeal that I stop, because I had turned into someone she no longer recognized.

But we were young, and so, dependent on each other, like orphans. By the time I left, at twenty-five, I knew I had been a fool, and had ruined everything, but I had to continue being a fool because it had been my odd misfortune to have stumbled onto kindness and tranquillity too quickly.

I moved to California in search of an earthly sexual paradise, and that year I tried hardest to make my peace with *joie de vivre*. I was sick but didn't know it—a diseased animal, Nietzsche would say. I hung around Berkeley's campus, stared up at the

Campanile tower; I sat on the grass watching coeds younger than I and, pretending that I was still going to university (no deeper sense of being a fraud obtainable), I tried to grasp the rhythms of carefree youth; I blended in at rallies, I stood at the fringes of be-ins, watching new rituals of communal love, someone being passed through the air hand to hand. But I never "trusted the group" enough to let myself be the guinea pig; or if I did, it was only with the proud stubborn conviction that nothing could change me—though I also wanted to change. Swearing I would never learn transcendence, I hitchhiked and climbed mountains. I went to wine-tasting festivals and accepted the wine jug from hippie gypsies in a circle around a beach campfire without first wiping off the lip. I registered for a Free School course in human sexual response just to get laid, and when that worked, I was shocked, and took up with someone else. There were many women in those years who got naked with me. I smoked grass with them, and as a sign of faith I took psychedelic drugs; we made love in bushes and beach houses, as though hacking through jungles with machetes to stay in touch with our ecstatic genitals while our minds soared off into natural marvels. Such experiences taught me, I will admit, how much romantic feeling can transform the body whose nerve tendrils are receptive to it. Technicolor fantasies of one girlfriend as a senorita with flowers in her impossibly wavy hair would suddenly pitch and roll beneath me, and the bliss of touching her naked suntanned breast and the damp black pubic hairs was too unthinkably perfect to elicit anything but abject gratitude. At such moments I have held the world in my hands and known it. I was coming home to the body of Woman, those globes and grasses that had launched me. In the childish fantasy accompanying one sexual climax, under LSD, I was hitting a home run and the Stars and Stripes flying in the background of my mind's eye as I "slid into home" acclaimed the patriotic rightness of my seminal release. For once I had no guilt about how or when I ejaculated.

If afterward, when we came down, there was often a sour air of disenchantment and mutual prostitution, that does not take away from the legacy, the rapture of those moments. If I no longer use drugs—in fact, have become somewhat antidrug—I think I still owe them something for showing me how to recognize the all-embracing reflex. At first I needed drugs to teach me about the stupendousness of sex. Later, without them, there would be situations—after a lovely talk or coming home from a party in a taxi—when I would be overcome by amorous tropism toward the woman with me. The appetite for flesh that comes over me at such moments, and the pleasure there is in finally satisfying it, seems so just that I always think I have stumbled into a state of blessed grace. That it can never last, that it is a trick of the mind and the blood, are rumors I push out of sight.

To know rapture is to have one's whole life poisoned. If you will forgive a ridiculous analogy, a tincture of rapture is like a red bandana in the laundry that runs and turns all the white wash pink. We should just as soon stay away from any future ecstatic experiences that spoil everyday living by comparison. Not that I have any intention of stopping. Still, if I will have nothing to do with religious mysticism, it is probably because I sense a susceptibility in that direction. Poetry is also dangerous; all quickening awakenings to Being extract a price later.

Are there people who live under such spells all the time? Was this the secret of the idiotic smile on the half-moon face of the painter Vartas? The lovers of life, the robust Cellinis, the Casanovas? Is there a technique to hedonism that will allow the term of rapture to be indefinitely extended? I don't believe it. The hedonist's despair is still that he is forced to make do with the present. Who knows about the success rate of religious mystics? In any case, I could not bring myself to state that what I am waiting for is God. Such a statement would sound too grandiose and presumptuous, and make too great a rupture in my customary thinking. But I can identify with the pre- if not the post-stage of what Simone Weil describes:

"The soul knows for certain only that it is hungry. The important thing is that it announces its hungry by crying. A child does not stop crying if we suggest to it that perhaps there is no bread. It goes on crying just the same. The danger is not lest the soul should doubt whether there is any bread, but lest, by a lie, it should persuade itself that it is not hungry."

So much for *joie de vivre*. It's too compensatory. I don't really know what I'm waiting for. I know only that until I have gained what I want from this life, my expressions of gratitude and joy will be restricted to variations of a hunter's alertness. I give thanks to a nip in the air that clarifies the scent. But I think it hypocritical to pretend satisfaction while I am still hungry.

— 13

The Brunch

I HAD BEEN INVITED TO A SUNDAY BRUNCH by an old friend of mine — I should say ex-lover — Jan, who wanted me to meet some of her friends. They were mostly politically engaged men and women. The women were all professionals, running day-care centers or getting advanced degrees. Some of them knew each other from being in the same Upper West Side women's group. There was lots of good food — omelets and bagels and whitefish and fruit salad and coffee and wine. By noon everyone was mildly drunk. Some of the guests were dancing to a rock 'n' roll record. I sat on a couch talking to a woman named Betsy who was going to social-work school, who had brought her little daughter, and who incidentally, I knew, had been an off-and-on lover of the hostess, when my friend Jan had decided to take lovers of her own sex. I hadn't been very comfortable with that period in Jan's life; but I had to admit that I was more disturbed by the thought of Jan's changing than by the tangible person next to me, Betsy, who looked so trustworthy. Betsy clearly wanted to talk to me, and there was nothing in her manner that seemed hostile to men. She was very open, pretty in a maternal, buxom way; and if I hadn't known she was otherwise inclined I might have made a pass at her.

Her little daughter began climbing around her lap and demanding her attention. Betsy ignored her at first, or stroked her hair while trying to ignore her. I turned to the kid to find out what she wanted. "Oh, that's right," said Betsy, "you're very good with kids, aren't you?" The thought that I had a reputation for being good with children, because I was a successful teacher, froze me. I found myself having to overcome a distaste for this child. She was whimpering about something, but basically had nothing to say. Soon her mother went to the bathroom, leaving us alone. "What grade are you in?" I asked her. "First," she said. I began to play a kind of game with her, threatening to cook her in a pot if she wasn't careful. She challenged me to do it — she was delighted at the idea. "Cook me!" she said. I grabbed her up and took her into the kitchen, where Jan was clearing away a few things. "We're going to put her in the stew," I said. "Oh, very good," said Jan, immediately falling into step. "Where's the seasoning?" "The spices are on the second shelf." I was still holding the girl in my arms, and by this time I noticed she was becoming a bit frightened. I reached for the basil and sprinkled a little on her stomach. "No!" she said, squirming to brush it off. "How about some cinnamon?" I asked. I took down the jar of cinnamon, and — this is the part I will never understand about me — poured some on her face, even though I guessed she would hate it. She began to cry. "Oh, what's the *matter?*" said Jan, taking the girl from me. "She must have gotten some in her eye . . . I was aiming at her nose," I said. "I know," said Jan; "some of it accidentally must have gotten in her eye. Poor baby!" At this, the girl began to cry twice as hard, and I thought to myself: Faker. If she was a well-brought-up child, she would know to be more stoical. She's just used to exploiting her mother's guilt as an only parent to get attention. We went back into the living room. "What happened?" asked her mother. "Oh, we were playing a game, and she started crying. . . . It's my fault," I said. Betsy apologized for her daughter and took her into the other room; and I thought it would be a long time before she said to me again, "You're so good with children."

_ 14

Modern Friendships

IS THERE ANYTHING LEFT TO SAY about friendship after so many great essay-
ists have picked over the bones of the subject? Probably not. Aristotle and Cicero,
Seneca and Montaigne, Bacon and Samuel Johnson, Hazlitt, Emerson, and Lamb
have all taken their cracks at it; since the ancients, friendship has been a sort of
examination subject for the personal essayist. It is partly the very existence of such
wonderful prior models that lures the newcomer to follow in the others' footsteps,
and partly a self-referential aspect of the genre, since the personal essay is itself an
attempt to establish a friendship on the page between writer and reader.

Friendship has been called "love without wings," implying a want of lyrical affla-
tus. On the other hand, the Stoic definition of love ("Love is the attempt to form a
friendship inspired by beauty") seems to suggest that friendship came first. Certainly a case can be made that the buildup of affection and the yearning for more
intimacy, without the release of sexual activity, keeps friends in a state of sweet-
sorrowful itchiness that has as much romantic quality as a love affair. We know that
a falling-out between two old friends can leave a deeper and more perplexing hurt
than the ending of a love affair, perhaps because we are more pessimistic about the
latter's endurance from the start.

Our first attempted friendships are within the family. It is here we practice the
techniques of listening sympathetically and proving that we can be trusted, and
learn the sort of kindness we can expect in return. I have a sister, one year younger
than I, who often took care of me when I was growing up. Once, when I was about
fifteen, unable to sleep and shivering uncontrollably with the start of a fever, I
decided in the middle of the night to go into her room and wake her. She held me,
performing the basic service of a friend—presence—and the chills went away.

There is something tainted about these family friendships, however. This same
sister, in her insecure adolescent phase, told me: "You love me because I'm related
to you, but if you were to meet me for the first time at a party, you'd think I was a
jerk and not worth being your friend." She had me in a bind: I had no way of testing her hypothesis. I should have argued that even if our bond was not freely cho-

sen, our decision to work on it had been. Still, we are quick to dismiss the partiality of our family members when they tell us we are talented, cute, or lovable; we must go out into the world and seduce others.

It is just a few short years from the promiscuity of the sandbox to the tormented, possessive feelings of a fifth grader who has just learned that his best and only friend is playing at another classmate's house after school. There may be worse betrayals in store, but probably none is more influential than the sudden fickleness of an elementary school friend who has dropped us for someone more popular after all our careful, patient wooing. Often we lose no time inflicting the same betrayal on someone else, just to ensure that we have got the victimization dynamic right.

What makes friendships in childhood and adolescence so poignant is that we need the chosen comrade to be everything in order to rescue us from the gothic inwardness of family life. Even if we are lucky enough to have several companions, there must be a Best Friend, knightly dubbed as though victor of an Arthurian tournament.

I clung to the romance of the Best Friend all through high school, college, and beyond, until my university circle began to disperse. At that point, in my mid-twenties, I also "acted out" the dark competitive side of friendship that can exist between two young men fighting for a place in life and love, by doing the one unforgivable thing: sleeping with my best friend's girl. I was baffled at first that there was no way to repair the damage. I lost this friendship forever, and came away from that debacle much more aware of the amount of injury that friendship can and cannot sustain. Perhaps I needed to prove to myself that friendship was not an all-permissive, resilient bond, like a mother's love, but something quite fragile. Precisely because Best Friendship promotes such a merging of identities, such seeming boundarylessness, the first major transgression of trust can cause the injured party to feel he is fighting for his violated soul against his darkest enemy. There is not much room to maneuver in a best friendship between unlimited intimacy and unlimited mistrust.

Still, it was not until the age of thirty that I reluctantly abandoned the Best Friend expectation and took up a more pluralistic model. At present, I cherish a dozen friends for their unique personalities, without asking that any one be my soul-twin. Whether this alteration constitutes a movement toward maturity or toward cowardly pragmatism is not for me to say. It may be that, in refusing to depend so much on any one friend, I am opting for self-protection over intimacy. Or it may be that, as we advance into middle age, the life problem becomes less that of establishing a tight dyadic bond and more one of making our way in a broader world, "society." Indeed, since Americans have so indistinct a notion of society, we often try to put friendship networks in its place. If a certain intensity is lost in the pluralistic model of friendship, there is also the gain of being able to experience all of one's potential, half-buried selves, through witnessing the spectacle of the multiple fates of our friends. Since we cannot be polygamists in our conjugal life, at least we can do so with friendship. As it happens, the harem of friends, so tantalizing a notion, often translates into feeling pulled in a dozen different directions, with the guilty sense of having disappointed everyone a little. It is also a risky, contrived enterprise to try to make one's friends behave in a friendly manner toward each other: if the effort fails one feels obliged to mediate; if it succeeds too well, one is jealous.

Whether friendship is intrinsically singular and exclusive, or plural and democratic, is a question that has vexed many commentators. Aristotle distinguished three types of friendship in *The Nicomachean Ethics*: "friendship based on utility," such as businessmen cultivating each other for benefit; "friendship based on pleasure," like young people interested in partying; and "perfect friendship." The first two categories Aristotle calls "qualified and superficial friendships," because they are founded on circumstances that could easily change; the last, which is based on admiration for another's good character, is more permanent, but also rarer, because good men "are few." Cicero, who wrote perhaps the best treatise on friendship, also insisted that what brings true friends together is "a mutual belief in each other's goodness." This insistence on virtue as a precondition for true friendship may strike us as impossibly demanding: who, after all, feels himself good nowadays? And yet, if I am honest, I must admit that the friendships of mine which have lasted longest have been with those whose integrity, or humanity, or strength to bear their troubles I continue to admire. Conversely, when I lost respect for someone, however winning he otherwise remained, the friendship petered away almost immediately. "Remove respect from friendship," said Cicero, "and you have taken away the most splendid ornament it possesses."

Montaigne distinguished between friendship, which he saw as a once-in-a-lifetime experience, and the calculating worldly alliances around him, which he thought unworthy of the name. In paying tribute to his late friend Etienne de la Boetie, Montaigne wrote: "Having so little time to last, and having begun so late, for we were both grown men, and he a few years older than I, it could not lose time and conform to the pattern of mild and regular friendships, which need so many precautions in the form of long preliminary association. Our friendship has no other model than itself, and can be compared only with itself. It is not one special consideration, nor two, nor three, nor four, nor a thousand: it is I know not what quintessence of all this mixture, which, having seized my whole will, led it to plunge and lose itself in his; which, having seized his whole will, led it to plunge and lose itself in mine, with equal hunger, equal rivalry. . . . So many coincidences are needed to build up such a friendship that it is a lot if fortune can do it once in three centuries." This seems a bit high hat: since the sixteenth century, our expectations of friendship may have grown more plebeian. Even Emerson, in his grand romantic essay on the subject, allowed as how he was not up to the Castor-and-Pollux standard: "I am not quite so strict in my terms, perhaps because I have never known so high a fellowship as others." Emerson contents himself with a circle of intelligent men and women, but warns us not to throw them together: "You shall have very useful and cheering discourse at several times with two several men, but let all three of you come together, and you shall not have one new and hearty word. Two may talk and one may hear, but three cannot take part in a conversation of the most sincere and searching sort."

Friendship is a long conversation. I suppose I could imagine a nonverbal friendship revolving around shared physical work or sport, but for me, good talk is the point of the thing. Indeed, the ability to generate conversation by the hour is the most promising indication, during its uncertain early stages, that a possible friendship will take hold. In the first few conversations there may be an exaggeration of agreement, as both parties angle for adhesive surfaces. But later on, trust builds through the courage to assert disagreement, through the tactful acceptance that differences of opinion will have to remain.

Some view like-mindedness as both the precondition and product of friendship. Myself, I distrust it. I have one friend who keeps assuming that we see the world eye-to-eye. She is intent on enrolling us in a flattering aristocracy of taste, on the short "we" list against the ignorant "they"; sometimes I do not have the strength to fight her need for consensus with my own stubborn disbelief in the existence of any such inner circle of privileged, cultivated sensibility. Perhaps I have too much invested in a view of myself as idiosyncratic to be eager to join any coterie, even a coterie of two. What attracts me to friends' conversation is the give-and-take, not necessarily that we come out at the same point.

"Our tastes and aims and views were identical—and that is where the essence of a friendship must always lie," wrote Cicero. To some extent, perhaps, but then the convergence must be natural, not, as Emerson put it, "a mush of concession. Better be a nettle in the side of your friend than his echo." And Francis Bacon observed that "the best preservative to keep the mind in health is the faithful admonition of a friend."

Friendship is a school for character, allowing us the chance to study in great detail and over time temperaments very different from our own. These charming quirks, these contradictions, these nobilities, these blind spots of our friends we track not out of disinterested curiosity: we must have this information before knowing how far we may relax our guard, how much we may rely on them in crises. The learning curve of friendship involves, to no small extent, filling out this picture of the other's limitations and making peace with the results. (With one's own limitations there may never be peace.) Each time I hit up against a friend's inflexibility I am relieved as well as disappointed: I can begin to predict, and arm myself in advance against repeated bruises. I have one friend who is always late, so I bring a book along when I am to meet her. If I give her a manuscript to read and she promises to look at it over the weekend, I start preparing myself for a month-long wait.

Not that one ever gives up trying to educate the friend to one's needs. I approach such matters experimentally: sometimes I will pride myself in tactfully circumventing the friend's predicted limitation, even if it means relinquishing all hope of getting the response I want; at other times I will confront a problem with intentional tactlessness, just to see if any change is still possible.

I have a dear old friend, Richard, who shies away from personal confidences. Years go by without my learning anything about his love life, and he does not encourage the baring of my soul either, much as I like that sort of thing. But we share so many other interests and values that that limitation seems easily borne, most of the time. Once, however, I found myself in a state of emotional despair; I told him I had exhausted my hopes of finding love or success, that I felt suicidal, and he changed the topic, patently embarrassed. I was annoyed both at his emotional rigidity and at my own stupidity—after all, I'd enough friends who ate up this kind of confessional talk, why foist on Richard what I might have predicted he couldn't, or wouldn't, handle? For a while I sulked, annoyed at him for having failed me, but I also began to see my despair through his eyes as melodramatic, childish petulance, and I began to let it go. As it happened, he found other ways during our visit to be so considerate that I ended up feeling better, even without our having had a heart-to-heart talk. I suppose the moral is that a friend can serve as a corrective to our insular miseries simply by offering up his essential otherness.

Though it is often said that with a true friend there is no need to hold anything back ("A friend is a person with whom I may be sincere. Before him I may think aloud," wrote Emerson), I have never found this to be entirely the case. Certain words may be too cruel if spoken at the wrong moment—or may fall on deaf ears, for any number of reasons. I also find with each friend, as they must with me, that some initial resistance, restlessness, psychic weather must be overcome before that tender ideal attentiveness may be called forth.

I have a good friend, Charlie, who is often very distracted whenever we first get together. If we are sitting in a cafe he will look around constantly for the waiter, or be distracted by a pretty woman or the restaurant's cat. It would be foolish for me to broach an important subject at such moments, so I resign myself to waiting the half hour or however long it takes until his jumpiness subsides. Or else I draw this pattern grumpily to his attention. Once he has settled down, however, I can tell Charlie virtually anything, and he me. But the candor cannot be rushed. It must be built up to with the verbal equivalent of limbering exercises.

The Friendship Scene—a flow of shared confidences, recognitions, humor, advice, speculation, even wisdom—is one of the key elements of modern friendships. Compared to the rest of life, this ability to lavish one's best energies on an activity utterly divorced from the profit motive and free from the routines of domination and inequality that affect most relations (including, perhaps, the selfsame friendship at other times) seems idyllic. The Friendship Scene is by its nature not an everyday occurrence. It represents the pinnacle, the fruit of the friendship, potentially ever-present but not always arrived at. Both friends' dim yet self-conscious awareness that they are wandering conversationally toward a goal that they have previously accomplished but which may elude them this time around creates a tension, an obligation to communicate as sincerely as possible, like actors in an improvisation exercise struggling to shape their baggy material into some climactic form. This very pressure to achieve "quality" communication may induce a sort of inauthentic epiphany, not unlike what happens sometimes in the last ten minutes of a psychotherapy session. But a truly achieved Friendship Scene can be among the best experiences life has to offer.

I remember one such afternoon when Michael, a close writer friend, and I met at a cafeteria on a balmy Saturday in early spring and talked for three and a half hours. There were no outside time pressures that particular afternoon, a rare occurrence for either of us. At first we caught up with our latest business, the sort of items that might have gone into a biweekly bulletin sent to any number of acquaintances. Then gradually we settled into an area of perplexing unresolved impressions. I would tell Michael about A's chance, seemingly hostile remark toward me at a gathering, and he would report that the normally ebullient B looked secretly depressed. These were the memory equivalents of food grains stuck in our teeth, which we were now trying to free with our tongues: anecdotal fragments I was not even sure had any point, until I started fashioning them aloud for Michael's interest. Together we diagnosed our mutual acquaintances, each other's character, and, from there, the way of the world. In the course of our free associations we eventually descended into what was really bothering us. I learned he was preoccupied with the fate of an old college friend who was dying of AIDS; he, that my father was in poor health and needed two operations. We had touched bottom—mortality—and it was reassuring to settle there awhile. Gradually we rose again, drawn back to the questions of ego and career, craft and romance. It was, as I've said, a pretty day, and we ended up walking through a new mall in Houston, gawking at the window displays of that bland emporium with a reawakened curiosity about the consumer treats of America, our attentions turned happily outward now that we had dwelt long enough in the shared privacies of our psyches.

Contemporary urban life, with its tight schedules and crowded appointment books, has helped to shape modern friendship into something requiring a good deal of intentionality and pursuit. You phone a friend and make a date a week or more in advance; then you set aside an evening, like a tryst, during which to squeeze in all your news and advice, confession and opinion. Such intimate compression may add a romantic note to modern friendships, but it also places a strain on the meeting to yield a high quality of meaning and satisfaction, closer to art than life, thereby increasing the chance for disappointment. If I see certain busy or out-of-town friends only once every six months, we must not only catch up on our lives but convince ourselves within the allotted two hours together that we still share a special affinity, an inner track to each other's psyches, or the next meeting may be put off for years. Surely there must be another, saner rhythm to friendship in rural areas— or maybe not? I think about "the good old days" when friends would go on walking tours through England together, when Edith Wharton would bundle poor Henry James into her motorcar and they'd drive to the South of France for a month.

I'm not sure my friendships could sustain the strain of travel for weeks at a time, and the truth of the matter is that I've gotten used to this urban arrangement of serial friendship "dates," where the pleasure of the rendezvous is enhanced by the knowledge that it will only last, at most, six hours. If the two of us don't happen to mesh that day (always a possibility)—well it's only a few hours; and if it should go beautifully, one needs an escape hatch from exaltation as well as disenchantment. I am capable of only so much intense, exciting communication before I start to fade; I come to these encounters equipped with a six-hour oxygen tank. Is this an evolutionary pattern of modern friendship, or only a personal limitation?

Perhaps because I conceive of the modern Friendship Scene as a somewhat theatrical enterprise, a one-act play, I tend to be very affected by the "set," so to speak. A restaurant, a museum, a walk in the park through the zoo, even accompanying a friend on shopping errands—I prefer public turf where the stimulation of the city can play a backdrop to our dialogue, feeding it with details when inspiration flags. True, some of the most cherished friendship scenes have occurred around a friend's kitchen table. The problem with restricting the date to one another's houses is that the entertaining friend may be unable to stop playing the host, or may sink too passively into his or her surroundings. Subtle struggles may also develop over which domicile should serve as the venue.

I have a number of chez moi friends, friends who always invite me to come to their homes while evading offers to visit mine. What they view as hospitality I see as a need to control the mise-en-scène of friendship. I am expected to fit in where they are mostly comfortable, while they play lord of the manor, distracted by the props of decor, the pool, the unexpected phone call, the swirl of children, animals, and neighbors. Indeed, chez moi friends often tend to keep a sort of open house, so that in going over to them—for a tête-à-tête, I had assumed—I will suddenly find the other friends and neighbors, whom they have also invited, dropping in all afternoon. There are only so many Sundays I care to spend hanging out with a friend's entourage before becoming impatient for a private audience.

Married friends who own their own homes are much more apt to try to draw me into their domestic fold, whereas single people are often more sensitive about establishing a discreet space for the friendship to occur. Perhaps the married assume that a bachelor like myself is desperate for home cooking and a little family life. I have noticed that it is not an easy matter to pry a married friend away from mate and milieu. For married people, especially those with children, the home often becomes the wellspring of all their nurturing feelings, and the single friend is invited to partake in the general flow. Maybe there is also a certain tendency on their parts to kill two birds with one stone: they don't see enough of their spouse and kids, and figure they can visit with you all at the same time. And maybe they need one-on-one friendship less, hampered as they are by responsibilities that no amount of camaraderie or discussion can change. Often friendship in these circumstances is not even a pairing, but a mixing together of two sets of parents and children willy-nilly.

What would the ancients say about this? In Rome, according to Bacon, "the whole senate dedicated an altar to Friendship, as to a goddess. . . ." From my standpoint, friendship is a jealous goddess. Whenever a friend of mine marries, I have to fight to overcome the feeling that I am being "replaced" by the spouse. I don't mind sharing a friend with his family milieu—in fact I like it, up to a point—but eventually I must get the friend alone, or else, as a bachelor at a distinct power disadvantage, I risk becoming a mere spectator of familial rituals instead of a key player in the drama of friendship.

A person living alone usually has more control over his or her schedule, hence more energy to give to friendship. If anything, the danger is of investing too much emotional energy in one's friends. When a single person is going through a romantic dry spell he or she often tries to extract the missing passion from a circle of friends. This works only up to a point: the frayed nerves of protracted celibacy can lead to hypersensitive imaginings of slights and rejections, during which times one's platonic friends seem to come particularly into the line of fire.

Today, with the partial decline of the nuclear family and the search for alternatives to it, we also see attempts to substitute the friendship web for intergenerational family life. Since psychoanalysis has alerted us to regard the family as a minefield of unrequited love, manipulation, and ambivalence, it is only natural that people may look to friendship as a more supportive ground for relation. But in our longing for an unequivocally positive bond, we should beware of sentimentalizing friendship, as saccharine "buddy" movies or certain feminist novels do, of neutering its problematic, destructive aspects. Besides, friendship can never substitute for the true meaning of family: if nothing else, it will never be able to duplicate the family's wild capacity for concentrating neurosis.

In short, friends can't be your family, they can't be lovers, they can't be your psychiatrists. But they can be your friends, which is plenty. For, as Cicero tells us, "friendship is the noblest and most delightful of all the gifts the gods have given to mankind." And Bacon adds: "it is a mere and miserable solitude to want true friends, without which the world is but a wilderness. . . ."

When I think about the qualities that characterize the best friendships I've known, I can identify five: rapport, affection, need, habit, and forgiveness. Rapport and affection can only take you so far; they may leave you at the formal, outer gate of goodwill, which is still not friendship. A persistent need for the other's company, for their interest, approval, opinion, will get you inside the gates, especially when it is reciprocated. In the end, however, there are no substitutes for habit and forgiveness. A friendship may travel for years on cozy habit. But it is a melancholy fact that unless you are a saint you are bound to offend every friend deeply at least once in the course of time. The friends I have kept the longest are those who forgave me for wronging them, unintentionally, intentionally, or by the plain catastrophe of my personality, time and again. There can be no friendship without forgiveness.

⌐ TEACHING AND WORK

_ 15

Hanging Out

from _Being with Children_

MRS. LOFTIN WAS SITTING in jeans and an embroidered smock on a corner couch, instructing two children in reading. I was not immediately sure whether she was the teacher or a school aide—she seemed rather subdued—but I looked around and there were no other adults in the room. I felt a kind of dryness or stillness, like a vacuum. Perhaps this vacuum made certain children extrasensitive to the stranger in their midst. A kid named Jamie engaged me right away in a conversation about monsters. He had some kind of speech impediment which made all his words difficult to understand but he spoke with such juicy enthusiasm that one got the point somehow. A girl named Karen, who was very emphatic, demanding of my attention, pushed Jamie out of the way and began telling me about the weirdoes in her neighborhood. Casually, children nearby started to gather around me patiently and ask my name, and I theirs. I never had to be introduced officially as the Poet. They made me feel welcome from the start—a reflection of their teacher's casual, accepting attitude.

As she walked around the room, checking on work assignments, Mrs. Loftin gave off a warm, steadying, calm vibration, which I can only describe as an inner hum. She was black with an Afro, a stunning figure, which was hard to ignore, and beautiful, high cheekbones. She moved through the school desks as if she were in her living room or had just gotten up from a nap. In her unhurried, well-rooted movements, there was a touch of the sleeper, but her eyes were actually very open; she never blinked.

I had the opportunity to witness a very curious transformation. Suddenly, without transition, she advanced to the blackboard, with her face set in determination, and began to teach a social-studies lesson on Transportation.

Everyone had to face front and pay attention to a trumped-up "class discussion" on fuel, which elicited the usual bottom-squirmings. "Juan, you especially need this," she snapped at a boy. Karen yelled out à propos of nothing in the discussion: "Oh look at that girl; she got a piece of paper stuck to her heinie!"—"Karen, I'm warning you; you watch yourself!" Under her threatening looks and stern disciplinary manner, it was still possible to feel Mrs. Loftin's warmth and easygoingness, but they had been absorbed by an impersonal, detached sense of Duty. It must have been Duty which prompted her to stage this very dull lesson. No one was really interested in the burgeoning list of transportation words taking over the blackboard; least of all herself, I suspect. Who was this list being made for?

Two days later I walk into the classroom to teach my first lesson and there is cheering and some applause. I've done nothing to earn this popularity but I like it. Three kids in front rush up to me; I start to introduce myself. "We know; you're the poet!" Somehow I realize that I am being watched carefully by the Spanish girls washing at the sink in back, by the various in and out groups, to see whom I will favor: the front desk, the whites, the blacks, the show-offs, the slow learners. One mistake in judgment and they will decide I am "not for them." For the time being, I am riding on a reserve tank of good will because I seem a novelty and a break from schoolwork. A real live poet—something I have to keep reminding myself I really am. The more I try to retain that notion, the more it slips from me. What is a poet supposed to act like?

Where does a poet stand in children's eyes? Not as high as an athlete, maybe above a teacher.

And now the teacher, Denise Loftin, comes forward to tell the class to give me their *full* attention. I wonder where I will locate myself: by her desk, in front of the blackboard, or somewhere completely unexpected. All these desks, these angles of vision, the stage feels wrong. Not my space. And it is the beginning of a struggle to build a comfortable space for myself in someone else's classroom. I start to talk about my background, how I came to be a writer, why I'm here—trying to sound natural. I'm conscious of being too tall: I want to bend in half to reach their level. I incline my head ostrich-like. I move around a lot. I read them a Yoruba poem about a monster God, with lines like:

Ogun has water but he washes in blood
Ogun is the needle that pricks at both ends
Ogun is the death who pursues a child until it runs into the bush
Ogun has four hundred wives & one thousand four hundred children
Ogun the fire that sweeps the forest
Ogun's laughter is no joke
Ogun eats two hundred earthworms & does not vomit.*

They like that part. Still, I sense their detachment: where is all this leading to? The teacher steps out to cover a disturbance in the hall. Side conversations begin . . . I'm

---

*In *Technicians of the Sacred*, anthology of poems edited by Jerome Rothenberg, Doubleday & Company, Inc., 1968, p. 164.

already losing some of my glamour! Then I pull it all together, WHAMMO, and before they know it I've sprung the assignment I had up my sleeve and yellow lined paper is being handed out. I write topics on the board. Boasts, Changing into a God or an Animal—ideas which don't particularly intrigue me (I wonder why I've started out so impersonally, with someone else's ideas), but you have to start somewhere.

I tell myself I want to get a sighting on their range of interests and writing abilities, though I am also thinking: They better be made to do some work the first time or they'll think I'm a pushover.

So the kids begin to learn the bitter truth, that this poet is merely another in a long series of adult foremen.

I bend down by the desk of one child who is having trouble, to explain the assignment and to help him. I feel relieved to be talking at eye level, one-to-one. Dolores, a provocative, cute-looking girl, keeps interrupting to show me her composition—"Don't let anyone see it!"—and covering it with elaborate gestures whenever anyone passes by. She has written a story about turning into a pig. I know she is testing me because of the line: "I leave shit all over the house." She asks me to read it aloud to the class and I say no, it's hers and she should read it aloud; if it embarrasses her, she should change it.

After a noisy public reading I collect the papers and promise to have them mimeoed by next week. Denise Loftin assures me it went well. "Usually they're *much* more distracted. They liked you." I don't know. I sensed they liked me before I opened my mouth, then I became just another salesman with a spiel to sell.

But I'm delighted I survived!

Over lunch, at the Eat Shop, Denise Loftin and I compared notes on different children. Her class seems skewed toward black and Spanish-speaking children, and I had noticed other classrooms which seemed to have a white, middle-class emphasis. Denise said the reason for this was that the parents were given a choice at the beginning of the year whether they wanted to place their children in an "open" or "more formal" classroom. The white, liberal parents of the Upper West Side tended to select open classrooms. The parents from ethnic minorities opted more for traditional classes, feeling that open education might be soft on basic skills at a time when their children needed a strong foundation in the three R's to crash through the racial barriers. The resulting class registers came out imbalanced. The school administration was caught between its commitment to integration, and its commitment to community control, which promised parents a greater say in the form of their children's education.

The ironic part was that these stereotyped categories were continually belied by the realities of the individual classrooms. I knew certain open classroom teachers who were quite inflexible and devoted to drill work. The only thing "open" about their classrooms was the clearing in the middle of the floor for the gerbil cages. On the other hand, someone like Denise, who listed herself as more formal, tended to be rather relaxed and broad-minded in spirit.

The white parents in her class had been up in arms, she admitted. They claimed their children were being held back academically by being placed with "slower learners" (euphemism for black and brown?). They wanted either to have their children transferred out of the class, or to trade five of Denise's non-whites for five whites in other classrooms. Denise thought such a trade was inevitable. She had already gotten attached to the class as it stood and thought the kids themselves could work out any difficulties among them, given more time. But the parents were insistent, and Mr. Jimenez, the principal, was eager to bring the crisis to an end.

I asked Denise if she thought her being black had anything to do with the parents' alarm.

"I don't think so. These parents aren't bigoted; they're just worried about their kids' safety. I don't really *blame* them. For instance, Janet's mother is a nice woman; I've known her a long time. She's afraid Janet will get into fights, or pick up street language from some of these kids—"

"But of course Janet already knows every word in the book."

"I wouldn't be too sure. Janet is *very* protected," said Denise.

I thought Denise was being uncommonly fair-minded and disinclined to cry "racism"—more than I would be in her shoes, probably.

Karen, one of Denise's students, handed me a story based on a conversation we had had the first day, and which I had asked her to write up. I could see she was proud of having finished it. The story is pretty harsh, especially when you consider that this is, at eleven years old, the way she sees life. Yet I couldn't help smiling a little at its gruesomeness.

The Lady Around My Block

Once upon a time there lived a lady around my block. She was not nice at all. She had to have a baby so one day she went to town to find herself a husband. She went all over town looking looking looking. So there was a man sitting on a step she said Mr. will you marry me so he was a fool to say yes. So then he went to court to ask could he get married and the court said yes. So when they got married she said give me a child so he did. When the child was born they was so happy when the child was two months old she nailed her on the wall. Happy days were over.

The End

It is almost a truism to observe that some of the most troubled, volatile children have enormous talent inside them. This seemed to be the case with Karen, if I could only find a way to work alone with her, or make her stop bullying the other children. Not a day went by that Karen didn't have two or three tantrums or fistfights; she was bidding hard for the title of class terror.

Karen conned me into overseeing her and two of her girlfriends, Stephanie and Gwen, practice a dance number in the Writing Room for some far-off auditorium performance. The three girls looked like budding Supremes as they went through their motions seriously, with studied arm rolls and hip twitches. I was enjoying the show, vaguely wondering what it had to do with my role as writing instructor but willing to chaperone. Unfortunately, Karen and Stephanie had a furious fight for the position of group leader while Gwen, the only real dancer of the three, watched with contempt. It turned rather ugly as Karen got impossibly bossy and short-tempered, and I had to take them back.

The second class went well enough, but I was still disturbed about the quality of attention, which declined after fifteen minutes. Of course I could figure out a way to condense everything I had to say into ten minutes, but that was no solution.

The classroom seemed spatially unsuited for holding a large group's attention. It was neither the old-fashioned arrangement of desks facing forward nor the free flow of the open classroom, but a loose confederation of tables. Each of the tables had a separate, social-club personality, with its own peer-group pressure. There were five or six of these large square tables placed at right angles to each other around the room, which meant that no matter where I stood I would always be facing a certain number of backs.

Some children made the courteous effort of turning their chairs around, but others simply continued to face their desks, their pencils, their inkwell, their dreams, their *assigned place*, and to keep their eyes lowered on the loose-leaf notebook, giving no indication whether they were listening or not.

I had the impression at times that I was a madman talking to a subway carful of indifferent travelers. Without that eye contact which registers the transfer of understanding, my own remarks struck me as a manic chain of desperate *non sequiturs*, a crazy plea for attention.

The table arrangement made it easy for the children to evade responsibility for participating and to dip in and out as neutral listeners without necessarily committing themselves to the enterprise. So long as they found me entertaining they would stick with me; otherwise they would change the channel.

I realized I had to find a way to get the students to accept their part in the lesson. They had to take more responsibility for the quality of the experience and stop relying on me as the sole performer. I would probably have to change my style of delivery to work in that space.

Perhaps my concern with the table arrangements was an alibi. I thought of that; but then the quickest way for me to get beyond an alibi to the real problems, whatever they might be, was to fuss with it until it stopped bothering me. By taking the alibi seriously and trying to eliminate it, I would find out the truth one way or the other.

The third time around I tried an experiment. I asked that only those children who wanted to work with me come to the back of the room. The rest could continue their work. A core group of ten arranged the chairs in a circle. With this volunteer structure no one would have an excuse for not paying attention; if he wasn't interested, he didn't have to stay.

The exercise I had prepared was one of my own devising, which promised to generate energy: Hypnotizing Poems. First they were to act out hypnotizing each other, two at a time. Then, once they had gotten the idea, they could write down a list of juicy commands, the sort you gave to some victim who was totally in your power!

I borrowed a gold locket from Roberto to use as a hypnotic pendulum. Roberto and Britt offered to try it first, with Roberto as the hypnotist. Britt was turned into a chicken, made to lay an egg (everyone roared at this innuendo) and worse. I filed away in my mind the information that Britt was a good actor.

The next two volunteers were not nearly as self-assured. Sammy swung the locket, and timid, baby-faced Gregory kept waiting to "go under." It was odd how some kids understood immediately that the game was make-believe, while poor Gregory actually expected to be mesmerized. I whispered to him the trick, and he started rolling his eyes and acting the swoon. Sammy could only think of a few commands, including the chicken routine—the success of the first actors was grasped at again and again.

The next duo came up with some variations and were rewarded with howls by their classmates. A few stragglers, drawn to the laughter, wandered by, including Adiel who was sucked into the excitement. Adiel: a peculiarly sober, phlegmatic kid with thick glasses and a porkpie hat. He started to hypnotize the explosive Karen. He was swinging the locket tentatively, not really sure what the game was about. Karen is not one to suffer insecure males. She grabbed the locket out of his hand and demanded to do the hypnotizing. I had unfortunately already promised the privilege to Xiomara. Karen blew up. I got her out of there before she had a fit.

A few moments later Christine said in a hushed voice: "I think you just made an enemy."

"Oh? Who?"

"Karen!" she said with dread. Christine is a red-haired, freckled girl who listens with wide incredulous eyes to everything that is said around her.

"I'm not worried about it," I replied. I handed out paper for writing. At this point several boys wandered away: game's over. The others stayed. I asked them to think not only of the kind of instructions they had given each other, but of more original, mysterious commands. And, to give an example, I read a few pieces from Yoko Ono's book, *Grapefruit*, which is written entirely in the imperative suggestive mode, e.g., "Watch the sun until it becomes square" or "Keep coughing a year." The kids listened absorbedly, bursting into laughter whenever they could. I noticed Christine especially taking it in with anxious fascination, as if it might possibly contain something against her religion.

After the kids had written their poems they wanted to act them out as we'd done before. So Gregory had to go up to Denise and say that he wanted to share his life with her; Jamie had to stroke my hair; Dolores had to run into the hallways and scream "I love you!" to the first person she saw. I can't say much for the writing as enduring literature, but it was good fun.

Feeling quite happy, I went to lunch with Denise. She was less exhilarated with the experience. She didn't like the way kids kept floating in and out of the fringes of the group. She thought that once they had agreed to join the group they should be obligated to stay and write.

I felt that if they didn't want to write a poem, I wasn't going to force them. And I was reluctant to close the group off to children who didn't see themselves as "writers," either by demanding that they write or by taking only the sign-up group out of the classroom into the Writing Room. Some of that fringe activity seemed to me a positive thing. Nevertheless, I could see her point about the raggedness of it, which made teaching harder at her end.

I suggested she set up a very definite alternative activity of an arts-and-crafts nature—anything too bookish might seem punitive by contrast—and corral the kids into one activity or the other.

"I don't know any crafts, do I?" Denise laughed with coy self-effacement. "Do I know any crafts? I haven't done anything like that with them all year."

"I'm sure you can come up with something," I said. My secret wish was that our working together would force her into more adventurous paths and generate a looser classroom.

Denise was at the point of demonstrating how to make God's eyes when I came by for my next lesson. God's eyes are diamond-shaped frames that you weave colored yarn in and around to make a pretty design. Denise had learned the technique as part of our agreement, from one of the teachers down the hall, and her eagerness to teach it was beautiful to watch. The kids were fascinated to try it too—this, their first crafts project of the year.

I had of course prepared my own writing lesson but I realized I would be an idiot to try to compete with the colored yarn. What was happening that day was God's eyes.

Outsmarted myself that time!

My carefully planned lesson would keep (what a letdown!), and I'd just as soon stroll around talking to the kids. The mood was more relaxed and pleasantly productive than any I had seen in this room so far. I siphoned off a few kids—Janet, Marissa, and Sammy—and we started talking about the idea of God having an eye. This led to the "third eye," which led to my showing them the eye on the pyramid of a dollar bill, and to feeling the bump on each other's foreheads (supposedly a test for spiritual insight), which led eventually to their writing a couple of stories. But this outcome mattered less to me than the naturalness of just hanging out, sitting alongside one kid after another, letting my hands be used for cat's cradle.

How I needed to cast aside the pressure of proving myself before a roomful of students, and become an ordinary Joe, a pair of eyes, a passive dope to play patty-cake with, a big giraffe, to tease, or punch, for no reason whatsoever. I had an appetite for soaking in the atmosphere of the school. I would come into Denise Loftin's class on a day off and sit at a desk in my raincoat, like a bum watching the world go by until one of the kids started up a conversation with me, which usually wasn't very long. The easiest way for me to get to know the kids was to talk to them when I had nothing up my sleeve, when I wasn't demanding any work from them.

There was one boy, Gene, who had been singled out by Denise as someone who needed extra help. He was bright, she said, but he hated to work at anything for more than two minutes, and he *loathed* writing, and he had no friends in the class. He was short, blond-haired, with a dirt-streaked face and a dirty football jersey which he wore every day. Through trial and error I got the impression he did not like to be looked in the eye. Sometimes you meet a child whom you have to approach obliquely, like a deer, and stand quietly until he gets a good chance to look you over and become used to your presence.

I sat next to him, looking at my hands for about a minute without opening my mouth. Then I said, still not looking at him, like two old-timers whittling on a porch: "What yer doin'?" "Makin' a drawing." "Let me see it?" It was something ghastly: a man's head being decapitated. "Nice. Looks like a horror movie," I said. "That's where I got the idea." "You like horror movies, eh?" "Yeah!" And now he began talking a blue streak about monsters, and mealworms, and his dog, whom he loved passionately. He talked with a feverish haste, one word falling on the next. We were still conversing through sidelong glances, which would have made an odd impression to a third party; but by the end of ten minutes I had slowly worked around to gazing directly at him, and he at me. It was a start.*

I found I did some of my best communicating on the days I wasn't there to teach. The key for me was having enough open, unscheduled time and making myself accessible to the children to fill it. I wanted to be available for their everyday inspirations and small talk. I tried not to let my schedule get so tight that I couldn't noodle around with the kids.

If only there was more slack time in the System! If only regular teachers had more of a chance to be with their children in an ordinary friendly way, to put aside the role of efficiency expert. I knew several classroom teachers who stayed after 3 P.M. just to have a chance to unwind with their students. During the school day these same good teachers would often become harassed automatons who blared out orders like public address systems.

I am aware that most hard-working, full-time teachers didn't have my scheduling advantages and might even resent the suggestion of hanging out. I only wish there were a way to demonstrate by cost-benefit analysis or other means that some of this slack time actually increases educational production. In my case I can swear

---

*Later we became much closer—he never did get to like writing but I used him in many videotapes and *West Side Story*.

that the time I spent roaming round the schoolyard and the lunchroom cafeteria led to the children's trusting me more and writing more honestly (as if that were the reason I did it!). In fact I had a little difficulty rationalizing why I was spending so much spare time around the school. I told myself it was an anthropologist's way of gathering clues to the underground culture of children. I told the other writers in the project that listening to kids outside of class time would give them new ideas for writing assignments. But it was pointless to try to elevate to an educational maxim what was largely a question of personal taste. I happened to like being in on the silly conversation of ten-year-old boys in the lunchroom as they made mush of their mashed potatoes. If at first I saw myself as a patient investigator gathering data, in the long run all this jostling with the kids is what sweetened the job, and stayed with me.

Dolores says to me: "Phillip, I hate you!"

"Why do you hate me?"

"I don't! I just like saying that!"

"One day you're going to make me cry if you say that."

"You can't CRY; you can only LAUGH."

"But that seems sad," I said, "never to be able to do anything but laugh. I'm not sure I like that."

"Well that's TOO BAD. You can't do nothing but laugh."

There are several girls in Mrs. Loftin's class who relate to me in this flirtatious, sweetly abrasive way. Lilli comes up and smacks me on the arm: "Where's my magazine, Phillip?"-"What magazine?" I ask, slapping her back. "*You* know," she says and walks away—only to return several hours later and smack my arm again. The kids tease me by matchmaking me with every female in the building. Lately the girls have started the rumor that I love Anna, a tall, quiet Spanish girl in the fifth grade. "How's An-na?" Dolores winks at me. This sends them into hysterics, and the funniest part about it is that Anna is the one student of Denise's whose name I could never remember. She is a silent, inconspicuous child who left so little impression on me that at last I took Denise aside with some embarrassment and asked her to furnish me with the name of "that tall girl" so that I wouldn't constantly be drawing a blank when I needed to call on her. Maybe the kids interpreted this speechlessness around her as lover's shyness! Anna became one of the five Spanish and black kids traded out of Denise's class to create a better racial balance. I probably would have forgotten her once she was gone if it weren't for hearing "How's *Anna?*" ten times a day. Sometimes I mutter, "I haven't seen Anna in weeks," which is true. Sometimes I answer, "We've never been happier!"

I can do with children what I have so much trouble doing with lovers and friends: I can watch their craziness without being pulled into it. I can take them or let them go. It isn't that I don't care about the children as much. I care about them. But if a child tells me he doesn't want to work with me that day or he doesn't like me any more, fine; I don't feel personally rejected. If he wants to work with me again some-time, good. Meanwhile I can turn my attention elsewhere.

Maybe it's because I am one and they are many, and they are more focused on me as a source of approval. The balance of power is so much in my favor that I can afford to let them go away from me and come back at their pleasure. I have only to shift my eyes from foreground to background to find some other child who wants my attention, or anybody's attention. But even among the children themselves, they seem to have a greater independence and—if I may use this word for once in a pos-itive sense—an enviable *promiscuity* in their social attachments. There is more of a free-floating affection which settles where it wants to, without the despondency and emotional blackmail which one adult so often uses to chain another.

I know that I often feel lighthearted around them, even when there is every good reason not to, and this minuet of teasing and flirtation is the dance I love doing with them the most.

Another Classroom

Walking through the halls one day, I looked into the door glass at Stanley Riegel-haupt's orderly, traditional classroom. I knew Riegelhaupt a bit because one of the writers had taught the previous year in his room. He had a reputation for being strict. He was bent over his register book; he had a crew cut and thick glasses. On an impulse I entered, presented myself to the class as a writer and asked merely if anyone wanted to be in a writing club with me. Fourteen kids signed up. They had no idea what they were getting in for; nor did I.

Stanley seemed pleased that I had chosen to work with his class. He was only dis-appointed that a boy named Clifford was absent. "This kid's a great writer—well, I'll sign his name to the list anyway. He won't mind." I got the idea that Clifford was the class intellectual. "He writes things that are practically over my head," Stanley laughed. "I have to use a dictionary to understand his compositions. Tommy here's also pretty good," he said, pointing to a boy near his desk, "not as good as Clifford."

It embarrassed me, this praise of one child above the others, and I tried to change the subject, but Riegelhaupt kept returning to it. I later realized that Riegel-haupt had nothing against embarrassing people. In fact, it was his stock in trade.

They wrote two kinds of stories in that class. One kind was the putdown of Riegelhaupt. The other kind was long, episodically plotted adventure stories: about Apollo V space missions, about winning a million dollars and spending it in differ-ent ways, about raising a horse to enter the Kentucky Derby, or about visiting the Land of Oz for the tenth time. The adventure stories were patterned closely on library books for children. They took several weeks to complete and the authors kept tabs on each other's progress, boasting how many pages they had done, which sometimes seemed to me their main interest in it all.

The writing was mechanical, in the sense of extending a narrative premise as far as it will go, without making a personal commitment to the subject. It was *facile*, jejeune, bloodless fantasy, cut off from the roots of experience and curiously unadventurous for all the plot. Sure, the kids were getting good practice at sentence-making, agile syntax, and logical transitions. But the price they paid was a loss of immediacy and passion. Their writing was affected by the same blight I had seen overspread other classrooms: the insidious take-over of the essay. By the sixth grade, training in composition-writing begins to color everything, poetry and fiction not excepted: everything starts to sound like a book report. Topic sentences, length for its own sake, impersonal diction, and the whole machinery of expository prose annexes the other literary territories as colonies.

I had divided the fourteen volunteers from Riegelhaupt's class into two writing workshops, Group A and Group B. At first many of the children assumed the workshops to be merely a free period to continue writing their episode stories. They would show me their latest chapter and ask me rather complacently how I liked it. I was in a difficult spot. Stanley had already written his approval in the margin. Nor did I want to discourage them—but I couldn't drum up much enthusiasm, either. All I could hope was that they would eventually get bored with this kind of demonstration and come around to trying a deeper approach.

Many of Riegelhaupt's kids were precocious, academically capable children from middle-class, professional homes, white and black, who were accustomed to receiving praise. They let you know their heritage right away. The first time the famous Clifford put in an appearance, he toured the Writing Room and announced in his cool way that it would make a "good meditation room." Another boy told a story about his parents' summer home in Fire Island and suddenly informed me: "I don't know if you know Fire Island. It's in Long Island Sound."

I confess that I was not drawn to these kids at first as much as I had been to Denise Loftin's. They struck me as privileged, competitive, and snooty. Perhaps I was going through my own form of reverse snobbism—or racism. I could not help contrasting them with Loftin's kids, many of whom had trouble writing a paragraph—but what finally came out was alive with the ache of living. Riegelhaupt's kids, the smarter class from the point of view of marks, had already learned how to pad. My problem here was different; it was not to get them to write. The problem was to get them to feel their writing.

An Aside

It may seem strange for me to be so critical of any children's writing, when tolerance and an appreciation bordering on gratitude are so often stressed in the literature as the proper reaction to a child's written expression. However, there is a great quantity of children's writing that is boring, shallow, unimaginative, unfelt. If one piece in five has vivacity, I feel grateful. Sometimes it is only a single line, or a surprising word, a solitary word, that momentarily leaps from a composition of distracted expediency. How to give recognition and support for that line or that word without fawning over every child's piece—which will only win his distrust anyway—is a discipline we need to begin to learn.

It used to be that children's literary products were ignored. Then the pendulum swung in the opposite direction: they became regarded as "the true poets"—*idiots savants*. A noted authority assures his public: "Children have a natural ability for poetry." This flattery of childhood passes for love of children, instead of what it really is, self-complacency. And it does harm by breeding an expectation, in parents and teachers, that their children are naturally gifted lyricists who have only to be touched lightly for sparkling verses to fall out. Then guilt ensues when this doesn't happen. Why not admit the truth? Some children write consistently well; most can achieve bursts of beauty; a few never do. The average poetic gift of children is probably no better or no worse than the average adult's gift for poetry.

To believe that every child is a natural poet is a form of democratic wishfulness gone awry. I am not trying to make poetry into an elitist activity; but the fact is that poetry or writing of any quality is hard work. Few children, and few adults, care to work that hard at it. Not everyone has the intellectual resources. We can discover virtues or charms in hastily written children's papers from now till Doomsday, but that will not necessarily bring the children any closer to electing the conscious pursuit of that hard road.

It is true, there are miraculous sessions which seem to draw out poetic writing from everyone. A St. Vitus's dance of contagious lyricism sweeps the room and all the children write down beautiful ideas and images. It seems as if they were all latent poets who simply awaited the right pedagogic touch. But then the next week the stimulus may be less "evocative": the results slump; those children who are gifted and inclined to writing continue to write while the others leave it alone.

The teacher who has stumbled on such an open sesame, only to find it close stubbornly a week later in his face, may wonder what he did wrong in not being able to sustain the high level of poetic expression; or may think, If only I could do as good a job as the experts. He should be aware that the experts don't admit their percentage of failure, and they don't publish the lifeless works by their kids. Before getting carried away with inflated expectations of a-poet-in-every-child, we should understand something of the odds involved in producing one good work.

"In Quest of Her Beauty"

One torpid morning, when Group A had not the slightest interest in literature, and nothing I said could entice them into writing, and I was considering giving up the profession, I noticed Tommy, who seemed as lost as myself. He was biting his fingernails for lack of anything to do and frowning as the other boys chased each other around the room. I asked him if he wanted to try writing a poem. He said he didn't think he could. And then he looked around unconsciously for Clifford, whose large literary shadow seemed to inhibit him. It had the effect of saying to me: Aren't you asking the wrong one?

I took out a poem in French by Apollinaire and asked him to write down a translation. "I don't know French," he said with understandable perplexity. I said I figured he didn't, but he should look at the words closely and say them over and over in his mind until they suggested some meanings. This is a technique called *mistranslation*, by which someone perfectly ignorant in a foreign language can "translate" it by sound associations, visual similarities and wild guesses. In another situation, with more outgoing children, I would have probably used a direct experiential approach; but with a child like Tommy, who was studious, self-conscious, timid about revealing his feelings, it was better to use a text—an objective starting point outside himself for inspiration.

The poem went:

Photographie

Ton sourire m'attire comme
Pourrait m'attirer une fleur
Photographie tu es le champignon brun
De la forêt
Qu'est sa beauté
Les blancs y sont
Un clair de lune
Dans un jardin pacifique
Plein d'eaux vives et de jardiniers endiablés
Photographie tu es la fumée de l'ardeur
Qu'est sa beauté
Et il y en toi
Photographie
Des tons alanguis
on y entend
Une mélopée
Photographie tu es l'ombre
Du soleil
Qu'est sa beauté

—Apollinaire

Tommy stared at it a long time. I urged him to put down any old idea for the first line; it didn't matter if it was silly or made no sense. When he realized that I was not going to help him with the translation, except in general ways like telling him he could add more words or syllables to make it read better if he liked, Tommy wrote down a tentative beginning. "The town squire's mattress came back to town." I nodded noncommittally. He was not a child given to irrationality of any kind, and I could see he was stretching himself. He kept stealing looks at my face with timorous excitement, not so much wanting suggestions as protection in this strange voyage through unknown waters. He seemed to know instinctively what to do but he proceeded very slowly. "It's weird," Tommy said, "how you could take words in a foreign language and translate them without knowing the language!" I wanted to say Shhh; I was afraid he would lose the spell; instead I nodded and murmured, "It's something like chemistry." Actually more like alchemy, I thought. The poem progressed; at each line he thought of and discarded several options; and after the first two lines (which unfortunately had little to do with the rest), he tried to make everything connect narratively. It was time to pick up Group B, but Tommy wasn't finished yet, and so I decided to let Group A stay in the Writing Room, though they were fooling around. I would have to rearrange my schedule to work with Group B in the afternoon. All these considerations were making me nervous, but I knew it was more important to sit with Tommy and be there for him until he finished his poem. As much for my own sake as for his. How often does one get a chance to be present at the birth of a poet? The whole process gave me shivers. Though the poem as a finished product would probably not convey to anybody else that shiver, I quote it as part of the record.

Photograph

The town squire's mattress came back to town.
Poor mattress fell on the floor.
She photographed the champion broom.
She found herself in the forest,
In quest of her Beauty.
The blankets shone.
Her chair was held up by balloons.
She found people dancing in jars.
As they were dancing they were making
some dough as flat as a plain.
She photographed some fumes from the
dust that rose in quest of her beauty.
She photographed tons of languages.
They entered a melody.
She photographed two lumps of soil
in quest of her beauty.
        —TOMMY

We went over Tommy's version from the beginning to see if he wanted anything improved. Did he like it? I asked.

"Well, it sounds like a real poem even though it doesn't exactly make sense."

I translated the original Apollinaire for him. Tommy listened with intense interest. Then he said modestly, "I think I like mine better."

"What about it do you like better?"

He thought for a while. "It's more like a story."

You make those choices: to hold the group's attention together, or go for a quiet moment with one student and let the group thing sag. Sometimes you're too tightly wound and defensive and supervisory even to detect the possibility of a quiet moment. Then something loosens you: a look or a stray remark is thrown at you like a clue, and you take it up.

A boy named Marvin was newly arrived from an all-black school in the South. He seemed stolid and more mature than the other children. One morning he came in late, near the end of a workshop, and sat in a chair with his coat on.

"Why don't you take your coat off?" I said.

He tossed his coat over mine, which happened to be lying on a desk. "Seems like my coat be in love with your coat," he said.

This remark made me turn around. Until he had said that I confess I had thought of him as a dull, "mulish" kid, but now it seemed there was more going on under his slow brown eyes than I had thought.

"Tell me more—how's your coat in love with mine?"

"I can't say, 'cause I don't know much about Coat Love," he said.

Now he really had me intrigued. I asked him if he thought objects, things, had actual feelings. He said he often talked to things that were lying in the street, tires and junk, carried on conversations with them. And now his mother was worried about him—she worked in a hospital as a nurse, she wanted to take him to the "Psych."

I told him I talked to myself, that all writers did, and it wasn't as unusual as he might think. Marvin brushed aside this reassurance with a worried look: "No, she's gonna take me to the Psych. I know something's wrong."

He seemed to want to talk about it, and I wanted to listen. But I didn't feel easy about adopting a therapist's role in relation to him. There had to be a way that he could talk, and that I could show him that his thoughts were not so bizarre or frightening (which I felt pretty certain that they weren't) *through* my ordinary role as writing teacher.

I took him to a far table and sat down with him and asked him to talk to himself as if he were in the street. I would write down everything he said. That way we could make what he said into a poem. "All right," he said skeptically. "Where should I start?" "Start the way you would if you were outside in the street, looking around, thinking to yourself." He began dictating to me. He seemed to be formulating it in his head, consciously editing out certain details and asking me to write down only those that would be good for the poem. At the end of his dictation I asked him what title he wanted to give it; and he said without hesitation, "The Sadness."

The Sadness

Helping my father wash the car
He tells me to get the water
Marvin turn on the hose pipe.
Turn on the hose
It's on.
All right that's good. Bring it here.
Now we splash the soap on
Marvin run the water on the car
All right that's good. Turn it off.
Now let's dry the car off
Gotta give me some money to go get a soda
Marvin you don't have to help me no more
Here's $5.
I go over to the wall.
Then I start staring.
I look down the street
I look up the street
What do I see?
I see one man coming with a carriage carrying junk
And a freight train running on its lane
There's no kids my size
Anyhow I'm outside
So I guess I'll talk to myself
Well I wish I had a horse
I look down the street and here come a mule.
They start clearing the junk house
So the mule can come and dump his load
I wish I had a darn horse.
I always wanted a horse and Dad know it
But I had to stop being afraid of horses first
Someone said they'll kick you to death
Mom & Dad say when we go down South
We'll get a horse.
And Dad say he'll get him one and me one too
So what am I worrying about
I'll be glad when I go down South
It is so warm there

—MARVIN

"It's very good, Marvin," I said when it was done. We were both a little stunned.

I took it to the second floor to show his teacher, Stanley Riegelhaupt, who happened to be in the teacher's lounge on his prep period.

"Marvin wrote that?" said Stanley. "That's terrific!"

"Well he told me what words to write and I wrote them down. . . ."

For all my enthusiasm about the poem, I still felt there was something less "legitimate" about dictated work. Wouldn't it be more useful for him to struggle through a written piece on his own? How much of the final product was shaped by my arranging it into lines?

After the second week's dictation from Marvin, I told him that next time he would have to write it himself. "But it doesn't come out so good as when you write it," he insisted. And it didn't. During the next few workshops, his eyes followed me with a hurt look as if I had betrayed his trust. He understood the trick—the same trick all the other teachers pulled. It was that universal *idée fixe* of adults: to get him to read and write. It wasn't enough apparently that a way had been opened for him to say what was on his mind.

So the weaning process took a step backward: I gave in and he dictated again. Was it the dictation itself that was so crucial to him, or the physical and mental closeness it brought between us? My hanging on to his every word? The next time, he gave in and wrote a page. For the rest of the year we were bound to each other by that first experience, glad when we met in the halls, embarrassed for no reason, as if looking to rediscover that same shock of intimacy.

Every week I brought in a new writing idea. The kids had come to expect it. I talked to friends who were also teaching writing; I bought materials; I compiled lists. Everything was turning into a writing assignment in my head. I would see a family walking together; we could do a lesson on families. I would get a headache; we could write about sickness and body sensations. The number of potential writing assignments was all too infinite. The night before going into class I would try to convince myself that one idea shone above the rest. I believed in it; I went to sleep on it. The next morning four other assignments seemed equally plausible. I would be riding the bus to school thinking lesson A, B, C, D? Or M? Suddenly I decided it has to be G, G, G. . . !

I am still walking to the front of the class mumbling to myself: G, G. . . or maybe A.

"Let me have your attention please," I would say to Mrs. Loftin's kids. (I had gone back to addressing the whole class.) "I'd like you to quiet down so we can begin."

How many times have I been struck, on uttering the words, "Today I thought we might write about. . . ", with the total unreality of my proposition. Why hypnosis and not favorite foods; or odes? Everything seems equally random. And in that split second between the getting of their attention and the telling of what it is they will have to do, as I stare down at thirty pairs of child's eyes, ready to inform me if

I have guessed well or badly, how often have I gone dizzy, wishing I could defer the judgment a little longer, and fallen into the abyss between the two halves of my sentence?

Some ideas would catch fire and not others, perfectly as good. Why? Was it my delivery? Or that certain ideas were narrower and less applicable to everyone? Or the mood of the class that day, the weather?

If only I could stick to a coherent plan week after week, a curriculum (magic crutch!). But I knew of no writing curriculum that was satisfactory; I would have had to make one up myself. I taught each class only once or twice a week, and the hope of drawing a continuity between the lessons kept getting thinner. When I tried to follow up a successful lesson, often it seemed that too much had intervened for the children in the week between and the idea already felt stale to them. I made attempts to force connections between lessons, but it was mostly for my own conscience. In the end I reassured myself that at least they were getting a "full spectrum" of writing experiences. They seemed to be satisfied with a random approach. But the *arbitrariness* of my assignments continued to gall me.

Rather than always second-guessing the kids' interests, I began asking them to volunteer writing subjects. But when you ask a class point-blank, "What do you want to write about?" the response is usually vacant stares, trivia, insincerity. The kids were still not ready to go without the initial writing stimulus that I brought in each week. Even if they rejected the bouquet, they felt better for having had it brought to them. I was the one who felt uncomfortable. There was something that didn't sit right with my educational philosophy, about programming thirty kids to write in a given form each week.

One day I tried an assignment that fell utterly flat. No relevance to anyone's imagination anywhere. Then I was surprised and moved to see certain children diligently carry it out—not because they were afraid of me but because we had been through a lot and they would humor me this time. They wrote almost out of a desire to make me feel better, with that kindness and childish diplomacy that mysteriously rises out of them. I began to realize I was banking on their love. Behind all the ideas and creative motivators was the unspoken appeal: Do it for *me*.

I was supposed to be teaching poetry and fiction writing to public school children; I saw this as my main job. At the same time I was being drawn to the different children as personalities. I wanted to communicate with them more directly but I couldn't, because the lesson stood in the way. Of course the lesson could be the very medium by which we spoke to each other. Sometimes it was; but sometimes I had the feeling that the lesson was only a *pretext* for us to enjoy each other's company.

The lesson was the tennis ball I hit to the kids every week, and their writing was the ball they hit back. The academic role structure between us was the net. Robert Frost once said that he didn't care to write free verse because it was "like playing tennis without the net." Maybe I'm perverse, but I've always been drawn to the notion of playing tennis without the net. So if the lesson were an indirect and, to some extent, hypocritical means for us to communicate with each other, wouldn't it be possible at some point to drop the pretext? Did we really need it? And if it proved impossible to do without (which I began to suspect it was, since my desires for something else were so vague that I could not imagine what I would put in its place), wasn't there some way to do it without as much artificiality?

What I was really looking for was a way to close the distance between my informal, hanging-around behavior and my regular teaching personality. I didn't want to be two people. It was painful to keep switching.

It was Riegelhaupt's kids who led me to a different approach. By their very indifference to writing games, they forced me to look elsewhere. Ideas that had worked like a charm with Loftin's kids failed to hold them. They had a tendency to use the Writing Room as a playroom. Their reluctance to write was understandable because they were already getting so much "creative writing" for homework. I saw it would be necessary to remake their whole attitude toward writing, by giving the act of writing a more existential ground. But that might take a long time. . . . Or else find another function and purpose for writing by connecting it like a balloon string to other arts: writing a script so that it could be acted onstage; or writing combined with artwork. Or forget about writing for a while. Maybe they were horsing around so much because they needed it.

I turned Group A loose with magic markers on the drab paper-covered closets of the Writing Room, to make graffitti, draw pictures, write messages to each other. I brought in adding-machine rolls for whoever wanted to write Endless Stories; magazines to be cut up for collage poems; fat, colored chalk for the blackboard. With arts materials, the atmosphere became more flowing.

The next time I had Riegelhaupt's kids write monologues and soliloquies for different characters and act them out. Then we combined the characters to make playlets. This led to a few weeks of tape-recorded radio plays: *The Prison Break, The Divorce Court.*

Radio plays are a beautiful form for promoting concentration and discipline. The technical limitation of one microphone focuses the group: everyone *has* to stand close around that microphone. If several people speak at once, the playback sounds like sludge. Whenever anyone starts making noise or jumping around, the others shush him because they want the sound to come out right. Riegelhaupt's kids adored radio plays. At last something had taken hold. I could feel their interest deepening with every advance into drama.

Theater was the activity they were starved for, the form toward which all their playing around had been pointing. The difference between "play" and "a play" is not very great in most children's minds. Theater reconciled their appetite for play with my desire to have them write something collaboratively and work hard at and care about an activity over a period of several months.

The next step was to write an actual play together. I began by having them improvise parts around a form that I always find appealing: the soap opera. Each child was to take the character of someone in a family and make up a disability or maladjustment for that character; or else play a neighbor or family doctor. From the first few weeks of sprawling, sloppy improvisations, we boiled down the best moments into a script, which was written by everyone in the ensemble. The result was our first play: *The Typical American Family with Problems.*

In a sense, I had put off the problem of teaching creative writing by expanding into other arts. It was not until the following year that I felt ready to attempt again a more coherent approach to the teaching of poetry.

16

Chekhov for Children

1

"And life itself is boring, stupid, dirty . . . it strangles you, this life. You're surrounded by weird people, nothing but country bumpkins, and after living
with them for two or three years, little by little you get to be weird yourself.
[Twirling his long mustache] Look how I've grown this enormous mustache
. . . it's a silly mustache. I've grown weird. Nurse . . . I haven't grown stupid-
er, my brains are still in the right place, thank God, but my feelings have
somehow gone numb. I don't want anybody, I don't need anything, I don't
love anybody . . . want anybody, except maybe you. [Kisses her head] When
I was little I had a nurse like you."
                    —*Dr. Astrov, to the Nanny, Uncle Vanya, Act I*

THE CHARACTERS IN CHEKHOV'S PLAYS are tormented by the thought that
they are misspending their lives and that perhaps it is already too late. Their ambitions have led nowhere; they are stagnating; they reach for a romantic solution but
fall in love with the wrong person; each thinks himself or herself the noble exception to a landscape of utterly monotonous banality. They can often be comic in their
self-deluded, manic bitterness, and they are capable of great animation in their talking jags, but invariably they lapse back into a state of passivity and remorse.

As Gorky wrote of Chekhov: "In front of that dreary, gray crowd of helpless
people there passed a great, wise and observant man: he looked at all these dreary
inhabitants of his country, and, with a sad smile, with a tone of gentle but deep
reproach, with anguish in his face and in his heart, in a beautiful and sincere voice,
he said to them: 'You live badly, my friends. It is shameful to live like that.'"

To no one's surprise, Chekhov is hardly a staple in the elementary school repertoire. With Shakespeare, there is a long, honorable tradition of elementary school
productions: some of the comedies, like *A Midsummer Night's Dream*, clearly have

potential to charm younger children, and a good sword-clanging drama like *Macbeth*, with its witches and magic spells, can also appeal to juvenile actors if cleverly abridged. True, Shakespeare's vocabulary is difficult, but this courtly language itself can be an attraction, lending a distanced charm of dress-up and fairy tales to the enterprise. The drama of Chekhov, on the other hand, is neither distanced enough to conjure up an exotic world nor contemporary enough to attract by its familiarity. Not only do the realism, the *ennui*, the pauses, the lack of physical action and spectacle all count against attempting Chekhov at this level, many would question whether such a view of life, such tableaux, are suitable for children at all. With Chekhov, it is not a matter of risqué material—of too much sexuality or violence, since the playwright is very moderate in these respects—but of a perspective so wholly, darkly adult in its awareness of time running out that some would argue it is unfair to subject children in their innocence to such gloomy prospects.

I must say right off that I think it is a very good thing for children to see what adult futility looks like (they see it anyway, whether we want them to or not), and to get an insight into the mistakes and the paralyses that hinder many grownups, so that they will not squander their own opportunities. To phrase the issue in larger terms, I think it good for children to gain a realistic view of life no matter what, and a harm for them to be "sheltered" from learning the truth and confined in an artificial world of cuteness. I realize this is part of a very touchy debate among parents and educators, and that each person who raises children draws the line at a different place, whether it is at letting them go to a funeral or allowing them to see certain movies. In this debate I generally take the side of John Holt, who argued in *Escape from Childhood*:

> Most people who believe in the institution of childhood as we know it see it as a kind of walled garden in which children, being small and weak, are protected from the harshness of the world outside until they become strong and clever enough to cope with it. Some children experience childhood in just that way. I do not want to destroy their garden or kick them out of it. If they like it, by all means let them stay in it. But I believe that most young people, and at earlier and earlier ages, begin to experience childhood not as a garden but as a prison. What I want to do is put a gate, or gates, into the wall of the garden, so that those who find it no longer protective or helpful, can move out of it and for a while try living in a larger space.

In June 1979 a dozen ten- to twelve-year-olds put on a full-length version of Anton Chekhov's *Uncle Vanya*, which was a gate to the larger world. They put it on before an initially indulgent but skeptical audience. Many who came to support the children in what they assumed would be an impossible undertaking were rather startled to find themselves pulled into the original drama as Chekhov had written it; they were unexpectedly moved by the characters. And I was in a sense the most surprised, knowing from having directed the play how catastrophically it could have gone.

What fascinated me all along about the *Uncle Vanya* project was that it pushed to the limits certain assumptions about proper educational practice, and continually butted against larger philosophical questions: What is the nature of childhood? Are children radically different from adults, or subtly different? What is "appropriate" for children at different ages, both from a developmental-learning and from a responsibly ethical point of view? Then came certain technical questions: Could this thing even be done? What were the capacities for memorization of ten- to twelve-year-old schoolchildren with no previous theatrical training? Granted that children understand a lot: What *would* be above their heads? Was there something they could not be made to understand? Could children connect with and feel compassion for issues they had never faced? What would be the difference between working on a play in which the children were highly motivated and familiar with the material beforehand (as with *West Side Story*, the production of which I had undertaken six years previous) and attempting a play in which the teacher's lone enthusiasm might have to overcome a good deal of indifference and resistance? What part ought a teacher's private obsessions and artistic tastes play in the educational process? Where does one draw the line between experimentation and self-indulgence?

I must say that I felt myself on firmer ground in answering the anxiety that I was robbing children of their "innocence" than I did in silencing personal doubts that this was nothing but an extravagant out-of-control whim, in which I might be using these children to satisfy my own pedagogic ambitions and need for excitement and escape. One thing is certain: I could have waited a million years before a group of sixth graders approached me and proposed that we do *Uncle Vanya*. No, the suggestion had to spring from me. It came about this way.

2

"Autumn roses, beautiful, sad roses. . . . "
—*Vanya, Act III*

In my creative writing classes at P.S. 90, I had been working on dialogue scenes with Monte Clausen's fifth/sixth-grade class. (P.S. 90 is a racially mixed school on the Upper West Side of Manhattan, where I had been directing an Arts Team full time for Teachers and Writers Collaborative.) Over the years I had noticed that, although the kids wrote capable stories and poetry, their dialogue scenes were no better than rudimentary, generally amounting to little more than exchanges of one-liners in which two characters drove each other to greater and greater degrees of exasperation. I was puzzled as to why even the most sophisticated of these child writers so rarely took advantage of the variations in speech length that are a natural part of conversation, instead clinging to a monotonous Ping-Pong of dialogue.

I thought I would also talk to this class about the manifest and latent levels of conversation: plant the suggestion that a person may be hiding his or her true meaning, or may even be unconscious of it. I wanted to explain how sometimes in plays the audience was conscious of a danger the character wasn't, which made for suspense; or how the audience saw one character coming to the truth while another was still in the dark (like the famous scene of the husband under the table in *Tartuffe*). The more I considered it, the more I saw that a good deal of dramatic interest in the theater derived precisely from the playwright's selective presentation and suppression of information. The audience was gradually put in the know and then was left to experience the delicious irony of each character's battle with self-delusion until the "recognition" or "discovery" scene finally occurred, which it did with twice the force because of the buildup.

All this is obvious to the average playgoer, but how to put such structurally complex ideas across to fifth graders? (Children love suspense, but it is precisely this kind of careful foreshadowing that they as writers are weakest at.) I decided I needed a long scene—and I thought of the sequence in *Uncle Vanya* when Sonia goes to Elena and tells her that she loves Dr. Astrov. Elena offers to sound out Astrov about his true feelings for Sonia. The problem is that Astrov is secretly in love with the beautiful Elena, and Elena . . . is a little taken with Astrov herself. After reassuring the homely Sonia that she will speak to Astrov on her behalf, Elena is left alone and delivers a monologue in which she makes it clear that she herself is tempted by Astrov. Astrov enters with some ecological charts (the ostensible pretext of this interview) and proceeds to expound at great windy length on the demise of flora and fauna in their district, all of which information leaves Elena cold. She brings the subject around to Sonia's crush. Astrov admits he does not "admire" Sonia "as a woman." But then he turns the tables on Elena and accuses her of toying with him. "You know why I come here every day," he cries. "And *who* I come to see. . . . All right? I'm conquered, you knew it even without the questioning. *[Folds his arms and bows his head]* I give up, here, eat me!" Elena protests, Astrov tries to trap her in an embrace and make an assignation, he declares his love in mumbled fragments, she is a picture of conflicted behavior, one moment saying go away, the next moment sinking her head on his shoulder. Vanya—also in love with Elena—comes in while they are embracing. He has seen it all.

A dizzying sequence of emotional transition—from friendship to love to ambivalence to contempt to loyalty to betrayal—all in ten pages. When I looked for the episode in my copy of *Uncle Vanya*, I somehow got sucked into reading the whole play again. It struck me as such a wonderful piece of writing. Oh, to be able to teach such a play! But that was getting ahead of myself; I doubted that the class would sit still even for a reading of this longish scene. I stalled for two weeks, meanwhile teaching other lessons. Then, finally, I went ahead, partly because I had already spent the money photocopying the scene for the class, and partly because I had to get this damn Chekhov lesson out of my system.

Their rapt interest surprised me as I read it aloud. What I hadn't bargained for was that the dramatic situation (X intervening for Y to find out Z's romantic feelings) was one they were going through at this particular stage of their boy-girl careers. No one in class had the nerve to ask someone out straightforwardly, so these matters were handled indirectly through a best friend. After the reading I analyzed the scene to the class as a triangle of unrequited love: John loves Marsha, Marsha loves Fred, etc. I had no doubt they would understand what I was talking about because unrequited love starts very early—even second graders can relate to these bruises. In any case, we went over the complexities of the action, and I asked them how each character felt about the others. The discussion was rich. Did they think Astrov really loved Elena? (Not sure.) What does Sonia mean by "Uncertainty is best"? Why does Elena say one thing and do another? They liked the scene because it was romantic and embarrassing—perfect for ten-, eleven-, twelve-year-olds. They roared at Astrov's lovemaking ("Here, eat me!"). Meanwhile, I was able to explain a few technical points about writing dialogue scenes. Mission accomplished. I might have left it at that.

But now I was thinking: What if I took a small group of interested students and started an *Uncle Vanya* study group. Just to read the play, mind you. ("And put it on!" a maniacal inner voice suggested.) No, I had to devise the project step by step, like a three-stage rocket, at each point ready to self-destruct if one of the parts fizzled. First stage, part one, was the lesson. That had worked out well, so we could move on to the second stage: a reading group. We would approach *Uncle Vanya* as a piece of literature. Perhaps that was even a more advanced and satisfying educational idea than this vulgar notion that we had to mount our own production. But if—if—the kids were interested, if the idea came from them, we then ... could consider ... look into ... see if it was even feasible. Ah, but what a coup it would be! What a march I would steal on all the other writers in the schools—forget the writers, even the theater people! Who had ever heard of an artist-in-the-schools pulling off such a thing? Chekhov by children. We could get the local TV stations to cover it. I would be modest at interviews: Please—the children did it all, speak to them....

Another restlessness was, I should admit, working inside me. After ten years of teaching children writing by using examples from one-page poems and choice prose fragments, the first few sentences of a novel, I yearned to sink my teeth into a complex, meaty, sustained piece of literature. One of the frustrations that writers face in working with children is that we always seem to be offering up slivers of literary models. But what made me fall in love with literature in the first place was fat novels, five-act plays. I loved the repetitions of themes, the rise and fall, even the doldrums, the calms, the tedium itself, and the big payoff, which could only occur when the writer had built up a meticulous architectural structure to house it. I felt like a fraud sharing lyrical bursts of expression with children and pretending that they were all there was to literature, while my own love was for the grand arch, the passage of time, the slow transformation of characters. Here at last would be a chance to dig in and demonstrate how a great literary work was like music, with patterns and refrains and variation, adagios as well as allegros. . . .

Hadn't I paid my dues already with years of meeting children on their own cultural terms—helping them make superhero comic books and vampire movies? Let them come to me this time, I thought. I was tired of scaling everything down to miniature size. On the brink of one of those periodic crises of staleness endemic to the teaching profession, I decided my only antidote might be a project of deep selfishness. *Uncle Vanya* was a play I liked and was reasonably sure I would not tire of. Therefore, we would study *Vanya*.

3

"It's a long time since I've played.
I'll play and cry—cry like a fool."
—*Elena, Act II*

I went to the Drama Bookshop and looked through all the *Vanya* translations. To my disappointment, none of them seemed exactly right. In some ways I liked the Stark Young version best, but it was rather stodgy and Victorian; the Tyrone Guthrie version was more modern but a bit too slangy and slick for my taste. In the end I settled for the Guthrie version because it was a cheaper paperback and because the bookstore had more copies.

Then I went to Monte Clausen, the classroom teacher, and we drew up a list of the dozen or so children who would be involved out of the pool of twenty who had already volunteered. I should say in passing that Clausen is an extraordinary elementary school teacher who has himself done science projects of immense scope and technical difficulty. At the moment he and his kids were building a model of the Brooklyn Bridge in the back of the classroom; the year before, he had lent his engineering expertise to our radio station project. Monte Clausen was one of a number of gifted, Ivy League-educated men drawn into elementary school teaching during the sixties by a combination of downwardly mobile idealism and the need to avoid the draft. With the thin, almost gaunt physique of a dedicated marathon runner, soulful eyes, a prematurely bald head, and a drooping mustache, this very popular teacher had a perfectionist streak tempered by a fatalistic sense of humor, reserved for inevitable snafus. I doubt if I would have attempted a project as farfetched as *Uncle Vanya* with any of the other teachers I was working with at the time. That he was someone like me who warmed to improbable schemes—we had once tried to build a waterfall in the Writing Room, a total fiasco, as it turned out—and that we were friends outside of school reassured me that he would be forgiving of the possible strains created by kidnapping his kids for so time-consuming a project. Monte knew already that I might want to put on the full-length play. He chuckled as he wrote in his Attendance Book: "Group for Uncle Vanya. (Uncle Vanya??!!!)"

These were the criteria for selection to the *Uncle Vanya* study group: (a) the probability that the particular child would be interested in this sort of venture; (b) my hunch that a kid would ultimately be good in a certain role—if ever it came to that; (c) racial balance; (d) intellectual capacity and maturity (there were a few exceptions to this); (e) Clausen's desire to include one or two kids who, thus far in the year, had been walking around lost in space.

Clausen's class held a goodly pool of intelligent and competent children, many of whom I regretted having to leave out. But it also had the peculiar limitation of a shortage of eligible boys. I could have cast the female parts in the play twice over, whereas it was really a struggle to find enough "mature" boys; the boys tended to be shorter and more babyish than the girls.

The core of the group I had chosen hung out together after school, frequented the same luncheonette, and came with its own pecking order. The clique included Lisa, Mylan, Slim, Jamal, and Sasha—if you went up against any of them you were accountable to the others. The rest of the eleven kids in the group were outsiders, loners; they looked to me for support and fair play whenever the clique got too pushy. The group broke down like this:

Angus was, already in my mind, a potential Uncle Vanya. He was a white fifth grader with large glasses and a thoughtful, deliberate way of speaking; something of a genius perhaps—in any case, very bright, with an unusual, technical mind—given to speculations; disliked by many of his classmates, considered "flaky" and "weird," he would sometimes raise his hand and then not remember by midsentence what he had started to say. His fourth-grade teacher was shocked when she learned I had given Angus the longest part in the play: "He blanks out!" she said. "He'll stare into space and forget where he is."

Mylan was tremendously popular, gracious, gushing with perceptions and energy. A good writer, dancer, actress, and pal. Half-black, half-white, the child of divorced parents, she seemed to have an unusual amount of insight for a sixth grader. And if a sixth grader can be said to possess glamour, Mylan had it.

Jamal was a mischief-maker and prankster. He wore a cat-that-ate-the-canary grin at all times. Often quite admirable and sweet, with a big Afro and handsome *café-au-lait* skin, he had the habit of slyly pushing one's patience to the brink, so as to ensure that one did not rely on him too much. He was one of my favorites, though not many shared my taste.

Slim, Jamal's best friend, was respected by the other children, though still a mystery to me. Even-tempered, white, nice-looking, with a shaggy dog haircut, just barely stopping at his eyes, he struck me as the strong and silent type.

Rebecca was a loner, bright, hypersensitive, upset by her parents' divorce; generally very cooperative; experienced. She had already trod the boards off-off-Broadway in a child role. A little plain of face, she would make an excellent Sonia.

Lisa was just a good kid to have around, the kind that teachers depend on to carry a new activity—capable, solidly intelligent, mature, a leader though still only a fifth grader. The rap on her was that she was coasting a little, had never been challenged to her fullest. Still, she would be good for any of the roles: she read well and with expression.

David was another fifth grader. I heard he had cried on the first day of school because he missed his fourth-grade teacher. But lately he was showing signs of mental growth underneath his baby fat. Who would ever have guessed at the beginning of the year that this rosy-cheeked cherub would be perfect as the Professor—an aged, sour, hypochondriacal intellectual?

Ayesha was highly theatrical, her mother was an actress. She had a powerful appearance, queenly, coal-black, flamboyantly baubled. She wrote beautifully, but she was also something of a bully, beating up on other children (especially boys), exploding, leading mutinies and walkouts. She would get tired suddenly, refuse to work anymore. I kept forgetting that this powerfully built girl had a fragile constitution, and had been in and out of hospitals with kidney problems.

Kioka was very sweet, matronly, black, and composed. A late transfer, she seemed never to have "joined" the class. She had no ambition to be seen by an audience and rather dreaded the idea. But Clausen had thought it would be a good experience for her to be part of this group.

Sasha wanted to be in on everything though she rarely initiated activity. Pint-sized, squeaky, she didn't have the charismatic presence of a principal lead, but I thought she would make a good extra and assistant director.

Randi was shy, humorous, and reliable. I pictured her as another extra and backstage organizer.

It helped that I had worked with a number of these children (Angus, Sasha, Mylan, Lisa, Jamal) on smaller plays and on films in past years. I knew their potential and their quirks, and they knew mine.

The reading of the play took up three afternoons. Lisa began, magically setting the scene in a calm, mature, respectful voice. Some of the other children, however, read so poorly that it unnerved me: I had assumed they were all reading at grade level at least. This did not bode well for putting on a full production. I stopped and explained the more difficult words, discussed some of the unfamiliar Russian details. On the whole, the reading aloud of the text offered cautious affirmation, if only because everyone was decently behaved. Maybe they simply wanted to get out of class, to be part of a privileged group. They neither liked nor hated *Uncle Vanya*: a few remarked that it was "boring" and "nothing really happens," but for the most part they took it at face value. They simply wanted the fun of putting on a play, any play, and asked when we could start holding tryouts. I grasped that the abstraction of a literary study group would have no meaning for them, and so proceeded timorously to stage three.

4

"It's funny—if Uncle Vanya says something, or that old idiot, my mother-in-law, it's all right, everybody pays attention. But if I so much as utter a single word, everybody gets upset. The very sound of my voice disgusts them."

—Professor Serebriakoff, Act II

Tryouts were held in mid-January. I encouraged everyone to read for as many parts as they liked. These readings were a lovely part of the process: the kids would divide up into groups of twos, threes, or fours and go off into the stairwell or hallway to practice the scene of their choice without my help. Then they would all come together and take turns performing the scenes for each other. It was fascinating to see three different Vanyas or Sonias in the space of an hour.

After a few weeks, the obviousness of certain choices became clear to all. Despite the fact that all the boys wanted the starring role and that Angus was maybe the least popular child in that group, everyone agreed that Angus *was* Vanya. Similarly, Mylan's flair for the part of Elena and David's surprising gift for recreating the invalidish, grumbling Professor were indisputable. Ayesha accepted with good grace that she made a wonderful old Nurse (her characterization was complete the moment she read for the part), in spite of her preference for the part of the beautiful Elena. Kioka was pressed into being Vanya's mother. Sasha and Randi agreed to be workmen in walk-on parts, and also to take charge of props and scenery. There was virtually no disagreement about these decisions. Children may lie, but they have an amazing honesty when it comes to recognizing objectively the competence of their peers.

I still had a problem casting two key characters, Astrov and Sonia. Neither Jamal nor Slim was particularly impressive as Dr. Astrov, and both Rebecca and Lisa would have made convincing Sonias. I decided to sound out the cast individually, to solicit their private opinions while also discussing with each one the character he or she had been selected to play. My first conference was with Mylan. She confided in me that she had gone out with Jamal the year before and that under no circumstances would she play love scenes with him. "I mean, I like Jamal and all, he's nice in his way, but he's just too immature, and I would be embarrassed to death to play a love scene with him and I *know* neither Lisa or Rebecca will." With that word of advice, I cast Slim as Dr. Astrov. The whole cast breathed a sigh of relief. Jamal got the comic role of "Waffles" Telegin, the obsequious family hanger-on.

Each of the potential Sonias was excellent in a different way: Rebecca had the injured, long-suffering, neurotic sensitivity of someone who has judged herself, in Sonia's words, "not pretty," and she was wonderfully expressive and had stage experience, but Lisa (who was, regrettably for the part, extremely pretty) had a gravity and a consoling adult quality that was also thrilling. Moreover, I dared not go against the power of the clique by depriving Lisa of a major role. Finally I decided to let them both be Sonia, in separate performances. I reasoned that role-doubling happens all the time in opera repertory companies. It led to headaches, and the girls were able to rehearse only half as much as the other actors, but somehow it still seems to me to have been the only choice.

I was discontented with the Guthrie translation; we needed our own version. I asked the kids to go through the scripts and suggest any changes or cuts. Then I sat down at the typewriter with the Stark Young, Tyrone Guthrie, and Marian Fell versions open to the same scene, the kids' recommendations in my lap, and chose what seemed to me the best translation of each phrase from the standpoints of literary power and "speakability" by the children. At times I paraphrased, using my own wording. With a foreign language dramatic classic you are never sure you are dealing with the pure text; this way we had more leeway for the children to put things in their own words without the guilt of violating the author's sacrosanct syllables. Had the text been in English—Shakespeare or Shaw—I would have been more hesitant about altering the language.

As for cuts, all I trimmed in the end were some of Astrov/Slim's longer speeches. If we were going through the trouble of putting on *Uncle Vanya*, we might as well do it whole.

In our first rehearsals we went slowly over the script, clearing up small points of meaning. I discovered that, sophisticated as these Upper West Side/Broadway kids appeared, they often did not know the meanings of ordinary words like "pompous," "uncertainty," "squabbling"—much less *samovar*. Sometimes we would rehearse a scene for weeks and the actor would develop just the right intonation and expression, then I would learn that he hadn't the foggiest notion what he was saying. Such was the case with David, who had spoken the phrase "to find yourself in this morgue!" many times over, until one day he turned to me and asked: "What *is* a 'morgue'?"

I also delivered a brief lecture on Russian history, with high points like the freeing of the serfs (contemporaneous with our Civil War), the assassination of the tsar, the flowering of Russian literature, the mood of post-heroic exhaustion and *ennui* around 1900 (the date of the play), and, looking ahead, the Russian revolution. I attempted to give a picture of the Russian social classes so the children would understand the economic position of the sort of people Chekhov was writing about, provincial landed gentry who were losing their wealth, and who, in this "hour of sunset," were torn between living in the big cities or in the country. Actually, I had visions of the play occasioning much more elaborate curriculum spinoffs:

Clausen and I would co-teach a unit on Russia, we would read other writings by Chekhov and the major Russian authors, I would have the cast write analyses of their characters and rewrite the ending of *Uncle Vanya*. Most of these schemes, educationally desirable as they may have been, never came to anything for the simple reason that rehearsals took up all of our time. In fact, the kids were already panicking from having to memorize lengthy parts and complete their regular homework every night. Some members of the cast did go to the library to look up Russian costumes. Some rewrote the ending of *Vanya*, and read other Chekhov stories and plays from the books I donated to the class library. They confessed to me that *The Cherry Orchard* was "too difficult," confirming my suspicion that *Uncle Vanya* was the sunniest, clearest, and, of Chekhov's four major plays, the most "do-able" for grade school children.

So much for curriculum tie-ins. We always came back to the text, understanding and reinterpreting it. Because my background is as a writer and not as a man of the theater (I have, in fact, no theatrical background or training to speak of), I approached *Vanya* primarily as a writer's play. Rather than spending a good deal of time on stage business and blocking, I focused instead on the words of the play, the double messages, the psychology, the patterns. Sometimes the children would spot them first, as when they pointed out how each character complains at one point or another that no one is listening to him. One day they noticed all the statements about weather; I tried to get them to figure out their dramatic function. Or, we could come to a line like "I have no hope, none, none." Does Sonia really mean it? Not exactly. Why does Sonia not understand in Act II that Dr. Astrov had rejected her? "Because she doesn't want to understand." Very good. Move on. I wish I had taped these discussions to verify just how much the children understood, how startling their insights were. I am convinced that in the end they grasped all the rich undercurrents in Chekhov, that they were not merely child-puppets mouthing incomprehensible lines, but it took a while. And it took even longer before they acquired a taste for this delicacy.

5

"Old people are like children, they want people to feel sorry for them. But no one feels sorry for old people."
—Nurse Marina, Act II

In the rehearsals, the children often struck, quite unselfconsciously, an amazingly Chekhovian note. One would wander off toward the window, another would be totally self-absorbed, a group would be atomized and looking in four different directions. It made me think that perhaps a stronger tangential connection than I had anticipated existed between Chekhov's world and the world of childhood: the lassitude, the petulance, the waiting for something to happen.

One of the theories I was testing—a theory I had concocted after a disastrous showing of *Citizen Kane* some years earlier to fifth and sixth graders—was that children had a hard time relating to the theme of life dwindling away. They could take sudden death with aplomb; catastrophe found them ever-willing spectators; but the slow dribbling away of potential, the diminution of vital powers, the compromises of integrity comprised by a sense of adult failure, irked them. Or so it seemed to me. Now this assumption was being called into doubt: there were moments when they seemed to get closer to a Chekhovian spirit than any professional production I had ever seen.

However, whole dimensions were still being missed. They played *Vanya* too darkly; it was *too* gloomy, *too* severe. The kids tended to take literally every character's "I'm so miserable" without understanding the Russian braggadocio in some of these assertions of suffering. They also seemed to miss half the irony. Slim would say "Thank you very kindly" in a friendly voice when a workman was pulling him away from his pleasant surroundings to attend a patient, without catching Astrov's acerbic side. Broad sarcasm was grasped a little better. But they had a hard time with self-irony (hard for any actor). Chekhov's characters, after all, are rather intelligent, conscious beings, for all their blind spots: they have a good sense of how they "sound" to others. Elena is both a shallow flirt and a much deeper woman criticizing the shallow flirt. If you play her only the first way you get cardboard.

There was still another level of irony to be grasped: the playwright's attitude toward his characters. Could the kids be made to appreciate that, while the characters may be complaining about their miseries, Chekhov is also inviting us to laugh at them? Would they understand the play as a *comedy?* This was hard for the children to see because there was very little comic stage business, aside from the pistol-shooting at the end of Act III. The humor in Chekhov's lines—those dry cackles of character observation that would eventually draw smiles and laughter out of our adult audience—was something the children still had to take my word for.

All this made me wonder about the developmental acquisition of the faculty of irony. Within this cast of ten- to twelve-year-olds, there was enormous variation. Angus, among the youngest in the group, led the way, as he so often did, in grasping the dynamic of self-irony (the actor standing off from his character, who is already standing off from himself—and then reintegrating the three). Slim brought up the rear. The others straggled in between. In order to lay a firmer foundation for these concepts, I devoted a lesson in Clausen's class to irony. I read from Swift's *A Modest Proposal*, got from the kids a list of things they hated, then asked them to select one and write an essay praising it. I was attempting to teach them to lie and tell the truth at the same time.

One way to lighten the tone of our production was to point out all of the text's humor and irony; another was to wean the children from a uniform tone of hopelessness. I told the cast: "You must play Chekhov for hope. Otherwise it won't work, there won't be any tension or suspense. Sonia must think she *might* get Astrov, Vanya must be at least momentarily optimistic about Elena, even though you as actors already know that in the end it doesn't work out."

To help them see some of these points, I rented a sixteen-millimeter print of Sir Laurence Olivier's *Uncle Vanya*, with Olivier as Astrov, Michael Redgrave as Vanya, Joan Plowright as Sonia, Rosemary Murphy as Elena, and Max Adrian as the Professor. I had seen this performance many years before on television and had loved it. I realized that I was taking a risk in showing them such a polished production—an actor friend warned that it might "crush them"—but it seemed to me that the kids were far enough along in their own characterizations to benefit from exposure to a superb model without necessarily being dominated by it. Ha! Not only were they not overawed by the Olivier version, but they went so far as to criticize it, and thought they could do *much* better. Everyone objected that Joan Plowright as Sonia was ridiculously "overacting" (a criticism I often hurled at them), with her quivering chin and wet eyes holding back the tears. Vanya/Redgrave was too "weak." Most thought Astrov "all right," but Slim *loathed* Olivier. He took to leaving the room whenever Sir Laurence came on-screen. And Mylan asked me afterward, "How come *you* said that I was supposed to make Elena sympathetic as well as flighty, but *she* just did the flighty business, la-de-da and all that?" "Well, you're right, Mylan, maybe we can do better. There are a lot of ways to play *Uncle Vanya*."

The funny part was that, perhaps because I was seeing it so much through the kids' eyes, I agreed with most of their objections. As I watched this production that I had been so moved by years before, it struck me now as stiff and English-repressed, at the same time hysterically forced and overtheatrical. Part of the problem may have been the transfer of a production originally designed for stage to the film medium, so that gestures like Olivier arching his brows, meant to be caught in the last row, tended to look very hammy on-screen. Also, *Vanya* is such a delicate ensemble play that a charismatic actor tends to smother it: this Olivier-directed production might have been more aptly titled *Dr. Astrov*. But the major problem was that we had already started our own *Uncle Vanya*, its seeds were growing inside us; as our inner vision conflicted with the Olivier version we had no choice but to declare it a "counterfeit."

A few practical improvements, which Ayesha, more respectful of professional acting craft, picked up from the film and urged successfully on the others, were: (a) that the characters laughed at each other's witty remarks and were not always in a dour humor; (b) that they sometimes moved around as they spoke. We did not have to *sit* quite so much.

The screening of the film reassured me, in a way; I realized how complex and mountainous a theater classic is, and how easy it is to fall short of it. If we should fail at *Uncle Vanya*, well, so had many others, among them actors of the highest caliber. Scarcely a production of Chekhov in the last twenty years had not been criticized for being forced, phony, trendy, overly neurotic, or false to the spirit of the playwright. It was finally in that sense, even more than in attempting a work rarely done by children, that we had taken on an infinite, staggering challenge.

6

"What still gets to me is beauty. I have an eye for beauty."
—Astrov, Act II

The major struggle was with memorization. The children had Act I and most of Act II down, but they bogged down in Act III, for what felt like months. It seemed that their heads could not hold any more. Angus and Slim had poor memories to begin with—and they had the biggest parts. Mylan discovered a method that worked for her: writing down speeches from memory and then comparing them with the script to catch her errors. Lisa invented a pictorial mnemonic device, connecting picture-symbols with arrows so that her diagram for a speech resembled a treasure map. Sasha drilled the kids when I was not around, they went to each other's houses and practiced. But it was never enough—no matter what they did, they didn't know their parts and we could hardly focus on nuances when they were still stumbling over their lines.

Eventually I understood that this was not just a mechanical problem, but a resistance to letting *Uncle Vanya* take over their lives. Perhaps they had never before known what it was like to be possessed by a task; there is inevitably a revulsion, a queasiness that occurs just before the moment of going under. The children were expressing in their eyes that imminent loss of independence. Ayesha raged that she had to rehearse so much. Slim would cry "Oh, no!" when I came to get him, whining that he had "no more time for math!" Scheduling tensions arose: another teacher wanted to use Mylan and Ayesha in a dance recital, the kids had to do their reports on the energy crisis. And not only was there competition from schoolwork: some of these children had a dizzying after-school agenda. Angus went to Boy Scouts, Stamp Club, Religious Instruction, Fencing, and who knows what else. No wonder he blanked out occasionally, pulled as he was in so many different directions between his parents' and his teachers' and my pressures. But still I was angry that he—they—did not give *Uncle Vanya* a higher priority. "You're the *star* of the *show*. When are you going to memorize it? *July?*" They had to understand, it seemed to me, that this was a unique experience in their lives, and that eventually they would have to put everything else behind them and everything they had into it if they wanted to get something out of it.

Clausen remarked astutely: "The trouble with doing *Uncle Vanya* is that it has to reach a very high level of success before people will even begin to take it seriously, whereas most school activities, however Mickey Mouse they may be, work on the basis of minimizing the chances of failure in order to build up self-confidence." I seemed to be moving in the opposite direction, making us all go out on a limb with a project whose risk of failure was great and whose probability of success slender.

Suddenly Kioka "quits," says she doesn't feel part of the group and is being picked on. I get down on my knees and coax her to remain. Ayesha and Jamal have a fight; she beats him up and he cries. Jamal is forever slipping out of the room with Slim to do mischief. Rebecca thinks I'm neglecting her, that I'm rehearsing Lisa more. Lisa is coasting. Moreover, she has started, in her cool way, to probe and raise doubts: "Maybe this is too difficult for us." Or, "Phillip, why did you pick *Uncle Vanya* in the first place?" "I wanted you to know how people can throw their lives away so that you won't make the same mistake," I snarl. "You mean," says Slim quietly, "like throwing your life away doing a play?"

Sasha is both efficient and officious. Half the time she is my right-hand man, an invaluable assistant; the other half she is planning months in advance for the cast party and considering whom to exclude. Angus is tense. And I myself am going through a sulk, because I have decided absurdly that the kids never show any "gratitude" to me. I am obsessed by their never saying thank you, always taking for granted the extra time and money I am putting into this. Of course, what I don't understand until much later—when the gratitude erupts almost embarrassingly from all sides—is that they are so dependent on me at this stage (I being the only one with a plausible map) that their symbiosis surpasses such petty acknowledgments. Since it is my dream to begin with, and it is I who have gotten them into this mess, I should be much more grateful to them than the other way around. Nevertheless, I am tired and miffed. When they want to get my goat they complain that the play is "boring." "It's *about* boredom, it's not the same as boring," I counter. "No, it's *boring!*"

Only David, that angel of cooperation, and Mylan are always there to support me. One day, when the rest of the cast leaves after a particularly turgid rehearsal, Mylan stays behind. She wants to talk about life with me, have a serious adult conversation. So we talk about depressions—she is in the middle of one, to my surprise—and about moods and her parents' divorce and the fact that she will have to spend the next few years with her father in Colorado. She will miss her little sister terribly, and her mother, of course. But she talks with humor and warmth: somehow, Mylan's "depression" is as sparkling as most other people's liveliness. I realize I am being—cheered up.

By now, both of us are in a good mood, and Mylan in her frisky way starts imitating all the adults at school. I ask her to do an imitation of me. She won't. I ask her what the kids think of me, why they seem to get such pleasure in provoking my anger. She says, "Most of the kids consider you more as a friend than a teacher and so they don't always listen, the way they don't listen to each other, and then they get surprised when you become like a disciplinarian." This surprises me. I doubt that they regard me on the same level as their friends, I have never tried to be other than an adult and a teacher, and yet I can appreciate how they might see my stern, demanding behavior as an irrational contradiction to my looseness at other times. I guess what I want them to know is that I am not demanding to be obeyed because I am the Boss, the figure of adult authority, but because the task demands it. Meanwhile, I am placated.

7

"The weather is charming, the little birds sing, we all live in this world in harmony—what more could we have! [Accepting a glass of tea] Thank you, from the bottom of my heart."

—*Waffles, Act I*

Full-cast rehearsals always carried the risk of discipline problems—a dozen kids to control. Duets and solos, on the other hand, were parts I could rehearse over and over: I'd pull a couple of kids out of class and we'd work on tiny details in a relaxed atmosphere. I particularly loved the beautiful two-women scenes, like the one in which Sonia and Elena make up and pledge their friendship. The feeling of comradeship in that scene, as Mylan and Rebecca or Lisa did it, was very strong and touching. I found myself having them redo it on occasion, not only to perfect some little detail but just to see it again. Those girls could take direction. What a thrill to tell your actors to change their approach and then actually watch them execute things according to your instructions! These small, closed rehearsals also gave each actor the chance to take risks, to experiment, without trying the group's patience.

One day, Lisa started twirling around as she was saying her lines about Astrov to Mylan. She thought her waltzing was a goof, and half expected me to get annoyed, but I was enchanted. It gave a nice lilting feeling to the scene. I encouraged them all to move whenever and wherever the spirit took them. Rather than blocking their movements in advance with chalk marks, which I thought would make them too self-conscious, I urged them to pay attention to the impulses in their bodies that told them to stand up or sit down or carry out a verbal phrase with a gesture.

This opened up a whole new play for them. They began wandering, pacing, retreating when their character was embarrassed, working off their nervous child-energy with spontaneous strolls. Angus showed genius at this, though sometimes he went too far, and one day while circling in his stockinged feet he made me seriously dizzy.

I had to tread a fine line between wanting them to be serious about rehearsing and encouraging them to "play" with the material, even if that was done in the spirit of sabotage. Some of these subversions were hilarious. There was their Robot *Uncle Vanya*, in which they surprised me by moving and talking like mechanical men. There was Horsey *Uncle Vanya*—Mylan had perfected a neigh and delivered all her lines whinnying. David and Angus had worked up a Donald Duck voice for the fight between Vanya and the Professor: "Quack quack you have quruined my life!" They had also rewritten the ending to their satisfaction: Elena is shot, Sonia marries Astrov, the Professor marries the Nurse, and all go off to Africa.

Perhaps the most satisfying rehearsals were the line readings, when I told them they didn't have to "act" but merely to recite the lines as a memory test. As they were speaking their lines, Lisa would be bouncing a rubber ball against the wall, Slim stretching out on the floor, Mylan pacing and chewing her nails, Angus reading a comic book on the radiator. This was truly the Child's *Uncle Vanya*. If only we could have put it onstage like that: I was tempted—we could have had one of the most true-to-life, natural performances of Chekhov in ages. But again, my actors had no idea how close they were to the spirit of the play. They thought they were being naughty.

Slim's *Frankenstein* portrayal of Astrov with stiff arm and leg movement was unfortunately not a parody. When he got nervous his whole body stiffened up. He seemed solemn and wooden to me; I despaired of ever seeing any of the charming, raffish, ironic side of Astrov shine through him. Perhaps it is easier to find cranky eccentrics like Vanya at sixth-grade level than jaded *roués* like Astrov. But I could not resign myself to having one of my main actors pull the whole production down. I began to think about getting a replacement from another class, like smooth-talking, debonair Robert Kowalski. As Easter approached, I even discussed with Monte Clausen the prospect of offering Slim the option of bowing out gracefully. Clausen talked it over with the boy, sounding him out tactfully as to whether the part was too much for him. Slim answered with dignity that he thought he would like to stick with it.

It occurs to me in retrospect that I had trouble appreciating Slim as much as he deserved because he was so different from the kind of child I had been. Slim was athletic, scientifically inclined, popular with girls—perhaps I was simply jealous of him. I had a much easier time identifying with Angus, whose large glasses and precocious manner reminded me more of myself as a boy. Let no one think that a teacher, even an experienced one, is immune to these types of transferences and unconscious rivalries with children.

The kids had been instructed to paraphrase if they forgot their lines. Angus was good at this, and sometimes could invent whole passages of Vanyaesque rant, so close was he to the character. Occasionally, though, he would end up completely confusing himself and everyone else; the beginnings and ends of his speeches were needed to cue the other actors. In time his co-actors, realizing that he had the largest burden of memorization and by now rather tolerant of his idiosyncrasies, adopted a jazzy flexibility in scenes with him. They would whisper key words to Angus when he forgot his lines, which usually set him on the right track again. But there was one speech that he always muddled—a speech that he would reparaphrase each time, and each time it would come out differently. Finally I told him he just had to know it cold.

"This is the only speech in the play that really gives me trouble," Angus said. "Let's take a look at it," I said. Vanya is attacking, in Act I, Elena's fidelity to her aged husband: "Because such fidelity is false from beginning to end. It has a fine sound to it but no logic. If a woman is unfaithful to an old husband whom she hates, that is considered immoral, but for a woman to silence in herself her poor youth and all her vital feelings—that is moral, I suppose." The speech is difficult first because it calls for sarcasm, second because, as Angus pointed out, Vanya is a moral man and therefore violating his principles when he advocates unfaithfulness. Angus put it this way: "He wants to do the wrong thing but he can't because he knows what wrong is. So he tries to fool himself by being clever."

Angus himself was changing through the experience of his starring role. For one thing, he had become more popular. For another he was less tightly controlled and premeditated, less likely to have to think over every word before saying it. His sense of humor had grown, too, or else he was more willing to let it show. His mother, coming by for rehearsals, was stunned to see him scampering around, playing the clown: "This is a side of Angus I have never seen!" One wisecrack of his neatly captured the paradox of our child-adult production. He was supposed to say of Elena: "Ten years ago, I used to meet her at my sister's. She was seventeen then and I was thirty-seven. Why didn't I fall in love with her and propose to her then?" Instead Angus gave the line as: "Ten years ago, I used to meet her at my sister's. I was twenty-seven and she was seven. Why didn't I fall in love and propose to her then? Goo-goo-ba-ba. Hey, wanta get married?" I realized that he was saying something about his own age, which was embarrassingly closer to infancy than to forty.

8

"There was a time when I thought that every person who was odd was crazy, abnormal, and now I'm of the opinion that the normal state of man is to be odd. So you're completely normal."
—*Astrov, Act IV*

One of the oddities of working with ten- to twelve-year-olds on *Uncle Vanya* was that the play began to sound more and more "childish" to me. Chekhov at times seemed to me a rather juvenile writer with a limited, repetitious mind, whose melodramatic plots had a silly side. For instance, the Professor's villainous attempt to sell the farm and boot its real owners out now seemed labored and contrived. Of course, I suspected that I had simply gotten too close to the play to see it fairly anymore, and that the children's behavior at rehearsals had infiltrated my perception of Chekhov. Still, for a week or two there I lost all feeling for *Uncle Vanya*. So did the kids, I imagine. I wonder how people put on ordinary plays for a living, if one can grow numb to such a treasure as this.

The kids had still not gotten Act III down, and with three weeks to go until our performance date, Act IV was nothing but a distant hope. I pleaded, scolded, raged. The one thing I wouldn't do was to praise them when they were merely mediocre.

Visitors who came by to watch rehearsals were very impressed, and a little surprised, I think, to find me so parsimonious with my praise. But it seemed to me we had passed the point of supportive "stroking"; any enthusiastic response had to be genuine or it would undermine the truth of future compliments. We were all co-workers now, and the mark of respect I paid them was to assume they could do the job.

One afternoon, the cast—as if playing a prank on me after having driven me crazy the day before—performed an Act II and Act III that was on such a high level that no one knew what to make of it. The actors who were not in the scene watched, for once, those who were with catlike absorption. We all learned something that day: mainly, that we could do it. I had seen bits and pieces of *Uncle Vanya* come alive at different rehearsals, only to watch the cast nervously kick it away and destroy the mood with self-protective frivolity, as though unwilling to raise expectations in me or themselves that they were capable of sustained intensity. Now we knew better.

I might add that some of these magic moments in rehearsals were never equaled in performace (though no rehearsal as a whole came up to the performances in consistency). How I would have loved to splice, like a film editor, the best Act II from one rehearsal with the best Act III from another. Such an assemblage would have made up the ideal production of *Uncle Vanya* by our cast, but that version exists only in my head, and will never be seen by anybody else. In compensation for the loss of those perfect interpretative moments, the theatrical process gives us—especially in amateur productions—the kamikaze thrill of diving into pure, terrifying surprise with every live performance.

Refusing to waste the production on the school auditorium, where the horrible acoustics and odor of old cheese sandwiches (it doubled as a lunchroom) would have strained the suspension of disbelief to the breaking point, I looked around for other halls. I managed to secure the nearby Symphony Space, a grand old movie palace that had been taken over by a nonprofit organization for use by local musical, theater, and community groups. They waived their usual fee since we had no money to pay them, asking only that they be given the whole box office gate for the evening performance. And they let us have four rehearsals on their stage—a generous amount, considering the demand for it among their performing groups.

Most of the time we still rehearsed in the Writing Room (an ordinary-sized classroom) or, occasionally, in the school auditorium. It was difficult to make the transition from one space to another. A tone of intimacy had been created in the Writing Room, which did not translate easily to the school auditorium stage, or to the even larger Symphony proscenium, with its mysterious ropes and wires and backstage passageways. The Symphony Space was in fact too big for us; it seated a thousand in the orchestra and balcony combined. I would have much preferred a little jewel box of a chamber theater seating two hundred, all close enough so that the children would not have had to raise their voices, but there was no such facility in the neighborhood, and we were lucky to be getting the Symphony. The day *Uncle Vanya* went up on the Symphony's theater marquee, it made the whole production seem more real to the kids. "We're going to be on Broadway!" bragged Randi, and in truth the Symphony was located on the Great White Way, only fifty blocks north of the legitimate-theater district. But it also raised the ante: we had to do well now. As one of our stars put it, "I wouldn't be so nervous but we're going to be in a real theater."

Now each one had to concentrate on facing the audience and throwing his voice. The small, cherished, naturalistic style of acting that had developed in the Writing Room seemed lost at first on the Symphony stage. It was pathetic; nothing came across. "Louder!" I kept calling. "Exaggerate more! Make it bigger!" In fact, I hated to force them away from their quiet underplaying and into that strident incisiveness which is so irritating to me when I go to the theater. I much prefer the more muted screen acting, where the audience seems almost to be eavesdropping, but the medium had its demands, and we had to bow to them. The kids had to be made at least somewhat aware of the necessity to project forward or the audience simply would not hear them, which, in a play so dependent on dialogue, would be disastrous. For a week, I entertained the possibility of stringing a set of microphones above the stage, but in the end the technical difficulties and cost forced me to give up this idea. Besides, it would be cleaner with natural sound. But no matter how many times I told the cast to speak louder, they had a hard time accepting the fact that they needed virtually to yell every line.

They loved the feeling of the larger Symphony stage, but in the beginning their wanderings always seemed to take them back, back into the sheltering regions of the stage where their voices were lost in the side flats and against the rear wall. I knew that they were afraid of the stark confrontation with an audience (even a hypothetical audience) downstage, and I sympathized. But they would have to overcome it.

In the meantime, the rest of Clausen's class was readying the scenery. Sasha took charge of scenery and props, and, with the aid of an art teacher, supervised the painting of several large backdrops. Sasha was everywhere, making lists of props, bossing around other children, throwing fits when something was out of whack. She had developed an enormous sense of responsibility for this production, one equal to mine, and I found myself leaning on her more and more as my lieutenant. I made her the prompter as well, which touched off an argument between us. One day she was in the wings and Jamal forgot his lines; the cast waited in silence for more than a minute. "Where's the prompter?" I yelled from the pit. Sasha stuck her head out: "He knows his lines, he's just pretending not to." "Sasha, don't get psychological on me. If they don't say their lines, just prompt! *Prompt!*" She ran into the pit and started weeping several rows behind me. "I quit!" she said. "I don't want to be prompter anymore." All the children onstage looked at me with solemn, accusing faces, as if to say, "You've gone too far this time." I knew I was partly wrong; in fact, I had told Sasha once before that she shouldn't give anyone his lines too quickly, she should let everyone have a chance to figure them out; but I could not bring myself to apologize to her immediately, as I would have done with another kid. She and I were so hitched to this production that we had started acting like an old married couple. At the end of the scene, I turned to her and begged her forgiveness. She accepted, but firmly refused to return to the prompting job.

9

"Such goings-on—shouting and yelling, shooting. . . . Shameful, that's what it is, shameful. . . . [Sighing] It's ages since I tasted any noodle soup."

—Nurse Marina, Act IV

By the first of June I had finished off all my other writing classes and was doing nothing but *Uncle Vanya*. I had decided to rehearse lightly in the last two weeks so as not to exhaust the kids. I was a little worried about the problem of their physical stamina, as we had never rehearsed all four acts together and the show would probably come to more than two hours. On top of that, I didn't want to push them too hard because they had to have some emotion left for the performances. So I concentrated on getting some of the other parts of the production ready. The scenery was going well; the kids had painted a large flowered wallpaper interior and then brown-washed it to make it look faded. There was also a pretty outdoor country scene, with birds and trees. We had gotten some old couches and a writing desk from Sasha's mother, and a real samovar from another parent. Three other kids from Clausen's class had worked out a pattern for the lighting; Angus's mother was helping with the costumes: babushkas, evening dresses, nightshirts, vests, and ties. We had printed up programs and flyers and sent children out to plaster the neighborhood with them. And we were starting to collect a number of volunteer kids who wanted to be in on the glamour and excitement of the final days.

I remembered this same momentum developing with *West Side Story*, some six years before. But that earlier production had had larger resonance: the whole school community had gotten excited, partly because more children were involved, partly because it was the first big theatrical at P.S. 90 (people were more jaded now); but more crucially, because *West Side Story* was a popular musical that everybody already loved, whereas *Uncle Vanya* seemed to be generating a lower order of curiosity. It was more like facing a cultural duty than an anticipated pleasure. I had to accept the fact that *Uncle Vanya* would probably go over the heads of many children and even some of the adults. Tickets for our evening show were not selling as quickly as they had with *West Side Story*. The principal, Mr. Jimenez, who had always shown an interest in our big creative projects, had already informed me that he would not be able to attend either performance, which hurt.

I also had a more private, protective feeling toward *Uncle Vanya*—as one might for an unsuccessful second novel—than I had had toward the crowd-pleasing

West Side Story. It seemed to me (how quickly we forget) that *West Side Story* had been easier to put on; no nuanced, sophisticated acting was necessary, just twenty seconds of dialogue, then a musical number. I did not remember having been afraid so far along in the *West Side Story* process that it might not come off, but I was having real fear of failure in the pit of my stomach right up to the last day of *Uncle Vanya.* In a sense I was competing with myself and that earlier success. To complicate things, the children themselves knew all about it: several of them had read the *West Side Story* section in my book *Being with Children* (it was in the school library). They even asked, "Are you going to write about *us*, Phil?" Certainly not, I said, and meant it. To imagine such commemoration in advance would jinx us.

We had scheduled two performances, one in the morning for all the upper grades of P.S. 90, one in the evening for the parents and community. I had been noticing that Slim seemed to be getting stronger as Astrov. No matter how much directing advice you give, the actor finally has to figure it out by himself, has to go off and think long and hard about the character. And this Slim had done. I told him how much more self-assured he sounded; he blushed, and Lisa said, "That's the first time you've complimented Slim in months!" They were keeping track of my compliments. One day Slim came in triumphantly and told me that he knew his entire part: his mother had been quizzing him every night and he had it down pat. It was true. I was so glad Slim had stuck with it: he taught me more about the progress a child was capable of than any of the others.

Mylan I knew I could depend on to do a good job; she seemed consistently professional. The two Sonias were a treat to watch. Angus was getting there. The final dress rehearsal went brilliantly through all of Acts I and II. "Uh-oh," said Sasha, conscious of the theatrical superstition. "It's going too well—and it's the dress rehearsal!" Fortunately, things fell apart in the second half: it was sloppy, slow, anarchic, dreadful.

The afternoon before the first performance, we had a low-key run-through of the still uncertain Act IV. We also had a quiet meeting, everyone sitting onstage, in which I listed the possible things that could go wrong (and the best ways to adjust to them). These ranged from stage fright and blank memory to duds in the cap pistol, falling scenery, tomatoes thrown, fights breaking out in the audience. I reminded them that during the love scene between Slim and Mylan they could expect an uproar from the kiddie audience. It was also possible that some children might be bored, and that a teacher might decide to take her class away during intermission. Significant looks were exchanged; everyone knew Mrs. Jacoby was the teacher I meant. They had already anticipated that the first performance, before their peers, would be the harder. Jamal surprised me by saying, "That's okay. They're just childish little babies. It's not our fault if this is too mature for them." He had already acquired the artist's advance defense mechanism for rejection by the public.

10

"I'm just as unhappy as you are, maybe, but I don't give up. I bear it and I'll go on bearing it till the end of my life. Then you bear it too, Uncle!"

—Sonia, Act IV

At seven-thirty the next morning I showed up at the Symphony with my bag of groceries (cheese, crackers, strawberry soda for the drinking scenes, and fresh roses) and waited for the bleary-eyed theater manager to open the doors. The kids arrived moments later. They hung the scenery, set up props for Act I according to the list we had made, inserted the caps into the cap pistol. Angus's mother took the nervous actors into the dressing room and applied their makeup.

The kids at the light board set the lights for Act I. The classes started arriving a few minutes to nine: all the fifth- and sixth-grade classes would be attending, and a few third/fourth-grade teachers had managed to sneak their classes in at the last moment, on the pretext that someone had a brother or sister in the cast. I doubted if the youngest kids would get much out of *Vanya*, but there was nothing much I could do at this point.

When the time came to start I sat in the front row, ready to dart backstage if needed. Our two "old women," Ayesha and Kioka, looked honestly wizened and grandmotherly. Lisa would be prompter, since it was Rebecca's turn to play Sonia. Their joking rivalry had given a new twist to the theatrical cliché as each encouraged the other to "break a leg."

Ayesha took her place onstage, sighing and knitting; the audience grew hushed; I signaled the lighting booth; the lights went dark in the pit; Slim/Dr. Astrov had already made his entrance and was pacing around, ready to respond to the first line in the play: "Have some tea, my boy."

So the first performance began. It was a restrained opening, until Angus came onstage, setting the play spinning like a top. Angus knew his lines pretty well by heart, and moreover he was giving it that extra something, improvising gestures and motions I had never seen him do before. He seemed possessed. The other actors reacted gratefully to his powerful lead, at the same time appearing a little in awe of his demonic stage presence. All except Mylan, who came on with her own energy, determined to project. Her Elena had taken on a little Mae West and Sadie Thompson in response to the live audience. There were already rumors backstage that some of the children were not speaking loudly enough, and Mylan was going to be heard. She practically directed the others while onstage by the emphatic way she placed herself and delivered her lines. I was glad for her take-charge air, even as I regretted the slight coarsening of, and remove from, her character.

When Act I ended, I ran onstage to help move furniture. The children were excited that they had gotten through the first part — "so far so good!" But they knew that they would have to speak a great deal louder to reach the classes in the back rows during the next act.

Act II began with one of my favorite scenes in the play: the reproachful duet between husband and wife, the Professor and Elena. Mylan brought her tone down (as I'd instructed) and David made the hypochondriac egoist as sympathetic as I have ever seen him played. Rebecca was very touching as Sonia. I was already beginning to wish I had cast her for the evening performance; I consoled myself with the logic of throwing the more professional actress to the tougher (children's) audience. Slim's somewhat herky-jerky interpretation of Astrov had grown on me. He did a great drunk scene, which bought waves of laughter from the kids. However, he and Mylan backpedaled away from each other like unicyclists during the love scene, disappointing the audience.

I was so hyperconscious of the audience's responses, super-sensitive to the backstage whispers and the footsteps of stage-hands during scenes, that the play itself, *Uncle Vanya*, passed me by. I couldn't feel it. The kids' fright had constricted their voice boxes so that the words came out correctly but without the full passion or authority I knew they were capable of delivering. Either that, or I was too numb with terror to notice how much *was* getting across.

Later, the cast was ebullient. "We did it!" they cried in the dressing room. "No one messed up his lines, Phillip. We did the whole thing perfect. Except for—" and they bubbled forth with the anecdotes of catastrophes skirted that all actors must tell to rid themselves of adrenaline: of how Sasha almost couldn't find the gun, how Angus forgot his line so Mylan made a bridge to her next speech, wasn't that clever? I congratulated them heartily, disguising the fact that I felt a little let down. Somehow, after all that work we had put in, I had expected it to be better. I was down on myself, too, for not being satisfied with the kids' best efforts. Teri Mack and Sue Willis, my Teachers and Writers colleagues, had loved it, but they were artists who had worked on plays with kids for years and could see the effort that had gone into the show. Some of the regular teachers were not sure what to make of the production. I might have allowed myself to be talked into ignoring my own inner doubts were it not for these others' puzzled responses. The performance had clearly not convinced everyone. I wanted it to be so strong that it made every spectator a believer.

A word should be said about the audience. They were remarkably attentive throughout, and as quiet as anyone can expect of five hundred children sitting for two and a half hours in the dark. Nor should it be assumed that P.S. 90 children were especially well behaved or always given to honoring the hard work of other children: I had seen pandemonium and fistfights break out during a visiting school's production of *Oklahoma*. But they watched *Vanya* with an eerie respectfulness, treating it as if it were a sober tragedy. All of the classes stayed until the end, which was itself a tribute. Some kids seemed deeply involved, others were no doubt bored and restless, but went no further showing it than a pantomime of yawns. Others leaned forward, straining to catch each actor's voice. All of the children seemed to understand that something "important" was going on before their eyes, even if they didn't quite get it. For many of them, it was probably their first experience of serious theater.

The first performance had, in short, its virtues and its partisans, but I still sensed we could do better. In the meantime, I was exhausted.

After everyone had gone, Mylan and her little sister stayed behind with me in the dressing room. Mylan wanted to get my honest impressions of how it had gone. Already so grown-up in certain ways, she had a love of postmortems that she knew I shared. But she also seemed to be checking to see if I was all right. Again, Mylan pulled me out of the doldrums by getting me to discuss everything with encouraging candor. I got the impression that she was also flirting with me—and I with her! It is a cliché in the theater that the director falls in love with his leading lady. Since adults are not supposed to fall in love with children, let us simply say that I appreciated Mylan's timely attentions.

11

"Second of February, vegetable oil twenty pounds. . . . Sixteenth of February, again vegetable oil twenty pounds. . . . "
—*Vanya, doing accounts, Act IV*

I had decided to regard the first performance as a dry run. This was, in effect, our one uninterrupted dress rehearsal before the real test. We still had a day intervening before the Thursday night performance to work out the kinks.

On Wednesday, I talked to the cast as a group. The kids were in great shape, they were telling me not to be so nervous. Clausen had instructed them to calm me down. He had gotten his own case of stage fever, of course, and was by now thoroughly involved in the production. On Thursday night he would direct traffic from the wings, freeing me to watch the performance from the audience. Clausen's pride in the project and in his kids was wonderful to see.

My speech to the group went as follows: first I complimented them, then I "calmly" pointed out areas for improvement. I spoke about the need for stillness: raising the shiver down their own backs and causing it in the audience. They had to rediscover the freshness of the play's emotions, take time to feel things, not be afraid to let a moment of silence spread, that's what Chekhov's pauses were put there for in the first place. Play with the pace if you feel like it. Not everything should be so even, so mechanically equal in importance, as on Tuesday morning. Stretch out a passage, give some words the emphasis they deserve. . . .

We still needed to work on the love scene between Astrov and Elena. Romance was an integral part of the play. A kiss would have been perfect, but barring that, the semblance of one would suffice. "You tell Slim he has to do it," Mylan whispered to me. "I'll do it if he does it. He's the one who's messing up." The rumor had already spread that Mylan liked Slim in real life. Slim, on the other hand, was very attached to Lisa, which also had to be corrected for onstage. He would follow Lisa with his eyes when, as Astrov, he was supposed to be utterly indifferent to her as a woman. I had to keep reminding him to neglect Lisa/Sonia for Mylan/Elena. The discordance between art and life was throwing this scene off.

I took Mylan and Slim into the assistant principal's office and locked the door. "These are your instructions. You must have five to ten seconds' contact. Slim, you must put your arm around her waist at the words, 'You can't escape.' Mylan, you put both arms around him then. And you put your head on his shoulder" (this wasn't easy, since Mylan was taller than Slim) "after you say 'Have mercy.' Now try it." I stood back and watched their all-thumbs attempt. "One must get the sense that electric currents are pushing you toward and away from each other, and that no matter what words you say to protest, your bodies are obeying their own laws. Slim, try to turn her more toward you."

"You don't know, Phillip. Slim really is a Dr. Astrov in real life!" said Mylan. "He's fresh!" Slim turned beet red and laughed. I demonstrated what I wanted with both partners, to reduce to a kind of dance step what had been too fraught with circumstance, but of course my intervention only led to more hysterics. Slim did not relish taking me in his arms, and Mylan cried "No kiss!" when I approached her as Astrov.

The night of the big performance, two telegrams were hanging on the dressing room mirror, one from the Parents Association and one from Mylan's father in Colorado.

Lisa was the only one who had not yet gone through the experience of acting her role before a live audience, and I was a little concerned about her, but she assured me she knew her lines. She had put her hair up in a bun and worn glasses and a dowdy blouse to make herself look less pretty. It was Lisa who started the kids "meditating" an hour before performance. I came backstage behind the side-flats and found them all kneeling or sitting alone, breathing deeply into themselves. What a sight! I tiptoed away; I could not have asked for a better way to focus them, though it would have seemed pretentious for me to ask them to meditate.

Sasha showed up late, on roller skates, with a tape recorder, a Polaroid camera, and every other imaginable gadget. It was her intention to "document" the play both by recording it in front of the stage on her rinky-dink tape recorder and by snapping flash photographs. I tried to explain to her that there was more than enough work to do backstage, getting the props ready for each act. Besides, my Teachers and Writers colleague, Teri Mack, had already set up a video camera in the aisle to tape the performance.

The audience began filing in a half hour early, while we were still putting up scenery. There was no curtain at Symphony Space, so all changes had to take place before the audience's tolerant view. I was too nervous to talk to the incoming crowd, but I recognized many reliable faces. About two hundred people, not as large a crowd as I had dreamed of (partly my fault, since I hadn't taken enough time away from the production to handle publicity or to delegate the responsibility for it properly), but certainly a decent turnout. The familiar greetings of many P.S. 90 playgoers with each other gave the theater a warm feeling of community. The director of Symphony Space made a welcoming speech and we were ready to begin.

12

"We shall rest! We shall hear the angels, we shall see the whole sky full of diamonds, we shall see how all earthly evil, all our sufferings, are drowned in a mercy that will fill the whole world. And our life will grow peaceful, tender, sweet as a caress. I believe, I do believe. . . . [Wipes away his tears with a handkerchief] Poor, dear Uncle Vanya, you're crying. . . . In your life you haven't known what joy was; but wait, Uncle Vanya, wait. . . . We shall rest. . . . We shall rest. . . . We shall rest!"

—*Sonia, final speech, Act IV*

The play was terrific. The acoustics were great; you could hear every word. The adults in the pit responded well to the ironic lines, and their laughter put the actors in a relaxed mood. They could feel a live audience enjoying every moment of them. As I watched the play in my seat, getting shivers from the drama, forgetting that these were children or even actors, receiving the full double-edged meaning of Chekhov's lines, I realized what people meant by "the miracle of the theater." That night was a miracle. I knew it was because I had seen that earlier daytime performance, which had been adequate but had not moved me at all. This time there was gooseflesh. I could see why theater folk are so superstitious and, more to the point, so often seem to have a personal relation to God. You start believing in divine intervention when all those random, unreliable elements cohere.

Lisa slowed everyone down; she was on edge, more so than the others, but her seriousness took the form of delaying and going inward, which quieted the cast. A sort of serene sadness played in her movements. There was one woman from Russia in the audience; she had nothing to do with P.S. 90 but had merely wandered in off the street to see *Uncle Vanya*. She told me later that all the children were good, but that Angus and Lisa had the real "Chekhov acting style."

It was Angus's evening. No one could stop talking about him afterward. And rightly so—this was an *Uncle Vanya* with Vanya at the heart of it. I watched him in total belief. So far as I was concerned, his was the definitive Uncle Vanya; as long as I live I will think of Vanya as a boy with a scowling, scrunched-up face and forlorn posture and imperious arm gestures. He and some of the other kids were 20 percent better than I had directed them to be. The truth is that they had peaked at just the right time, in the evening performance. Mylan, having gotten her role down long before the others, had added exuberant *femme fatale* flourishes. She was having a great time onstage. They were all learning enormous amounts about acting each time they performed before a live audience.

One of the curiosities of this production was that the children still seemed to be acting for themselves, rather than to the audience. As often as I had urged them not to show their backs, in the end I stopped nagging about it, because I preferred them to react naturally to each other even if it meant momentarily turning away. The audience became, in effect, eavesdroppers on a world that was not staged for them. Such a solution, coming as it did out of the children's instinctive preferences as well as their amateur limitations, enhanced the purity of the Chekhovian mood.

I kept moving from seat to seat in the large hall, to make sure that the voices were carrying everywhere, but also to be part of different sections of the audience. The play so absorbed me that it was as though I were hearing *Uncle Vanya* for the first time, wondering how it would turn out. Only one funny moment jarred the illusion of life: in the middle of Mylan and Lisa's poignant duet, which was going perfectly, Sasha appeared at the apron of the stage and snapped what must have been two of the longest and loudest Polaroid flash exposures in the history of tactlessness. Mylan froze. The whole audience waited for Sasha to get out of the way, but she stood her ground. It occurred to me that she had never quite accepted not getting one of the major roles and that this was her unconscious revenge.

During intermission the audience seemed collectively to pinch themselves in happy surprise at how well it was going. They were happy, too, I thought as they jammed the lobby, to be escaping momentarily that morbid world of provincial Russia. Angus's name was on everyone's lips. And suddenly, the star himself appeared in the lobby, as did the other actors—racing down the aisles to hear their praises sung. They were forgetting my orders about staying in character! But the audience loved this touch of unprofessionalism. They could return to clucking over the kids as cute.

People were shaking my hand as though it were already over. I worried that the tension might seep out of the second half but was too elated to stay away from congratulations. One parent, who had supported our activities over the years, said to me: "Phil, I have to admit that when I heard you were doing *Uncle Vanya* with the kids, I thought, 'This time he's really flipped his lid.' Forgive me, I owe you an apology." His comment gave me an uneasy, sickening feeling, as I realized how close I had come to destroying their confidence in me. All it would have taken—would still take—was one panicky actor.

The second half maintained the high quality of the first. The love scene between Mylan and Slim was neither the backpedaling race of the first performance nor a real clinch, but some compromise in between. The last act, when Elena, the Professor, and Astrov leave the farm one by one and Sonia and Vanya are left alone, turning to "work" as a momentary anodyne for their abandonment, had a nice hushed floatiness. I had wanted Lisa to take Sonia's magnificent "We shall rest" speech slowly, so that the audience would know the end had come. The ending had been too sudden on Tuesday morning, partly because Rebecca had rushed her lines, partly because the lighting crew had forgotten to fade out slowly. This time we had worked out a new staging where both Angus and Lisa would stand at the edge of the stage for her long speech, and the lights would begin their slow fade in the middle of it. Lisa pulled a blank, a few lines into the speech, but then her groping through it, her pauses, her difficulty in trying to remember made the speech sound even more sincere and moving. It was as though she were struggling to find the right words with which to console Vanya and herself.

The lights went out and Lisa's father stood up with tears in his eyes. Then everyone applauded. We had rehearsed the bows and they were fairly neat. Mylan called me onstage (as I had asked her to, not trusting to spontaneous acclamation) and I thanked everyone behind the scenes and ended by proposing, tongue in cheek, "Next year, *The Cherry Orchard*." Inwardly I thanked God for saving my skin: I promised myself this was the limit, that I would never try anything so difficult with children again.

"We did it! We did the Impossible!" cried Angus to anyone backstage who would listen.

13

"They're gone!"
                    —Mme. Voitskaya (Vanya's mother), Act IV

The next day I had arranged to take the cast as a treat to the Russian Tea Room, after three o'clock. This sounds more generous than it was: I had asked them to bring their own money, about five dollars each, but promised that I would escort them and treat anyone who couldn't swing the finances. (Somehow, certain adults still got the idea that I was paying for everyone; their eyes misted over, so great is the need for people to find "Mr. Chips" figures in everyday life.)

An essential part of the cast by now, Monte Clausen came with us. On the subway the kids were making uneasy jokes about not being let in, and when they entered through the Russian Tea Room's revolving doors and gazed up at the swank interior I could see them go stiff with fright. True to their nightmare, the hostess took one look at the gang of children and refused to seat us. "But I made a reservation for thirteen yesterday," I said, retreating toward the back of the restaurant. "You stay there!" she added. "I'll go ask the manager." I saw them conferring and the manager frowning. I advanced toward them and started to explain that this group had just put on *Uncle Vanya* and wasn't it appropriate that they have tea at the Russian Tea Room—but apparently I had already committed a great sin by passing beyond the *maître d's* red sash, since they both looked up in horror and motioned me back, caring not at all to hear my sentimental explanation.

They finally decided to seat us. So the great menus were brought and the waitress put on her children-serving smile. I had expected the kids to be full of talk about their triumph the night before. But for the first half hour they were so intimidated by the fancy surroundings that they compensated by playing a game of Rich People. Ayesha said, "I almost drowned in my bathtub yesterday. Gracious! A hundred feet is really too big for a bathtub." David cracked, "I only sold two yachts yesterday." These were mostly middle-class kids, but they had evidently never been in a joint like the Russian Tea Room before. One more educational experience. I drew their attention to the polished samovars and the paintings and the waiters' red peasant smocks: "If only we could have had some of those for the play!" Gradually, they settled comfortably into the surroundings, and stuffed éclairs and swan-shaped cakes into their mouths, and drank tea in a glass, à la Russe. I ordered an "Uncle Vanya," a sweet cocktail which happened to be listed under that name on the menu, and let them each take a sip. "My mother's going to kill you when she finds out, Phil!" Mylan said.

"It's finished!" cried David. "I feel so sad about it. We worked for so long, and now there's no more Uncle Vanya. . . ."

Jamal, meanwhile, was stealing every sugar cube and matchbook in sight. The kids stocked up on free postcards on the way out. They had promised they would take me out once or twice during rehearsals, and I had made the same promise to them, but in the end we went Dutch, as was fitting. They were still handing me crumpled dollar bills as we headed up 57th Street past Carnegie Hall, happy to be in the warm sun again. Some were running ahead, mixing with the five o'clock crowd, while others continued to feed me bills from their pockets.

The dollar bills that children give you are different from other people's currency. They are bunched up and folded six times over and very, very sweaty. They don't know how to lie flat. They made my wallet bulge for days afterward.

I could go on to justify Uncle Vanya in traditional educational terms by saying that it increased the children's vocabulary, reading, and memorization skills, taught them a good deal about acting, literature, and Russia, and helped instill the values of patience, endurance, and team cooperation. I also recognize that it represented a kind of luxurious excess: it was educationally inefficient and labor-intensive, took too many hours away from other endeavors, involved only a third of the class, and was never organically integrated into the rest of the curriculum. It did not resolve, one way or the other, those large philosophical questions about the nature of childhood I posed in the beginning, however tantalizingly it brushed against them. Nor, given the typical constraints of the American school day and the myriad pressures put on teachers, would I expect such an effort to be easily replicated. I had a uniquely advantageous set of circumstances, and I feel intensely grateful to the P.S. 90 community for having given me the latitude to take such a risk of failure with their children. I wish there were more room allowed in the educating of our young for attempting such follies, such adventures that challenged children to the limits of their (surprisingly expandable) capacities.

That summer I went away to the country for vacation. I was sharing a house in Wellfleet with several people, and we would often meet in the course of the day for a few moments on the sun deck, exchanging pleasantries about the weather or non sequiturs accented with glints of confession in a manner that reminded me uncannily of *Uncle Vanya*. Snatches of *Vanya* would come back to me as my housemates and I sat facing the pond, looking not at each other but outward toward that external point, where the audience would have been. In the architecture of the summer cottage, with visitors coming and going, each of us entering and exiting group scenes from his or her world of privacy, the wisdom of Chekhov's observations struck me time and again. I would mumble Vanya's irritable lines to myself as I retreated to my room, annoyed at some social snub or aroused by some amorous triangulation. And I could have sworn that, miles away, on their own vacations, the kids were also remembering the lines of the play, and connecting them with the life they were seeing all about them.

17

Suicide of a Schoolteacher

ALL THIS HAPPENED A WHILE AGO, IN 1979. At the time I had been working for close to ten years as a writer-in-residence at P.S. 90, a public school on Manhattan's Upper West Side. My situation there was unique: unlike most writers-in-the-schools, who are sent into scattershot residences all over the map, I was allowed—thanks to the receptive staff of P.S. 90 and my sponsoring organization, Teachers and Writers Collaborative—to sink roots in one place and to teach anything I wanted. The children and I made films together, put on plays, produced novels and poetry magazines and comic books, ran a radio station. I became entwined with the life of the school, went to Parents Association meetings and staff parties, and felt for the first time in my life a productive member of a community.

If the elementary school world was far more earthbound, less glamorous, than the downtown literary/art circles (around which my career and erotic fantasies still revolved), it nevertheless felt warmer, more communal, richer in drama, and more willing to make a fuss over me personally. This dream of the grade school as maternally nurturing community may have been in part, I see now, a naïve family romance, or a narcissistic projection of my own need to play the favorite son. That not everyone who taught at P.S. 90 was so well served by, or contented with, the milieu was a fact I certainly took in but tended to downplay. In any case, my dream received a jolt of reality one night when Monte Clausen, the schoolteacher I was closest to at P.S. 90, phoned me at home.

"Did you hear about Jay Becker yet?" asked Monte, cautiously.

"No. What about Jay?"

"He killed himself."

I turned off the television. "How?"

"He jumped from his apartment window. The twenty-seventh floor, something like that, of the Amsterdam Towers."

"Jesus." All my life I had prepared myself for a phone call telling me that someone I knew had committed suicide. Now that one had finally come, I was at a loss. "The Amsterdam Towers, that's right around me."

"You knew he'd moved into your neighborhood. . . ?"

"Sure. We used to get off at the same bus stop together." This seemed so inadequate a claim of connection with the victim that I immediately felt ashamed for having said it. I pressed Clausen for details, and we had one of those *Dragnet* exchanges: What time of day did it happen? How did you find out? Underneath my sober tone I sensed a spark of excitement at the gaudiness of the news—perhaps survivor's superiority or simply the pleasure of sharing a choice bit of gossip, which did not seem real to me yet. It was almost as though, now that Jay had made his point, he could dust himself off and go about his business. Side by side with that reaction was the unwanted understanding, like a punch in the gut, that Jay Becker was gone forever.

Jay always seemed bigger than life. One simply didn't expect such a vivid person to die, period, much less kill himself. On the other hand, in some subterranean way, I had sensed this was going to happen. I didn't dare explain the reasons for this feeling to Clausen, not yet.

We talked for a few minutes, and I seem to remember mouthing clichés about the shallow relationships of people in the big city, where everyone rubbed elbows constantly but took no real responsibility for each other. This was bullshit: New York City was not to blame. In any locale I could have imagined, even a little mountain village, I would have kept my distance from Jay Becker.

Don't get me wrong, I genuinely liked Jay. I liked him, at the same time as I congratulated myself for being fond of someone who could be very hard to take. He had a shrillness about him that telegraphed a large hurt. One felt life's intensity in his presence, much as watching the dentist approach, drill in hand, quickens one's perceptual apparatus. Sometimes I was not in the mood for the challenge of his clangorousness, and had to steel myself before entering his orbit.

I had made an early attempt at describing Jay in *Being with Children*, the book I wrote in 1975 about my experiences as a writer-in-residence at P.S. 90. At the time I had changed Jay's name to Stanley Riegelhaupt:

Riegelhaupt had the loudest teacher's voice I had ever encountered. Children ducked under their desks when they heard that voice; they held their ears like dogs whining at passing fire engines. The strangest part about his voice was that it was not malicious or cruel. Only loud. He seemed to enjoy demonstrating the power of the organ for the fun of it. While escorting his students through the halls he would unleash it, then turn around and smile at the cringing spectators. It did manage to keep the class in line; but only, I think, because they were irritated at the volume, not because they were afraid of him. Once they discovered that underneath that voice he was something of a softie and rather benign, they found ways of getting around him.

Coming into that charged atmosphere as an outsider, it was not always easy for me to know how to react to him. Every time I picked up the kids to go to the Writing Room, he would use my entrance as an occasion for a practical joke. One morning I came in wearing a red-flowered shirt; some kids complimented me on it. Stanley, picking up the murmur, demanded in his loud voice: "All right, class, who has the more colorful shirt on today, Phil or me?" He happened to be wearing an utterly bland tan wash and wear shirt. The kids cried overwhelmingly: "Phillip does!"

"What's that?" he roared. "All right, who wants to stay after school and get extra homework? You should know that I *always* have the most colorful shirt." He took another vote, and this time he won.

What embarrassed me was not the subtle hostility against me but the hostility against himself. But like all Dostoevskian buffoons, he seemed to imply that his time would come. On another occasion, he took the opportunity to make me blush by announcing that I had just gotten married. As the kids crowded around me, offering handshakes and congratulations, I was covered in confusion and kept trying to tell them that it wasn't true! Finally I had to run out of the room, with a few kids chasing down the halls yelling the news to everyone, and I got teased for days with that apocryphal story.

A love-hate relationship had grown up between Riegelhaupt's students and him, provoked by Stanley's own inclination to self-ridicule. Stanley liked to trade gross insults with his students. But often as not, he was the butt of his own jokes. The room was papered with compositions which told of Riegelhaupt's animal genealogies and uncertain parentage, his lack of wit, his failure at every endeavor, his alleged nasty habits—and on top of each one he had written in red ink, "Excellent!" or "Very Funny, Great Imagination!"

In fact they were not so funny; they were a little hard to take. But the kids liked doing them. He had managed to sell them the idea of creative writing by offering himself as a target. Every week he assigned "Creative Writing" for homework, and every week they came back with pages and pages of sarcastic, juvenile fantasies about their teacher.

I shudder when I read this now. In a book otherwise filled with affectionate or at least diplomatic portraits of the schoolteachers I worked with, I had allowed myself a certain ridiculing sport in Jay's case; even the pseudonym, Stanley Riegelhaupt, was chosen for its comic, Jerry Lewis *shlemiel* sound. Not that what I wrote was untrue, but the passage falsifies through its cheerfulness; it denies an anguish I was trying not to see. Disturbing, too, is the ominous phrase, "he seemed to imply that his time would come."

Jay Becker had a tight, compact body and an erect military bearing, an impression furthered by his crew cut, which he wore throughout the entire period when long hair was the male fashion. He had thick glasses with dark rims. His nose drew your attention: it was always shiny, beaded with sweat, large-pored, hooked, and aggressive. When he didn't like something his nostrils would pull in and the nasal ridge-bone protrude. Sometimes his nose alone would turn white or blush pink—dilate with pleasure or look suddenly pinched—betraying his secret emotion, while the rest of his face remained frozen in geniality. He had a ferocious grin that seemed partly intended to undercut the effect of his vocal blasts. The edges of his mouth would tremble in warning just as he was about to crack a joke, especially one at the listener's expense.

Nowadays, there are many people who seem vague and watery, and whose search for identity troubles themselves and those around them. Jay Becker was the opposite; if anything, he seemed overdefined. Like a Harold Lloyd or Pee-wee Herman assembling a recognizable persona from props and mannerisms, Becker proudly displayed the barking voice, the Mr. Square costume, the towering, put-on rage before a malfeasant student—all the while shielding his inner turmoil from sight.

Teachers are actors: little by little, like barnstorming Shakespearians, they acquire exaggerated *shtiks*, routines to get them through. So what if some children regard them as battle-axes or grotesques? They know they still have within themselves the same complexities, the same youthful dreams. It seemed to me that Jay had become a victim of his overdrawn persona. By collaborating in your perception of him as a "character," he invited you not to take him seriously. When we say of someone "He's a character!" we disarm him; we don't expect anyone so categorized to be in such intense inner pain that he takes the measure of his own peculiarity and pronounces the death sentence, any more than we would expect it of a Dickens caricature like Mrs. Jellyby.

Yet there were times when Jay shed that overdrawn character. I remember particularly one relaxed June afternoon in 1972, a year after I had begun working at the school, when he and I took his class on a picnic to Central Park. We were sitting next to each other on the crosstown bus, and the kids were behaving well so there was no need to keep after them, and we settled into a quiet confiding conversation. He told me about his childhood. It seems his parents had operated a seaside hotel: he had never had his own room, and was forced to move to whichever one was unoccupied. It had given him a permanent anxiety about security, which was why, he thought, he had taken a civil service job.

After college, he told me, he had studied law at the University of Pennsylvania, and even gained his degree. But then the problem of military service arose; he did a stint in the air force. "Stay out of the armed services, Phil," he told me, grinning crookedly, "if you're anything like me." He couldn't take it, and was discharged, though I never did learn why the Air Force had been so harrowing for him. He was a good athlete, and, with his carefully creased pants and military posture and the value he placed on discipline, he almost seemed to belong in the service. Or else he had internalized a part of its training, even after it had proved inimical to him.

In any event, he became a teacher on leaving the service. I wondered if the relatively low status of elementary school teacher bothered him. He seemed to feel no regrets about not having practiced law. "I basically like teaching," he told me. And now he was getting married; he thought that might solve his problems of rootlessness and insecurity.

There was a beautiful, trusting sweetness in Jay as he spoke to me on the bus. I noticed it at other times as well, a tenderness that leaked out of his gruff mask in so pure and undefended a form it was almost jarring to watch. His return to "normal" a few hours later struck me as a kind of betrayal. While we were walking home across Central Park, I ran into an old acquaintance of mine, sitting on a park bench with her new baby. Since I had not seen her in some time, I stopped to chat while the group moved on. Later, when I caught up with them, I took a merciless ribbing from Becker. "Whose baby was that, Phil? Don't you think you ought to marry the lady? At least give her a place to live, so she doesn't have to sleep on a park bench!" Back to the armor.

Jay's marriage did not last a year. I never met his wife; when I asked him after the breakup what had gone wrong, he got a hard concentrated stare and a grimace around his mouth, as though he were eating some acidic fruit. He told the truth when he wore that expression, though he told the short version, shrugging between sentences. "There were problems with the in-laws. And she . . . she wanted to live in a suburb in New Jersey and I didn't like it out there. I felt more comfortable in the city. So now I'm a bachelor again." No doubt there were other problems, but Jay's telegraphic style did not encourage probing.

He moved into a high-rise apartment in the Lincoln Center area, not far from where I lived. One night I ran into him at Cherry's, a local diner that served Chinese food. He told me he was on his way to a Unitarian Church singles mixer. I could never go to those mixers or singles bars, preferring to do without rather than risk the humiliation of being rejected by a stranger. Jay, on the other hand, subjected himself regularly to the harshness of the singles scene. When he described the outcomes, he had a way of comically disparaging his capacity to attract and to hold. But behind the shrug, I imagine, was the ball of anger that grows in the stomach from being sexually rejected. "So how are *you* doing, Phil?" he would ask, quickly turning the subject away from himself. "You must be getting a lot of women."

He never told me what he thought about the portrait I had drawn of him in *Being with Children*. I wonder if it caused him grief. All he ever said was, "Congratulations, Phil. When are you going to write a best-seller? When are you going to leave us for Hollywood?" He always tried to give the impression that his life was unimportant compared to mine. At first I would attempt to compete with him in failure, but eventually I would rise to the flattery, and tell him a tidbit of recent literary fortune. "That's great! You're really going places," he would say, his sweat-coated nose quivering in what I guessed must be at least partly chagrin. But perhaps it wasn't: Jay read a lot and had a simple admiration for writers. Sometimes I would brag about the projects I was doing around P.S. 90, like the *Uncle Vanya* production, and again he would respond with unmixed praise. "Today Chekhov, tomorrow Shakespeare or

George Bernard Shaw. Who knows? You can start your own repertory company here."

Did he ever boast about his own teaching achievements? Not that I remember. But he had a reputation for getting good results. One could always tell Becker's students' compositions because the grammar, punctuation, syntax, and spelling were generally on a much higher level than the other classes'. Becker would drill his class on the fundamentals: paragraph indentation, quotation marks, topic sentences. His creative writing assignments stressed fantasy over experience: boys often wrote about adventures in space, girls about raising Kentucky Derby winners. They had learned to exercise their imaginations glibly, but there were too few moments of true feeling or authentic observation for my taste.

Over the years, the written work that came out of Becker's classes had an odd thematic consistency. Besides the wish-fulfillment stories, there was that high quota of student attacks on their teacher, which I took to be a sort of guerrilla retaliation against Becker's efforts at embarrassing them. (For instance, he'd call a girl with dental retainers "Braceface.") There was also a surprising—for sixth graders—amount of toilet humor. Becker would consistently be flushed down the toilet, first having been suitably miniaturized, and would end up in a lady's apartment. I never could figure out what element of his classroom style prompted this obsession, but I do remember that getting a bathroom pass in that class was sometimes an ordeal, and cause for much smirking.

Even colleagues who found Jay's approach too strict or rote-based had to admit that the children learned under his command. When parents were dissatisfied with their kids' grammar, reading, or math skills, they would lobby for a transfer to Becker's class in senior year, as a sort of prep for the rigors of junior high school. If the child had not only learning but discipline problems, he would more than likely be assigned to Becker. Many successful young adults walking around today consider Jay Becker the teacher who changed their lives. Jay had always been a savior for certain kinds of kids—rowdy boys who lacked a sense of direction, shy intellectual girls who loved to read. But big rowdy girls, especially black girls, he rarely knew how to treat. His penchant for public embarrassment found a match in their sassiness, and often they would trade him decibel for decibel, their sense of dignity refusing to allow anyone to "yell at me that way" without equivalent comeback. It is safe to say that no teacher possesses a style that works for all students. But in the last year before his death, Jay began to get more agitated by the ones he couldn't reach.

One morning in June, four months before his suicide, I bumped into Jay inside a coffee shop on Broadway, where, a creature of habit, he ate his breakfast every morning before school. As we sat side by side on counter stools, I asked him how his class had gone that year. He started to stutter: "Some-some of these kids . . ." He stared off into space, searching for the right words. "Most of these kids are bright and want to work. They're good kids basically. I'm having trouble with a few of them. I don't know; I can't seem to get through to a few." His eyes glazed over.

It was the pain of every teacher, the unsureness about ever doing a good enough, a thorough enough job. "I guess I've been teaching too long. I'm running out of solutions. Maybe I should get out of the profession."

"Look, no one bats a thousand."

"Sure, I know that, but I can't seem to get enthusiastic about teaching anymore. There's no kick in it for me. Anyway, we should probably get going before we're late," he said, picking up his check.

After learning of his suicide I remembered this conversation, but at the time it didn't leave much of an impression on me. I may have thought that Jay was suffering a little teacher burnout; 1979 was the year of "teacher burnout." It had become a catch-phrase; everyone was talking about the nagging frustrations that wore schoolteachers down, physically and spiritually, year after year, as though this common knowledge had suddenly become a scientific discovery. On the positive side, teachers could finally speak about their weariness as a systemic problem rather than a private, guilty secret. But "burnout," which had started as a useful shorthand for the complex of forces attriting schoolteachers, eventually came to possess an independent identity of its own, like a mysterious virus in a horror movie striking victims at random. Just as every decade turns up a new disease (mononucleosis, hypoglycemia, Epstein-Barr syndrome) to which not only its legitimate sufferers but all those afflicted with *tedium vitae* lay claim on the basis of having read a magazine article, so "teacher burnout" became the fashionable panacea of the moment, rationalizing all the unhappiness teachers were holding inside them in lieu of actually reforming the root educational problems.

The new school year was barely a month old when Jay Becker stayed home for a week. He was extremely conscientious; he had almost never taken a sick day; so we were all surprised when the week turned into an indefinite leave of absence. One of his colleagues, Cesar Gomez, called him at home to see what was wrong. Becker answered readily that he had "emotional problems." Gomez asked Becker whether or not he wanted people in the school to call him, and Jay, after a pause, said yes, he'd like to hear from them.

A teacher who did phone reported that Jay seemed to be getting his problems under control: he had invited his mother to move in temporarily to take care of him.

Sometime in the evening of Monday, October 22, 1979, Jay jumped out the window of his twenty-seventh-story apartment. One assumes his mother was out at the time. Did she return to find her son on the pavement? Many of these police-blotter details were never clarified, since no one at school felt he or she had the right to ask his relatives for the full story. Not that it is of any importance whether he jumped at eight or nine o'clock, climbed out the window onto a ledge or crashed through it. In any event, there must have been many curious strollers from Columbus Avenue gathered around the body on that warm October night.

I see two stories here. The first is about a man who couldn't take it anymore, which is of necessity a mystery story without a satisfying solution, since the motives and last thought processes of a "successful" suicide are for the most part denied us. I might speculate in my own way why he killed himself, but anyone else's guess would be as good as mine. The second is about a public school, and how everyone (including myself) dealt with the disturbing private challenge to institutional life that suicide proffers. Here at least I can record what I personally witnessed about the community's response to this crisis.

Around midnight, Eduardo Jimenez, the principal of P.S. 90 received a distraught call from Jay's stepfather telling him what had happened. By the next morning, the news had spread through the staff. A gloomy Tuesday morning, many teachers were in shock. "It can't be," they kept saying. "I just can't believe Jay is dead." Some students had begun to hear rumors, but when they asked for details they got little response. The adults seemed to be afraid of a panic breaking out among the children. One fourth-grade teacher, Kate Drucker, who often held long discussions with her class about the most serious topics (including death), and who herself is a very analytical, honest woman, told them evasively that she wasn't sure what had happened. She admitted later that a truthful discussion would probably have been the best approach, but she didn't feel like talking about it just yet, she was too shaken up. (That night, Kate told me later, she called everyone she knew, people she hadn't spoken to in years, to see if they were still alive.)

The other staff members were equally reticent, as though they were waiting for a policy statement from the main office about how to phrase it—or, even better, an expert opinion from a developmental psychologist on what amount of truth the children could absorb at each grade level.

Becker's own class, of course, would have to be informed. Mr. Jimenez went into Room 234, along with the Parents Association president, and told the students that their teacher had died. When they asked the principal how, all he would answer was that it had been an "untimely death," which was tantamount to telling the kids that he had died of death.

An emergency lunchtime staff meeting was called to discuss the crisis. Ed Jimenez, somber on the best of days, seemed especially grim, as well as uncharacteristically subdued. He admitted that he was at a loss, and solicited the advice of his staff. To those who had watched Jimenez laying down the law at staff meetings over the years—sometimes judiciously, sometimes wrongheadedly, but always forcefully—his uncertainty came as a surprise.

A parent suggested that we bring someone in from the nearby Columbia Teachers College or Bank Street School of Education to do a workshop on handling death and grief in the classroom. Someone else remembered that Dr. Myra Hecht, the director of the New York Center for Learning, had once given a valuable talk on this subject. Perhaps she could be prevailed upon to deliver it again, this time with special attention to suicide. "For the kids or the staff?" it was asked. "For both, maybe," came the tentative reply. "You mean two separate workshops?" Someone volunteered to phone Dr. Hecht and see what she was amenable to doing.

After the meeting, Kate Drucker commented: "How screwed up we are that we have to bring in someone from the outside to tell us what we should be feeling and how we should respond at a time like this."

It had taken honesty for the principal to admit that he could not be the leader, the Father-knows-best figure, that everyone seemed to want in the situation. The cause of death may have had something to do with his hesitancy. Jimenez was not at his best when on the receiving end of strong emotional display; given to temperamental outbursts himself, he was nevertheless made profoundly uncomfortable by others' eruptions. He once told a female teacher, who burst into tears after he had severely scolded her, that if she cried one more time in his office he would put a letter in her file for unprofessional behavior.

The second reason he had trouble leading the school in its grief was that he and Jay Becker had been on opposite sides politically for many years. What had begun as an educational difference of opinion had taken on the nuances of a personal feud. But to understand their quarrel, it is necessary for me to backtrack a bit and explain some of the school's history.

The trouble goes back to the big citywide school strike in 1968, during John V. Lindsay's mayoralty. Though any veteran of New York City's "school wars" will tell you that it started long before that, I prefer the 1968 cutoff date because that strike, the bitterest and most interesting of recent decades, left deep ideological scars. It was a strike, as you may remember, that pitted the teachers' union against the ethnic minorities, liberals against radicals, one half of the civil service bureaucracy against the other. It started when black and Hispanic parents, who felt their children were getting cheated educationally, demanded more community control over their schools, and gained it in a few experimental areas; then the United Federation of Teachers (UFT), the most powerful teachers' union, rose up and said that the integrity of the teaching profession was being undermined by community interference. The minority parents accused the largely Jewish union of racism, the union replied with charges of anti-Semitism, and the battle was joined. In that quarrel, leftists crossed picket lines for the first time in their lives and volunteered to keep the schools open as teachers and principals (the Association of Supervisors having taken the side of the striking teachers). It was a period when some reputations were damaged for good (including Mayor Lindsay's), while others rose astonishingly swiftly. When the dust settled, the union had gained ground from the community groups; both kept long memories of who had done what to whom.

On the Upper West Side, however, the concentration of reformers and community activists helped to produce results that were different from those in the city at large. A coalition of minority parents and white progressives installed three "community principals" chosen by the community school groups rather than taken from an approved list of potential supervisors. One of the three men was Eduardo

Jimenez at P.S. 90. The unorthodox selection process was disputed, and led to a court case in which Jimenez and a black principal successfully challenged the Association of Supervisors list as racially unfair and an instrument to inhibit minority principalships.

Ever since, P.S. 90 had been divided into two camps: the traditional or "more formal" (as they were called on the organization sheet) teachers, who had sided with the union in the strike; and the neo-Deweyite or "open classroom" teachers, who had allied with the community forces. The dominant philosophy of the school and its principal was the open classroom. Jimenez is an educator immensely sympathetic to creative ideas. A tall, bearded man with thick glasses and an electric-socketed bush of hair, he had studied painting in his youth, and he brought to the school an almost artistic vision of a dynamic educational environment. He set about recruiting like-minded staff and ensnaring outside resource programs. In very little time the school became an experimental laboratory in which science museums, theater troupes, philosophers, opera workshops, and artist-in-residence programs (such as my own Writing Team) all tried out ambitious curricula. P.S. 90's open corridor and bilingual programs became models, drawing visitors from all over the country and abroad. Convenient to the downtown television stations and newspapers, the school also became a media favorite. It was no surprise to see a TV crew hanging around the colorful open classrooms on the first floor when a visual filler was needed on children's reactions to a holiday or current event.

Understandably, the traditional teachers felt bitter about what they perceived as second-class treatment; and in terms of resource allocation—the open classrooms had parents' committees that raised funds for special materials, as well as an adviser from Dr. Hecht's Center for Learning—and the boss's positive approval, they were right. Most of the traditional teachers had been on staff prior to Jimenez's appointment in 1970; they were the old guard, and the principal made no secret of his desire to be rid of them. His very appointment had entailed a fight, he was embattled from Day One, and it was his personal style to struggle against, rather than to accommodate, those he took to be his enemies. There is a certain kind of humanistic activist whose values are impeccably compassionate but whose own human skills at handling people leave much to be desired. The teachers frequently complained that Jimenez ignored people's wants and needs and rode roughshod over them. Since he did not, according to contract rules, have the right to fire teachers he disapproved of as long as they were functioning adequately, he tended instead to make life hard for them, with the hope that they would eventually leave of their own accord. They reciprocated by plotting against him and undermining him whenever possible.

The traditional teachers' stronghold was a corridor on the second floor where Edna Jacoby, Jay Becker, Harriet Ullman, and Millie Brown all had classrooms. These four teachers shared resources, co-taught subjects, and kept their strength up, as good friends and allies will. Harriet Ullman and Millie Brown usually taught classrooms that combined third and fourth grades, while Edna Jacoby and Jay Becker handled the "big kids," the eleven- to twelve-year-olds in fifth- and sixth-grade class-rooms. It was the bitter contention of some of these teachers that the children in the open classrooms were not getting a good education, that their teachers were too permissive and were thus harming the children's chances for advancement at a later date. Conversely, the open classroom teachers accused the traditionalists of being stodgy, unimaginative, lackluster "lifers" who would never get involved in school-wide activities, and who punched out at three o'clock on the dot. Though I myself felt closer to the open classroom philosophy (and was perhaps even seen in the school as one of Jimenez's boys), I made a point of working in both settings; I could see that each side had misjudged the other. I knew that Jay Becker stayed late many afternoons, tutoring students who needed help, and I knew that the open classroom teachers ran a much tighter ship than the traditionalists had assumed.

In any event, to return to their personal feud, Jimenez and Becker would go at it during staff meetings. Both were capable of violent self-righteousness, though from different directions: Jimenez was a revolutionary who bullied those around him "for their own good"; Becker was a stubborn stickler for procedure who had been in the school system a million years and knew "the way things had to be done." To add to the tension, Becker was elected UFT chapter chairman. In his vigilance over the potential erosion of teachers' privileges, in his advice to colleagues on filing griev-ances against their principal, he often came into conflict with Jimenez. Between them, they revived again and again the acrimony of the 1968 strike.

When Jay's term as chapter chairman ended, he was ironically faced with having to ask the principal for a favor. He wanted to take a rest from his regular assignment, to give up the running of a classroom for a year and become a cluster teacher. A cluster is someone who goes around from class to class, spelling the regular teach-ers during their prep period breaks and presenting a short lesson in some specialty of his or her own. Jay's would have been history, a field he knew better than anyone at P.S. 90. Jimenez reviewed his available personnel in the face of extensive budget cuts that year—and ruled against the request.

Each year there were teachers who complained about Jimenez's assignments, claiming that he gave preferential treatment to his favorites. Others, like Monte Clausen and Doris Friedman, both open classroom teachers, were quietly of the opinion that as principal he had the right to make whatever assignments he saw fit. But in the days following Jay Becker's suicide, even Jimenez's staunchest supporters felt resentful retrospectively over the denial of Jay's cluster request. The temptation to blame someone for the tragedy (other than the perpetrator himself) was strong, and who better to point the finger at than the boss?

By Tuesday afternoon, around the lunchroom and the school-yard, the kids' rumor mill was already in full operation. Some children thought Mr. Becker may have been hit by a car. Another rumor, unfounded but tenacious, was that Becker had been suffering from skin cancer, and that he had decided to kill himself rather than prolong the incurable disease. The cancer rumor had probably been started by a well-meaning adult who had sought to justify Becker's suicide (as if unbearable emotional suffering were not enough justification). Some of the parents who knew the circumstances of Becker's death let their children in on the facts; but the next day, when their children told other kids, many of these kids refused to believe them, thinking it a wild, made-up story. Gradually, they would approach their teachers and say, "Somebody told me this crazy thing that Mr. Becker jumped out the window. That's not true, is it?"

Meanwhile, the school continued to handle Becker's suicide in the way they would a death from natural causes. On Wednesday morning the usual public address messages were canceled, and instead the announcement was made that the school had suffered a great loss. Mr. Becker, a man who had taught and helped children for fourteen years, was no longer with us, and the classes were asked to observe a minute of silence. It was the first of many such moments of silence, a ritual that became almost droll in its ecumenical utility.

What fascinated me was the *denial* of suicide, the reluctance to speak its name publicly. It put me in mind of another situation I had encountered at the school. In 1976, after the debacle of Senator Eagleton withdrawing from the vice-presidential race because of previous psychiatric treatment, I thought of doing an educational unit on mental illness. How did the idea of "crazy" differ from society to society? What was the historical evolution of insane asylums? What about Freud's ideas? I could see the creative writing possibilities, using literary models like Gogol's "Diary of a Madman." It seemed a rich subject, one which afforded a chance to reduce the children's fears of their own deviations from the norm. So I was a little surprised when everyone at school—even Clausen, who usually indulged my zaniest notions—reacted with discomfort and total resistance. Since the idea would never work without my colleagues' cooperation, I abandoned it.

I kept thinking about this earlier constraint in connection with the adult reticence to tell the kids about Jay's suicide. How far did the taboo extend? Were we still so close, I wondered, to the barbaric medieval stigma attached to suicide? Perhaps the theological and legal sanctions that continue to surround the deed, such as refusing to bury the victim in hallowed ground, or requiring hospitals to file a police report, accounted for some of the reticence. But not all: no, there was something unique about suicide, I began to feel, that made a public school singularly ill-equipped to handle it. Schools are dedicated to helping children find their way into life, and an adult self-doubt so deep it denies the worth of life itself cannot help but threaten that environment. Since little children often regard their teachers as semi-parents, and since the offspring of suicides have a greater tendency than others to follow that self-destructive path, the suicide of a schoolteacher could seem a dangerous model. Beyond that, suicide is a defiantly private expression, a dissonance jamming public discourse, like a monotonously insistent burglar alarm that no one can shut off. The radical nature of the suicide act is that it both draws attention to a distressing problem and simultaneously obliterates the possibility of ameliorating it. By rejecting all human assistance, by announcing in advance that any relief will have arrived too late, it negates the whole *raison d'être* of those in the "caring professions": teachers, nurses, social workers, psychotherapists.

Implicating his or her survivors in guilt, the suicide (strange how the word fuses doer and deed) mocks the shallow understanding of those who thought he or she was doing all right, who mistook a calm scornful smile for adjustment. Revenge, spite, anger, stubborn willfulness all have their part in suicide. The suicide insists on having the final word. No wonder people at the school found themselves unable to talk freely.

The most frightening part of suicide is its reminder that we are none of us so far from it. Suicide has a suggestive, contagious dimension, as Durkheim showed long ago with his charts, or the suburban teenagers in Texas and New Jersey more recently. But why go so far afield? I had only to look within myself to know my own vulnerability.

At seventeen I had tried to kill myself with pills, and, botching the job, had landed in a locked psychiatric ward. Though this was my only bona fide suicide attempt, it began in me a lifelong relationship with that temptation. It seemed to me I had a "virus" inside me like malaria that could flare up at any moment, and I needed always to be on guard against it. On the other hand, I would court it, even in times of seeming tranquillity. I seemed to derive creative energy from the assertion of suicide as an option. This morbidity left me freer to act or write as I wanted, as much as to say: No one understands me, I'll show them. It also became my little secret that, while going about in the world, and functioning equably as expected, several times a week I would be batting away the thought of killing myself. How often have I thought, in moods of exasperation or weariness: "I don't want to go on anymore. Enough of this, I don't want any more life!" I would imagine, say, cutting my belly open to relieve the tensions once and for all. Usually, this thought would be enough to keep at bay the temptation to not exist. So I found myself using the threat of suicide for many purposes: it was a superstitious double hex warding off suicide; it was a petulant, spoiled response to not getting my way; and it was my shorthand for an inner life, to which I alone had access— an inner life of furious negation, which paradoxically seemed a source of my creativity as a writer.

Added to this was an element of loyalty to youthful positions. Just as a student protester might vow never to become conservative in middle age, similarly, after they released me from the psychiatric ward and people said to me, "Now wasn't that a stupid thing to do?" I swallowed my pride and nodded yes; in my head, however, I swore allegiance to the validity of my decision. If nothing else, I vowed that I would always respect the right of an individual to kill himself. Whether suicide was a moral or immoral act I no longer felt sure, but of the dignity of its intransigence I was convinced.

In any event, I came to believe, rightly or wrongly, that I had a sixth sense in these matters, which is why Clausen's phone call with the news did not entirely surprise me. I had started seeing a look of constant pain in Jay's eyes; I knew more or less what the look meant. I think because he could not bear to have another person see him that way—hunted from within—his eyes fled mine. Whenever our gaze did lock for a moment, it was odd and unbearable. A sympathetic vibration exists between "suicide-heads" that is dismaying, to say the least. After Jay killed himself and everyone kept saying how astonished they were, I felt isolated by having had a presentiment along these lines. It's hard to tell whether the uncanny shiver that comes from sensing, after an act of violence, that one may have foreseen it is mere vanity or something more valid. The matter was complicated by a memory fragment that suddenly surfaced after Jay's death; I was not a hundred percent sure whether it had actually happened this way, whether this was a hallucinatory vision, or a combination of both. Here is what I "remembered," from the previous spring:

We had been standing by the time clock, where we often bumped into each other at the end of a school day. Jay was getting ready to punch out. (As a consultant I was not required to, but I hung around the time clock out of solidarity and a need to imagine myself in the regular teachers' shoes.) I asked him: "How goes it?" He said: "Not so good." "Why, what's the matter?" Then I remember that twisted smile of his, as he faced the time cards, and his saying, "Everything," and adding under his breath, "I'm even thinking of killing myself." His tone had just enough of that pessimistic New York irony for me to try to dismiss it as hyperbole. "Cheer up," I said, patting his shoulder, trying to make light of it, "hang in there. Death comes soon enough on its own."

I next remember fleeing the schoolhouse, shaken by what one might call the paranoia of empathy. I had had a glimpse at a pain so palpable it could not be denied, and was revulsed by my patronizing pat on the back, as though a colleague's reassurance could somehow assuage it.

This sensing of Jay's suicidal capacity went no further than species recognition. I did not feel impelled to warn those close to him, or to speak to his therapist if he had one, or even to draw him out about the fantasy, as one is supposed to do with suspected suicides. If anything, I'd been scared away from him. In my defense, we did not have the kind of relationship that could have easily permitted my extracting other confidences; he told me exactly as much as he wanted and then clammed up. Beyond that, I did not really consider myself to have the power to change his feelings. It was his decision to make, to live or die. All I could do was be a witness, and file away my impressions for a later date when I might be able to help him more, if the situation arose. Was this a cop-out? Does it show the error of my frequent position of detachment? Or is it megalomaniacal now to horn in on his death and act as though it was up to me to alter the trajectory of his history? I don't know what my responsibilities are to alleviate the suffering of others. Let me add that barely a day goes by without my picking up uncanny hints of someone's urgent misery beneath the social mask. I am never sure how much of this "intuition" is trustworthy and how much is projection, a distortion for the sake of promoting melodrama or feelings of superiority. I have sniffed suicide in the air a dozen times or more and been proven wrong. This time, however, I was right, and it spooked me.

The funeral was on Wednesday, around noon, and some of the teachers who had been closest to Jay switched their lunch hours with other staff so that they could attend. They piled into taxis and rode the twenty blocks down to Riverside Chapel, on 75th Street and Amsterdam Avenue.

As usual, tabs were kept on who showed up. The principal's absence was duly noted. On the other hand, some of Becker's traditionalist allies, who were very protective of him, made caustic remarks about certain open classroom teachers who did attend. "What's she doing here? She always gave him trouble when he was alive."

The funeral lasted fifteen minutes.

Jay's mother and stepfather wept. The rabbi spoke of the special relationship between the mother and her departed son, which was unusually close and devoted; of the deceased's having helped children; of his years of dedicated service to the community; his love of fresh air. Not a word about suicide. True, it was a religious service, and since Judaism views suicide as a sin, the rabbi perhaps felt unable to mention it. Nevertheless, it seemed ironic that Jay, who had finally spoken of his pain in a manner impossible to ignore, was still not getting through.

After the funeral, most of the teachers returned to school. A few, who had student teachers covering their classes, went out for coffee, along with some ex-P.S. 90 teachers who had been notified of the service. Two of these "alumnae" were now teaching in other schools; several had gone on to downtown jobs like copywriting or bank-telling, which seemed elegant to them compared with working in an elementary school. They defended their decision to leave teaching.

"Let's face it," said one ex-teacher bitterly. "Kids are takers, not givers."

"No, kids can give you a lot," said a woman still at P.S. 90. "But you have to know how to receive it from them."

"And if you know that, you're probably secure enough not to need their support in the first place," replied the first woman.

Lilly Chu, a more formal teacher who was on sabbatical that year, spoke to me with feeling about how good Jay had been to her. "Once there was a mouse running around the classroom and I was scared stiff. He came in and took care of it. His door was always open. He was such an important part of that school! He was like a rock, always there when you needed him. I'm afraid I got more from him than I ever gave him. . . . If only I had reached out more."

"But he made it hard to reach out," I answered. "He never asked for help. There has to be something in the person that you can grab on to."

"That's true, but still I think we could have done more. Everyone's in their own world, their own problems. So much sadness in him. Nobody pays attention." Lilly's eyes began watering.

There was much talk, after Jay's death, about "reaching out." As one teacher put it, "To work in the same school and not know he was suffering like that . . . and all he needed was a little friendship." Everyone took it as a given that Jay had died of loneliness, that his death could have been prevented by more human contact. I was not so sure. P.S. 90 is not a particularly cruel, unfeeling environment—quite the opposite. Most suicides have people around them who do say a kind word, offer a helping hand, but it seems to come from a great distance away, and they don't know how to read the gesture. Often they don't want to. The suicide has to screen out or misinterpret a great deal of the kindness that comes his way if he is to get on with the business at hand. He must concentrate all his energies on keeping the tenuous flame of suicide alive inside and feeding it day by day. Sometimes it is not loneliness so much as the need to act decisively, for once, in one's uncontrolled, errant life.

The words "reach out," with their telephone-commercial sappiness, began to get on my nerves. In contradistinction to that line from *Under the Volcano*, "*No se puede vivir sin amor,*" I believed it *was* possible to live without love. Many do in this world, and we mock their endurance by pretending otherwise. Of course it could be argued that I am using the word "love" in too narrow a sense. There are many kinds of love besides human companionship: love of place, love of work, love of culture and beauty, love of God. In my view Jay had known some or all of these. I guessed that he had gotten fatigued, exhausted from some unremitting inner struggle, or from a tormenting superego that told him he could do much better, and that somehow he had crossed the line between the tolerable and the unbearable. Yet even as I balked at the kitschy explanation, "All you need is love," what if an important truth did lie under its sentimentality? Perhaps my old need to defend suicide as a valid action was getting in the way of my understanding the obvious: that Jay Becker had not been cared about or loved enough.

After the funeral I went back to school. In the teachers' lounge, where Jay had so often held forth, loudly and raucously turning innocent remarks into double entendres (he had, by his own cheerful admission, a "dirty mind"), he continued to dominate by his absence. As we discussed him, I had the feeling that each of us was fingering a private guilt.

"I was so surprised about Jay Becker," said the elderly librarian, Sophie Arens, who shook with palsy. "I couldn't help thinking about it all night. I mean, he seemed to be doing all right, he had a girlfriend—"

"What's that got to do with it?" I said testily.

"Well, you figure if someone has a girlfriend or a boyfriend, they're a little happier. These days, you don't have to get married. You can live with your girlfriend or your boyfriend and no one says anything about it anymore," Sophie noted, with a trace of shock.

"Wasn't Jay living with someone?" asked Debby Trabulski, a younger teacher.

"Yes, but she moved out."

"Well, maybe that's what did it," said Sophie. "He got depressed about the breakup."

Cherchez la femme.

"His girlfriend did not break up with him," informed Frieda Maura. Frieda was big as a house, slow-moving, shrewd, with thin gray hair dyed red: her beady little eyes set in her fat, canny face reminded me of a Politburo functionary. I could never figure out what Frieda Maura's real job was; she seemed to just sit around drinking coffee and *kibitzing* all day. Frieda had probably gotten closer to Jay Becker than any of his other colleagues; in the last two days she had become a *maven* of Jay-ology. "His girlfriend moved out when he got too despondent. But she was on the phone with him every day."

"Then what was he unhappy about?" asked Sophie Arens.

"There were all kinds of things. He didn't like what was happening to the school, with the administration," said Frieda, lowering her voice significantly. "When Jay fought, it was good. This year he didn't fight."

"It was three years ago when *he* started in on me. And that was when my tremors started," said Sophie. In a public school, whenever an unidentified *he* or *she* enters the conversation, it is always understood to be the principal.

"I remember how, when I came back after my illness," said Frieda Maura, "Jay came over to me and offered to pick up my kids at lunchtime and have his monitors run errands. Because it was hard for me to climb the stairs."

"When I filed my grievance," said Sophie, "Jay wrote a very strong letter in my behalf against Jimenez. He stuck his neck out for me. And I know I wasn't the only one he did that for."

"I don't know if you know this: Jay had an earlier breakdown. But he went to a shrink and he got over it," said Frieda.

"I had no idea."

"Sure," Frieda continued, shifting her remarkable bulk in the chair. "I knew he had this illness for years. He spent a fortune on psychiatrists."

Kiko Fuzuwa, a petite Japanese-American who taught third-fourth grades, volunteered that she thought Jay had great difficulty relating to women.

Everyone nodded, each mulling this over in his own way.

It seemed strange, I thought, that Jay, whom everyone was diagnosing as starved for the love of a woman, should have worked in such a female environment. Of the thirty-four classes in P.S. 90, only four had male teachers. The rest were women, many of them as lonely as Jay. Yet the "logical" solution of getting together with one had never seemed a possibility—for him any more than it had for me. I suspected Jay's suicide had touched the single teachers in a rawer way, reminding them of the fragility of living alone.

"I spoke to him just last week," Kiko Fuzuwa was saying. "He told me that when this emotional problem was over he would go on a hike with me. We both belonged to the same hiking club, you know. I'm being honest, he sounded pretty good!"

"You know, I keep thinking of something his mother told me at the funeral," said Frieda Maura. "She told me that all during the last week of his life he kept saying to her, 'I love you, Ma. I love you.' His mother said to him, 'I know you do, honey.' He was just being considerate. He didn't want her to feel guilty after he did it."

"Isn't that nice."

"I wonder what will happen to his pension," said Sophie Arens. "Will the money go to the state, or . . . "

Doris Friedman, a veteran teacher who had been in a sad daze all this time, awoke and answered: "His beneficiaries will get it."

"I don't think the union will try to claim it."

Long silence.

"It takes guts," said Debby Trabulski.

"No it doesn't. It takes desperation," Doris Friedman replied with conviction.

"You don't think jumping out of a twenty-seventh-story window takes strength?"

"The strength is to go on living. All it requires is desperation."

A brief argument followed on the subject.

That day I saw two girls I knew in the hallway. They were from Becker's class, and I asked them how his students were taking it. They giggled and said most of the kids were glad! Then they did an imitation of the adults: "We should all talk about this. Mr. Becker died yesterday. Now on to math." They mocked the public address announcements, the solemnity of the principal, everything. These were both fairly sweet, sensitive, and intelligent girls, for the record. Their merry refusal to grieve, chilling and unfeeling as it was, bespoke a survivors' will to be themselves in the face of what they perceived as adult intimidation. I asked the girls if they knew how their teacher had died. "We don't! Someone said—he *killed himself,* but that's probably wrong." They giggled at the scandal of it. I listened without answering: I was too intrigued by their response to reprimand them; besides, I needed to think about it more.

On Wednesday night the annual bake sale was supposed to take place at the school. Some had argued that it should be canceled in deference to the recent tragedy, but others answered that the children and parents had gone to a lot of effort, and why should they be punished? So the bake sale was held in the school cafeteria as planned.

A large crowd swarmed around the tables and bought cake slices and cupcakes, the proceeds of which were to go for the school's legal battle to get back its Title I funding.* It was a happy crowd, with the children running around the cafeteria and the parents chatting, and everyone waiting for the judges to award the prizes. Before the judging began, the new Parents Association president, Dave Naumann, a friendly shaggy-bearded man with a huge belly, rose to make an announcement.

---

*For years, the federal Title I monies, earmarked to support compensatory education programs for disadvantaged children and desegregation, had provided Jimenez with the discretionary funds to improve the educational product. They paid for, among other things, the cluster teacher positions of the sort that Jay Becker had wanted. As P.S. 90 stabilized and improved, the neighborhood

He said that the school suffered a deep loss. "And I don't mean the loss of our Title I designation. A teacher who had served in the school for sixteen years—"

"Fourteen years!" corrected several pedantic children.

"—Jay Becker, who had been suffering from an illness . . . died of that illness on Monday night. Now I'd like us to have a moment of silence—a minute is a long time, I know, so I'm only asking for a moment—to honor the memory of Jay Becker."

Everyone stood at attention, facing different directions, perhaps wondering how long a moment was in Dave Naumann's mind. I thought it a shame that, having gotten everyone's attention, he had waffled at the crucial moment. But later I agreed with others that Naumann had done a brave thing under the circumstances. After all, many had opposed his making any announcement, on the grounds that it would mar a festive event.

Several parents spoke to me that evening. They were worried about the kids in Becker's class. No one seemed to be talking to them, working through whatever problems they might be having with the tragedy. Some of the other teachers had held honest discussions with their classes by this time, but Becker's kids had only been treated to a succession of substitute teachers, starting with his leave three weeks before. The mood in that class had grown anarchic. Becker's kids were being avoided, almost like pariahs contaminated with the unpleasantness of suicide. Maybe, in some unconscious way, people blamed them for what had happened, or—and this, the parents stressed, was particularly dangerous—the children felt themselves to blame. Meanwhile, Jimenez had gone away for a few days on business, and, due to the budget cuts, there was no assistant principal around that year to deal with the problem.

I decided that it was up to me to go into Jay's class the next morning and level with the kids. Over the years I had developed the conviction that it was wrong to shield children from the truth; to the extent that we could even know the truth (and in this case we did), we must tell it to them. What worried me was the thought that this high-minded position might have also satisfied some sadistic impulse in me—the side of truth-telling that takes pleasure in pulling the mask off hypocrisy and disenchanting innocence. Also, I hesitated because I was not a trained psychologist or counselor, only a writing teacher. But this qualm finally seemed cowardly to me: What else was being a teacher but trying to respond as humanly as possible to problems that would not wait for an expert? Besides, I would get them to write. On Thursday morning I came into school early. I was shaking, as though I were about to teach my first lesson at P.S. 90. I ran into Monte Clausen in the main office. I told him that I would probably be criticized like hell for this but that

---

around it started to gentrify, at which point the government decided that its disadvantaged population had dipped slightly below federal guidelines, and cut off its Title I funds.

I was going to discuss Becker's death with his class. "Why criticized?" he said. "It's about time someone did. People will most likely be grateful to you. What are you afraid of?"

I couldn't explain my fear. I had the sense that I was about to touch something very explosive and dangerous, partly because my own feelings about suicide might not be under control. "Oh, I guess I'm worried that parents will write letters protesting my exposing their kids to such ugly matters. . . . "

"But you have a role in this school of articulating feelings that no one else will come out and say."

"I do?" I felt relieved that what I thought might be interpreted as provocation had come to be considered approved behavior—my "role," in fact. Articulating the unspoken feelings of a community seemed a much more interesting function for a writer-in-the-schools than the narrower one of imparting writing techniques. I thanked Clausen for saying what he had said, and he wished me good luck.

I spoke to the substitute teacher and asked if I could take over her class for about an hour to discuss Becker's death. She said they were in the middle of long division, but if I came back in half an hour, they would be ready for me. I went down to the teachers' lounge and had a cup of coffee, and when I came back I was shaking a little less.

First I introduced myself to the class, said my name, and reminded them that I was the writing teacher. A third of the kids had worked with me in previous classes; the others recognized me from the halls, or in any event acknowledged my right to be there. I said I wanted to "clear the air" about Mr. Becker's death. When something important happens like that, you just can't sweep it under the rug. You need to bring it out into the open, talk about it, not let it stay bottled up inside. (I heard myself resorting to cliché after cliché, but I clung to them for support; these trite, soothing figures of speech seemed to be absolutely necessary to get me started.)

"First of all, how did Mr. Becker die?" I asked.

A few hands. "My father told me he committed suicide."

"That's right. He did."

"How did he kill himself?" several kids called out.

"He jumped out of a twenty-seventh-story window."

There were several gasps. "See, I told you!" one boy cried as he smacked another. "Was there blood on the sidewalk?"

"Get outta here!" cried David, a sensitive blond-haired kid who was embarrassed at his classmates' gory curiosity.

"I didn't see the spot where he fell," I answered.

"When did it happen?"

"Monday evening."

"What time Monday evening?"

"I don't know, about eight or nine, thereabouts. . . . "

"Somebody said he had cancer."

"To the best of my knowledge, he didn't have cancer. He killed himself for emotional reasons."

The students began talking loudly among themselves.

"What kind of teacher was Mr. Becker?" I asked over the noise.

An explosion of hands.

"He was funny," two girls said, laughing together.

"How, funny?"

"He would always tell corny jokes like—if a boy was talking to a girl, he would say, 'Flirting with the girls, Damon?' And one time he said that Julie shouldn't worry about Damon liking her, because Damon liked only dogs!"

"No, he said Damon only liked girls who looked like dogs!"

"And he brought in a picture of a collie and said that was Damon's girlfriend."

"And he used to say, 'When I talk about my two friends, I mean Danielle and Julie.' And they would get em*bar*-rassed."

"He liked the girls better than the boys."

"No he didn't."

"Hold it! Quiet. One at a time. What else about Mr. Becker?" I asked.

"He screamed at you."

"Yeah! We had to put our fingers in our ears and dive under the desks. And one time he yelled at Tracy and Tracy yelled right back at him. He hollered '*Aren't you doing your assignment?*' and Tracy hollered back '*No!*'"

Tracy beamed with pride. She was a cute black girl who had a reputation for fearlessness and trouble.

"What did he do when he wanted to reward you for being good?"

"He would let us go to the park. He would give us extra recess."

"And how did he punish you for being bad?"

"By screaming at us!"

"That's all?"

"That was enough! He would scream till you were sick to your stomach."

I paused a moment. So far, the kids seemed to regard their teacher as a one-dimensional figure. As yet they showed no feeling that a real man had died.

"How did he seem in class?"

"He seemed happy!"

"Did he ever seem not happy? Did he ever do anything that seemed strange to you?"

One little black girl near the front said softly: "Sometimes, when everyone was doing their work in silent period, he would stare out at nothing and look real sad."

"Yeah, he would stare out the window. But only during reading period."

"Or he would look down at his shoe and sorta frown."

"Uh huh," I nodded encouragingly, but there was nothing more forthcoming on the topic. "Why do you think someone would want to kill himself?" I asked.

"Somebody said he was married and his wife divorced him."

"That's true, she did, but that was many years ago."

"Somebody said his wife was still bothering him, even after the divorce."

"I wouldn't know," I said. "But lots of people get divorced. Why would someone go so far as to kill himself?"

"Can't take it anymore," one boy shrugged.

"Uh huh. . . . Why not?"

"Maybe he's depressed," said one child.

"Maybe he has emotional problems," said another.

There was something glib, almost disinterested in the tone of their responses. I've taught certain lessons with children that attained a deep spiritual quality, where each of their answers sounded forth like a bell in a thoughtful silence. This was where I had hoped to bring the discussion, but for the most part the kids were extroverted, noisy, too impatient to listen to each other or take the pain of the subject seriously. I understood there must be a terrific need to avoid that pain at all costs. I was torn between pushing further into it and letting them get away.

"I knew a girl, she hung herself because she got an F on her report card," mentioned the same soft-spoken little black girl in front.

"I once wanted to kill myself," said a boy in the middle rows, "because I did something wrong, and I thought my mother was going to kill me!"

"*She* tried to kill herself!" Tracy pointed happily at a plump white girl across the aisle from her.

"Shut up, Tracy," muttered the girl.

"How?" someone else asked.

"She took a whole mess of pills."

"You and your big mouth, Tracy," said the girl, looking daggers at her supposed friend.

I asked the class how many had ever thought about killing themselves. About ten raised their hands (including the substitute teacher!). It was odd how they could admit to suicidal feelings in themselves but still not identify enough with Becker to feel very sorry for him.

One boy said disenchantedly: "Mr. Becker always told *us* to be good and then he went and jumped out a window!"

"I don't think that it's like 'being bad' to kill yourself," I said. "It's a tragedy, it's a sad thing, but I don't think it's a crime or a sin."

"It is a sin," said a tall Hispanic boy in back. "It's breaking one of the Ten Commandments."

I quickly went through the list in my mind, not having remembered any against suicide. "Which one?"

" 'Thou shalt not kill,' " he answered.

"But doesn't that mean you shouldn't kill someone else?" asked a boy near him. "Not: you shouldn't kill yourself?"

"I honestly don't know," I said.

"What does 'adultery' mean?" asked one of the girls.

"It's . . . when you're married and you sleep with someone who's not your husband or wife." I turned to the substitute teacher apologetically, as if to say: Well, they're getting an education at least. Then I went to the blackboard, out of some pedagogical instinct (or perhaps to shift the subject from theologically hazardous waters) and showed them the etymological breakdown of the word "suicide," along with homicide, fratricide, parricide, and regicide.

Some children wanted to discuss what happens to a person when he dies: the worms versus heaven. There was a lot of cross-conversation at this point, not all of it germane; those with short attention spans were getting impatient with the strain of a long discussion and tried to sabotage the focus.

"When someone is dead—" I began to phrase the question.

"Don't use that word!" cried a girl.

"Why not?"

"It sounds awful! Gives me the creeps. Use something else."

"Which would you prefer?"

"Passed on."

I began to make a list on the blackboard, based on their suggestions, not sure where this was leading: passed on/retired/into the blue/on vacation/gone but not forgotten. To these, at the bottom, I added my own word: dead.

"Do you think Mr. Becker is in heaven, or in the other place?" asked a boy whimsically. This got a big laugh.

"I don't actually believe in heaven or hell," I answered, "but everyone is entitled to have his own ideas on the subject."

I had noticed that there was a group of children who had been silent for most of the discussion. Just out of curiosity, I asked how many children had had Mr. Becker in class all of the previous year as well as this term. Most of the silent ones, sixth graders, raised their hands. I asked how many of the children had had Mr. Becker only since September. This time most of the noisiest students raised their hands. It was clear that the children who had been in his class the longest felt most complexly about him, and as yet were unable to put their feelings into words. The taboo against sentimentality in this age group may also have deterred them.

"Of those who had Mr. Becker last year," I asked, "do you think your attitude toward him changed over time?"

Yes, several volunteered. One Chinese-American boy explained how he had come to like the man because, when Mr. Becker explained things, he made sure you understood them. He was strict but he really cared if you learned. He, personally, had learned a lot from Mr. Becker.

"Some of the teachers in this school let you get away with murder," said another sixth grader. "But Mr. Becker really taught you. He was the best teacher in the school."

Now the tide seemed to be turning.

"I liked him because, even when he made fun of you, he always knew if he hurt your feelings," said a scholarly girl with glasses. "And then later he would try to cheer you up. I *liked* having Mr. Becker as a teacher, only I didn't like being in this class because of the other kids who spoiled it for me, like—" Her recitation of names was drowned out by the classmates' boos.

I asked them whether they thought that, overall, Mr. Becker was a good teacher, a bad teacher, or in between. For some reason, this question made Becker's critics most uncomfortable. They were unwilling to say out loud that they thought he had been a bad teacher, although some obviously felt it.

I told them I didn't think there was a single teacher who worked well with all kids. There were bound to be some kids who would thrive under one teacher while others would do better with someone else.

"What about Mrs. Reilly?" asked a boy. "I had her in the first grade and she was good with all the kids."

A little wide-eyed girl begged to differ: "She *hits* kids."

Rather than get into a discussion of the merits of Mrs. Reilly, I asked them how they had felt when they heard that their teacher had died.

"I was shocked!" said Danielle, one of Jay's favorites.

"I felt sad the way I would if any man had died," said a fifth-grade boy soberly, "like if someone had been shot on the battlefield. But I didn't really know the man."

Many of the newcomers to the class agreed. They had barely known him, how could they feel much about his death?

I explained that it was not a question of right or wrong feelings. Feelings were like the cards you were dealt in a game; you just had to go with those cards. Sometimes everyone might be crying at a funeral and you might be feeling nothing; that was the card you had been dealt that time. Sometimes a person died and you felt angry at him for leaving you. The important thing was to be honest and know what you were feeling. There was no point in faking it.

I told them I wanted them to write, a request that was met with the usual groans of protest. I threw out two suggestions: One idea was to write a portrait of Mr. Becker as they remembered him, a truthful portrait, not making him look either better or worse than he did while he was alive. The second idea was to write about how they felt and were still feeling about his death.

Paper was handed out, the children set to work. Some worked in pairs, most wrote singly.

I approached the substitute teacher, who had helped maintain some order during the discussion, which was not always easy. She had technically supported my efforts, but at the same time I had sensed something like disapproval in her—not exactly disapproval, but a scowling, hard-bitten quality, an angry wall. Substituting does that to some people.

"How has this class been?" I asked, under my breath.

"Rough," she said. "It's a tough situation."

"I'll bet it is."

"I wouldn't have been able to get that much out of them. I didn't think it was my place to talk to them about it."

"Were you surprised," I asked, "at the . . . amount of indifference they expressed at first?"

"I'm always surprised by their amount of indifference. I've been teaching for years and I've never seen a group of kids like this. They're cold. They have no hearts."

"They're avoiding a lot," I countered.

"Maybe you could excuse them that way. To me they're just cold. The other day we were at gym and I said at the end of the period, 'Aren't you going to put away the mats?' 'We didn't take them out, so we're not going to put them back!' I tried to explain to them that if you do something nice for people in this world, it will be better for you in the long run. 'Don't you believe in helping others?' I asked them. They all said, 'No. It's every man for himself.'"

What bad luck these kids had, I thought: on top of everything else, they had ended up with a rather narrow-minded substitute teacher who could see no farther than their manners. Oh, I knew what she meant, I've felt that way about kids at times. But this class didn't seem so extraordinarily vicious. A little rowdy, perhaps, having escaped the strict disciplinary hand of Mr. Becker. A class that starts to get a maverick reputation often takes perverse pride in confirming its notoriety; something of that "bad seed" swagger was detectable here.

About half of the children wrote short pieces, a few generalized, perfunctory sentences that were followed by a drawing of their former teacher. I don't know if our discussion had already exhausted what they had to say, or if the challenge of judging an authority figure objectively on paper was too threatening, or if they were just being lazy. The other half wrote papers that were more interesting—at the very least, shot through with revealing flashes. I offer these examples not so much as gems of children's creative writing, but as documentation that may shed some light on the various ways children come to terms with an unusual situation:

On the first day of school, all my friends and I were waiting to see what classes we were in. After about fifteen minutes, everybody in my class went to their new classes, all except me. I was not on the list. I told the principal, and he went to all the classes to see if I was listed. Finally one of my friends came to tell me that Mr. Becker had called my name when he was calling roll. I was a little disappointed that I had Mr. Becker because he had a bad reputation of yelling so much. When I got into the room and of course he was yelling, I said to myself, "it's going to be a long year." After about a week of school I liked Mr. Becker, and I thought that everybody was wrong about him. Then he started coming on strong with his yelling. I once heard that he was a little deaf, that's why he had to yell so loud. When Mr. Becker died I felt sad but not too sad because I didn't know him that well.

—David

At times he acted very strange. When he walk he puts his hands in his pockets and looks down at the floor like if he was very very sad.

He was a very good teacher. He knew when he was going to be absent. He was absent every day and Mr. Jimenez said he'll be back next year and then 3 weeks later Mr. Jimenez came in with 2 parents and said that he died but he didn't want to tell that he committed suicide.

—Lorraine

Mr. Becker was much more different than the other teachers I had and know about. He was very positive. He had a special touch to make kids like himself. Mr. Becker had no right to kill himself, he should have been proud of his work. Many amount of kids since the last 14 years have gone to fantastic schools. His pupils had a lot of liking for him.

Mr. Becker might of yelled a lot but the kids he yelled at deserved it. Every kid in school except for kids in his class think he's a loudmouth but he really isn't what kids think he is. He let us do things that no other kids got. We went outside and every time we went out we went to the park! Personally I liked him.

—Jonah

When I heard Mr. Becker died I was really surprised almost shocked. I couldn't believe it. Mr. Becker will be gone forever. You won't hear him yell or scream again.

Most people didn't like him. I admit I didn't like him that much but not enough to hate him or be happy he died.

I'm very unhappy he died. I wish he hadn't.

—Kim

Mr. Becker was a very strange man he always wanted things done his way. When we had a spelling test if you made a certain mistake like if you added a s he would count it wrong. And he always squinted his eyes like he couldn't see and he always put his hands in his pockets. And yelled like he couldn't hear his self.

—Wendy

When I heard that Mr. Becker died, I was very surprised because he had been with this school for 14 years, and now when I come into this class he jumps out the window. Last year when I was just going into fifth grade, Mrs. Goldstein got hit with a block. The girl that threw the block, meant to throw the block at a boy named Donald, but he ducked and it hit Mrs. Goldstein and she fell off her chair and was knocked out. Mrs. Goldstein went to the hospital and never came back to our school. And the girl that threw the block was in lots of trouble and got transferred to another school.

So the same thing happened this time but Mr. Becker jumped out a window.

—Damon

Mr. Becker is a very good or you could say was a very good teacher. It's a shame that I could not have written is, but I hate to say I had to write was.

I wish he did not kill himself because he was the best teacher in the school.

—Ian

We felt surprised and upset cause something died. We never expected it but in a way we appreciated it. But it was very interesting, cause if it were on the 100th floor that would be more interesting, cause then he would die before he reached the ground. But even though Malina is so sad, and Mrs. Hoffheinz cries, we on the other hand clap, clap, clap, while Malina is saying boo we're saying Yeah and we mean YEAH!

—Dara and Michelle

Chapter 1: The truth about Noodlenose Greasy Fingers!

This may be a strange name for Mr. Becker but if you saw him you'd agree. Noodlenose stands for his noodle shaped nose. Greasy Fingers means that when he thinks he puts his index and middle finger up his nose and pushes his nostrils up. So this makes his fingers greasy because snot gets all over them.

Chapter 2: In the beginning of the year

When I came in the first year in his class I was glad to sit in the back. Because he screams so loud. When he screams nobody seems to listen.

Chapter 3: His looks

Now he is a very odd looking thing. His hair looks like toothpicks. His nose is so big that it weighs more than his body does and it makes him walk bunched over. His mouth can open as big as an ocean when he yells, but still big when it's closed tightly.

Chapter 4: Our thoughts of him

Sometimes we get so mad at him, that we wish he gets hit by a car on his way home. So he'll have to stay in the hospital with 2 broken arms, legs. And he'll stay in the hospital for the rest of the year.

—Tanya and Danielle

When I heard that Mr. Becker died, I was sad at first. Later on I decided it wasn't so bad. That night, I just stared at my bedroom ceiling over my bed. As I was lying there, I thought about all the jokes he always made.

I really do miss him. He was mean sometimes, but usually, he knew that he had hurt your feelings, and he would cheer you by making jokes. He was a nice teacher.

—Julie

When I heard that Mr. Becker died I thought he died of a sickness in a hospital. Then I heard rumors that he commited sewerside. Then when I heard that it was true I felt pretty shocked.

—Jason

I felt like I was going to cry but when I heard he killed himself I was mad because they said he died of a sickness.

—John

When I heard about Mr. Becker I almost fainted because it happen all of a sudden. When I heard he committed suicide I said shut your mouth because my mother said that he jump out 27 floors. Mr. Becker was a nice and mean man but he was a good one. I am glad I was in his class.
 —Sonia

Mr. Becker was a very nice teacher when I was in the class for the first 7 days. Mr. Becker showed me how to fill out my label and he showed me where to put my Glossary in my spiral notebook and he yelled at me only 5 times.
 —Pierre

When I heard that Mr. Becker was dead I felt so surprised that I had to go to his funeral. When I went to the funeral it was the saddest funeral. I never could go in and see other funerals cause you need to be a certain age.

 I thought they were going to open part of the coffin but they didn't. In the funeral a Jew was preaching and some ladies started crying.
 —Nikola

All in all, I felt pleased with the way the lesson had gone and told myself I had risen to the occasion. My chronic need to be the hero of my life story had resulted in making myself take action, which temporarily silenced my frustration at the *fait accompli* of Becker's suicide. So we console ourselves with having "done something" by turning out a well-phrased eulogy on a friend, or seeing that his obituary gets in the *Times*.

Myra Hecht said no to a workshop for us; she had lost a sister to suicide the previous year and wasn't sure she could conduct it without breaking down. Dr. Hecht did advise Jimenez on the phone that they could not afford to look at suicide as an isolated aberration—in other words, getting rid of it by putting it in a category. We had to realize, she said, that we were all quite close to it a dozen times a day. On the other hand, she thought that in this jittery period we should emphasize "continuity and connection": both Jay's connection to the school through his good works as a teacher, and the ongoing life of the school community itself.

This word "community" began to seem more and more abstract to me each time it was invoked as a worthwhile counterweight to Jay's self-destructive act. Is one alone or in a community? I was not so sure anymore. And what was so special about this "community" that it could absorb any number of human sacrifices without having its ongoingness disturbed? Apparently I was not the only one visited by these thoughts.

On Friday, amid the brown-bag lunch eaters of the teachers' lounge, Kate Drucker voiced in her usual skeptical manner the doubts she'd been having. "Everyone says, 'Life must go on.' But what's so good about life going on as always? I feel there's something terribly wrong about this business-as-usual attitude. Couldn't the factory be stopped for just a little while? Shouldn't this tragedy be acknowledged in some way?"

"We need a ritual. Come on, Phil, think of a good ritual, you're the creative one around here."

"Bullshit," I said.

"At least some sort of memorial service," muttered Kate Drucker.

"That's a good idea. Who'd take charge of it?"

"I don't know. Not me, I feel shot," Kate said.

"I think we should put a plaque in the library," said Doris Friedman, "and buy history books and donate them to the library in Jay's name."

"Yes. And we should celebrate the birthdays of Claude and Jay every year!" suggested Cesar Gomez.

There had been another death in the P.S. 90 "family" a few years before: Claude Hardwick, the beloved assistant principal, a young man who played jazz and loved a good time, had died of cancer at age thirty. Out of that death came annual memorial evenings and a Claude Hardwick scholarship fund; his photo was cheered during the graduation exercises' slide show, his black-bordered portrait hung permanently by the main entrance door; and there was even a movement to rename the school after him. One sensed that there would be none of that groundswell of iconographic devotion in Becker's case. As Monte Clausen, my P.S. 90 guru, explained later: "There are two complicating factors why it won't happen. The first is the manner of Jay's death, which some people feel very turned off by. The second is that Jay was not exactly the most popular teacher with kids in this school." Still, it seemed the least we could do was to go ahead with a memorial service.

On Sunday afternoon, Ed Jimenez called me at home. It was a surprise, since he rarely phoned me at home; on the other hand, our paths crossed often enough outside school. I would run into him around town, usually at gallery openings or book signings, and once every few years we would meet for a colleagual drink. I really liked Ed, and admired what he was trying to do, though I was well aware of his difficult, moody side, which rubbed people the wrong way. I figured he must have needed to talk with someone who could sympathize with his point of view. Irrationally or not, I had been angry at him since Jay's death, making him out to be the villain of the piece. Therefore I welcomed the chance to hear him out.

Over the past week I had been keeping fairly lengthy diary entries about everything connected to Jay's suicide I took notes while Ed spoke on the phone.

"Thank you for going in and working with Becker's kids. I checked with one of them on Friday and he said the discussion with Phil Lopate really cleared the air."

"I'm very glad to hear it."

"This morning, it hit me," he said, sounding tired. "It must have been a delayed reaction. I was making French toast and I started to cry. Now I can't remember when I did that last. I didn't even cry when my father died. But it must have been linked in my mind to my father's recent death and Claude Hardwick's. It was like that extra water in the glass that makes the whole thing overflow."

We talked about his father's death for a minute, and then I asked why he hadn't told the kids the facts about how Jay died.

"I got the news from Becker's stepfather, who was so hysterical over the phone I wasn't sure whether to believe him even. I mean, he wasn't making any sense. Also, I didn't know if the stepfather wanted everyone to know it was suicide. Tuesday I consulted with everyone: the teachers, the parents, the district office. No one had much guidance to offer. I read a book on death for young people, but there was no advice on how to handle suicide. I told his class it was an 'untimely death.' I figured it was enough of a shock for them to deal with that and it would be too much of a shock for them all at once to know it was suicide as well. . . . Some of the reactions of people, particularly the parents, were so weird. This one parent grabbed hold of me and she said her son was a potential behavior problem and she had placed him in Becker's class because he needed a strong traditional male teacher to stabilize him and could I guarantee a replacement? This woman knows the school staff and she knows there isn't any other male traditional teacher at the fifth-sixth level. Some of the other people's reactions were so selfish. It was hard having to play the role of the calm person consoling everyone. I had to go out of town for two days, to a minimum competency conference in Philadelphia. I was glad to get out because the atmosphere around the school was so depressing. When I came back on Friday the atmosphere was still depressed. Monte Clausen confirmed to me that everyone had been down."

I asked Kate Drucker's question: Then why encourage business to go on as usual?

"I didn't want there to be business as usual. I was against holding the cake sale. I figured, who would want to go to a festive occasion after what had happened? But the parents insisted. Most of the traditional teachers respond with business as usual because they're trained in that authoritarian manner. But we have a humanistic school here, with concern about the individual, so it doesn't make sense. If someone else had died, let's face it, Becker would have gone on with business as usual. He was a very rigid guy. I'm not saying he wasn't a dedicated teacher, because obviously he was. He would tutor kids after school on his own time. If a kid came to him and said, 'I really care about learning,' he would go all out for him. But if a kid cut up and seemed indifferent to learning, he had no use for him. I don't like to have to say this about the dead, but I'm trying to be honest. Often Jay was nasty, he was abrasive, he was rigid. He would have recurring periods where he was feeling bad and then he would take it out on me. He gave me a tough time with union matters. In the ten years or so that I've been principal, I've gone through several of those phases with him. After his marriage broke up, and after the breakup of another serious relationship. . . . But you had to be a prophet to know when these phases would recur. . . . He had asked me for a cluster position, and because of the budget cuts I couldn't. So I designed a class for him that would be easy, with no troublemakers. That's why they've held together so well."

"Do you feel guilty now because you denied him the cluster request?"

"No, I don't feel guilty. It was the only decision I could have made. I had to balance the good of the institution with the available staff."

"I don't know how to say this without making you angry," I plunged in, "but sometimes people feel that your administration overlooks the needs and wants of individual staff, and usually makes decisions for the good of the institution rather than the person. Eventually someone has to pay the price."

He was silent. "Look, who knows what it takes to push someone over the edge? Maybe if there hadn't been those budget cuts . . . maybe if we hadn't lost Title I he could have become a cluster teacher, and maybe gone on to find a new lease on life. On the other hand, maybe none of it would have made any difference. The last year or so, I knew something was wrong because he was finding it increasingly harder to handle troublesome kids. The kind he used to handle easily. After he took the first three days off, he came back and he was depressed. But sweet. Not nasty like usual toward me. Frieda Maura was the only one who knew how sick he was. Look, it's a closed society. They don't tell the principal who's having severe emotional problems, who's in therapy, who's under stress. Can you blame them?"

We talked for a few minutes more. I was touched by Jimenez's willingness to listen to whatever challenges I threw his way. On the one hand, who was I to sit in judgment? On the other hand, I wanted to use the opportunity to mediate a little between him and his enemies, by expressing their point of view in the words of someone he respected, and I wanted to clear up my own resentments. By the end of the conversation it was impossible to hold a grudge against him. What struck me, in fact, was that Jay, Jimenez, and I had been the three bachelors of P.S. 90. We were each peculiar in our own ways, each a solitary, and now one had quit the ranks and the two of us were left to commiserate.

The following week, Cesar Gomez emerged as the natural leader to organize the memorial service. In many ways, Cesar—young, handsome, outgoing, married, a bilingual open classroom teacher, and gung-ho organizer of the kids' basketball tournament—seemed Jay's antipode; but he had succeeded Jay Becker as the UFT chapter chairman, and this transfer had established a bond between the men. "Let's stress the positive!" Cesar told everyone now. "His life should be the topic of the service, not his death."

Cesar called up Jay's relatives and confreres and invited them to the service, which was scheduled for the evening of November 7. A strange listlessness, no doubt a secondary symptom of grief, was affecting everyone else, however, to the point that even getting the stencil for the memorial program typed began to seem a Sisyphean effort. Then there was the stalemate over which budget to use for the cake and cookies. Jimenez pulled forty-five dollars out of his pocket, settling the bureaucratic tangle with his characteristic brusque impatience, and sent his assistant off to the bakery. Still, there seemed none of the usual last-minute competition among parent volunteers to make the coffee. The community was not pulling together; people began to express fears about an embarrassingly poor turnout.

Myself, I had other anxieties: I had been asked to deliver one of the eulogies. I could appreciate that the decorum of memorial services dictated a stylization of virtues and that any alteration of that genre might prove offensive to some. On the other hand, it always seemed to me a mockery of the dead person's complexity as a human being to portray him or her as a flawless saint. If there is, underneath all, comfort in hearing the truth, would not a balanced description prove more healing?

As usual, I talked things over with Monte Clausen. "The one thing you can't do," he told me, "is to link pathology with behavior in the classroom. People won't stand for it." In other words, I could not so much as hint that the emotional distress that made Jay kill himself might have carried over, however slightly, into his professional conduct. For this reason, Clausen even advised against my reading the Riegelhaupt passage from *Being with Children*.

Sophie Arens, the librarian, wasn't sure whether to tell the story of how Jay went to bat for her as UFT chapter chairman. Specifically, she wondered whether she should use the word "grievance"—whether it would be too divisive, or would violate the spirit of the occasion. I told her I thought it would be all right.

A few kids from Becker's class were supposed to read the portraits they had written for me. Word had come down that Jimenez was worried I might let them get away with "inappropriate" observations; he wanted to take a look at their pieces before the program. I was becoming annoyed at the spirit of censorship, or self-censorship, that seemed to be descending on the memorial service from all sides. So I refused to turn the kids' compositions over to Jimenez—not by arguing him down, but by lying low and staying out of his sight.

A hundred people showed up, a respectable crowd. They settled in the first ten rows of the school auditorium. The memorial service began with a reading of the Emily Dickinson poem, "After great pain, a formal feeling comes." Frieda Maura served as M.C. She introduced Ed Jimenez, who spoke briefly, stressing how much Becker had cared about children. "He was connected to our school. He was connected to our children. He was connected to all of us. He became isolated, and he went away from us." In these words I heard Myra Hecht's advice to Jimenez somewhat gingerly and formulaically applied.

Harriet Ullman, a traditional classroom teacher, spoke touchingly about Jay's sense of fairness, his wanting everyone to be treated with justice.

Sophie Arens, the librarian, said, "I came to him with a problem and he treated the problem as if it were his own" (a nice end-run around the g-word).

Cesar Gomez gave a flowery oration in the Latin American mode, emphasizing Jay's moral stature, dedication, and love for what he did, ending with: "It is up to us to make Jay Becker immortal—through continuing his work! Let us not mourn his death, let us simply celebrate his life."

Then a serious-looking fifth grader, Jessica, played a classical violin piece. She played it so well that one's adult indulgence, held in readiness for any mistakes she might make, proved unnecessary. Her music reverberated in the auditorium, giving me goose bumps.

I was next on the program. I read aloud the two-page statement I had written in which I described Jay physically, analyzed the rather stereotypical persona he had developed as a teacher, and then went on to show his contradictory aspects, concluding:

> One could see a secret tenderness in him, which was not only his vulnerability to hurt, but his sensitivity to other people's suffering minus the usual protective screening device. And one could see an anger which he worked so hard to control, popping out with surprisingly harsh reproach or malice in public situations. This anger was his other secret. Manfully he wrestled to subdue it, and in the end, perhaps also manfully, he turned it against himself.

> One of his students, when I asked them to write about their teacher last week, wrote a sentence that stuck in my head. "He talked so loud like he couldn't hear hisself." He couldn't hear his self. If Jay's death tells us anything tonight, on the eve of winter, it is that we need to listen more patiently and lovingly to the chaos in ourselves, and we need to attend more carefully to the pain in others.

I was not at all sure what I meant by this pious last sentence, but it had a rhetorical ring, so I let it stand. "Children from Class 5–6/234" were listed next in the program, and strangely, none of the delegated student readers had shown up. Perhaps they were ashamed of what they had written, perhaps they simply couldn't be bothered to come at night. In any case, I breathed a sigh of relief. We proceeded to Dave Naumann, president of the Parents Association. "He has touched many lives," said Naumann. Specifically addressing Jay's mother in the first row, he said, "I congratulate you on a remarkable, remarkable son."

The final speaker was Virginia Cramer, a first-second-grade open classroom teacher who had written a poem for the occasion. It was Virginia who had pointed out to me earlier the typo on the program:

In Memoriam
Jay Becker
1935–1979

"If I die, check the spelling, Phil," she said, with her dimpled smile. A woman of great heart, with the matronly soothing appearance of a veteran first-grade teacher, Virginia had turned out to be one of the most prolific poets in the writing workshop I had given for teachers and parents the year before. Now she began reading her three-page poem:

Goodbye, Jay.
I never said goodbye to you before;
I always said, "Hi, Jay!"
Or "Have a good weekend, or holiday, or summer."

Goodbye, Jay.
Goodbye to running into your room for a signature
Or an opinion, or to borrow a window pole for gym.
Goodbye to the erect way you sat up close to your desk
And the sensitivity I watched in your hands and fingers
As you received a paper from a kid,
Or returned one.

Goodbye, Jay.
Goodbye to your loud voice and your abrasiveness
At staff conferences and UFT meetings.
Sometimes you grated on me, I'd get annoyed, impatient, aggravated.
Sometimes I'd think, "I wish he'd shut up!"
And sometimes I'd think, "Good for him! He said what we were
All thinking but couldn't say straight out."
And goodbye to your laughter.
To the boyish, rascally way you sometimes kidded
And exaggerated a funny idea or a line of sarcasm;
Laughing and talking fast with the excitement of saying it all
Before it got lost.

Goodbye, Jay.
Goodbye to seeing you in the district office corridor every day
Coming from leaving your class for lunch,
Walking your usual pace, hands in pockets,
Head slightly tipped, glasses glared by light.

Goodbye to your medium size, middle age, thinning hair,
Your rough, tweedy sports jackets
And dark shirts.
To the tempo at which you always moved
(I never saw you rush or run).
Goodbye to the question drawn across your eyes
That never came out when you talked.
Goodbye to your positions from which you rarely bent,
To all the statements of conviction I heard and knew you believed.
Goodbye to your professionalism
That protected a space in this school

For kids and staff,
A space I never worried about; I knew it was safe;
You kept it so.

Goodbye, Jay.
Goodbye to the little I knew of you
And to the larger part of you I missed.
You were here for fourteen years
But you're not here now
And your not-here-ness is heavy, hard and palpable
In my chest, stone-like behind my sternum.
The back of my head stings at the words sharply reminding me:
You were one of us; as thick and richly colored and strong
As any of the fibers in the fabric of this school.
We go on, school goes on, life goes on,
The cloth holds.
The tears are repaired, the lost threads replaced,
But there is memory.

Goodbye, Jay.
Goodbye to your physicalness,
To your sounds, your shapes, colors and movements.
And Hello to you as a member of my memory,
A membership I clutch closely now,
Some solace amid the disarray of death.

Hello, Jay.
Goodbye, Jay.
Hello, Goodbye, Hello.

I was proud of Virginia. Yes, her poem included lines I might have wanted to edit out or strengthen; but she had caught a piece of Jay in it. I was moved by her deciding in the first place that her own fledgling poetry could be the proper vehicle for responding to his death. As soon as the memorial service was over, I went up to her and we hugged.

At the reception afterward, I went up to several strangers who introduced themselves to me as Jay's neighbors, "part of the Amsterdam Towers family." They hadn't known Jay much, he rarely spoke in the elevator, but they had wanted to come because they felt "involved somehow." (Indeed, he had jumped from their building.) Someone from the Appalachian Mountain Club, who had led hikes with Jay, came up to me. He said Jay and he had clashed at times, but they'd shared a love of nature. Denise Loftin one of my favorite P.S. 90 teachers, remarked that my speech had been "hard-hitting," which made me wince. "What do you mean, hard-hitting?"

"Just—hard-hitting," she said, looking me squarely in the eye: "It was good and honest but it was a little close for comfort."

There was far too much cake left. No one seemed in the mood for noshing. I hesitated about introducing myself to the family, in case they had taken offense at my portrait. But Jay's younger brother Roger (handsome, curly-haired, a successful attorney, I had been told, which made me wonder about their sibling rivalry) was very gracious, asking for a copy of the speech. "You really caught him, down to the shiny nose," he said.

"If you don't mind my asking, why do *you* think he . . . "

"Jumped? Jay didn't believe in halfway measures. That's why he chose that way. He never did anything half-assed. He was very thorough: he left two notes, one to me, one to our mother. And he left all his bank statements and effects perfectly taken care of."

"He always had a sense of order."

"There's something else you might not know," said the brother. "Jay was on antidepressant drugs, and he'd had an adverse reaction to them shortly before he died. Maybe, with a different drug, he might still be alive. I'm convinced these things are partly chemical."

In the next few days, I heard some indirect negative feedback about Virginia's and my eulogies, all of it originating from the "more formal" teachers. Among other things, they were particularly outraged, it seemed, with one detail of our physical descriptions, which they thought we'd misrepresented: "Why did they both say he was medium height? Jay wasn't medium height, he was tall! I remember seeing him and Mario standing next to each other, and he was as tall as Cesar, not counting Cesar's Afro. Why do they go out of their way to belittle the man?"

Had I really meant to belittle Jay, unconsciously or otherwise? I didn't think so. . . . As for his height, it was hard for me to summon an exact physical impression of him any more. Perhaps I'd gotten that part wrong—and if that part, who knows what else.

Slowly the ache began to recede.

A month after his suicide, people had stopped talking about Jay. Everything had been said. And resaid. What was the point of dwelling morbidly on it? seemed to be the general sentiment. I could see their point. When all was said and done, the school staff had done everything that could be expected and more.

Still, Jay's suicide continued to preoccupy me. By now I had begun to wrestle with Becker—to identify with and argue with him. If he had waited longer, things might have gotten better for him. What arrogance, to assume it would all stay the same. I kept trying to enter his consciousness to understand why he did what he did. How does one arrive at a final conviction that there is no hope? What part of the decision was rational, mental, and what part physiological? I imagined a psychic pain growing inside him (myself) that demanded some physical outlet. Suicide must have been his attempt to give Pain a body, a representation, to put it outside himself. A need to convert inner torment into some outward tangible wound that all could see. It was almost as though suicide were a last-ditch effort at exorcism, in which the person sacrificed his life in order that the devil inside might die.

At the simplest level, I imagined Jay a victim of a screaming inside his head. When the screaming grew too intense, he jumped.

I had no such inner scream, but a continuous subvocal nattering, and at times I pretended to turn the volume up on it so that I might experience what Jay's distress would have been like. With the cold weather and shrinking of daylight, I felt a contraction of hope. That fall I decided to go to Yom Kippur services; the main sin I confessed to on Kol Nidre night was despair. (Didn't Catholicism also consider it the sin against the Holy Ghost?) I was experimenting with suicidal consciousness, walking for a while in Jay's footsteps. From the outside everyone saw me as tranquil, productive, satisfied; I had so tricked them into believing my confident act that they could not perceive the suffering underneath. Was suicide the only way I could ever get them to take my pain seriously? I wondered melodramatically. Of course, part of the reason people could not "credit" my misery was that it didn't go that deep, compared to others'. Yet I supposedly had all this friendship and good fortune coming toward me, and then I would turn the corner and not feel it.

Why did I, who, if I wanted to be honest about it, had a much wider support network of love and admiration than Jay, keep trying to minimize the difference between us? Perhaps if he and I were equally bereft, then I no longer had to feel guilty about being more advantaged; my debt would be cleared toward him. In part, my flirtation with suicide was also a way to absorb the shock of his passing. Sometimes we mime on a minor level the death of someone we know—take to our beds with a lingering cold when a friend has died of AIDS. I also needed to manufacture grief (or sorrow, which kept turning into self-pity) because I felt bad about not being more upset by his not being around. Maybe I was also competing with Jay Becker on some unconscious level, jealous of the attention he had gotten by killing himself.

Though I preferred to think of Jay as in some sense my opposite (shrill, inflexible), he kept turning up in my head as an undesired aspect of myself, an alter ego I was trying to push down. His self-contempt held up a frightening mirror to my own tendencies toward self-dislike. I suspect, too, that, because he was older and stronger-voiced than I, I was projecting onto him some of my feelings toward my older brother. Though in daily life I get along well with my older brother, we have had at times a very troubled, treacherous, competitive relationship, and in dreams he still often threatens to harm or kill me; the obverse is that subconsciously I have wished him dead on occasion. Who knows whether there was not some disguised relief experienced at Jay's (my brother's) death, for which I felt doubly culpable?

Preoccupied by all this, I tried my usual method of coping with distress, which is to write about it. I had in mind an objective reportorial essay, with myself kept firmly in the background, for some magazine like *The Atlantic* or *The New Yorker*. But as soon as I put pen to paper I felt my insides shaken up. I couldn't find the right entry-way into the story, I couldn't get enough distance from it; everything was so inter-connected mentally that hundreds of possibly irrelevant details begged to be writ-ten down. I was also disgusted at the idea of capitalizing on Jay's suicide, making something opportunistically, journalistically "topical" out of still open wounds. So I put away my notes for a little while, until I could feel calmer, more objective. That little while stretched into eight years; and it is only now, at forty-four—Jay's age when he jumped—that I am at last ready to take it up again.

I think there was another reason for my having been unable to write the essay then. I had come to a decision, around the middle of the school year, to leave P.S. 90. Running the P.S. 90 project for Teachers and Writers had been the best job I'd ever had, maybe ever would have, but after ten years of doing it, I felt "burned out," if you will. I had exhausted my pedagogic fantasies; I couldn't think of any new projects. On the one hand, I needed to break away from a place in which I felt almost cloyingly, undeservedly loved, and try new risks; on the other, I was tired of being so poorly paid, getting less after twelve years as a consultant than a starting teacher's salary. It was time to "graduate" to a university post.

Jay's death had seemed a warning sign to get out—of P.S. 90, of New York City, of my solitariness, if possible—before it was too late. I heard from a poet friend, Cynthia Macdonald, about a job that had opened up in the new creative writing department at the University of Houston; I applied for it, was interviewed in March, and was accepted. Knowing I would be leaving, I did not feel I could in good con-science write about P.S. 90 as though still an inside member of that community. I had already said good-bye to it. Like Jay, I, too, was walking out on the kids, the school. Any attempt to write about my connection to that ongoing institution would be dogged by elegy and guilt.

A permanent teacher had been hired to take over Becker's class. Hildy Weiss was young and pretty, an ex-stewardess, I was told. I said hello to her in the halls; she had a pretty smile. Before I got around to trying anything, the grapevine informed me she was getting married.

Sometime in the spring, we had a long chat. Hildy Weiss (now Korman) told me how she'd been recruited for the job. She had done some pinch-hit teaching at P.S. 90 several years before, but had left to become a stewardess. Apparently the admin-istration had liked her and had kept her résumé on file. After Jay's death, Jimenez's assistant, Marian Morrone, phoned her repeatedly to ask her to come back. "I wasn't sure I could teach again," she said, "because I'd been away from it so long. But Marian kept saying, 'These kids *need* you.' Finally I went into my Pan Am supervi-sor's office and told her I was thinking of going back to teach school. 'You're crazy!' she said to me. 'You have to live your own life. In two years they won't even remem-ber you. You should be having your own family, your own children!' I was torn. I loved flying more than anything, and I kept changing my mind about whether I could give it up, until finally Jimenez told Marian I was probably too immature for the job anyway. The next morning he called me on the Coast: one last time, yes or no? I said I would do it. On the flight home that night I was crying. I thought, 'I'll never be in a plane again, this is the last time!' But when I walked into that class, I couldn't leave them. They were my class.

"At the beginning, I didn't feel comfortable. I didn't know whether I was supposed to do an extension of Jay's curriculum or start my own. I felt very insecure. I was doing what my parents or the principal wanted, I was being a 'good girl.' Then eventually it all came together."

"You should be proud of having done such a good teaching job," I said, thinking of her having stepped into a difficult situation and gotten the class to cohere, with a lively production of *Oliver*.

She shrugged off the compliment. "I'm not a good teacher. I'm a good human being, but I'm not a good teacher."

"At that age level maybe they need a good human being more than a pedagogic whiz."

"I still wish I knew what I was doing more. Half the time I'm bluffing."

"What do you think the net effect of Jay's suicide has been on the class?" I asked.

"The kids don't talk much about Jay. At first they were angry because they were the last ones told how he died. But then they stopped talking about it. Around December, a social worker from Mount Sinai Hospital started coming in. I think the administration hired her because they were worried about buried feelings and traumas. It may also have been to protect themselves legally, in case parents said later on, 'My child suffered a deep emotional scar.' Anyhow, by the time she started visiting it was probably too late. This social worker had a very psychiatric approach. She'd sit there and say, 'What's bothering you? How do you feel? What do you want to talk about?' There were great silences. The kids really resented her. She visited the class once a week for forty-five minutes or so—three or four sessions, all told. In between her visits, the kids would say, 'Why does she have to come again? We don't want to talk about it anymore! That happened so long ago.' It would take the kids an hour to settle down each time after she left.

"Anyway—I get a real kick out of this—the last time she came, she said to them in the final minutes, 'Are there any questions *you'd* like to ask *me?*' One kid raised his hand: 'Are you pregnant?' And she was! Somehow they'd guessed it. That's what they were interested in. Meanwhile, Jimenez was pleased: he wrote her a rave letter about the great job she'd done. . . .

"I think for the most part they don't brood about his death. A few of them probably feel guilty because they didn't like him when he was alive. I have to say I didn't like Jay that much myself. He was strange. A few years back, when I was student-teaching here, we would be in the subway and he would talk really loud, the way he did to the kids. Maybe he had a hearing problem. I would move two steps away to show that it was too loud. He never seemed to notice. There was a rigidity about him that transferred to the classroom. It was stark. Bare. When you're a teacher you collect all sorts of junk through the years. But when I took over his class there was nothing. A few books lined up. Nothing on the walls. There was an emptiness."

In May I told Jimenez I was leaving. But the program would continue: Teachers and Writers would replace me with another writer.

In Tolstoy's *Death of Ivan Illych*, one of the noblest works of fiction, the protagonist is "redeemed" by his mortality. Before dying he learns what he was put on earth for, and by extension, so do we, the story's readers, at least for a wrenching, consoling moment. But I keep forgetting the Tolstoyan point. What *is* it that we are put on earth for? After all these pages, I can redeem neither Jay Becker's life nor his death.

That June the school was featured on the cover of *New York* magazine under the headline "Twelve Public Schools That Really Work." The photograph, which showed every kid in class with his or her multi-ethnic hand straining to the bursting point to answer, had obviously been staged. To me there was something ludicrous about a city magazine's consumerist mania to find the twelve best of everything, be it late-night rib joints or neighborhood schools. But while we took the compliment with a grain of salt, knowing how inaccurate such media hype can be, we also acknowledged that P.S. 90 was a pretty good public school, all things considered. Typical was the defensive pride of one speaker at graduation exercises: "We didn't need *New York* magazine to tell us we were special. We knew that already."

At graduation, Ed Jimenez said in his principal's address: "This school prides itself on being a caring community. That's one thing that never changes. We care about the children, we care about each other. We continue to hold a belief in humanistic education, the importance of the individual in the learning process." True, but on the other hand, I mused (in the way one has of framing objections to any speaker's rhetoric), what about the vitriolic tensions among the staff, or an individual like Jay, who slipped between the cracks of our caring?

Nine months after the warm October night of Monte Clausen's phone call, a staff party was thrown to celebrate the end of the school year. Jimenez, with his ill-at-ease attempts at facetious banter, was trying to circulate, play the gracious boss, though his very presence made certain staff members deeply uneasy. They had not even wanted to invite him. He had, however, been so kind to me at graduation exercises, reading aloud one of my poems and wishing me the best in my new, post-P.S. 90 life, that I made it a point to chat with him for a long while, conspicuously distancing myself from those who were getting their revenge by cold-shouldering him at the staff party. By the same token, making small talk with Jimenez could be an arduous affair, and some of my friends on the Malcontents' sofa were giggling at me, and I longed to join their bitchy confab.

By the time I finally did make it over there, the mood had grown quiet.

Kate Drucker was saying what a hard year it had been. The staff hadn't organized anything like the previous year's fun activities: no Vest Day (when everyone had dressed elegantly and worn a vest), no lunch-hour volleyball game for teachers. Somehow the spirit just hadn't been there this year.

"Why is that, do you think?" I asked.

"Because there were no prep periods," said Kate. "Once the budget cuts eliminated our preps, we didn't have any time to visit each other's classes or talk during the day."

"And then everyone in *our* crowd got assigned different lunch periods. Not unintentionally, I might add," said Denise Loftin, with a significant arch of the eyebrow in Jimenez's direction.

Judy Hoffheinz, one of the few cluster teachers left, said: "It was just a very rough year. Hard. Grueling. Relentless. Grim. I found it that way at least."

"Do you think," I asked, "it might have had something to do with Jay Becker?"

Kate Drucker seemed surprised to hear that name from the past. Then she answered, with her sad ironic little smile, "No, I honestly think it had more to do with their taking away the prep periods."

Reproduced baldly, her remark may sound callous, but in that living moment it felt the opposite—warm with the perplexed gallows humor of truth-telling—so much so that we all laughed. It was an uncomfortable laugh, to be sure. We were all thinking of Jay at that moment. Like the group's bad conscience, I had forced us to, but having done so, a bit self-righteously, I had no more to say on the subject than any of the others. I had hoped *they* would come up with the right, miraculously eloquent response. Someone had passed away whom we had known, liked, and worked alongside for years, and yet—how can it be that a man's death does not matter more? It could have been a leaf falling in the background. Was it because of Jay's exasperating nature, or our own impotence to mourn? Leave it alone, I thought. Beneath our rueful collusive chuckle lay a plea for forgiveness and a recognition that this is finally how we do deal with the death of someone not central to our lives: we absorb it, we hurt over it, we forget it, we move on.

— POLITICS, RELIGION,
MOVIES, BOOKS, CITIES

18

Resistance to the Holocaust

WHEN I WAS SMALL, a few years after World War II had ended, my mother would drag me around Brooklyn to visit some of the newly arrived refugees; they were a novelty. We would sit in somebody's kitchen and she would talk with these women for hours (usually in Yiddish, which I didn't understand) to find out what it was like. After we left, she would say in a hushed voice, "Did you see the number on her arm? She was in a concentration camp!" I didn't understand why my mother was so thrilled, almost erotically excited, when she spoke these words, but her melodramatic demand that I be impressed started to annoy me. I had only to hear about those lurid arm numbers to experience an obstinately neutral reaction and begin digging in my heels. Maybe I was picking up some of her own ambivalence; beneath my mother's sympathetic sighs, I sensed a little distaste for these victims. Years later she confessed that, when the camp survivors first started coming into her candy store, they were the most difficult customers to please; they had—and here she paused, realizing how insensitive her appraisal might sound, given their tragic backgrounds—a "chip on their shoulders."

Actually, I was touched by her honesty; just because someone has suffered a lot doesn't mean you have to like them, has always been my motto. I used to go into a neighborhood hardware store run by a concentration camp survivor with thick wire-framed glasses, whom I did like but whose superior bitterness gave all transactions an air of mistrust. Once I heard this proprietor say after he had thrown a customer out of his store: "What can he do, kill me? I already died in Auschwitz." This advantage of the living dead over the rest of us seemed unfair.

But I am getting ahead of myself. I want to return to that moment when my mother and I were leaving some poor woman's kitchen and I froze at the demand for my compassionate awe. Let me try to explain by way of anecdote. I once heard of a very liberal Jewish couple whose child would scream whenever she saw a black person. The parents were distressed that their little girl might be learning racist attitudes from somewhere, so they went to a child therapist and asked his advice. After questioning the little girl alone and learning nothing, the doctor suggested that he go for an outing with the family so that he might observe them in an everyday setting. As they were walking along the street, he noticed that whenever a black person approached, the mother would unconsciously tighten the grip on her daughter's hand and the girl would, naturally, cry out. In my case, whenever my mother uttered those magical words "She was in a concentration camp!" the music on our emotional sound track got turned up so loud that I went resolutely numb. Maybe this is the seed of that puzzling resistance I have felt toward the Holocaust all my life.

Before I give the wrong impression, let me interject that I am not one of those revisionist nuts who deny that the Nazis systematically exterminated millions of Jews. On the contrary, I'm convinced that they committed an enormous and unforgivable evil, about which I would feel presumptuous adding my two cents of literary grief or working myself into an empathic lather through the mechanics of writerly imagination. I was not there, I am not the one who should be listened to in this matter, I cannot bear witness. It is not my intent to speak at all about the atrocities of the Nazi era, but only about the rhetorical, cultural, political, and religious uses to which the disaster has been put since then. Of these, at least, I do have some experience.

When I was growing up, we never spoke of a Holocaust; we said "concentration camps," "the gas chambers," "six million Jews," "what the Nazis did." It might seem an improvement over these awkward phrases to use a single, streamlined term. And yet to put any label on that phenomenal range of suffering serves to restrict, to conventionalize, to tame. As soon as the term "Holocaust" entered common circulation, around the mid-sixties, it made me uncomfortable. It had a self-important, strutting air—a vulgarly neologistic ring, combined with a self-conscious archaic sound, straining as it did for a Miltonic biblical solemnity that brought to mind such quaint cousins as Armageddon, Behemoth, and Leviathan.

Then, too, one instantly saw that the term was part of a polemic and that it sounded more comfortable in certain speakers' mouths than others; the Holocaustians used it like a club to smash back their opponents. Lucy S. Dawidowicz states, "The Holocaust is the term that Jews themselves have chosen to describe their fate during World War II." I would amend that to say "some Jews" or "official Jewry"; but in any case, it is one of those public relations substitutions, like *African-American* for black or *Intifada* for Palestinian troubles, which one ethnic group tries to compel the rest of the world to use as a token of political respect. In my own mind I continue to distinguish, ever so slightly, between the disaster visited on the Jews and "the Holocaust." Sometimes it almost seems that "the Holocaust" is a corporation headed by Elie Wiesel, who defends his patents with articles in the "Arts and Leisure" section of the Sunday *New York Times*.

"Shoah" carries over the same problems as the term "Holocaust," only in Hebrew. Both "Shoah" and "the Holocaust" share the same self-dramatizing theological ambition to portray the historic suffering of the Jews during World War II as a sort of cosmic storm rending the heavens. What disturbs me finally is the exclusivity of the singular usage, *the* Holocaust, which seems to cut the event off from all others and to diminish, if not demean, the mass slaughters of other people—or, for that matter, previous tragedies in Jewish history. But more on these topics later.

We need to consider first the struggle for control of the Holocaust analogy. All my life, the *reductio ad Hitler* argument has been applied to almost every controversy. If it is not always clear what constitutes moral action, it is certain that each controversial path can be accused of initiating a slide that leads straight to Hitler. Euthanasia? Smacks of the Third Reich. Abortion? Federal payments make it "possible for genocidal programs as were practiced in Nazi Germany," according to Senator Orrin Hatch. Letting the Ku Klux Klan march? An invitation to Weimar chaos. Forbidding the march? Censorship; as bad as Goebbels. The devil can quote Scripture and the Holocaust, it would appear. We see in the Middle East today how both Israelis and Palestinians compare the other side to Nazis. The Hitler/Holocaust analogy dead-ends all intelligent discourse by intruding a stridently shrill note that forces the mind to withdraw. To challenge that demagogic minefield of pure self-righteousness from an ironic distance almost ensures being misunderstood. The image of the Holocaust is too overbearing, too hot to tolerate subtle distinctions. In its life as a rhetorical figure, the Holocaust is a bully.

The Holocaust analogy has the curious double property of being both amazingly plastic—able to be applied to almost any issue—and fantastically rigid, since we are constantly being told that the Holocaust is incomparable, in a class by itself, sui generis, must not in any way be mixed up with other human problems or diluted by foreign substances.

When President Jimmy Carter made a speech commemorating all those liquidated by the Nazis, which he put at a figure of 11 million, the eminent Holocaust scholar Yehuda Bauer accused Carter and his adviser Simon Wiesenthal of trying to "de-Judaize" the Holocaust. "The Wiesenthal-Carter definition appears to reflect a certain paradoxical 'envy' on the part of non-Jewish groups directed at the Jewish experience of the Holocaust. This itself would appear to be an unconscious reflection of anti-Semitic attitudes . . ." warned Bauer. We Jews own the Holocaust; all others get your cotton-picking hands off.

"How dare they equate using napalm in Vietnam or even dropping the bomb on Hiroshima with the Holocaust?" one often hears. The underlying sense is: "How dare they equate anything with the Holocaust?" The Holocaust is a jealous God; thou shalt draw no parallels to it.

The problem is that drawing parallels and analogies is an incorrigibly natural human activity. I, too, find it deeply offensive and distasteful when flippant comparisons to Nazi genocide are made. But on the other hand, it does not seem to me unreasonable to regard the Holocaust as the outer limit of a continuum of state-sanctioned cruelty, other points along the spectrum of which might include the French torture of Algerians, Idi Amin's liquidations, My Lai and other Vietnam massacres, the slaughter of the Armenians, Pol Pot. I realize it may appear that I am blurring important distinctions among a genocide, a massacre, and other horrors; but I am not asserting that any of these atrocities was as *bad* as the Holocaust (whatever *that* means), only that the human stuff, the decisions and brutal enactments that followed, may have had much in common. I find it curious for people to speak of the murder of 6 million Jews as a "mystery" and the murder of several million Cambodians as perhaps a more run-of-the-mill open-and-shut affair. The truth is, unfortunately, that there are few things less mysterious and unique in the history of the world than genocide.

It is true that the Holocaust was singular in its hideous anti-Semitism, which made the mere fact of being a Jew grounds for death. But as the historian Irving Louis Horowitz argues in his essay "The Exclusivity of Collective Death": "To emphasize distinctions between peoples by arguing for the uniqueness of anti-Semitism is a profound mistake; it reduces any possibility of a unified political and human posture on the meaning of genocide or the Holocaust. . . . Insistence upon separatism, that the crime was Jewish existence and that this makes the Jewish situation different from any other slaughter, whatever its roots, contains a dangerous element of mystification."

A good deal of suspicion and touchiness resides around this issue of maintaining the Holocaust's privileged status in the pantheon of genocides. It is not enough that the Holocaust was dreadful, it must be seen as *uniquely* dreadful. Indeed, the catastrophe of the Jews under Hitler is sometimes spoken of as an event so special as to sever history in two—breaking the back of history, in effect. "Holocaust stands alone in time as an aberration within history," states Menachem Rosensaft. And Elie Wiesel writes that "the universe of concentration camps, by its design, lies outside if not beyond history. Its vocabulary belongs to it alone." What surprises me is the degree to which such an apocalyptic, religious-mythological reading of historical events has come to be accepted by the culture at large—unless people are just paying lip service to the charms of an intimidating rhetoric.

In attempting, for instance, to resolve the recent "historian's dispute" in West Germany, President Richard von Weizsäcker declared: "Auschwitz remains unique. It was perpetrated by Germans in the name of Germany. This truth is immutable and will not be forgotten." The *New York Times's* reporter Serge Schmemann goes on to report (October 22, 1988): "Speaking to a congress of West German historians in Bamberg, Mr. von Weizsäcker rejected the attempts by some historians to compare the systematic murder of Jews in Nazi Germany to mass killings elsewhere—like those in Cambodia under Pol Pot or in Stalin's purges—or to seek external explanations for it. Such approaches have been assailed by other historians as attempts to frame the German crime in 'relative' terms."

Mr. von Weizsäcker has been rightly praised for his integrity and statesmanship in this matter—and yet I can't help thinking that he has also engaged in a certain amount of magically placating incantatory language: unique, immutable, never forget, antirelativism. I would have thought that a relativistic perspective was part of the discipline of competent modern historians. Not that history writing is ever entirely value-free or objective; but attempting to situate an era in a larger context still seems closer to normal historical methods than expecting historians to believe there is such a thing as an absolute historical event or an absolute evil. There seems to be a fear that, if we admit there are similarities between the Nazis' war against the Jews and other genocidal atrocities, we will be letting the Germans off the hook. On the contrary, we will be placing them on the same hook with other heinous criminals. And we will be asserting that the forces in history and human nature that brought about the death camps are not necessarily a fluke, so—be on guard.

As Yehuda Bauer has astutely observed:

> If what happened to the Jews was unique, then it took place outside of history, it becomes a mysterious event, an upside-down miracle, so to speak, an event of religious significance in the sense that it is not man-made as that term is normally understood. . . . If what happens to the Jews is unique, then by definition it doesn't concern us, beyond our pity and commiseration for the victims. If the Holocaust is not a universal problem, then why should a public school system in Philadelphia, New York or Timbuktu teach it? Well, the answer is that there is no uniqueness, not even of a unique event. Anything that happens once, can happen again: not quite in the same way, perhaps, but in an equivalent form.

Let us look at some of the cold figures on genocide in this century. According to Roger W. Smith, in *Genocide and the Modern Age*:

> Turkey destroyed the lives of a million or more Armenians; Nazi Germany destroyed 6 million Jews, but it is often forgotten that it went on to murder other groups as well, so that a reasonable estimate for the total number of victims, apart from war deaths, is 16 million; Pakistan slaughtered 3 million Bengalis; Cambodia brought about the death of 3 million persons; and the Soviet Union first destroyed 20 million peasants in the 1930s and then went on to take hundreds of thousands of other lives in the 1940s with its assaults on various nationality groups suspected of disloyalty.

These numbers may be somewhat high. Barbara Harff, who provides both lower and upper estimates in the same book, rounds out the picture with other twentieth-century genocides: Nigeria's extermination of 2 to 3 million Ibos; the Indonesian slaughter of supposed Communists, 200,000–500,000; the Indonesian action in East Timor, 60,000——100,000; Idi Amin's murder of fellow Ugandans, 500,000; the Tutsis' massacre of 100,000–200,000 Hutus in Burundi; Sudanese against the Southern Sudanese, 500,000; and so on.

The position that the Jewish Holocaust was unique tends to rest on the following arguments: (1) scale—the largest number of deaths extracted from one single group; (2) technology—the mechanization of death factories; (3) bureaucracy—the involvement of the state apparatus at previously unheard-of levels; (4) intent—the express purpose being to annihilate every last member of the Jewish people. Thus it is argued that, although Hitler killed many, many Poles, he still intended to use the majority of Poles as slave laborers. Some scholars counter that it was Hitler's goal also to eliminate the entire Gypsy population; others dispute this claim. The fact that one's group was not targeted for extermination in toto is a serious distinction, but hardly much consolation to the Gypsies, homosexuals, radicals, Poles, Slavs, etc., whom the Nazis did wipe out.

Alan Rosenberg asserts that the uniqueness of the Holocaust lies above all in "the Nazi abuse of science and technology, the application of bureaucratic techniques, principles of managerial efficiency and 'cost-benefit' analysis." This assessment, with its obvious implications for the present, dovetails with Theodor Adorno and Max Horkheimer's philosophical argument that the systematic, orderly, "Germanic," if you will, manner in which the killings were carried out shows the ultimately debased heritage of Western Enlightenment reason. Certainly much of our abiding fascination with the Holocaust rests on its dystopian, nightmarish use of rational, mechanized procedures. But I wonder how much of the importance we ascribe to these factors represents the narcissistic preoccupations of our Western technological society. Does it really matter so much if millions are gassed according to Eichmann's timetables rather than slowly, crudely starved to death, as in Stalin's regime, or marched around by ragged teenage Khmer Rouge soldiers and then beheaded or clubbed? Does the family mourning the loved one hacked to pieces by a spontaneous mob of Indonesian vigilantes care that much about abuses of science and technology? Does neatness count, finally, so damn much? (And what about the tragic fiasco—not genocide, true, but equally fatal—of the Great Leap Forward during the 1959–60 famine in China, when "anywhere between 16.4 to 29.5 million extra people died during the leap, because of the leap," according to Harvard political scientist Roderick MacFarquhar.)

I find it hard to escape the conclusion that those piles of other victims are not so significant to us North Americans as Jewish corpses. Is it simply because they are Third World people of color? How much is social class itself a factor? In so many books and movies about the Holocaust, I sense that I am being asked to feel a particular pathos in the rounding up of gentle, scholarly, middle-class, civilized people who are then packed into cattle cars, as though the liquidation of illiterate peasants would not be so poignant. The now-familiar newsreel shot of Asian populations fleeing a slaughter with their meager possessions in handcarts still reads to us as a catastrophe involving "masses," while the images of Jews lined up in their fedoras and overcoats tug at our hearts precisely because we see the line as composed of individuals. Our very notion of individuality is historically connected with the middle class; on top of that, Jews have often stood for individuality in modern culture, by virtue of their outsider status and commitment to mind and artistic cultivation. I am by no means saying that all the Jews who died in the camps were bourgeois (on the contrary, the majority were poor religious peasants); I am suggesting that, since the bulk of the narratives focus on middle-class victims swept up in the slaughter, this may help account for why the murder of European Jews plays on our sympathies so much more profoundly in this culture than the annihilation of Bengalis, East Timorese, or Ibos. The most obvious explanation may be demographic: there are many more Jews in the United States than there are Ibos or Bengalis.

"What's wrong with you?" I hear certain Jewish readers ask. "Are you not closer to your own dead than to those others? It's understandable for blacks to care more about slavery than about the Holocaust, or Armenians to mourn more for their massacred than for ours. But why do you, a Jew, insist on speaking as if these others mattered the same as our own flesh and blood killed in the gas chambers?" I don't know; I must be lacking in tribal feeling. When it comes to mass murder, I can see no difference between their casualties and ours.

That we must continue to come to terms with the Holocaust is obvious. The questions are: What forms will these commemorations or confrontations take? And addressed to whom? And who will be allowed to speak? And what is the permissible range of discourse?

There exists at present the urgent sense that we must keep up the pressure of commemorating the Holocaust to counteract the poisons of the extremist "revisionist" historians, like Robert Faurisson. To be truthful, I don't believe that the Faurissons and their ilk, who deny that a mass extermination of Jews ever took place, pose a serious threat to altering the world's perception of the historical record. They are the lunatic fringe, which we will always have with us. It makes sense to be vigilant about them, but not so paranoid as to exaggerate their real persuasional powers.

As for the more moderate revisionist historians—such as Andreas Hillgruber, who has tried to link the collapse of the eastern front with the death camps' greater activity and to propose that many German soldiers were heroically doing their duty—their views may set our teeth on edge with their insensitive tone or alarm us with their usefulness to the far right. But the greater threat they pose to the purity of our outrage is that some of what they say could hold a grain of truth. Is it reasonable to deny that some German soldiers in World War II may have been decent men victimized by the situation? Are we to divide the guilt by battalions—determine, as many are wont to do, that an ordinary German foot soldier may not have been entirely vicious, but that anyone in the S.S. was a sadistic criminal? I can well imagine a kid who didn't know better getting swept up in the mood of the day and joining the S.S. out of idealism. (One may scoff at the seeming oxymoron, Nazi idealist, yet every political movement generates its youthful idealists.)

I know of no event in recent years that has so united educated people in incredulous disgust as President Reagan's visit to the military cemetery in Bitburg, West Germany. At the time, glad to heap scorn on a President I despised, I heartily joined the chorus, although with a slight inner uneasiness that I was too cowardly to express. Now, thinking it over, I would say that it may not have been such a dastardly thing for the visiting President of a victorious nation to lay a wreath on the tomb of his defeated enemy's soldiers. The gesture contains a certain old-fashioned Homeric nobility. *But don't you understand? There were S.S. troops buried in that cemetery! Reagan was "signaling" the neofascists that all is forgiven.* Yes, yes, I remember that argument. To be fair to Reagan, he has also made tributes to the Holocaust. So what was really being objected to was appearances. We could not allow any reconciliation to appear to cloud the distinction between victims and culprits, radical good and radical evil, even if was perfectly obvious to all of us that Reagan was not condoning Nazism. The Holocaust has become a public issue around which Jews must Save Face, must spot anti-Semitism and decry it even when we know that the substance underneath is rather different.

A similar reaction occurred recently when the speaker of the West German parliament, Philipp Jenninger, made a speech in which he tried to show how the Germans were taken in by Hitler. In attempting to re-create the psychology of the typical German fascinated by Hitler's air of success, his irony was misunderstood—in some cases intentionally so by his political opponents—and he was forced to resign. Jenninger, a longtime supporter of Israel, was taken to task for saying honest things at the wrong time and, specifically, for quoting from Nazi speeches and reports without systematic, repudiating interruptions. Yet how is it possible to understand this complex historical phenomenon of the Holocaust without reexamining the Nazi point of view? What sort of intellectual grasp can we have of a historical situation if it is presented only from the standpoint of the horrors inflicted on the victims?

The "sensitivity" quotient operating around the Holocaust has begun to preclude any public discourse that goes beyond expressions of mourning and remorse. And even within that constricted discourse, how greedily we watch for signs of imbalance. Will the Pope single out sufficiently the tragedy of the Jews in his remarks about World War II? If not, Jewish organizations are quick to get on his case. There is something so testy, so vain, so divalike about this insistence that we always get top billing in any rite of mourning. Must every official statement that does not mention the Jews first among the dead be treated as an ominous sign of forgetting? Even if it were true that a certain resentment against the Jews, an incipient form of anti-Semitism, was lurking behind these official wordings or omissions, the result of all our monitoring and suspicious rebuttal is only to leave the impression of a Jewish lobby seeking to control like a puppeteer the language of politicians and Popes.

Whenever I see in the newspaper a story about the opening of yet another memorial or museum dedicated to the Holocaust, complete with photograph of distinguished backers surrounding a cornerstone or architectural model, my stomach gets nervous. What I need to figure for myself is how much this discomfit derives from legitimate doubts and how much it is simply the old fear of making ourselves too visible, drawing too much attention to Jewish things in a world that will never be anything but anti-Semitic. I would like to think, naturally, that there is more to it than cowardice. All right, then, what could possibly be wrong with a Holocaust memorial?

We will start with an obtuse response: I just don't get why both New York City and Washington, D.C., should have to have Holocaust memorial museums. Or why every major city in the United States seems to be commemorating this European tragedy in some way or another. An Israeli poet on a reading tour through the States was taken into the basement of a synagogue in Ohio and proudly shown the congregation's memorial to the 6 million dead: a torch meant to remain eternally lit. The poet muttered under his breath, "*Shoah flambé.*" In Israel they can joke about these matters. Holocaust monuments seem to me primarily a sign of ethnic muscle-flexing, proof that the local Jewish community has attained enough financial and political clout to erect such a tribute to their losses.

In the past, monuments commemorated victories and glory; they were a striving for immortality in the eyes of the polis. But with the very survival of the planet in doubt, eroding our confidence in a future public realm, and in light of our disenchantment with the whole ideal of glory after Vietnam and Watergate, a patriotic equestrian monument raised at this moment would seem embarrassing. Myself, I can easily live without more cannons and generals on pedestals. On the other hand, the dethroning of glory has brought about a tendency to erect monuments to shame and historical nightmare. These monuments have an air of making the visitor feel bad, at the same time retaining a decorously remote and abstract air—all the more so when they are removed geographically from the ground of pain. Auschwitz is one thing: the historical preservation of the death camps in situ makes perfect sense. But it is quite another to allocate the leftover land from a new luxury apartment tower in Lower Manhattan to a Holocaust museum, for which the developer will receive the usual tax abatement.

Snobbish as this may sound, I view museums as primarily places for the exhibition and contemplation of interesting objects. Institutions like Yad Vashem (the Holocaust Heroes and Martyrs Museum) and the Museum of the Diaspora in Israel, which have few artifacts—consisting mainly of slide shows, blown-up photographs, and accompanying wall texts—are, in my view, essentially propaganda factories, designed to manipulate the visitor through a precise emotional experience. They are like a Tunnel of Horrors or a Disneyland park devoted to Jewish suffering. The success of the exhibit depends entirely on entering in a properly preprogrammed state and allowing one's buttons to be pushed.

A woman I know, the child of camp survivors, had grown up with tales of Hitler and Buchenwald at every meal. Finally she got to visit Yad Vashem. She was so bursting with emotion, so ready to be wiped out by the experience that, shortly after entering, she saw a lampshade and thought, Oh my God, that could be my uncle Morty! and ran in tears from the museum. Her companion caught up with her to try to calm her down. "But, Hilda," he said, "those lampshades are part of the exhibit showing a typical Jewish scholar's study, before the Holocaust even began."

In my own visit to Yad Vashem, I was part of a group of Jewish American academics who thought it so "heavy" that I didn't dare open my mouth. Some of the exhibits were undeniably interesting, but it was not an overwhelming experience for me; rather, I was disturbed by what seemed a theatrically partisan misuse of historical methods. I also found it hard to summon the 6 million dead in the face of such ennobling strain. The grounds were a sort of monument park filled with sentimental-expressionist statuary. Our tour guide explained that the steel pillar symbolized a smokestack as well as a ladder of transcendence. All this artistic symbolism talk reminded me of the remark of an Israeli friend: "If bad sculpture could be turned into food, then Israel could feed the world."

Yad Vashem's memorial hall did have a bleak architectural elegance of stone and concrete; but the fire (another "eternal flame") was upstaged by an ugly black organic relief, symbolizing charred bones, I suppose. Someone in my group produced a mimeographed poem, which we read aloud. It was all about the flame being a symbol for the slaughter, of eternal memory, of oppression—a list of pious abstractions clunkily metered and redundant. Why does the poem have to be so bad? I found myself thinking. It is at that level of kitsch doggerel that I start to rebel.

Will the above seem the ravings of a finicky aesthete? I apologize. But remember that it is an aesthetic problem we are talking about, this attempt to make an effective presentation of a massive event. The dead of Auschwitz are not buried in Yad Vashem; believe me, I am not insulting their memories. Yad Vashem is the product of us the living and as such is subject to our dispassionate scrutiny and criticism. To project religious awe onto this recently built tourist attraction is idolatry, pure and simple.

In a brilliant essay called "The Kitsch of Israel," which appeared in the *New York Review of Books*, Avishai Margalit wrote:

> Israel's shrine of kitsch is not, as may have been expected, the Wailing Wall, but a place that should have been furthest away from any trace of kitsch: Yad Vashem, the memorial for the Holocaust. A "children's room" has been dedicated there recently. . . . The real significance of this room is not in its commemoration of the single most horrible event in the history of mankind—the systematic murder of two million children, Jewish and Gypsies, for being what they were and not for anything they had done. The children's room, rather, is meant to deliver a message to the visiting foreign statesman, who is rushed to

Yad Vashem even before he has had time to leave off his luggage at his hotel, that all of us here in Israel are these children and that Hitler-Arafat is after us. This is the message for internal consumption as well. Talking of the PLO in the same tone as one talks of Auschwitz is an important element in turning the Holocaust into kitsch.

Another method of Holocaust remembrance takes the form of educational instruction in grade school. The pedagogic problem I have with these Holocaust study units is that they are usually parachuted into the classroom with very little connection to anything else in the curriculum. As someone who worked in elementary and secondary schools for twelve years, I've had many occasions to see how the latest concession to each ethnic lobbying group—be it Puerto Rican Week, Black History Month, or Holocaust Week—was greeted by the students as a gimmick, not to be taken seriously. I remember the morning that the local Holocaust curriculum person came into a fourth-grade classroom at P.S. 75 and in her sweet, solemn voice began describing the horrors of a concentration camp. The children listened with resentful politeness, distracted not necessarily because the subject matter was unsuitable for their age group but because any subject matter introduced in so artificial a manner, with so little relation to their other studies, would be treated as an intrusion.

I realize it may be asking a lot, but we should be attempting to teach the Holocaust within a broader context, as part of an invigorated, general strengthening of historical studies. Why isolate Hitler completely from Bismarck, Kaiser Wilhelm, Adenauer, Stalin? Why teach children about Buchenwald and not other genocides? The Holocaust becomes their first, sometimes their exclusive, official school instruction on death and evil. Of course, kids daily see war and gore on the six o'clock news, but in school we seem to want them to encounter the horrors of mass killing solely through presentations about the fate of the Jews. It is almost as if we Jews wanted to monopolize suffering, to appropriate death as our own. But as Irving Louis Horowitz points out, while Judaism as a way of life is special, there is no "special nature of Jewish dying. Dying is a universal property of many peoples, cultures and nations."

I cannot help but see this extermination pride as another variant of the Covenant: this time the Chosen People have been chosen for extraordinary suffering. As such, the Holocaust seems simply another opportunity for Jewish chauvinism. I grew up in Williamsburg, Brooklyn, surrounded by this chauvinistic tendency, which expressed itself as an insecure need to boast about Jewish achievements in every field, the other side of which was a contempt for the non-Jews, the gentiles, who were characterized as less intelligent, less human, less cultured, humorous, spicy, warmhearted, whatever. All my life I've tried to guard against the full force of this damaging tribal smugness, to protect myself from the weakening lies of group *amour propre* (not that I don't succumb regularly to my own form of it).

"Secularization," Hannah Arendt has written, ". . . engendered a very real Jewish chauvinism, if by chauvinism we understand the perverted nationalism in which (in the words of Chesterton) 'the individual himself is the thing to be worshipped; the individual is his own ideal and even his own idol.' From now on, the old concept of chosenness was no longer the essence of Judaism; it was instead the essence of Jewishness."

There are reasons other than chauvinism why Jews might be loath to surrender the role of the chief victim. It affords us an edge, a sort of privileged nation status in the moral honor roll, such as the Native Americans have enjoyed for some time. Following Hitler's defeat, Jews had a short grace period in world opinion, pitied as we were and valued as an endangered species. Given the world's tendency to distort and demonize Jews in the past, it would almost seem as though there was no middle ground: either continue to fight for persecuted, good-victim status or else watch the pendulum swing the opposite way, to where we would be regarded as exceptionally wicked. But in my opinion, there must be a middle ground, and it is worth fighting for. In the meantime, is it not possible for us to have a little more compassion for the other victimized peoples of this century and not insist quite so much that our wounds bleed more fiercely?

Theodor Adorno once made an intentionally provocative statement to the effect that one can't have lyric poetry after Auschwitz. Much as I respect Adorno, I am inclined to ask, a bit faux-naively: Why not? Are we to infer, regarding all the beautiful poetry that has been written since 1945, that these postwar poets were insensitive to some higher tact? Alexander Kluge, the German filmmaker, has explained what Adorno really meant by this remark: any art from now on that does not take Auschwitz into account will be not worthy as art. This is one of those large intimidating pronouncements to which one gives assent in public while secretly harboring doubts. Art is a vast arena; must it all and always come to terms with the death camps, important as they are? How hoggish, this Holocaust, to insist on putting its stamp on all creative activity.

On the other hand, reams have been written arguing that you *can't* make art out of the Holocaust. Elie Wiesel once declared, "Art and Auschwitz are antithetical." Perhaps people would like to believe that there is some preserve, some domain that ought to be protected from the artist's greedy hands. Actually, a whole body of splendid art about the tragedy of the Jews under the Nazis has been made. One thinks right away of Primo Levi's books, the poems of Paul Celan and Nelly Sachs, Tadeusz Kantor's theatrical pieces, films like Resnais's *Night and Fog*, Ophüls's *The Sorrow and the Pity* and *Hotel Terminus*, Losey's *Mr. Klein*, Corti's trilogy *Where To and Back*. . . . Maybe not a lot, true, but then not much great art came out of the debacle of World War I. We should not forget that 99 percent of all art-making attempts are failures, regardless of subject matter.

It has also been argued that the enormity of the Nazis' crimes against the Jews calls for an aesthetic approach of an entirely different order than the traditional mimetic response. This seems to me nothing more than a polemic in favor of certain avant-garde or antinaturalist techniques, hitched arbitrarily to the Holocaust. Yes, Paul Celan's cryptic, abstract poems are powerful approaches to the concentration camps, but so are Primo Levi's direct, lucid accounts. I would not like to think that every stage piece about the Holocaust must perforce follow the stripped, ritualized strategies of Grotowski's or Kantor's theatrical works—effective as these may be by themselves—out of some deluded idea that a straight naturalistic approach would desecrate the 6 million dead.

Art has its own laws, and even so devastating an event as the Holocaust may not significantly change them. For all its virtues, the longeurs, repetitions, and failures of sympathy in Claude Lanzmann's *Shoah* are not exonerated, no matter what its apologists may argue, by the seriousness of the subject matter, as though an audience must be put through over eight hours of an exhaustingly uneven movie to convince it of the reality of the Holocaust. A tighter film would have accomplished the same and been a stronger work of art. Lanzmann might reply that he is indifferent to the claims of art compared to those of the Holocaust; unfortunately, you can't play the game of art and not play it at the same time.

What is usually meant by the statement that the Holocaust is unsuitable for artistic treatment is that it is too vast and terrible to be used merely as a metaphor or backdrop. Certainly I understand the impatience of serious people with the parade of shallow movie melodramas and television docudramas that invoke the milieu of Nazi Germany as a sort of narrative frisson. Indeed, where would the contemporary European art film be without the Holocaust? As a plot device it is second only to infidelity. For the fractured European film market, the trauma of World War II is perhaps the only unifying historical experience to which narratives can appeal commercially. Yet the mediocrity of such "prestige" movies as Truffaut's *The Last Metro*, Visconti's *The Damned*, Zanussi's *Somewhere in the Night*, Malle's *Lacombe, Lucien*, De Sica's *The Garden of the Finzi-Continis*, Szabo's *Hanussen*, among others, illustrates the degree to which—even for talented directors—the Nazi terror has ossified into a stale genre, a ritualized parade of costumes and sentimental conventions, utterly lacking in the authentic texture of personally observed detail. Now we have the Third Reich as dress-up: all those red flags with swastikas, those jeeps and jackboots suddenly flashing in key-lit night scenes, the tinkle of broken glass—accoutrements that seem considerably less menacing in Technicolor, by the way, than they used to in black and white. We have endless variations of the *Cabaret* plot, as characters flounder in frivolous, "decadent" sexual confusion before the evil Nazis announce themselves at midpoint and restore order and narrative suspense in one blow. The Gestapo represents the principle of Fate rescuing the story from its aimlessness— a screenwriter's best friend. The Jewish protagonists are pulled, at first unknowingly, into that funnel of history, then gradually learn that there is something larger than their personal discontents. Meanwhile, the Christian characters sort themselves into betrayers and noble selfless neighbors, thanks to the litmus test of the Holocaust plot; and the audience readies itself for that last purgative scene, the lineup before the trains. . . .

To enumerate the clichés is not to agree with the viewpoint that no art can be made about the Holocaust. Quite the contrary; it is only to demand that the artist go beyond a sentimental, generic approach to the subject and find a more complex, detailed, personal, and original path.

I have a former student, Bella, whose father was always trying to get her to see Resnais's *Night and Fog,* an admittedly fine film about the death camps. The father believed that we must all deal in one way or another with the Holocaust, and his way, as befit an educated man, was to read as many books and to see as many films on the subject as possible. This approach he urged on his daughter. But Bella did not want to see *Night and Fog.* As a child she had had many phobias, and even after she had outgrown them, there was something about the way her father talked up the film that made her leery. He would try to get her to meet him at a movie theater where it was showing. He kept saying, "But you owe it to *them* to see it." Them: the ghosts, the 6 million.

Bella refused. Since that time she has moved to Israel and is leading, in her own way, a good Jewish life.

What are our obligations to *them?* Whatever they may be, no living person can tell us.

While I also read books or see movies on the Holocaust, I do it more out of a sense of cultural curiosity and desire to learn about history than a religious debt to the victims. I am not convinced that learning history means trying to put oneself emotionally through the experience—or blaming oneself if one is not feeling enough.

I am trying to put my finger on a problem regarding empathy. A Jewish educator recently wrote that we must find a way to make our young people "feel more anguishingly the memory of the dead." But the effort to project oneself into the Holocaust, to "undergo" for a few minutes what others have suffered in the transport trains and the camps, to take that anguish into oneself, seems—except in rare cases—foredoomed. That way generally lies tourism and self-pity. It is hard enough in psychoanalysis to retrieve affectively one's own past, one's actual memories; to expect to relive with emotion invented memories seems overly demanding. Or gimmicky: like those black history courses that made the students crawl along the floor "chained" to each other to give them an existential feel for conditions in the hold of a slave ship.

False knowledge. Borrowed mysticism. By blackmailing ourselves into thinking that we must put ourselves through a taste of Auschwitz, we are imitating unconsciously the Christian mystics who tried to experience in their own flesh the torments of Christ on the cross. But this has never been part of the Jewish religion, this gluttony for empathic suffering. Though Jewish rabbis and sages have been killed for their faith, and their deaths recorded and passed down, Judaism has fought shy in the past of establishing a hagiography based on martyrdom. Why are we doing it now?

In certain ways, the Jewish American sacramentalizing of the Holocaust seems an unconscious borrowing of Christian theology. That one tragic event should be viewed as standing outside, above history, and its uniqueness defended and proclaimed, seems very much like the Passion of Christ. Indeed, in a recent book, *The Crucifixion of the Jews*, Christian theologian Franklin H. Littell has argued that the true crucifixion *was* the Holocaust, not the death of Jesus on the cross, and that the subsequent establishment of the State of Israel was the Resurrection. Littell asks, "Was Jesus a false Messiah? . . . Is the Jewish people, after all and in spite of two millennia of Christian calumny, the true Suffering Servant promised in Isaiah?" And John Cardinal O'Connor of New York wrote, "To say to the Jews, 'Forget the Holocaust,' is to say to Christians, 'Forget the Crucifixion.' There is a sacramentality about the Holocaust for Jews all around the world. It constitutes a mystery, by definition beyond their understanding—and ours." Soothing as all this may sound, it worries me because it shows how easily Judaism can be Christianized—or at least co-opted into a Christian vocabulary—by mythologizing the Holocaust experience.

The theological uses to which the Holocaust has been put by an assimilated American Jewish community are so diverse that the Holocaust has begun to replace the Bible as the new text that we must interpret. There is the danger that the "glamour" of the Holocaust will eclipse traditional religious practice in the eyes of American Jewry—that, in effect, the Holocaust will swallow up Judaism. In the vacuum where God used to be, we are putting the Holocaust.

I first began to notice the usurpation of the traditional Passover service by Holocaust worship at a large communal seder in Houston, around 1982. Though rewritings of the Haggadah were nothing new to me (in the late sixties, the Vietcong were compared to the Jews in Egypt trying to throw off their oppressors), the introduction of references to the Holocaust in every second or third prayer seemed to have a different function. For many of the people at that seder in Texas, the Holocaust *was* the heart of their faith; it was what touched them most deeply about being Jewish. The religion itself—the prayers, the commentaries, the rituals, the centuries of accumulated wisdom and tradition—had shriveled to a sort of marginally necessary preamble for this negative miracle. The table conversation turned to accounts of pilgrimages to Buchenwald and Bergen-Belsen and Auschwitz, package tours organized by the United Jewish Appeal. The ancient Jewish religion was all but forgotten beside the lure of the concentration camp universe.

The importance of the Holocaust for such assimilated Jews must be considered within the broader framework of the erosion of Jewish group memory in the modern period. By group or "collective" memory, I mean simply all the customs, rituals, ceremonies, folkways, *Yiddishkeit*, cuisine, historical events, and so on, that used to be the common inheritance of every Jew. The desperation to hold on to the

Holocaust is informed by this larger decay. Underneath these anxious injunctions never to forget, what I hear is "We must never forget the Holocaust because we're rapidly forgetting everything else, so let's hold on at least to this piece."

At first glance it seemed to me a paradox that Jews, ostensibly "the historically minded people" par excellence, should be so resistant to placing the Holocaust in a comparative historical context. But then I came across an illuminating little book by Yosef Yerushalmi, *Zakhor: Jewish History and Jewish Memory*, which argues that anti-historical currents are nothing new within Jewry. The oft-repeated injunction to "remember" is not the same as urging a historical perspective: "Not only is Israel under no obligation whatever to remember the entire past, but its principle of selection is unique unto itself. It is above all God's acts of intervention in history, and man's responses to them, be they positive or negative, that must be recalled."

Yerushalmi points out that for nearly fifteen centuries after the death of Josephus, during the Talmudic period so fertile for commentary about the patterns and meaning of the Bible, there were no Jewish historians. The rabbis felt it unnecessary and perhaps even impious to keep contemporary historical records (except for sketchy rabbinic genealogies), precisely because the Bible was already "sacred history." A brief flurry of Jewish history writing occurred in the sixteenth century, partly touched off by the need to understand the catastrophic expulsion from Spain and Portugal; but these chronicles were not so scientific as Christian histories of the same era; they had elements of messianism and followed a somewhat apocalyptic approach, examining the past for signs and prophecies of an approaching redemption. Even this limited historical activity was submerged, at the end of the sixteenth century, by the greater appeal of Lurianic Kabbalah, which offered Jews "a unique interpretation of history that lay beyond history ... an awesome metahistorical myth of a pronounced gnostic character. That myth declared that all evil, including the historical evil that is Jewish exile, had its roots before history began, before the Garden of Eden was planted, before our world existed, in a primal tragic flaw that occurred at the very creation of the cosmos itself" (Yerushalmi).

In the modern era, of course, a plethora of Jewish histories and historians came into being, but the new objective methods of analysis have been on a collision course with providential history. "To the degree that this historiography is indeed 'modern' and deserves to be taken seriously," notes Yerushalmi, "it must at least functionally repudiate" two cardinal assumptions of traditional Judaism: "the belief that divine providence is not only an ultimate but an active causal factor in Jewish history, and the related belief in the uniqueness of Jewish history itself."

Forgive this digression; it actually has a point. Our response to the Holocaust must be seen within this broader framework of the ancient Jewish ambivalence toward a historical outlook, which threatens the religious one. The hostility toward anything that questions the uniqueness of the Holocaust can now be seen as part of a deeper tendency to view all of Jewish history as "unique," to read that history selectively, and to use it only insofar as it promotes a redemptive script. Thus, the

Holocaust's "mystery" must be asserted over and over, in the same way as the "mystery" of Jewish survival was through the ages, in order to yield the single explanation that God "wants" the Jewish people to live and is protecting them. Being a secular, fallen Jew with a taste for rationalism and history, I cannot help but regard such providential interpretations as superstition. Against them I would place the cool, cautionary wisdom of Spinoza about his own people: "as for their continuance so long after dispersion and the loss of empire, there is nothing marvelous in it."

Sometimes I see the Jewish preoccupation with the Holocaust, to the exclusion of all other human disasters, as uncharitable, self-absorbed, self-righteous, and— pushy. On the other hand, it makes no sense to counsel putting it aside for a while. How can we expect to get over so enormous a tragedy in only forty or fifty years? It takes time, centuries. It took over a thousand years for the Jews as a people to get over the destruction of Jerusalem by Titus, and we may still not have recovered from that. My problem is not that the grief is taking too long but that the orchestration of that grief in the public realm sometimes seems coercive and misguided.

Jewish history is filled with disasters, from which some redemptive meaning has ultimately been extracted. The Holocaust is proving to be a large bone to swallow; it does not turn "redeemable" so easily, and when we try to hurry up that process with mechanical prescriptions and ersatz rituals, compelling governments and churches to pay verbal tribute to our losses in narrowly defined terms, and browbeating our young people to feel more anguishingly the memory of our dead, something false, packaged, sentimentally aggressive begins to enter the picture. Perhaps the problem is that for many alienated, secularized Jews who experience themselves as inauthentic in a thousand other ways, the Holocaust has become the last proof of their own authenticity. If so, they should realize that even this proof is perishable stuff; the further one gets from personal experience, the harder it is to take the spilled blood of history into one's veins.

19

The Movies and Spiritual Life

It is the flattest and dullest parts that have in the end the most life.
—Robert Bresson

THE EARLIEST FILM I REMEMBER SEEING was *The Spanish Main*, made short-ly after World War II had ended. I must have been all of three or four—which is to say, too young to offer the auteurist apology I would now, that the wonderful romantic director Frank Borzage was simply misused in a swashbuckler. I remem-ber a good deal of blushing orange-pink, the color of so many movies by the time a print got to our local theater. But what irritated me were the love scenes, especial-ly the long clinch at the end, when the hero held Maureen O'Hara in his puffy sleeves. "Cut out the mushy stuff!" I yelled.

What children want from movies is very simple: a chair smashed over the gun-man's head, a battle with a giant scorpion. They get restless through the early devel-opment scenes that give background information, the tender glances, the land-scapes. But then a knife is hurled through the air and they are back into it. The kinet-ic at its most basic captivates them.

This was the initial charm and promise of the medium, as a somewhat astonished Georg Lukács reflected in 1913 after a visit to the motion picture emporium:

The pieces of furniture keep moving in the room of a drunkard, his bed flies out of his room with him lying in it and they fly over the town. Balls some people wanted to use playing skittles revolt against their "users" and pursue them uphill and downhill. . . . The "movie" can become fantastic in a purely mechanical manner . . . the characters only have movements but no soul of their own, and what happens to them is simply an event that has nothing to do with fate. . . . Man has lost his soul, but he has won his body in exchange; his magnitude and poetry lie in the way he overcomes physical obstacles with his strength or skill, while the comedy lies in his losing to them.

What Lukács could not have predicted was that, side-by-side with this fantastic cinema of movement, would develop a cinema of interiority, slowness, contemplation. Certain directors of the so-called transcendental style, like Dreyer, Bresson, Ozu, Mizoguchi, Rossellini, Antonioni, Hou Hsiao-Hsien, would not be content until they had revealed the fateful motions of their characters' souls on film.

I remember the first time I saw such a movie, in college: Robert Bresson's *Diary of a Country Priest*. The picture follows the misfortunes of a young priest, alienated from his worldly and cynical parishioners, who undermines his health in a quest for divine communion by eating nothing but bread soaked in wine. At the end he dies, attaining grace on his deathbed. Bresson frustrates conventional expectations of entertainment by denying the audience melodrama, spectacle, or comic diversion, offering instead an alternation of tense theological discussions and scenes of the priest alone, trapped by landscape or interiors in psychic solitary confinement. No doubt I identified, in my seventeen-year-old self-pity, with the hero's poetic heartache. But what affected me so strongly at the time was something else.

There was a solitary chapel scene, ending in one of those strange short dolly shots that Bresson was so fond of, a movement of almost clumsy longing toward the priest at the altar, as though the camera itself were taking communion. Suddenly I had the impression that the film had stopped, or, rather, that time had stopped. All forward motion was arrested, and I was staring into "eternity." Now, I am not the kind of person readily given to mystical experiences, but at that moment I had a sensation of delicious temporal freedom. What I "saw" was not a presence, exactly, but a prolongation, a dilation, as though I might step into the image and walk around it at my leisure.

I'm sure most people have at one time or another experienced such a moment of stasis. If you stay up working all night and then go for a walk in the deserted streets at dawn and look at, say, a traffic light, you may fixate with wonderment on the everyday object, in an illumination half caused by giddy exhaustion. Recently, while watching *Diary of a Country Priest* on videotape, I confess I kept dozing off, which made me wonder whether that first celluloid experience of eternity was nothing more than the catnap of a tired student faced with a slow, demanding movie. But no, this is taking demystification too far. Bresson's austere technique had more likely slowed down all my bodily and mental processes, so that I was ready to receive a whiff of the transcendent.

In Paul Schrader's *Transcendental Style in Film*, he accounts for this phenomenon by arguing from the bare, sparse means of Bresson's direction, which eschews drama and audience empathy: "Stasis, of course, is the final example of sparse means. The image simply stops. ... When the image stops, the viewer keeps going, moving deeper and deeper, one might say, *into* the image. This is the 'miracle' of sacred art."

All I know is that I was fascinated with the still, hushed, lugubrious, unadrenalated world of *Diary*. I kept noticing how the characters gravitated toward windows:

could not the panes' transparency be a metaphor for the border between substance and immateriality? "Your film's beauty," wrote Bresson to himself in *Notes on Cinematography*, "will not be in the images (postcardism) but in the ineffable that they will emanate." Perversely, it seemed, he was struggling to express the invisible, the ineffable, through the most visually concrete and literal of media. Yet perhaps this is less of a paradox than it might at first appear; perhaps there is something in the very nature of film, whose images live or die by projected beams of light, that courts the invisible, the otherworldly. The climax of Murnau's *Nosferatu*, where the vampire, standing before the window, is "dissolved" by the rays of morning light, must derive some of its iconic power from self-reflexive commentary on the medium itself.

I noticed at the time that Bresson was also very fond of doors—in much the same way that Cocteau used mirrors in *Orpheus*, as conductors from one world to another. *Pickpocket*, Bresson's greatest film, has a multitude of scenes of a door opening, followed by a brief, tense dialogue between well-meaning visitor and protagonist (the pickpocket), and ending with the frustrated visitor's exit through the same door. This closed-door motif suggests both the pickpocket's stubbornness, his refusal of grace, and the doors of spiritual perception, which (Bresson seems to be saying) are always close by, inviting us to embrace salvation. Bresson's world tends to be claustrophobic, encompassing a space from the door to the window and back, as though telling us how little maneuvering room there is between grace and damnation. Curious how such a chilly idea, which would be appalling to me as a precept to follow in daily life, could prove so attractive when expressed in cinematic form. But part of its attraction was precisely that it seemed an intensification, a self-conscious foregrounding of problems of cinematic form.

A director must make a decision about how to slice up space, where to put the camera. Jean Renoir generously composes the frame so that it spills toward the sides, suggesting an interesting, fecund world awaiting us just beyond the screen, coterminous with the action, if momentarily off-camera; a Bresson composition draws inward, implodes, abstractly denies truck with daily life, cuts off all exits. In many scenes of *Diary*, the priest, let into a parishioner's house, encounters almost immediately a painful interview in which his own values are attacked, ridiculed, tempted. There is no room for small talk; every conversation leads directly to the heart of the matter: sin, suicide, perversity, redemption, grace.

I wonder why this forbidding Jansenist work so deeply moved me. I think it had something to do with the movie's offer of silence ("Build your film on white, on silence and on stillness," wrote Bresson) and, with it, an implicit offer of greater mental freedom. A film like *Diary of a Country Priest* was not constantly dinning reaction cues into me. With the surrounding darkness acting as a relaxant, its stream of composed images induced a harmony that cleansed and calmed my brain; the plot may have been ultimately tragic, but it brought me into a quieter space of serene resignation through the measured unfurling of a story of human suffering.

I could say a good deal more about Bresson's *Diary*, but, first of all, the film has already been picked clean by scholars and academics, and, second of all, rather than fall into the prolixities of scene-by-scene analysis, I want to concentrate on the challenge at hand: to explain how this one movie changed my life.* It did so by putting me in contact with a habit of mind that I may as well call spiritual, and a mental process suspiciously like meditation.

The monks in Fra Angelico's order were each assigned a cell with a painting on which to meditate. It may sound far-fetched to speak of watching a movie as a meditative discipline, given the passivity of the spectator compared with the rigors of Zen or monastic sitting; but parallels do exist. There is a familiar type of meditation called one-pointedness, which focuses the meditator's attention through the repetition of a single sound or mental image. Yet another meditation practice encourages the sitter to let thoughts fall freely and disorientedly, without anchoring them to any one point. The films of Mizoguchi, say, seem to me a fusion of these two methods: by their even, level presentation of one sort of trouble after another, they focus the viewer's mind on a single point of truth, the Buddhist doctrine of suffering; and by their extreme cinematographic fluidity, they arouse a state akin to free fall.

At first I used to resist my mind's wandering during such films, thinking I was wasting the price of admission. But just as in Buddhist meditation one is instructed not to brush aside the petty or silly thoughts that rise up, since these "distractions" are precisely the material of the meditation, so I began to allow my movie-watching mind to yield more freely to daily preoccupations, cares, memories that arose from some image association. Sometimes I might be lost to a personal mental thread for several minutes before returning with full attention to the events on-screen; but when I did come back, it was with a refreshed consciousness, a deeper level of feeling. What *Diary of a Country Priest* taught me was that certain kinds of movies— those with austere aesthetic means; an unhurried, deliberate pace; tonal consistency; a penchant for long shots as opposed to close-ups; an attention to backgrounds and milieu; a mature acceptance of suffering as fate—allowed me more room for meditation. And I began to seek out other examples.

In various films by Ozu, Mizoguchi, Naruse, there will be a scene early on where the main characters are fiddling around in the house and someone comes by, a neighbor or the postman (the traditional Japanese domestic architecture, with its sliding shoji, is particularly good at capturing this interpenetration of inside and outside); a kimono-clad figure moves sluggishly through the darkened interior to answer, some sort of polite conversation follows; and throughout this business, one is not unpleasantly aware of an odd aural hollowness, like the mechanical thud-thud of the camera that used to characterize all films just after sound came in; and it isn't

---

*This essay was originally published in an anthology entitled *The Movie That Changed My Life*, edited by David Rosenberg.

clear what the point of the scene is, except maybe to establish the ground of dailiness; and at such junctures I often start to daydream, to fantasize about a movie
without any plot, just these shuttlings and patient, quiet moments that I like so
much. Ah, yes, the lure of pure quotidian plotlessness for a writer like myself, who
has trouble making up plots. But then I always remember that what gives these
scenes their poignant edge is our knowledge that some plot is about to take hold, so
that their very lack of tension engenders suspense: when will all this daily flux coa-
lesce into a single dramatic conflict? Without the catastrophe to come, we probably
would not experience so refreshingly these narrative backwaters; just as without the
established, calm, spiritual ground of dailiness, we would not feel so keenly the
ensuing betrayals, suicide pacts, and sublimely orchestrated disenchantments.

I tried to take from these calm cinematic moments—to convince myself I
believed in—a sense of the sacredness of everyday life. I even piously titled my second poetry collection *The Daily Round.* I wanted the security, the solace of a constant,
enduring order underneath things—without having to pay the price through ecstasy
or transcendence. My desire had something to do with finding an inner harmony in
the arrangement of backgrounds and foregrounds as I came across them in real life;
an effort, part spiritual, part aesthetic, to graft an order I had learned through movies
onto reality. How it originally came about was this way: watching a film, I would
sometimes find myself transfixed by the objects in the background. I remember a
scene in Max Ophüls's *Letter from an Unknown Woman,* when the heroine is ironing in
the kitchen, and suddenly I became invaded by the skillets and homely kitchen-ware
behind her. For several moments I began to dream about the life of these objects,
which had become inexplicably more important to me than Joan Fontaine.

Certain directors convey a respect for rooms and landscapes at rest, for the world
that surrounds the drama of the characters and will survive it long after these struggles are over. Ozu frequently used static cutaway shots of hallways, beaded curtains
in restaurants—passageways made for routine human traffic, which are momentarily devoid of people. Bresson wrote: "One single mystery of persons and objects."
And: "Make the objects look as if they want to be there. . . . The persons and objects
in your film *must walk at the same pace, as companions.*" Antonioni also engaged in a tactful spying on objects, keeping his camera running long after the characters had quit
the frame. Why these motionless transitions, I thought, if not as a way of asserting
some constant and eternal order under the messy flux of accident, transience,
unhappiness?

I tried, as I said, to apply this way of seeing to my own daily life outside movie
theaters. I waited on objects to catch what Bresson calls their "phosphorescence."
In general, these exercises left me feeling pretty pretentious. Just as there are people
whom dogs and children don't seem to trust, so objects did not open up to me,
beyond a polite, stiff acquaintance. They kept their dignified distance; I kept mine.

Once, I took Kay, a woman I had been dating for several years while steadfastly
refusing to marry, to see Dreyer's *Ordet.* It has been as hard for me to surrender spir-

itually as conjugally; I have long since become the kind of skeptic who gets embarrassed for someone when he or she starts talking about astrology, out-of-body experiences, past lives, or karma. I don't say I'm right, just that I'm rendered uncomfortable by such terms. And if the exotic vocabulary of Eastern religions makes me uneasy, the closer-to-home terminology of Christ the King and Christianity makes me doubly so—perhaps for no reason other than that I'm an American Jew. In any case, there we were at the Carnegie Hall Cinema, Kay (who is Presbyterian) and I; we had just seen the magnificent final sequence, in which Dreyer "photographs" a resurrection: the mentally disturbed Johannes, invoking Jesus Christ, raises Inger from the dead—which is shown not by any optical trick, mind you, but simply by filming the event head-on, unadorned. One moment the woman is lying in her bed; the next moment she sits up and kisses her husband. I don't know which moved me more, Dreyer's own seeming faith in miracles, his cinematic restraint, or the audacity of his challenge to the audience to believe or disbelieve as we saw fit. The lights went up, and, just as I was wiping away a tear, Kay punched me. "You see, you can take it in films, but you can't take it in life!" she said.

Sometimes I think I am especially inclined to the spiritual, and that is why I resist it so. At other times this seems nothing but a conceit on my part. You cannot claim credit for possessing a trait you have run away from all your life. This does not prevent me from secretly hoping that spirituality has somehow sneaked in the back door when I wasn't looking, or was miraculously earned, like coupons, through my "solitary struggles" as a writer. (It would not be the first time that making poetry or art was confused with spiritual discipline.)

Every once in a blue moon I go to religious services or read the Bible—hoping that this time it will have a deeper effect on me than merely satisfying some anthropological curiosity. I do not, by and large, perform good works; I do not pray, except in desperation. I have never pursued a regular meditative practice, or even meditated under a learned person's guidance (though I have many friends and relatives who described the experience for me). No, the truth is I probably have a very weak (though still alive) spiritual drive, which I exercise for the most part in movie theaters.

It is, I suppose, a truism that the cinema is the secular temple of modern life. A movie house is like a chapel, where one is alone with one's soul. Film intrinsically avows an afterlife by creating immortals, stars. In its fixing of transient moments with permanence, it bestows on even the silliest comic farce an air of fatalism and eternity. All well and good. What I want to know is: Did I purposely seek out the spiritual in movies in order to create a cordon sanitaire, to keep it from spilling into the other facets of my life?

Films have been a way for me to aspire to the spiritual, without taking it altogether seriously. *Diary of a Country Priest* may have helped shape my sense of beauty, but I notice that as a writer I have never striven for Bressonian purity. I am too gabby; such austerity is beyond me. In fact, when I encounter Bresson on the page, in interviews and in his writings, he sometimes seems to me insufferable. Even some of his films, especially the later ones like *The Devil, Probably*, and *Lancelot du Lac*, have passages that strike me as moronically solemn. And, as I am not the first to observe, there is often something mechanical in the plots of Bresson, along with those of other modern Catholic storytellers—Graham Greene, Mauriac, Bernanos (who supplied the novel on which *Diary of a Country Priest* is based)—that stacks the deck in favor of sin, perverse willfulness, and despair, the better to draw grace out of the pile later on. I think even as a college student I suspected this, but the very air of contrivance, which alluded to theological principles I ill understood, filled me with uncertainty and awe.

Another reason why I did not build more on the glimpses of spiritual illumination I received in movies occurs to me belatedly: All the films I was attracted to were either Christian* or Buddhist. I could not travel very far along this path without becoming disloyal to Judaism. Though I haven't been a particularly observant Jew, I retain an attachment to that identity; put bluntly, it would horrify me to convert to another faith. What, then, of Jewish models? Was there no Jewish transcendental cinema? I think not, partly because modern American Judaism doesn't appear to be very big on transcendence. There may be transcendental currents in the Old Testament, the Kabbalah, or Kafka, but Judaism doesn't seem to me to put forward a particular theology of transcendence. Catholicism asserts that death can bring redemption and an afterlife, but it is unclear whether Judaism even believes in an afterlife. In my experience of Judaism, there is only morality, guilt, expiation, and satisfaction in this life. Catholicism insists on the centrality of a mystery. Bresson quotes Pascal: "They want to find the solution where all is enigma only." And in Bresson's own words: "Accustom the public to divining the whole of which they are only given a part. Make people diviners." This language of divination and mystery seems to me very far from the analytical, Talmudic, potentially skeptical methods of Jewish study; as it happens, it is with the latter that I have come to identify.

One of the most beautiful passages in motion pictures is the ending of Mizoguchi's *Ugetsu*, when the errant potter returns to his cottage after long travels and a 180-degree pan finds his old wife sitting there, preparing him a meal. He falls asleep happy, only to wake up the next morning and learn from neighbors that his wife is dead: the woman who had tended him the night before was a ghost. The 180-degree movement had inscribed the loss all the more deeply through its play on absence and presence, invisibility and appearance. Such a noble presentation of the spirit life, common in Buddhist art, would be extremely rare in Jewish narratives, where ghosts are not often met.

---

*Even Buñuel, another early favorite whom I took to be antireligious by his parodies of the transcendent, seems, in films like *Nazarin, Viridiana, Simon of the Desert*, heavily shaped by a Catholic world view. To turn something inside out is still to be dependent on it.

If you were to think of a "Jewish cinema," names like the Marx Brothers, Woody Allen, Ernst Lubitsch, Jerry Lewis, Mel Brooks, Billy Wilder spring to mind—all skeptical mockers, ironists, wonderful clowns, and secular sentimentalists. Yiddish films like *Green Fields* and *The Light Ahead* do have scenes of religious piety and custom, but even these celebrate the warmth and sorrows of a people rather than the spiritual quest of a lonely soul straining toward God. Whatever the virtues of Yiddish movies—humanity and humor in abundance—they are not aesthetically rigorous: indeed, it is the very muzziness of communal life that seems to constitute the core of their triumphant religious feeling.

As I look back, I realize that I needed to find something different, something I did not know how to locate in my watered-down Jewish background. I took to the "transcendental style" immediately; it was obviously the missing link in my aesthetic education. Movies introduced me to a constellation of ritual and spiritual emotion that I could willingly embrace so long as it was presented to me in the guise of cinematic expression, but not otherwise. At that point these appeals, these seductions, came into conflict with a competing spiritual claim, indefinitely put off but never quite abandoned: to become a good Jew, sometime before I die.

20

Detachment and Passion

NOW THAT I AM SECURELY MARRIED, I often think back to my bachelor days, indulging in this candy store of my imagination an occasional mental infidelity with an ex-girl friend who will come around to haunt me for a few days. I will picture her face or skin, recall a scent, try to revive the shock her beauty gave me the first time she undressed; or else the opposite, certain annoying tics, dry Sunday brunches, her betrayals or my cruelties. Lately I have been thinking about Claire. I find her floating in my consciousness more than others who had far more connection with me. Perhaps the very fact that ours was a middling affair makes me brood about her, as over an unsolved riddle. But more likely, it is simply because she died young.

I first met Claire through my sister Molly: they were "dharma buddies" and best friends. Neither Claire's Buddhism nor her friendship with my sister would have been recommendations to me, being a skeptic in both spiritual and familial matters. My inclination was not to go out with any of Molly's social circle. In the best of circumstances, it is a loaded situation: there is something humiliating, not to mention bordering on incestuous, about an older brother preying on his younger sister's friends. If the romance takes, then the sister may feel she has lost a friendship; if it sours, she may have to choose sides.

Added to these qualms were my complicated feelings about Molly. Briefly: My sister is almost exactly to the day a year younger than I am. At times we've been as close as twins. During the period I'm writing about, however, her Billie Holiday, femme fatale, and Kerouac adventuress stages behind her, she was going through a rather shrill, strident period, rationalizing disappointments in love or work with what sounded to me like spiritual eyewash. She had developed the neophyte convert's verbal armor, which gave her answers for every occasion. Granted, I was not as open as I might have been to receiving lectures about compassion from a younger sister; but inwardly I distanced myself from her, against those moments of possession by her Buddhist dybbuk.

Underneath the rigid sunniness of my sister's new-found wisdom, I sensed, she was lonely and depressed. In fact, I liked her much better when she was *openly* depressed: only then did she seem her old, cynical, Marquise de Merteuil self, freed from those Pollyanna smile-faces of her manic positive mode. Of course, it was easy for me to say, "Just be *sad*, for God's sake, stop acting." Perhaps with Molly, the pain ran so deep, the self-criticism was so severe, that any display of serenity, even the most synthetic, should have been preferred.

If I suspected my sister was deluding herself, what did it say about Claire that she hung around Molly? Eager though I was to discount this Claire, the few times I met her at social gatherings I liked her quick, amusing, unimpinging manner. There was a pleasing, ladylike coolness about her, embodied by her smooth, creamy skin. Whatever doubts I may have had did not stand a chance, finally—especially after my steady girlfriend and I had broken up and I was once again "available"—before the fact that Claire was so pretty. She had long black hair that fell in symmetrical plaits to her shoulders, and a sympathetic, perky, forties face with a dimpled lipsticked smile, and—this especially caught my attention—a gorgeous figure. I am sorry to have been so superficial about it, but there it is. At the time, I was led into many cha-grins and contretemps, allegedly beneath my level of intelligence, by the attempt to sleep with beautiful women whenever possible. I have since repented.

In any event, Molly brought her friend, looking particularly ravishing in a blue silk dress, to the book party for my novel *Confessions of Summer*, and Claire bought a copy, got me to sign it, and kissed me on the cheek. That was all the stimulus I needed.

Having made up my mind to go after her, however, I suddenly felt hesitant about the difference in our aesthetic stations: she was a beauty and I was—a passable-looking intellectual with glasses. Shortly after the book party, I called Molly and asked if her friend was seeing anyone at the moment. As far as she knew, Molly said Claire was seeing several guys, but none seriously. Not quite the answer I'd hoped for, yet it left the door open. Did she know if—*were* I to ask Claire out—she would be receptive or not? Molly guaranteed nothing. "She's in the phone book. Ask her yourself. What's the worst that can happen? If she turns you down, it has nothing to do with your attractiveness; she may be sexually programmed to go for certain types of guys." This sisterly sagacity irked me; what I'd wanted was inside informa-tion. "Couldn't you at least—sound her out? Oh, forget it. I'll make the call."

So I asked Claire to dinner, she accepted, and we began to get to know each other. I found her remarkably easy to talk to. Claire was a freelance magazine writer and, like most journalists, up on just about everything. She played smoothly the tra-ditional feminine role of drawing out the male's concerns and listening flatteringly and flirtatiously, however boorish she might think him. In short, she knew how to "date," as an activity enjoyable in itself, without being consumed, as I was, by the suspense of whether or not we would go to bed together.

It was the winter of 1979. I had just turned thirty-six, Claire was thirty-one; we were both veterans of the liberated sixties. She told me she'd even been a waitress at Max's Kansas City, the downtown art bar, in its heyday; I could picture her wearing a long braid, turning heads wherever she went. "I was never a groupie, but I did have a rock musician boyfriend." How could I compete?

Sometimes, at the beginning of an affair—or to make it *be* an affair—one has to leap into another persona. On our third date we went to an expensive disco supper club, Regine's, on Park Avenue, a place for international jet-setters that ordinarily I wouldn't be caught dead in; but I was trying to show that I could be "fun," not just the bookish highbrow I seemed to be. And Claire told me she liked to dance. So we danced; we drank; we watched with superior amusement the short gray-haired South American (ex-dictator?) rhumba with his statuesque blond starlet partner, the European investment brokers stationed in America trying to boogie, the account executives grinding away like day laborers to Gloria Gaynor's "I Will Survive." New York had narrowly averted bankruptcy in 1975; the memory of that near catastrophe still fresh, we were feeling the start of the Boom, artificially fueled by foreign investments; the bacchanale of the eighties was approaching; and Regine's, now defunct, harbingered an era that promised to be as indestructible as vulgarity itself.

Our amused mood persisted in the taxi, driving through the lamplit Park Avenue snow to Claire's house (she had given the cabbie her address, half the answer to the question I wanted answered), and lust proved a natural outgrowth of margaritas and mirth. But even after we had slept together that first time, I still wondered if Claire was attracted to me or simply being a gracious hostess. Always pleasant, sexy, responsibly conversational, good-humored, she never abandoned her impersonal self-composure. It was not so much what she expressed as what she didn't: urgency, hunger. She seemed more intent on offering me the continuing integrity of solitude and privacy.

For the most part, I took my cues from her, which meant returning tenderness for tenderness, moderation for moderation. We continued to go out, to enjoy ourselves, to perform the act of greatest potential intimacy between human beings; and it continued—not to matter very much.

One night, after we'd made love and I'd fallen asleep, I was awakened by her hand on my penis. It surprised me: not that I'd failed to satisfy her completely, but that she'd brought herself this once to admit a need. I would like to think I honored her request, but memory draws a veil. . . . What I do recall is my overall puzzlement at not being more excited about sleeping with this *dish*. I began to cast about for some way to blame her for my own lack of intense desire; I watched her for subtle indications of "putting me off," as though she were responsible for extruding an aura around herself, like a seducing Circe, but in reverse, a cloud of unexcitement that neutralized her beauty's effect.

I noticed that if, for instance, I complimented Claire on the way she looked, she would reply "You're such a dear" or "You're sweet" with an abstracted, dismissive air, as though she thought I'd been laying it on too thick. Was this simply the reaction of a pretty woman for whom compliments had become boring? Or perhaps she was saying, "What do looks mean, after all, in the larger, karmic scheme of things?"

On the other hand, maybe she was self-conscious and critical of her appearance, so that "You're sweet" might be interpreted as "*You* may think I look like a model, but *I* know I have tons of flaws, a bumpy nose, too hippy," etc.

I began to notice also, at first because it seemed another form of resistance to me (as in: "Don't kiss me, my mouth must taste like an ashtray") but later, as a curious phenomenon in and of itself, that she would often complain about something somatically off-register, which kept her from optimum functioning: she had sinus headaches; the pressure of deadlines and caffeine was making her jumpy, or the lack of work, sluggishly woozy; she had slept too much, too little, had insomnia, got up too late, was tired all the time, watched too many late-night movies on the tube, smoked too many cigarettes, hadn't eaten a decent meal all week, felt fat, queasy, bloated, the greasy English muffins were sitting on her stomach, refusing to digest. At first I responded sympathetically, suggesting Coca-Cola to settle the stomach; later, I treated these anxieties as an ongoing subvocal burble that periodically rose to the surface. Were they not also her shield, or a garbled text whose gist was: *You don't understand me, all sorts of thoughts and sensations are going on constantly inside me of which you haven't the faintest idea.* Any woman might think that of any man, and be correct.

Once, out of the blue, she said to me, "You seem like a happy person."

"Happy is hardly the way I look at it," I replied, immediately on guard. Was she trying to assuage her guilt toward me? Getting ready to dump me? "I feel I'm in the middle of my life. I'm absorbed, I'm doing the work I want to do, and that's almost enough for me. What about you?"

"Hmm?" she asked absentmindedly, as if responding to a faulty long-distance connection.

"Are you happy?"

"Oh, sure. I'm basically a happy person. I just wish I felt like you, that I was in the middle of my life."

"Well, it took a while to get there," I said smugly.

"I know. I didn't mean you were lucky. I'm sure you're very good at what you do."

"I don't know about very good, but I'm good enough."

We had fallen into the oldest of male-female scripts: I was the grown-up, she the fumbling late bloomer. Had I not been so passive, I might have challenged this flattering schema, which allowed her to hide so effectively from me.

Claire lived in an old building in the East Twenties, near Lexington Avenue, with a slow, tight little elevator that held the curried smells of takeout delivery bags from nearby Indian and Turkish restaurants. We usually stayed at her place; she felt more comfortable there. Even so, she would often express her impatience to fix up the place.

"What's so bad about it? Looks okay to me," I would say, glancing around at the gray felt chairs, the Mission-style daybed, the plants, the altar, the stacks of magazines. The place had a shabby-genteel air, small, dark, crepuscular: essentially it was one large room divided into four, with the amenity of a Parisian-style skylight.

"The chairs are ratty. I need some blinds. People can look in and see everything. . . . I don't know what to get my mother for Christmas. Look at this plant, it's really pathetic. You should get more sun, baby."

"Maybe the steam heat dries it out."

"No, this one's sick even in the summer. I think it's some sort of scaly disease. Like my chapped lips. Everything's scaly here. I wish I had some new books. I've been reading too many magazines, they're like junk food."

What are people saying when they speak? What are they actually trying to say? It is my lifelong project to figure this out, but I never can decide if someone is speaking literally or metaphorically. With Claire, I tried to follow the emotional thread beneath her random remarks—was she feeling insecure about her reading because she thought me a brain, or did it have nothing to do with me, was she recalling some deferred ambition, or was she hinting she wanted a book for Christmas? By this time Claire would wander into the bathroom and begin blow-drying her wet hair. She had a strong Roman profile, like Penelope in the tapestries. I would relish the flesh peeping through her terrycloth robe—aroused suddenly by her being preoccupied.

"Fascinating, isn't it?" she'd say, catching me spying on her through the door.

"I like to watch you making your *toilette*, like a Degas painting."

"I'm thinking of cutting my hair. It's ridiculously long, don't you think?"

"I like long hair."

"Would you believe I used to have it cut like Cleopatra? Shorter in back, with bangs straight across the front. What a riot. Actually, it didn't look bad. All right, hair, that's enough for you guys," she'd talk to a strand, then switch to a high, squeaky "No, no, we're not dry yet!"

Claire did these comic voices, often addressing inanimate objects. Nothing stayed serious for long. But gradually, in spite of her rapid shifts, I learned a partial itinerary of her concerns. She felt bad about taking money from her parents. Not that there were any strings attached; but as long as they paid her rent and she only had to earn her expense money, she could remain in this freelance, odd-job life, which felt at times like a trap. She wondered if she shouldn't get a *job* job, a nine-to-five. Also, she had been writing articles for a city magazine for over four years, and wasn't it time they put her name on the masthead? She brooded a great deal about how to approach the editor-in-chief to give her a contributing editor title. The next minute she would talk about throwing over her magazine work and writing a book about Tibetan medicine (a project that struck me as far-fetched, given her lack of both medical training and Tibetan), or else leaving the city entirely and going into retreat, to a Buddhist monastery/convent in France.

What interested me about these intermittent anxieties was that they offered an alternative, a counter-Claire (if one could but understand it) to the calm, detached perspective she, for the most part, upheld. I was also detached. It had long been my habit to stand apart from myself, observing, and to "borrow" excess emotion from the woman, who was usually more ardent or angry or involved in the prospect of relationship. But this time we were both detached: who was there to keep us emotionally honest?

I knew that my own detachment had come from the need to preserve myself, while growing up, within a family given to operatic hysteria, and later, from a need to protect my writing. But what were Claire's reasons? Had Buddhist practice given her a ground of detachment and poise, or was she drawn to Buddhism because she wanted to find a larger system that would support her characterological equanimity?

Claire kept, as I've said, an altar in her living room, with photographs of her guru, Dujam Rinpoche, surrounded by jewelry and flowers. I assume she meditated regularly before it. She also attended classes at the Tibetan Buddhist center near her house. Yet she never proselytized (as Molly tended to do) or even spoke about her practice, her spiritual progress, her setbacks. Whatever I learned had to be dragged out of her reluctantly. "You don't want to know about all that," she would say, and apologize self-mockingly for her "shrine." She knew exactly how a cynic might regard such trappings; many of her friends were, indeed, cynical journalists, and she tended to keep separate the two spheres of her life. But the less Claire talked about her Buddhist involvement, the more I eyed it for clues to her nature—especially the part I felt her withholding from me.

Here we may invoke Lopate's law of relationships: The less one is getting what one wants from the other person, the more one is apt to fill in the vacuum with interpretation. Claire's mystifying neutrality or reserve inspired several theses in turn: that she was slow to trust men (an all-purpose explanation, always true, up to a point); that she was distracted by various career and personal worries; that there was simply not that much to her, she was bland; that her affect had been "flattened out" by a spiritual practice that valued nonattachment. Others would follow; but for the moment the Buddhist thesis intrigued me the most.

Even without Claire and Molly, I had been coming up against the Buddhist challenge. All during the seventies the New York cultural scene was saturated with Buddhism: benefit poetry readings with Allen Ginsberg, Anne Waldman, and John Giorno; concerts by Philip Glass and other musicians of tantric orientation; conferences at the New School on what Buddhist psychology had to offer Western psychotherapies. Writer friends of mine were conscientiously studying Tibetan grammar. There was a definite upscale chic attached to Buddhism, especially the Tibetan strand—a pedigreed intellectual respectability such as had never burnished, say, the Hare Krishna or Guru Maharaji sects.

The first Buddhist wave had been Japanese: the Zen of the fifties and sixties, introduced by Alan Watts and D. T. Suzuki. The next influx was Tibetan, dominated by the flamboyant, Oxbridge-educated Chogyam Trungpa, whose poet-disciples established the Naropa School in Boulder, Colorado. Molly and Claire looked askance at whiskey-drinking, philandering, bad-boyish Trungpa, preferring instead their aged, gentle lama, Dujam Rinpoche. The old man lived mostly in France; but his American followers had established a center in New York, and every few years he would visit it—to the immense excitement of his devotees.

Socially on the fringes of this scene, I would sometimes be pulled in by curiosity, the chance to witness one more Manhattan subculture. Once, Molly invited me to hear the Dalai Lama address a packed church. I could barely understand a word of His Holiness's talk, due to the thick accent of his translator and bad acoustics, and the little I heard sounded like platitudes about our need for love and world peace. Now, it may well be that platitudes ultimately contain the highest wisdom attainable. But I was looking for evidence to debunk the scene. I never doubted that Buddhist practices had great efficacy for Tibetans; I was only dubious that the beaming middle-class Americans in the pews around me would ever get beyond their consumerist pride in fingering esoteric traditions.

The American devotees I knew also displayed a parvenu fascination with Tibetan aristocracy (the Dalai Lama and his retinue, the ranks of lamas) that I can only compare to the way Texas moneyed society grovels before the British royals. One night I was taken to an event, at a Soho loft, honoring a group of Tibetan lamas who had just arrived in the States from India. The lamas sat on a raised platform and conversed among themselves, while an awed, handpicked, mostly Ivy League audience, kneeling and lotus-squatting below, watched them eat. What struck me was the determination of the devotees to wring spiritual messages from the most mundane conduct. If a lama belched, it became a teaching: "Don't take anything too seriously." If several lamas laughed (at a private Tibetan joke), the audience would join in gratefully, as though being taught the mystery of joy. Meanwhile, a bevy of *dahinis*, attractive young women chosen to serve the lamas, advanced with dishes and finger bowls. These American women, probably all willing to be identified as feminists, who would have been shocked if asked to perform such duties for their countrymen, were blushing with happiness at the chance to serve the robed contingent. Other women in the audience gasped as one of the tall young head-shaved priests stood up, his saffron robes leaving his muscled arms bare. The monks inspired rock star crushes.

Shortly after the feast had ended and the entire lama delegation had left to go to another party, those remaining milled about, still processing the privilege they'd been given. The Princess of Bhutan and her seven-year-old son were pointed out to me. Much was made of the little boy's playing with a top, as though it were a precocious demonstration of spiritual powers; when the top skittered over the loft floor, everyone oohed and clapped. I wasn't sure whether the child was being drooled over because he had royal blood, because he was mischievous (high spiritual marks for that in *this* crowd), or because he was of an age when future Dalai Lamas are customarily detected.

I was glad not to be won over by this display; it saved me an enormous bother. On the other hand, I could not simply reject an immensely complex, sophisticated tradition just because of some sycophantic behavior on the part of certain follow-ers. The little I knew of Buddhist doctrine actually appealed to me, by virtue of its insistence on the void, on mindfulness, and on the universality of suffering. In fact, I could go along with at least two of its four "noble truths": the first, that existence is suffering, I could accept wholeheartedly; the second, that the cause of suffering is craving and attachment, I was less sure about, but willing to concede. I balked only at the final two: that there is a cessation of suffering, called Nirvana, and that the way to Nirvana lies in dissolving the self and following the "eightfold path." As with Marxism, I agreed with the analysis of the problem, only not the solution.

Buddhism was continually being put forward to me as a doctrine suitable to the agnostic modern age. To my doubts about the necessity for any religion, my sister would repeat, "I *hate* organized religions. But Buddhism isn't a religion. It doesn't even have a god!" I wasn't sure I liked this, and I had even more problems with Molly's insistence that Buddhism "superseded" Freud, was "vastly superior" to psy-choanalysis. It seemed to me she was really saying, in an upwardly mobile, assimila-tionist vein, that she had no further use for the religion we were born into, Judaism (as represented in my mind by Freud). Not that I pored over the Talmud either; but *were* I to feel spiritual twinges, I would first give my own heritage a chance.

In that sense, I had less problems with Claire's Buddhism, because she was Catholic. It was not for me to judge the theological wanderings of Roman Catholics; moreover, Claire still accompanied her father to Mass like a good daughter. What did it *mean*, though (back to square one), that she was a Buddhist? It seemed such a strenuous, willful act for an American—whose background was Catholic, Jewish, Presbyterian, whatever—to "become" a Buddhist. Did she see herself as a *dakini* (one step away from a Buddhist chorus girl, in my mind)? Or was she actually seek-ing—what an odd, ambitious idea!—to become enlightened, an illuminated being, to suffer compassionately with all living things, like the bodhisattva? If so, I could well respect her abstracted preoccupation.

Or was there another explanation?

Based on my sister's unforgotten remark, I thought I might not be the only "guy" Claire was still seeing. New Year's Eve, the test, began to loom. When I asked her at the beginning of December, her first response was to hedge: she was thinking she might go out of town, to her parents' house in the mountains. "Can I get back to you in a few days? I won't hang you up. I know, you want a hot date for New Year's Eve," she said, disparaging herself and me in one sentence. I waited a week, darkly imagining her efforts to secure a better offer. The next time, she answered sweetly: "Sure. What did you have in mind?"

I had in mind a movie, Preston Sturges's *Unfaithfully Yours* at Theater 80 (which proved as delicious as I'd hoped), dinner at a good restaurant, and a New Year's Eve party, where I knew there'd be plenty of interesting types. I remember that almost as soon as we entered the party, Claire and I went our separate ways, talking to different people till the time came to leave. This independence was a sign either of a couple supremely comfortable with each other or of one that would soon break up.

Mutual glibness aside, we actually had very little in common to talk about. One of our few conversational mainstays was Molly. Having overcome any scruples about frankly discussing my sister with her best friend, I communicated my worries over Molly's get-rich schemes, which changed weekly, or her then harsh social manner, which turned off men. Claire, to my surprise, agreed. The difference was that when she spoke about Molly, it was not with the overidentifying conflictedness of a family member but with genuine tolerant affection. Her attitude seemed to be "Molly's Molly, that's just the way she gets at times. She'll figure it out—and anyway, isn't she great, on the whole?" Yes, exactly, *that* was what I had meant to say—or feel.

Was it Claire's Buddhist training in compassion that allowed her to enjoy people just the way they were, without troubling about their nuttiness? Or had she simply a good heart?

She rarely spoke ill of anyone; her sympathy was so evenly spread out that I felt, in the end, slighted. She saw the good in me as she would in the next person. I never had the sense she had *chosen* me, or thought of us as an *us*. (Whether I wanted us to be an *us*, in the long run, was a question I put off, too busy being offended that she had not raised it.)

My distrust of Claire grew also from her journalistic work, which caused her to marshal a spurious fascination for the assignment of the moment, and a dazed indifference to the matter once copy had been handed in. I was not the first to suspect this vocation of a built-in shallowness, by virtue of its opportunistic obsession with topicality and trivia. Since then, having been forced to try my own hand at journalism, I have acquired a much healthier respect for the work habits, intrepidity, and antennae necessary to excel at it. At the time, however, I was still appalled at the superficiality of the journalistic enterprise, and I saw Claire's cool aplomb, which kept me at arm's length, as a function of her métier. But even to say that she "kept me at arm's length" falsely implies that I was the ardent, unrequited suitor, when the truth was, I was keeping my distance in my own way, by not respecting what she did.

Our relationship seemed in a holding pattern; and yet it was pleasant enough. Even when Claire became slightly less available than before, begging off because of deadlines and out-of-town trips, we would still get together about once a week. This spared me the necessity of finding a new girlfriend. Busy with my own projects, I viewed our affair as a sort of minimal romantic insurance policy. Then it suddenly ended.

Claire had gotten the assignment to write a story about old, freestanding movie houses in New York. She invited me to come along on her research; as a film buff, I might find it interesting. When the Saturday for our scheduled tour arrived, I had the flu. I told her I felt too awful to go out. "Oh, we'll just wrap you in lots of sweaters. It'll be fun! You'll get to see the inside of all those wonderful old movie houses and it'll cheer you up." I was about to remark that it wasn't a question of moodiness, but flu, as in "germ theory of illness," when I realized she was determined—she had arranged this and I was coming along, period. I suspected she was on deadline and needed my input. Her selfishness seemed a revelation to me: I thought I was finally seeing the true, insensitive Claire. For the first time I got angry with her (though in hindsight, I may have been repressing some anger toward her all along). This bile accompanied me throughout the day while I shivered in the subway up to Washington Heights, felt my throat swell bronchially under the February rain, stood on my feet for hours, spitefully and self-pityingly getting sicker by the moment while perversely pretending to be all right, as the movie managers took us around with flashlights to explore the art deco moldings and cornices in what were now grimy fleapits. I asked the right questions about the old days, and Claire seemed pleased. "See? It was fun after all." We took a cab down to my apartment, where I hoped she would make it up to me by tucking me into bed. But when we got to my door, she held on to the cab, saying she had an appointment downtown and really couldn't come inside, even for a few minutes. Once I was alone, my anger and fever merged in a blaze. Here I was dying, delirious, and this ***** couldn't even come inside and make me a cup of tea.

That did it. We were through.

The oddest part was that there was no breakup scene. I simply never called Claire again, and she never got around to calling me either. It was symptomatic, I thought bitterly, of how little the affair had meant, that it didn't even need a denouement; we just drifted away like steam vapor.

Shortly after that incident, I was offered a university teaching post down at Houston. I took it, vowing I would find some nice, sweet Texas girl; I would get away from those hard, self-serving New York women like Claire, too careerist and too stingy to love. How could I have thought there was a mystery about her? Claire became the newest target of my immature anger, always ready to flare up at women for not giving me the affection I felt due me.

In the years that followed, I would occasionally hear news from Molly about Claire. She had completed her book on Tibetan medicine, the first such in English on the subject, and a small press interested in Eastern religions had published it. She had quit her magazine work and gone into retreat in France for several years, fulfilling the required term for Buddhist novitiates at her guru's center. All this dedication and follow-through could not help but impress me. The closest I had ever come to making such a commitment was to writing; but writing fed my ego rather than extinguishing it. Self-knowledge I pursued, at best, without benefit of system, defensively interrogating my experiences after the fact, so that whatever wisdom might stick to me was accidental, like a burr in a forest walk. I lived for myself, within myself; I had never been able to locate some Whole or Cosmic Mind that was higher than the individual, inspiring contemplation and admiration. Not that I *wanted* to locate any such principle; I was content to follow my discontented path for the rest of my life. But I tipped my hat to Claire.

The spark of anger I had seized upon to exit from our floundering relationship in fine, self-righteous fettle had long passed; and I mainly recalled Claire's graciousness. Playing back our affair in my mind, I began to think that I may have gotten the whole thing wrong: probably she had liked me more than I'd thought (though clearly not loved me), and the price she had had to pay for getting to know me better, given the only terms I offered her, was to sleep with me and pretend a romantic involvement. This she had done like a good sport. The fact that we had not gone through a breakup scene might be less an indictment of our relationship than a subconscious recognition by our adult selves that there was no need to besmirch with inflationary animosity what had never been more than a courteous, friendly liaison.

So, when Molly informed me that Claire was in New York for a few months, just as I was, and had mentioned she would "love" to see me sometime, I was pleased at this second chance for a more successful closure. I called her and we arranged to have dinner. On the phone Claire sounded much the breezy way I'd remembered her; but as our reunion approached, I began to worry. What had all that meditation work and French country retreat done to our Claire?

She opened the door, attractive as ever, and quickly put me at ease by detailing the latest struggle to hold on to her apartment, which she'd been subletting. The building had been sold to a pair of shysters: a typical New York realty story of the eighties, which reassured me that her street smarts remained intact. Then we went out to dinner together and caught up. Her descriptions of the Buddhist group in France were all amusingly down-to-earth; but she seemed more eager to report gossip about her old American friends, the ones she'd seen in the past two weeks. Fortunately, her practice had not yet purified her of gossip. She also wanted to know everything I had done the past few years; she was hungry for thick narrative detail. Eventually we got around to the subject of romantic involvements. By then we had repaired to a bar in order to prolong the evening's discussion, and were sitting at the railing. I told her about the woman I'd been dating in Houston. She said she was, alas, not in love at the moment, but added that she still saw "various men from time to time." I took this to mean some of the journalist friends she had mentioned earlier. I was working up the courage to ask her about—us.

"What went wrong?" I wondered aloud. "Why didn't we work out as a couple?"

"Well, there was no passion between us," she answered, as though it were the simplest matter in the world. I was glad to hear her put it this way: to distribute the lack equally. She went on to say that passion was rare for her, but of the highest importance. During the period of our affair, she now admitted, she *had* been in love—wildly, reciprocally, with a handsome foreigner, a very important diplomat (she refused to tell me his name) who was, unfortunately, married. Whenever he was in the country, they resumed their secret passion. This affair had gone on for years, until the time that she entered Buddhist retreat.

So! She *had* been keeping a part of herself back. This explained everything—even her stall around New Year's Eve; she was probably waiting to hear from her dashing emissary if he planned to be in the States. I felt a warm contentment, approaching happiness, at receiving this piece of the missing puzzle. I always feel strengthened by learning the truth (however unpleasant) after long being kept in the dark. Besides, it was far too late to feel jealous resentment of this "rival"; happily, he was a diplomat, not a fellow writer, and it pleased me that, by her description, he was very handsome. I made him into Louis Jourdan in *Letter from an Unknown Woman*. It was aesthetic justice that a woman as pretty as Claire should be swept off her feet by an equally good-looking man. I could admire, from outside, the amours of these beautiful people, like a fairy tale one has always believed in. And it exonerated me from any mistakes I may have made in our affair: how could it have worked, she was already in love with someone else?

Finally, there was sweet vindication of sorts in learning that Buddhism hadn't given her any detached perspective toward love, but that—like several other women I had known—she had worshipped at the altar of Passion, kept a votive candle lit to the secret, demon, phantom lover who came and went, holding her in thrall. It pleased me that I recognized the pattern, had encountered it before, and was not alarmed by it, whereas true Buddhist nonattachment would have remained much more opaque and threatening.

Claire drew me out in turn. As she listened shrewdly to my stories of romantic folly, and contributed her own, there was so much good humor back and forth between us that the night took on a sparkle; it became one of the dozen or so charmed evenings in my life. I felt in perfect rapport with Claire. At last, we were meeting as equals, survivors, on a common ground of mutual delight in each other's company. I walked her home; I would have gladly "jumped her bones," as the saying now goes, but I sensed no such invitation. And besides, I feared that making a sexual pass would spoil the mood of the evening. Even if it had succeeded, we would be back in that dry polite corner of two uninfatuated lovers instead of the much richer space (for us) of old friends, which we had achieved for the first time that night. I realized I'd liked Claire far more before and after our time of "intimacy," than during. A love affair, it was borne in on me again, is sometimes the worst way to draw out the best in another.

Claire went off again to her retreat in France. We agreed that we would get together, with pleasure, whenever she came into town. It would be wonderful to leave the story like that, on a high note. But in 1988 my sister told me, trying to keep her voice calm, that Claire was back in New York "for health reasons." Brain cancer had been discovered. She was in Doctors Hospital, receiving chemotherapy treatments.

That Saturday, I made up my mind to visit her. I suddenly recalled all of Claire's complaints about bodily symptoms; could they have been advance warnings? On my way to the hospital, I experienced faintness; there was a "sympathetic" buzz in my head, a fibrillation in my legs. Of course, I often felt that way when I got near hospitals. Still, I seemed to be much more upset about Claire's illness, I was not sure why, than I had expected.

I had debated what sort of reading matter to take someone with brain cancer, deciding in the end to buy a stack of glossy fashion magazines. So I entered the ward, the bearer of frivolous goodies about how to stay young or keep your figure, wondering if Claire had been shaven bald yet or grown emaciated. I first ran into Claire's mother, an Upper East Side matron, looking distressed in the most abject way: she had become deindividualized, the archetypal mother fearing the loss of her only child. Her eyes were already grief-stricken. Claire, she told me, was downstairs in X-ray but would be up shortly.

I waited and looked around the solarium, with its amazing 360-degree views of Manhattan. This was certainly the cheeriest, poshest hospital facility I had ever been in.

A half hour later, Claire entered the ward wearing a quilted robe, moving slowly, gingerly. She still had her beautiful long hair and her striking Penelope profile. But she was thinner; her angles had been purified into ascetic lines, there was now nothing sexual about her. She invited us into her room and sat on the edge of her bed, like a teenage girl. I gave her the magazines. "You're such a dear," she said in that vague way, only this time I was happy to receive the compliment.

I asked her to fill me in. She told me when the pains began; how the diagnosis was made; what her chances were—not good, but not hopeless either. She had discovered a whole network of cancer patients across the country and, like the trained journalist she was, had been keeping up with them via computer, learning all about the latest experimental cures. If she survived this, she quipped, she would go for a medical degree; she'd done three quarters of the work already. I could not help noticing that she bore her suffering with a placid, evolved dignity and determination that were in stark contrast to her mother's panic. Claire was taking it all so calmly that I felt more sorry for her mother at that moment than for her.

I did not want to tire her, so I said good-bye and left. Walking from the hospital, I had the sense of having been in contact with something large—larger than myself. I felt dissolved, borderless, dizzy. A part of me was happy to have seen Claire irrespective of the circumstances. But I was almost certain the cancer would kill her. She would die at forty, still alarmingly fresh and beautiful.

The memorial service was at Frank Campbell's, a traditional Catholic funeral parlor on Park Avenue on the Upper East Side. Nearly all of New York Buddhism's elite showed up, and there was a touching, if awkward, attempt to mix Catholic and Tibetan ritual, all worked out painstakingly beforehand by the family and Claire's dharma buddies. Many speeches were made, attesting to the deceased's considerateness for others and zestful, life-loving personality. I cannot remember clearly a single thing that was said; in my daze, it was enough to take in that Claire had been one of those popular people, like Frank O'Hara, about whom each best friend learns at the funeral that there were a hundred others. Afterward, at the party at someone's house, I wandered around, eavesdropping on various groups, all of whom were reminiscing and telling Claire stories. I wanted to join in, yet what could I say to them? I never had had the illusion that I was one of her closest friends. I had no way to fathom her deepest commitments. But I mourned her nonetheless.

— 21

CONTEMPT: The Story of a Marriage

THIRTY-FOUR YEARS AFTER ITS PREMIERE, one of the masterworks of modern cinema, Jean-Luc Godard's *Contempt*, long unavailable, has been ravishingly restored and is back in town. The film has inspired passionate praise—*Sight & Sound* critic Colin McCabe may have gone slightly overboard in dubbing *Contempt* "the greatest work of art produced in post-war Europe," but I would say it belongs in the running. It has certainly influenced a generation of filmmakers, including R. W. Fassbinder, Quentin Tarantino and Martin Scorsese (who paid his own homage by quoting from the Godard film's stark, plangent musical score in *Casino*, and cosponsoring its re-release). Scorsese has called *Contempt* "brilliant, romantic and genuinely tragic," adding that "It's also one of the greatest films ever made about the actual process of filmmaking."

In 1963, film buffs were drooling over the improbable news that Godard—renowned for his hit-and-run, art house bricolages such as *Breathless* and *My Life to Live*—was shooting a big CinemaScope color movie with Brigitte Bardot and Jack Palance, based on an Alberto Moravia novel, *The Ghost at Noon*. It sounded almost too good to be true. Then word leaked out that Godard was having problems with his producers, Carlo Ponti and Joseph E. Levine (the distributor of *Hercules* and other schlock), who were upset that the rough cut was so chaste. Not a single nude scene with B.B.—not even a sexy costume! Godard obliged by adding a prologue of husband and wife (Michel Piccoli and Bardot) in bed, which takes inventory of that sumptuous figure through color filters, while foreshadowing the couple's fragility: when she asks for reassurance about each part of her body, he reassures her ominously, "I love you totally, tenderly, tragically."*

Beyond that "compromise," Godard refused to budge, saying: "Hadn't they ever bothered to see a Godard film?"

---

*I say "ominously," because this triumvirate of adverbs signals Paul's absolutist romanticism, his masochistic eagerness to embrace the tragic notion of fate, rather than make the compromises necessary for the mundane everyday balm of growing old together.

Ironically, *Contempt* itself dealt with a conflict between a European director (Fritz Lang playing himself) and a crude American producer, Jerry Prokosch (performed with animal energy by Palance), over a remake of Homer's *Odyssey*. Prokosch hires a French screenwriter, Paul (Michel Piccoli), to rewrite Lang's script. Paul takes the job partly to buy an apartment for his wife,* the lovely Camille (Bardot); but in selling his talents, he loses stature in her eyes. Through a series of partial misunderstandings, Camille also thinks her husband is allowing the powerful, predatory Prokosch to flirt with her—or at least has not sufficiently shielded her from that danger. Piccoli, in the performance that made him a star, registers with every nuance the defensive cockiness of an intellectual-turned-hack who feels himself outmanned.

According to Pascal Aubier, a filmmaker who served as Godard's assistant on *Contempt* and many of his other sixties pictures, "It was a very tormented production." Godard, unused to working on such a large scale, was annoyed at the circus atmosphere generated by the *paparazzi* who followed Brigitte Bardot to Capri. B.B., then at the height of her celebrity, arrived with her latest boyfriend, actor Sami Frey, which further irritated Godard, who liked to have the full attention of his leading ladies. The filmmaker was also not getting along with his wife (and usual star) Anna Karina, and seemed very lonely on the shoot, remembers Aubier; "but then, that's not unusual for him. Godard also has a knack for making people around him feel awkward, and then using that to bring out tensions in the script." He antagonized Jack Palance by refusing to consider the actor's ideas, giving him only physical instructions: three steps to the left, look up. Palance, miserable, kept phoning his agent in America to get him off the picture.** The only one Godard got on well with was Fritz Lang, whom he idolized. But Lang was not feeling well, and had to cut short his participation.

No sign of the shooting problems mars the implacable smoothness of the finished product. Godard famously stated that "a movie should have a beginning, a middle and an end, though not necessarily in that order." *Contempt*, however, adheres to the traditional order: it is built like a well-made three-act tragedy. The first part takes place on the deserted back lots of Rome's Cinecittà studios† and at the pro-

---

*Incidentally, this Rome apartment made more sense in the novel, where all the characters were Italian, than the film, where we never learn why this French couple is so keen on buying a co-op in Rome.

**Palance also despised his co-star, Bardot, for her diva-like requirement that she be allowed to sleep late and work only in the afternoon. But this hostility worked in the film's behalf: the sexual spark betwen Camille and Prokosch seems all the more based on animalism and attraction to power, stripped as it is of the least tenderness.

†"Italian cinema is not doing so well these days," observes one character. Indeed, the fate of cinema is a persistent theme in the film, from the Lumière Brothers' quote painted on the screening room wall ("The cinema is an invention without a future") to Paul's counterstatement that "I think the cinema will last forever." Godard himself wrote a few years later, in 1965: "I await the end of cinema with optimism."

ducer's house. The second part—the heart of the film—is an extraordinary, lengthy sequence in the couple's apartment: a tour de force of psychological realism, as the camera tracks the married couple in their casual moves, opening a Coke, sitting on the john, taking a bath in the other's presence, doing a bit of work, walking away in the middle of a sentence. (This physical casualness is mimicked by a patient, mobile camera that gives the artful impression of operating in real time.) Meanwhile, they circle around their wound: Paul feels that Camille's love has changed since that morning—grown colder and contemptuous. She is indeed irritated by him, but still loves him. With the devastating force of an Ibsen play, they keep arguing, retreating, making up, picking the scab, until they find themselves in a darker, more intransigently hostile space.

The third part moves to Capri—the dazzling Casa Malaparte, stepped like a Mayan temple by a disciple of Le Corbusier—for a holiday plus some *Odyssey* location shooting. Capri is an insidious, "no exit" Elysium where luxury, caprice and natural beauty all converge to shatter the marriage and bring about the inevitable tragedy.*

Part of *Contempt*'s special character is that it exists both as a realistic story and a string of iconic metaphors, connecting its historical layers. Palance's red Alfa Romeo sweeps in like Zeus's chariot; when he hurls a film can in disgust, he becomes a discus thrower ("At last you have a feeling for Greek culture," Lang observes dryly); Bardot donning a black wig seems a temporary stand-in for both Penelope and Anna Karina; Piccoli's character wears a hat in the bathtub to imitate Dean Martin in *Some Came Running* (though it makes him resemble Godard himself); Piccoli's bath towel suggests a Roman toga; Lang is a walking emblem of cinema's golden age and the survival of catastrophe, his anecdotes invoking Dietrich and run-ins with Goebbels; the Casa Malaparte is both temple and prison. Meanwhile, the CinemaScope camera observes all; approaching on a dolly in the opening shot, it tilts down and toward us like a one-eyed Polyphemus. Or is it Lang's monocle? ("The eye of the gods has been replaced by cinema," observes Lang.) Primary colors are intentionally used as shorthand for themes. Bardot in her lush yellow robe on the balcony in Capri incarnates all of paradise about to be lost.

What makes *Contempt* so unique a viewing experience today, even more than in 1963, is the way it stimulates an audience's intelligence as well as its senses. Complex and dense, it unapologetically accommodates discussions about Homer, Dante and German Romantic poetry, meditations on the role of the gods in modern life, the

---

*This tragedy is promised from the first by a multiplicity of signposts: the brooding musical score of Georges Delerue; the allusions to Greek tragedy; the passage Paul quotes from Dante ("Already death looked down from the stars/ and soon our joy was turned to grief"). No attempt is made to prolong suspense over whether things will turn out well or ill: rather, an unhappy fate is asserted with overdetermined insistence, and the only question becomes what form it will take.

creative process, the deployment of CinemaScope (Lang sneers that it is only good for showing "snakes and funerals," but the background-hungry, color-saturated beauty of cinematographer Raoul Coutard's compositions belies this).

It is also a film about language, as English, French, Italian and German speakers fling their words against an interpreter, Francesca (admirably played by Georgia Moll), in a jai alai of idioms which presciently conveys life in the new global economy, while making an acerbic political comment on power relations between the United States and Europe in the *Pax America*. (More practically, the polyglot sound track was a strategy to prevent the producers from dubbing the film.)

"Godard is the first filmmaker to bristle with the effort of digesting all previous cinema and to make cinema itself his subject," wrote critic David Thomson. Certainly *Contempt* is shot through with film buff references, and it gains veracity and authority from Godard's familiarity with the business of moviemaking. But far from being a smarty-pants, self-referential piece about films, it moves us because it is essentially the story of a marriage. Godard makes us care about two likable people who love each other* but seem determined to throw their chances for happiness away.

Godard is said to have originally wanted Frank Sinatra and Kim Novak for the husband and wife. Some of Novak's musing, as-you-desire-me quality in *Vertigo* adheres to Bardot. In her best acting performance, she is utterly convincing as the tentative, demure ex-secretary pulled into a larger world of glamour by her husband. Despite Godard's claim that he took Bardot as "a package deal," and that he "did not try to make Bardot into Camille, but Camille into Bardot," he actually tampered with the B.B. persona in several ways. First he toyed with having her play the entire film in a brunette wig—depriving her of her trademark blondness—but eventually settled for using the dark wig as a significant prop. More crucial was Godard's intuition to suppress the sex kitten of *And God Created Woman* or *Mamzelle Striptease*, and to draw on a more modest, prudishly French-bourgeois side of Bardot** for the character of Camille. In her proper matching blue sweater and headband, she seems a solemn, reticent, provincial type, not entirely at ease with the shock of her beauty.

---

*Do they in fact love each other? Some would argue that they seem to have been merely infatuated enough to get married, but never really knew each other; hence "love" is a misnomer. But the way I read the movie is that there is some genuine love between them (despite their differences) and the potential for lasting love, which makes the outcome all the more sorrowful.

**For instance, when Bardot remarked to Godard that she had trouble saying dirty words aloud, he purposely wrote in a speech for Camille to utter a string of profanities ("*Trou de cul ... putain ... merde ... nom de Dieu ... piége a con ... saloperie ... bordel ...*"), which she does, but so awkwardly that it only accentuates the character's basically prudish unworldliness. This side of Bardot survives in the doyenne who today proclaims her disgust with modern society's "decadence, moral and physical filth ... and the spread of pornography," never acknowledging her own contributions to the record of sexual iconography.

When she puts on her brunette wig in the apartment scene, she may be trying to get Paul to regard her as more intelligent than he customarily does—to escape the blond bimbo stereotype. (Her foil, Francesca, the dark-haired interpreter, speaks four languages and discusses Hölderlin's poetry with Lang.) At one point Paul asks Camille, "Why are you looking so pensive?" and she answers, "Believe it or not I'm thinking. Does that surprise you?" The inequalities in their marriage are painfully exposed: he sees himself as the brain and breadwinner, and her as a sexy trophy. Whatever her newfound contemptuous feelings may be, his own condescension seems to have always been close to the surface. "You're a complete idiot," he says when they are alone in Prokosch's house, and later tellingly blurts out, "Why did I marry a stupid twenty-eight-year-old typist?"

On the face of it, her suspicion that Paul had acted as her "pander" by leaving her with his lecherous employer seems patently unjust. Clearly he had told her to get into Prokosch's two-seat sports car because he did not want to appear foolishly, uxoriously jealous in the producer's eyes; and we can only assume he is telling the truth when he says his arrival at Prokosch's house was delayed by a taxi accident. Still, underneath the unfairness of her (implicit) accusation is a legitimate complaint: he would not have acted so cavalierly if he were not also a little bored with her, and willing to take her for granted. Certainly he is not particularly interested in what she has to say about the minutiae of domesticity: the drapes, lunch with her mother. All this he takes in as a tax paid for marrying a beautiful but undereducated younger woman. Her claims to possessing a mind (when she reads aloud from the Fritz Lang interview book in the tub) only irritate him, and he becomes significantly most enraged when she has the audacity to criticize him for filching other men's ideas (after he proposes going to a movie for screenwriting inspiration).

Camille also says she liked him better when he was writing detective fiction and they were poor, before he fell in with that "film crowd." His scriptwork does put him in a more self-abasing position, since screenwriting is nothing if not a school for humiliation. We see this in the way Paul, having watched Prokosch carry on like an ass in the projection room, nevertheless pockets the producer's personal check, after a moment's hesitation. (It is precisely at this moment in a Hollywood film that the hero would say: Take your check and shove it!) Paul compounds the problem by seeming to blame her for turning hack, saying he is only taking on the job so that they can finish paying for the apartment. It is important to remember that we are not watching the story of an idealistic writer selling out his literary aspirations, since "detective fiction" is not so elevated a genre to begin with, and since Paul's last screenplay was some junky-sounding movie called *Toto Contra Hercules* (a dig at Joseph E. Levine), so that, if anything, the chance to adopt Homer for Fritz Lang is a step up.

More important than issues of work compromise is that Camille has come to despise her husband's presumption that he can analyze her mind. Not only is this unromantic, suggesting she holds no further mystery, but insultingly reductive. She

is outraged at his speculation that she's making peace for reasons of self-interest—
to keep the apartment. As the camera tracks from one to the other, pausing at a
lamp in between, Paul guesses aloud that she is angry at him because she's seen him
patting Francesca's bottom. Here the lamp is important, not only as an inspired bit
of cinematic stylization, but as a means of hiding each from the other, if not from
the audience. Camille shakes her head in an astonished no at Paul's misinterpreta-
tion, then catches herself. She scornfully accepts his demeaning reading of her as
jealous, saying, "Okay, let's admit that it's that. Good, now we're finished, we don't
have to talk about it anymore."

After he speculates that she no longer loves him because of his dealings with
Prokosch, she tells him: "You're crazy but . . . you're intelligent." "Then it's true?"
he presses, like a prosecutor. "I didn't say that . . . I said you were intelligent," she
repeats, as if to link his "craziness" with his intellectual pride, as the thing responsible for his distorted perceptions.

More than anything, the middle section traces the building of a mood. When
Paul demands irritably, "What's wrong with you? What's been bothering you all
afternoon?" he seems both to want to confront the problem (admirably), and to
bully her out of her sullenness (reprehensibly). At first she evades with a character-
istically feminine defense: "I've got a right to change my mind." We see what he
doesn't—the experimental, tentative quality of her hostility: she is "trying on" anger
and contempt, not knowing exactly where it will go.* Her grudge has a tinge of play-
acting, as though she fully expects to spring back to affection at any moment. She
even makes various conciliating moves, assuring him she loves him, but, because of
his insecurities, he refuses this comfort. Paul is a man worrying a canker sore.
Whenever Camille begins to forgive, to be tender again, he won't accept it: he keeps
asking her why she no longer loves him, until the hypothesis becomes a reality. Paul
is more interested in having his worst nightmares confirmed** than in rehabilitating
the damage.

Perhaps we can understand this Godardian dynamic better by referring to a lit-
tle-known but key short of his, "Le Nouveau Monde," which he shot in 1962 as part
of the compilation film *ROGOPAG*.† The protagonist goes to sleep and wakes up
to find everything looking the same but subtly different. Pedestrians pop pills nervously, his girlfriend tells him she no longer loves him—just like that. "The New
World" has a sci-fi component: while our hero slept, an atomic device was exploded

---

*Her voice-over interior monologue accentuates this reading: "Why did I talk to him like that?
To get revenge somehow. Paul had hurt me terribly. Now it was my turn to make him suffer. So I
hinted at this and that . . . without saying anything specific."

**As his own interior monologue confirms: "I had often thought that if Camille left me, it
would be the worst possible catastrophe. Now I am in the midst of that catastrophe."

†The movie's title was an acronym of the participating directors' names: Rossellini, Godard,
Pasolini and Gregoretti.

above Paris, which may account for his girlfriend's spooky, affectless indifference. But the short is also a dry run for *Contempt:* one day you wake up and love has magically disappeared.

All through the sixties, Godard was fascinated with the beautiful woman who betrays (Jean Seberg in *Breathless*), withdraws her love (Chantal Goya in *Masculin-Féminin*), runs away (Anna Karina in *Pierrot le Fou*) or is faithless (Bardot in *Contempt*). What makes *Contempt* an advance over this somewhat misogynistic obsession with the femme fatale is that here, Godard seems perfectly aware how much at fault his male character is for the loss of the woman's love.

The film's psychology shows a rich understanding of the mutual complicities inherent in contempt, along with the fact that trying to alter another person's contemptuous opinion of yourself is like fighting in quicksand: the more you struggle, the farther in you sink. As William Ian Miller wrote in his book *The Anatomy of Disgust:* "Another's contempt for or disgust with us will generate shame and humiliation in us if we concur with the judgment of our contemptibility, that is, if we feel the contempt is justified, and will guarantee indignation and even vengeful fury if we feel it is unjustified." Paul responds both ways to his wife's harsh judgment: 1) he agrees with her, perhaps out of the intellectual's constant stock of self-hatred, 2) he considers her totally unjust, which leads him to lash out with fury. He even slaps her—further damaging her shaky esteem for him. In any film today, a man slapping a woman would end the scene (spousal abuse, case closed); but in *Contempt* we have to keep watching the sequence for twenty-five more minutes, as the ramifications of and adjustments to that slap are digested.

In assessing the film, much depends on whether one regards the director's sympathies as balanced between the couple, or as one-sidedly male. Some women friends of mine, feminists, report that they can only see the male point of view in *Contempt:* they regard Bardot's Camille as scarcely a character, only a projection of male desire and mistrust. I see Godard's viewpoint as more balanced. True, Piccoli's edgy performance draws a lot of sympathy to Paul; even when he is being an ass, he seems interesting. But Camille also displays striking insights; her efforts to patch things up endear her to us; and her hurt is palpable.

Pascal Aubier told me point-blank: "Godard was on Camille's side." In that sense, *Contempt* can be seen as a form of self-criticism: a male artist analyzing the vanities and self-deceptions of the male ego. (And perhaps, too, an apology: what cinematographer Coutard meant when he called the film Godard's "love letter to his wife," Anna Karina.)

Still, it can't be denied that in the end Camille does betray Paul with the vilely virile Jerry Prokosch. It has been Prokosch's thesis all along that Homer's Penelope was faithless. Lang, and Godard by extension, reject this theory as anachronistic sensationalism. Godard, you might say, builds the strongest possible case for Camille through the first two acts, but in Act III this Penelope proves faithless.

Bardot's Camille is a conventionally subservient woman, brought up to defer to her man. "My husband makes the decisions," she answers Prokosch when he invites her over for a drink. Later she tells Paul, "If you're happy, I'm happy." It is her tragedy that, in experiencing a glimpse of independent selfhood—brought about through the mechanism of contempt, which allows her to distance herself from her husband's domination—she assumes she has no choice but to flee into the arms of another, more powerful man.

Contempt is an ironic retelling of Homer's *Odyssey*. At one point Camille wryly summarizes the Greek epic as "the story of that guy who's always traveling." But Paul's restlessness is internal, making him ill at ease everywhere. In modern life, implies Godard, there is no homecoming, we remain chronically homeless, in barely furnished apartments where the red drapes never arrive. Paul's Odysseus and Camille's Penelope keep advancing toward and retreating from each other: never arriving at port.

But the film also resembles another Greek tale, *Oedipus Rex*. Paul is infantilely enraged at the threatened removal of the nurturing breast, and jealous of a more powerful male figure who must be battled for the woman's love. The way he keeps pressing to uncover a truth he would be better off leaving alone is Oedipal, too. His insistent demand to know why Camille has stopped loving him (even after she denies this is the case) helps solidify a tentative role-playing on her part into an objective reality ("You're right, I no longer love you"). Anxious for reassurance, he will nevertheless only accept negative testimony which corroborates his fears, because only the nightmare has the brutal air of truth, and only touching bottom feels real.

Even in Capri, when the game is up, Paul demands one last time: "Why do you have contempt for me?" She answers: "That I'll never tell you, even if I were dying." To this he responds, with his old intellectual vanity, that he knows already. By this point, the reason is truly unimportant. She will never tell him, not because it is such a secret, but because she has already moved beyond dissection of emotions to action: she is leaving him.

Godard spoke uncharitably about Alberto Moravia's *The Ghost at Noon*, the novel he adapted for *Contempt*, calling it "a nice, vulgar read for a train journey." In fact, he took a good deal of the psychology, characters and plot line from Moravia—a decent storyteller, now neglected, who was once regarded as a major European writer. Perhaps Godard's un-generosity toward Moravia reflects an embarrassment at this debt, or a knee-jerk need to apologize to his avant-garde fans.

The exigencies of making a movie with a comparatively large budget and stars, based on a well-known writer's novel, limited the experimental-collage side of Godard and forced him to focus on getting across a linear narrative. In the process he was "freed" or "obliged" (depending on one's point of view) to draw more psychologically shaded, complex characters, whose emotional lives rested on overt causalities and motivations, more so than he had ever demonstrated before or since. Godard himself admitted that he considered Paul the first fully developed character he had gotten on film. Godardians regard *Contempt* as an anomaly, the master's most "orthodox" movie. The paradox is that it may also be his finest. *Pierrot le Fou* has more epic expansiveness, *Breathless* and *Masculin-Féminin* more cinematic invention, but in *Contempt* Godard was able to strike his deepest human chords.

If the film records the process of disenchantment, it is also a seductive bouquet of enthrallments: Bardot's beauty, primary colors, luxury objects, nature. *Contempt* marked the first time that Godard went beyond the *jolie-laide* poetry of cities and revealed his romantic, unironic love of landscapes. The cypresses on Prokosch's estate exquisitely frame Bardot and Piccoli. Capri sits in the Mediterranean like a jewel in a turquoise setting. The last word in the film is Lang's assistant director (played by Godard himself) calling out "Silence!" to the crew, after which the camera pans to a tranquilly static ocean. The serene classicism of sea and sky refutes the thrashings of men.

— 22

Confessions of a Shusher

I AM A SHUSHER, which is to say a self-appointed sergeant-at-arms who tells noisemakers in the theater to be quiet. You take your life in your hands when you shush a stranger, since he may turn out to be a touchy psychopath who is reminded of an admonishing schoolteacher he detested. But having been in the past a grade-school teacher, I cannot shake the idea that I am somehow responsible for the correction of these breakdowns in the assembly.

My usual procedure is to start with a glare at the offender. Glares are unfortunately quite ineffective when the noisemakers sit in front of you. Even if they are to the side or behind, a glare may be misinterpreted as rubbernecking. I then proceed to clear my throat, hoping that this signal of civilized discomfit will be understood as a reproach. It almost never is. I then usually undergo an internal struggle, asking myself, Who am I to set myself up as a policer of public behavior? Can't I simply ignore the nuisance? Is it really worth it to emit an ugly sound, which grates on my ears as well, which may distract others from the movie and may draw on my head some physical retaliation against which I am ill-prepared to defend myself, or else some unpleasant curse? These questions are merely a way of biding my time in the hope that the problem will disappear by itself. If it doesn't, I am compelled to graduate to Stage 2: a good hearty "Shhh!" Much as I might want to soften the aggressiveness of this susurration, experience has taught me that a tentative shush is a waste of time—too easily mistaken for some private sigh.

But then, even a lusty shush is frequently ignored. Perhaps it is too comic-sounding, has too much of the sneeze about it, the hyperactive radiator or the ready kettle. In any event, a shush does not obligate its target to recognize that he or she has been addressed, the way normal speech does. What shushes do have in their favor is that, being such a universal signal, they make the reprimand seem less a personal confrontation and more the bubbling up of a communal superego. However, if the offenders continue to talk after several shushes (perhaps even issuing some derisive mimicking shush of their own as a witty riposte), then there is no choice but to come out from behind the anonymity of the shush and, heart in mouth, escalate to a crisp verbal "Please stop talking." This is sometimes followed by "You're not in your living room, you know," if one is feeling pedagogically self-righteous. Whatever statement one makes is likely to produce a furious twisting in the chair by the chief gabbler, to see what puritanical nerd has had the temerity to question his freedom of speech. It is necessary to return the fellow's look with a cool, frowning stare of one's own. Sometimes the shusher senses a small ripple of curiosity among those nearby, like schoolchildren drawn to a playground fight. Their lack of support for law and order is not the least irritating facet of the situation, since you had thought you were intervening at least partly for everyone's sake, and now realize that to them you are merely one more lunatic releasing commands into the indifferent dark.

By now the movie's spell has been broken. I sit boiling, feeling helplessly angry and at the same time frightened of the offender's potential rage. If he falls into a resentful silence, I can calm my heartbeat and tell myself that I have struck a blow for moviegoers everywhere. The problem is that the request to shut up is often taken rather personally. It seems to touch a sore spot in the requestee's dignity. Particularly, I have noticed, if the chief talker is showing off for his date, or his group of buddies, he may continue to jaw all night as a point of machismo, so that what had started out as unconscious rudeness graduates, via shushing, to defiant policy.

At such turns I compose speeches to myself, along the lines of "We did not pay good money to listen to your asinine conversation" or "How can we expect to have a democracy if . . ." But I usually spare them the civics lesson, because by this point I decide to write these people off as hopeless morons. I sweep up my coat and belongings, ignoring the victorious hoots, and allow myself a slow, censorious abandonment of the row. Perhaps a grain of guilt, I tell myself, will lodge itself in their subconsciousness and come to ripening next time.

It would be agreeable to report that the problem ends there. But many times my newly chosen section is also contaminated with talkers, so that I may be forced to move three times in the course of a feature film. In doing so, I incur the risk of being mistaken for a restless flasher, but it is a small price to pay for cinematic peace of mind.

The crux of the problem is that I want to watch movies in movie theaters, as they were designed to be seen, and I like having the company of other bodies, other spectators around me; but at the same time, I have become preternaturally sensitive, during years of devoted filmgoing, to distractions: not just to the conversationalists but to the foot-kickers or those who nervously cross and uncross their legs behind me, each time pressing into the back of my seat; the latecomer who compounds the first fault by making what seems like a deliberately elaborate coming to rest, removing her coat slowly and rearranging her department store bags; the doting parent who keeps feeding his child sourball candy wrapped in maximally crackling cellophane. ... I don't even like to sit behind bald-headed men, because their domes reflect too much light and detract from the screen's luminescence. (The fact that my own hairline is receding at a rapid pace makes me hope that others are not so pathologically picky.)

The truth is, I can live with the kickers, the candy-unwrappers, the baldies, etc., but I draw the line at prattlers. Is it just my luck to attract them, or have today's movie audiences declined across the board in their capacity to keep silent?

We can always blame television for altering movie-viewing habits. A good many people who attend movies today do seem convinced that they are sitting on the couch at home; others must believe they are in the bedroom, as they snore or make love. You would expect that young people, who have grown up in the channel-hopping, short-attention-span era, would be the worst offenders. But the noisiest, from my observation, are elderly couples, who keep comparing notes on what is happening and why. Maybe hearing loss makes them talk louder, but it is also as if submission to the film experience were a threat to their dyadic bond, and in the end they choose togetherness over immersion.

Audiences of the twenties and thirties were famous—indeed, they were so criticized by intellectuals—for their mass somnambulism as the lights dimmed. Today's audiences are like patients hard to hypnotize; they resist the oneiric plunge. Accustomed to seeing modest-sized images in the convivial, lamp-lit surround of family life, they do not fully participate in the ritual of a sudden, engulfing nightfall. And today's theater owners further dilute the darkness by letting in considerably more ambient light—usually for security reasons—and scaling down the grandeur with smaller, multiplexed screens. The result is an uneasy suspension above the film narrative, the equivalent of a light sleep.

Audience chatter has also been affected by a shifting perception of when a movie actually begins. I was sitting in a movie house recently, waiting for the show to start (I like to get there early, to absorb the atmosphere and compose myself for the descent), and in front of me were two women having a discussion about apples. Granny Smith versus Macintosh, fresh versus baked. It was one of those tedious conversations you cannot help but eavesdrop in on. The lights lowered, the coming attractions started, the women chatted on. Now they were discussing which restaurant they would go to after the show. Coming attractions can be fascinating cultural artifacts, and, in any case, I have a fondness for their tantalizing promise, but I recognize that they are, in a sense, only advertisements, and so the audience has the right to talk through them, resisting these solicitations with skeptical remarks, such as "They couldn't pay me to see that one." However, the titles of the feature film started to appear, and the women continued conversing. Should they go to a French bistro or eat Chinese? But—you will say—it was only during the titles. *Only* the titles? I am curious who is in the cast, who wrote the screenplay, produced it; and even if I were not, I would still think the labor of these collaborators deserved a respectful silence as their names passed before my eyes. Then there is the choice of typeface, no small matter. . . . Above all, the title sequence often introduces the key visual and musical leitmotifs in the film. One school of criticism even argues that the title sequence is a miniature model—encoded, of course—of the movie to follow. All right, I see I haven't convinced you about the significance of the title sequence; but surely you will agree that the first shot of the film is highly important in arousing our expectations—as important, say, as the first sentence of a novel. Yet the women kept talking. This particular opening shot panned across the rooftops of a Sicilian city huddled in the landscape, establishing the drama's larger social context while at the same time expressing certain aesthetic choices (camera movement, angle, lighting) that allowed us to sense the tempo at which Fate would be distributed to the characters. It was a particularly engrossing, well-composed mood-setting shot, undermined by the chatter of my neighbors, and I felt I had no option but to shush. One of the women replied, "Nothing's happening yet!" Mood, location— this was nothing. It was only during the first *dialogue* sequence that they decided something was happening, and finally fell silent.

I want to make a distinction here between what I regard as justifiable audience noise and the kind of chatter I have been describing. I do not expect utter silence in a theater, nor do I necessarily want it. Comedies obviously gain from being seen in a packed, roaring house. If I am at a horror movie and during a frightening sequence some teenagers start yelling "Watch out!" or "Oh, gross!" it's in the spirit of the occasion. If my fellow moviegoers rejoice at a chainsaw dismemberment or at so-called "street slime" being blown away in *Death Wish IX*, I may fear for their souls and their politics, but I do not fault them for improper audience behavior. They are still reacting as a public to the events on-screen, are swept up in the drama. What I cannot accept is the selfishness of private conversation. Even when nothing is audible from a nearby tête-à-tête but a whispering buzz, the mere knowledge that my neighbors are not watching with their full attention dilutes and spoils my own concentration.

For all that one is still a crowd member, moviegoing is essentially a solitary process. To refuse that solitude is to violate the social contract that should be written on each ticket stub. If, indeed, movie audiences of today chatter more during films than they used to, I can only surmise that it has something to do with, on the one hand, a spreading fear of solitude and, on the other, an erosion of what it means to be a member of the public.

There have been times, over the years, when my roles as cinephile and swain have come into conflict. I have had to make it clear to my date, however much I may have doted on her, that I actually did want to watch the movie. I have made it clear to the gabblers around us as well, though one woman who was a perfect lady and to whom I was especially devoted, hated my shushing, which she found an embarrassment and a breach of manners. One time I went so far as to shush *her* when she was talking to a friend who had come with us to the movies, and afterward she let me know, with uncharacteristic directness, that if I ever did that to her again, she would break my arm. She was right, of course—or at least I pretended she was right, because I knew that if I attempted to defend my quixotic position, it would only make things worse. Nobody loves a shusher.

_ 23

Reflections on Subletting

MY FIRST NIGHT BACK IN NEW YORK, I generally arrive from the airport just as the regular tenants are about to leave. An awkward changing of the guard takes place, initiation into the mysteries of pilot light and keys. They do not want to seem impolite by rushing off too soon, and I don't want to seem to be kicking them out of their own home, but the truth is, I am dying to be left alone. Finally they depart and I am alone. In fact, too alone; I roam around this strange apartment wondering where to place myself, like an actor feeling out a new stage set. Sounds from the street remind me how vast the city's business is, how little it knows or cares about my reentry. There is no place on earth that hits me with as keen and cosmic a loneliness as New York City on the first night back. I feel myself at the bottom of a steep concrete well. It is not just the monumental scale of the city, but the fact that New York really is my hometown, and lacks the adventurous camouflage of an exotic port that one knows in the end one will betray. I am homesick precisely because I have come home, but not to any house of mine.

Compulsively I begin to make phone calls. "I'm back in town!" I say to those friends I happen to catch in. "Great! Give me your number, I'm in the middle of something, I'll call you back around elevenish?" Wounded narcissism: they are always in the middle of something in New York; why can't they just rush over and embrace me? But even if they had offered, I would have shied away, wanting this first evening to myself, to experience head-on the excitement and the fear. How can I be afraid of a city where I've spent at least three fourths of my life? Mine is not the out-of-towner's dread that he'll be mugged or get on the wrong train, but the fear that this time New York will prove too much, that I've become soft away from the city, that I've already forfeited my place in it, like a latecomer to a game of musical chairs.

I start to unpack, laying claim to my new space. Animals piss on trees to establish territoriality; I unpack. The tenants have left me the requisite two empty dresser drawers and half a closet, storing their overflow in shopping bags on the closet floor. I hang up my travel-creased suits and shirts, spitefully shoving their hangered clothes tighter together to make more room for my own. (Why this spite? These people have kindly allowed me to live in their home.) I turn on the radio and fortuitously find a Mets game, which I listen to for a few innings while unpacking. Syllogistic comfort: I am still a Mets fan, therefore I must still be a New Yorker.

Finally I am ready to tackle the streets. My plan is a late dinner and a stroll around Greenwich Village. The streets don't alarm me; they are, in fact, what always lure me back. Prodigal son returning, I accept my patrimony of street life, this home-coming feast of gritty passing faces. What a privilege to be a member of a crowd again, wrapped in that downbeat anonymous sense of oneself. At the newsstand I buy a few papers and begin looking for a restaurant. There are five on every block, I can't make up my mind. I enter what seems a reasonably priced trattoria and am seated at a dark table by the rest rooms. Why are tables for one always shunted off in the blackest corners? It's precisely those of us who eat alone who need the best light to read by, while the romantic dates could use some chiaroscuro. "Sorry, it's too dim," I mutter to the waiter and abruptly leave, looking for another restaurant. Any one will do, I'm no fussy gourmet, and yet . . . the first meal back in New York is meant to be something better than a cheeseburger in the Greek coffee shop (admittedly brightly lit) whose window menu I study next. Finally I settle for an overpriced French bistro; its candlelight just enables me to make out the movie listings in the *Voice*. I start circling with a pen: Tuesday, the Film Forum; Friday, Japan Society. A regimen, a schedule, a life begins to suggest its trajectory above the ache of undifferentiated newcomer's time.

Back on the avenue, fed, I feel exhilarated, happy to be back in New York again. I follow the crowd's amoebic tropisms. Pulled along by the vortex of Sixth Avenue, doubling back to check the video rental store's display, edging past the teenage bikers and NYU show-offs, looking over the shoulder of the sidewalk portrait artist. . . . It is only when I turn in for the night that the panic returns: I am sleeping in another man's bed.

"There are roughly three New Yorks," E. B. White observed. "There is, first, the New York of the man or woman who was born here, who takes the city for granted and accepts its size and its turbulence as natural and inevitable. Second, there is the New York of the commuter—the city that is devoured by locusts each day and spat out each night. Third, there is the New York of the person who was born somewhere else and came to New York in quest of something . . . the city of final destination, the city that is the goal." To these I would add a fourth: that of the native New Yorker, self-exiled either through better job opportunities elsewhere or wanderlust, who now seeks to regain his paradise lost through a subletter's foothold.

Ever since I moved from New York to accept a teaching job in Houston, I have been sneaking back to the mother city for summer vacations or occasional leaves of absence. Since I had to give up my old Manhattan apartment when I first moved away, I've been obliged each time to find a sublet.

If a *pied-à-terre* is a foot on the ground in town, then a sublet must be a *pied-en-l'air*, the most tenuous of all claims to hearth and home. This is particularly true in New York, given the legally gray status of many sublets here. Sometimes the tenant's lease clearly stipulates the right to sublet his apartment (with the landlord's permission), but relations between tenant and landlord have grown so antagonistic that the tenant is loath to ask for this favor. I have been assured via long distance that a sublet is legitimate, only to be told on arrival not to put my name on the mailbox, "just to be on the safe side." In one apartment, where a tenant had no right to sublet except to a relative, I was asked to pose as his half-brother. I was once kept secret by a co-op apartment owner who had illegally walled off a section of his flat for rental income; threatened by a co-op board inspection, he said I might have to move out for a few weeks while he busted a hole in the wall again, "just temporarily." Fortunately, it never came to that. Still, unable to announce my citizenly existence in the standard manner, I started to feel vaguely on the run, like an outlaw or an illegal alien, although I was paying quite a hefty rent.

In the present avaricious New York market, it is certainly easier to find a sublet than a permanent apartment. Tenants now lease out their pads for slivers of time— two weeks, ten days, even a long weekend. They will always find takers: I have known fellow seekers who came to the city and, unable to secure an affordable apartment with a lease, have spent years moving from one sublet to another. In their own less extreme way, they are part of the city's homeless problem.

Each time I sublet, I land on a new box on the city's Monopoly board. My lodgings have gravitated from the Upper West Side to Tribeca to Stuyvesant Town to Chelsea to Herald Square to the West Village to Soho to the Upper East Side. I have learned the Sunday moods, dry cleaners, supermarkets, greasy spoons, slants of light, and vest-pocket parks of each. Streets I had only passed through as a visitor before, on my way to a restaurant or movie, have become, however briefly, my home turf. I have told myself that this vagabondage would make me into a more complete New Yorker, as I was learning the city—or at least mid-to-lower Manhattan—far better than when I lived here year-round. On the other hand, these relocations have left me uncentered, with no firm attachment or loyalty to any one section of town. I feel like an adolescent shifting from youth hostel to crash pad at a time when I should be settling into the householding wisdom of middle age. Maybe this subletting binge is my last-ditch attempt to forestall middle age.

Each time I have been quick to assure the regular tenant that I would not need much in the way of comforts. No air conditioner? No problem; the veteran subletter takes pride in his/her chameleonic ability to adjust. A worldly person can fit in anywhere, presumably: into a Scottish castle or a prison cell.

Yet once I have taken over a sublet, a tricky period of matching my sense of habitational order (or disorder) to the alien environment begins. It is part of the larger struggle to impose enough of my personality on the borrowed lodgings so that my spirit won't feel extinguished or overwhelmed. At the same time I am well aware that my main task is to adapt, not interfere. I may reverse the positions of couch and easy chair, but the objects remain obdurately themselves. Sometimes I become abnormally sensitive to light and lighting in these early stages: a long cavernous loft with windows only at both ends may give me a sense of wintry desolation.

Inevitably the practiced subletter develops both an ability to adjust and a finicky ideal of domestic space, based on accumulated awareness of one's peculiar little habits and one's discomfort when they are thwarted. For instance, I happen to like a hook or nail in the bathroom for my robe when I shower, and while we're at it, a nail or two inside the closet, so that if I should happen to come home at night too sloshed to hang up my clothes properly I can always suspend them temporarily on a nail. But some designer purists consider it a sin to despoil their walls with anything so mundane as a nail. I have stayed in apartments that were as austere as art galleries, where I sensed a chilling frown of disapproval each time I left my socks bunched up on the hardwood floor.

There are sublets I have entered and felt immediately, gratefully at home in, and others that never stopped fighting me, like a transplanted organ the body keeps trying to reject. My feelings toward the people I am displacing enter into this, naturally. Whenever possible I sublet from friends: they don't profiteer by charging me more rent than they pay—the very definition of a friend in these dark times—and they are glad to have someone they know guarding their home. But even so, my sojourn is inevitably colored by the history of our relationship. If I am very fond of the regular tenants, I tend to delight in their little domestic ways. They become my ideal parents, taking care of me, guarding me, from afar. Conversely, if I have developed ambivalent feelings toward people who are subletting to me, living in their house only confirms prior doubts: a narrow squeeze between bed and chiffonier that condemns me to banged-up knees becomes a corroboration of their tight, unforgiving natures.

Subletting can be compared to that period of adjustment when a newlywed couple first sets up house and each begins to discover the little quirks and nesting habits of the other. The difference is that, in the subletting relationship, one of the parties is never around, while the one who remains on the premises still feels the tug of relationship, with its ups and downs, irritations, compromises, and insights. You learn more about a person by living in his house for a week than by years of running into him at social gatherings. This information is sometimes as tiny and precise as the dry goods kept in the pantry, which constitute his or her notions of emergency solace. I once sublet the loft of an admirable elderly couple, two artists who clung to a Spartan simplicity learned in their days of bohemian poverty, though they had become well-off recently. In the pantry were such homely, unepicurean staples as lentils, cornstarch, cocoa, a box of Mueller's spaghetti; when I ferreted around in their shelves, I felt empathic sensations of old age, a not unpleasant mixture of lumbago and historic memory rising in my bones.

Another time I sublet in Tribeca from a stylishly pretty woman: her silk kimonos, her peignoirs, her sachets cohabited with my undershorts and T-shirts in the limited dresser space. Not only did I have the pleasure of sleeping in this glamorous woman's bed, albeit without her, I also experienced myself for fractions of a second as a glamorous woman. The low angle of her showerhead, the scent of her oval bath soap, the pegboard arrangement of her pots and pans, all subtly feminized me: by going through her daily motions I was camping in her psyche, my muscles mimicking her reach, my eye level learning to emulate hers.

Trying on other lives is the privilege of the actor, the novelist, the schizophrenic—and the subletter. When I first started subletting I experienced this borrowing of identity only as a freedom. A temporary holiday from stewing in my own daily life. Both the subletter and the hotel customer have merely to lay out the cash to be absolved from the burdens of homemaking and repair. The hotel speaks more to our need for mediocre taste: conventional, consoling, the mass culture of travel. While the impersonal hotel bedroom conjures up a long parade of imagined licentious acts, erased as effortlessly in the mind as the squiggles on a child's "magic pad" when its plastic oversheet is lifted, the erotic relation to a sublet space is necessarily more tender, unrequited, prolonged. The subletter fingers day after day the combs, spoons, personal effects of another; the rooms he moves through are saturated with narrative; he has only to rest his absentminded gaze somewhere—like the detective in *Laura* falling in love with a portrait—to fantasize about the inner lives of the lady or man of the house.

With a mixture of stewardship, voyeurism, longing, and parasitic contempt, I haunt the rooms I have borrowed. As subletter I am the tamest of poltergeists, vowing to shake nothing permanently from its spot. Of course, I may temporarily remove the ugly nuclear-freeze poster from the hallway or the grandparents' pictures from the mantel, and store them under the bed, flaunting in their place some reassuring *kitsch* of my own. Or I may casually glance through the check stubs in the desk, or read the carbon copy of a letter left faceup, then the one underneath that. . . . But even if I bring myself to resist (as decent people should) the deplorable temptation to snoop through old diaries, to examine the shopping bags in the back of the closet for fetishistic clues, I may still experience guilt for having crossed some indeterminate line of privacy. Subletting revives psychologically the voluptuous shame of the child dressing up in Mother's clothes. One might say, in fact, that the subletter is a habitational transvestite, wrapping the self in decors that belong to another.

And, just as a drag costume insinuates an element of satire, however mediated by admiration, so, too, the first time I welcome a guest to my borrowed quarters and show him or her about, with the ironic pride of a nonpossessor, the urge to mock the taste of the original tenants is very strong. I detach myself from their follies, their pretenses, their art deco solemnities or country-quilt homilies, like a Peter Pan floating above nesting finalities. Not that I hesitate to show off the deluxe elements—the fireplace, the French doors—since they bestow status on me as well, prompting from my guests those expressions of apartment envy that in New York have become as much a conversational opener as inquiries about one's health used to be.

Subletting is a species of tourism, and offers opportunities to sample life-styles far above or below one's accustomed socioeconomic level. In the same way that a favorable currency fluctuation may suddenly allow a middle-class traveler to book a suite in the Grand Hotel, I once lucked into a light airy apartment with a beautiful art collection which I pedantically ciceroned for each of my visitors. On the other hand, I have sublet tiny sweatboxes in seedy, smelly, noisy, dilapidated six-story walk-ups. Since I grew up poor, "slumming" holds no adventurous novelty for me, only the sense of a nightmarish regression.

Rule of thumb: it is easier to expand into an abode larger and more luxurious than one is accustomed to than it is to contract into a smaller. I have found that the reduction of my normal domestic space by so much as a room may induce a claustrophobic twinge, like the throbbing awareness of a missing limb to which amputees testify.

Though I have had my share of fortunate sublets, somehow it is the misadventures that linger in the mind. One time I sublet from a rather short academic couple, whom we'll call the Lilliputians. The rent was too cheap to pass up; the apartment, in an old tenement building, had the quaint moldiness of a rabbit burrow, with small, low, cell-like rooms off a main foyer. All the rooms, including the narrowly passable foyer, were crammed with double-stacked bookcases. To a bibliophile like myself, this looked to be heaven, at first. I have always felt uneasy—no, threatened, negated—in sublets with barely any books. Where books abound, there is a particular thrill to that initial stroll through the collection, discovering what rarities lie in store, what serendipitous encounters with authors you had always intended to read but never had got around to. As subletter, you have license to eat of the Tree of Knowledge, to ravage the forbidden fruit of your lessor's bookshelves. A scholar who might have hesitated to loan you a prized volume now has no choice in the matter.

However, in this particular case, I found myself depressed by the overwhelming number of books around me; moreover, the collection seemed theory-greedy, leaning toward phenomenology, structuralism, ethnopoetics, Marxism, linguistics, and Buddhist philosophy. In fiction, which I always check out first, there was Broch, Musil, Sarraute, Beckett, Pynchon, all laudable in their way, but not exactly pleasurable old-fashioned stories with which to while away a summer's afternoon. A certain puritanical modernist taste was in operation here. So I took it upon myself to become familiar at last with Musil's trilogy, with Husserl and Polanyi, with Scholem on kabbala, with Jakobson's poetics, but most of it went way over my head: I would read a passage of Scholem on the toilet, and dutifully pick up Habermas or Gramsci at the breakfast table, without finishing anything.

I always seemed to be getting a headache in that apartment, partly because of the dense prose I was trying to riddle, and partly from the poor ventilation, but mostly, I think, because I kept banging my head. I am pretty tall and this couple, as I have mentioned before, were not: they had constructed an entire interior universe to suit their stature, so that I got shiners from cupboard doors and had to genuflect while washing dishes. The greatest menaces, however, were the loft beds, which seemed everywhere. It was the second marriage for both Lilliputians, and as each had several grown-up children from previous unions, their idea seemed to have been to encourage these young people to sleep over by offering them a plethora of lofts and bunk beds.

A further complication should be mentioned here. One of my subletter's tasks was to water the plants, of which there were some twenty-eight hanging, sitting, or potted, scattered around the apartment. This necessitated several trips back and forth to the sink with a watering can. But the real inconvenience came in reaching the plants on the upper windowsill, behind the bunk beds, in the woman's study. I would often knock my head against the protruding loft ledge while ascending the ladder, or else, having gained the upper berth and belly-whopped onto it with can tilted at an angle such that no water would spill until I had crawled forward to reach the geraniums, I would forgetfully straighten up and bang my head on the ceiling.

Now it should also be mentioned that these people kept a Buddhist altar at the front of this bunk bed. Various *chotchkes* of a ceremonial nature were carefully set on a prayer rug, below a framed portrait of their guru. I imagine they practiced sitting meditation there, though the one time I tried to get into a lotus position before the altar, just to see what it would be like, there was very little leg room. I also need to point out that this shrine was next to a window with an air conditioner—the only cooling device in the apartment. It was a summer of record heat; the electrical wiring in the building was very old; and I had been warned that if I did not hit the buttons on the unit at precisely timed intervals several minutes apart (each sequence increasing the cooling capacity), a fuse would blow and I and my neighbors would be plunged into darkness. Indeed, part of my subletter orientation session had consisted of a visit to the basement, flashlight in hand, to get acquainted with the fuse box. Since I had no desire ever to reexperience that urinous, rat-friendly catacomb, I quickly leaped up whenever the air conditioner sounded ready for its next cycle, usually knocking my head against the upper loft's ledge in my effort to avoid stepping on the altar and crunching its sacred objects, and I would lurch or corkscrew forward, gashing my hand against the torn metal of the air conditioner's facade, while groping in the dark for the right button. The whole apartment seemed to me a booby trap to which I never became accustomed.

I suppose the final straw was the place I sublet from a young investment banker who was being posted abroad to Paris. I had waited until the last minute, trusting to the network of friends' contacts, but this time they had turned up nothing, and the advertised sublets I dialed always seemed to be busy, and so I pounced on this place as a last resort. It was a grim white cube of a studio in Chelsea, quite expensive, decorated with various Francophilic touches like a Paris street sign and a tricolor baguette wrapper. When I discovered that the toilet was in the outer hall, not in the studio itself, I almost balked, but the young man assured me that this was very "European."

So I took it. Try as I might to imagine that I was staying in a continental hotel in Budapest, the indignity of not having my own bathroom at my age and in my own hometown kept eating at me. Moreover, I could never manage to relax in that apartment, to loll around with my clothes off late at night, because I was always worried that the call of nature would oblige me to throw on something before going off to the hallway toilet.

However, the toilet situation was nothing compared to the problem of the garbage trucks. The street was divided between manufacturing and residences—an enlightened urban practice in theory, but one that causes unexpected abrasions in practice. Among other things, mixed usage generates a lot of garbage, apparently too much for the city's sanitation department to handle. Instead of doing the logical thing, which would be to hire one truck to pick up for everybody, each building contracted with a separate carting firm. After midnight the street belonged to these private carters. The drivers would stand outside their trucks, joking and drinking from brown-bagged pints like the first guests to arrive at a party. Then the symphony of garbage collection would ensue. Being a native New Yorker, I do not mind a little city noise, nor am I normally an insomniac. But insomnia was the only possible response to the crash of upended dumpsters, the grinding of gears, the garbage masticated through the rumps of trucks hour after hour, until 5:00 A.M., when the last truck drove away and I was able to drift off....

After a week of near sleeplessness, I had come to know the various beasts in the jungle. There was the high-pitched *breep-breep!* of the sea-green mastodon backing up in reverse; there was the dark blue dinosaur with its *jrowrr-jrowrr* gnashing mechanism; there was that mutant creature that went *garock-kikguh!*... Sometimes the drivers left their motors running for an hour while they went across the street to Lanza's Cafeteria (*vrip!* the metal grille of the cafeteria front lifting and closing) for a few rounds. Lying awake, I thought of opening sniper fire on the trucks; I thought of importing special Italian ear stoppers (the American ones did nothing); of buying thick drapes and rugs to deaden the sound (was it worth it for a three-month sublet?); I thought of organizing all the businesses on the block into a cooperative to pool their carter services; I thought of sleeping elsewhere and using this place as a daytime office; I thought of trying to become a night person by shifting my biological clock, or adapting to the noise through Zen mind control or sheer habituation; I thought of forfeiting my deposit and moving to another sublet. And I thought of Baudelaire's prose poem, "Anywhere Out of This World," about being contented nowhere. Surely it was partly my fault, my restlessness, the difficulty I had of living in my own skin. I am getting too old for this, I thought. One more sublet, I thought, will send me around the bend.

And yet, even as I finished off the season in this studio with the W.C. down the hall, as I went about shipping my books back to Houston and filing a change-of-address card at the post office I experienced the usual wistfulness. I had been occasionally peaceful here, and productive at times; there was creaturely regret at being unseated from any nest, however uncomfortable

It is the subletter's duty to leave no trace of himself. On the day before departure, I washed the dishes, scrubbed the bathtub swabbed the floors, returned all photos to their original situation on the mantelpiece. Like that a robber who makes sure to remove fingerprints, I was destroying all evidence of my tenure. Like of a lover who, in "possessing" a woman's flesh, possesses nothing in the end but a memory, my hold on the sublet was starting to evaporate. I noticed, however, that I had left a few bruises on the body of the place. Some little erosion has always taken place: a chip on a coffee mug's lip, a bureau handle that fell off and that I have clumsily Scotch-taped back in position. My subletter's calling card.

— THE STYLE OF MIDDLE AGE

24

Portrait of My Body

I AM A MAN WHO TILTS. When I am sitting, my head slants to the right; when walking, the upper part of my body reaches forward to catch a sneak preview of the street. One way or another, I seem to be off-center—or "uncentered," to use the jargon of holism. My lousy posture, a tendency to slump or put myself into lazy, contorted misalignments, undoubtedly contributes to lower back pain. For a while I correct my bad habits, do morning exercises, sit straight, breathe deeply, but always an inner demon that insists on approaching the world askew resists perpendicularity.

I think if I had broader shoulders I would be more squarely anchored. But my shoulders are narrow, barely wider than my hips. This has always made shopping for suits an embarrassing business. (Françoise Gilot's *Life with Picasso* tells how Picasso was so touchy about his disproportionate body—in his case all shoulders, no legs—that he insisted the tailor fit him at home.) When I was growing up in Brooklyn, my hero was Sandy Koufax, the Dodgers' Jewish pitcher. In the doldrums of Hebrew choir practice at Feigenbaum's Mansion & Catering Hall, I would fantasize striking out the side, even whiffing twenty-seven batters in a row. Lack of shoulder development put an end to this identification; I became a writer instead of a Koufax.

It occurs to me that the restless angling of my head is an attempt to distract viewers' attention from its paltry base. I want people to look at my head, partly because I live in my head most of the time. My sister, a trained masseuse, often warns me of the penalties, like neck tension, that may arise from failing to integrate body and mind. Once, about ten years ago, she and I were at the beach and she was scrutinizing my body with a sister's critical eye. "You're getting flabby," she said. "You should exercise every day. I do—look at me, not an ounce of fat." She pulled at her midriff, celebrating (as is her wont) her physical attributes with the third-person enthusiasm of a carnival barker.

"But"—she threw me a bone—"you do have a powerful head. There's an intensity . . ." A graduate student of mine (who was slightly loony) told someone that she regularly saw an aura around my head in class. One reason I like to teach is that it focuses fifteen or so dependent gazes on me with such paranoiac intensity as cannot help but generate an aura in my behalf.

I also have a commanding stare, large sad brown eyes that can be read as either gentle or severe. Once I watched several hours of myself on videotape. I discovered to my horror that my face moved at different rates: sometimes my mouth would be laughing, eyebrows circumflexed in mirth, while my eyes coolly gauged the interviewer to see what effect I was making. I am something of an actor. And, as with many performers, the mood I sense most in myself is that of energy-conserving watchfulness; but this expression is often mistaken (perhaps because of the way brown eyes are read in our culture) for sympathy. I see myself as determined to the point of stubbornness, selfish, even a bit cruel—in any case, I am all too aware of the limits of my compassion, so that it puzzles me when people report a first impression of me as gentle, kind, solicitous. In my youth I felt obliged to come across as dynamic, arrogant, intimidating, the life of the party; now, surer of myself, I hold back some energy, thereby winning time to gather information and make better judgments. This results sometimes in a misimpression of my being mildly depressed. Of course, the simple truth is that I have less energy than I once did, and that accumulated experiences have made me, almost against my will, kinder and sadder.

Sometimes I can feel my mouth arching downward in an ironic smile, which, at its best, reassures others that we need not take everything so seriously—because we are all in the same comedy together—and, at its worst, expresses a superior skepticism. This smile, which can be charming when not supercilious, has elements of the bashful that mesh with the worldly—the shyness, let us say, of a cultivated man who is often embarrassed for others by their willful shallowness or self-deception. Many times, however, my ironic smile is nothing more than a neutral stall among people who do not seem to appreciate my "contribution." I hate that pain-in-the-ass half-smile of mine; I want to jump in, participate, be loud, thoughtless, vulgar.

Often I give off a sort of psychic stench to myself I do not like myself at all, but out of stubborn pride I act like a man who does. I appear for all the world poised, contented, sanguine when inside I may be feeling self-revulsion bordering on the suicidal. What a wonder to be so misread! Of course, if in the beginning I had thought I was coming across accurately, I never would have bothered to become a writer. And the truth is I am not misread, because another part of me is never less than fully contented with myself.

I am vain about these parts of my body: my eyes, my fingers, my legs. It is true that my legs are long and not unshapely, but my vanity about them has less to do with their comeliness than with their contribution to my height. Montaigne, a man who was himself on the short side, wrote that "the beauty of stature is the only beauty of men." But even if Montaigne had never said it, I would continue to attribute a good deal of my self-worth and benevolent liberalism to being tall. When I go out into the street, I feel well-disposed toward the (mostly shorter) swarms of humanity; crowds not only do not dismay, they enliven me; and I am tempted to think that my passion for urbanism is linked to my height. By no means am I suggesting that only tall people love cities; merely that, in my case, part of the pleasure I derive from walking in crowded streets issues from a confidence that I can see above the heads of others, and cut a fairly impressive, elevated figure as I saunter along the sidewalk.

Some of my best friends have been—short. Brilliant men, brimming with poetic and worldly ideas, they deserved all of my and the world's respect. Yet at times I have had to master an impulse to rumple their heads; and I suspect they have developed manners of a more formal, *noli me tangere* nature, largely in response to this petting impulse of taller others.

The accident of my tallness has inclined me to both a seemingly egalitarian informality and a desire to lead. Had I not been a writer, I would surely have become a politician; I was even headed in that direction in my teens. Ever since I shot up to a little over six feet, I have had at my command what feels like a natural, Gregory Peck authority when addressing an audience. Far from experiencing stage fright, I have actually sought out situations in which I could make speeches, give readings, sit on panel discussions, and generally tower over everyone else onstage. To be tall is to look down on the world and meet its eyes on your terms. But this topic, the noblesse oblige of tall men, is a dangerously provoking one, and so let us say no more about it.

The mental image of one's body changes slower than one's body. Mine was for a long while arrested in my early twenties, when I was tall and thin (165 pounds) and gobbled down whatever I felt like. I ate food that was cheap and filling, cheeseburgers, pizza, without any thought to putting on weight. But a young person's metabolism is more dietetically forgiving. To compound the problem, the older you get, the more cultivated your palate grows—and the more life's setbacks make you inclined to fill the hollowness of disappointment with the pleasures of the table.

Between the age of thirty and forty I put on ten pounds, mostly around the midsection. Since then my gut has suffered another expansion, and I tip the scales at over 180. That I took a while to notice the change may be shown by my continuing to purchase clothes at my primordial adult size (33 waist, 15 1/2 collar), until a girlfriend started pointing out that all my clothes were too tight. I rationalized this circumstance as the result of changing fashions (thinking myself still subconsciously loyal to the sixties' penchant for skintight fits) and laundry shrinkage rather than anything to do with my own body. She began buying me larger replacements for birthdays or holidays, and I found I enjoyed this "baggier" style, which allowed me to button my trousers comfortably, or to wear a tie and, for the first time in years, close my top shirt button. But it took even longer before I was able to enter a clothing store myself and give the salesman realistically enlarged size numbers.

Clothes can disguise the defects of one's body, up to a point. I get dressed with great optimism, adding one color to another, mixing my favorite Japanese and Italian designers, matching the patterns and textures, selecting ties, then proceed to the bathroom mirror to judge the result. There is an ideal in my mind of the effect I am essaying by wearing a particular choice of garments, based, no doubt, on male models in fashion ads—and I fall so far short of this insouciant gigolo handsome-ness that I cannot help but be a little disappointed when I turn up so depressingly myself, narrow-shouldered, Talmudic, that grim, set mouth, that long, narrow face, those appraising eyes, the Semitic hooked nose, all of which express both the strain of intellectual overachieving and the tabula rasa of immaturity . . . for it is still, underneath, a boy in the mirror. A boy with a rapidly receding hairline.

How is it that I've remained a boy all this time, into my late forties? I remember, at seventeen, drawing a self-portrait of myself as I looked in the mirror. I was so appalled at the weak chin and pleading eyes that I ended up focusing on the neck-line of the cotton T-shirt. Ever since then I have tried to toughen myself up, but I still encounter in the glass that haunted uncertainty—shielded by a bluffing shell of cynicism, perhaps, but untouched by wisdom. So I approach the mirror warily, without lighting up as much as I would for the least of my acquaintaInces; I go one-on-one with that frowning schmuck.

And yet, it would be insulting to those who labor under the burden of true ugli-ness to palm myself off as an unattractive man. I'm at times almost handsome, if you squinted your eyes and rounded me off to the nearest *beau idéal*. I lack even a shred of cowboy virility, true, but I believe I fall into a category of adorable nerd or absentminded professor that awakens the amorous curiosity of some women. "Cute" is a word often applied to me by those I've been fortunate enough to attract. Then again, I attract only women of a certain lopsided prettiness: the head-turning, professional beauties never fall for me. They seem to look right through me, in fact. Their utter lack of interest in my appeal has always fascinated me. Can it be so sim-ple an explanation as that beauty calls to beauty, as wealth to wealth?

I think of poor (though not in his writing gifts) Cesare Pavese, who kept chasing after starlets, models, and ballerinas—exquisite lovelies who couldn't appreciate his morose coffeehouse charm. Before he killed himself, he wrote a poem addressed to one of them, "Death Will Come Bearing Your Eyes"—thereby unfairly promoting her from rejecting lover to unwitting executioner. Perhaps he believed that only beautiful women (not literary critics, who kept awarding him prestigious prizes) saw him clearly, with twenty-twenty vision, and had the right to judge him. Had I been more headstrong, if masochistic, I might have followed his path and chased some beauty until she was forced to tell me, like an oracle, what it was about me, physi-cally, that so failed to excite her. Then I might know something crucial about my body, before I passed into my next reincarnation.

Jung says somewhere that we pay dearly over many years to learn about ourselves what a stranger can see at a glance. This is the way I feel about my back. Fitting rooms aside, we none of us know what we look like from the back. It is the area of ourselves whose presentation we can least control, and which therefore may be the most honest part of us.

I divide backs into two kinds: my own and everyone else's. The others' backs are often mysterious, exquisite, and uncannily sympathetic. I have always loved backs. To walk behind a pretty woman in a backless dress and savor how a good pair of shoulder blades, heightened by shadow, has the same power to pierce the heart as chiseled cheekbones! . . . I wonder what it says about me that I worship a part of the body that signals a turning away. Does it mean I'm a glutton for being abandoned, or a timid voyeur who prefers a surreptitious gaze that will not be met and challenged? I only know I have often felt the deepest love at just that moment when the beloved turns her back to me to get some sleep.

I have no autoerotic feelings about my own back. I cannot even picture it; visually it is a stranger to me. I know it only as an annoyance, which came into my consciousness twenty years ago, when I started getting lower back pain. Yes, we all know that homo sapiens is constructed incorrectly; our erect posture puts too much pressure on the base of the spine; more workdays are lost because of lower back pain than any other cause. Being a writer, I sit all day, compounding the problem. My back is the enemy of my writing life: if I don't do exercises daily, I immediately ache; and if I do, I am still not spared. I could say more, but there is nothing duller than lower back pain. So common, mundane an ailment brings no credit to the sufferer. One has to dramatize it somehow, as in the phrase "I threw my back out."

Here is a gossip column about my body: My eyebrows grow quite bushy across my forehead, and whenever I get my hair cut, the barber asks me diplomatically if I want them trimmed or not. (I generally say no, associating bushy eyebrows with Balzackian virility, *élan vital*; but sometimes I acquiesce, to soothe his fastidiousness). . . . My belly button is a modest, embedded slit, not a jaunty swirl like my father's. Still, I like to sniff the odor that comes from jabbing my finger in it: a very ripe, underground smell, impossible to describe, but let us say a combination of old gym socks and stuffed derma (the Yiddish word for this oniony dish of ground intestines is, fittingly, *kishkas*). . . . I have a scar on my tongue from childhood, which I can only surmise I received by landing it on a sharp object, somehow. Or perhaps I bit it hard. I have the habit of sticking my tongue out like a dog when exerting myself physically, as though to urge my muscles on; and maybe I accidentally chomped into it at such a moment. . . . I gnash my teeth, sleeping or waking. Awake, the sensation makes me feel alert and in contact with the world when I start to drift off in a daydream. Another way of grounding myself is to pinch my cheek—drawing a pocket of flesh downward and squeezing it—as I once saw JFK do in a filmed motorcade. I do this cheek-pinching especially when I am trying to keep mentally focused during teaching or other public situations. I also scratch the nape of my neck under public stress, so much so that I raise welts or sores which then eventually grow scabs; and I take great delight in secretly picking the scabs off. . . . My nose itches whenever I think about it, and I scratch it often, especially lying in bed trying to fall asleep (maybe because I am conscious of my breathing then). I also pick my nose with formidable thoroughness when no one, I hope, is looking. . . . There is a white scar about the size of a quarter on the juicy part of my knee; I got it as a boy running into a car fender, and I can still remember staring with detached calm at the blood that gushed from it like a pretty, half-eaten peach. Otherwise, the sight of my own blood makes me awfully nervous. I used to faint dead away when a blood sample was taken, and now I can control the impulse to do so only by biting the insides of my cheeks while steadfastly looking away from the needle's action. . . . I like to clean out my ear wax as often as possible (the smell is curiously sulfurous; I associate it with the bodies of dead insects). I refuse to listen to warnings that it is dangerous to stick cleaning objects into your ears. I love Q-Tips immoderately; I buy them in huge quantities and store them the way a former refugee will stock canned foodstuffs. . . . My toes are long and apelike; I have very little fellow feeling for them; they are so far away, they may as well belong to someone else. . . . My flattish buttocks are not offensively large, but neither do they have the "dream" configuration one sees in jeans ads. Perhaps for this reason, it disturbed me puritanically when asses started to be treated by Madison Avenue, around the seventies, as crucial sexual equipment, and I began to receive compositions from teenage girl students declaring that they liked some boy because he had "a cute butt." It confused me; I had thought the action was elsewhere.

About my penis there is nothing, I think, unusual. It has a brown stem, and a pink mushroom head where the foreskin is pulled back. Like most heterosexual males, I have little comparative knowledge to go by, so that I always feel like an outsider when I am around women or gay men who talk zestfully about differences in penises. I am afraid that they might judge me harshly, ridicule me like the boys who stripped me of my bathing suit in summer camp when I was ten. But perhaps they would simply declare it an ordinary penis, which changes size with the stimulus or weather or time of day. Actually, my penis does have a peculiarity: it has two peeing holes. They are very close to each other, so that usually only one stream of urine issues, but sometimes a hair gets caught across them, or some such contretemps, and they squirt out in two directions at once.

This part of me, which is so synecdochically identified with the male body (as the term "male member" indicates), has given me both too little, and too much, information about what it means to be a man. It has a personality like a cat's. I have prayed to it to behave better, to be less frisky, or more; I have followed its nose in matters of love, ignoring good sense, and paid the price; but I have also come to appreciate that it has its own specialized form of intelligence which must be listened to, or another price will be extracted.

Even to say the word "impotence" aloud makes me nervous. I used to tremble when I saw it in print, and its close relation, "importance," if hastily scanned, had the same effect, as if they were publishing a secret about me. But why should it be my secret, when my penis has regularly given me erections lo these many years— except for about a dozen times, mostly when I was younger? Because, even if it has not been that big a problem for me, it has dominated my thinking as an adult male. I've no sooner to go to bed with a woman than I'm in suspense. The power of the flaccid penis's statement, "I don't want you," is so stark, so cruelly direct, that it continues to exert a fascination out of all proportion to its actual incidence. Those few times when I was unable to function were like a wall forcing me to take another path—just as, after I tried to kill myself at seventeen, I was obliged to give up pessimism for a time. Each had instructed me by its too painful manner that I could not handle the world as I had previously construed it, that my confusion and rage were being found out. I would have to get more wily or else grow up.

Yet for the very reason that I was compelled to leave them behind, these two options of my youth, impotence and suicide, continue to command an underground loyalty, as though they were more "honest" than the devious strategies of potency and survival which I adopted. Put it this way: sometimes we encounter a person who has had a nervous breakdown years before and who seems cemented over sloppily, his vulnerability ruthlessly guarded against as dangerous; we sense he left a crucial part of himself back in the chaos of breakdown, and has since grown rigidly jovial. So suicide and impotence became for me "the roads not taken," the paths I had repressed.

Whenever I hear an anecdote about impotence—a woman who successfully coaxed an ex-priest who had been celibate and unable to make love, first by lying next to him for six months without any touching, then by cuddling for six more months, then by easing him slowly into a sexual embrace—I think they are talking about me. I identify completely: this, in spite of the fact, which I promise not to repeat again, that I have generally been able to do it whenever called upon. Believe it or not, I am not boasting when I say that: a part of me is contemptuous of this virility, as though it were merely a mechanical trick that violated my true nature, that of an impotent man absolutely frightened of women, absolutely secluded, cut off.

I now see the way I have idealized impotence: I've connected it with pushing the world away, as a kind of integrity, as in Molière's *The Misanthrope*—connected it with that part of me which, gregarious socializer that I am, continues to insist that I am a recluse, too good for this life. Of course, it is not true that I am terrified of women. I exaggerate my terror of them for dramatic effect, or for the purposes of a good scare.

My final word about impotence: Once, in a period when I was going out with many women, as though purposely trying to ignore my hypersensitive side and force it to grow callous by thrusting myself into foreign situations (not only sexual) and seeing if I was able to "rise to the occasion," I dated a woman who was attractive, tall and blond, named Susan. She had something to do with the pop music business, was a follower of the visionary religious futurist Teilhard de Chardin, and considered herself a religious pacifist. In fact, she told me her telephone number in the form of the anagram, N-O-T-O-W-A-R. I thought she was joking and laughed aloud, but she gave me a solemn look. In passing, I should say that all the women with whom I was impotent or close to it had solemn natures. The sex act has always seemed to me in many ways ridiculous, and I am most comfortable when a woman who enters the sheets with me shares that sense of the comic pomposity behind such a grandiloquently rhetorical use of the flesh. It is as though the prose of the body were being drastically squeezed into metrical verse. I would not have known how to stop guffawing had I been D.H. Lawrence's lover, and I am sure he would have been pretty annoyed at me. But a smile saying "All this will pass" has an erotic effect on me like nothing else.

They claim that men who have long, long fingers also have lengthy penises. I can tell you with a surety that my fingers are long and sensitive, the most perfect, elegant, handsome part of my anatomy. They are not entirely perfect—the last knuckle of my right middle finger is twisted permanently, broken in a softball game when I was trying to block the plate—but even this slight disfigurement, harbinger of mortality, adds to the pleasure I take in my hands' rugged beauty. My penis does not excite in me nearly the same contemplative delight when I look at it as do my fingers. Pianists' hands, I have been told often; and though I do not play the piano, I derive an aesthetic satisfaction from them that is as pure and Apollonian as any I am capable of. I can stare at my fingers for hours. No wonder I have them so often in my mouth, biting my fingernails to bring them closer. When I write, I almost feel that they, and not my intellect, are the clever progenitors of the text. Whatever narcissism, fetishism, and proud sense of masculinity I possess about my body must begin and end with my fingers.

25

The Moody Traveler

TRAVELING ALONE HAS ITS PLUSES: you can go where you want when you want, and you are spared that runaway irritation which comes of suddenly spotting all the little flaws in your companion (who alone seems to be detaining you from perfect enjoyment) and the tension of having to keep that knowledge secret. However, the minus is that you will have no one to blame but yourself for the occasional rotten mood. The ecstasies and lone epiphanies of the morning museum eventually evaporate, and by late afternoon, after a mediocre, overpriced lunch has made you sluggish, you are ready to turn the big guns on yourself. To travel is to brood, and especially if you are your sole company. I would go so far as to recommend traveling alone as an excellent way of catching up with all the poor opinions of yourself that you may have had to suppress during the busy, camouflaging work year, when it is necessary to appear a self-approving, winning member of society.

I remember one such afternoon in beautiful Florence when the charm I derived from my personality was at a low point. I had mapped out my agenda for a visit to the nearby hill town of Fiesole. Though I could have taken the excursion bus near my hotel, I commanded myself to hike, ostensibly because it was good exercise, and because you see so much more on foot, but in actuality, I realize now, to punish myself.

As I slogged uphill past "rows of cypresses and sumptuous villas" (Michelin guide), my mind was so filled with worthless thoughts that broke off and told me so little—that I had the impression not of a walk through a real landscape but of one continuous spiteful déjà vu. It was a playback of all those times I had walked enviously and stupidly through the world of rich houses where I didn't belong. Nothing less than owning a villa, *any* villa, on this Italian hill would satisfy me. Yet I saw so little of the actual residences I coveted, their gardens or marble sculptures or whatever I was supposed to look at, that even in my surly mood this envy struck me as comic. Envy for a landscape I took so little trouble to observe? Perhaps we only envy that which we look at superficially; and a deeper look would take care of our urge for possession? Nah. In any case, I kept walking.

I arrived at a flat village square cut into the hill, where tourist buses were parked in the afternoon heat. Fiesole. Was it sunny? Clouded over? I wasn't interested enough to notice. I headed for a café that seemed to exist on the trade of tourists waiting for their bus driver to return from who knows where and start his engine. I sat down at the nickel-plated soda fountain, with the momentarily satisfied sense of having stumbled on a "find." Not that the stopover was attractive, but it was at least an oasis of decrepitude: there were dusty cutout doll books and movie magazines, and a faded Italian novelization of Erich Segal's *Love Story*. I ordered a Campari, hoping for a mindless respite. Yet just as soon as I had drained it, a spasm of restlessness overcame me and I paid and walked out.

By now I was thoroughly fed up with my impatience. I was determined to slow down and practice "the discipline of seeing." It was a sometime conviction of mine that, wherever one found oneself, the world was rich enough to yield enjoyment if one but paid close attention to the details. Or, as John Cage once said, when something bores you, keep looking at it and after a while you will find it intriguing. Inside, however, I rebelled against this notion, which struck me as forced quietism—an aestheticizing trick to bring about the opposite of what one knows to be true. The day is boring, horrible? Very well, that's the card I've been dealt. Let's not pretend it's any better.

I was still arguing these two positions when I sat down on a bench overlooking what I knew most people would think a magnificent vista. All of the Arno Valley and Florence were stretched before us. The city fathers had wisely provided benches. Not only was this undeniably and obviously a magnificent vista, but it was an "officially recognized" magnificent vista, even more annoying. But then, what *had* escaped the tourist industry's exploitative eye in Italy? Where could one find any beauty in this country that was fresh and unframed?

This line of thinking soon struck me as foolish petulance. The truth is, I loved Italy, so what was I whining about?

I literally forced myself to concentrate on the Italian family a few benches over. The son was leaning semidangerously over the hilltop. That could be interesting. But then he sat down next to his father, who was cutting an orange rind circularly with a fruit knife. I wondered if this orange paring was an Old World custom. (Vapid anthropologizing to replace self-ennui.) The mother was taking thick sandwiches out of a plastic bag and handing them all around. They seemed a big, warm, friendly family—two daughters, one son, a father, a mother—speaking casually to each other, eating their picnic lunch, playing with the dog.

To fathom the secret of that Italian familial harmony, I watched them covertly for ten minutes, dividing my attention between their interactions and the landscape below, and came to the conclusion that they weren't as warm as I had originally given them credit for. They simply ate a great deal. The more I watched them, the more it dawned on me that there was absolutely nothing exceptional about them. That in itself was unusual. Most families yield up fairly rich pathologies, but this one did not interest me in any conceivable way. My hypothesis about steady attention to detail was being contradicted.

At about this time an elderly Italian man, tall, angular, bald, toothless save for one top incisor, looking in his mid-seventies—about the age of my father, in fact—came up and asked with gestures if he could sit on my bench. This seemed a little odd, as there was another bench completely unoccupied, but who was I to deny a fellow-man my company if he thought he could reap some nourishment therefrom? Had I not been complaining of the burden of my solitude? Perhaps this old guy would amuse me or turn into a *vivid anecdotal experience*, the goal of all tourists at loose ends.

"What is your name?" he asked me in halting English. I told him. "And yours?" Nicola. He tried out his few English questions on me, I answered him in my limited Italian. It was the sort of conversation one has on the road often, and which seems to exist in order to prove that the stiff dialogues of phrase books are, in fact, the height of naturalism. The old man began to talk about his work in a garage (I think he said he was a retired mechanic) and to complain that now he had nothing to do. He told me about his sons, his wife, his vineyard. These Italians, I reflected, are unquenchably sociable, they love to chatter. True, I had my doubts that this was going to lead to a vivid anecdotal experience, and was already feeling bored, since I understood only one out of every three sentences, but I congratulated myself on being such a good and patient listener. The man is obviously lonely, I thought; he reminds me of the aged pensioner in De Sica's *Umberto D*; perhaps I can reap from him some necessary lesson in humility and human dignity. Meanwhile, he was talking my ear off in Italian, and I was nodding and pursuing some interior reverie about how sad it is that society is so afraid of the old, how wrong that we back off squeamishly from them, and he had just gotten to the part where he told me his wife had died when he seized my hand in an iron grip.

At first I did nothing, pretending it was a sort of international brotherhood handshake; but then I tried to pull away, and discovered that the old man was not letting go. I stared at his frayed white shirt, buttoned to the top, pulled taut by his chest; he was like a wooden plank, not a scrap of fat on him. I looked around for help to the picnicking family, but they had apparently wandered off without my noticing. Now he grinned in what seemed a possibly rather lecherous manner—at the same time trying to reassure me that he was not going to hurt me. He only wanted to hold my hand. So we sat there, my hand sweating in his. He had very large brown fingers, liver-spotted around the webs.

I immediately recalled a strange incident that had once happened to my sister. She had entered a subway car in New York and sat down next to a blind man. He had a braille book open in his lap. She stared without embarrassment at his face, which was lined, blotched as if from poison ivy. There was no reason to assume he felt her interest. It so happens that my sister is very pretty, but how could the blind man know that? Suddenly he took hold of her arm. She thought he wanted her to help guide him out of the train or across the platform, and began to explain that it wasn't her stop yet, but he paid no attention. She felt his hand working down her arm until it had captured her hand. He began squeezing each of her fingers separately, all the while kneading her palm. She could not take her eyes off their two hands, like starfish swimming locked together. She felt she should scream, but no sound came out; she just sat there, paralyzed, ashamed and, my sister admitted candidly, fascinated. "This man was an artist of hands," she recalled. He had supreme tactile sensitivity. Finally his grip loosened, he closed his eyes, and she looked down at his brown pants, which were stained near the fly. It outraged her that he might ride the subways daily and molest women and they would probably say nothing, just because he was blind.

Anyhow, this old toothless Italian next to me was by no stretch of the imagination an artist of hands. He simply had a very powerful grip. I began to speculate about his secret life, in and around his role as good family man and laborer, of chance pickups. I didn't even know if he was gay necessarily, or if he was so starved for human touch, the memory of young flesh, that it didn't matter which sex he accosted. How many tourists before me had he done this with? Were we all Americans? I wondered. If he did try any funny stuff, I thought I could hold him off. But all he seemed to be doing so far was holding my hand and smiling—every so often he would wriggle the wrist a little in the air and grin at me, as if we were both relaxing from a good arm-wrestle.

By this time other tourists had joined us on the hilltop (to my relief) and were consuming the landscape. I, too, looked down at the vista, since I had nothing better to do and was tired of trying to figure out the old man's game. Now the shifting pattern of light over the valley—a dusky evening light that brought out the muted pinks, the muddy browns, the raked greens of cultivated countryside and, in the distance, Florence, all salmon and white walls—seemed to me extremely fetching. For the first time all day, I was able to enjoy the physical world around me. Were I given to looking on the bright side, or religious allegories, or megalomania, I might say that the old man was an angel sent down by God to handcuff me to one spot and force me to attend the earth with pleasure.

I suppose part of what kept me from retrieving my hand was the flattering knowledge that *someone* at least desired me, needed me at that moment, in this place through which I had taken it upon myself to travel alone. For the longest while, neither of us said anything. Then he got up, gave me a courtly bow, muttered *"Grazie"* in a hoarse, dry voice, and strode off. Watching his bald brown head and stiff back recede, I laughed disbelievingly at what had just happened. The weirdness of it had driven away my black mood, and I kept laughing all the way home on the tourist bus. For those who do not like happy endings, my apologies.

— 26

THE DEAD FATHER: A Remembrance of Donald Barthelme

DONALD BARTHELME HAD A SQUARISH BEARD that made him look somewhat Amish and patriarchal, an effect enhanced by his clean-shaven upper lip. It took me a while to register that he had a beard but no mustache; and once I did, I could not stop wondering what sort of "statement" he was trying to make. On the one hand, it connoted Lincolnesque rectitude and dignity, like that of the ex-Surgeon General, C. Everett Koop. On the other hand, it seemed a double message: bearded and shaven, severe and roguish, having it both ways. Finally I got up the nerve to ask him, in a kidding way, why he shaved his mustache. He told me that he couldn't grow one because he'd had a cancerous growth removed from his lip. This reply made me aware of all I didn't, probably would never, know about the man, and of my inclination to misjudge him.

I loved to watch Donald. In a way, I could never get enough of him (which is something one says about a person who always withholds a part of himself. I know, because it has been said about me). We worked together for the last eight years of his life, and were close colleagues, friends, almost-friends—which was it? I found Barthelme to be an immensely decent, generous, courtly, and yet finally unforthcoming man. He was difficult to approach, partly because I (and I was not alone here) didn't know what to do with his formidable sadness, partly because neither did he. Barthelme would have made a good king: he had the capacity of Shakespearian tragic monarchs to project a large, self-isolating presence.

The combination of his beard, bulk, and steel-rimmed eyeglasses gave him a stern Ahab appearance that he was perfectly happy to let intimidate on occasion—only to soften it with a warm glint in his eye, like a ship's captain putting his trembling crew at ease. Having read Barthelme's whimsical miniatures, I had expected a smaller, more mercurial, puckish man, certainly not this big-shouldered, hard-drinking, John Wayne type. I couldn't get over the discrepancy between his physical solidity and the filigreed drollness of his art. Somewhere locked inside that large cowman's frame must have been a mischievous troll; and I kept stealing glances at

Donald to see if the little man would put in an appearance. As time went by, how-ever, I learned to read his jeweled sentences in the manly baritone my ear came to identify as intrinsically Barthelmean, and the sense of contradiction all but disap-peared. It became natural that our fin de siècle exhaustion and cultural despair should be enunciated by a tall Texan with cowboy boots.

I had been teaching in the University of Houston's creative writing program for a year—the program, started by two poets, Cynthia Macdonald and Stanley Plumly, had recruited me from New York in 1980 as their first fiction writer—when the great news came down that Donald Barthelme would be joining us. Barthelme's arrival caused universal rejoicing: this would really put our program on the map, not only because Barthelme was a "name" writer but because he was one of the handful who commanded a following among graduate writing stu-dents. Indeed, probably no other short story writer, with the exception of Raymond Carver and Anne Beattie, was more imitated by M.F.A. students in the seventies and early eighties.

I was initially surprised that a writer of Barthelme's stature would relocate to Houston. True, he had been offered an endowed chair, a hefty salary, and regular paid sabbatical leaves, but that would not normally be enough to pry most estab-lished fiction writers from their comfortable lives. The key to the "seduction" (recruitment is the eros of academia) was that Barthelme was coming home. Though by birth a Philadelphian, he had grown up in Houston and was educated at the University of Houston, the same school that would now employ him. Barthelme was still remembered around town for his youthful cultural activities, reporting for the Houston *Post*, launching the UH literary magazine, *Forum*, directing the Contemporary Art Museum in the early sixties. Then he'd gone off to New York with regional upstart energy to make his mark (like Robert Rauschenberg, Andy Warhol, Merce Cunningham: our avant-gardists almost always seem to come from the provinces), and a few decades later was returning famous—or as famous as seri-ous writers become in America. It was also a family move: his aging parents, his three brothers—Pete, Frederick, and Steve—and his sister Joan still lived in Houston or near enough by. Marion Knox, Donald's second wife, was pregnant, and they both thought Houston might be an easier place to raise a child than Lower Manhattan.

I had no idea what to expect from Barthelme as a colleague: whether the weight of such a star might throw off-kilter the fragile balance of our program. But Donald proved not to have an ounce of the prima donna in him. On the contrary, he was the ultimate team player, accepting his full share of the petty, annoying bureaucratic tasks, sitting on boring departmental committees, phoning our top applicants to convince them to choose our program, lobbying university bigwigs with his good-ole-boy communication skills. A would-be graphic artist ("the pleasure of cutting up and pasting together pictures, a secret vice," he once wrote), he designed all our posters and letter-heads. Donald had one of the most pronounced civic consciences I have ever come across, and was fond of exhorting us with the Allen Ginsberg line: "Come, let us put our queer shoulders to the wheel."

Each Tuesday noon we would have a meeting of the creative writing staff to determine policy. These lunch meetings took place on-campus in the Galaxy Room of the School of Hotel Management; eating there was like going to a barber school for a haircut. Donald would be the first to arrive. He would order a large glass of white wine, which he would ask to have refilled several times during lunch. After we had all settled in and ordered (trial and error had convinced me that, despite poignant attempts to retool the menu, only the grilled cheese sandwich was reliable), Cynthia Macdonald, the program's founding mother and an ex-opera singer, would, with her operatic sense of urgency, alert us to the latest crisis: either our graduate students were in danger of losing their teaching stipends, or some English professor was prejudiced against our majors, or the university was hedging on its budget commitments, or a visiting writer had just called to cancel a reading.

Barthelme, who abhorred stinginess, preferred to settle the smaller crises by dipping into the "Don Fund," as the discretionary monies attached to his academic chair came to be called. He thus made it possible to circumvent the bureaucracy, save the students' literary magazine, advertise an impromptu reading, or preserve the program's honor when a visiting literary dignitary like Carlos Fuentes came to town, by taking him out to a fancy restaurant.

Sometimes, however, the problem was stickier and had to be thrashed out by Cynthia, Donald, Stanley Plumly (who left after a few years, replaced by the poet Edward Hirsch), and myself, as well as a rotating visiting cast that included Ntozake Shange, Rosellen Brown, Richard Howard, Joy Williams, Jim Robison, Mary Robison, Meg Wolitzer. In the familial dynamic that developed over the years, Cynthia and Donald were Mommy and Daddy, with the rest of us siblings contending for their favor. During heated discussions Donald would often wait until everyone else had declared a position, and then weigh in with the final word, more like an arbiter than an interested party. He was good at manipulating consensus through democratic discussion to get his way; and we made it easy for him, since everyone wanted his love and approval. At times he would inhibit opposition by indicating that any further discussion on an issue he regarded as settled was extremely dumb and ill-advised. Still, when a vote did go against him, he bowed sportingly to majority will. He often seemed to be holding back from using his full clout; he was like those professional actors who give the impression at social gatherings of saving their energy for the real performance later on.

Sometimes in the midst of the meeting, I would raise my eyes and find Donald's gaze fixed on me. What did he *see?* I wondered. He would immediately look away, not liking to be spied in the act of exercising curiosity. At other times I would catch Donald at this funny habit: he would sniff his sleeve a few inches above the wrist, taking a whiff of his arm, either because he liked the smell of his sweat or because he needed to ground himself, establish contact with his body when his mind was drifting toward Mars.

Though we usually agreed on specifics, Donald believed more fully in the mission of writing programs than I could. There was much talk about having to maintain our position as one of the top three writing programs in the country. By what standards, aside from wishful thinking, this ranking had been determined I never could ascertain: presumably it had something to do with the faculty's repute, the number of applications we received, and the publishing fortunes of our alumni. In any case, Donald was ever on guard against anything that might "dilute the quality of the program." Sometimes I would recommend bringing in visiting writers who might be less well-known but who could give our students a broader perspective stylistically or multiculturally. "But are they any *good?*" Donald would demand, and I knew what he meant: if they were any good, why hadn't he heard of them?

Donald was a man with a great sense of loyalty to family, neighborhood, academic institution, and publisher. *The New Yorker* had published him throughout his career, and he believed in the worth of those who appeared in its pages; ditto, those authors active on the executive board of PEN, the international writers organization. The other side of the coin was that he showed a massive incuriosity toward writers outside the mainstream or his personal network. If a novelist was recommended to us for a teaching post by his brother Rick—arriving under the familial mantle, as it were—he would display serious interest. But if you mentioned a good living writer he didn't know, his response was a quick veto. There was something of the air of a Mafia don about Barthelme's protection: he treated his own circle of friends (Grace Paley, Ann Beattie, Roger Angell, Susan Sontag) as family, and he proposed their names for our reading series year after year. His refusal to consider literary figures who were not inside his particular spotlight used to drive me up the wall, partly because it seemed to leave out many worthy small press/experimental writers and partly because I had not escaped the hell of anonymity so long ago or so conclusively as not to identify with these "unknown" wretches. But from Donald's point of view, I had nothing to worry about; I was good enough to be on the writing faculty team, therefore I was one of the saved.

Ironically, Barthelme was himself an experimental, iconoclastic writer, so that there was a certain contradiction between his antitraditional literary side and his involvement in rank, the Establishment, continuity. (What else is being a teacher but an assertion of belief in continuity?)

There was always a formal side to Barthelme that I associate with the English— a Victorian dryness he used to comic effect. It crops up in his earliest stories, like the "The Big Broadcast of 1938": "Having acquired in exchange for an old house that had been theirs, his and hers, a radio or more properly radio *station*, Bloomsbury could now play 'The Star Spangled Banner,' which he had always admired immoderately, on account of its finality, as often as he liked." This qualifying, donnish quality was accompanied by an equally British terseness in social situations. "I think not," he would say in response to some proposal he considered dubious, and that would be that.

Or he would signal the conversation was at an end for him by taking your arm at the elbow and guiding you off on your rounds. I was at first astonished by this gesture, which seemed like an eruption of regal impatience. At the same time, I found something reassuring in his physical steering of me, like a father picking up his child and placing him out of harm's way.

Much of Donald Barthelme's fiction consists of witty dialogue. Yet when I think of Donald in real life, I recall few bon mots; I remember rather his underlying silence, which has now, in death, prevailed. Silence seemed his natural condition; his speech had very little flow: you never knew when it was going to dry up. Of course, Donald talked well, in the sense that he chose his words economically and with care. His listeners would often smile at the sardonic spin he gave to well-worn figures of speech. (Among others writers, I've known only John Ashbery to take as much delight in fingering clichés.) But the pearls of wit or wisdom one might have expected from him were rare; and this was because, I think, fundamentally he did not view speech as the vehicle for expressing his inner thoughts. Rather, he treated speech as a wholly social medium, to which he subscribed as a solid, dues-paying citizen, dipping into the common fount.

What one looks for in the conversation of writers is a chance to be taken back into the kitchen where they cook up their literary surprises: a sudden flash of truth or metaphor. Around Donald, what you got was not so much the lyrical, imaginative Barthelme as the one who re-created social intercourse like a game, a tennis match, with parrying one-liners keeping the interlocutor off-balance. His remarks tended to stop rather than advance conversation.

When you waxed serious around Donald, you would expect to have your wings clipped, since he regarded getting worked up about anything in public as inappropriate. "Down, boy," he frequently mocked if I started to expatiate on a subject. These interventions felt more like a fond head-pat than anything malicious. But I never could figure out if he consistently played the referee in order to keep everyone around him at a temperature suitable for his own comfort, or out of some larger sense of group responsibility, which, in his eyes, conflicted with solo flights of enthusiasm.

Barthelme clearly considered it bad form to talk about books or the writing process in public. Perhaps he thought it too pedantic a topic to bring before intellectually mixed company. It also appeared that, toward the end of his life, he was bored with literature, much preferring the visual arts.

I had hoped, given the countless intellectual references sprinkled throughout Barthelme's stories, that the author of "Kierkegaard Unfair to Schlegel" and "Eugénie Grandet" would be as eager as I was to discuss our favorite authors. As it turned out, asking Barthelme what he thought was like demanding a trade secret, though I never gave up clumsily trying to pry loose his literary opinions. Once, at a brunch, on learning that the Swiss writer Max Frisch, who interested me, was a friend of Donald's, I immediately asked, "What do you think of Frisch's work?" I had either put the question too directly or shown too naked a desire for a glimpse at a higher circle (those writers of international stature, Frisch and Barthelme included) to let my curiosity be indulged, or Donald's feelings toward the Swiss writer were too complex or competitive for him to untangle them in public. Such speculations proliferate in the absence of a definite answer. Donald managed a grudging few syllables, to the effect that he thought Frisch's work "substantial," though "the fellow has a pretty big ego." He seemed much more comfortable discussing the rumor that Frisch might be buying an expensive loft in Soho.

This professional reticence, I should add, was by no means singular to Donald. Part of the larger loneliness of our literary life stems from the fact that writers, especially those who have reached a successful level, tend to shy away from discussing the things one would think mattered to them most—the other authors who continue to inspire them or the unsolved obstacles in their day-to-day composition—preferring instead to chatter about career moves, visiting gigs, grants, word processors, and real estate, all of which become, in effect, the language of power.

Once, when I managed to get Donald off by myself (we were driving to some forlorn suburb in outer Houston to make a fund-raising presentation), he indulged my hunger for candid literary talk. I asked him what he thought of several recent novels by Texas writers of our acquaintance. He didn't mince words; his assessments were extremely pointed and shrewd. It was exhilarating to gain admittance to the inner tabernacle of Barthelme's judgment—not to mention the fact that two writers dissecting the flaws of a third contemporary can bond them in a deliciously fratricidal way. But, to my regret, the experience was never repeated.

Perhaps because Donald had begun as a newspaperman, he still had a fair amount of the journalist left in him, which included not only a topical alertness to fashions but a heavy-drinking, hard-boiled, almost anti-intellectual downplaying of his own identity as practitioner of serious literature. I remember his boasting once that he'd dashed off a review on a *Superman* sequel, a "piece of hackwork for some glossy for a nice piece of change." Yet when the review came out, I saw that Donald had, as usual, given good weight, with an elegantly amusing, well-constructed essay. Barthelme always worked conscientiously to get the least piece of prose right. But like the A student who hates to admit he studied for a test, he preferred the pretense that he was a glorified grub working to pay the bills. I think he would have *liked* to have been a hack; it was a persistent fantasy of escape from his literary conscience. He fit into that debunking, up-from-journalism tradition of American satirists: Twain, Bierce, Ring Lardner. The problem was that his faux-hack pose made it difficult for you to take your own writing seriously in front of him, or discuss other literature with any seriousness.

Barthelme also seemed uncomfortable with psychological conversation, which was either too intimate or too tattling for his taste. His writings make it clear that he was quite astute at character analysis; and yet there was a curious antipsychological side to him, or at least a resistance to discussing such things aloud; in this he was both a gentleman of the old school and a postmodernist. One time Donald and I were talking after a meeting about one of our colleagues, who had thrown a fit over some procedural matter. I remarked with a smile that she seemed to take a certain pleasure in releasing her wrath all the way. Donald replied that he'd known people who had had temper tantrums just for the fun of it, but surely not someone as mature as our colleague. This seemed a perfect instance of Donald's loyalty: having decided that someone was a "good guy," he did not like to acknowledge that that person might still be capable of childish or self-indulgent behavior.

Once or twice a year Marion and Don would invite me to their house: they'd either give a dinner party or ask my girlfriend and me over for a two-couple evening. Sometimes, after a particularly happy night of warm, sparkling talk and wonderful food (both Barthelmes were superb cooks) and plentiful wine, I would think, Donald and I are actually becoming friends. I would fall under the spell of the man's gruff charm, morality, intelligence; it was like having a crush; I couldn't wait to see him again soon and take it further. But there never was any further.

I would run into him at school and say, "I really enjoyed the other evening at your house, Don."

"Well, good, good," he would reply nervously, which was his favorite way of dismissing a topic. Perhaps he was simply being modest about their hospitality; but I also thought his uneasy look expressed concern that I would start to get "mushy" on him, and make demands for a closeness he had no inclination or ability to fulfill. What I wanted was to remove the evening from the category of "dutiful community socializing that had turned out well" and place it under the file of "possible developing friendship." But the story of Barthelme's and my friendship seemed forever stalled in the early chapters; there was no accrual of intimacy from one time to the next.

In trying to account for this stasis, I often wondered if it was a question of age. Twelve years separated us, an awkward span: I was too old and set as a writer to inspire the parental fondness he bestowed on his favorite graduate students, but too young to be accepted as a peer. I was the same age, in fact, as his younger brother Frederick, who was enjoying considerable success; if anything, insurgent writers twelve years younger may have seemed to him enviable pups, breathing down his neck. Then again, the appetite for shared confidences often dwindles after fifty; at that point some writers begin to husband their secrets for the page. In any case, I sensed that he'd become used to accepting rather passively the persistent courtship by others (which is not my mode). As a woman novelist said to me: "Donald sits there on the couch and expects you to make a pass at him."

I got a deeper glimpse into his own thinking on friendship one night at a dinner party at the Barthelmes' apartment in Houston. After dinner, Donald and I settled into a rare personal conversation. I asked him if he showed his work to anyone before he sent it off for publication. He said he showed Marion; that was about it. I then inquired if he had any close friends who were his peers with whom he could talk writing. He surprised me by saying he didn't think so. He said he had had two good friends, and they had both died. One was Thomas B. Hess, the other Harold Rosenberg, both well-known art critics. "I started hanging around them in the sixties. They were older than me and they were my mentors, and it was great that we could talk about art and not necessarily about literature. They taught me a whole lot. I haven't learned anything since. I'm still working off that old knowledge. It was distressing how they both died around the same time, which left me feeling rather . . . odd," he said. "What I really want are older men, father figures who can teach *me* something. I don't want to be people's damn father figure. I want to be the baby—it's more fun. The problem is that the older you get, the harder it is to find these older role models."

A reluctant patriarch, still looking for the good father. Having been on that same search off and on, I understood some of Donald's loneliness. It doesn't matter how old you get, you still have an ache for that warm understanding. He began talking about his own father, Donald Barthelme Sr., a highly respected architect in Texas. His father, he said, had been "very uptight" with them when they were growing up: "I think he was terrified of children." As an architecture professor, Barthelme senior always tried to get the better of his students and demonstrate his superior knowledge. "Well of course we know more than our students, that's not the point!" said Donald.

I thought of his novel *The Dead Father* and wondered whether that title had irked Barthelme senior, who was (and is still) very much alive. The book is Barthelme's best novel and one of his finest achievements. In this part parody, part serious Arthurian romance, the Dead Father is an active character, boasting, complaining, demanding attention. Like a corpse that will not acknowledge its demise, this patriarch who has been "killed" (or at least put in the shade) by his more successful son seems to represent the dead weight of guilt in the Oedipal triumph. *The Dead Father* is an obsessive meditation on generational competitiveness, the division between younger and older men, and the fear of time's decaying hand.

Many of Barthelme's short stories revolve around Oedipal tensions implicit in education, mentorship, and the master-flunky tie. Take, for instance, "The King of Jazz," where Hokie Mokie blows away the young Japanese challenger in a jam session, or "Conversations with Goethe," where the narrator-flunky is triumphantly put in his place at the end:

> Critics, Goethe said, are the cracked mirror in the grand ballroom of the creative spirit. No, I said, they were, rather, the extra baggage on the great cabriolet of conceptual progress. "Eckermann," said Goethe, "*shut up*."

I always winced when I heard Barthelme read that story aloud (as he often did), partly because of the glee he seemed to express at maintaining the upper hand and partly because of the hint—at least I took it that way—that any friendship with him would have to grow out of an inferior's flattery.

Sometimes it seemed that Donald not only was bored with everyone around him but had ceased to expect otherwise. In Houston he drew his social circle from mildly awed professionals—doctors, lawyers, etc.—who could produce a soothing harmonious patter into which he would insert an occasional barb to perk things up. Mostly Donald preferred to stand back, making sure the social machinery was running smoothly.

In his distance from us, he seemed to be monitoring some inner unease. I suppose that was partly his alcoholism. No matter how sociably engaged alcoholics are, one corner of their minds will always be taking stock of the liquor supply and plotting how to get in another drink without being too obvious about it. I never saw Donald falling-down drunk; he held his liquor, put on a good performance of sobriety; but, as he once admitted, "I'm a little drunk all the time." Sometimes, when he drank a lot, his memory blacked out.

Example: During a spring break Cynthia Macdonald delegated me to phone Donald in New York and find out which students he wanted to recommend for a prestigious fellowship. I called him around eight in the evening, and he gave his recommendations, then asked me a series of questions about departmental matters, raises, courses for next year, etc. A few days later Cynthia called him and mentioned in passing the telephone conversation he had had with me. Donald insisted he had not spoken to me in weeks. Cynthia told me to call him again, this time making sure it was before five o'clock, when the chances for sobriety were greater. The odd part is that when I did call him, we had the identical conversation: he put the same questions in the same order, with the same edgy impatience, quickly voicing one question as soon as I had answered the last. I never let on that he was repeating himself, but it struck me that he must often have been on automatic pilot, fooling the world with rote questions while his mind was clouded by alcohol.

At times he gave the impression, like a burn victim lying uncomfortably in the hospital, that there was something I was neglecting to do or figure out that might have put him at greater ease. Perhaps there is always a disappointment that an alcoholic feels in a nonalcoholic: an awareness that, no matter how sympathetic the nondrinker may seem, he will never really "get" it. That was certainly true for me: I didn't get it. I knew Donald disapproved of my not drinking—or not drinking enough. He once objected to our holding a meeting at my house, saying, "Phillip never has any liquor on hand." Which wasn't true, but interesting that he should think so. The noon meeting took place at my apartment anyhow; Donald arrived with a bottle, just in case.

I also think he disapproved, if that's the word, of my not philandering. When an artist in town began openly having an extramarital affair and most of the Houston arts community sided with his wife, Donald reassured the man that these things happened, telling him comparable experiences from his past. One of the ways Donald bonded with someone was through a shared carnal appetite—what used to be called a "vice," like drinking or womanizing.

In keeping with his Southwestern upbringing, Donald combined the strong, silent dignity of the Western male with the more polished gallantry of the South. He liked to be around women, particularly younger women, and grew more relaxed in their company. I don't think this was purely a matter of lechery, though lust no doubt played its classical part. The same enchantment showed in his delight with his older daughter, Anne, a vibrant, outgoing girl from an earlier marriage, who had been brought up largely by her mother in Scandinavia and who came to live with the Barthelmes while studying theater at the University of Houston. Given Barthelme's own (to use his phrase) "double-minded" language, hemmed in by the ironies of semantic duplicity, girl talk must have seemed a big relief. In his novel *Paradise* (1986), the hero, a middle-aged architect named Simon, shares an apartment with three beautiful young women and seems to enjoy listening in on their conversation about clothes, makeup, and jobs as much as sleeping with them.

In *The Dead Father*, Barthelme shows an awareness of the way a fifty-year-old's interest in young women might look to one's wife:

> Fifty-year-old boys . . . are boys because they don't want to be old farts, said Julie. The old fart is not cherished in this society. . . . Stumbling from the stage is anathema to them, said Julie, they want to be nuzzling new women when they are ninety.
>
> What is wrong with that? asked the Dead Father. Seems perfectly reasonable to me.
>
> The women object, she said. Violently.

Certainly some of the women in the writing program objected to what they felt was Barthelme's preference for the pretty young females in class. I ended up being a sort of confidant of the middle-aged women students, who had raised families and were finally fulfilling their dreams to become writers; several complained to me that Barthelme would make short shrift of their stories, for being too domestic and psychological. Of course, these were the very materials I had encouraged them to explore. It's true that Donald once said to me if he had to read another abortion or grandmother story, he would pack it in. I understood that what he really objected to was the solemn privileging of certain subjects over linguistic or formal invention; but I was sufficiently competitive with him for the students' love that it pleased me to hear their beefs. They also claimed that his real pets were the talented young men. This is a standard pattern in the writing program, with its hierarchies of benediction. I, too, observed how certain of our top male students would gravitate to Barthelme, and how he not only would help edit their books—and get them publishers and agents—but would invite them to hang out with him as his friend. Perhaps "jealous" is too strong a word, but I was certainly a little envious of their easy access to Donald.

In the classroom Donald could be crusty, peremptorily sitting a student down after a few pages of a story that sounded unpromising to him—a practice his favorites endorsed as honest and toughening-up; those less sure of their abilities took longer to recover. His true generosity as a teacher shone, I thought, in individual conferences, where he would go over students' manuscripts he had line-edited as meticulously as if they had been his own. Often, as I was leaving, I would see a queue waiting outside his office; he put many more hours into student conferences than I did. I sensed that in the last years his main reading was student work—or at least he led me to believe that. When I would ask Don what he'd been reading lately, he replied, "Class stories, theses. Who has time for anything else?"

Donald loved to play talent scout. When one of his graduate students finished a manuscript he thought was publishable, he would call up his agent, Lynn Nesbit, and some New York editors, maybe start a few fires at *The New Yorker*. I was reluctant to take on this role with students: both because I wasn't sure I had the power to pull it off and because I didn't like the way the writing program's success stories generated a bitter atmosphere among the unanointed. But Donald acknowledged no such side effects: to him, each book contract drew more attention to the program and simply made us "hotter." The students, whatever qualms they may have had about the hazards of Brat Pack careerism, wanted a Godfather to promote them. They were no dummies; they knew that one word from Barthelme could lead to publication.

It's embarrassing to admit, but a few times I also tried to get Donald to use his influence in my behalf. That he had a measure of power in the literary world became steadily clearer to me from remarks he would drop at our lunchtime meetings: how he had helped so-and-so receive a lucrative prize, or had worked behind the scenes at the American Academy of Arts and Letters to snare honors for the "good guys." The Prix de Rome, given out by the Academy, went to several of his protégés in the space of a few years. Well, if goodies were being handed out, what the heck, I wanted some too. Once I asked him shamelessly (trying to make it sound like a joke), "Why don't you ever recommend me for a Prix de Rome or one of those prizes?" After a stunned pause, he answered, "I think they're interested in younger men, Phillip."

Flattering as it was to be told I was past the point of needing such support, I suspected more was involved. During the eight years we taught together, two of my books were published; I sent them to Donald for advance quotes, but he always managed to misplace the galleys until long after a blurb would have done any good. By then I'd had enough good quotes; what disappointed me more was that Donald had not responded to my work.

Months after the time had passed for Donald to "blurb" my novel *The Rug Merchant*, I continued to hope that he would at least read the book and tell me honestly what he thought. I asked him a few times if he had gotten to it yet, and he said, "Regrettably, no." Finally, I must have made enough of a pest out of myself to have an effect. We were sitting together at a party, and by this point in the evening Barthelme was pretty well in his cups. His speech slurred, he said he had read my novel and "it was a good job." He was sorry the main character, Cyrus, had not gotten round to marrying the girl in the end. "Anyway—a good job," he said again, tapping my knee.

In that neurotic way we have of probing a loose tooth, I brooded that Donald didn't like my writing. More likely, he simply felt indifferent toward it. A few times he did compliment me on something I'd written, usually after having seen it in a magazine. But I was insatiable, because his approval meant so much to me—a long-awaited sign of love from the emotionally remote father. The irony is that I so longed for approval from a writer whose own work I didn't entirely accept. Our aesthetics were worlds apart: I was interested in first-person confessional writing and the tradition of psychological realism, whereas Barthelme seemed to be debunking the presumptions of realist fiction. I suppose the fact that this blessing would have come from someone who was not in my literary camp but who represented the other orthodoxy, formalism, seemed to make it all the more desirable. I imagined—craved—a reconciliation, a pure respect between his and my style in some impossible utopian space of literary exchange.

For a long while I felt secretly guilty toward Donald because I did not love his work enough. I respected it, of course, but in a detached way. When I first began reading Donald Barthelme in the sixties, he struck me as a trickster, playfully adjusting a collection of veils, impossible to pin down. Later, when I got to know Donald, I saw that almost every line of his was a disguised personal confession—if nothing else, then of inner weather and melancholy: he was masterful at casting deep shadows through just the right feints, a sort of matador courting and dodging meaning, sometimes even letting himself be gored by it for the sake of the story. Recently, the more I read him, the more I come to the conclusion that he *was* a great writer. Minor, yes, but great at his chosen scale. He could catch sorrow in a sentence. A dozen of his stories are amazing and will last.

The bulk of his best work, to my mind, was done in the sixties: we sometimes forget how energized Barthelme was by the counterculture, the politics and playful liberatory urges of that period. His peak lasted through the early seventies, up to and including *The Dead Father* (1975). After that, his fiction lost much of its emotional openness, devolving on the whole into clever, guarded pastiche. Always the professional, he could still cobble together a dazzling sentence or amusing aperçu, but he became increasingly a master of trifles. There is, however, something noble in a great talent adapting itself to diminished capacities. His 1986 novel, *Paradise*, is a sweet if thin fabrication. Between the lines of its sportive harem plot, one can read an honest admission of burnout. Donald confessed to me that he thought the book "pretty weak," and I hope I had the hypocrisy to hide my agreement. *Paradise* is honest, too, in departing from his earlier intellectual references and in reflecting the creature comforts that engaged him mentally during his last years: food, decor, and sex.

As he got older and was drawn more to comfort, Houston seemed an appropriate choice of residence. It is an easy city to live in—not as stimulating as one might like at times, but pleasant. The Barthelmes lived on the second floor of a brick Tudor house in one of the city's most beautiful areas, the oak-lined South Boulevard. Just across the street was Poe School, an excellent elementary school where his little girl, Katharine, started to go when she was old enough. Nearby were the tennis courts where Marion played regularly. In Houston the Barthelmes enjoyed more of a black-tie, upper-middle-class life than in New York, going regularly to the opera, the symphony, the ballet; Donald became a city booster, telling outsiders that the Houston performing companies were good and getting better every year. Houston proved an ideal place for him to act out his civic impulse: of the ten established writers in town, each one called upon to do his or her community share, Donald was the most famous and most cherished, being a native son. This was what his compatriots in the New York literary world, for whom his resettlement in Texas seemed a perverse self-exile, found so hard to understand.

I remember telling one of Don's Manhattan friends, who was worried that he might be wasting away down there, how packed the literary life was in Houston, how needed he was. Secretly I asked myself whether living in Houston had indeed dried up some of his creative juices. Having never known Barthelme during his "conquering years," I had no way to compare; but I suspect that Houston was not a factor. His creative crisis had already started in the late seventies, when he was still living in New York; if anything, he may have accepted the move to Texas partly in the hope of being shaken out of stagnation and personal loss.

Barthelme's sardonic, Olympian use of brand names in his fiction led me to the mistaken idea that he took a dim view of consumerism, whereas I found him to be more a happy captive of it. He would often talk to me about new types of VCRs or personal computers, a sports car he was fantasizing buying, or the latest vicissitudes with his pickup truck—assuming incorrectly that I knew as much as the typical American male about machines. He was also very interested in food: I would run into him shopping at the supermarket, wicker basket in hand, throwing in a package of tortellini; one time he began talking about the varieties of arugula and radicchio, then added that he could never leave the place without spending a fortune. "They create these needs and you can't resist. They've figured out a way to hook you," he said.

These disquisitions on arugula were not exactly what I had hoped for from Barthelme. I kept waiting for him to give me more of his innermost thoughts. But later I began to think: suppose I had been misinterpreting him all along, because of my own Brooklyn-Jewish expectations of conversation—that mixture of confiding anecdote, analytic "delving," and intellectual disputation—when in fact he was disclosing his inner self with every remark, and I was too dumb or incredulous to perceive it. Maybe he was not trying to frustrate me by holding back the goods of his interior life, but was confiding his preoccupation with things, comforts, sensual pleasures.

And why couldn't I accept that? I seemed to have to view it as a copout, a retreat into banality; I wanted him to stand up and be the staunch intellectual hero-father. Part of me responded with a line from Ernest Becker's *The Denial of Death*: "The depressed person enslaves himself to the trivial." Another part suspected that I, longtime bachelor, was merely envious of his settled domestic family life. It should be clear by now that Donald Barthelme was an enormously evocative figure for me. The difficulty is distinguishing between what was really Donald and what he evoked in me—not necessarily the same thing. If I came to regard Donald as the prisoner of a bourgeois lifestyle dedicated to discreet good taste, down to the popular Zurburán reproduction of fruit above his dining room table, this probably says less about Donald than about my own pathological attraction-repulsion vis-à-vis the Good Life, or what passes in today's world for joie de vivre.

No doubt Barthelme *was* often depressed and withdrawn, underneath all that fixation on obtainable pleasures. But he also seemed reasonably contented much of the time, at home with Marion and his two daughters. The younger Barthelme had written scornfully about married life: "The world in the evening seems fraught with the absence of promise, if you are a married man. There is nothing to do but go home and drink your nine drinks and forget about it" ("Critique de la Vie Quotidienne"). The later Barthelme, now remarried, wrote in "Chablis":

> I'm sipping a glass of Gallo Chablis with an ice cube in it, smoking, worrying. I worry that the baby may jam a kitchen knife into an electrical outlet while she's wet. I've put those little plastic plugs into all the electrical outlets but she's learned how to pop them out. I've checked the Crayolas. They've made the Crayolas safe to eat—I called the head office in Pennsylvania. She can eat a whole box of Crayolas and nothing will happen to her. If I don't get the new tires for the car I can buy the dog.

The tires, the baby, the Crayolas, the dog: the tone seems more fondly engaged with domesticity. If the later stories seem to have lost an edge, it's also possible that Donald was simply happier.

His moments of joy seemed most often connected with his child of middle age, Katharine, whom he was smitten by and who was in truth a remarkably adorable, lively, bright little girl. I remember once hailing him as he carried Katharine on his shoulders across the street. "We're just setting off for an ice cream cone," he explained, blushing to his roots as if I had come upon a guilty secret. I had indeed caught him at his most unguarded, a doting father-horsie, without his irony or gravity buckled on.

When Donald went back to New York for the summer months, he became slightly more nervous and speedy—or, as Marion put it ruefully, he "reverted to Type A"; but for that very reason, I think, I felt closer to, more in harmony with him there. In New York, also, we were removed from the demands of the writing program, and so I found it easier to pretend that we were not only colleagues but friends. The Barthelmes had retained, after protracted warfare with the landlord, their great floor-through apartment on West Eleventh Street: the walls were painted Pompeiian red; a large framed Ingres poster greeted the visitor; the radio was usually tuned to jazz; on the coffee table were oversized art books, often with texts by friends, such as Ann Beattie's *Alex Katz*. Barthelme may have been a postmodernist, but his furnishings held to the scrupulous purity of high modernism, the leather and chrome of MOMA's design galleries. As soon as you entered, Donald offered you a drink, and it was bad form to refuse, if only because your not having one undercut his pretext for imbibing. He was an extremely gracious host, perhaps overdoing the liquor refills, but otherwise attentive as a Bedouin to your comfort.

In May of 1987, by a coincidence having nothing to do with Donald, I sublet an apartment in the same brownstone on West Eleventh Street where the Barthelmes lived. Kirkpatrick and Faith Sale, their writer-editor friends, occupied the garden apartment below them, and I was two flights up in a tiny studio, sublet from an ailing Finn who had gone back to his native country for medical treatment. Though the building had more than its share of literary vibrations and timeworn, rent-stabilized charm, I quickly grew dissatisfied with my bare studio cubicle. It overlooked the street and was very noisy, especially on weekends, when the rowdy packs spilling out of Ray's Pizza on Sixth Avenue clamored up the block.

Donald knocked on my door the day he arrived in New York (I had preceded him by three weeks) and immediately began rearranging my room. "That bed doesn't belong there," he said, pointing to the Finn's futon. "The lamp's in the wrong place too." The interior decorator side of Donald took over; I became passively content to let him dictate the proper placement of objects. He insisted on loaning me some excess furniture from his apartment, and in no time at all I had an attractive Scandinavian rug, a chair ("You can borrow my Wassily chair—it's a facsimile of the Breuer"), a typewriter table, a trunk that would do as a coffee table, and some art posters for the walls. He kept running up and down stairs, hauling pieces from the basement storage.

Donald was a true good neighbor, and I could see he was delighted to have hit upon a way to help me. As long as I expected any sort of intimacy from him, it made him uncomfortable, but if I approached him as one generic human being to another, with a problem that needed fixing, he would be there instantly. If I had a flat tire, if my car engine needed a start-up, if I lacked home furnishings, I knew I could come to Donald for help. This neighborliness and common decency struck me as very Texan. Once, when my apartment in Houston had been burglarized and all my appliances stolen, Donald offered to loan me the little black-and-white television he and Marion used to keep in the kitchen for the evening news while they were preparing dinner. The generosity of this sacrifice I understood only when I returned the set three months later and saw how happy they were to get it back.

In any case, that summer Donald continued to take an active interest in my housing situation; and when I found a charming one-bedroom apartment on Bank Street, three blocks away, and signed a two-year lease, he went with me to have a look. By now I had accepted him as my habitational guru. Through his eyes I suddenly saw it as much smaller than I'd remembered, but he passed over that in silence. "Very nice. Very nice. If I were you, though, I'd have these wall stains removed," he said. "It's simple to do. I can help. Also, if you decide to paint the place, I'm good at paint jobs."

Here was a man who had barely addressed ten sentences to me during the past six months in Houston, and now he was volunteering to paint my house and wash the stains from my walls. I tabled the repainting idea, but I did enlist Donald's help in lugging my belongings the three blocks from West Eleventh to Bank Street. On the Saturday I moved, it was ninety-four degrees, naturally, and several trips were required, and we must have looked a sight, Sancho Panza and the Don with his scraggly beard, pulling boxes roped together on a small dolly. At one point it tipped over and spilled half my papers onto the sidewalk. After that, I let Donald carry the lion's share of the weight, he having a broader back and a greater liking (I told myself) for manual labor, as well as more steering ability. He was hilarious on the way over, joking about the indignity of being a beast of burden, and I must admit it tickled me to think of using one of America's major contemporary writers as a dray-horse. But why not take advantage when he seemed so proud of his strength, so indestructible, even in his mid-fifties?

When I was set up in my new apartment, I invited the Barthelmes over for Sunday brunch. It was both a return for the many dinner parties they had invited me to and a way of asserting that I was now a responsible adult entertaining on my own. Marion, who had just been in Vermont with Katharine, showed up looking radiant and tanned in a sundress. Donald was ill-at-ease that day, as though having to get through an unpleasant obligation—or else hung-over. I remember there was a direct overhead sun out on the terrace that bothered him into changing his seat several times, and made me worry about the food melting. I had overdone the spread, with so much lox and bagels, quiche, focaccia, orange juice, fruit, pie, and coffee as to leave little room for our plates. But I pulled out all the stops to be amusing, and gradually Donald began to unbend as we sat out on the terrace gabbing about the latest plays and movies and art shows and people we knew. Meanwhile, Katharine had discovered the hammock, and was having a great time bouncing in and out of it and performing "risqué" peekaboo fandangos. As usual, she and I flirted, Donald pretended to look paternally askance, and Marion was ladylike, furthering the conversation with her journalist's bright curiosity while supervising Katharine with a light hand.

Whenever, in the face of his opaque silence, I began wondering if I had fallen out of Barthelme's good graces, someone would reassure me: "Oh, but Don's very fond of you. He always asks after you in an interested way." During the spring semester of 1988, however, I kept having the feeling that Donald was becoming cooler toward me. Interactions that used to take up thirty-five seconds were now clipped to twelve. Nor had I been invited to the Barthelme house for their customary dinner. Had I done something to offend him? I raised the question to Ed Hirsch, who was closer to Donald than I was, and Ed told me that he had detected the same curtness in Barthelme of late—which consoled me, I must admit.

Then on April 15 we received the awful, sickening news that Donald had had to go to the hospital for throat cancer. His doctor, we learned now, had been treating it with antibiotics, but eventually decided an operation would be necessary, as the tumor turned out to be larger than originally thought. All along Donald had kept his illness secret from us, whether out of privacy or stoicism scarcely matters. I was ashamed that I had been taking his withdrawal personally. We were told he would be in the hospital anywhere from five to fourteen days, but not to visit him there, as he didn't want people seeing him in such condition.

About a week after he had come home from the hospital, and we were informed it was all right to pay a brief visit, I dropped by the Barthelme house. Knowing his love for jazz, I had bought him five archival jazz albums as a get-well present. With his newly shaven chin, Donald looked harshly exposed and rubicund. His eyes were dazed. He had a tube running from his nose to his mouth like an elephant's proboscis; its purpose was to feed him liquids, as his throat was still too sore to take in solids.

We sat in his living room, staring across at each other, having nothing to say. When I handed him the stack of jazz records, he patted them wordlessly, without bothering to examine what they were. Though I knew he must be extremely weak, I still felt hurt: wouldn't he have at least read the titles if someone he liked more had brought them? I told myself I was being ridiculous, the man was gravely ill—put ego aside for once!—and began cranking up conversation. As usual, Donald was the master of one-liners. "Demerol is great stuff." And: "I'm tired of sounding like Elmer Fudd." The tube pinching his nose did make his speech sound gurgled.

He asked testily about our having moved to offer someone a teaching position for next year while he was in the hospital. Though Donald definitely liked the writer, I sensed an undercurrent of breached protocol. I explained that it was an emergency and we couldn't keep the man waiting any longer. "Well, good, good," he said. I apologized for our having acted without his final input. Barthelme nodded. His daughter Katharine ran into the room, naked and wet. "Don't look at me!" she commanded. "I just took a showw-er!" Donald smiled, followed her with his eyes. I excused myself after another minute or two. A painful half hour.

The next week, though there was really no need for him to do so, Donald came to our Tuesday lunch meeting. He said he was bored hanging around the house. He also seemed to be telling us with this visit: I may be sick but it doesn't mean I'm giving up my stake in the program. Perhaps because he was up and about, and therefore one expected an improvement, his pasty, florid appearance shocked me more than when I had seen him at home. He looked bad. We wanted him to go home and lie down, not sit through our boring agenda.

I could only agree when someone said afterward, "That just wasn't Donald." Not only had he lost his beard, but his glass of white wine. The doctors had told him that from now on he was to give up all alcohol and tobacco; these two habits had probably contributed to the throat cancer in the first place.

Over the next few weeks Donald began to enjoy a remission, and we let ourselves hope that he was out of danger. That summer I moved back to New York, quitting the job at Houston, but I kept tabs on him from mutual friends. They told me he was becoming the old Donald again, except that he seemed miraculously to have given up liquor and smoking—oh, every now and then cadging a cigarette or sneaking a sip of wine at a party when Marion's back was turned.

During the spring of 1989, Barthelme went to Italy, visiting Ed Hirsch, who was there on a Prix de Rome. From all accounts, Donald was in good spirits in Rome. Passing up sightseeing, he preferred to spend his days marketing, cooking, and working on his new novel, *The King*. So in July, when I ran into someone who told me Donald was in bad shape, I wanted to argue that that was old news, no longer current. But it was current. I was stunned, yet at the same time not: when you learn that someone in remission from cancer has had a relapse, it is never a total surprise. I prayed that Donald would somehow be strong enough to pull out of it again.

A week later, waiting by the cash register for a breakfast table at the Black Labrador Inn in Martha's Vineyard, I was turning the pages of the *New York Times* and came across Donald Barthelme's obituary. There was that familiar face, staring at me with unruffled calm. It wore the same expression he wrote about in his story "Critique de la Vie Quotidienne": "you assume a thoughtful look (indeed, the same grave and thoughtful look you have been wearing all day, to confuse your enemies and armor yourself against the indifference of your friends) . . ."

I suddenly remembered the time I had written an essay on friendship for *Texas Monthly*, and I had described a "distinguished colleague" (transparently Donald) whom I liked but with whom I could never establish a real friendship. To my surprise, since Barthelme generally shunned confrontation of any sort, he confronted me on it. "I saw what you wrote about me in that *Texas Monthly* piece," he said, letting me know by his ensuing silence that if I felt there was anything needing to be cleared up, he was willing to give me the opportunity.

"Did it . . . distress you?" I asked.

"I was a bit distressed, yes. But I recognize that that's your style as a personal essayist. You write about people you know; I don't."

"Did you think that what I wrote was . . . inaccurate?"

"No, no, not necessarily. I grant you it's hard for me to make friends. Ever since my two best friends, Tom Hess and Harold Rosenberg, died . . ." and he repeated substantially what he had told me the first time.

After his death a wise man who knew us both said, "Maybe Donald couldn't be a friend, but I think he had deep feelings for all of us." It was hard for me sometimes to distinguish between the taciturnity of deep feeling and unconcern. On my side, I felt guilty for having been one of those indifferent friends who didn't take the trouble to call near the end and ask about his condition. I had told myself, Don't bother them, you're not in the inner circle anyway—a poor excuse.

I have been assessing him in these pages through the prism of my needs, hence probably misjudging him. Certainly it is perverse of me to have manufactured a drama of being rejected by Barthelme, when the objective truth is that he was almost always kind to me—distant (such was his character) but benevolent.

It has not been easy to conjure up a man who, for all his commanding presence, had something of the ghost about him even in his lifetime. My relationship to him all along was, in a sense, with a rich, shifting absence. Donald is still hovering on the page, fading, I am starting to lose him. I had hoped to hold on to him by fixing his portrait. And now I hear him knocking, like the statue of the slain Commendatore in *Don Giovanni*, warning me that I will be punished for my sins, my patricidal betrayals of his privacy.

I have one more memory to offer: the night of the first fund-raising ball for the creative writing program. When the ball had ended, I could sense an air of letdown afterward as Donald and Marion, Cynthia and I drove in the Barthelme's pickup truck to their house for a nightcap. The event had been pretty successful, but not as large a windfall financially as we had fantasized, after the year's work we had put into it. I tried a few jokes, but I could see the others had invested too much in the evening to jest about it. When we arrived, instead of sitting around having a postmortem, we—began singing songs. Cynthia has a fine trained voice, and Donald had a lovely baritone and a great memory for lyrics: Cole Porter, musical comedy, jazz ballads. It turned into a wonderfully pleasurable evening. Each of us alternated proposing songs, and the others joined in, to the best of our memories. Slowly the tension of organizing the ball seeped away. Donald seemed particularly at ease. There was no need to articulate his thoughts, except in this indirect, song-choosing fashion. It was another instance of Barthelme expressing himself most willingly through an outlet other than his chosen vocation: Donald the would-be graphic artist, the moving man, the decorator, the pop singer.

— 27

The Story of My Father

Is it not clearer than day, that we feel within ourselves the indelible marks of excellence, and is it not equally true that we constantly experience the effects of our deplorable condition?
—*Pascal*

1.

OLD AGE IS A GREAT LEVELER: the frailer elderly all come to resemble turtles trapped in curved shells—shrinking, wrinkled, and immobile—so that in a roomful, a terrarium, of the old, it is hard to disentangle one solitary individual's karma from the mass fate of aging. Take my father. Vegetating in a nursing home, he seems both universalized and purified, worn to his bony essence. But as LSD is said to intensify more than alter one's personality, so old age: my father is what he always was, only more so. People meeting him for the first time ascribe his oddities (the withdrawn silences, sloppy eating habits, boasts, and pedantic non sequiturs) to the infirmities of time, little realizing he was like that at thirty.

A man in his thirties who acts the octagenarian is asking for it. But old age has set his insularities in a kinder light—meanwhile drawing to the surface that underlying sweetness that I always suspected was there. Dispassionate to the point where the stoical and stony meet, a hater of sentimentality, he had always been embarrassed by his affections; but now he lacks the strength even to suppress these leakages. I have also changed and am more ready to receive them. These last ten years—ever since he was put away in old age homes—have witnessed more expressions of fondness than passed between us in all the years before. Now when I visit him, he kisses me on sight and, during the whole time we are together, stares at me greedily, as though with wonder that such a graying cub came from his loins. For my part, I have no choice but to love him. I feel a tenderness welling up, if only at the sight of the wreck he has become. What we were never able to exhibit when he had all his wits about him— that animal bond between father and son—is now the main exchange.

Yet I also suspect sentimentality; and so I ask myself, How valid is this cozy resolution? Am I letting both of us off the hook too quickly? Or trying to corner the market on filial piety, while the rest of my family continues mostly to ignore him? Who is, who was, this loner, Albert Lopate, neglected in a back ward? I look at the pattern of his eighty-five years and wonder what it all adds up to: failure, as he himself claims, or a respectable worker's life for which he has little to be ashamed, as I want to believe? We spend most of our adulthoods trying to grasp the meanings of our parents' lives; and how we shape and answer these questions largely turns us into who we are.

My father's latest idea is that I am a lawyer. The last two times I've visited him in the nursing home, he's expressed variations on this theme. The first time he looked up at me from his wheelchair and said, "So, you're successful—as a lawyer?" By my family's scraping-by standards, I'm a worldly success; and worldly success, to the mistrustful urban-peasant mind of my father, befogged by geriatric confusion, can only mean a lawyer.

Lawyers, I should add, are not held in the highest regard in my family. They are considered shysters: smooth, glib, ready to sell you out. You could say the same about writers. In hindsight, one reason I became a writer is that my father wanted to be one. An autodidact who started out in the newspaper trade, then became a factory worker and, finally, a shipping clerk, he wrote poetry in his spare time, and worshipped Faulkner and Kafka. I enacted his dream, like the good son (or usurped it, like the bad son), which seems not to have made him entirely happy. So he turns me into a lawyer.

Not that my father's substitution is all that far-fetched. I had entered college a prelaw major, planning to specialize in publishing law. Secretly I yearned to be a writer, though I did not think I was smart enough. I was right—who is?—but bluff got the better of modesty.

The last time I visited my father, he said, "I know what you want to be. *Abogado.*" He smiled at his ability to call up the Spanish word you see on storefronts in barrios, alongside *notario.* So this time I was not yet the successful attorney, but the teenage son choosing his vocation. Sometimes old people get stuck on a certain moment in the past. Could it be that his mental clock had stopped around 1961, right about the time of his first stroke, when he'd just passed fifty (my present age) and I was seventeen? *Abogado.* It's so characteristic of my father's attachment to language that a single word will swim up from the dark waters of dotage. Even before he became addled, he would peacock his vocabulary, going out of his way to construct sentences with polysyllabic words such as "concomitant" or "prevaricate." My father fingers words like mahjong tiles, waiting to play a good one.

Lately he has been reverting to Yiddish phrases, which he assumes I understand, though I don't. This return to the mother tongue is not accompanied by any revived interest in Judaism—he still refuses to attend the home's religious services—but is all part of his stirring the pot of language and memories one last time.

I arrive around noon, determined to bring him outside for a meal. My father, as usual, sits in the dining room, a distance apart from everyone else, staring down at his chin. There are a group of old ladies whom he manages to tantalize by neither removing himself entirely from their company nor giving them the benefit of his full attention. Though he has deteriorated badly in recent years, he still remains in better shape than some, hence a "catch." One Irish lady in particular, Sheila, with a twinkle in her cataracted eye, is always telling me what a lovely man my father is. He pays her no attention whatsoever.

It was not always thus. A letter he dictated for my sister Leah in California, when he first came to this home, contained the passage: "There's a woman by the name of Sheila who seems to be attracted to me. She's a heavyset woman, not too bad-looking, she likes me a lot, and is fairly even-tempered. I'm not sure of my feelings toward her. I'm ambivalent." ("Ambivalent" is a favorite Albert Lopate word. Purity of heart is for simpletons.) "Should I pursue this more aggressively, or should I let things go along at a normal pace?" The last line strikes me as particularly funny, given my father's inveterate passivity (what would aggressive pursuit entail for him?) and the shortage of time left to them both.

It took me a while to give up the hope that my father would find companionship, or at least casual friendship, in a nursing home. But the chances were slim: this is a man who never had nor made a friend for as long as I can remember. Besides, "friendship" is a cuddly term that ill describes the Hobbesian enmity and self-centeredness among these ancients.

"Don't push anything out of the window!" yells one old woman to another. "If anything's pushed out the window, it's going to be you!"

"I want to get out of here, I want to forget you, and I won't forget you unless I get out of this room!" yells the second.

"You dirty pig."

"You're one too."

So speak the relatively sane ones. The ward is divided between two factions: those who, like my father, can still occasionally articulate an intelligent thought, and those with dementia, who scream the same incoherent syllables over and over, kicking their feet and rending the air with clawed hands. The first group cordially detests the second. *Meshuge*, crazy, my father dismisses them with a word. Which is why, desperately trying to stay on the right side of Alzheimer's, he has become panicked by forgetfulness.

Asked how he is, he responds with something like: "It worries me I'm losing my memory. We were discussing the all-star pitcher the Dodgers used to have. Koufax. I couldn't remember Koufax's first name. Ridiculous!" For a man who once had quiz-show recall, such lapses are especially humiliating. He has been making alphabetical lists of big words to retain them. But the mind keeps slipping, bit by bit. I had no idea there could be so many levels of disorientation before coming to rest at senility.

This time he has forgotten we've made a lunch date, and sits ready to eat the institutional tray offered him. In a way, I prefer his forgetting our date to his response a few years ago, when he would wait outside three hours before my arrival, checking his watch every ten minutes. As usual, he is dressed too warmly, in a mud-colored, torn sweater, for the broiling summer day. (These shabby clothes seem to materialize from nowhere: where does his wardrobe come from, and whatever happened to the better clothes we bought him? Theft is common in these establishments.)

I am in a hurry to wheel him outside today, before he becomes too attached to his meal—and before the atmosphere of the nursing home gets to me.

I kiss him on top of his pink head, naked but for a few white hairs, and he looks at me with delight. He is proud of me. I am the lawyer, or the writer—in any case, a man of accomplishment. In another minute he will start introducing me to the women at the next table, "This is my son," as he has already done a hundred times before, and they will pour on the syrup about what a nice father I have, how nice I am to visit him (which I don't do often enough), and how alike we look. This time I start to wheel him out immediately, hoping to skip the routine, when Sheila croaks in her Irish accent, "Don'tcha say hello to me anymore?" Caught in the act of denying my father the social capital a visitor might bring him, I go over and schmooze a bit.

Meanwhile, the muskrat-faced Miss Mojabi (in the caste division of this institution, the nursing staff is predominantly Pakistani, the attendants mainly black, and the upper management Orthodox Jewish) reminds me that I must "sign the form" to take legal responsibility for our outing. Were Armageddon to arrive, these nurses would be waiting pen in hand for a release signature. Their harsh, officious manner makes me want to punch them. I temper my rage with the thought that they are adequate if not loving—that it was we, the really unloving, who abandoned him to their boughten care.

My father's nursing home, located in Washington Heights, is perched on the steepest hill in Manhattan. After straining to navigate the wheelchair downhill, fantasizing what would happen if I let the handlebars slip (careening Papa smashing into tree), I bring us to a Chinese-Cuban takeout place on Broadway, a hole in the wall with three formica tables. It's Sunday, everything else is closed, and there are limits to how far north I am willing to push him in the August heat. My father seems glad to have made it to the outside; he wouldn't mind, I'm sure, being wheeled to Riverdale. Still, he has never cared much about food, and I doubt if the fare's quality will register on him one way or the other.

After asking him what he would like, and getting an inconclusive answer, I order sesame chicken and a beef dish at the counter. He is very clear on one thing: ginger ale. Since they have none, I substitute Mountain Dew. Loud salsa music on the radio makes it hard to hear him; moreover, something is wrong with his false teeth, or he's forgotten to put in the bridge, and he speaks so faintly I have to ask him to repeat each sentence several times. Often I simply nod, pretending to have heard. But it's annoying not to understand, so, as soon as he clears his throat—signaling intent to speak—I put my ear against his mouth, receiving communiqués from him in this misted, intimate manner.

From time to time he will end his silence with an observation, such as: "The men here are better-looking than the women." I inspect the middle-aged Dominican patrons, indoor picknickers in their Sunday best—the men gray-templed and stout, wearing dark suits or brocaded shirts; the women in skirts, voluptuously rounded, made-up, pretty—and do not share his opinion, but nod agreement anyway. I sense he offers these impressions less to express his notion of reality than to show he can still make comments. Ten minutes later another mysterious remark arrives, from left field, like the one about *abogado*. I prefer this system of waiting for my father to say something, between long silences, rather than prying conversation out of him. If my wife Cheryl were here, she would be drawing him out, asking him about the latest at the nursing home, whether he had seen any movies on TV, what he thought of the food, if he needed anything. And later she would consider the effort a success: "Did you see how much better he got, the longer we spoke? He's just rusty because nobody talks to him. But he's still sharp mentally. . . ." I'm glad she's not here, to see me failing to keep the conversational shuttlecock aloft.

You must have heard that corny idea: A true test of love is when you can sit silently next to the beloved without feeling any pressure to talk. I have never been able to accomplish this feat with any woman, howsoever beloved, but I can finally do it with one human being: my father. After fifty years of frustration as this lock-jawed man's son, I no longer look on his uncommunicativeness as problematic or wounding. Quite the contrary: in my book, he has at last earned the right to be as closemouthed as he wants, just as I have earned the right to stare into space around him, indulging my own fly-on-the-wall proclivities.

He eats, engrossed, engaged in the uneven battle between morsel and fork. With the plastic utensils they have given us, it is not easy for a man possessing so little remaining hand strength to spear chicken chunks. So he wields the fork like a spoon to capture a piece, transport it to his mouth, and crunch down, one half dropping into his lap. Those dark polyester pants, already seasoned, absorb the additional flavor of sesame sauce. He returns to the plate with that morose, myopic glare which is his trademark. My wife, I know, would have helpfully cut up the pieces into smaller bits. Me, I prefer to watch him struggle. I could say in my defense that by letting him work out the problem on his own, I am respecting his autonomy more. Or I could acknowledge some streak of cruelty for allowing him this fiasco. The larger truth is that I have become a fly on the wall, and flies don't use utensils.

Eventually I, too, cut up everything on my father's plate. So we both arrive at the same point, my wife and I, but at differing rates. Cheryl sizes up a new situation instantly, and sets about eliminating potential problems for others—a draft, a tipsy chair—as though all the world were a baby she needed to protect. My tendency is to adjust to an environment passively, like my father, until such time as it occurs to me to do what a considerate Normal Person (which I am decidedly not, I am a Martian) would do in these same circumstances: shut the window, cut up the old man's meat. My father is also from Mars. We understand each other in this way. He, too, approaches all matter as obdurate and mystifying.

My father drops some broccoli onto his lap. "Oh Al, how could you?" my mother would have cried out. "You're such a slob!" We can both "hear" her, though she is some eight miles downtown. As ever, he looks up sheepish and abashed, with a strangely innocent expression, like a chimp who knows it is displeasing its master but not why.

It gives me pleasure to spare him the expected familial reproach. "Eat it with your hands, Pop. It's okay," I tell him. Who can object to an old man picking up his food? Certainly not the Dominicans enjoying themselves at the next table. Many African tribes eat with their fingers. The fork is a comparatively recent innovation, from the late Middle Ages; Ethiopians still think that the fork not only harms the food's taste, imposing a metallic distance, but also spoils the sociability of each eater scooping up lentils and meat with soft porridgy bread from the common pot. Mayhap my father is a noble Ethiopian prince, mistransmigrated into the body of an elderly Jew? Too late: the tyranny of the fork has marked him, and he must steal "inadvertent" bits for his fingers' guilty pleasure.

I empathize with that desire to live in one's head, performing an animal's functions with animal absentmindedness. Sometimes I, too, eat that way when I'm alone, mingling culinary herbs with the brackish taste of my fingers, in rebellious solidarity with his lack of manners. Socially, my older brother, Hal, and I have striven hard to project ourselves as the opposite of our father—to seem forceful, attentive, active, and seductive. But when no one is looking, I feel my father's vagueness, shlumpiness, and mania for withdrawal inhabit me like a flu.

Across the street from the café, a drunken bum about sixty is dancing by himself on a park bench to Latin jazz. He has no shirt on, revealing an alkie's skinny frame, and he seems happy, moving to the beat with that uncanny, delayed rhythm of the stoned. I point him out as a potentially diverting spectacle to my father, who shows no interest. The drunk, in a curious way, reminds me of my dad: they're both functioning in a solipsistic cone.

Surrounded by "that thick wall of personality through which no real voice has ever pierced on its way to us," as Pater phrased it, each of us is, I suppose, to some degree a solipsist. But my father has managed to exist in as complete a state of solipsism as any person I have ever known. When he gets into an elevator, he never moves to the back, although by now he must anticipate that others will soon be joining him. Inconsiderateness? The word implies the willful hurting of others whose existence one is at least aware of.

I once saw an old woman in the nursing home elevator telling him to move back, which he did very reluctantly, and only a step at a time for each repeated command. (Perhaps, I rationalized for him, he has a faulty perception of the amount of space his body takes up.) The old woman turned to her orderly and said, "When you get on in years, you have to live with old people. Some of them are nice and some are— peculiar." Meaning my father. When we got off the elevator, he said loudly, "She's such a pain in the ass, that one. Always complaining. I need her like a *luk im kopf*." His statement showed that he *had* been aware of her, but not enough to oblige her.

My father has always given the impression of someone who could sustain very little intensity of contact before his receptive apparatus shut down. Once, after I hadn't seen him in a year, I hugged him and told him how much I loved him. "Okay, okay. Cut the bullshit," he said. This armor of impatience may have been his defense against what he actually wanted so much that it hurt.

"Okay" is also his transitional marker, indicating he has spent long enough on one item and is ready for new data. If you haven't finished, so much the worse for you.

My sister Molly is the only one who can challenge his solipsism. She pays him the enormous compliment of turning a deaf ear to his self-pity, and of assuming that, even in old age, there is still potential for moral growth. Years ago, hospitalized with pneumonia, he was complaining to her that nobody cared enough to visit him, and she shot back, "Do you care about anyone? Are you curious about anyone besides yourself?" She then tried to teach him, as one would a child, how to ask after others' well-being. "When you see them, say, 'How are you? What have you been up to lately? How are you *feeling*?'" And for a while it took. My father probably said "How are *you*?" more times between the ages of seventy-five and seventy-nine than in all the years preceding. If the question had a mechanical ring, if he speedily lost interest in the person's answer, that ought not to detract from the worthiness of my sister's pedagogy.

My father's solipsism is a matter of both style and substance. When I was writing an essay on the Holocaust, I asked him if he had any memories of refugees returning from the camps. He seemed affronted, as though to say, Why are you bothering me with that crazy business after all these years? "Ask your mother. She remembers it."

"But I'm asking you," I said. "When did you find out about the concentration camps? What was your reaction?"

"I didn't think about it. That was them and this was me," he said with a shrug.

Here was solipsism indeed: to ignore the greatest tragedy of modern times—of his own people!—because he wasn't personally involved. On the other hand, my father in his eighties is a hardly credible witness for the young man he was. What his reaction did underline was the pride he takes in being taciturn, and in refusing to cough up the conventionally pious response.

As I ask the Chinese waiter for the check, my father starts to fiddle with several napkins in his breast pocket. He has developed a curious relationship to these grubby paper napkins, which he keeps taking out of his pocket and checking. I've never seen him blow his nose with them. I wonder if old people have the equivalent of what clinical psychologists call "transitional objects"—like those pacifiers or teddy bears that children imbue with magical powers—and if these napkins are my father's talismans.

Just to show the internalized superego (God or my wife) that I have made an effort to Communicate, I volunteer some news about myself. I tell my father that Cheryl and I are soon to have a baby. His response is *"C'est la vie."* This is carrying philosophic resignation too far—even good news is greeted stoically. I tell him we have bought a house, and my teaching post is secure. None of these items seems to register, much less impress. Either he doesn't get what I'm saying, or he knows it already and is indifferent.

Hal called him recently with the news that *he* had had his first baby. On being told he was a grandfather, my father's answer was "Federico Fellini just died." This became an instant family joke, along with his other memorable non sequiturs. (If indeed it was a non sequitur. The translation might be "What do I care about your new baby when death is staring me in the face?") Though I could sympathize with Hal's viewing it as yet another dig to add to his copious brief against our father, who has always tended to compete with his sons rather than rejoice in their good fortune, this Fellini response seemed to me more an expression of incapacity than insult. The frown on his face nowadays when you tell him something important, the repetition of the phrase *c'est la vie*, is a confession that he knows he can't focus enough to hold on to what you are saying; he lacks the adhesive cement of affect.

Even sports no longer matter to him. They used to be one of our few common topics: I was guaranteed a half hour's worth of conversation with my father, working my way through the Knicks, Mets, Rangers, Giants, Jets. . . . His replies were curt, yet apt: "They stink. They got no hitting." He it was who taught me that passionate fandom which merges with disenchantment: loyalty to the local team, regardless of the stupid decisions the front office made; never cross a picket line, just stick with the union, for all their corruption; vote Democratic no matter how mediocre this year's slate. I would have thought being a sports fan was part of his invincible core, as much as his addiction to newspapers. He continues to have the *Times* ordered for him, but now it sits on his lap, unopened, like a ship passenger's blanket.

Back at the home, I bend down and kiss him on the cheek before leaving. He says, "I still got more hair than you do." This statement—untrue, as it happens—no longer can provoke me. He shakes my hand, to demonstrate how strong his grip is: it's a stunt he's learned, no indication of his actual strength, but, like the occasional big word, all that is left in his armatorium of self-esteem.

"Do you need anything, Pop?"

"Well, I do and I don't."

Not knowing what to make of this enigmatic response, I say, "Do you need any money?" I hand him two twenty-dollar bills. He takes them uncertainly and bunches them in his hands without putting them away, which makes me think they will not stay long in his care. My father seems much more solicitous of his old napkins than these greenbacks.

"Do me a favor," he says hoarsely.

"What's that?"

"Try to see me more regularly. Once every few weeks."

This request takes my breath away. He's right, of course.

"I'll try. I *will* try. I was insanely busy this past month, but from now on . . ." I lie. Then, to shift the burden elsewhere, I ask, "Did you get any other visits recently?"

No, he shakes his head. I know this is not true: my brother visited him last Sunday. He gets no brownie points; Pop's already forgotten. Which means he won't remember my visit either by tomorrow.

2.

"If I wrote my life down, I would have to title it *The Story of a Failure*." This is, in old age, my father's idée fixe. Ask him for particulars, he will reply tersely, "I was a failure. What else is there to say?" Being a failure apparently grants one the privilege of taciturnity (just as being a success must condemn me to garrulity).

Many times I have argued with him: "What makes you so presumptuous or so arrogant as to judge yourself a failure, when you accomplished no less than ninety-five percent of the rest of humanity?" He will not hear of it. He thinks I am trying to reassure him. Besides, he seems at times proud to be labeled a failure, to partake of its peculiar romance. Nineteenth-century Russian fiction perfected this defense of the failure as the underground man, the marginal, economically redundant, passive intellectual, for whom superfluousness was a mark of superiority. The less you accomplished, the more you built up your store of latency, and the purer your integrity remained.

About a year ago my wife and I were driving my father to a midtown restaurant, just to give him an excursion. In the car he was telling us he considered his life a failure.

I had heard this too many times to comment, but Cheryl said, "Why? You worked every day of your life, and you raised four children and they turned out fairly well."

"But I was always doing what I shouldn't have been doing, and not doing what I should have," he replied.

"What do you mean? You were supposed to go to work and you did."

"Yeah, but even though my bosses said I was a good worker, they didn't pay me well."

"Then it's their failure, not yours," said Cheryl. "They failed to do the right thing."

"What do you think you should have been doing?" I interrupted.

"Writing," he said.

"What kind of writing?"

"Fiction."

I never knew he thought of himself as a failed *novelist*. "Fiction?" I demanded.

"Or semifactual," he reconsidered. "I always wanted to be a writer, or something of that sort, and in some respects you fulfilled my ambition. Vicariously, I am *kvel-ling* in your success as a writer." He added that lately he had been having "hallucinations" that he wrote a book, or rather, stole it from me, and in so doing brought shame and dishonor on us all.

This confusion between his and my writing achievement has been there right from the start. Growing up, I was impressed by my father's large vocabulary, his peculiar, formal, crisp feeling for language. I submitted my first short story (about a gangster shot in a dark alley) for his criticism, and watched as he struck out the unnecessary words and told me, "Write what you know." Still trusting his infallibility in writing matters, I was graduating from junior high school when my teacher asked me, along with four other students, to compete for valedictorian by writing a speech. Since I had the highest grade average in the school, everyone assumed I would win the contest. But I had no idea what a valedictorian's speech was supposed to sound like, and so—oddly enough—I asked my father to write mine for me. He complied, employing his fanciest vocabulary and dwelling on the *parents'* feelings during such an occasion (using words like "vicarious" and "progenitors"). The speech laid an egg, and a chubby girl named Andrea Bravo, who expressed herself earnestly if tritely, got chosen instead. After that, I was warier about asking for his writing help.

I remember when I told my father back in 1971 that my first book of poems was about to come out. His only response was "I haven't been writing any poems recently." I was struck then by how little feeling he seemed to have for me. Yet my siblings claim that I am my father's favorite—that he brags about me more to strangers, or, to put it another way, that he pays even less attention to them than he does to me.

"The possum," my mother calls him. "He plays dead. It's an act, he thinks the Angel of Death won't notice him if he lays low. The old man's stronger than you think. He'll outlive me, you, everybody."

All my life, it seems, I have been rehearsing prematurely for the death of my father. At eleven years old I woke from a dream in which he had been killed; I got up like a sleepwalker and, as if by dictation, wrote down a poem of grief over the vision of him laid out on a bier. My mother took it to her analyst, Dr. Jonas in the Bronx, and he told her that dreams were wish fulfillment. She broke the hard news to me: it wasn't that I loved my father so, it was that I wanted him dead in order to marry her. This made little sense at the time, but I have always been willing to believe the worst about myself, and began to accept the possibility of harboring a parricide within.

("Parricide," incidentally, was a concept very much in the air when I grew up. My father had no love for his father, and his favorite book was *The Brothers Karamazov*.)

I must say, never for a conscious instant did I wish my father dead. But that may be because he seemed, as long as I can remember, already suffering from a mortal wound. One of the movies that left the deepest impression on me in my youth was *Odd Man Out*, in which the sympathetic IRA operative, Johnny, played by James Mason, has been shot and spends the rest of the movie trying to stay alive. Somehow you know just by looking at him that he is bleeding to death. James Mason (cerebral, ironic, solitary, drawn) was a sort of idealized version of my father. Wiry and gaunt, my father would come home, his job having consumed his stamina, and sit like a zombie, half-dozing, letting the cigarette ash grow dangerously, while a ballgame sounded on the radio.

Avoiding pain and love, he withdrew into that dreamy, numbed zone that Schopenhauer (one of his favorites) called "the lost paradise of nonexistence." These withdrawals, this maddening, arms-folded passivity of his, infuriated my mother, goading her into ever-stronger provocations. We, his four children, also provoked him, wanting him to notice us. It was like baiting a bear; occasionally he would treat us to a smack, but for the most part he shrugged us off, with a half-smile that said, You can't get to me.

I have never known a man who was criticized as severely as my father. You would think he had committed some heinous crime. Hour after hour, he would be told he was uncouth, insensitive, thoughtless, gross. It made no difference in his behavior: he didn't get it, or he didn't want to get it. He continued to do things in what seemed like an alien, oafish manner—not to mention the things he didn't do, such as: talk to us, buy us birthday presents, show us affection, compliment us, even go to the hospital when my mother gave birth. By today's sensitive-male standards, he was certainly a washout. On the other hand, I wonder if he was really so different from many men of his generation.

Just for variety's sake, if nothing else, I would defend him in the family circle. But then he would say something mean to me as well that would catch me up short and make me realize what hostile bitterness had collected behind that carapace of silence. It was the custom for my father to take us to the museum on Saturdays when he didn't have to work—usually after much badgering by my mother, who wanted some time to herself alone. One Saturday morning when I was about ten years old, we were all hounding him because he wouldn't take us anywhere; and this time I joined in the assault. Suddenly he lashed out at me with rabid fury: "You! You stay out of it, you're a cold fish." It was as if he were rebuking me for not having attacked him "warmly" enough in the past. I think he liked being attacked, or at least knew how to convert that coin into love more dependably than direct expressions of affection.

"Cold fish" is an awful judgment to hang on a ten-year-old kid. But give him his due, he could have had a prescient insight: I often think there is something cold and "fishy" about me. Or perhaps he was really saying, "You're like me, detached, unemotional." An inverted compliment.

So I became a writer.

But this is not about me; I must restrain myself from turning my father into a repository of clues to the genesis of my own development. I must get back on track and try to tell the story of this tight-lipped man's life, attempt to discover its under-lying meaning. Why had he gravitated toward death-in-life? What made him throw in his hand so quickly? Or did he, really? There are organisms, such as barnacles, that manifest the most dogged willpower through a strategy that looks initially like weakness or dependency.

Albert Donald Lopate was born on September 2, 1910. He grew up in Jamaica, Queens, with three older half-siblings and one full brother. He felt unloved by both his mother and his father, with good cause.

My grandmother Sophie died before I was born, so I cannot describe her from experience. (I am told that she spent her last years looking out the window spotting car makes, went mad, and died in a mental hospital.) But I remember my grandfa-ther Samuel Lopate quite well. He was a *character*, a Jewish Fyodor Karamazov in his appetite for women and money, and his utter indifference to children.

My grandfather was born in Russia; when he was about ten, his parents fled the pogroms, via Turkey, to Palestine. Family legend has it that they were thrown out of Palestine because he pissed on the Wailing Wall. My father says, more conservative-ly, "He did something which caused the Arabs to expel them. He made fun when the Arabs were praying at the wall, and they were outraged."

The next we hear of my grandfather, he has come to New York and married, for love, a woman who dies in childbirth. Soon after, for economic security, he latches on to an older widow, Sophie—a second cousin of his—with three children and a dry goods store. He goes to work in the store and wrests it from her. He sires two sons, Arthur and Albert.

Sophie was almost fifty when she had my father, and felt so lukewarm toward this child, whom she had tried unsuccessfully to abort, that she would not even look at him. Afterward she used him as her servant, making him wash the floors every Saturday. She favored the offspring from her first husband, the love of *her* life.

My father's parents fought openly. Sophie called Samuel a *trumernik* (loafer, bum, philanderer). My grandfather was, in truth, something of a ladykiller. He had one talent that would knock women dead: he could cry at will. The sight of those plump crocodile tears rolling down his émigré cheeks melted many a female heart. (This led my father to the unfortunate conclusion that being emotionally undemonstrative was a mark of sincerity.) All told, Samuel buried three wives, which gave him the reputation of the family Bluebeard. The last wife, Esther, I knew as a child. She was sweet, gave us oatmeal cookies, and was a reader (by which I mean she subscribed to the Book-of-the-Month Club). My mother, who despised her lecherous father-in-law, used to say, "He'll drive her into a grave too, like the others." Sure enough, Esther died, leaving Samuel a chunk of money, and us a box of books, which included Goren's *Contract Bridge, Thirty Days to a More Powerful Vocabulary,* and Henry George's tracts on social economy, which I tried in vain to penetrate.

I remember Samuel in his widower dotage: a cranky, cold, bald-headed, fat old man who would sit on his porch in Ozone Park, his bulging pants held up with suspenders. The only time I ever saw him pleased was when he took out a rainbow-speckled Irish Sweepstakes ticket, ornate as a stock certificate, and stared at it. He was convinced he would win, and not have to enter an old-age home; but he didn't, and soon he was complaining from the much smaller confines of half a room in the Rogers Avenue Nursing Home. My father would take us there to visit, perhaps in the hope that Samuel's grandparental warmth would be belatedly awakened and he'd leave us something. We were all very conscious that the longer he stayed in that nursing home, the more our possible inheritance was being eaten up.

I tried to encourage Grandpa to go out into the little garden and take a constitutional. He never listened to me, any more than he did to my father. My sister Molly alone knew how to handle Grandpa. Whenever she needed money for the movies, she would pay him an impromptu visit and wheedle a dollar bill out of him. This game he understood; he had played it on women often enough.

But to return to my father's youth. He used to sit in the back of his parents' dry goods store and read for escape. Dumas, Hugo, *The Count of Monte Cristo.* At school he was skipped ahead, and a sympathetic teacher helped him to catch up with the older kids; by the end of the term he had the highest average in the new class.

The next year my father, a natural lefty, had a less understanding teacher, who tried to force him to write right-handed. He developed a stammer, and his grades suffered when the teacher couldn't decipher his penmanship. Defiantly, he went back to writing left-handed.

In high school he continued to read voraciously on his own, meanwhile ignoring the assigned schoolwork. Later in life he would brag about his scholastic exploits in high school: acing a Latin test he hadn't studied for, or frustrating teachers with his nonchalance. "I had a math teacher who would open up the class with a question, 'Lopate, did you do your homework?' And I would say, 'No, ma'am.' And she'd write down a zero in front of my name. Then I got 96 on the final, and she gave me a 69 for the course. I said to her, 'How could you give me a 69, when I got 96 on the final?' So she showed me all the zeroes and when she averaged them out, I got a 34. I said, 'Why don't you give me a 34, then? What you're doing is dishonest.'"

He was proud of being an intellectual dark horse—a "gifted underachiever," as it would later be called. I asked him once why he took such pleasure in flouting the teacher's authority, when he must have known he would get punished for it. He said, "I didn't give a good goddamn what she thought, so long as I knew I understood the math."

His rebellion extended to rejecting his own family's Orthodox Judaism and Republican politics. They thought him a Socialist, and at least temperamentally he was pointed that way. "I thought of money as evil. I became an intellectual snob. *I eschewed* financial gain," he boasted. He wanted to go on to college and asked his mother for a loan, and she turned him down, "although she had the dough," and although she had already subsidized his brother Arthur's higher education. He knew enough not to ask Samuel. "My father never treated me with the proper respect." The only one in his family who saw he had a brain, and encouraged him to continue learning, was an older half-brother, Charles. But Charles obviously could not foot his tuition bill, so my father went to work, with the notion that eventually he might save enough to pay for his own college education.

He was drawn to newspapers. His first job was taking ads and running the switchboard for the *Long Island Press*. From there, he tried out for a job at a trade magazine, *Editor and Publisher*. Typical of my father's somewhat self-destructive integrity is that he made a point of telling the interviewer he was Jewish (he does not look noticeably so), at a time when discrimination against Jews was widespread. They hired him anyway. After that, he became a reporter for the *Queens Evening News*: his beat was to cover the political clubs and civic organizations in different neighborhoods and drum up stories. Though I find it difficult to imagine my father engaged in anything so extroverted, these cub reporter days were happy times for him. His terse style suited the newspaper format.

Having saved enough money, he enrolled in night school classes in journalism. But, after the long workday, he would fall asleep in class. So he dropped out of college in his freshman year, focusing on reporting instead.

"Then the Depression came, and the paper folded up, and there were no more journalistic jobs to be had." (Whenever my father would say, "Then the Depression came," the historical, capital *D* event always carried an echo of clinical, small *d*.) He took the only job he could get: a stock clerk for six dollars a week. As this was not enough to live on, he augmented his salary by playing poker at night. My father has always disliked gambling; but he was blessed with a poker face, and always believed himself smarter than others, and so, by cautious, close-to-the-vest playing, he would pocket a few extra dollars.

It was still not enough to make ends meet, so he asked his boss for a raise. "I was told, 'I can replace you with a college graduate who will willingly take your place for the same salary.'" My father answered, "In that case, you can get someone else." Years later he recalled vividly the boss's utter power over him; in that encounter, despite his shaky bravado, he was traumatized into a lifelong fear of unemployment.

He reluctantly took the step of going to work for his older brother Arthur, on the assumption that a family member, at least, would never fire him.

At this moment in the story we may pause and note two things: (1) my father's capacity for defiance and self-assertion was still operating; he had not yet joined the legion of the defeated; (2) his explanation that the Depression had closed down his journalistic options, true as it may be, does not explain why he never tried to reenter this beloved milieu when the economy improved. His fatalistic statement, "Then the Depression came," became one of those family myths that remains to this day sacrosanct, unquestioned. On the other hand, I have no business judging him on this score, never having lived through such an ordeal. The critic Manny Farber once told a younger man, "You know, I'm not someone who ever survived the Depression. It's not the sort of experience you ever really get over."

In any event, my father despised his powerful older brother, so that to go to work in his ribbon-dyeing factory, Parkside, meant no small swallowing of pride. The source of this fraternal dislike must have had roots in childhood, but my father always harps on a later incident. "When my brother Arthur got married, he started catering to my mother, he played up to her, and he got a good present for the wedding. I thought he had prostituted himself to get some dough, because he didn't give a damn about her. I don't think he cared at all about her, he didn't have one iota of feeling."

"Did *you* care about your mother?" I asked him.

"Not really. But I wasn't ready to prostitute myself."

As people are rarely entirely unselfish or sincere, I could never understand my father's enduring shock at this bit of filial pretense (if it was that). His outrage had something primitive about it: Arthur had stolen the "blessing" of their mother, through guile, and Albert had gotten nothing. Jacob and Esau all over again.

It was also said in my family that Arthur "cheated" my father by skimping on his salary. I have a feeling he paid him the going rate, no more, no less. My father liked certain manual labor aspects of the job: lifting hundred-pound bales, going out with the drivers on delivery. One time, however, the workers struck; my father was sympathetic to their cause, but felt an overriding family loyalty. When the labor trouble was settled, everyone got a raise, except my father, who was not in the union and was treated, conveniently in this instance, as management. To compound the indignity, Arthur "threw me a few extra dollars from time to time, to keep me quiet."

If Uncle Arthur had that family knack of treating Albert with insufficient respect, my father also seemed quick to take offense. In recent years he would tell of running into Arthur at the funeral of a relative. Arthur took him aside and said, "We're the only ones left. Let's stay in touch. Give me your phone number." My father pulled himself up with dignity: "You should know my phone number. It has been in the book for years." He offered this story as proof of Arthur's hypocrisy: "He was phony as a three-dollar bill." Of course, my father could have just as easily phoned Arthur all those years, and didn't.

It strikes me as curious that, though my family has been willing to mock my father at every turn, it has never questioned his judgment of Arthur. In our family myth, Uncle Arthur is the Evil One, the vulgar Capitalist, like the figure of the watch-chained plutocrat in left-wing cartoons. On the few occasions we visited Arthur in his spacious Queens home, usually for his children's bar mitzvahs or engagement parties, he struck me as a typical hail-fellow-well-met type. I remember his prosperous, well-fed look, the rosy spots on his cheeks—and the well-founded report that he had a mistress.

That he kept a mistress made me like him. I dreamed of attaining the same worldliness as a man. Over the years, in fact, I developed a blasphemous feeling of identification with Uncle Arthur, partly because I did not myself "eschew" financial success and partly because I took with a grain of salt my impoverished family's self-serving antagonism toward him. Maybe Arthur really was a shithead, maybe he was a decent guy, I have no idea. All I know is the role he played in the family mythology. After he sold the ribbon-dyeing plant, he went into "the oil business." Probably what was meant was some sort of fuel delivery, but I always liked to fancy him an oilman, the Queens equivalent of a Texas millionaire. If I secretly identified with Uncle Arthur, I also suspected my father associated me with his older brother. He had been told when they were growing up that Arthur was the handsome one, and he, not; he has often described me, with mixed pride and rue, as "a good-looking guy." At such moments I feel myself lumped with his nemesis. The glib-tongued charmer. The lawyer.

My father, from the photographic evidence of his young manhood, seems to me to have been quite good-looking, in that brooding, sunken-cheeked way of Lincoln, Joseph Wiseman, Jack Palance, Cesare Pavese, and an Appalachian farmer in a Walker Evans photograph. But what matters is what my father thought; and when my father met my mother, he thought himself ugly. At twenty-seven, he had never been in love; he had never slept with a woman who was not a prostitute. My mother, Frances, was working in a beauty parlor when they met. She was sexy, she had a voluptuous figure, and all the guys wanted her, or at least, as she puts it, wanted to fool around with her. But she was attracted to brains; and in their Jamaica, Queens circle, Albert was the intellectual. He wooed her with talk about politics, books, art, Bach. He taught her. He saw in my mother an unformed intelligence—but an intelligence. "All of Fran's siblings kept saying she was the dummy in the Berlow family. I took one look at her family, and I said, 'You're not stupid. They are.'"

Bonding on the resentful basis that they were both insufficiently respected by their families, they married. Many good marriages have been founded on less. In their case, however, it was not enough.

My father tells it one way, my mother another. The difference is that my mother's version is livelier and more voluble; my father's, extremely laconic. (I once tape-recorded my mother telling her life story: it took six sessions and twenty-two sides. My father's took less than an hour.) As long as I can remember, my mother has been honing and expanding the story of his husbandly wrongs. According to her, the problems began while they were still courting; he had laughingly allowed a jibe at her by Arthur's son ("Gee, you got a big nose!") to stand, and she never forgave him his lack of gallantry. My mother had notions of a gentleman's behavior toward women that my father violated at every turn: he did not pay enough attention to her on their honeymoon, he lacked the proper romantic approach to lovemaking. Later, back in the city, he would come home from the factory, reeking with sweat; the odor turned her off. She would make him take a bath immediately. His personal hygiene standards, she felt, left much to be desired; his sexual technique, likewise.

My father says: "Look, Fran was not a virgin when I married her. She insisted that I wasn't 'liberated' enough, that we weren't sexually 'compatible.' Although we managed to have four kids, supposedly we weren't 'compatible.'"

Juxtaposing their testimonies, I can still hear the sound of two people not listening to each other—the sound that dominated my childhood.

My mother says now that my father missed out on the joys of fatherhood by not involving himself in changing diapers, preparing bottles, cradling us, and so on.

By his own account, he kept a distance from childrearing: "When Hal was born, we used to have a next-door neighbor named Herman. And Hal would say 'Herman, Herman' before he said 'Daddy.'" My father's deadpan voice on the tape betrays only a quiver of the pain this memory must have caused him.

"How come?" I hear the interlocutor (myself) ask.

"I don't know. Maybe I wasn't exactly a loving father like most fathers are. And this man paid a lot of attention to the kid, and the kid reacted to it."

"Do you think it was because you hadn't gotten any example of love from your own father?"

"Probably. Same thing happened all over again."

By my father's admission, he was ambivalent about having children. The first one he accepted philosophically. "When we had the second and third, I became a little leery."

Understandably, since there was never any money, and he had found himself indentured to the economic burdens of a large family. He took them on without complaint, working six days a week. At home he was both an ineffectual and a scary figure. I remember as a boy being physically frightened of my father. He was much more prone to hit my older brother than me, being more jealous of Hal, I suppose. And Hal was more willing to trade blows with him: they would go at it, crashing into furniture, with my mother in the background, screaming at them to stop. I felt it taboo, unthinkable, to raise my hand against my father. He could have killed me. I kept my distance, knowing he could hurt just as easily through absent-mindedness as intention. One time we were waiting to be served in a bakery, and he accidentally let a cigarette ash drop down my back. For years I felt that ember on my back with wincing reflex.

By the time I was six, the fighting between my mother and father had become so severe they almost split up. This is how he told it to me on tape:

"Let's get to the nitty-gritty. When I was first married, your mother was unfaithful to me. And I found out. And one day I found myself choking her. Then, in the middle of it, I stopped short. Because I said to myself, 'Why am I doing this? This is not me. I am not a violent person. I'm not a person of action.' And I stopped. That's when your mother had me. Because she had something she could always hold against me, that I tried to choke her."

My father had very consciously set up this experience as the key point in his oral autobiography, although, with his usual self-absorption, he was unaware of the repugnant effect this confession—that he wished he had strangled my mother—might have on me, her son.

"Why didn't you leave her instead?"

"That's the story of my failure. Because I couldn't leave her. I'm not saying this in defense of myself. I *said* I made my mistake: I should have killed her, and it would have ended then and there. I would have been tried and sent to prison, and that would be that. This way I let everything linger on, and solved nothing."

"So your greatest regret in life is that you didn't kill her?"

"Yes. That I didn't stop the thing—the condition."

"And that would have been the only way to stop it?"

"I don't know whether it was the only way, but it was a solution. Whereas what ensued was not."

"How would you characterize what ensued?"

"Years of nothing. Of numbed nonexistence." (I was surprised to hear my father himself acknowledge this death-in-life state.) After a long pause, he said, "I want to amend that. The only encouraging thing was that we engendered four children whom I think in some ways have embellished my life." He paused. "I realize, of course, that Leah is not my kid. But I never told her, and I never acted as if I knew. I acted as fairly as possible, because I said to myself, 'This is not her fault, why should I hold it against her?'"

In fact, he succeeded, to the degree that he showed more fondness for Leah as a child than for the rest of us. What does it say about this man, that he would dote on the one child that was not his own? Self-hatred? But Leah was also the youngest, she was very winning, she was a girl (hence less threatening to him than his sons), and she was quiet, soft-spoken like him. Whatever the reasons, his decision to treat her as his own, without ever letting her know she had a different father (the truth came out eventually, but not through him), seems admirable in retrospect. It may be the most noble, disciplined-heroic thing he ever did. A shame we never gave him sufficient credit for it.

But something was bothering me: "How is it that you and Mother were so sure Leah wasn't your kid?"

"I wasn't that sure until your mother told me. . . . Look, it doesn't make any difference, that's the way I felt."

"Still, it's a hard thing to know for sure unless you take blood tests."

"At first she looked a little different than the Lopates. Don't get me wrong, I think Leah is, in her way, a wonderful girl."

He spoke about the summer that had led up to her birth. "We went upstate on vacation, and we lived in a bungalow colony—a *kuchalein*, they called it, because you did your own cooking. At that time I used to play cards. I spent a little more time with cards than I should have. That's when your mother took up with this fellow. Benno. He was supposed to be related to one of the big-shot families in the Israeli government. He was a nice guy. He must have aroused a spark in the old lady. He didn't seem too bright to me. But that judgment may be qualified by the fact that I resented him. Actually, I spent too much time with cards, and I shouldn't have."

"So you blame yourself partly?"

"Oh, yes. The old lady wasn't entirely wrong."

This responsible, mature perspective somehow manages to coexist with the regret that he did not kill her.

My father's emphasis on the choking incident spooked me because I had already used that episode as the climax of my story "Willy." After the story appeared in my book *Bachelorhood*, my mother informed me that I had exaggerated the ferocity of his beating. "I wasn't afraid of him for one second. If he'd really tried to hurt me," she boasted, "I could have broken him in half." (My mother is a stout woman and, in fact, outweighs him.) My father, on the other hand, was so impressed with the story's denouement that he seemed to have appropriated it as his central myth. I'm not at all convinced he saw his whole life as leading up to and away from this failed homicide until he read my story, which could have put the notion into his head.

Around the same period that I tape-recorded him, when he was in his mid-seventies, my sister Molly asked him, point-blank, "When did you decide to become a vegetable?"

He answered her: "When I had my hands around your mother's throat, I was so horrified at the violence this evil woman had provoked in me, when my nature is not violent, that I decided then and there to punish her by becoming passive."

To Molly, this answer confirmed her belief that he had deliberately created a passive persona—out of spite. I remained skeptical. For one thing, it was almost word for word what he'd said to me, and sounded too canned. For another, I could never accept the family's idea that my father had sinisterly willed himself to be a "vegetable." This gave him too much credit for intent; he was trying in the final hours to pretend he had caused the shambles of his life, rather than acknowledging the more common fate of limitation and deterioration.

But Molly took him at his word. Her response was funny if harsh: "If you want to be a vegetable, you gotta be sent to the farm!" (i.e., the nursing home).

My mother's tendency was always to speak of my father as a needy child. "I got five kids at home, you four and Al. He's the biggest baby of all." Or: "He doesn't want a wife. He wants a mother. A nursemaid," she would say bitterly. She is a large-bosomed woman, and I took her comment to mean she found something infantile about my father's fixation on that part of her anatomy. But what is so unusual about a man looking for Nirvana at a woman's breast? Freud argued that fantasy had its origins in an irrecoverable experience of bliss at the mother's breast, and that all later gratifications, including sex, are bound to be incomplete. In my father's case, his own mother had been cold toward him, so his search was all the more imperative, if tinged with the expectation of rejection.

Many of the dozen or so poems my father wrote my mother, in an effort to win her back when she was seeing another man, speak to this pathos of unsatisfied desire, the distance between coitus and possession.

Dilemma of Love

I made love to you and you sighed
And violently clawed my heaving flesh.
This should have been ecstatic joy,
But both you and I know that
Tho I possessed your body, I had
Penetrated only to your outer shell.
Deep inside there remained the
Suppressed mask of discontentment
The ever-present search for
I know not what. But not for me.

I make no claims for my father's verse—he was clearly a self-taught, Sunday poet—but what mesmerizes me is the Cavafyan dryness, the refusal of consolation that pops up in the last line. Another poem is again about sex; this time he is the onlooker. It begins:

Last night you were entwined with another.
I saw your passionate embrace
And heard your deeply contented sighs,
And I fondly remembered that there
I had once joyously nestled.

"Nestled"—so fitting a word for the infant at the breast. He then seeks to recall her to their happy hours together: meanderings through Central Park and Coney Island, long conversations on her stairs. The poem ends:

Even tho you presume not to remember,
And your thoughts are concentred on him,
I can never obliterate them from my mind—
And neither can you.

That menacing last line—no wonder these poems did not do the trick of winning her over! Reading through them, I am struck by their narrow range of lament at love's inconstancy. However, as Faiz once said, "the proper subject of poetry is the loss of the beloved." Certainly there is something moving about a pain so unbearable it could find expression only in poetry—and then only once, during the initial marital crisis.

That early threat of losing her had elicited, then, two extraordinary responses: the poems and the choking, that violent aggression finally coming to the surface. After that, he was spent, for the rest of his days, or so he says. But isn't this too pat, too "literary" an interpretation of a man's life? Are there really such crossroads of decision in life, like a well-made Chekhov story, after which the person who has chosen unwisely drags on to the end like a ghost of himself? Is there such a limited supply of life force in a human being that it can be consumed at one go?

Interestingly, my mother dates his giving up to an earlier point: the marriage itself. "He didn't read as much after he got married. He started quoting what he'd already read." Since she had married him for his brains, this relaxing of mental striving caused her understandable chagrin. Still, it means he stopped trying to expand his range not from jealous spite but from relief of the sort that follows accomplishing a goal. Supposing this lonely, cerebral young man had yearned for "normalcy," marriage and family, and, having attained this plateau—like the woman who lets her looks go after marriage—he had less need to develop his intellect as a lure.

All the while that he was working at his brother Arthur's factory, my mother was always goading him to improve his situation in life. Among other things, she urged him to become a life insurance salesman. One of her beaux sold insurance, and said he would put in a good word for Al. My father went so far as to enroll in a training program. At night he would practice the standard pitch, the euphemisms sticking in his craw ("Should one of your loved ones drop out of the picture . . . "), using his children as audience. But he had such a mournful countenance that one could not imagine him selling anything, much less insurance. When he took the aptitude test, he scored high on the intellectual portion, as expected, then was disqualified by a disastrous personnel interview.

According to my mother, he kept resisting advancement. After he left his brother's plant to work in another factory, he took a test for a foreman's position and scored very high, only to see a man with a lower grade but more seniority hired. "Instead of telling himself, 'Okay, I'll get it on the next opening,' he gave up. He was defeated before he started," she says.

My mother is, if anything, the opposite: she had a lifelong dream to become an entertainer, and, after she was fifty, did succeed in getting acting jobs, doing commercials, playing Golda in road productions of *Fiddler on the Roof.* Perhaps she had so much life force, so much determination, that he receded before it, feeling that that department was already being looked after. He was content to support her efforts to enter show business.

I think another reason for his resistance to climbing the managerial ladder was that he already had an ambition—to write—and, failing to achieve it, didn't wish to substitute a less compelling one. All this is speculative; my father himself has offered only the murkiest explanations about this area. I asked him once, "Did you *want* to be promoted to manager at the plant?"

"I didn't know what the hell I wanted. I was so confused at the time."

Eventually he followed my mother into the white-collar side of the textile industry, becoming a shipping clerk in midtown Manhattan. He was an excellent clerk, perfectly suited for the duties of keeping track of numbers and shipments, by virtue of his phenomenal memory. Sometimes he could not resist showing off his intellectual superiority, as when he sent a telex to the North Carolina plant in Latin: *"Que usque, Catilina, abutere patientia nostra?"* ("How long, Catiline, will you abuse our patience?") That must have gone over big.

Though my father continued to read, often picking up the novels my brother and I introduced into the household, his main intellectual activity became doing the crossword puzzle. Increasingly, the less respected he felt in the world, the more he took to boasting about his mathematical shortcuts or word power. Or he would go on about how he was the first in our family to appreciate, say, Bessie Smith or Stroheim's *Greed*. Even as a child I was embarrassed by these threadbare boasts; for if this was all a grown man had to feel good about himself, he was clearly in trouble.

As he grew older, the boasting anecdotes began to substitute for an active memory. He would tell for the thousandth time how he had responded to *Greed* before anyone else knew it was good. "The thing that made it so unusual was that they cast against type. They took ZaSu Pitts, who was known as a dizzy comic, and made her play the mean, calculating bitch. Then they got George O'Brien, this romantic lead, and made him play a stupid lunk."

(One time, overcome by impatience at hearing this broken record, I interrupted: "Actually, it was Gibson Gowland who played McTeague, not George O'Brien, and what makes *Greed* so great is the physical detail of the film—the direction, not the casting." He looked miserable. "I don't know, I probably got it confused." Instantly I regretted not having let him ramble on. It was too easy to slay this father.)

Bragging is a Lopate family trait; not only my mother and siblings, but I succumb to it all too often—especially under stress. As soon as I start to brag, though, I hear my father's voice, and flinch at the futility of bestowing on oneself the admiration one craves from others.

The other negative of his bragging was that it deepened his obsession with being a failure. Had he not insisted so on his superiority, he might not have been so hard on himself about the way his life had turned out.

3.

Each year the nursing home invites family members to a staff meeting to discuss the resident's overall condition. I have been to several of these: the psychologist always says, with concern, "Your father seems depressed," as though such reaction to being locked away in a nursing home were peculiar. Each year I answer, "My father has been depressed all his life." The statement is greeted with meaningful nods, but has little lasting effect: the training of those in the caring professions seems to obligate them to treat melancholy as a temporary aberration. The psychologist working with my father is a behavior-modification enthusiast who is convinced that if you can get people to frame their statements in a positive form, they will feel better about themselves. The clinical equivalent of a "Smiles" face. It is even more futile in this case, given my father's vanity toward his pessimism. But I appreciate that they are trying their best: the concern and good intentions of the staff are evident. They tell me (first the good news) that my father is an "attractive," well-liked resident, who makes a strong impression. But (the bad news): "He does not eat. He is losing weight. He shows very little appetite, and he won't even let us feed him." All present look frowningly in the direction of the wheelchaired old man, head sunk on his chest, who, as it happens, has been there throughout his case discussion.

I do my part to scold as well. "Pop, you're intelligent enough to know that if you don't eat, you'll get sick. Do you want to be sick?"

He's heard it before. Unimpressed. He keeps his counsel: silent, deep, unfathomable.

"Mr. Lopate," asks a social worker sharply, in such a way as to demand an answer, "what do you make of all this?"

"I'm trying to figure out," says my father, "how the hell to get out of here."

When he was in his early fifties, my father had his first stroke. I was still living at home, going to college, and I remember the shrieking in the middle of the night as my mother tried to restrain him from getting out of bed. "Please, Al, don't move, the ambulance is coming!" He had it in his head that she was trying to kill him, and he had better get up or he would never rise from the bed again.

Tanizaki's novel *The Key*, which had been making the rounds of our house, lay on his night table: this perverse story of husband and wife plotting to do each other in may have fueled his suspicion. Then again, my mother had so often declared she wished he was dead that I, too, watched her uneasily that night.

After the stroke he never recovered the full strength on his right side. And it threw a fear of death into him that made him even more inert, as though by doing next to nothing he would conserve strength and live longer: the possum strategy.

On the plus side, he was no longer frightening to me after his stroke. His new harmlessness enabled me to nurture feelings of affection and pity for him: I came to a fondness for the idea of my father, especially in the abstract. I admired his dutiful work ethic, his dry sense of humor, his love of reading, his gentle, long-suffering air, his ethical values, his progressive politics. Moreover, we looked a lot alike—had the same rangy build, shy grin in company and set grim mouth when alone, along with several dozen physical gestures we shared or, I should say, he had imprinted on me.

After I was set up in my own life, I had a persistent if undeveloped fantasy that I would somehow rescue my father. It seemed to me I was the only one in the family who actually liked and understood him. So I would go out of my way on occasion to be nice to him, or to treat him with the deference and respect to which I imagined a "normal" father might be entitled. These good intentions were fine as long as they stayed largely in the abstract and were not tested by reality.

In the spring of 1969, when I was living in California, I invited him to stay with me for a week. My first marriage had collapsed, I had run away to Berkeley, and I was trying to throw myself into teaching children creative writing, while waiting for the pieces of my shattered ego to reknit. My father arrived, and soon let it be known that he was unimpressed with the Bay Area: it had fewer pizza parlors, barbershops, and newsstands than New York. On Saturday afternoon I took him to Candlestick Park to watch a ballgame. His response was lukewarm: too windy. A classically provincial New Yorker, little-traveled, he shielded himself against feelings of unworldliness by making a point of appearing unimpressed with new experiences. I knew this. Still, his phlegmatic sourness began wearing me down: after the first few days I left him more and more to himself, especially during the day, while I went off to my teaching job at a private school. At night I would come home bearing excited tales of battles with the school administration and of the kids' responses to the creative writing assignments I had just cooked up. My father cut off my enthusiasm with the comment "Those who can, do. Those who can't, teach." It had not occurred to me—so sure was I that all this pedagogic turmoil would one day be grist for the literary mill (as indeed it was)—that, at twenty-six, I was already a failure in his eyes. Like him.

He continued to work at the textile firm of M. Lowenstein & Sons, rarely missing a day, until he turned sixty-seven and the company forced him to retire. It was retirement that withered him. Without the focused identity that his desk and shipping orders brought, he became hollowed-out. About a year after his retirement, he came down with pneumonia. I visited him in the hospital, where he was hoarding a pile of hospital menus—long green slips with boxes for checking off the desired entrées. Disoriented, he thought they were shipping orders, "work" he had to finish while recuperating.

I remember the urgent phone call from my mother at the start of that illness. "Come quickly, he's very ill." I thought, This is it. On my way over, I began preparing for the worst, rehearsing my funeral oration, letting my stomach's churn dredge up the proper words. His death, I secretly hoped, would deepen me. I was always waiting for life to become tragic, so that I would merely have to record it to become a powerful, universal writer.

"He's always been such a stoic," my mother said, greeting me at the door. "So when he said he felt a little pain, I knew it must be bad. Poor Pop, it hurt him so much he was doubled over, he couldn't lie down, he had to sleep all night in the chair. I can't bear to see it happening to him. He's like a—great tree withering in its branches."

A great tree? My mother, a professional actress, tends to dramatize. Still, I was pleased to hear her invoking this sequoian imagery in his behalf, instead of the usual scorn. We helped him on with his trousers; I kneeled at his feet to strap on leather sandals over phlebitis-swollen ankles, enacting my Cordelia fantasy. There *was* something grand, Lear-like about him that morning, a frail, bundled-up survivor lifted into a taxi in the freezing cold, skittering across iced sidewalks.

Once stationed in a ward, however, he became a hospital thing. I visited him two days later: sunk in a bed-wet trough, he was gray-stubbled, bone-protrudingly thin, his complexion white as celery. Amber traces oscillated on the EEG screen: which will it be, life, death? life, death . . . ?

"If I don't talk, it's not because I'm not happy to see you," he said.

"Please, no need to talk. You can even sleep; I'll still be sitting here." Frankly, I would have preferred he slept; talking was never easy between us. His eyes kept opening and staring at me—accusingly, I thought, though perhaps this was only his myopic stare.

"Don't worry, Pop, tomorrow they'll give you a shave. You'll look a million times better. You want your glasses?" No, he shook his head. "Why don't you put on your glasses?" I repeated. Somehow it seemed to me that everything would be fine if I could just get him to wear his glasses.

"I'm saving my eyes," he said.

"What are you saving them for? A rainy day?" I joked.

The glasses were smudgy with thumbprints; I washed them off with water from the tumbler and placed them on him.

"What are you thinking?" I asked, in the silence.

"I'm thinking, Why me?"

In those days I still hoped for some sort of wisdom from my father, poised at the maw between life and death. "Why me?" was not the illumination I had in mind. But "Why me?" was a curt summary of what he felt.

"Gimme that thing." He pointed his bony finger toward a plastic bottle that he kept by his side constantly.

I watched, heard him, pee into the bottle.

"Got any pretty nurses?" I asked. "I saw one outside your door, she looked like a cutie."

He stared at me sternly, reproachfully, with sea-green eyes. "Take my word for it, this is the most—emasculating experience you could ever have," he said. He swallowed hard; then he rubbed his forehead, looking pained.

"What's wrong, Dad, got a headache?"

No, he shook his head.

"Do you want to hear the news?"

"What difference does it make?"

"What do you think about, lying here all this time?" I tried again.

"Nothing. When you're in pain, that's all you think about."

Again, he was telling me something important, but I didn't know how to listen to it.

4.

My mother and father had once taken a magazine quiz: "Do You Know Your Mate?" She had been able to fill out everything about him, from his Social Security number to his mother's maiden name, whereas the opposite was true for him. "He didn't even remember my mother's maiden name! I realized I was living with a stranger, who didn't care at all about me as long as I fulfilled his creature comforts." What my mother says is true, up to a point. My father is a stranger to everyone. On the other hand, his not knowing her Social Security number does not negate the fact that he was completely attached to her, and would have undergone any amount of humiliation to keep living in her presence.

Ten years ago, when my father was seventy-four and my mother sixty-eight, she divorced him so that she could put him in a nursing home. She was candid about not wanting to spend her remaining years nursing an old man she didn't love, and it was clear that he could no longer take care of himself. Apparently the nursing home's regulations stated that a prospective lodger could have no other recourse before being taken in: hence, the necessity for divorce.

After the divorce went through, there was an interim period when my parents continued to live together, waiting for an opening at the nursing home. During this time my father was "on probation," as it were, and if he behaved well, it seemed my mother might reverse herself and allow him to stay with her. In the midst of that limbo period, I was in New York for a few weeks (I had taken a regular teaching job in Houston) and called on them. My mother sent us out to breakfast together so that we could talk "man-to-man." Since he is so laconic and apt to drift into withdrawal, I could only smile at my mother's fantasy of a "father-son powwow." We stopped at the corner stand to buy a newspaper; I was tempted to buy two newspapers, in case we ran out of things to say. It was raining as we walked across the street to the coffee shop, a greasy spoon joint, for breakfast. The breakfast special was $ 1.55, "Hot Pastrami Omelette." Since he was treating, I had chosen the cheapest place around.

"How's . . ." my father began, then lost his train of thought.

"How's Helen?" I prompted, offering the name of my then-current girlfriend.

"I thought the other one was prettier."

"What other one?" I asked irritably, knowing he meant Kay, a previous flame who had two-timed me and whose prettiness I did not relish being reminded of at the moment.

"You know, I had a funny dream last night," he said, changing the subject. "I dreamt I was sick and there were about ten people in the hospital room who came to see me. One of them was my brother Bernie. Now, I know my brother's been dead for years. I don't understand the significance of his being there."

"I don't either. What happened in the dream?"

"Nothing. Your sister Leah was in the room, and her friends. That's another thing I couldn't understand. Why wasn't Molly in the dream? Or you and Hal? Your mother would have an interpretation."

"Probably." A long silence fell. "So, you and Mom seem to have made peace with each other."

"You know, your mother and I got divorced."

"I know. Does it feel strange, living together after you're divorced?"

"Yes it feels strange."

"Did you sign the papers too, or—"

"I signed it," he said. "It was a joint divorce. Because your mother was going to go through with it anyway. One of the reasons for the divorce was to get a better tax break. And now they've changed the law, so it wouldn't have made any difference anyway."

"I thought the divorce was so that they wouldn't take Mother's income if she put you in a nursing home."

"Yes. But I don't want to go into a nursing home. My father, my brother, and my sister all went into nursing homes, and I don't have fond memories of them."

I liked the understated way he put it. "What I don't understand is, is it your legal right to stay in the apartment now, or are you there at Mother's sufferance?"

"I think it's the second. Besides, she doesn't want to have me forcibly removed."

"So you're on your best behavior now? And you're getting along?"

"Well. . . . There have been some peculiar things lately."

"Like what?"

"We were at a gathering, and your mother was talking as if I had nothing to do with the way you kids turned out," he said, holding his fork in midair and glancing up at me sideways. "She was saying 'My son does this' and 'My other son does that' and 'My daughter is such-and-such.' She was taking all the credit, as if I had no influence on you."

"Well, that's not true. We all feel you had a big influence on us." For better or worse, I added in my mind.

"I'm not saying I was the only influence. But I did have a little."

"Of course. She was just bragging, Pop. Like you do."

Another long silence, during which I watched the flies buzzing around the Miller beer sign.

"What have you been thinking about lately?" I asked.

"Nothing. I've been slightly depressed," he said.

"About what?"

"Nothing special."

"Your health all right?"

"My health is as good as can be expected for a man my age. I'm actually in good physical shape, except I have emphysema. I haven't smoked for years, but I still have emphysema from all the smoking I used to do."

"Are you still on medication?"

"Just vitamin pills."

"That's great!" I said with false, hearty enthusiasm.

"And half an aspirin a day for my heart."

"You get any exercise at all? Do you walk?"

"No, I don't walk much." He shook his head.

"You used to love walking."

"But now I walk so slowly. I used to walk real fast. Now your mother walks faster than I do, and she gets impatient."

"You can take walks alone."

"But I walk so slowly that it bugs me. Put it this way: My *halcyon* days are over," he said, grinning at his use of the unusual word.

"When were your halcyon days, Pop?" I asked skeptically.

"Before I got my stroke. I thought I was immortal. I was healthy as a horse. I used to work all day and night without stopping. I never even took a sick day. Then I got the stroke and I couldn't get out of bed. I don't know if you could understand unless it happens to you. You try to stand up and you can't. That frightened the hell out of me." Now he was warming up. "And I had this internist. Supposed to be one of the top internists in the city. At least that's what he told me. He prescribed Dilantin and something else. The two medications canceled each other out. Later on, someone told me that I could have sued him for malpractice. But someone else said that if he was such a big internist, then I couldn't win. So I didn't sue."

"Just as well."

"He's still practicing. Cut down on his hours, though," he added.

"But that was over twenty years ago. A long time to get over a fright."

"A lot of people at the Senior Center had strokes. So they understand. That's one good thing about that place. The problem is . . . that the two men I played canasta with, one is sick and the other man . . ." he mumbled.

"I'm sorry, I didn't hear."

"The other man passed on."

"That's too bad. So you have to make new friends."

"It's not easy for me. I'm not the gregarious type."

You could say that again. "Why is that, I wonder?"

"Your mother was the gregarious type, but I wasn't."

"What about when you were younger, before you met Mom?"

A pained look. "I didn't have too many friends."

"Were you shy?"

"Probably I am shy."

"Why is that?"

"I didn't have any confidence in myself."

The truth in a nutshell. Another silence. "Well, you don't have to make friends with the people at the Center, you just have to play cards."

"I do. I play rummy. And I find I'm better at rummy than I was at canasta— Eat slowly, take your time," he told me. My French toast was so awful that I was trying to get through it as fast as possible.

"Does the Center ever go on outings?" I asked.

"They go to Atlantic City. That's not my style. I don't bother going."

"I was once in Atlantic City," I reminisced, "and I enjoyed it. The ocean, the Boardwalk."

"The hotels expect you to gamble. I'm not a gambler."

When he was finished, he started to get up, and reached ever so slowly into his raincoat, which was hanging on the hook behind him, for some money. He found only a dollar. Puzzled. His hand traveled with incredible hesitation across to the other pocket. Nothing in there. A look went across his face, like that of a child who has accidentally lost something and expects a beating. He put his hand in his shirt pocket. Pulled out a twenty-dollar bill. Satisfaction. The check came to $5.60.

"You pay the tip," he said cheerfully.

A week later I asked my mother how Pop was doing. "He fell out of bed again. I didn't help him up either. He's got to learn to do for himself. What if I go on the road again? It's what I learned when I was working with those retarded kids—same principle. You've got to teach them to be independent."

"It's not very nice to compare him to a retarded kid."

"Don't worry," she sighed, "I'll do what's right. Because I don't want to live with guilt. I've lived with guilt before and it's no fun."

But fighting broke out between my parents constantly. Before I left the city, I visited them again. My mother was telling me about her stocks. Considering how poor we had been, and how she is still living in government-subsidized housing, having stocks, even worthless ones, is a status symbol. "This stock went from fifty cents to four dollars, I didn't sell, and now it's down to a dollar."

"If it reaches four dollars again, you'd better sell," I said cautiously.

"What's the difference? It only cost me a few hundred bucks. If I can't afford to risk that much, forget it."

My father interjected, in his phlegmy growl, something about the Mindanao Mother Lode.

She blew up at him: "You'll see, you're not getting a cent of that money! Even if the lawyer did say you were entitled to fifty percent of our property after the *divorce*. I'll fix your wagon!"

My father shrank into himself. I was shocked at the venom with which she had yelled at him, even after all these years of hearing it. I asked, "What's this about the Mindanao Mother Lode?"

She said, "Aw, I invested a lousy hundred dollars in this oil drilling outfit in the Pacific a few years ago, and never heard a word about it. But from him I never *stop* hearing it! If he keeps rubbing it in, he's the one who's gonna suffer."

Much as I had wanted to protect him in the moment against her temper, after I left them I realized the passive-aggressive cunning of my father in employing just those words which would set her off. (It showed the same quiet ability to insert a dig as calling my previous girlfriend prettier than my current one. For all his solipsism, he was observant enough when he wanted to be, and had a feel for other people's exposed areas.)

A few months later the parental truce was irrevocably shattered. It seemed the toilet had overflowed while my father was using it, and he didn't clean it up. He had phoned my sister Molly to report the toilet had flooded, and she, not having any time that day to stop by, gave him practical advice: Call the maintenance man. He didn't; instead, he sat there for eight hours "with his arms folded," as Molly put it. My mother came home, saw his turds on the floor, the sight of which pushed her over the limit for good.

It was the two women's interpretation that he was not "out of it" at all but had contrived to punish his wife by his passivity, because only by provoking her fury could he get the attention he wanted from her. I suspected geriatric debility to be the greater cause and was irked at my mother and sister for showing so little understanding of human frailty. On the other hand, most of the burden for taking care of him had fallen on them, not me. It was easy for me to play the compassionate relation at a distance.

My father called me himself in Houston, a rare event, to say that he would not be living at home anymore. My mother was putting him in an adult home near Far Rockaway. I said maybe it was for the best. He said, "Yes, well, in the sense that we weren't getting along."

Desperate for some optimistic note, I added, "And it will be near the beach. That's nice."

"Well, that part doesn't matter to me. I don't swim."

"Still, it's nice to see the ocean." He did not deign to reply to this inanity. "And maybe you can make friends there," I added.

"I didn't make any friends at the Senior Citizens Club. Although there, the people were walking in off the streets. Maybe here there'll be more people—of substance."

Around the time of the divorce, my family tended to split along gender lines. My brother Hal and I sympathized more with our father's eviction from his home, while the two girls shared my mother's point of view. Molly, a practicing Buddhist who usually preached compassion, surprised me by her adamance. "Why should I feel guilty for not visiting him regularly? He abandoned the family long ago." She had taken to calling him Mr. Ross, because, she explained, if you say "Albert Ross" quickly, it comes out "albatross."

After he was deposited in the home, my mother went around depressed for a while. Hal thought it was guilt; I thought it was being faced with a void. Whom would she blame now for her unhappy life? She had never admitted how dependent she might be on him, only the other way around.

My own impulse had been to sympathize more with my father, both because he seemed the weaker party and because my mother had cheated on him. As a young man, I had taken her infidelity very personally, as though she had somehow betrayed me. Objectively, I could appreciate that—being the young woman she was, lost in a miserable marriage—it was absolutely necessary for her to reach out to other men. Nowadays it isn't her affairs I hold against her, but the fact that, in justifying herself, she felt compelled to demean my father before his children's eyes. I know, I know, I am being unfair in blaming her for not "allowing" us to venerate him more, as though it were ever possible for her to lie about her most intense feelings—to situate him, by some *trompe l'oeil* of maternal tact, on the patriarchal throne.

I dropped in at my mother's before leaving New York. She was going on about how he'd got what he deserved. My mother, for all her psychological astuteness, is someone who speaks and acts out of a self-righteous wound. Her recognition that she may have hurt someone can proceed only from the perception that she was hurt first.

"Supposing there were two other people you were looking at whose marriage was this bad," I said, "wouldn't you be inclined to assume they were both a little at fault?"

"Yeah, I suppose," she said. "But he blew it."

"If he was so terrible, why did you stay with him so long then?"

"I wish I knew. That's the $64,000 question. He had so much promise! What happened to it? He just didn't have the drive. After he retired, I tried to get him to be interested in things, I took him with me to the community college. But he thought he was smarter than everyone else, and if they didn't appreciate that immediately . . . He dropped out, and I got my degree. To me, it was a challenge. To Al, a challenge was already a defeat."

My mother has so much life force it's hard to imagine what it must have been like to live with her opposite all those years. Vitality like hers, ever on tap, has been a constant delight for me but not a mystery. The mystery has been my father and his deep reserves of inanition.

5.

After my father was put in the nursing home, the next family crisis occurred when my mother announced she didn't want him at the Passover seder at her house. I was outraged. Then my friend Max, the soul of kindness, said he sympathized with her. She had suffered for years in an unhappy marriage, and now she was divorced. Why should she be hypocritical and welcome him? Why pretend we were an intact family when we weren't? Each of the children would have to learn how to adjust to this new arrangement; each would have to make a separate deal with our father.

I began going out to the Belle Harbor Adult Home in Far Rockaway. It took forever on the subway; you had to catch a spur train over Broad Channel the last couple of stops. Once off the train, you found a calm residential neighborhood, one- or two-family homes with hedges, an old-fashioned New York lower-middle-class feeling, with quite a few senior citizens residences and funeral homes in the vicinity. My father didn't like the area because the nearest newsstand was seven blocks away; he was used to a denser city life.

His half of the room contained a bed, a night table, some pictures of the family, and—I was both flattered and obscurely ashamed to see—my books. His roommate was deaf, a hundred years old, spoke only Yiddish, and was paranoid; when I tried to bring the empty chair near his side of the room over to my father's bed so that we could sit together, he barked at me. No words, just guttural attack-dog sounds.

My father, each visit, would fill me in on the deathwatch. "There's a guy here who dropped dead the other day from a coronary. Fell over into his soup. He seemed in okay health, too."

I wanted to make him feel better. So, one day I took it into my head to buy my father a pair of swimming shorts. Since he lived only a block away from the beach, surely there might come a time, even if he didn't swim, when he'd want to warm his legs in the sand. We walked the seven blocks to the retail street, taking over a half hour to do so. At the shop my father wouldn't let me get him swimming trunks but insisted on Bermuda shorts. He went into the dressing room to try them on.

"Do they fit, Pop?"

"Yeah, they fit." This was his highest accolade—the acme of enthusiasm—coming from my father.

On the way home I asked, "Do you think you'll wear them?"

"Not very often," he said, honest to a fault.

During this time I kept trying to buy my father gifts. First I bought a TV for his room (which he never watched, preferring the common room's), then a half-refrigerator for snacks, because he didn't like the food they served. I was doing this partly to lift his depression and partly to administer a lesson to my family on the right way to treat him—I did not like all their talk about his being an "albatross" or a "vegetable." The problem was, I kept coming up against my own upset at his lack of appreciation. The man had no talent for accepting gifts.

I needed to see my father as a poor, maligned Père Goriot abandoned in old age, who deserved our love as a matter of course and custom, and to dismiss the others' beefs against him as petty. I wanted to start with him on a clean, tender page. But to do so, I had to hide my own scars and keep my buried angers against him in check. And sometimes I could no longer overlook the meaner side of the man, which Molly insisted was holding together the works.

One weekend I checked him out of the adult home to spend a few days at the loft I was subletting. In a sense, I was trying out my fantasy of what it would be like to have my father move in with me. I had bought us baseball tickets at Shea Stadium so that we could watch Doc Gooden go for his twentieth victory. The morning of our planned outing was drizzly, and Father moped that the game was going to be rained out. Luckily, the weather cleared up long enough for Doc to pitch—and win; but still my father seemed morose. All weekend I had cooked for him, taken him around, arranged dinner at a fancy restaurant, and nothing pleased him: the coffee was too weak, too strong. By the end of the weekend I was completely sympathetic with my mother. Every time he complained about something—say, wanting another radio station on the car radio—I could hear her voice in my thoughts: WHY DON'T YOU CHANGE IT YOURSELF? Though he didn't know how to drive, he was sure I was going the wrong way, and insisted we ask directions at the gas station. Moreover, he seemed completely uninterested in my life—every few hours asking, "When is Hal coming back from vacation?" Prolonged, continuous exposure to the man was eroding my idealized defense of him, making me see him exactly as the other family members did: infuriatingly passive, selfish, hurtful, uncouth.

Looking back at that weekend, I see now what it might have been like for him. He couldn't give himself over to the pleasures offered when they were so temporary, and when they came at the humiliating price of my expecting his gratitude. If this was indeed a test—a dry run for some possible future living arrangement—he could not afford to be on best behavior. My father would rather disappoint quickly and get the suspense over with.

6.

The trek out to Far Rockaway was too long, the family members were visiting him less and less, and it was agreed that we should try to find a home for him closer to town. My brother was able to relocate him in an ultradesirable "adult residence" on the Upper West Side, near Lincoln Center. Once again he could walk to the corner and buy a newspaper. We could take him out to a variety of restaurants, all within a stone's throw of his building. He could look out the window and see Broadway, Citarella's fish store, Fairview's produce stand. He could get himself a haircut. He began perking up again, making observations. One of his repeated bon mots was "When it says 'hair salon' instead of barbershop, that means you're paying extra." Another: "When you see a cloth napkin, that means you're paying extra." This was his streetwise peasant side letting us know, You can't fool me, it's still the same baloney.

The new residence home seemed, at first, a paradise for seniors. There were classical music concerts, daily video screenings, poetry workshops (to which my father brought his half-century-old poems on onionskin about his wife's defection)—all in a building that felt more like an apartment house than a prison. Each resident had his own separate "apartment" (a room, really), while enjoying the social life of the common parlors. The pretense was that of dignified, autonomous seniors who just happened to need the additional services of a specialized hotel. The problem in such a place was that you could not falter. If you got too sick, too frail, too out of it, you were told you didn't belong in this establishment but in a nursing home, and were summarily kicked out.

After a while, there was no kidding ourselves: my father was on a slow, inexorable path downward. It was not just that he had cataracts (they could be corrected with surgery) or that he was a loner, acting, by the residence staff's standards, un-communally. It was that he began to experience "incontinence problems"—in short, wet his pants, making him an undesirable presence in the dining room. The family took a crash course in adult Pampers, rubber diapers, prostate surgery, and behavioral modification training.

Incontinence was the precise metaphor to galvanize family arguments about my father's willpower. "He's doing it on purpose!" said Molly. "He can hold it in if he wants to."

"I don't think so," I said. Meanwhile, my father went around looking utterly hesitant to travel any distance farther than a half-block from the nearest bathroom.

I remember one particular night I had planned to take him to a screening at Lincoln Center. When I got there, he was so sloppily dressed that I decided to forgo the movie and just have dinner with him across the street, at a newly opened Italian restaurant.

We had the usual tepid time of it, neither hostile nor affectionate. The most interesting moment was when Father volunteered this short summary of his marriage: "I felt that I loved your mother more than she loved me." Undoubtedly true, and I realized I had probably contrived my whole romantic life until then so as not to be caught in the same situation.

He also said, "She always attracted dykes. She must have done something for that to happen."

I told my father that my mother's older brother, Uncle George, had died. There was a silence. He finally said, "I have mixed feelings about him."

"Why?"

"Well, I think he played around with her when she was a kid. And then she was madly in love with him, all during the time when we were first married. I couldn't prove anything, but . . ."

It seemed to me he was casting about wildly for rivals, to explain why my mother had come to dislike him.

When the meal ended, he tried to get up and couldn't seem to rise, so I gave him a hand and walked him to the men's room, one flight down. He had become very unsteady on his feet, especially managing stairs. "Why do they always put the men's room where you have to go up or down a flight?" he said. I waited outside the toilet door for ten minutes. After a while I thought maybe he had died in there. "Pop, you all right?" I called out. He grunted something in reply, so I knew he was still among the living. "Can I help?" I asked. "No," came his foggy voice uncertainly. Ten more minutes passed. "Pop, what's going on?" Finally I went inside to have a look. "I had an accident," he said. I noticed the tiled floor was smeared with shit. "I made in my pants. I couldn't get them off in time."

"Okay. Let's get outa here." I helped him up the stairs and we left quickly, before the waiters could see the bathroom floor. It's their problem, I thought. I'll never go back to that restaurant anyway.

"I'm sorry," he said as we crossed the street.

"It's not your fault, Pop. It's old age." I was already thinking ahead to what I would have to do. Get him undressed and into a shower. I was very calm, patient, the way I used to be when I was working with kids. We took the elevator upstairs to his room, and he immediately sat on the bed and took off his pants, smearing the bedspread in the process. I helped him off with his shirt and led him into the bathroom across the hall. Two minutes later I still hadn't heard the sound of running water.

"Pop, what's the matter?" He was standing outside the shower stall, dry and dirty.

"I can't get my socks off."

"Oh for crying out loud!" I said, sounding just like my mother. "The socks can get wet. Just go in the shower!"

I pushed him in.

"I can't get the hot water to work," he said. Now his total helplessness was getting on my nerves. He had turned on the hot water; it would just take a minute to warm up. Didn't he know that, after all these years on the planet? I gave him soap and told him to rinse well and left him there. Back in his room, I threw away his soiled underpants. I stripped the bedspread and bunched it on the floor, hoping his attendant would deal with it tomorrow. And I turned on the Mets game so that he would have something to watch when he returned.

He came back. One of his legs was still covered with shit. I cleaned it off as best I could with water and toilet paper. Wiping off my father's ass wasn't what I'd expected from the evening, but—all in the nature of reality. I tried to tell myself it was good for my spiritual development. As soon as he was lying down comfortably, however, I said good-bye. I could have stayed longer, but I didn't. He could have said thank you, but he didn't. He made his usual "okay" grunt. As I fled the building onto Amsterdam Avenue, a junkie was vomiting against the side of the car. What a night!

There was some hope that a prostate operation might improve the incontinence situation. In any event, he had to have one. After it was done, I received a call from the hospital to pick up my father. Molly was also there to help, but she seemed in a foul mood.

"How about if I go down to pay for his TV and phone," I said, "and meanwhile you can see that he gets ready."

"I've got to speak to you," said Molly. Taking me outside the room by the arm, she told me in a fierce whisper, "Look, I didn't get any sleep last night because I have a splitting headache and a cold, and I absolutely don't want to have to dress that old man and touch his body and see his old balls, I can't handle it today."

I was surprised to hear my sister sounding so squeamish, since she is a professional masseuse; but as usual I admired her bluntness. "Fine, I'll take care of it." I went back into the hospital room and found an elderly German-Jewish woman in a white hospital coat, who told me she was the social worker. I started to help my father on with his underwear when she told me, "Don't! He has to do it for himself." She then explained to me that the West Side Residence Home had told her they refused to accept responsibility for him unless he could dress himself and walk. The hospital, for their part, refused to keep him there any longer because "this is not a nursing home" and his operation was over and he'd had a few days' rest. So she would have to determine for herself whether he was capable of dressing himself. If not, the family would have to hire an attendant eight hours a day to take care of him in the residence home.

Molly lost her temper with the woman and yelled, "Why did they tell me yesterday that he could go? Which is it supposed to be, go or stay? Why don't you make up your frigging minds?!" She was carrying on like a street tough, and the social worker, who had probably seen it all (maybe even the camps), was undaunted.

I took Molly aside and told her, "She can't say which it is to be until she ascertains whether Father can take minimal care of himself."

"Oh fine! And he's going to play helpless because he wants to stay here, where they do everything for him."

The woman kept repeating what her responsibilities in the current situation were. Finally I said to her, as calmly as I could, "Look, we're all pretty bright here, we understand what you're saying."

She blinked her eyes and left the room.

I turned to Father and said under my breath, "Pop! Try very hard. Don't give up. It's important that you show her you can dress yourself. Otherwise they won't let you out. So give it your all."

"All right, I'll try," he said. And proceeded to do just that, dressing himself slowly, manfully, with dignity.

Not to be dissuaded by the evidence, Molly started hectoring him from the hallway. "What's the matter, you like it here, so you don't want to try to get out?"

"Sure. I'm crazy about the place," he answered sarcastically. "Show me someone who don't mind staying in a hospital and I'll show you a schmuck."

"You think if you just give up, everyone will wait on you hand and foot—right?" retorted Molly.

"Leave me alone! Stop giving me the business."

I caught my sister winking at me: this was her version of reverse psychology. I realized that the social worker, now nowhere in sight, might not believe he had dressed himself, so I hurried to fetch her. When I spotted her, I explained my errand, adding, "One thing you have to understand: my father has always been the kind of man who becomes more dependent when there are people around to do for him. But he was like that at thirty."

She nodded, with an appearance of understanding. I was trying to establish rapport with her. The stakes were high; we could never afford a full-time attendant. And where would he go if they kicked him out of his residence home?

The social worker returned just in time to see Molly buttoning my father's pants! Molly said, "That's the only thing he couldn't do for himself." But he still didn't have his shoes on. The three of us watched as Father, with agonizing slowness, tried to get his foot into the Velcro-strap sneakers that Hal had bought him. I tried to smooth the way by explaining, "He always has trouble putting his shoes on. Even before the operation."

"I wasn't told that," sniffed the social worker.

"The attendant at the home does it for him every morning," Molly said. Fortunately, he got his shoes on by himself, for once, and now the test was his walking ability. He started down the hallway past the nurses' station, the social worker walking alongside to monitor his progress.

"Maybe he needs a cane," she said. "Why does he take such small steps?"

"He always walks like that."

As he approached the nurses' desk, he quipped, "She's too old for me. Get me a younger one." The nurses cracked up. They all seemed to like him. (I'm fascinated by the fact that many people do take to my father right away.)

"Your dad has a great sense of humor," a nurse said.

"He's a riot," said the other.

"Good-bye, Mr. Lopat. You don't want to stay here with all these sick people, do you?"

He waved to his fan club. We bid adieu to the social worker, who reluctantly agreed that he was ambulatory.

An Academy Award performance. Molly and I got him quickly into a taxi, before he could collapse.

Shortly after that, the inevitable happened. He fell down one morning, and in consequence was kicked out of the West Side Residence (whose hoity-toity airs I had come to despise) and sent to his present nursing home. This is no doubt the Last Stop. There is nothing he can do here that will disqualify him from the right to sit in the common room with the TV on.

Recently, during a period when he had been feeling too despondent to eat, I visited him there and wheeled him out to nearby Fort Tryon Park. He noticed a magnificent elm overlooking the Hudson River. "That's a beautiful tree," he said.

"You see, Pop? It's not so bad being alive. Which would you prefer—tell me honestly: to be dead or alive?"

"Alive, of course." He was annoyed to be asked such a childish question.

For the next few minutes his senescent-poetic mind spliced the word "tree" into different sentences. "They don't brag so much about the trees. Especially since they had that . . . Holocaust."

Later I tell his social worker that, from my observation, my father likes to be placed in front of ongoing scenes of daily life. Especially activities involving youth: teenagers playing basketball, tots splashing through the fountain, pretty girls walking by.

She says skeptically, "You caught him at a good moment. We took him to the park, there were plenty of children around, and he dozed through it all, no interest whatsoever. You know what he wants? He wants you."

I hang my head guiltily.

"But in today's way of life . . ." she adds, that vague, exonerating statement.

I ask myself, Would it be possible to take him in? Where would we put him? The basement? The baby's room? A shed on the roof? We could manage, somehow, couldn't we? In the midst of this deliberation, I know that I will never do it. I take consolation from what a scientist friend tells me: "Societies choose differently what to do with old people. The Eskimos choose the ice floe, we choose the nursing home."

How much does my father understand? Has his mind become permanently loosed from its logical moorings—like that comment about trees and the Holocaust? At other times he seems to make perfect sense. During the staff meeting I had tried to explain the reasons for his depression, adding, "He's taken a lot of abuse from his family."

My father picked his head up and said, clearly, "I was also responsible for the discord."

A final word on failure. I once read an essay by Bill Holm, the gifted Midwestern writer, called "The Music of Failure," in which he tried both to argue against the hollow American obsession with success and to redeem failure, to find beauty in it. In effect, Holm was attempting to invert commonplace values and turn failure into a victory, or at least show how it could be better, more human than its opposite. Intriguing as the essay was, I finished it with a sigh, thinking, But there is such a thing as failure. There *are* failed lives, which no amount of rhetorical jiujitsu can reclaim as triumphs.

Maybe my father's insistence that he is a failure does not signal the obsessions of senility but grows out of a long, enforced, reluctant meditation at the end of his life, which has obliged him to take responsibility for some of his very real errors. In that sense, there is hope for all of us. I would like to give him the benefit of the doubt.

Postscript

Shortly after I had completed writing this, on June 26, 1995, my father passed away. He was a few months shy of his eighty-fifth birthday. The official cause of death was pneumonia and sepsis. As far as I could tell, he remained unconscious the whole time he was in the hospital; at least he did not die, as he had dreaded, in the nursing home itself. When I visited him during that last week, at the Allen Pavilion (his room overlooked Baker Field football stadium), the attending physician urged me to sign a "Do Not Resuscitate" form, and I did so.

About the exact time of his death, I was driving home and my car overheated and I had to pull over by the side of the road. I opened the hood and a plume of steam escaped. I like to think this was my father's spirit escaping from his body.

That night, after having been notified of his death, I called the hospital again and asked if I could see my father one last time. They said it would not be possible that evening, but I could come by in the morning and view him. The next morning they told me that, due to some bureaucratic mix-up, they had already sent his body off to be cremated.

First Love

To the child, Love is both real and a pretense: a necessity sometimes, a role at other times; instinctive, yet learned behavior. I see my little girl offering her hand to be kissed, in a very la-di-da manner. She is trying on the gallantries of love, just as she tries on the petulance of childhood. How quickly they master the social codes of love, hugs and kisses, and hearts—as quickly as they learn to manipulate the heartstrings by refusing such tokens. All around children, there are cultural signals, prompts to express and receive love: in fairy tales, it is the ultimate reward for being discovered as who you really are, the beauty under the cinders, the prince beneath the frog. In advertisements, every product is sold with the promise that its purchase will bring or enhance true love.

At the same time that these diaphanous romantic feelings are being planted, there is the hot, urgent need of the child to be listened to, have needs attended to, right away. "Mommy I need a pair of scissors *ANTZ* is coming out on videotape I'm hungry I pooped in my pants change me no stupid daddy not that kind of crayon the other kind!" All demands are on the same plane of importance, and worthy of tears. The child does not prioritize but asks only to be obeyed, pronto—with all due respect to the "magic words" please and thank you, those road-bump nuisances placed by parents, who are slow-witted and don't understand that they are your servants. It's frustrating sometimes that they won't acknowledge it; they do so much for you as it is, why won't they just come clean and admit they are your abject slaves? And in return you love them, distractedly, wholeheartedly, ambivalently ("I hate you Mommy! I'll never kiss you again for the rest of my life!"), and in the best possible way, organically, like a heliotropic plant.

So your first love as a child is for your parents. The thermodynamic model seems to be: love in, love out. If the parents' love has been expressed cleanly, without mixed messages or scary anger or abandonment (it almost never is, the psychologists tell us), the child will grow up into a serene, unconflicted adult; and if there are complications (there almost always are), the child will probably grow up to have "unresolved issues." But some confusion is inevitable: before you even reach kindergarten, you may very well have conceived the idea of marrying one of your parents later on (and why not?—he/she is so conveniently present, so attractively devoted to your needs); and you may have experienced jealous annoyance at their displays of affection to each other. As my four-year-old daughter Lily said to me this morning, when I had the nerve to kiss her mother in front of her, "That was the longest, rudest kiss I ever saw!"

My daughter went through a quandary around the time she turned three. Who should she marry? she began to fret. I was an early candidate, I am happy to say. She enjoyed slow-dancing with me to Ella Fitzgerald and got a dreamy look in her eyes when I held her aloft in my arms. But she accepted (all too sanguinely, it seemed to me) the information that she could not marry her daddy because it just wasn't done.

So her attention turned to other suitors. Her principal beau was the boy next door, Dominick. This kid is a lout. He barely speaks except to grunt, he is fixated on trucks, he regularly gets into trouble at play school for fighting. I tell you frankly, he is beneath my daughter in intelligence and deportment. Yet she professes to love him and plans to marry him. She tells me he will not always be so wild, he will make a good man when he grows up. He seems to possess that masculine *je ne sais quoi*, that essence of machismo that even four-year-old girls are attuned to. I try to interest her in the more intellectual boys in her circle, but she pays them no mind. I will say this for young Dominick: he does seem to behave better around Lily, and, in his own way, appears fond of her. Still, I wonder how to protect her from the pain of unrequited love.

The other day, Lily wanted to go to the neighborhood park because she thought Dominick might be there. "He loves the park, almost as much as he loves me," she said confidently. When we finally caught up with him, he seemed, from my vantage point, to ignore her—tearing back and forth on his bike, while she pretended he was chasing her. When she got tired of running from his approach, she sat on a bench and watched him. She was in no way put off by his self-absorption; rather, she seemed able to weave his mere presence into her ongoing fantasy that he is crazy about her.

When she first began asking "Who should I marry?" I was not the only one to tell her the question might be a little premature. Our assurances did nothing to quell her sense of urgency. Obviously she had reached a developmental stage in her own mind when the act of deciding about something big—the choice of a life partner—had to be undertaken, at least in practice. I knew where some of the romantic suspense was coming from. She had chronically watched five different versions of *Cinderella* on tape, from Betty Boop to Brandy, then had graduated to obsessions with *The Sound of Music, Funny Face, Gigi,* and *My Fair Lady.* One day, she remarked, like a precocious narratologist, "You know, they're all the same story." It was true: in each variation, a lowly girl had been plucked from the chorus, so to speak, to marry the top man.

A few other candidates for Lily's hand had to be evaluated. Lily's great-uncle Reuben regularly proposed that they run away and get married, but he was over seventy and had a hearing aid; and besides, there was Aunt Florence, his wife of forty-five years, to consider. Then her pediatrician, Doctor Monti, expressed interest, but he was always so busy. No, it would have to be Dominick. Now that that dilemma was settled, Lily began mulling over her wedding gown, tiara, pumps, jewels, boa, tutu. Wedding announcements would have to be sent out, ribbon bows tied, handwriting of name practiced. She began to tell everyone who came to visit: "I have a boyfriend named Dominick and we're going to get married."

Did this mean that she was infatuated with Dominick? On the contrary, during this time she had little contact with the actual boy, nor did she seem to want more. Meanwhile, I witnessed her daily eruption of intense feelings for another love object altogether: her cat, Newman. She could not get enough of catching him, snuggling with him, holding him captive by the paws, tying kerchiefs on his head, strapping blankets to his body, tormenting him in every possible fashion, and sobbing when he ran away. Here, I thought, was the real thing: love without the romantic gauze, but with the cruelty and appetite of attraction that one sees in film noir. She would kill for him—or kill him! How often my wife and I have had to intervene to protect the creature, removing from his neck harnesses and cravats that could have easily turned into nooses. Yet he always comes back to her, like the poor sap Glenn Ford used to play in those films noir, for more punishment. He craves her attention; and she, in turn, relates to him fearlessly, accepting whatever scratches may come her way.

Lily loves Newman in a deep, passionate manner. It is like a cross between her instinctual, inadvertent love for her parents and her elective affinity for the little boyfriend next door. Though the Abyssinian has been with her all her life, her feelings have increasingly focused on and matured toward him: she talks to him regularly as though he were her child, her honey, her one and only. The problem is that Newman is twenty years old—ancient by cat standards. Already he is arthritic, cataracted, and worrisomely skinny. He sleeps for much of the day, curled up in a ball, until Lily comes around to prod him into motion. As parents, we can try to protect our child from viciousness and harm, but not from the consequences of tender attachment. We shudder to think of what will happen when he dies. Then she will really know the sorrow that is so often inextricable from first love.